The Palace File

The
Palace File

Nguyen Tien Hung
and
Jerrold L. Schecter

PERENNIAL LIBRARY

Harper & Row, Publishers, New York
Cambridge, Philadelphia, San Francisco
London, Mexico City, São Paulo, Singapore, Sydney

Grateful acknowledgment is made for permission to reprint:

From *RN: The Memoirs of Richard Nixon*. Copyright © 1978 by Richard Milhous Nixon. Reprinted by permission of Warner Books, Inc.

From *Years of Upheaval* by Henry Kissinger. Copyright © 1982 by Henry A. Kissinger. Reprinted by permission of Little, Brown and Company.

From *White House Years* by Henry Kissinger. Copyright © 1979 by Henry A. Kissinger. Reprinted by permission of Little, Brown and Company.

A hardcover edition of this book was published in 1986 by Harper & Row, Publishers.

THE PALACE FILE. Copyright © 1986 by Nguyen Tien Hung and Jerrold L. Schecter. All rights reserved. Printed in the United States of America. No part of this book may be used or reproduced in any manner whatsoever without written permission except in the case of brief quotations embodied in critical articles and reviews. For information address Harper & Row, Publishers, Inc., 10 East 53rd. Street, New York, N.Y. 10022. Published simultaneously in Canada by Fitzhenry & Whiteside Limited, Toronto.

First PERENNIAL LIBRARY edition published 1989.

Library of Congress Cataloging-in-Publication Data

Nguyen, Gregory Tien Hung, 1935–
  The palace file.

  "Perennial Library."
  Bibliography: p.
  Includes index.
    1. Vietnamese Conflict, 1961–1975—Diplomatic history.   2. Vietnam—Foreign relations—United States.   3. United States—Foreign relations—Vietnam.   4. Nixon, Richard M. (Richard Milhous), 1913–   —Correspondence.   5. Ford, Gerald R., 1913–   —Correspondence.   6. Nguyễn, Van Thiêu, 1923–   —Correspondence.   I. Schecter, Jerrold L.   II. Title.
  DS557.7.N42 1989   959.704′32   86-45333
  ISBN 0-06-091572-2 (pbk.)

89 90 91 92 93   RRD   10 9 8 7 6 5 4 3 2 1

To our children:

Christine, Daniel, and Michael Hung
and
Doveen, Evelind, Steven, Kate and Barney Schecter
May they continue to enjoy security and freedom
and take neither for granted

Contents

Illustrations

(following page 272)

The Independence Palace *(AP/Wide World Photos)*
Hung and Thieu *(Collection of Nguyen Tien Hung)*
Nixon and Mao Zedong *(National Archives, Nixon Project)*
Kissinger and Zhou Enlai *(National Archives, Nixon Project)*
Nixon and LBJ meet *(George Tames, New York Times)*
Nixon and Mrs. Chennault *(Collection of Mrs. Anna Chennault)*
Ngo Dinh Diem *(Paris Match/Camus)*
Humphrey congratulates Thieu *(Ted Van Dyk)*
Thieu and Bunker *(UPI/Bettmann Archive. By David Hume Kennerly)*
Thieu and Nixon *(National Archives, Nixon Project)*
Thieu addresses troops *(UPI/Bettmann Archive. By David Hume Kennerly)*
South Vietnamese armored vehicles *(Larry Burrows)*
Kissinger talks with Le Duc Tho *(National Archives, Nixon Project)*
Hoang Duc Nha greets Kissinger *(Collection of Hoang Duc Nha)*
Lord, Rodman and Negroponte *(National Archives, Nixon Project)*
Kissinger announces peace *(National Archives, Nixon Project)*
Nguyen Phu Duc meets Nixon *(AP/Wide World Photos)*
North Vietnamese and U.S. delegations *(National Archives, Nixon Project)*
Kissinger and Le Duc Tho *(National Archives, Nixon Project)*
Rogers and Tran Van Lam *(AP/Wide World Photos)*
Thieu in mandarin robe *(UPI/Bettmann Archive)*
Kissinger meeting with Pham Dong *(National Archives, Nixon Project)*
Tran Van Lam *(UPI/Bettmann Archive)*
Duong Van Minh *(UPI/Bettmann Archive)*
Tran Van Huong *(UPI/Bettmann Archive)*
Tran Van Don *(Tran Van Don)*
Ngo Quang Truong *(Collection of General John Murray)*
Vuong Van Bac *(AP/Wide World Photos)*
Nutter *(Collection of Jane Nutter)*
Laird *(UPI/Bettmann Archive)*
Schlesinger *(UPI/Bettmann Archive)*

ix

Haig *(AP/Wide World Photos)*
Martin *(David Hume Kennerly)*
Vogt *(U.S. Air Force photo)*
Ford with Thieu *(UPI/Bettmann Archive)*
Hung *(Collection of Nguyen Tien Hung)*
Hung addresses diplomatic corps *(Collection of Nguyen Tien Hung)*
Military cemetery at Bien Hoa *(Yves Billy/Sygma)*
Nixon welcomes Vietman POWs *(National Archives, Nixon Project)*
Nixon greets Thieu *(National Archives, Nixon Project)*
Reagan and Nancy Reagan *(AP/Wide World Photos)*
Truong Thi Bich Diep and McCloskey*(Collection of Nguyen Tien Hung)*
Hung, Martin and Thieu *(Collection of Nguyen Tien Hung)*
The Weyand Mission *(David Hume Kennerly)*
Refugees fleeing *(Collection of Eric Von Marbod)*
South Vietnamese soldiers *(Buffon-Darquennes/Sygma)*
Tan Son Nhut airfield *(Collection of Eric Von Marbod)*
Ford and Weyand *(David Hume Kennerly)*
Kissinger, Ford and Von Marbod *(David Hume Kennerly)*
Ford addressing Congress *(Courtesy Ford Library)*
Kissinger et al. *(David Hume Kennerly)*
Vietnamese refugees *(Collection of Eric Von Marbod)*
Kissinger, Nessen and Scowcroft *(David Hume Kennerly)*
North Vietnamese tank *(Buffon-Darquennes/Sygma)*

Preface

NGUYEN TIEN HUNG, a professor of economics at Howard University and an economist at the International Monetary Fund, returned to South Vietnam in 1973 to serve as a Special Assistant to President Nguyen Van Thieu. He later became Minister of Economic Development and Planning in Thieu's cabinet. During their association, Thieu showed Hung a file of letters which Presidents Nixon and Ford had written him over a period of five years. Even a cursory examination of the file by Hung revealed that the letters, secret memoranda, and messages were a remarkable unpublished documentation of the relationship between South Vietnam and the United States during this period. In April 1975, as the end was approaching for South Vietnam, Thieu sent Hung to Washington in a last-ditch effort to secure more American aid. Thieu was torn between the American demand that he keep the letters secret and the need to tell the world that he had been promised help by Presidents Nixon and Ford; if he did not use the letters now, it would be too late. Just before Hung departed, Thieu entrusted the letters to him.

On April 30, 1975, the day Saigon fell, Hung was still in Washington. In an appeal to save South Vietnamese refugees, he released two of the letters in a press conference in Washington, D.C., but they attracted only brief attention at that time from an American press and public that wanted to put the war behind it. Despite congressional requests for the record of secret American commitments to South Vietnam, the letters were not released by the Ford administration.

After the fall of Saigon, Hung returned to his position at Howard University and began to write a history of what happened in South Vietnam during the last years of the war. Almost ten years later, he was still working on the book when he was introduced to Jerrold L. Schecter by a mutual friend. Schecter had been a *Time* magazine correspondent in Vietnam from 1960 to 1963, and on special assignment there in 1965. From 1971 to 1975 he observed Vietnam diplomatic and political developments from Washington, first as a White House correspondent, covering Nixon and Kissinger, and then as diplomatic editor of *Time*. Hung showed the letters to Schecter, who was so impressed by the scope of their commitment that he felt they should be published in full and their significance examined critically. They decided to collaborate on the story behind the letters, recording from the Vietnamese vantage point what happened in South Vietnam and to President Thieu's government from the time of the 1968 presidential election between Humphrey and Nixon until the end of the Republic of Vietnam in 1975.

The twenty-seven letters from President Nixon and four from President Ford to President Thieu form the core of this book. They were maintained by Thieu in a file to which only he had access in his personal suite in the Palace. Although excerpts from some of the letters have been quoted, they have never been disclosed in their entirety; the full extent of the correspondence and the exact nature of its contents were denied in the final days of the Vietnam War. The book describes the decisions, actions, and events that resulted from the letters. It also includes Hung's notes from cabinet sessions and meetings in the Palace, his extended conversations with Thieu since 1975 and extensive research into both published and original sources, some of them only recently made available or declassified. Finally, there are interviews with the leading participants in the events of this period who would agree to see the authors, including Presidents Thieu and Ford; former Foreign Minister Vuong Van Bac and former Information Minister Hoang Duc Nha; Generals Cao Van Vien, Tran Van Don, and Ngo Quang Truong; Secretaries of State Henry Kissinger and Alexander Haig; Defense Secretaries Clark Clifford, Melvin Laird, James Schlesinger, and Elliot Richardson; Ambassador Graham Martin, Mrs. Anna Chennault, and numerous other Vietnamese and American officials, both military and civilian, who made and executed policy in Saigon and Washington. President Nixon declined repeated requests to be interviewed.

The presidential letters are an important part of the story of the U.S.–South Vietnamese relationship. They contained specific assurances of American commitments and how they would be carried out, yet they remained secret and were never shared with the Congress even on a selective restricted basis. Members of Presidents Nixon and Ford's cabinets, Defense Secretaries Melvin Laird, James Schlesinger, and Elliot Richardson, disclosed in interviews that they were not aware of the letters until the final days of the war when Hung made them available. By then it was too late for the pledges they contained to play a meaningful role in congressional action. The letters shed a disturbing light on America's behavior toward its closest Asian ally, with whom it fought an undeclared war for more than ten years at the cost of more than one million Vietnamese deaths and casualties and 58,000 American lives.*

---

* South Vietnamese civilian casualties were estimated at 1,435,000, of which there were an estimated 430,000 deaths. See *Congress and the Nation*, Vol. IV, 1975.

They raise sobering questions for the future about the role of secret diplomacy in an open, democratic system that requires the support of the President's own cabinet, the Congress, and the public for any policy to succeed.

Acknowledgments

NGUYEN TIEN HUNG is grateful to the Earhart Foundation for providing summer research grants in 1977 and 1980. We thank Professor Nguyen Manh Hung, Chu Xuan Vien, John Negroponte, Richard Solomon, Philip Schwartz, Miriam G. Schecter, Evelind Schecter, Steven Schecter, Kate Schecter, Ari Roth, Doveen Schecter, Barney Schecter, Christine Hung, Daniel Hung, Michael Hung, Judy Protas, and Michael Shafer for their careful reading and discussion of portions of the manuscript. Catherine Bamberger's efforts to type and edit an early version of the manuscript are greatly appreciated. We thank Harley Hindrichs for introducing us. N. Van Dao, Nguyen Ngoc Bich, Cung Tien and Le Lai made helpful suggestions and encouraged our efforts. Seymour Hersh, Tad Szulc and David Hume Kennerly were generous in their professional cooperation. Professor and Mrs. Lien Fu Huang and Professors Yuan li-Wu, Leland B. Yeager, George R. Horton and Jane Nutter offered the benefit of their experience and support. Francine Krasowska transcribed most of the taped interviews. Martha Albershardt helped us organize the final manuscript and end notes.

At Harper & Row we would like to thank Michael Bessie and Edward Burlingame, who encouraged our efforts. Buz Wyeth, our editor, offered graceful guidance and unerring soundness in suggesting style and structure. Debra Orenstein made helpful suggestions as did Ann Adelman.

Therese Hung and Leona Schecter, our literary agent, provided the support and criticism which were essential for sustaining us through the writing. By combining ideas with elegant meals they enhanced our collaboration, lessened the drudgery and stimulated our understanding of the human as well as historical dimensions of the book. Without their criticisms this book would have been finished much sooner.

We appreciate all the criticisms and suggestions, but the final responsibility, of course, remains with us.

The large kingdom declared, ''You have failed us.'' But we have given everything to the large kingdom. There is nothing more we can do. As the ancients have said, while serving a larger state, the small state is treated either as a human or as a hunted deer. As a human when the larger state feels virtuous; as a deer when it does not. What risks must we assume? The fate awaiting us is not ours to choose.

—Extract from a letter written by
Prince Tzu-chia of Cheng
to Prince Hsun of Chao, circa 600 B.C.

From *Selections from History and Classics,*
edited by Lee Hung Chang,
foreign minister in the late Manchu dynasty.

左傳鄭子家與趙宣子書
寡君即位三年召蔡侯而與之事君九月蔡侯入於敝邑以行敝邑以侯宣多
之難寡君是以不得與蔡侯偕十一月克減侯宣多而隨蔡侯以朝於執事十
二年六月歸生佐寡君之嫡夷以請陳侯於楚而朝諸君十四年七月寡君又
朝以蕆陳事十五年五月陳侯自敝邑往朝於君往年正月燭之武往朝於君
八月寡君又往朝以陳蔡之密邇於楚而不敢貳焉則敝邑之故也雖敝邑之
事君何以不免在位之中一朝於襄而再見於君夷與孤之二三臣相及於絳
雖我小國則蔑以過之矣今大國曰爾未逞吾志敝邑有亡無以加焉古人有
言曰畏首畏尾身其餘幾又曰鹿死不擇音小國之事大國也德則其人也不
德則其鹿也鋌而走險急何能擇命之罔極亦知亡矣將悉敝賦以待於倏唯
執事命之文公二年六月壬申朝於齊四年二月壬戌為齊侵蔡亦獲成於楚
居大國之間而從於強令豈其罪也大國若弗圖無所逃命

CHINA

Red River

BURMA

Dien Bien Phu

Hanoi ★

NORTH
VIET NAM

Haiphong

Mekong River

Thanh Hoa

GULF OF
TONKIN

LAOS

Vinh

Truong Son

Vientiane ★

Tchepone

DEMILITARIZED ZONE

Dong Ha
Quang Tri

THAILAND

Lam Son 719 Operation Area
February-April, 1971

Khe Sanh

Hue

Da Nang

MILITARY REGION 1

Que Son
Tam Ky

Mekong River

HO CHI MINH TRAIL

Mountains

Dak To
Kontum

BINH
DINH
PROV.

★ Bangkok

Central
Highlands

Qui Nhon

MILITARY REGION 2

CAMBODIA

SOUTH

Ban Me Thuot

VIET NAM

SOUTH CHINA SEA

Nha Trang

Cam Ranh

Loc Ninh

GULF OF
THAILAND

Phnom Penh ★

An Loc
Tay Ninh

MILITARY REGION 3

★ Saigon

Phu Quoc I.

MILITARY REGION 4

Mekong Delta

Con Son Is.

Indochina
Before the
Cease-Fire

→ NVA attacks in the
1972 Easter Offensive

| 0 | 50 | 100 | 150 | 200 | 250 km |

| 0 | 50 | 100 | 150 mi |

Prologue

THE WHITE HOUSE
WASHINGTON

October 16, 1972

Dear President Thieu:

I have asked Dr. Henry Kissinger to convey to you this personal letter regarding our current negotiations with North Vietnam which now appear to be reaching a final stage.

As you know, throughout the four years of my Administration the United States has stood firmly behind your Government and its people in our support for their valiant struggle to resist aggression and preserve their right to determine their own political future. . . .

As far as I am concerned, the most important provision of this agreement, aside from its military features, is that your Government, its armed forces and its political institutions, will remain intact after the ceasefire has been observed. In the period following the cessation of hostilities you can be completely assured that we will continue to provide your Government with the fullest support, including continued economic aid and whatever military assistance is consistent with the ceasefire provisions of this agreement.

Sincerely,
[s] Richard Nixon
November 14, 1972

. . . But far more important than what we say in the agreement on this issue is what we do in the event the enemy renews its aggression. You have my absolute assurance that if Hanoi fails to abide by the terms of this agreement it is my intention to take swift and severe retaliatory action.

Sincerely,
[s] Richard Nixon
January 5, 1973

. . . As we enter this new round of talks, I hope that our countries will show a united front. . . .

Should you decide, as I trust you will, to go with us, you have my assurance

I

of continued assistance in the post-settlement period and that we will respond
with full force should the settlement be violated by North Vietnam.

Sincerely,
[s] Richard Nixon
January 17, 1973

. . . I must repeat what I have said to you in my previous communications:
The freedom and independence of the Republic of Vietnam remains a paramount objective of American foreign policy. I have been dedicated to this goal
all of my political life, and during the past four years I have risked many grave
domestic and international consequences in its pursuit. It is precisely in order
to safeguard our mutual objectives that I have decided irrevocably on my present course. . . . Let me state these assurances once again in this letter:
    —First, we recognize your Government as the sole legitimate Government
of South Vietnam.
    —Secondly, we do not recognize the right of foreign troops to remain on
South Vietnamese soil.
    —Thirdly, the U.S. will react vigorously to violations of the Agree-
ment. . . .

Sincerely,
[s] Richard Nixon

    This book is a study of the relationship between the top officials of the
United States and South Vietnam during the last eight years of South Vietnam's existence. Because the two presidents, Nixon and Thieu, met face to
face only three times during the period, and Ford and Thieu never met after
Ford became president, the highest levels of contact were through the
American ambassador in Saigon, or special envoys sent on missions to
either capital, especially the visits of Assistant to the President for National
Security Affairs Henry Kissinger and his deputy Alexander Haig. Now it
has been revealed fully for the first time that there was another level of
contact, the exchange of private letters, that were the formal validation of
America's commitments to South Vietnam.
    The letters dated October 16, 1972, November 14, 1972, January 5,
1973, and January 17, 1973, from Richard Nixon to Nguyen Van Thieu
which are excerpted here are four of the twenty-seven letters and messages
that Nixon wrote to Thieu over a period of three years. While these letters
address many issues and concerns, almost all of them repeat the theme of
America's unswerving material, military, and political support for its hard-
pressed Asian ally. Within twenty-four hours of succeeding to the presidency after Nixon's resignation on August 9, 1974, Gerald Ford wrote Thieu
affirming that "the existing commitments this nation has made in the past
are still valid and will be fully honored in my administration." Ford subsequently wrote three more letters in which, while addressing other points, he
reaffirmed this pledge.

Only a few of Thieu's letters to Nixon and Ford are known to exist outside the still classified files of the U.S. government, the Nixon and Ford presidential papers, and the Henry Kissinger Papers. One of these was written by Thieu and sent to President Ford via the American Embassy in Saigon on March 25, 1975—a month before the fall of Saigon. It reads:

Dear Mr. President:

Thank you for your letter of March 22, 1975.

As I am writing to you, the military situation in South Vietnam is very grave and is growing worse by the hour.

The serious disequilibrium in the balance of forces in favor of the North Vietnamese as well as their strategic advantages accumulated over the past two years, have led to the present critical situation, especially in MR [Military Region] I and II, as you already know. Heavy pressures are being exerted on all the rest of our national territory and Saigon is itself threatened.

It has become evident that it would be extremely difficult for us to contain the advance of the communist forces to hold the line in order to push back the invaders without drastic and prompt measures on your part to redress the balance of forces.

Hanoi's intention to use the Paris Agreement for a military takeover of South Vietnam was well known to us at the very time of negotiating the Paris Agreement. You may recall that we signed it, not because we naively believed in the enemy's good will, but because we trusted in America's solemn commitment to safeguard the peace in Vietnam.

Firm pledge was then given to us that the United States would retaliate swiftly and vigorously to any violation of the Agreement by the enemy.

We consider those pledges the most important guarantee of the Paris Agreement. We know that the pledge is most crucial to our survival.

Mr. President:

At this crucial hour when the fate of free South Vietnam is at stake and when peace is severely threatened, I hereby solemnly request that you take the two following necessary actions:

To order a brief but intensive B-52 air strike against the enemy's concentration of forces and logistic bases within South Vietnam, and

To urgently provide us with necessary means to contain and repel the offensive.

Only with these two actions can we stop the enemy *from tearing off* the last remnants of the *Paris Agreement*.

Mr. President,

Once again, I wish to appeal to you, to the credibility of American foreign policy, and especially to the conscience of America.

I am heartened that upon assuming the Presidency, you were prompt to renew to us the assurance of the continuity of American foreign policy and the validity of its existing commitments. I am grateful for your determination to honor these commitments in full in your administration. As you so rightly noted, these assurances are particularly relevant to the Republic of Vietnam.

Generations of South Vietnamese who will be living free from the horror of North Vietnamese domination will be indebted to your prompt actions and to the steadfastness of the great people of America.

> Sincerely,
> [s] Nguyen Van Thieu
> President of the Republic
> of Vietnam

This is the last letter Nguyen Van Thieu sent to an American President. It was never answered.

1

The Turning Point

THE SAIGON MORNING was hot and bright, the air heavy with decay, a combination of exhaust fumes, rotted sugar cane, and traces of jasmine. Nguyen Tien Hung, dressed in his best dark blue suit, walked out of his mother's house on Phan Dinh Phung Street, where he had been staying since his return from America, and stepped into the back seat of an official black Peugeot. It was September 15, 1971, and Hung was on the way to his first meeting with the President of South Vietnam at the Independence Palace.

As his car passed the giant tamarind trees that lined Thong Nhat Boulevard, Hung recalled times when, as a young refugee from North Vietnam, he had had to wait in the hot sun on his small French Mobylette motorbike while movable barbed-wire roadblocks were thrown across the street to halt traffic and make it easier for dignitaries to enter the Palace.

Today, he would not wait. Now a professor of economics at Washington's Howard University, Hung had been writing to Thieu for nearly two years offering his support, his personal assessments of how the war was seen in America, and suggesting new ways for South Vietnam to improve its image there. Thieu had sent back word that he found Hung's impressions a valuable supplement to the official reports he received from the embassy in Washington, and he had asked Hung to come to see him.

When they saw the official car, the Palace guards, carefully chosen for their unusual height, and dressed in crisp white cotton uniforms with gold braid, white gloves, and black berets, opened the massive iron front gate of the Palace. The gate was the last vestige of colonial days when the Palace housed the French High Commissioner for Indochina. The Palace had been rebuilt after being badly damaged during a coup attempt against President Ngo Dinh Diem in November 1962.[1] President Thieu himself, then a colonel commanding the 5th Division, had led the final attack against Diem in 1963.

The guards' American-made M-16 rifles sparkled in the scorching sunlight, which reflected off their pagoda-shaped posts along the Palace wall. There were two helicopters parked on the Palace lawn. On the ramp leading

5

to the entrance the guards snapped to attention and saluted Hung in his car, as if he were an ambassador or a cabinet minister. The bespectacled chief of protocol, dressed in a black suit, greeted him and accompanied him up the curved, heavily carpeted staircase that led to the glass doors of the second-floor reception room.

As they stepped inside, the chill of the air conditioning accented the silence surrounding an opulent display of antique furniture. Ornately carved blackwood chairs, lacquer tables, and chests adorned the anteroom; an inlaid Chinese screen formed a backdrop for a pair of giant elephant tusks on blackwood stands. Crystal vases, filled with orange and red gladiolas, marked the way to President Thieu's office.

In the formal atmosphere of the Palace, Hung felt a sense of awe. Then thirty-five years old, dapper and intense, with brown eyes that sparkled when he spoke, Hung had an air of youthful eagerness and sincerity. However, he was uneasy as he approached Thieu. As a military man, he wondered how President Thieu would respond to Hung the economics professor. Would he be the cold, aloof dictator, as portrayed in the American press; or would he offer nothing more than his own monologue, as was the custom with the late President Ngo Dinh Diem?[2] Even after thirteen years in America there remained in Hung the traditional Confucian respect for the leader—the leader to whom he would be making policy suggestions.

A uniformed guard opened the door to Thieu's office. The chief of protocol stepped inside and introduced Hung to President Thieu as Professor Hung. This pleased him, since scholars traditionally have the highest rank in the Vietnamese social hierarchy of scholar, farmer, artisan, businessman, and soldier (sy, nong, cong, thuong, binh). Thieu stepped forward and shook Hung's hand firmly. "So we finally meet," he said with a broad smile.

Thieu was alone. Hung had expected other aides to attend the meeting. One-on-one he felt more comfortable; he could speak directly, without intermediaries. His first impression of Thieu was one of strength, but also of a deep reserve and an aura of seriousness, befitting a traditional Vietnamese leader. Thieu's eyes had a diamond-hard edge, with an inner luminescence. He looked directly at Hung, searching his face. Hung imagined Thieu trying to assess his character and whether he was working for the CIA or had come for a political favor. Vietnamese educated in the United States were often suspected of having been recruited by the Agency.

Hung answered the inspection by looking straight back into the president's eyes. Thieu's features were very smooth, with no wrinkles or stress signs on his clear skin. Only a few strands of silver graced the sides of his carefully combed black hair. He was dressed in a short-sleeved khaki bush jacket and matching slacks. Now he motioned Hung to one of two brocade-covered armchairs that faced each other on the far side of the room opposite a mahogany desk. Both men sat down to begin a personal relationship that would permanently alter Hung's life.

Hung was born in Thanh Hoa Province in North Vietnam, where his father, a devout Catholic, owned more than three hundred acres of rice fields in the district of Nga Son. The family of nine children lived in the only three-story brick house in the village of Dien Ho. In May 1954, at the time of the French defeat when Hung was only eighteen, he learned that the Viet Minh were about to descend on the village from the nearby hills. As a landowner and a Catholic Hung's father was in jeopardy: Hung warned him that the family had to flee within the hour. On foot, they joined the mass of retreating troops and peasants swarming through sniper fire to the coast twelve miles away. After an all-night march the family was dazed, and Hung, the eldest son present, took charge. At dawn he removed the gold cross from his neck and traded it for rice to feed the family. Then he hired a fisherman in a small sampan to row them out to the open sea in exchange for two gold bars. After hours of bobbing in the swells, they spotted a French freighter and were taken aboard, climbing a rope ladder thrown over the side. Along with nearly a million other refugees, they began their journey south to Saigon, where Hung would live for the next four years as a student before leaving for the United States in 1958 on a Smith-Mundt scholarship to study economics.

He earned his Ph.D. at the University of Virginia, where he studied under Warren Nutter and James Schlesinger, rival stars in the Economics Department before they moved to Washington for careers in government. In America, Hung used his given Catholic name, Gregory. He had not used the name of the famed Pope Gregory I the Great (590–604) since it was bestowed on him by the village priest when he was baptized. After graduation, Hung stayed on to teach economics at North Carolina Wesleyan College. In 1963 he was set to return to Saigon, in line for the post of director of Foreign Exchange in Saigon, but the coup against Diem changed his plans. Instead of returning home, he moved first to Trinity College, and then to Howard University in Washington, D.C., for the academic year 1965–66. In 1966 he joined the International Monetary Fund (IMF), where he worked on economic programs for former French colonies in Africa. While in Washington he married a colleague, Catherine Bamberger, an American woman from Denver, Colorado, and they had three children, a daughter, Christine, and two sons, Daniel and Michael.

In March 1968, Hung was traveling in Gambia on an International Monetary Fund mission when he turned on his short-wave radio and heard over the Voice of America that Lyndon Johnson would not seek reelection. He sensed a major change in American policy toward South Vietnam. When he got back from the trip, he decided to leave the IMF and return to academic life where he could be politically active on behalf of his country—as an international civil servant he was barred from politics. In the summer of 1969, Hung became an associate professor of economics at Howard University, and he wrote his first letter to President Thieu. He described student opposition to the war and the hostility of the American media to Thieu and his generals, accused of corruption. The letter was delivered for Hung by

General Tran Van Don, a family friend and a figure in the National Assembly whom Thieu called on to serve as an unofficial roving ambassador.

Thieu was impressed with Hung's memorandum and asked him to continue reporting and advising him. Hung had frequent meetings with Warren Nutter, who had now become Assistant Secretary for International Security Affairs in the Defense Department and Defense Secretary Melvin Laird's key man on South Vietnam's economic problems. Hung sent Thieu a series of memoranda recommending austerity measures to stabilize Saigon's war-inflated economy. Hung knew from his contacts that the momentum for American disengagement was accelerating. He explained to Thieu the strong pressure on Nixon from draft-age students and anti-war activists to end the war. The shooting to death by National Guardsmen of four students and the wounding of nine others at Kent State University in Ohio on May 4, 1970, during a protest against Nixon's decision to invade Cambodia the previous month, became a symbol of the martyrdom of American youth in the anti-war cause. To the protestors it did not matter that militarily the "incursion" was a success, pushing the North Vietnamese timetable for the war against the South back by two years.[3] Such action only fanned new and violent opposition to the war, as did the publication of the Pentagon Papers, leaked to *The New York Times* and other newspapers in June 1971 by anti-war defense analysts for the government.

Then, on July 15, 1971, President Nixon surprised the world by announcing the secret trip to the People's Republic of China by Henry Kissinger, his Assistant for National Security Affairs, which would pave the way for a visit to China by President Nixon himself seven months later, in February 1972. The years of public Chinese denunciations of America as a "paper tiger" and "the leader of world imperialism" were about to end. America was to supplant its fear of Soviet-supported Chinese aggression in Southeast Asia with a new three-pronged policy of detente with the Soviet Union, exploitation of Sino-Soviet rivalries, and normalization of American-Chinese relations.[4] Nixon's design, to be executed by Kissinger, was to engage China in a new constructive relationship and withdraw from the Vietnam War. He would enlist the help of the Soviet Union and China to convince North Vietnam of the sincerity of American proposals to end the war.

This daring reversal by Nixon of twenty-two years of Sino-American enmity, a major turning point in American policy, shocked and disconcerted America's allies who had not been consulted. (There were also repercussions within the conservative wing of the Republican Party, whose loyalty was to the Republic of China on Taiwan.)

The news shook Thieu deeply. He was anxious to know how Nixon's new strategy would affect Vietnam. Above all, Thieu had to determine whether or not Nixon had lost heart and abandoned his anti-communism. Thieu had kept a file of Nixon's speeches, and he got it out and looked up the one he remembered.[5] The words stuck in his memory. The Vietnam War, Nixon had stated in 1965, is a confrontation—not fundamentally between Vietnam and the Vietcong or between the United States and the Vietcong—but between the United States and Communist China.

If the United States gives up on Vietnam, Asia will give up on the United States and the Pacific will become a Red Sea. These are the stakes.

Do we stop Chinese Communist aggression in Vietnam now or wait until the odds and the risks are much greater?"[6]

Until Nixon's surprise announcement, the American commitment in South Vietnam had been equated with the containment of Communist China in Indochina and Southeast Asia. This had been American policy since Eisenhower had ended the Korean War in 1953 and aided the French against Ho Chi Minh in 1954. It was known as the Domino Theory, as outlined by Eisenhower: If one nation in Asia fell, the others would tumble like a row of dominos. Now Thieu was concerned that America's broader strategic interests with the Soviet Union and China would be served at the expense of South Vietnam. Thieu realized that the Americans would no longer look upon the Chinese as their primary adversary in Asia, that their fear of Chinese expansionism, which was at the root of U.S. intervention on the side of South Vietnam against the Communist North, would evaporate. No longer would the United States base its Asian policy on the fear that the Chinese would foment revolutions and intervene in regional wars in Asia on the Communist side. The United States would want to withdraw from Vietnam, leaving the South Vietnamese to fight the North alone. If this happened, the Republic of Vietnam could survive only if the Soviet Union and China stopped supporting Hanoi.

Thieu's unease at the new U.S. policy was increased by Kissinger's behavior during his recent visit to Saigon in July (on his way to China), ostensibly part of a familiarization trip in Asia, his first as Assistant to the President for National Security Affairs. Arriving in the midst of the preparations and positioning for the Vietnamese presidential election in the fall, Kissinger followed the official U.S. position of neutrality and not openly supporting any candidate. To implement this position, he met with Thieu's rivals and opposition leaders among the Buddhists and labor unions. For Thieu, Kissinger's behavior meant that American support for him had been withdrawn; he recalled the violent events of 1963 when, following American Ambassador Henry Cabot Lodge's meetings with Buddhist monks who opposed President Ngo Dinh Diem, Diem was overthrown and murdered in a coup. Thieu saw Kissinger's intervention in the Saigon political process as an effort to undercut his authority, and he put his security troops at the Independence Palace on alert.[7]

Now, after the announcement of the China trip, Thieu's suspicions increased. Had Kissinger made a secret deal with Zhou Enlai? Had he stopped off in Hanoi prior to visiting Beijing? What role would South Vietnam play in America's new global balance of power strategy after Washington resumed normal diplomatic relations with Beijing? All these questions were on his mind.[8] Although they met only briefly, the foundation for distrust between Kissinger and Thieu was solidly in place. Thieu was to tell Hung and his close associates, "America has been looking for a better mistress and now Nixon has discovered China. He does not want to have the old mistress hanging around. Vietnam has become old and ugly."[9]

A few days after Nixon's announcement of Kissinger's secret trip to China in July, Thieu received a letter from Hung urging him to begin his own peace initiative toward North Vietnam before Nixon's scheduled visit to China, and warning that the Republic of Vietnam must avoid being swept away by America's drastic change in policy. It was for this reason that Thieu had invited Hung to Saigon.

Facing each other for the first time in Thieu's office, Thieu asked Hung in his husky Central Vietnamese accent: "You are a professor in America. What are they up to?"

"Well, Mr. President, I think they are giving up on us," replied Hung.

Thieu stared hard at Hung, jolted by his openness.

"The Americans assess problems with a balance sheet listing assets and liabilities and they come to a bottom line on which they determine their policy," said Hung, using the English words "balance sheet."

Thieu seemed puzzled. Hung took out his notebook and drew up a balance sheet for Thieu, listing in two columns examples of Vietnam's assets and liabilities for American foreign and domestic policy. Up to now Vietnam had been considered an asset, Hung explained; now it had become a liability. With a sweeping gesture he shifted Vietnam from the assets column to the liabilities column. Thieu smiled and nodded. "Nixon is a strong supporter of yours and of South Vietnam, but he is under heavy pressure," Hung explained. "I'm not certain how long President Nixon can keep on resisting that pressure. Vietnam has become a personal burden to him. The public pressure to end the war is so strong that South Vietnam has to take its own initiatives to move toward peace. Only by taking such initiatives will we not appear recalcitrant and will we gather American public support."

Hung was keenly aware of Thieu's stated policy of Four No's to North Vietnam: No recognition of the enemy, no neutralization of South Vietnam, no coalition government, and no surrender of territory to the enemy. To suggest that President Thieu propose the resumption of trade between North and South Vietnam as a first step leading to peaceful reunification was a major policy change. He had raised the idea in his letters to Thieu. Now Hung was determined to elaborate on how it would work, based on the German formula of "two zones in one economic entity."

"Politically," Hung told Thieu, "there will be two parts of Vietnam; but economically we will move toward one market." Hung was careful not to speak of one country, but only of a joint market for all of Vietnam. Thieu had to take the diplomatic offensive himself or become overwhelmed by great power politics. Hung wanted to convince Thieu that he must position himself as flexible and imaginative, seriously willing to negotiate with the North on the basis of mutual self-interest. Hung argued that even if the North Vietnamese rejected the trade initiative, it would reverse Thieu's image of being rigid and uncompromising.

Thieu began to make notes on 4 by 4 squares of thin notepaper taken from a small box on the table between their two chairs. Encouraged, Hung suggested to the president that Saigon take the first step by inviting North Vietnam to jointly rebuild the North–South railroad for the resumption of trade and to engage in the development of the Mekong River projects. This plan, which was supported by the United Nations, would cost an estimated $2 billion but would supply electric power to all the countries of Indochina including North Vietnam.

Hung was surprised at how easy it was to talk to Thieu. In the American press, Thieu was portrayed as stern and corrupt. Alone with Hung, he did not act superior. Hung was impressed by the president's self-confidence and self-possession, his qualities of command bearing.

However, Hung also perceived a guarded, suspicious character in Thieu. Despite his seeming calm, he often blinked his eyes while talking, indicating to Hung an inner turbulence and anxiety. The president did not volunteer his own views on Hung's proposal other than to say, "Your ideas are promising," and to ask him to incorporate them in a speech to be used during the election campaign. Thieu asked Hung to check out the idea of trading with North Vietnam with American officials when he returned to Washington. The trade initiative should be a unilateral gesture not dependent on the Americans, thought Hung, but he readily agreed to Thieu's suggestion. Thieu said he would be in touch with him soon.

The meeting was over. Hung could see the concern in Thieu's mood over the threats to South Vietnam that they had discussed. In the past Thieu had always looked upon trade with the North as the bridge to a coalition government; he knew that every coalition with Communists meant the systematic elimination of the non-Communist parties. But now Thieu needed a new strategy to deal with his allies. Hung watched Thieu withdraw into himself and cut off the communication that had flowed between them. "Such is the weight of leadership," he thought. Yet he left the Palace elated. He would be working directly for the president. He knew that Thieu needed help in America; it was a measure of his desperation that he would grasp at the straw of trade and turn to an obscure professor like himself to plead his case.[10]

Hung's visit came in the midst of Thieu's heavy-handed campaign for a second term. In spite of the strong American objections to a single candidate, Thieu did not back down from his plan to run unopposed in the 1971 election. His aides maneuvered the pro-government National Assembly to pass a law requiring each presidential candidate to obtain the signatures of thirty-one province chiefs before he could run. Vice President Nguyen Cao

Ky obtained the necessary number of signatures, but was late in filing. He was upheld by the Supreme Court but decided not to run, as did General Duong Van Minh, known as Big Minh, who did not obtain the required number of signatures. The Americans were deeply concerned that there be an opposition candidate to oppose Thieu and offered General Minh the funds to run his campaign. President Thieu had proof that Big Minh transferred funds to Paris from his account with the Bank of Tokyo in Saigon. When it became apparent to Big Minh that he could not beat Thieu, he kept the money and did not run.[11]

Thieu claimed he would have to change the election law to allow more candidates to run once the deadline had passed. He argued with Ambassador Ellsworth Bunker that it would take three months to change the law, then three more months of campaigning, which would undermine law and order during wartime. Thieu decided to face American wrath rather than give way to a candidate he felt would lead South Vietnam to a coalition government and a Communist takeover.[12]

Thieu and those close to him did not really believe in the usefulness of elections in a backward, war-ravaged country. They maintained that the country should be at peace first, otherwise the election process was subject to manipulation by the Communists. They looked on power in terms of a Mandate from Heaven, the Confucian sign that the leader should rule and maintain his power, not unlike the Calvinist belief in God's grace and predestination. Any means for holding onto the Mandate of Heaven are considered fair. For the Vietnamese, the concept of an American election was alien and difficult to comprehend. "Often we went along with the Americans to please them," explained one cabinet minister.[13]

For Hung, Thieu's actions were understandable. Thieu had told him that the generals did not want an election after they took power in 1965, but the Americans had insisted. One day Marshal Nguyen Cao Ky, then prime minister, was visiting the delta and a journalist asked him "When are you going to move toward a civilian government?" Ky replied: "In two years. We will continue a military government for two years." That frightened the Americans, recalled Thieu; they thought it was too long to wait. Two weeks later, Thieu said, there were demonstrations by Buddhists and students demanding a civilian government. "Any time the American ambassador came to see me and asked me to do something and I refused, you could count two weeks before the demonstrations erupted," said Thieu.[14]

Hung wrote the speech setting forth the proposal for trade between North and South, and Thieu gave it in Saigon on October 1, 1971, two days before the election. It was widely reported in the Saigon press, where it was viewed as a long-overdue and welcome initiative by Thieu, but one that had probably come too late. The idea received scant attention from the American news media. Back in Washington, Hung lobbied for the idea and was introduced to Philip Habib, then Assistant Secretary of State for East Asian and Pacific Affairs. Habib told him: "It is interesting, but it is too late." At the time Hung did not understand what Habib meant. Later, when he learned about Kissinger's secret negotiations with Hanoi, he realized that the time had passed when there could be any direct meaningful exchanges between Thieu and the North Vietnamese.

In an effort to placate Nixon and improve his image in America, badly tarnished by the lack of opposition candidates, Thieu announced that if peace were achieved he would return to civilian life.[15] Running unopposed, Thieu received 94 percent of the votes from a turnout of 87 percent of the eligible voters, according to a government announcement, but there were questions raised over the numbers claimed.[16]

Thieu thought he had renewed the Mandate of Heaven for four years. He did not realize the high price he would pay in the loss of American congressional and media support because of the way he thwarted all opposition.

In December, Thieu invited Hung to Saigon again. An officer from the Palace came aboard his plane, saluted, and cleared him through Customs. On this second trip Hung had more time to rediscover the city. After thirteen years in America everything in Saigon seemed smaller because it was now measured against American highways and skyscrapers. The city, with its broad boulevards and grand French colonial public buildings, seemed to have shrunk. Only the war loomed large. When he had seen Saigon for the first time in 1954, as a refugee from North Vietnam, the city had possessed for him vitality, grace, and the promise of opportunity. The yellow-and-ochre stucco residences with terracotta roof tiles marked the style of Cochin China, the traditional French name for the southern part of Vietnam. Saigon was the capital of the rich South, which drew its easy lifestyle from the largesse of the waters of the Mekong River, the *Cuu Long Giang,* river of the Nine Dragons. In Vietnamese mythology, the dragon is a benign, life-giving force. As the Mekong ends, 1,100 miles from its source in the Tibetan plateau beyond the Himalayas, it divides to form the many mouths of the Mekong Delta, curving in shapes that the Vietnamese conjure to be the outlines of dragons. Its abundant waters provide as many as three crops of rice in the richest parts of the delta. There was always enough food to eat and some left over to sell to the poor North.

Before Hung left for America in 1958, only a few places such as the U.S. Information Service Library and the French doctors' offices were air-conditioned. Now, most offices and even his mother's apartment had air conditioning. Refrigerators, once placed in the living room as a piece of status-symbol furniture, were now common appliances found in the kitchen.

Hung was convinced that an essential part of the roots of the war stemmed from the economics of North and South Vietnam. From his childhood in North Vietnam, Hung had seen the pressures created by the need for food and the lack of it north of the 17th parallel.

At a luncheon meeting in the Palace on the day after Christmas, Hung told Thieu he was convinced that one of the major reasons Hanoi shifted from a relatively low level of warfare to its all-out effort to conquer the

South was that the North had been cut off from the South's rice after 1954. He reminded Thieu that shortly after the partition, Hanoi tried, but failed in getting President Diem to enter into a rice trade deal with them, and he told him a story about what happened in his own district of Nga Son in Thanh Hoa Province in the North when he was a child.

In 1945, because of the disruption of internal trade during World War II, the traditional flow of rice from the South to the North was cut off. An estimated 1.5 to 2 million people, 12 percent of North Vietnam's population at the time, died from starvation or its effects, most of them from Thanh Hoa and the surrounding poverty-stricken provinces, including Nghe An Province, the birthplace of Ho Chi Minh and the revolution.[17] Hung was nine years old that year, and every Sunday his father ordered him to stand at the gate of their house to regulate the flow of hungry peasants coming into the yard for a bowl of rice soup in the afternoon after prayers in the church. He was surprised that he, a skinny, small youth, succeeded in keeping order; but the starving peasants, foraging for food, obeyed his orders to stand in line. The "soup" consisted of about ten bowls of dry rice cooked with lots of water in a giant clay jar. Each person, regardless of age, was given one bowl of rice soup so he could keep on moving to the next village in search of another Good Samaritan. Some of them were so weak they did not make it to the next village.

One evening after feeding the peasants, Hung and his family sat down for their own dinner of boiled chicken and rice. Hung's younger brother threw a bone on the ground so their dog would have something to eat. Suddenly, a skinny old man who had been standing outside the fence watching jumped over the fence and rushed into the kitchen. He grabbed the bone out of the dog's mouth and fled into the night.

Another day, after Hung's father woke the children up for the daily mass at the parish, he had to go out to the gate ahead of them to move the dead bodies piled up during the night so that they could walk through the door on the way to church. At church, his father used to tell them they had to pray for a good harvest, no more dikes breaking, and no more floods. Above all, they were to pray for the rice from the South to quickly return to the North.

On this particular day, however, a few young revolutionaries outside the church would have nothing to do with the praying. Instead, armed with a homemade loudspeaker, the biggest and toughest-looking fellow among them waited until the priest was deep in silent prayer, then shouted into the loudspeaker:

> Stand up! Stand up!
> Follow Uncle Ho
> Tenants will have land
> Poor men will be rich
> Rice will be plenty
> Down with the landlords!

The priest ordered the children inside the church to sing louder to drown the sounds from outside. At the end of the mass all the young revolutionaries quickly disappeared into the nearby mountains, but their message remained behind in the village. Hung's father grew more and more concerned with the revolution; he stayed at the church longer and longer to pray after mass as the frequency of the revolutionaries' appeals increased.

When the August 1945 revolution came and the peasants responded fully to Ho's promise of more rice, it seemed to Hung that it was this promise that had brought the Vietnamese Communists to power. And it was thanks to those bowls of rice soup that his father's head was saved. The peasants, remembering his help, did not bring him to the People's Court set up to try landlords. Because of his great desire to get rid of the French, Hung's father responded to the Viet Minh appeals during the first year and allowed his children to follow "Uncle Ho" and promote the revolution by singing revolutionary songs at village meetings. Hung told Thieu he could still remember singing "Who loves Uncle Ho Chi Minh more than we children?" His mother donated her gold jewelry and became chairwoman of the district's Gold Week committee to collect jewelry for Ho Chi Minh, to buy weapons to fight the French, and, it turned out, to bribe the Chinese Nationalist general who controlled the northern part of North Vietnam in the fall of 1945.[18]

Thieu showed great interest in Hung's story and told him that he too had witnessed the great famine of 1945. But Thieu's village, which was in Phan Rang Province in Central Vietnam, 218 miles from Saigon, had been lucky because it was close to the sea coast and the villagers could rely on fish to eat.

"What made you think that Hanoi might respond to our proposal for a resumption of trade?" Thieu asked.

"Because they made several attempts to negotiate for rice after the partition in 1954. Back in the summer of 1955 I was one of a group of students who marched through the streets of Saigon shouting 'Down with trade with the North!' We attacked the Majestic Hotel where the North Vietnamese delegation was staying and the head of the delegation, General Van Tien Dung, narrowly escaped." When President Diem turned them down, they got angry and established the National Liberation Front in 1960. (He swore that he would return to Saigon with tanks, and he did. In April 1975, Dung was Chief of Staff of the Vietnam People's Army and led the attack on Saigon.)

After their discussion, Thieu instructed the Vietnamese delegation at the formal Paris Peace Talks to include the possibility of resumption of trade between the two Vietnams in its latest proposal to Hanoi.

At this time—early January 1972—the secret talks between Kissinger and the North Vietnamese in Paris, while known to Thieu, had not been made public. As far as the world knew, there was only a formal meeting between North Vietnam, South Vietnam, the Provisional Revolutionary

Government of the Viet Cong, and the Americans once a week at the French Foreign Ministry's International Conference Center on Avenue Kléber in Paris—a propaganda forum that accomplished nothing. The North Vietnamese never replied to Thieu's proposal to resume trade.

In fact, Kissinger had been meeting secretly with Le Duc Tho since September 1969. Even though Thieu had agreed to the talks, he grew very concerned because Kissinger supplied him with only sketchy reports of the discussions through briefings from Ambassador Bunker. Thieu had sent Kissinger a series of memoranda outlining the South Vietnamese insistence on the mutual withdrawal of troops as a condition for a cease-fire, but Kissinger's response was vague. The vagueness of his responses served to confirm Thieu's suspicions that Kissinger would make agreements with the North Vietnamese without consulting him.

His worst fears had been confirmed only a few days after Thieu and Hung's first meeting the previous September. General Alexander Haig, Kissinger's deputy, came to Saigon at President Nixon's direction to advise Thieu of a new secret American negotiating position to be presented to the North Vietnamese in Paris on November 20. (Actually the proposal was given to the North Vietnamese earlier and Thieu was not advised.[19]) After months of frustration at the North Vietnamese insistence on linking the political and military aspects of the talks, the United States had given in.[20] Kissinger proposed, and Nixon approved, a provision for a new presidential election in South Vietnam within six months of signing the final peace agreement. The election would be run by an electoral commission representing all the political forces, including the Communists, under international supervision. One month before the election, President Thieu would resign and his function would be assumed by the president of the Senate.

Although he had failed to create any opposition candidates to face Thieu, Kissinger had now fashioned a peace plan to force his resignation. It would be a less obvious way than insisting directly on Thieu stepping down. Thieu considered the American proposal an outrage, but he felt compelled to accept it at the time because he was trapped by Kissinger. If he behaved too stubbornly before the election, Kissinger could still upset his plans with a coup or worse. The negotiations between Kissinger and Le Duc Tho were still secret; he would not be publicly embarrassed if he went along and bought time until he had won the election mandate. Besides, he doubted that the North Vietnamese would agree to a presidential election. The Communist one-party system did not provide for presidential elections. The Politboro appointed the leaders. Nobody would publicly know of the indignity that had been foisted on him by Kissinger. Thieu felt he could deal with the American proposal later. He believed that the American plan was only a negotiating position and that the North Vietnamese would reject it.[21] Although he was bitter at Kissinger for this move, which would undercut his authority, Thieu held his tongue with Haig and sought his own leverage against the North Vietnamese. It would not do to argue in public with his major ally. He still did not think he was being abandoned by Nixon, despite his growing suspicions of Kissinger.[22] He could not allow himself the luxury of an open rift with the Americans.

Thieu often likened his problems with the United States to the relationship between husband and wife. "Can't there perhaps be quarrels between husbands and wives? And do they become enemies for that? Not only that, quarrels between a husband and wife should take place in the bedroom and after the door has been locked. Children should never see their parents in a hair-pulling match. It's the same for friends. And it's in my interest, in the interest of the United States, to avoid any public row that serves the Communists."[23]

Kissinger's meetings with Le Duc Tho were reported in brief summaries to Bunker, who then briefed Thieu. Kissinger avoided regular State Department channels to prevent leaks, but also to prevent the professionals from criticizing his actions. He was able, with Nixon's approval, to control the secret talks in a tight circle, making promises and concessions on his own without the constraints of the bureaucracy. The South Vietnamese delegation in Paris was not briefed on Kissinger's meetings with Le Duc Tho until after President Nixon announced publicly in January 1972 that the secret talks had been held. Even then, the South Vietnamese complained that the briefings from Kissinger were sketchy and frustrating.

The South Vietnamese did not know that in the secret talks between Kissinger and Le Duc Tho, on August 16, 1971 the United States had already promised to withdraw American troops within nine months of an agreement. If agreement were reached by the end of November 1971, the Americans would be out by August 1, 1972. Thieu was unaware of the full details of Kissinger's proposal, but he had grown wary of Kissinger.

Ever since General Haig presented him with the secret plan which called for his resignation, Thieu realized that the peace negotiations with North Vietnam, carried on secretly by Henry Kissinger in Paris, showed a disturbing weakening of the American position. Kissinger was not keeping him informed in any detail of the substance of the talks and this made him very uneasy.

Now, with Nixon's trip to China approaching, Thieu grew even more anxious. He suspected that Kissinger's concessions to the North Vietnamese were linked to Nixon's hopes for success in Beijing. Thieu had asked Hung how much Nixon relied on Kissinger, and Hung had told him that ever since the secret trip to China, Kissinger was "riding high." "Let me know if you hear of anything he is planning," Thieu replied. Thieu wrote privately to Nixon restating his concerns about a cease-fire, and also expressed his reservations to Ambassador Bunker. Bunker reassured him there would be no change in American policy, but Thieu wanted to hear this directly from Nixon. He began to suspect that Kissinger was reporting to Nixon only after he had made concessions to the North Vietnamese, and was not conferring with Thieu or Nixon beforehand. He also feared that Nixon was not directly involved in the details of Vietnam policy.

Thieu was anxious to reach Nixon directly. He hoped that his personal letter to him, drafted by his private secretary Hoang Duc Nha, would open a channel that could bypass Kissinger, or at least keep Nixon directly advised of Thieu's concerns. The letters were a direct link to Nixon. He knew that even if Kissinger read them, they would reach Nixon, who would read them and reply to him. There would be no filtering through Ambassador Bunker or Kissinger. Thieu believed Kissinger must remain in his role as a presidential retainer, rather than becoming the dominating force in the relationship between Saigon and Washington. Kissinger could provide ideas and information, but Thieu would fight to prevent the President's adviser from separating him from Nixon, who Thieu believed would not betray Vietnam.

On January 2, 1972, Thieu received his first personal letter from President Nixon. He considered the arrival of the letter from Nixon at the beginning of the year in the Western calendar auspicious.

Courtly, elegant Ellsworth Bunker came to deliver it himself, and Thieu was pleased to receive him. In the Confucian manner, Thieu respected Bunker because of his age (Bunker was then seventy-seven) and experience. Wise, courteous, Bunker never let personal emotions intrude on his instructions from Washington. Thieu knew he was a man of integrity. Although he realized Bunker had no power and "was only a messenger," he held him in high personal regard.

After the exchange of New Year's greetings, Ambassador Bunker settled his six foot, four inch frame in an oversized armchair in Thieu's office and said: "As you know, Mr. President, President Nixon will soon be visiting China. Before his trip, he wants to share with you some of his thoughts. He also wants me to assure you that his trip to China will be beneficial to Vietnam as well as the rest of Asia. I have just received a letter from President Nixon for you."

Bunker then handed Thieu the original letter, which had arrived in the diplomatic pouch from Washington. Thieu thanked him and cut open the envelope with a black lacquer–handled letter opener. He read the letter in a few minutes. It was the first time Thieu had seen Nixon's signature on the heavy rag bond presidential stationery with "The White House" engraved at the top. Bunker again assured Thieu of President Nixon's good intentions. After Bunker left, Thieu reread the letter carefully.

Dear Mr. President:

As I prepare for my forthcoming trip to Peking to meet and talk with the leaders of the People's Republic of China, I would like to share with you some thoughts concerning the conversations I expect to have there.

The main purpose of these conversations will be to clarify the positions of our Government and of the Chinese Government on the issues that separate us, and to establish a means for continuing communications. The differences between us are deep and complex and they will not yield to easy solutions. I hope, however, that the conversations in Peking will be a first major step toward easing the long standing tensions between the People's Republic of China and the United States, a development which would bring lasting benefits for all of Asia and for all of the world.

The talks will focus on bilateral questions between the Chinese and ourselves, of which there are many. Given our differences, the question of formal diplomatic relations will not arise. You may be absolutely certain that I will make no agreements in Peking at the expense of other countries or on matters which concern other countries. You should also know that the treaty commitments which the United States has established with other countries will not be affected by my visit to Peking.

Should the question of the Vietnam war arise in Peking, I want to assure you that I will set forth clearly and forcefully the position of the United States and the Republic of Vietnam that the war in Vietnam must be ended through direct negotiations with Hanoi, or failing that, by the growing ability of the Republic of Vietnam to defend itself against Hanoi's aggression.

I want the Chinese leaders to understand clearly that our two governments stand firmly together on this vital issue.

With respect to my visit to Moscow in May 1972, I wish to make it clear that the United States has no intention of dealing over the heads of its friends and allies in any manner where their security interests might be involved. For example, there have been no, and there will be no, bilateral United States–Soviet negotiations on mutual withdrawal of forces from Europe. I hope, however, that some concrete progress might be made, either before or during my Moscow visit, in such bilateral areas as arms control and economic relations.

Please accept my best wishes for the continued success of your economic and military programs as you embark on your second term in office. You can continue to rely on the assistance of the United States in your efforts to bring peace to Vietnam and to build a new prosperity for the Vietnamese people.

Sincerely,
[s] Richard Nixon

At first, Thieu liked the tone of the letter. The last paragraph, promising continued U.S. support for his second term, was particularly reassuring after all the bad feeling generated over American resistance to his running unopposed. Nixon had not referred to the tensions over the new proposal to Hanoi offering Thieu's resignation once a settlement was reached. Rather, the presidential letter placed a heavy emphasis on "conversations" between the United States and China and easing tensions. There was no talk of substance. Nixon had stated that there would be no question of formal diplomatic relations and "no agreements in Peking at the expense of other countries or on matters which concern other countries."

Thieu recalled his first meeting with Nixon in 1967. In those days Nixon was a lawyer representing Pepsi-Cola, traveling through Asia on a fact-finding trip in preparation for the 1968 presidential campaign. He asked to see Thieu, who was then chairman of the Military Council. They met in Thieu's office in the Gia Long Palace, where Thieu told Nixon of his dream to unify the nation to fight communism and become self-sufficient and self-reliant. At that time Nixon had not spoken of the need for America to reconcile its differences with Communist China. He had stressed his anti-Communist beliefs and reminded Thieu how he had supported the French in their struggle against the North Vietnamese and even advocated the U.S. bombing of Dien Bien Phu when he was Vice President under Eisenhower in 1954.[24] They had hit it off well and Thieu was impressed by Nixon's grasp of the issues in Asia and his sophistication with foreign policy in general. Thieu saw Nixon as a man of honor, and told his closest advisers: "If he says he is helping somebody, he will deliver. He will do his best to deliver."[25]

At the same time as he pondered what Nixon meant by bilateral issues, Thieu realized that Vietnam was the most basic of bilateral issues between China and the United States. American policy, based on the premise of containing Chinese expansion into Southeast Asia, was changing. Now the Americans were courting the Chinese, and all the signs pointed to an American shift away from South Vietnam, belying Nixon's promises and reassuring words. Thieu speculated that in the eyes of American foreign policy makers, South Vietnam had metamorphosed from being an asset to a liability.

Nixon's trip to China was an unexpected blow, perhaps the danger Thieu would be forced to face in the year of the Rat, his zodiac sign; the astrologers had warned him to be careful in the year of his own sign. Still, Thieu had a letter from Nixon promising to "stand firmly together" on the question of settling the Vietnam War and assuring him that the United States would not deal "over the heads of its friends and allies in any manner where their security interests might be involved." Thieu showed Nixon's letter to his cousin and private secretary Hoang Duc Nha and they reviewed the bidding. Thieu was beginning his second term, his second Mandate From Heaven.[26] Thieu's relationship with Nixon as President was entering its fifth year and in 1972 Nixon would run for a second term. The China trip was a major part of Nixon's bid for reelection and Thieu knew an American presidential election meant vigorous efforts to end the war. To Thieu and those close to him, Nixon's week-long journey to Beijing was to become the week that changed Vietnam.[27]

2

Nixon and Thieu: A Political Debt

NGUYEN VAN THIEU believed that Richard Nixon owed him a political debt as a result of his refusal to support President Lyndon Johnson's peace initiative just before the U.S. 1968 election. Although he never said so publicly, Thieu was certain that his refusal to take part in the peace talks with the North Vietnamese and the Viet Cong when President Johnson halted the bombing of North Vietnam on October 31, 1968, just five days before the election, played a decisive role in Nixon's victory over Hubert Humphrey.[1] When Hung became a special assistant to Thieu in 1973 and moved to Saigon, Thieu described these feelings to him. They spent long hours over meals together analyzing American motives and behavior. Hung began to understand Thieu's perspective and how, despite his dependency on the United States, he fought the American demands on him.

Thieu believed that a Humphrey victory would mean a unilateral halt in the bombing of North Vietnam and a softening of the American position on the Viet Cong, the National Liberation Front (NLF). "A Humphrey victory would mean a coalition government in six months," Thieu explained; "with Nixon at least there was a chance."[2]

Thieu had a very distinct impression of Hubert Humphrey, based on their meeting in 1967 when Vice President Humphrey attended Thieu's inauguration as president. After the ceremonies Humphrey met with Thieu in the Independence Palace, accompanied by his assistant Ted Van Dyk and Ambassador Ellsworth Bunker. Humphrey told Thieu that he was concerned by the Americanization of South Vietnam's military and its economy. "You need to know the political picture in America: time is running out and a transition is needed to greater Vietnamese self-help," said Humphrey. Thieu replied: "Yes, we understand, but we also understand it will be necessary for you to remain here at the present levels." Humphrey then repeated his concerns and told Thieu: "Several years more of the same aid levels, militarily and economically, are not in the cards." Thieu listened carefully as the ash from his Gauloise dropped onto the heavy carpet, but he made no further reply and the meeting ended.

Outside on the Palace steps, Humphrey asked Bunker: "Was I too tough on him?"

"No," replied Bunker, "he needed to hear that."

At that moment a mortar round, fired by the Viet Cong at the Palace, exploded on the lawn. Humphrey and Bunker ducked into their waiting limousine and the motorcade rushed back to the embassy. Thieu and Humphrey had become enemies.[3]

Six months later, in May 1968, Cyrus Vance, for the United States, and Ha Van Lau, representing Hanoi, had held a "procedural meeting" to work out details for peace negotiations in Paris. Bunker spent long hours persuading Thieu to join in the talks with North Vietnam and their surrogates, the National Liberation Front, in the South. Thieu agreed to talk with the North Vietnamese, but not with the NLF. To negotiate with the NLF, he told Bunker, would be to give the NLF a status equal to the Saigon government, a status it did not merit. The Viet Cong were a creation of Hanoi. If they took part in the negotiations as a separate entity, it would be the first step toward a coalition government, and the end of democracy in South Vietnam. Thieu would not accept a coalition or any formula that hinted of one. He thought the Americans wrong when they suggested to him in the mid-sixties that he should talk to Hanoi. "In 1966 Ambassador Cabot Lodge came and put his arm around me and said: 'Ho Chi Minh is not that bad. Maybe he will be another Tito.' The Americans wanted us to form a coalition government with the Communists. They saw the solution in Laos applying to Vietnam, but it was not the same." Thieu thought the Americans were naive. In 1967, on one of his visits to Saigon, Defense Secretary Robert McNamara told Thieu: "We (the U.S.) need an election in order to negotiate with North Vietnam." Bunker knew the history of the North Vietnamese Communists, but he continued to press Thieu. "Public pressure in the United States has forced the President's hand. There must be a peace negotiation to show the U.S. Congress and the American public that we— both Washington and Saigon—want peace," he told Thieu.[4]

In 1968 when Bunker approached Thieu on the bombing halt, Thieu never said no, but always gave a conditional yes. In a television talk to the South Vietnamese people, he repeated: Saigon would agree to a U.S. bombing halt if Hanoi would give assurances that this would lead to productive negotiations. When Bunker pressed Thieu to sign a joint communiqué with Johnson to proclaim the bombing halt, Thieu became elusive. He sent word back to Johnson through Bunker that although he agreed in principle, he wanted firm assurance that Hanoi would join in deescalating the war. Second, he wanted a pledge from Hanoi to negotiate directly with the Saigon government. Finally, he wanted Hanoi to agree that the Liberation Front would not attend the conference as a separate delegation.[5]

Thieu worried that Washington had sprung Hanoi's trap to force Saigon to negotiate directly with the Viet Cong as an equal partner. Keeping the NLF out of the talks as an equal partner was an essential element of Thieu's negotiating strategy. He had carried it with him to Honolulu when he had met there in July 1968 with Johnson. It was his firm belief that he had to negotiate directly with Hanoi, not with a proxy created by Hanoi to rule in the South.

Throughout October 1968 Thieu tried to delay the Johnson bombing-halt decision and an announcement of Paris Talks as long as possible to buy time for Nixon. Thieu said he had to check with his National Security Council and his Congress as part of the democratic process he had learned from the Americans. He knew that Johnson would proceed on his own, so he did not openly object to Johnson's proposal but only to the specifics of its terms. He fed speculation in the press that the halt might eventually take place; he prepared himself and public opinion for the halt.

Thieu's contacts in Washington included his ambassador, Bui Diem, and his friend Anna Chennault, the Chinese-born widow of General Claire Chennault, commander of the Flying Tigers, the American volunteer group that fought against the Japanese during World War II. After her husband's death in 1958, she took his place as an officer of the Flying Tiger Airline and kept close ties with Chiang Kai-shek in Taiwan. She traveled through Southeast Asia for the Flying Tiger Airline and often visited Saigon, where she usually met Thieu.

Thieu was fascinated by Anna Chennault's political and business acumen and her Washington contacts. She played a major role in the China Lobby and raised funds for the Republican campaign. An intelligent, stunning woman, Mrs. Chennault moved freely in Washington's political circles and was proud of her Washington contacts. She first met Nixon in 1954 when he traveled to Taiwan as Vice President. In 1960 she worked for the Nixon presidential campaign against Jack Kennedy.

Anna Chennault visited Saigon frequently in 1968 to advise Thieu on Nixon's candidacy and his views on Vietnam. She told him then that Nixon would be a stronger supporter of Vietnam than Humphrey. "Thieu was under heavy pressure from the Democrats. My job was to hold him back and prevent him from changing his mind," Mrs. Chennault said.

Mrs. Chennault was chairwoman of the Republican Women for Nixon in 1968 and she had arranged for South Vietnam's Ambassador Bui Diem to meet Nixon at his Fifth Avenue apartment in New York in the winter of 1967. Nixon had told Bui Diem to pass on any information to Mrs. Chennault and for her to report directly to John Mitchell, Nixon's campaign manager. At the meeting Nixon promised to make Vietnam his top priority if he won and "to see that Vietnam gets better treatment from me than under the Democrats."[6]

Thieu was leery of Bui Diem whom he considered to be primarily loyal to Vice President Nguyen Cao Ky. Thieu sent his own messengers to Washington to contact Mrs. Chennault, and he relied heavily on his brother Nguyen Van Kieu, who was South Vietnamese Ambassador to Taiwan. Mrs. Chennault often sent messages to Thieu through aides of his brother.

During the closing week of the election, Nixon's campaign manager, John Mitchell, called her "almost every day" to persuade her to keep Thieu from going to Paris for peace talks with the North Vietnamese. They knew their calls were being tapped by the FBI and she joked about it, asking Mitchell playfully: "Who is listening on the other side?" Mitchell did not find it funny and told her, "Call me from a pay phone. Don't talk in your office." Mitchell's message to her was always the same: "Don't let him go."[7]

A few days before the election, Mitchell telephoned her with a message for President Thieu. "Anna, I'm speaking on behalf of Mr. Nixon. It's very important that our Vietnamese friends understand our Republican position and I hope you have made that clear to them."[8]

At the same time that Mrs. Chennault was telling Thieu to "hold on," Henry Kissinger was advising Nixon that Johnson was preparing a bombing halt as an "October Surprise" before the election. In his memoirs, Nixon reveals a memorandum from Haldeman quoting Kissinger's report to Mitchell: "Our source [Kissinger] does not believe that it is practical to oppose a bombing halt but does feel thought should be given to the fact that it may happen—that we may want to anticipate it—and that we certainly will want to be ready at the time it does happen. . . . Our source is *extremely* concerned about the moves Johnson may take and expects that he will take some action before the election."[9] Kissinger was working for Nelson Rockefeller as a foreign policy adviser at the time and offered his services to the Nixon team.[10]

Johnson, who was receiving full reports on Mrs. Chennault's calls to Saigon from the CIA and the FBI, decided not to make her efforts public, but to proceed with his initiative.[11] Thieu continued to dig in his heels, yet always gave an enigmatic hint of hope that he could be persuaded to go along. Bunker reported to Washington that given a little more time, the Saigon government could be brought to the conference table. In a diversionary tactic, Thieu dispatched a three-man advance team to Paris to arrange quarters and communications facilities for eventual South Vietnamese participation in the talks.

After a meeting with New Zealand's Prime Minister Keith Holyoke in late October, Thieu issued a joint communiqué with Holyoke asserting that the NLF "cannot be considered as an independent entity distinct from North Vietnam in international peace negotiations." Thus, Thieu did not completely rule out the Viet Cong's participation, as long as it remained part of the Hanoi delegation and did not have equal status with South Vietnam.[12]

Thieu continued to bob and weave, raising new objections and dropping tactical roadblocks, each consuming from one to three days to resolve. Always he was the model of sweet reasonableness, indicating that if only his objections were overcome and his advisers could be brought on board, all would be well for the bombing halt and the peace talks to start after the election.

Nixon's frustration mounted as he felt Johnson taking the initiative and continuing "to hold the whip hand."[13] On October 26, Nixon decided to issue a statement on the peace talks:

In the last thirty-six hours I have been advised of a flurry of meetings in the White House and elsewhere on Vietnam. I am told that top officials in the administration have been driving very hard for an agreement on a bombing halt, accompanied by a cease-fire, in the immediate future. I have since learned that these reports are true. I am . . . told that this spurt of activity is a cynical, last-minute attempt by President Johnson to salvage the candidacy of Mr. Humphrey. This I do not believe.[14]

As the election neared and pressure increased, Johnson summoned his military commander in Vietnam, General Creighton Abrams, to Washington for consultations. Abrams arrived at Andrews Air Force Base shortly after midnight on October 29 and came immediately to the White House. At the unlikely hour of 2:30 a.m. Johnson convened a meeting of his top advisers in the Cabinet Room. After reviewing the military situation in detail, the President looked hard at Abrams for a few moments and said: "This is a critical period here. In the light of what you know, do you have any reluctance or hesitancy about stopping the bombing?"

"No, sir," he said firmly.

"If you were President, would you do it?"

"I have no reservation about doing it," Abrams said. "I know it is stepping into a cesspool of comment. But I do think it's the right thing to do. It is the proper thing to do."

Word arrived during the meeting that Ambassador Bunker was having trouble getting in touch with Thieu to nail down the final agreement. The South Vietnamese insisted they needed more time, that they would be unable to organize their delegation and get it to Paris in time for the November 2 meeting that Johnson hoped to arrange.[15]

At 5:00 a.m. the meeting was adjourned. Abrams went to sleep while Dean Rusk returned to the State Department to call Bunker in Saigon, since it was twelve hours later there and Bunker would tell him what had happened during the day. At 6:15 a.m. Johnson called another meeting in the Cabinet Room to discuss Mrs. Chennault's activities on Nixon's behalf with his top advisers, including Secretary of State Dean Rusk and Secretary of Defense Clark Clifford.

Clifford was outraged, and in his best lawyer's manner said that the last-minute South Vietnamese delay was "reprehensible and utterly without merit."[16] Johnson instructed Rusk to tell Bunker that Washington planned to proceed with the meeting with the North Vietnamese on November 2, without Thieu.

Bunker urged the President to hold off announcing the bombing halt for twenty-four hours and to delay the Paris Peace Talks from November 2 to November 4, giving Saigon more time to organize its delegation. "I would be willing to postpone things a day or two before I broke up the alliance," Johnson told his advisers. Johnson then sent Thieu a personal message urging him to join the United States in Paris. At noon on the 30th he received Thieu's answer. It was a masterful dodge: Thieu would accept only if his conditions were met.[17]

At that point Johnson decided to proceed on his own, setting 8:00 p.m. October 31 for his announcement that the bombing halt would become effective in twelve hours. The date for the first meeting in Paris was set for November 6, the day after the election. Johnson still hoped throughout the day that he would be able to make a joint announcement with Thieu's concurrence. Bunker spent seven hours with Thieu, Vice President Ky, and Foreign Minister Thanh trying to eliminate differences. Johnson notified the presidential candidates of his plans; an hour before he was to go on the air, he learned from Bunker that Thieu still was insisting on revisions. Unable to delay his move any longer, Johnson went on television to announce the bombing halt. He tried to cover the situation by saying that "representatives of the government of South Vietnam are free to participate."

In Saigon, Thieu reacted to the announcement by disassociating himself from the bombing halt, declaring that it was a "unilateral" decision by the United States. His response softened the political impact of the President's dramatic move on American voters and raised doubts about peace. At the same time Thieu privately told Bunker that he would not do anything to upset the President's initiative. He indicated to Bunker that he would join the conference if the Viet Cong were not a separate negotiating delegation. His final card was to be his speech on National Day, November 1 (October 31 Washington time).

Humphrey was elated with Johnson's move. It was the support to end the war for which he had been maneuvering during the last months of the campaign. Johnson's firm prosecution of the war had driven a wedge between them. Humphrey wanted to end the war and quiet the anti-war movement, which had succeeded in severing large segments of the American population from its leaders. Now, in the final hours, Johnson had pulled a masterstroke to both end the war and elect a Democratic successor. The day after the President's speech, *The Washington Post* reported that "the initial reaction of political leaders of both parties was that President Johnson's announcement last night of a bombing halt in Vietnam would strengthen Democratic chances of retaining the White House and Congress in Tuesday's election." Humphrey was described as "somber and relieved," hoping the President's action would bring an "honorable peace." The *Post* said that, "in public and private, he made clear his belief that an enormous burden had now been lifted from his candidacy."

If Humphrey was elated, Nixon should have been saddened; but this was not the case. With his intimate knowledge of what Thieu was contemplating in Saigon, he was glad to see the Democrats sinking into a self-created trap. Nixon knew that Thieu would not go to Paris, yet the Democrats were inflating the prospects for peace by linking the bombing pause to expanded Paris Peace Talks scheduled for November 6. On October 21, the Gallup Poll had given Nixon an eight-point (44% to 36%) lead over Humphrey. By the time Gallup had completed his poll on November 2, two days after Johnson's announcement of the bombing halt, "an upheaval had taken place and Nixon led Humphrey by only two points (42% to 40%)."[18]

In a cunning move, Nixon turned the seeming disadvantage to his favor. He inflated peace hopes even higher, knowing they would be deflated by Thieu and he would benefit politically from the disillusion and doubt over President Johnson's initiative. Nixon responded to the bombing-halt announcement at a Madison Square Garden rally on October 31 by insisting that neither he nor his vice-presidential candidate would "say anything that might destroy the chance to have peace." Nixon said he trusted the total bombing halt would "bring some progress" in the Paris Peace Talks scheduled for November 6. In fact, Nixon knew that Thieu would not participate in the Paris talks and he was setting up Humphrey and Johnson for a fall.

Thieu was scheduled to address a joint session of the two houses of the Vietnamese National Assembly on the morning of November 1. The evening before his speech, Thieu gave a reception for the diplomatic corps at the Independence Palace. As he described it, "Ambassador Bunker spent very little time socializing. Instead, he ran into me frequently and discussed my forthcoming speech. Several times he asked me, 'Is everything okay now, Mr. President?' 'Of course, of course, everything is okay,' I told him."

Bunker was pleased and offered a toast to the freedom of the Republic of Vietnam. Thieu trapped Bunker to advise Washington that Thieu would join in the Paris Talks and that the announcement would come in his speech the following day to the National Assembly. Thieu went to extraordinary lengths to keep the contents of his speech to the National Assembly a secret, writing the draft himself and employing three secretaries to prepare the text for delivery, each working from random pages so that no one of them could read the full text.[19]

November 1 was a quiet Saturday morning during the dry and pleasant time of the year in Saigon, just after the rainy season. On his way to the National Assembly from the Independence Palace, Thieu feared that he might be assassinated by the CIA if Johnson and Humphrey found out in advance that he was to reject the President's peace plan and undermine Humphrey's chances to defeat Nixon in the election on Tuesday, November 5. By making his announcement publicly, Thieu not only believed he would more effectively undercut President Johnson, but he would also help make himself immune to an American decision to act against him personally and remove him from office.

Seated prominently in the front row of the National Assembly, Ambassador Bunker, whose serious and aloof demeanor had earned him the Vietnamese nickname *ong dai su tu lanh* ("Mr. Ambassador, the Refrigerator"), now appeared relaxed and smiling, after a month of difficult and prolonged negotiations with the Vietnamese president.

When President Thieu arrived, television cameras from the three American networks turned to cover him, and the audience rose and applauded, halting as the national anthem was played.

Thieu was visibly moved and resolute as he began to speak. After a brief introduction, his voice rose; in a loud, sharp tone he demanded that

North Vietnam enter into direct talks with his government. The Viet Cong would participate only as part of the North Vietnamese delegation. Then, slowly emphasizing each word, he said: "The government of South Vietnam deeply regrets not being able to participate in the present exploratory talks." The chamber exploded in applause and a long, standing ovation. The television lights and cameras focused on Bunker. Thieu recalled: "I could see Bunker trying hard to control his emotions. He began to sweat. As I looked at his face I felt sorry for him, but there was nothing I could do. I could not accept a situation that would bring us into a coalition with the Communists."[20] Thieu's speech lasted for twenty-seven minutes and was interrupted eighteen times for extended applause; his decision was major news.[21]

Thieu's National Day speech was the key move Nixon had plotted and anticipated to compound confusion over President Johnson's action. Thieu's declaration made headlines, raising doubts about prospects for the peace talks. "S. VIETNAM SPURNS NOV. 6 TALKS," read *The Washington Post* headline, while the news story noted that "the result [of Thieu's action] was to leave in doubt the next moves in the American effort to get to substantive talks with the Communists on how to bring an end to the Vietnam war."

Thieu's action, three days before the election, he believed had a decisive impact on the outcome. His decision not to take part in Johnson's "October Surprise" led to doubts about the effectiveness of Johnson's ploy and raised questions about the President's integrity. Perhaps it was a political ploy first and a peace ploy second. As Theodore White noted in *The Making of the Presidency 1968:*

> Had peace become quite clear, as fact, in the last three days of the election of 1968, Hubert Humphrey would probably have won the election; he would have been a minority President, but President nonetheless. Through the confusion of those last three days, however, it became apparent that the bombing halt, begun on Friday morning, would not end the killing of Americans in Asia; and the tide of opinion that had begun to flow to Hubert Humphrey began, at the end of the weekend, to flow back to Nixon.[22]

"The bombing halt unquestionably resulted in a last-minute surge of support for Humphrey," wrote Nixon in his memoirs, adding that "the Democrats' euphoria was dampened on November 2, when President Thieu announced that his government would not participate in the negotiations Johnson was proposing."[23] By holding back his support for Johnson in his National Assembly speech, Thieu "fostered the impression that Johnson's plan had been too quickly conceived and too shakily executed."[24]

"It was not easy for us to try to cope with Hanoi and Washington at the same time," Thieu recalled. "To resist the tremendous pressure from the Americans and then to hold on until the last minute was very difficult and risky."[25] During the three critical days before the election, the pressure increased and LBJ sent a personal message to Thieu urging that "we do not abandon each other at this critical hour."[26]

Thieu had long suspected that his office was bugged by the CIA. Now he used the bugging to his own advantage. In his discussions with Vietnamese politicians in his office, Thieu knew he was also speaking to the "secret" microphones. He told the politicians of his plans to enter into negotiations with the Communists eventually and to send Saigon's delegation to Paris, hoping this would convince the Americans that he might go along. Thieu was treading a narrow line. Open opposition, he believed, would have led to his ouster, like President Diem.

After the speech Thieu was extremely nervous, fearing that Humphrey might still win the election. Because of the twelve-hour time difference it was not until late in the evening of the day following the election that word came to Saigon that Nixon had definitely won. Hoang Duc Nha, his private secretary and confidant, rushed into Thieu's private sitting room where he was smoking a cigar after dinner and reported the news. Thieu was very pleased. "This is nice. Now at least we have bought ourselves some time. When the new President comes in, he has to learn something, and we have some more rope to play with," he said to Nha. There was no jubiliation for Thieu, only the realization that he had won a high risk hand. Now he would start anew with Nixon.[27]

Nixon received 43.40 percent of the total national vote versus 42.72 percent for Humphrey. Nixon's margin of victory over Humphrey was only 499,704 votes. The opinion of the Nixon leadership was that if the election had been held on Saturday or Sunday, Nixon might have lost; had it been held a week later, Nixon's margin of victory might have run as high as 2 million to 5 million votes.[28] Thieu had played a major role in undercutting Johnson's effort to help Humphrey.[29] Thieu's victory came in Paris: the day after the election the Paris Talks were postponed.

Thieu's elation did not last long. Ambassador Bunker and the State Department were deeply upset with him. He sensed that he had overplayed his hand. A week after the election, on November 11, President-elect Nixon visited LBJ at the White House and received a foreign policy briefing. At the end of the meeting, Nixon, referring to Vietnam, said that he had given assurance to the President and Secretary of State "that they could speak not just for this Administration but for the Nation and that meant for the next Administration as well." The press immediately interpreted the move by Nixon as "pressuring" Thieu.[30]

Mrs. Chennault was furious and felt that Nixon had betrayed Thieu after the latter's critical support during the campaign.[31] When Mitchell called and asked her to tell Thieu he should join the peace talks in Paris, Mrs. Chennault refused. She recalled how Mitchell had called the talks in Paris "phony" and now suddenly it was important for Thieu to send a representative to Paris. Nixon had completely reversed his position.[32] Nixon asked Senator Everett Dirksen to speak with Ambassador Bui Diem and Dirksen made the call. Bui Diem returned to Saigon with the message. In Saigon, Thieu and Nha were less concerned. "We saw Nixon as biding his time until he took office, letting Johnson do the dirty work. Politicians are politicians and we did not expect miracles from Nixon. They are going to help you only if it serves their purposes," explained Nha.[33]

On November 12, Defense Secretary Clark Clifford publicly displayed his displeasure with Thieu by warning that unless he joined the peace talks in Paris, the United States would consider proceeding without him. In Saigon, the Clifford signal was taken as a serious warning that Johnson was raging against Thieu and might act on his own to oust him. How far he would go, and how quickly, was the subject of the Saigon rumor mill. Thieu was deeply concerned with the possibility of a *coup d'état* against him before Johnson left office. He took special precautions with his elite Palace Guard and advised Hoang Duc Nha to sleep in the Palace so as not to be isolated and subject to assassination if a coup was mounted. Thieu's own cabinet, including his rival, Vice President Nguyen Cao Ky, stood firmly behind him when he defied Johnson, but now there were new pressures. Clifford's public criticism of Thieu implied to all of Saigon and the North Vietnamese that the Americans were preparing to remove him. "If Johnson overthrew me before Nixon took office, it would have been a most elegant solution for Nixon," recalled Thieu. "He would not have to overthrow me. I did not base my policy on a single personality but on the U.S. policy. I understood that U.S. policy was to negotiate a coalition for South Vietnam, not to win a military victory. I never had any illusions that Nixon's policy was for us to achieve a military victory over the North Vietnamese." Nixon took office without any further efforts to intimidate Thieu, but the threat of being deposed and assassinated in the manner of the Ngo brothers lingered and became an unspoken but key element in the equation for political survival. Thieu believed his actions in thwarting LBJ and Humphrey had saved Saigon from a Communist takeover for at least four years. He was proud of his efforts to help defeat Johnson's peace plan in 1968; and later recalled "those difficult days in 1968; the American pressure on us was not small."[34]

In Nixon, Thieu saw an anti-Communist American leader with wide foreign policy experience and a record that commanded respect. He had carefully read Nixon's October 1967 article in *Foreign Affairs,* "Asia After Vietnam," in which Nixon had warned:

> Without the American commitment in Vietnam, Asia would be a different place today. . . . Vietnam has diverted Peking from other such potential targets as India, Thailand and Malaysia. It has bought vitally needed time for governments that were weak or unstable or leaning toward Peking as a hedge against the future—time which allowed them to cope with their own insurrections while pressing ahead with their political, economic and military development.

Nguyen Van Thieu looked forward with high hopes to meeting Richard Nixon on Midway Island June 8, 1969, for the first time after Nixon's election. Thieu felt certain that he was in a strong position, that he could count on Nixon's support and some acknowledgment of his role in helping Nixon win the presidency. Now there was a strong anti-Communist in the White

House, and one who was politically indebted to him. Although Thieu realized Nixon was under pressure to reduce the American commitment in Vietnam, he thought there would be room to maneuver and that Nixon would remain constant in his support.

It had been a difficult spring. At the end of February the North Vietnamese launched a countrywide offensive in the South, killing 453 Americans in the first week, 336 in the second week, and 351 in the third. The South Vietnamese lost more than 500 soldiers a week. While Nixon and his advisers debated whether to respond by bombing North Vietnamese bases in Cambodia, the North Vietnamese increased the pressure and fired rockets on Saigon. Finally, on March 18, Nixon ordered a B-52 attack on the area suspected of being the North Vietnamese base in Cambodia, three miles from the border with South Vietnam.

On April 14, a U.S. Navy EC-121, an unarmed propellor-driven Constellation used for routine reconnaissance over the Sea of Japan, was attacked and shot down over international waters ninety miles from the coast by North Korean MiG fighters. The plane carried a crew of thirty Navy men, one Marine, and six tons of monitoring equipment to provide information about North Korean troop dispositions vital to prevent a surprise attack on South Korea. There were no survivors.

Nixon was facing his first major crisis. On the first day, the President was presented with two options: To retaliate by bombing the North Korean airfield where the attacking planes were based, or to continue the EC-121 flights with combat escorts. There was no consensus within the government on how to respond. The State Department, led by Secretary William Rogers, pressed for replying in a nonconfrontational tone. There was no real determination to use force.[35] At a White House press conference on April 18, Nixon announced that the flights would be continued. He was immediately praised by Congress and the press for his restraint. Actually, among the options Nixon, Kissinger, and Alexander Haig discussed was "taking a page from Eisenhower's book to end the Vietnam war." Eisenhower had threatened the North Koreans with escalation if they did not agree to an armistice after he became President in 1953.[36] Nixon could order the bombing of the airfield in Pyongyang and pass the word to the North Vietnamese that they could expect a similar escalation unless they agreed to serious negotiations in Paris. The Soviet Union would also be notified that the United States was taking strong action not to escalate the war, but to end it. Finally, Nixon compromised. He decided not to bomb North Korea, but to order another raid on the North Vietnamese base in Cambodia. There had been no response from Hanoi or Phnom Penh to the first raid, which, like the second, was not made public by the government.[37]

Nixon regretted his failure to act directly against the North Koreans, telling Kissinger: "They got away with it this time, but they'll never get away with it again."[38] Later, Nixon told Haig that the failure to respond quickly and strongly to the North Korean attack on the EC-121 "was the most serious misjudgment of my Presidency, including Watergate." Nixon, explained Haig, realized that he had missed the opportunity that comes in the first weeks in office to take dramatic initiatives.[39] Although the EC-121 experience was to shape Nixon's approach to dealing with North Vietnam in the future, at Midway it appeared that he was seriously winding down the war.

Nixon chose Midway because he feared anti-war riots would prevent a successful meeting in Washington. Thieu requested the meeting be held in Honolulu, but Kissinger and Nixon bypassed Honolulu because Thieu had met Lyndon Johnson there.[40] Midway, best known for the World War II victory of the U.S. Navy over the Japanese Pacific Fleet, is today an isolated, desolate refueling stop whose main inhabitants are gooney birds. The house of the U.S. naval commander, the site for the meeting, received a fresh coat of paint and new furniture; but the arrangements did not go well. First, they had argued over the location site for the meeting. Then they had asked Thieu to arrive before Nixon. He had refused, insisting that Nixon, as the host, should be on hand to greet him. The Americans had also suggested he would be tired and should come to Midway the night before and sleep there, but Thieu said no. "I'll bring a bed and sleep on my plane," he insisted.

Finally, the schedule was arranged so Nixon would arrive first and welcome Thieu. When Nha spoke to presidential press secretary Ronald Ziegler on Air Force One, Ziegler assured him that President Nixon would land first. In fact, when Thieu arrived, Nixon's plane was still fifteen minutes from Midway.

Four chairs were lined up in a row in the living room for the meeting; the fourth, a taller chair with a higher back, was the one in which Richard Nixon would sit. President Nguyen Van Thieu was both amused and outraged. He didn't say a word, but walked into the dining room, grabbed a chair the same size as Nixon's, and placed it opposite Nixon. Then Thieu sat facing the President of the United States at eye level. "After Midway," recalled Thieu, "I heard from my American friends that Kissinger never foresaw that President Thieu was the man he was."

Thieu had proposed that he and Nixon should meet alone, but President Nixon insisted on being accompanied by his National Security Advisor, Henry Kissinger. "I need Dr. Kissinger," he said.

"Then I will bring my adviser, too," said Thieu. They compromised and Thieu was accompanied by his Special Assistant for Foreign Affairs, Nguyen Phu Duc.

Thieu knew before he went to Midway that Nixon would ask for the beginning of American troop withdrawals from Vietnam. He had read from daily press summaries that Nixon was planning to begin a troop withdrawal from Vietnam. "It was an American trial balloon," Thieu told his advisers, "but it helped us plan our own strategy." To forestall a conflict over what he knew was inevitable, Thieu took the initiative and suggested to Nixon the "redeployment" of American troops in the spirit of Nixon's recent

May 14 speech proposing mutual withdrawal of North Vietnamese and American forces. Thieu's action was very much in character. He often sought to preempt others—"I felt it was important to speak of redeployment, not withdrawal, to minimize the impact of the move on the North Vietnamese." Nixon agreed, but explained to Thieu that he needed to buy time to develop his strategy for Vietnam.[41]

According to Hoang Duc Nha, who handled arrangements for the visit and accompanied Thieu, Thieu knew that "time was running out for us. We had to do something. We knew that the Americans were on an inexorable course of action. They had to get out. It was at Midway that Thieu told Nixon: 'I know that you are going to go, but before you go, you have to leave something for us as friends. Leave something to help me out.' "[42]

At Midway, Thieu asked Nixon to provide funds and equipment to create two new reserve divisions, a Marine and an Airborne division. Thieu needed reserve forces that could move rapidly from one part of the country to another to counterattack North Vietnamese forces crossing the Laotian or Cambodian border into South Vietnam. The two new divisions were to compensate in part for the American troops being withdrawn. They were to be mobile, elite forces deployed as a fire brigade to crush enemy attacks. They were never formed.

Nixon and Thieu played political poker. Thieu tried to get as much as he could without giving way to a plan for total American withdrawal. He hoped for a gradual American withdrawal that would end with a residual American force in South Vietnam. Visualizing a Korean-type solution with the demilitarized zone acting as a buffer between North and South Vietnam, Thieu hoped that two divisions of American troops, about 40,000 men, would be stationed there to act as a deterrent to a North Vietnamese invasion.

Nixon proposed that secret, private contacts be started with Hanoi by the Americans at the presidential level. Thieu agreed, provided he was informed about any political discussions. Thieu believed the private American talks would be aimed at bringing the North and South to the conference table, not that the Americans would have the South's proxy to create a settlement on American terms.[43]

Nixon then told Thieu they would go to the navy base's movie theater to make a statement to the press. After a short walk in the hot sun Thieu found himself inside a sheet-metal building with a makeshift stage. From a podium with the presidential seal, Nixon answered questions for fifteen minutes from the White House correspondents traveling with him. Then President Thieu was called on, with no preparation or advance warning, to take questions in English. Thieu found the procedure strange. He was surprised and annoyed, but he made no protest and answered questions in English for nearly fifteen minutes.

Nixon was jubilant with the results of the meeting. For the first time since the Marines landed at Da Nang on March 6, 1965, American troops were to be withdrawn from Vietnam.[44] Thieu, for his part, found the meeting disconcerting and it left him uneasy. He expected better treatment in return for his political debt. The meeting had been troublesome, as if he had been there only to enhance Nixon's and Kissinger's image and to solve their political problems.

He was uneasy about what might follow. After the meeting Thieu thought of the Vietnamese saying: *"dau xuoi duoi lot"* ("If the head slides through easily, the tail will follow").

On his way back to Saigon, Thieu stopped in Taipei to meet with Chiang Kai-shek, president of the Republic of China, the first casualty in the wars against communism in Asia and long experienced in the ways of living with an American ally. It was a hot, muggy afternoon when Thieu's chartered Pan American jet landed in Taipei and the motorcade proceeded to the Grand Hotel where he would stay overnight. Rarely did President Chiang come to call on visitors, but Chiang had a high regard for Thieu and his coming to meet Thieu that afternoon was seen as a gesture of support.

After a firm handshake, when the two leaders were left alone, Chiang told Thieu he was anxious to find out what really happened at Midway. Chiang, who had often met with Thieu, asked in a whispering but clear voice, "So the Americans are going to withdraw from Vietnam? Why did you let them do it?" Chiang was deeply concerned that an American pull-back from Vietnam would have an adverse effect on Taiwan.

"You know," Thieu replied in an assured tone, "when Nixon decides to withdraw, there is nothing I can do about it. Just as when Eisenhower, Kennedy, and Johnson decided to go in, there was very little my predecessors had to say about it.[45]

"Once you know that you cannot change the American decision, it is better to make the best of it. I even took the initiative and suggested a possible withdrawal when Nixon began to explain how difficult it was for him to maintain the current level of troops in Vietnam. He outlined how painful and difficult it was to have to face a hostile Congress, the press, and demonstrating students. I agreed to the first American troop withdrawal because President Nixon told me he had a domestic problem and the withdrawal of 25,000 troops would only be symbolic. Nixon told me he viewed it as a public opinion ploy and he agreed to call it a 'redeployment' instead of a 'withdrawal.' He told me he needs the support of public opinion and the Congress. But I also told him, you have to make sure that Hanoi doesn't see the troop withdrawal as a sign of American weakness."

"What did you make of Nixon?" asked Chiang.

"He promised me eight years of strong support. Four years of military support during his first term in office and four years of economic support during his second term. He spoke of military Vietnamization in the first term and economic Vietnamization in the second. By the time most of the Americans have withdrawn, so will the North Vietnamese; by then Saigon should be strong enough to carry on its own defense with only material support from the United States," Thieu replied.

Chiang nodded his head in approval.

Thieu explained that Nixon had firmly agreed to the condition that withdrawal of American and North Vietnamese troops would have to be mutual. Thieu felt that this was a major concession because only six months earlier at his meeting with President Lyndon Johnson in Manila, they had agreed that Hanoi had to withdraw its troops from South Vietnam six months before the Americans left. Thieu then opened his briefcase and took out a small file.

"Mr. Nixon agreed with me on the basic and essential principle of negotiation," said Thieu. He showed Chiang the text of Nixon's May 14, 1969, television speech on Vietnam proposing compromise terms for negotiations. Thieu pointed to the lines he had underlined: "We have ruled out a one-sided withdrawal, or the acceptance in Paris of terms that would amount to a disguised defeat."

The conversation was unhurried and intimate. Chiang recalled his own experiences with the Americans, twenty years earlier, when he had been defeated by the Communists and forced to flee to Taiwan. Before he left, he had been under American pressure to enter into a coalition government with Mao Zedong's Communists, Chiang recalled. Both men understood the peril of coalition with the Communists. Chiang did not need to impress Thieu with the dangers of a coalition government that contained Communists. Thieu's whole experience with the North Vietnamese had taught him that ruthless elimination of all opposition was the first rule of Ho Chi Minh.

The history of the Vietnamese independence movement contains repeated examples of nationalist leaders being betrayed or eliminated by the Communists. In the formative years of the Vietnamese Communist movement Ho Chi Minh betrayed Phan Boi Chau, a respected Nationalist leader, to the French Security Service. In 1925 Chau was active in Shanghai, advocating a democratic republic for Vietnam through his political organization, the Vietnam Duy Tan Hoi, or Association for the Modernization of Vietnam. The group agitated for an end to French colonialism and independence for Vietnam.

Chau reached out to build links with other Asian militants and was better known than Ho Chi Minh at the time. His organization was a formidable rival to Ho's newly formed Vietnamese Revolutionary Youth Association. Ho infiltrated Chau's organization in Hong Kong and joined with Nguyen Cong Vien, another revolutionary, to subvert Chau and his Nationalist group. Ho arranged to have Chau invited to a meeting in the French concession of Shanghai. When Chau arrived, he was immediately arrested by the French police. Ho and his co-conspirator, Nguyen Cong Vien, split a reward of 100,000 piastres (equivalent to $56,000 at the time) from the French. Chau was brought back to Vietnam, tried, and sentenced to house arrest in Hue, where he died fifteen years later.

Ho had established this pattern for neutralizing or annihilating any group with which he might have to share power in the earliest days of the Communist movement. It was to continue until three months after the Communist victory over Saigon in April 1975, when Hanoi's Politburo began to eliminate all traces of the National Liberation Front (Viet Cong) and the Provisional Revolutionary Government.[46] From the early days until the present the pattern has never changed.

Ho continued to subvert Chau's Nationalist movement by betraying young Vietnamese patriots. It was the practice of the Nationalist movement to bring young men to China for revolutionary training. Those selected were required to send two photographs of themselves to Nguyen Cong Vien before their departure. Those who responded to Ho Chi Minh's appeals and joined the Revolutionary Youth Association were returned secretly and safely to Vietnam. The others, who rejected the Communist appeals and remained faithful to the Nationalist cause, were arrested when they crossed the frontier into Vietnam by French Security Service officials who invariably possessed a copy of the photographs they had sent to Hong Kong. Nguyen Cong Vien, when he informed Ho of the impending return of an "unsuitable" student, provided the French Consulate in Hong Kong with details of the route and a photograph, for which he received a monetary reward.[47]

When Ho took power in August 1945, he systematically and forcefully eliminated the Nationalist, non-Communist leadership of Vietnam.[48] From July 11 to 13, 1946, General Vo Nguyen Giap conducted a nationwide roundup of Nationalist leaders and the Viet Minh police seized the head-quarters and other facilities of opposition parties.[49]

So, when Thieu heard the word "coalition," it recalled for him the North Vietnamese record of destroying all opposition movements and per-sonalities by force and stripping away all civil liberties.[50] Thieu knew that the National Liberation Front in the South was only an instrument of North Vietnam. He feared that forming a coalition with the Viet Cong would build a bridge making it easy for Hanoi to cross into the South and take control. Before there could be any talk of a political settlement, the North Vietnam-ese troops had to be withdrawn from the South, Thieu insisted. A coalition government without the removal of North Vietnamese troops from the South was tantamount to a Communist victory. Thieu often reminded Amer-ican officials that during the Korean War North Korean troops had to be withdrawn above the 38th parallel before negotiations began. Whenever the North Koreans were below the 38th parallel, the war continued. "You have to insist that the North Vietnamese leave South Vietnam—as LBJ did—before negotiations can start, rather than negotiating about the withdrawal itself," Thieu stressed.[51]

Thieu's basic policy, as we have seen, was that of the Four No's: No recognition of the enemy, no neutralization of South Vietnam, no coalition government, and no surrender of territory to the enemy. He was prepared to negotiate on Hung's proposal to resume trade if there was a favorable response from the North, but told Chiang that a coalition, with the presence of North Vietnamese troops in the South, was absolutely nonnegotiable for him. He had pre-empted Nixon a week prior to his meeting on Midway by laying out his views in a major speech in Saigon. Nixon did not mention coalition at Midway. It was best, Nixon had told him, to separate the military issues from the political issues. The key military issue was how to negotiate mutual withdrawal of both North Vietnamese and American troops in order to reduce the size of the American presence in Vietnam to a level acceptable at home. And that would also buy time for the strengthening of the South Vietnamese forces. In any case, Nixon promised, when the American troops left, the North Vietnamese troops would leave at the same time.

Thieu and Chiang's conversation ran more than an hour over the scheduled period; Chiang did not have enough time to return to his residence to change for the state dinner. He ordered his uniform to be sent to Thieu's rooms so he could change there and continue their talk.

At the state dinner that night Chiang toasted to the freedom of the Republic of Vietnam, to the courage of Thieu and his determination to keep Southeast Asia free of Communist domination. The elegant Chinese banquet and the rice wine relaxed Thieu, and the two leaders discussed the merits of Chinese cuisine compared to that of Taiwan, deciding that the island's foods were just a tamer version of those on the mainland. Chiang was gracious, but retired early because of his poor health. Thieu was grateful for an early end to the evening after the grueling meeting he had been through.

Yet when Thieu lay down, he had difficulty falling asleep. The conversation with Chiang that afternoon played itself over in his mind again. Yes, maybe he would eventually have to face Chiang's warning of the American penchant for resolving military problems through political coalitions. Why, Thieu asked himself, with Nixon as President, was Chiang still so concerned about Vietnam? Clearly, Chiang was questioning Nixon's intentions.

In retrospect, the Midway meeting had been worse than he first acknowledged to himself. Why had Nixon rejected his proposal for a meeting in Washington or Honolulu? Honolulu was much pleasanter than Midway and the Commander in Chief Pacific's (CINCPAC) headquarters, overlooking the blue Pacific with a view of Pearl Harbor and the might of the American Navy, would have been ideal to project American power. Isolated and impoverished, Midway was a strange and desolate choice.[52]

Only a year earlier, in July 1968, Thieu had met with Lyndon Johnson in Honolulu. The President had pledged support for South Vietnam "as long as the help is needed and desired." Johnson had also acknowledged the pledge of "not imposing a coalition government on Saigon." Had Thieu erred in backing Nixon over Humphrey? Thieu did not have to be reminded by Chiang of the perils of a coalition government; the problem was to convince the Americans. He wondered how to convey to Nixon and Kissinger the lessons of his own experiences with the North Vietnamese Communists.

Thieu had been born of humble origins on December 24, 1924, in the hour, day, month, and year of the Rat, an auspicious moment according to the astrological signs of the Chinese lunar calendar.[53] (Kissinger, the Vietnamese were fond of noting, while being born in the year of the Rat, had only one rat sign.) The youngest of seven children, he was called Number Eight for as long as he could remember, since his father was known as Number One and his eldest brother as Number Two.

His father, orphaned at age eleven, lived with an uncle on a small farm in the countryside and drove cattle from one province to another to make a living. "He became kind of a cowboy," said Thieu. "In those days there were no roads and often he would start with twenty to thirty cows and lose half of them on the rugged journey." Eventually he earned enough money to buy a two-acre plot in Phan Rang and marry. His family of four boys and three girls worked hard. From age five Thieu began to sell rice cakes from a bamboo basket in the village market. His mother made the cakes and Thieu carried them to market early in the morning. He sold enough to buy new materials for the next day's sales and make a small profit. As a boy he loved soccer and he hoarded his small earnings so that one day a week, on Sunday afternoon, he could skip the market and go to watch the soccer games. That day he ate the rice cakes himself or gave them to his friends. After soccer he went home and gave his mother the same amount of money as on other days, never telling her he had been to the game.

Thieu grew up liking the hot weather and fishing in the South China Sea. He was an excellent student in high school, studying French and English. He was raised in a traditional household, where his father stressed the Confucian virtues of loyalty, righteousness, filial piety, courage, respect, magnanimity, sincerity, earnestness, and kindness.[54] His father also taught Thieu to calculate in advance and not to take chances. One day his father set off on a trip to the North. He packed and went to the train station early in the evening and stayed overnight, despite the swarms of mosquitoes and the fact that the train would not leave until noon the following day. Why had he gone to the station so early, Thieu asked his father on his return. His father replied, "People wait for trains. Trains do not wait for people." It was from his father that Thieu learned to be certain of every move, to be suspicious and wary—traits he carried with him throughout his career.

Thieu's first experience of American power came in 1945 at the end of the war when a wave of American bombers attacked his village, which was occupied by the Japanese. There were heavy casualties and Thieu still recalls joining a rescue team to sift through the rubble for survivors.

It was also shortly before the end of World War II that he joined the Viet Minh resistance movement against the French and began to learn about the ruthlessness of the North Vietnamese Communists. For a time the Viet Minh made him a local youth leader and later a district chief in his own province, Ninh Thuan, in Central Vietnam. He was one of hundreds of thousands of Nationalists fighting side by side with the Viet Minh against the French, but he often questioned Communist doctrine. As a result he was warned that he was on a Viet Minh assassination list, and he had to flee his village.

After Thieu broke with the Viet Minh and fled to Saigon, he enrolled in the first officer class of the Vietnamese Military Academy in Hue. Bao Dai was chief of state and the instructors at the academy were French. The cadets at Hue were told that the French were there to help the Vietnamese fight the Viet Minh; once the task was done, complete independence would be granted to Vietnam.

Thieu earned a reputation as a bright, skilled, ambitiuos officer, who was brave in combat and accepted responsibility. Among his peers he was known for his ability to plan operations and handle staff work well. He married Nguyen Thi Mai Anh in 1951, the daughter of a prominent Catholic, and was baptized in 1957. But he never became a favorite of Ngo Dinh Diem, Vietnam's first Catholic president. Thieu had a different patron saint from Diem. Nor did he join Diem's Can Lao political party. Instead, he joined the old Dai Viet (Greater Vietnam) Party, one of the major nationalist parties fighting the French during the colonial era.

He was considered a rising star in the military when the coup was organized against Diem in 1963. A colonel, Thieu was based in Bien Hoa as commander of the 5th Division, and his support was considered critical to a successful coup. In the post-coup jockeying for power Thieu was a leading member of the Young Turks, a group of young generals who controlled the armed forces and forced the older generals to retire. After the ouster of General Nguyen Khanh in February 1965, Thieu carefully maneuvered himself to be chosen chairman of the junta, then chief of state with General Nguyen Cao Ky as prime minister. Thieu had thus worked himself into a position to be chosen to run for President in the September 1967 election.[55]

On the short flight from Taiwan to Saigon, Thieu again reviewed the Midway meeting. No, he decided, he had nothing to fear. Nixon would not sell out Vietnam, he would fight communism even harder than Lyndon Johnson. Thieu had met with Johnson at Manila and Honolulu and found dealing with him difficult. Johnson did not listen and he had an imperious air. There was no discussion. Johnson made up his mind and that was that. At Manila, LBJ sat in a special chair, bigger than those in which the other presidents sat.[56] LBJ reminded Thieu of the American general John W. (Iron Mike) O'Daniel, designated in 1954 by President Eisenhower as the first head of the American military advisory group in Vietnam. In 1955, during a disagreement with his Vietnamese counterpart, O'Daniel barked: "Who pays, commands."[57] There was no exchange of letters between Thieu and LBJ.

Nixon was different. He had a lawyer's style and method, making his case in a logical, orderly manner with a clear grasp of the issues. He listened and seemed to understand the problem well, coming up with a realistic course of action. Thieu felt that Nixon understood foreign policy and Asia better than Johnson. However, he did not get as favorable an impression of Kissinger. His role in the making of Vietnam policy was still unclear; but Nixon was in charge.

After all, Nixon's whole career had been built on anti-communism. He was one of the advocates for containing China. Nixon was the one who first advocated the use of American airpower to lift the siege of Dien Bien Phu in 1954 when he was Vice President. Above all, Thieu felt that Nixon owed him a debt from the 1968 election. The two men did not discuss the election at Midway, but Thieu continued to feel that his role had been critical in Nixon's victory.

Soon after the Midway meeting, Thieu learned that Nixon was about to visit the Far East, and asked him to stop in Saigon as a symbol of his support. Nixon did not answer immediately, but then decided to make a surprise stop in Saigon on his round-the-world trip in July 1969, only a month after the Midway meeting. The stop in Saigon, the first—and only— visit of an American President to the Independence Palace, was a big boost for Thieu's political popularity and underwrote his Mandate from Heaven as defined by Washington. In their private talks, however, Nixon repeated to Thieu what he had told him at Midway: He had to start troop withdrawals to maintain the support of the American public.

"I understood Nixon," Thieu recalled. "But he never said to me that it would be a systematic timetable of withdrawals at America's initiative. He only spoke to me of the domestic difficulties he was having in the United States, and asked me to help him. He said to me, 'Help us to help you.' I replied: 'I will help you to help us.' At that meeting we again talked about gradual withdrawal. Mr. Nixon pledged again that such a with- drawal must be reciprocated by North Vietnam, and be in accordance with the defense capability of South Vietnam, and in accordance with the continuous military and economic aid given to South Vietnam." Thieu recalled Nixon saying, "We have gone as far now as we can or should go in opening the door to peace, and now it is time for the other side to respond."[58]

Thieu said that he suspected a unilateral American withdrawal, despite Nixon's promises, yet "at that time I still felt confident in and still trusted a great ally." After all, in his May 14 speech announcing a new peace plan Nixon had declared:

> A great nation cannot renege on its pledges. A great nation must be worthy of trust. When it comes to maintaining peace, "prestige" is not an empty word. I am not speaking of false pride or bravado—they should have no place in our policies. I speak rather of the respect that one nation has for another's integrity in defending its principles and meeting its obligations. If we simply abandoned our effort in Vietnam, the cause of peace might not survive the damage that would be done to other nations' confidence in our ability.[59]

Yet Thieu's suspicious nature always made him dwell on the prospect of betrayal; it had become second nature for him since the assassination of President Diem. He wondered how long this new mood of trust would last. In his memoirs, Kissinger confirmed Thieu's premonition, saying that after

Nixon's meeting with Thieu in Saigon, "we were clearly on the way out of Vietnam by negotiations if possible, by unilateral withdrawal if necessary."[60]

Thieu wanted to give Nixon a small but elaborate reception at the Palace, but for security reasons he waited until only a few hours before Nixon's arrival to invite a handpicked list of key officials and their wives. For the women it was a gala occasion and they put on their best dresses and jewelry. After the champagne toast to the Republic of Vietnam, the helicopter engines began to turn over, their blades rotating with the thumping, quickening rhythm that was the symbol of American power and presence in Vietnam. Thieu accompanied Nixon and Kissinger to the landing pad on the Palace lawn and waved with a smile as the helicopter rose rapidly over the red tile rooftops of the city.

On that day, July 30, 1969, Nixon had not told Thieu that Kissinger would immediately be heading for Paris to begin secret negotiations with the North Vietnamese. He would not inform him until after Kissinger had completed the meeting.

3

No Secret Deals

IN SPITE OF KISSINGER'S SECRET *di dem* (walks in the night) with the
North Vietnamese in Paris, the first two years of Nixon's presidency
had been good for South Vietnam. During 1969 and 1970, Nixon appeared to be positioning himself favorably with Thieu and defending South
Vietnam on all fronts. Morale rose with the Vietnamization program and
arms flowed into the South from the increased American commitment.
Thieu seemed to be fitting into the new American strategy of the Nixon
doctrine by which the United States would help its allies with sufficient
economic and military aid—but not manpower—to defend themselves
against aggression.[1] Thieu, buoyed by his support from Nixon, had taken
the initiative at home to pacify the countryside and instigate a land reform
program that had won widespread approval.

The memory of Tet 1968, when Communist troops entered Saigon and
attacked the American Embassy during the time set aside for New Year
celebrations, had faded away. The Viet Cong and North Vietnamese sustained heavy losses and had not been able to replace their men and equipment. The American–South Vietnamese incursion into Cambodia in the
spring of 1970, although it caused a political firestorm against Nixon by anti-
war demonstrators in America, had been a military success for Saigon. The
North Vietnamese headquarters in the Parrot's Beak between Cambodia
and South Vietnam had been destroyed. For a fleeting moment at the end of
1970 Thieu's confidence rose to the point that he declared South Vietnam
was "crossing over into the postwar era."[2]

As 1971 began, Thieu sensed that there were to be new tests and challenges but felt confident he could meet them. To demonstrate his rising
optimism in the Vietnamese New Year, he allowed the use of traditional
firecrackers to chase away the devil spirits for the first time since the North
Vietnamese Tet Offensive in 1968.

The first test of 1971 was Operation Lam Son 719, a code name derived
from the famous battlefield in North Vietnam where the Vietnamese won an
overwhelming victory against an invading Chinese army in 1427. Although

Vietnamization was two years old, it had still to be tested, and the Americans called upon the Army of the Republic of Vietnam (ARVN) to pursue an aggressive "search and destroy" operation against the very heart of the North Vietnamese supply bases and offensive staging grounds for the Ho Chi Minh Trail at Tchepone in northern Laos. Thieu felt he had to demonstrate to the Americans, who proposed the operation, that the ARVN had matured and could take over offensive operations, until then conducted primarily by American forces.

Even though he had his doubts, Thieu committed two of Vietnam's best divisions, the Airborne and the Marines, to the operation.[3] The Americans only provided air support. After the first four days the ARVN forces met stiff resistance from battle-tested North Vietnamese forces and the operation bogged down. The ARVN failed to get the American close-in air support it had been promised because nobody had tested the use of Vietnamese air controllers, speaking in heavily accented broken English, trying to call in air strikes. North Vietnamese General Vo Nguyen Giap called for reserves and brought in 36,000 troops, including two armored divisions equipped with Russian tanks, to combat the attacking South Vietnamese force of 25,000 men. Wherever the South Vietnamese attacked, northern troops seemed to be ready and waiting for them.

The head of the Psychological Warfare Department of the Vietnamese army told his aides at the time that the operations plan for Lam Son was prepared by the Americans and given to General Cao Van Vien, chairman of the Joint General Staff, to sign. There was no real joint planning and coordination between the Americans and Vietnamese. The delays in approving the plan by the Americans led to security leaks that allowed Giap to disrupt the operation.[4] Thieu wanted to prevent the North Vietnamese from being able to attack his forces at Tchepone by moving a division into North Vietnam above the 17th parallel near Vinh as a diversion, but the Americans refused to approve this. Thieu felt such a move would have assured victory at Tchepone and forced the North Vietnamese to keep more troops in the North for fear of an attack from the South.[5]

If Thieu was slow to make decisions to commit his forces, he was quick to sense a trap. He ordered his commander, General Hoang Xuan Lam, to seize Tchepone but not to try to hold it. Thieu could see a repetition of Dien Bien Phu with his forces committed to an indefensible outpost without any possibility of resupply. "You go in there just long enough to take a piss and then leave quickly," Thieu ordered General Lam.[6] The operation was over forty-four days after it had begun. The high rate of casualties, nearly 8,000 men, was a debilitating factor for South Vietnamese morale. For Thieu, it was the Americans who bugged out first, not the ARVN. To the Americans, the ARVN had not passed its test.

In his assessment of the Lam Son operation in his memoirs, Henry Kissinger noted that General William Westmoreland had rejected an attack on Tchepone with four American divisions as too risky while the South Vietnamese had allotted less than two divisions to seize and hold Tchepone.[7] Kissinger charges that President Thieu had ordered his commander to be careful in moving west and to stop the operation altogether as soon as they had suffered 3,000 casualties.[8] Thieu insists he never gave such an order. "It is illogical for a military man to fix in advance a number of casualties. Dr. Kissinger is being very imaginative when he says that. We could not go too far west because we could not be too much beyond the radius of the medical evacuation. Kissinger says we withdrew our troops without telling the Americans. How could we withdraw more than ten thousand troops without them noticing it?" Thieu explained.

To Thieu, what went wrong was the lack of American helicopters. "Three days after the beginning of the operation the Americans had suffered too many casualties among their helicopter pilots, and without air cover and suppressive fire against the enemy they were reluctant to continue a timely and adequate evacuation. That created a big problem for the South Vietnamese troops. We could not evacuate our dead and we could not evacuate our wounded. It not only affected morale, but also the progress of the operation."[9]

General Alexander Haig was sent to Vietnam by President Nixon in the middle of the Lam Son operation to assess what was going wrong. Haig recalls that "Lam Son destroyed the cream of the South Vietnam army and was far more serious and detrimental than was believed at the time. Our handling of that was very bad. The whole American role of guidance and support was hands off because of bureaucratic mischief in the Pentagon."[10] As a test of Vietnamization, the Pentagon refused to let Americans take part in the operation; the support the Vietnamese had been used to and expected to continue was no longer forthcoming.

Thieu tried to avoid any recriminations with the Americans. He was shown a picture that appeared in the American news magazines of a South Vietnamese soldier trying to flee from the battlefield like a scared rabbit by clinging to the skids of a rescue helicopter. It was captioned: "Rabbit." "I just smiled," Thieu recalled. "I despised that. You cannot prevent just one single soldier from doing something like that, yet the press accused the South Vietnamese soldiers of being rabbits. Meanwhile they completely suppressed the truth about the lack of fighting spirit of American helicopter pilots in this operation."[11]

The New Year's mood of confidence disappeared as the wounded from Operation Lam Son filled all available hospital beds. In Saigon, the failure of Lam Son generated rumors in the cafés and coffeehouses that Thieu's days were numbered. Amidst the sad songs of war the word was spreading that the Americans would promote a "peace candidate" in the Vietnamese presidential elections scheduled for October. Late into the night the gentle voice of Khanh Ly, Saigon's favorite ballad singer, could be heard in the tea house on Tu Do Street lamenting:

> I have a lover who just died!
> He died at Ashau Valley,
> lying curled on the frontier

pass! Body blackened, no clothes
on, his face still dreaming!

And a few blocks away in the poorer area of the Old Market, Duy Khanh, the folk singer, reflected the sinking spirits of the moment:

Today, Ben Het Outpost I shall guard.
Tomorrow, Laos jungles I will cross!
Gun on my shoulder, helmet on my head,
I never dared to ask you to wait.
Future? I have nothing for your dreams!

Thieu's political fortunes had survived Lam Son. Now in the New Year, 1972, he would be serving a four-year term and the Americans would have to deal with him or remove him forcibly. Thieu awaited the next American move.

On January 25, 1972, in preparation for his trip to China in February and a summit with Brezhnev in May, Nixon publicly offered a new comprehensive political and military peace proposal to the North Vietnamese. The secret talks with Hanoi had bogged down, and with the presidential election coming up in the fall Nixon decided to take the offensive. For the first time he revealed that Kissinger had held twelve secret talks with the North Vietnamese in Paris beginning in August of 1969.[12] To Thieu, the most disturbing part of Nixon's speech was the revelation that the United States had dropped its formal demand for the mutual withdrawal of forces by both sides. Nixon's military plan called for the complete withdrawal of "other outside forces."[13] In addition, he made public the secret proposal Haig had brought to Thieu the previous September for the resignation of the South Vietnamese president and vice president one month in advance of new elections, which would be held within six months of a cease-fire.

Although Nixon refused to accept the North Vietnamese political demand that President Thieu be ousted as a precondition to a settlement, Thieu felt that the American proposal, in effect, served the same purpose. While Nixon did not say so in his television address, he planned to recruit the Russians and the Chinese to exert their influence on North Vietnam by reducing arms shipments to Hanoi and urging the North Vietnamese to negotiate.[14]

Thieu had been told by Ambassador Bunker two days before Nixon's speech that the United States was going to make the record of the secret talks public, but it was not until 7:00 p.m. the day before that Bunker presented him with a copy of the text and asked for his concurrence and comment. Thieu told Bunker he wanted to study it. Then he called his private secretary, Hoang Duc Nha, at home and asked him to join him in his private quarters at the Palace.

Thieu had relied on Nha as his American expert from the time he took office as president in 1967. A second cousin who had lived as a member of

Thieu's family when Thieu was commandant of the military academy in Dalat, where Nha attended high school, Nha always addressed Thieu as "Elder Brother," and to Thieu he was indeed a surrogate son. Nha had finished his secondary schooling in Paris, then gone on to spend four happy years at Oklahoma State University where he obtained a degree in mechanical engineering, enjoyed the open atmosphere of the campus, the company of tall blonde co-eds, and picked up American mannerisms and slang. Later he went to the University of Pittsburgh for a master's degree in development economics, taking courses in international economics, political science, and administration. In his American education Nha was taught to question, to develop the pros and cons of a problem, and to find a rational answer.

Nha is tall for a Vietnamese (six feet), and handsome, with smooth, graceful features. He has an easy, open manner, carefully cultivated in America. A bit of the savvy Oklahoma country boy rubbed off on him; so did the ambition that came from visiting the homes of American businessmen. He took part in American family life in Tulsa, Oklahoma, and in Riverdale, New York, where one of his best friends took Nha to a synagogue. He learned Yiddish expressions and the word "kosher" became a part of his vocabulary.

When he returned to Saigon in 1968, Nha was offered the position of private secretary to President Thieu. For Thieu, Nha filled two important needs: he wanted someone he could trust who knew the Americans, and in the Asian tradition of appointing one's relatives to important positions, Nha's appointment would balance appointments he had given to members of his wife's family. Nha became Thieu's eyes and ears. Because of his closeness to Thieu, he understood Thieu's feelings, habits, and logic. As a military man, Thieu had learned to analyze battle situations from a detailed intelligence, logistics, and operations plan presented to him by aides before making a military decision or developing strategy and he carried this training with him to the presidential Palace. Nha's ability to work through a problem and reach a solution by outlining a series of possible answers was scarce in the Vietnamese bureaucracy—immobilized by the French *fonctionnaire* system, which passed all decisions slowly up to the top for action—and was extremely helpful to Thieu.

Nha shared his duties with Nguyen Phu Duc, a Harvard graduate who was Thieu's special assistant for foreign affairs, but it was primarily Nha who sat with Thieu and participated in drafting his letters to Nixon during 1971 and 1972, was privy to Thieu's private dealings with the Americans, and knew Thieu's thinking on how to deal with the North Vietnamese Communists. Later this would be Hung's role.

But despite his skills, Vietnamese politicians and American diplomats alike considered Nha inexperienced, arrogant, and often abusive of his powers. They felt he had gained his position only by being a relative of Thieu's, and his brash, American-acquired style drew heavy criticism. He drove a Mustang convertible and then a Mercedes sedan through the streets of Saigon in the midst of the war, a symbol of ostentation and privilege. He did not follow the standard behavior of checking his ideas out first with the Americans for their approval and he did not defer to his elders in the cabinet if he thought their ideas foolish.

When Nha arrived at the Palace on the evening of January 24, Thieu handed him a copy of Nixon's eight-point peace plan and puffed on a thin Schimmelpennick cigar while Nha read the text. Nha realized that Thieu could not openly reject the proposals.[15] What would the Americans say if Thieu rejected them? Nha asked himself. Besides, Nixon was going to make the speech in a few hours and there was no time to discuss the contents with Washington. "Let's not say anything now," Nha advised Thieu; "if we say anything against the proposal, we will be portrayed as the bad guys with the American public. They'd say, 'This is a very constructive idea that would solve the whole problem. Why do you object to that? You care more for your own power than for peace.' Let's not do anything. Let's wait until tomorrow."

"What do you think are the intentions behind the American move?" asked Thieu.

"I think this is the beginning of a breakthrough in the peace talks. I think they've got something already. They've got to have agreed on something, otherwise they would never come out with this kind of thing. This is a balloon they are floating just to see how we react and what the U.S. public opinion and Congress will say. If they get a showing of support, they will come back to us like gangbusters all right. So I say, let's not give them reasons to doubt our sincerity. In the morning, after the speech, we'll have our own comment," urged Nha.

Thieu decided not to challenge Nixon openly because he did not believe the Communists would accept the Nixon plan for new presidential elections and it still mentioned the withdrawal of "other outside forces," the code words for the North Vietnamese in the South. As Nha explained: "To please the Americans we went along with Nixon's proposal, but we never changed our position on mutual withdrawal. Thieu was supremely confident that the Communists would never negotiate a political settlement without a military settlement tied to it. So why should Thieu stand in front of an American steamroller?" Nha presented three choices to Thieu: Stand in front of the steamroller, stand aside, or go along for the ride. For the moment, they would go along for the ride and see where it took them.

When Nha left Thieu, he went to his office in the Palace to draft a brief response to the Nixon speech. He woke Thieu at 6:00 a.m. and showed him a paragraph that said: "In light of the peace plan being announced we offer our wholehearted support and will do our best to assure that peace comes."

Despite his gracious public acceptance of Nixon's proposals, Thieu was deeply disturbed by what Nha described as "the cavalier way in which it was handled. Thieu was not consulted in a meaningful manner; he was only informed. He is a pragmatic enough man to realize that in this negotiation the Communists wanted him out. He harbored no illusions of clinging to power as has been portrayed; but he got pissed off. He was told only a few hours in advance of the speech that Nixon was making the secret proposals public and he had no time to really respond. Remember," stressed Nha, "that was the first time we knew the details of Kissinger's secret meetings with the North Vietnamese and Nixon's plans." [16]

Thieu knew only too well that 1972 was another American election year and that pressure would grow rapidly to end the war. From the more than half million Americans in Vietnam when Nixon and Thieu met on Midway in 1969, the number had been reduced by 65,000 that year, 50,000 in 1970, and 250,000 in 1971. By the end of January 1972, there were 139,000 Americans in Vietnam. Then Nixon approved the withdrawal of 70,000 more, so that by May 1, 1972 there would be only 69,000 Americans remaining in Vietnam.

Thieu was ready to go along with Nixon if the American President would increase the amount of American aid. Thieu needed to increase the size of his armed forces to compensate for the Americans who were being withdrawn. He was still trying to get the funds and equipment to establish two additional reserve divisions. He had only the Marine division and an Airborne division as reserves—some 20,000 men. The rest of his troops were tied down in the four corps areas and Saigon. There were no reserves to counter North Vietnamese thrusts across the border. The withdrawal schedule had been accelerated much faster than Thieu was led to believe at Midway, and there was nothing he could do to slow it down. In a conversation with Bunker one day, Thieu offered to send every departing American soldier to a Saigon tailor for a new suit of civilian clothes if the G.I. would leave his uniform, boots, and rifle to equip a Vietnamese soldier. He also offered to lease Cam Ranh Bay to the United States for ninety-nine years. Bunker declined politely, explaining that the United States did not want a permanent base in Vietnam. Thieu warned: "You have it now. Don't throw it away or the Russians will grab it." [17]

It gnawed at Thieu that in his new peace initiative, Nixon had eased away from the agreed-upon position on mutual withdrawal. The wording of Nixon's speech was vague, leaving room for a formula to permit the North Vietnamese to keep their troops in the South. He had shifted from a firm "ruling out a one-sided withdrawal" to a softened, vague position on the withdrawal of "other outside forces." [18] Nixon was very specific that the Americans would withdraw their troops "six months before other outside forces." America had come full circle. From LBJ's insistence that the North Vietnamese withdraw before the Americans, Nixon now offered to pull out before the North Vietnamese.

The offer had been made privately to the North Vietnamese in the secret talks in Paris eight months earlier, on May 31, 1971. [19] In his memoirs, Kissinger insists that Thieu "knew of—and had approved—our May 31 proposal, which had abandoned it [mutual withdrawal]; he now claimed that any public formal change would weaken his domestic situation." [20]

Thieu was in a difficult position having Kissinger as his proxy in the negotiations. He still believed that he was not being abandoned by Nixon despite his growing suspicions of Kissinger.[21] But Thieu never got the kind of detailed briefings he expected.[22] Until Nixon's speech, Thieu believed that the secret meetings in Paris were part of the overall formal negotiations that were taking place in Paris and that Kissinger "was only trying to get the North Vietnamese out of the South as the Americans withdrew." Thieu expected that Kissinger would be representing the South Vietnamese position to the North. Instead, he found that Kissinger had come up with his own agenda. To Thieu, Kissinger's proposals—put forth by Nixon—appeared to be moving closer to the North Vietnamese position. Aware of the weakening American posture, the North Vietnamese on January 27 rejected the American proposal and published their own nine-point peace plan, demanding more specific concessions from the United States.[23] The United States must set a firm date for total American withdrawal, and the entire Saigon government, not only President Thieu, must be ousted. In an effort to divide Saigon and Washington, the Communists called a press conference in Paris suggesting it had an "elaboration" of its nine points. They turned out to be another call for Thieu's resignation and dismantling the ARVN, the police, and the pacification program before negotiations for a coalition government could begin.

After the blow of the January speech, Thieu sought further reassurances from Nixon that there would be "no secret deals." Shortly before Nixon departed for China, Thieu wrote to him again appealing to him not to accept Hanoi's demands and indicating his own willingness to cooperate. Thieu wanted to show Nixon that he would cooperate with the United States and that a solution was possible. In his letter, Thieu cautioned Nixon against a coalition with the Communists, because it was only a step toward Hanoi's ultimate goal of conquest of all Indochina. Thieu warned Nixon that the Communist side in Indochina—which in Thieu's mind included China, the Soviet Union, and North Vietnam—would regard any solution short of their total domination of Indochina only as "a strategic pause." Thieu also emphasized that whether or not there was a signed peace agreement with Hanoi, the ability of the Republic of Vietnam to defend itself was the key to a lasting peace in the area. As a sign of his good faith and intentions Thieu, in writing, offered to step down from the presidency prior to a new presidential election, thus formally accepting Nixon's January proposal.

President Nixon visited China from February 21 to February 28, 1972 —a week, he said, "that changed the world." In his talks with Chairman Mao Zedong and Premier Zhou Enlai, Nixon had made it clear that the Vietnam War should be ended as soon as possible.

The United States and China had each stated their views separately on Vietnam in the Shanghai Communiqué, but in private Nixon made it clear to Premier Zhou that he wanted to withdraw from Vietnam in return for the release of American prisoners of war and a cease-fire. "If I were sitting across the table from whoever is the leader of North Vietnam and we could negotiate a cease-fire and the return of our prisoners, then all Americans would be withdrawn from Vietnam six months from that day,'' Nixon told Zhou in Beijing.[24] The Chinese carefully refrained from directly attacking the American views on Vietnam in the communiqué, but the Chinese did not indicate they would stop supplying military and economic aid to Hanoi.[25] The negotiating record would later show that Kissinger in his talks with Zhou prepared the way for the end of American insistence on mutual withdrawal of armed forces from Vietnam.[26]

The new U.S. relationship with China was based primarily on American power in Asia serving as a deterrent to Soviet expansionism against China.[27] The private talks emphasized the strategic nature of renewal of Sino-American relations, another way of saying that the Chinese viewed the Soviet Union as a greater threat to China than the United States. The United States would be a counterweight to Soviet influence in Asia. Politically the pressure was off the United States, but it was increasing on South Vietnam to accept a coalition government as a solution. The Chinese were supporting the Provisional Revolutionary Government in the South, and while Zhou carefully refrained from criticizing the North Vietnamese, it was the Chinese desire to see a coalition government in the South so that Hanoi would not totally dominate the South as well as Laos and Cambodia. Although the Chinese did not criticize their ostensible ally, they were now in a position to encourage the United States. For the Chinese, the American presence was clearly a lesser evil than the Soviet presence in Southeast Asia.

When he returned from China, Nixon knew he had to reassure Thieu. He dispatched Assistant Secretary of State for East Asian and Pacific Affairs Marshall Green to brief Thieu on the China trip and sent a personal letter replying to Thieu's January letter. Green arrived in Saigon on March 2, 1972, and met with Thieu at the Independence Palace.

Both Green and Secretary of State William Rogers had been excluded by Kissinger and Nixon from the meetings with Premier Zhou and Chairman Mao. The State Department was relegated to negotiating economic and cultural agreements while Kissinger and his National Security Council staffer Winston Lord joined Nixon for the sessions on global strategy and U.S. Chinese political rapprochement.[28] Thieu was not unaware of Green's peripheral role, but he was determined to put a good face on the Nixon trip and greet Nixon's emissary cordially. After a cabinet meeting on March 1, Foreign Minister Tran Van Lam announced that "we fully approve of Mr. Nixon's trip. No one can deny that it helped create an atmosphere of eased tensions." The Vietnamese were pleased by the U.S. support for their position in the Shanghai Communiqué.[29]

Green found Thieu in an optimistic frame of mind. Although he had not been included in the meetings with Mao and Zhou, Green was authorized to assure Thieu that no secret deals had been struck. Thieu read the letter from Nixon rapidly and then he and Green discussed its contents. It was the only letter to a head of state that Green carried on his tour of Southeast Asia to report to American allies on Nixon's visit to China.

In his letter, Nixon praised Thieu for his "generous and statesmanlike offer" to resign prior to a new presidential election, "which can only be regarded as a major move in the search for peace in Indochina." Nixon agreed with Thieu's point that the ability of the Republic of Vietnam to defend itself "is the key to a lasting peace in the area. I want to assure you that I hold the same view." The President also shared Thieu's view that the Communist side sought nothing less than total domination of Indochina as "a possibility against which we must indeed be on guard."

Nixon went on to tell Thieu that in the Shanghai Communiqué of February 28,

> I defined the United States objective in Asia and the world as a peace which is both just and secure—just to fulfill the aspirations of peoples and nations for freedom and progress, and secure to remove the danger of foreign aggression. It is for such a just and secure peace that our two countries have been fighting. You may be certain that I will do all in my power to insure that the enormous sacrifices of the Vietnamese and American peoples do not come to nothing.

Nixon said that his talks with the Chinese leaders had been "highly successful," and that "our lengthy and searching discussions concentrated on bilateral issues between the United States and the People's Republic of China." The meetings were "marked by honesty, candor and directness, and there was no attempt to pretend that major differences did not exist." To reassure Thieu, Nixon then added:

> We negotiated nothing behind the backs of friends of the United States; there were no secret deals. In talking with the Chinese we based our position firmly on the principle that the United States stands by its commitments. When our talks touched on Indochina, I set forth the United States position clearly and forcefully, as reflected in the February 27 communiqué. The Chinese could not have mistaken our sincere desire for peace or our dedication to the principle of self-determination for the people of South Vietnam.

In conclusion, Nixon reiterated his support for Thieu: "You may be confident that you will continue to have the understanding, support, and material assistance of the United States as the people of South Vietnam work to attain security against aggression and to build a just and enduring peace."

Green left Saigon pleased with the public Vietnamese response to the Nixon visit to China and Thieu's high spirits. "President Thieu in our meeting even seemed more optimistic than the facts justified," said Green.[30]

For Thieu, Nixon's words that he would do "all in my power to insure that the enormous sacrifices of the Vietnamese and American peoples do not come to nothing" had a strong impact. Thieu until then had been receiving oral assurances of American support. Now he had a presidential promise in writing based on the blood of American and Vietnamese soldiers. This was to be a theme that Nixon would repeat as his correspondence with

Thieu continued. Thieu weighed the American lives and treasure that had been spent on the war, and concluded that the American investment in Vietnam was too high for a change in policy. The Vietnamese could not imagine that the most powerful nation in the world would accept defeat at the hands of North Vietnam, a nation of twenty-two million people without an industrial base.

The South Vietnamese were deeply impressed with the extent of the American presence in Vietnam and the infrastructure that the Americans laid down on top of the existing Vietnamese society. The Americans had their own communications system, supply depots, airlines, and highways. The American base at Cam Ranh Bay was seen as a strategic anchor holding the United States to South Vietnam. Here was the base that the Russians desired and that historically had been their refueling port during the Russo-Japanese War of 1904–05. The Americans had spent an estimated $2 billion to build a naval and air base around the natural harbor, which has been coveted by Western powers since the nineteenth century. It was a perfect site, with deep-water piers, POL jetties, airfields, and club houses. Cam Ranh had everything from ice-making equipment to a custom-built bungalow for presidential visits. In all there were some 5,000 buildings in the complex. With radar coverage in the highlands at Ban Me Thuot protecting the base, it had a strategic advantage unparalleled anywhere in Southeast Asia. Vietnamese General Lu Lan, former commander of Military Region II, called the Cam Ranh–Ban Me Thuot link "a military beauty."

The four-lane highway from Saigon to Bien Hoa, some twenty-five miles long, was another engineering miracle frequently mentioned by Vietnamese as part of America's strategic commitment to South Vietnam. In case of war with China, so the story went, the highway would be used as a landing field for American jet aircraft. The fifty American-built airfields throughout the country impressed the Vietnamese that the Americans were there to stay.

For the Vietnamese, aside from American lives lost and dollars spent, there was the basic issue of honor, prestige, and saving face. The Vietnamese could not imagine that the United States would be prepared to accept defeat in South Vietnam or withdraw under unfavorable conditions. Hung recalls people in Saigon using the phrase, *My khong the bo Vietnam* ("The Americans cannot abandon Vietnam"). The Vietnamese viewed America as the great victor in World War II and again in the Korean War. America was the superpower that had forced the Soviet Union to back down in the Cuban missile crisis. Most generals shared this perception. Air Force Commander General Tran Van Minh said: "I never dreamed that our friends would betray us and drop us. I thought of Berlin and Korea. And I saw how the Americans protected them. I thought that we, too, were one of the outposts of freedom in the world."[31]

Yet Thieu remained worried about Nixon's Beijing trip and thought Nixon protested too much that no secret deals had been made. The Chinese, in their efforts to gain influence in Vietnam, supported the Provisional Revolutionary Government, and the Shanghai Communiqué carried a Chinese statement in support of the PRG.[32]

Thieu was so concerned to find out what had happened in China that he sent Hoang Duc Nha to Washington in February to get a reading on American intentions toward South Vietnam and to sound out the Americans on Nixon's new China policy. When he came to Washington, Nha met with Hung and asked him for an assessment of the American attitude toward South Vietnam and reactions to Nixon's January 25 peace plan. "We are like frogs looking up from the darkness at the bottom of a well," said Nha, using the Vietnamese proverb to describe a situation where one is completely in the dark about another's motives or intentions.

When Hung asked why Thieu had agreed to step down before new elections, Nha replied: "Tremendous pressure from the Americans."

Returning to Saigon, Nha conveyed Hung's observations to Thieu that the China trip had been enormously successful for Nixon and no longer was China considered the primary threat in Southeast Asia. The United States had taken advantage of China's fear of the Soviet Union. South Vietnam was caught in the squeeze play the United States was developing between the Soviet Union and China. Hung had told Nha that Vietnam would command less attention from the United States and was no longer an important asset on the strategic global balance sheet. He urged Nha to convince President Thieu that Saigon needed to present its case better in America. Nha reported that he and Hung got on well together and Nha was impressed with Hung's grasp of the American scene.

Thieu sought a diplomatic initiative of his own following Nixon's China trip. After studying Nixon's letter, and the findings of Nha's visit to Washington, President Thieu decided to ask Hung to come to Saigon for consultations.

As Hung approached Saigon from the air on March 30, 1972, the ordered green rice paddies seemed peaceful. Only the presence of new cemeteries around the city made him realize how the intensity of the war had increased since his last visit just a few months earlier. Usually the plane arrived after dark; now as the sun was setting he could see the panorama of the city spread below him: the red tile of the rooftops and the yellow and tan of the buildings lying gracefully amid the giant tamarind flame trees with their bursts of bright orange flowers.

At Ton San Nhut Airport the weather was hot and muggy, the heat so intense it left a steamy haze even after the sun set. The airfield was filled with C-130 cargo planes painted in camouflage brown and green. Hung felt the increased tempo of the war as he watched helicopters rise and descend in a far corner of the airfield, the heavy whine of their engines and the thumping beat of their rotors reverberating in the red sky.

In the middle of the night a giant explosion woke Hung from his sleep in the family's house on Phan Dinh Phung Street in central Saigon. His mother told him to get under the bed because she thought it was a Communist rocket attack. The sound of the explosions reminded Hung of his childhood in North Vietnam, when his mother used to order him and his brothers and sisters to get under their beds if they heard shellfire. The sound of aircraft circling the city continued through the night, but after the initial explosion there was no more firing.

Saigon starts the day early: by 5:00 a.m. the sound of motor scooters in the street was loud and continuous, waking Hung up. He laughed when he found himself under the bed instead of on top of it. When he called to the Palace to report his arrival, he was told that the North Vietnamese had invaded the South across the demilitarized zone at Dong Ha and were advancing rapidly. His meeting with Thieu had been postponed—he was to call at the end of the day to be advised of military developments. Shocked at the news, Hung quickly realized that all his hopes for a trade initiative with North Vietnam had vanished with the invasion.

The North Vietnamese action was taken to prevent the Chinese and the Russians, whom Nixon would visit in May, from compromising Hanoi's interests by supporting U.S. efforts to move toward meaningful peace talks. The North Vietnamese knew from their experience in Geneva in 1954 that they could not win at the conference table what they had not gained on the battlefield.

In November 1971, after Nixon's visit to Beijing was announced, Prime Minister Pham Van Dong of North Vietnam, hoping to forestall the U.S. initiative toward improving relations with China, visited Beijing, where he had a tense meeting with Mao Zedong and urged him not to receive Nixon. Mao said that the North Vietnamese successes had forced Nixon to come to China. Then Mao quoted an old Chinese proverb: "If the handle of your broom is too short, you cannot wipe out a spider high on the wall of a closet. So you must allow it to stay." The message was clear: Hanoi should not seek a total victory in the South. The North Vietnamese, implied Mao, did not have the resources to get rid of the Americans and should settle for less than total American withdrawal. Pham Van Dong replied: "Excuse me, but the handle of the Vietnamese broom is long enough to sweep all these dogs out of Vietnam."[33] Ignoring the Chinese warning and Nixon's forthcoming summit with Brezhnev, the North Vietnamese decided to proceed on their own.

Nixon was furious when word of the North Vietnamese attack across the DMZ reached the White House on March 30. It had not been expected; Vietnamization had been going well, and during the first three months of 1972 the United States thought that Hanoi would not be able to launch a spring offensive. The South Vietnamese, however, were less surprised. Thieu recalled the pattern of increased North Vietnamese activity during an American election year. The Tet Offensive in 1968 had had a major influence on the American political scene and Thieu was expecting a similar major move.

Three North Vietnamese divisions, an estimated 30,000 men, supported by more than 200 Soviet T-54 tanks, spearheaded the attack. The North Vietnamese then struck on three other fronts. In all, fourteen divisions and twenty-six independent regiments totaling an estimated 150,000 men attacked. Nixon ordered massive bombing of the North Vietnamese supply lines and storage depots. In a meeting in the Oval Office, Nixon complained to Haldeman and Ehrlichman of the poor flying weather in Vietnam. "Damn it, if you know any prayers, say them. . . . Let's get that weather cleared up. The bastards have never been bombed like they're going to be bombed this time, but you've got to have the weather."[34]

On the evening of April 1, Hung was briefed at the Palace. The Communists had seized ARVN's M-48 tanks in Loc Ninh near the Cambodian border and near Dong Ha. At gunpoint, they had forced the South Vietnamese drivers to turn their tanks against their own troops. It was also the first time that the North Vietnamese were able to mount a conventional attack with their own tanks. The guerrilla war entered a new phase, transformed into conventional warfare. The equipment was primarily Soviet-made and had come to North Vietnam in 1971.[35] Nixon and Kissinger could speak of detente, but the Russians had already played their card for Hanoi by providing new war supplies.

Thieu met with Hung after the first week of the offensive, when military conditions were at a low ebb. Thieu recalled Lyndon Johnson's understanding with Hanoi as part of the 1968 bombing halt: Hanoi would not cross the DMZ with its troops as long as the United States suspended its bombing. Because of that understanding, Thieu stationed the newly formed and weak 3rd Division below the DMZ. It was quickly overwhelmed by the North Vietnamese invasion force, which captured Dong Ha, Quang Tri, and overran the outer defenses of Kontum City. The scale of the North Vietnamese attack and the scale of firepower had changed the balance of forces. Negotiations were out of the question until the balance of forces could be redressed. Vietnamization was on trial.

At Hung's meeting with Thieu, they discussed the invasion. There was no talk of trade with the North. Thieu told Hung that North Vietnam's invasion force was using advanced weaponry, such as 133mm recoilless artillery and Soviet-made T-54 tanks. "We desperately need new equipment quickly. The Americans should send M-48 tanks, TOW* anti-tank missiles, and 175mm howitzers. Worst of all, we have no reserve forces. We need American support to establish two new divisions as reserve forces. Try your best to talk to all our friends in Washington and I will approach the President through my own channels," Thieu said.

The reports coming back to Washington on the performance of the South Vietnamese armed forces were discouraging. General Creighton Abrams, the U.S. commander in Vietnam, cabled that it was quite possible that the South Vietnamese had lost their will to fight and that all might be lost.[36] Nixon decided to buoy President Thieu's spirits in an effort to stiffen

* Tubular-launched, Optically tracked, Wire-guided.

the South Vietnamese will. He sent him a brief message, which was delivered by Ambassador Bunker. The text read:

> At this trying time for you and your brave forces, you can be assured of our continued support for the people of South Vietnam in the courageous defense of their homeland. What will ultimately determine the outcome of this struggle is the will and spirit of the South Vietnamese people. Hanoi cannot win unless they break the spirit of the free people of South Viet-Nam.
>
> I am confident that you will continue to provide the inspired leadership which will guarantee the survival of South Viet-Nam as an independent country.

In his diary for May 2, Nixon wrote: "I think it is vitally important that we not be responsible for his losing his courage at this very difficult time when bad news is coming in from the war front. The real problem is that the enemy is willing to sacrifice in order to win, while the South Vietnamese simply aren't willing to pay that much of a price in order to avoid losing. And, as Haig points out, all the air power in the world and strikes on Hanoi-Haiphong aren't going to save South Vietnam if the South Vietnamese aren't able to hold on the ground." [37]

On April 5, Nixon wrote to Thieu assuring him of his support and trying to stiffen the South Vietnamese morale. The letter was a prime example of Nixon's careful use of American encouragement while urging Thieu to perform better. It read:

> Dear President Thieu:
>
> I want you to know that in this moment of great trial for the Vietnamese people, you have my fullest support as President of the United States and Commander-in-Chief of our armed forces.
>
> Hanoi's invasion across the provisional demarcation line of 1954 is a flagrant and outrageous violation of both the Geneva Accords of 1954 and 1968 understandings which led to the cessation of bombardments and all other acts involving the use of force by the United States against North Vietnam.
>
> You can be sure that the United States stands fully behind the heroic efforts of your people in the defense of their homeland. I can assure you that in the days and weeks ahead we will not hesitate to take whatever added military steps are necessary to support the intense and valiant struggle in which your country is now engaged. We cannot allow Hanoi's intensified and blatant aggression to go unpunished.
>
> Allow me to take this opportunity to express my continuing and profound admiration for the leadership you are providing your people in these moments of difficulty and the bravery they have shown in resisting Hanoi's attacks. I am confident that with our assistance you will succeed in overcoming the present threat posed by Hanoi's forces to your people and that ultimately we will achieve our mutual goal of a just and lasting peace.
>
> Sincerely,
> [s]Richard Nixon

For Thieu, the letter was a much-needed stimulant, and he showed it to the Chief of the Joint General Staff, General Cao Van Vien, and his prime minister, Tran Thien Khiem. This was his third letter from Nixon and it had come at an opportune time. Nixon had praised his leadership, spoken of ultimately achieving "our mutual goal," and promised not to allow "Hanoi's intensified and blatant aggression to go unpunished."

The letters afforded Thieu a mystique of power to be used with his generals and cabinet ministers. They demonstrated that Thieu could deal as an equal with the American President, since they represented the highest form of communication between heads of state and government. They possessed a legitimacy that overpowered the transitory nature of conversations and oral instructions delivered by an ambassador or an emissary. In an exchange of letters Thieu and Nixon were equals. The American President's word on behalf of the most powerful nation in the world was formally recorded and his promise sealed. The letters were tangible proof of Thieu's modern Mandate from Heaven from the American gods, who could supply bombers, ammunition, and one billion dollars a year in economic and military assistance.

Nixon backed his words to Thieu with strong actions. On April 1, the U.S. President ordered the bombing of North Vietnamese territory within twenty-five miles of the demilitarized zone. Within two weeks he ordered air strikes up to the 20th parallel. American airpower provided massive support for the ARVN. Helicopters with the capability of destroying enemy tanks were flown to the battlefield to counter the North Vietnamese. Two cruisers and eight destroyers were sent to Vietnam for sea bombardment of the invading forces.

Thieu wrote back in reply to Nixon on April 17, thanking him for the "prompt response" to the North Vietnamese invasion. Thieu told Nixon, "it seems to me that the current offensive is the beginning of a supreme effort made by Hanoi before it would decide either to accept a negotiated settlement or to fade away. Therefore it is likely to last throughout this year, which is the electoral year in the United States." He emphasized the new sophisticated weapons being used by the North Vietnamese—tanks, surface-to-air missiles, and long-range artillery—and asked for "increased and accelerated help from the United States" for modernizing the Vietnamese armed forces, particularly the air force.

Now was the time for military action. Thieu had to rally his forces and halt the North Vietnamese. He turned to the best professional soldier he had, General Ngo Quang Truong, and appointed him the new commander in I Corp at the northern front. Truong was a dynamic combat leader with a reputation for integrity and honesty—a rarity among the top generals—who had proved his ability in crushing the Viet Cong during the 1968 Tet Offensive. Tall, lean and intense, Truong was like a coiled spring, eager to attack the enemy. Despite his success as a general he remained a professional soldier with no political ambitions. A southerner, born in the Mekong delta, Truong worked well with his American advisers. He went into the field with

his men and showed compassion for them. Under Truong's leadership the
ARVN forces stiffened and bloody fighting with high casualties on both
sides took place in May.[38]

As the South Vietnamese sought to stem the North Vietnamese invasion, Nixon's mind was on his upcoming summit with Brezhnev in Moscow.
He could not negotiate with the Soviet leader from a position of strength if
the American commitment to Vietnam was crushed by the North Vietnamese invasion. Nixon was determined to punish the North Vietnamese before
he visited Moscow. He began to consider the mining of Haiphong Harbor
and the bombing of prime military targets in North Vietnam. Kissinger was
scheduled for a secret pre-summit trip to the Soviet capital to pave the way
and work out major issues on the agenda with the Soviet leader from April
20 to April 25. So secret was the visit by Kissinger and his team that the
American ambassador in Moscow, Jacob Beam, was not informed of Kissinger's presence in the city until he was preparing to leave.

Nixon instructed Kissinger to insist upon a Vietnam settlement with
Brezhnev "as a prerequisite for discussion on any other subject."[39] There
could be no agreements until Moscow prevailed on North Vietnam to end
the war through negotiations. Kissinger however disobeyed his instructions
from Nixon, pressing ahead with negotiations for an agreement on the control of strategic nuclear weapons that was "considerably more favorable"
than Nixon and Kissinger expected and became SALT I.[40]

During his secret talks with Brezhnev at the Dom Pryomov, the official
guest house in the Lenin Hills overlooking the Moscow River, Kissinger
offered the North Vietnamese, through the Russians, a series of concessions
that would form the basis for the final Paris Agreement in January 1973.
Kissinger told Brezhnev that the United States would be willing to accept a
cease-fire in place in exchange for the removal of only those North Vietnamese forces that had entered the South since the start of the offensive on
March 31. Those who had entered the South before the offensive, an estimated 200,000, could remain in place. This was the first time that the United
States explicitly agreed to allow North Vietnamese troops to remain in the
South. This specific American concession was made without Thieu's agreement, and for the first time the United States sent a message to Hanoi via
Moscow that it was retreating from the principle that had been agreed upon
with South Vietnam for mutual withdrawal.[41]

In the past, when the United States used the expression "cease-fire in
place," it had meant that a cease-fire would be the starting point for negotiations that would include "mutual withdrawal" of forces. President Thieu
found the American logic baffling. He said he repeatedly told Bunker and
Kissinger that "only after Hanoi agreed to withdraw its troops from the
South should there be a cease-fire."[42] Until Kissinger's Moscow trip, the
United States had only hinted at allowing the North to maintain its troops
in the South. The January 25, 1972, American proposal had been deliberately vague, calling for "the withdrawal of outside forces from Indochina,
and the implementation of the principle that all armed forces of the countries
of Indochina must remain within their national frontiers."

When Kissinger returned from Moscow, he brought with him an indication from Brezhnev that the North Vietnamese were prepared to negotiate a settlement. "We have to see what unfolds, but some expectation of serious talks turned our position around," Kissinger said. White House aides indicated that "Brezhnev has given us more than a signal."[43] Nixon in a nationwide television address on April 26 said, "We are resuming the Paris Talks with the firm expectation that productive talks leading to rapid progress will follow through all available channels."

By May 1, Nixon, deeply engrossed in preparations for the forthcoming summit with Brezhnev, received a letter from the Soviet leader asking him to refrain from further actions in Vietnam because "they hurt the chances of a successful summit."[44] Nixon sent a stiff reply, noting that "promised Soviet influence if it has been exercised at all has proved unavailing."[45]

That evening, after attending the White House Correspondents' dinner, Kissinger flew to Paris to meet with the North Vietnamese for a secret negotiating session. He found them so "insolent and unbearable" that he broke off the talks. For Nixon, "that was Hanoi's last chance. I decided that now it was essential to defeat North Vietnam's invasion."[46] Nixon was determined to go ahead with the mining of Hanoi and Haiphong. Although the summit with Brezhnev was at stake, Nixon decided he could not go to Moscow while losing the war in Vietnam. He saw the bombing and mining as the best course to follow—one that would not put the Russians in a corner, but would exercise continual pressure on the North Vietnamese invasion by interdicting supplies.

Nixon discussed the action and its impact on a summit with Kissinger, H. R. Haldeman, Treasury Secretary John Connally, and Alexander Haig, Kissinger's deputy. Nixon told them: "The summit isn't worth a damn if the price for it is losing in Vietnam. My instinct tells me that the country can take losing the summit, but it can't take losing the war."[47] Kissinger and his staff were almost certain the Russians would cancel the summit. He told Nixon there was only a 20 or 25 percent possibility of noncancelation. Kissinger was overshadowed by John Connally and Attorney General John Mitchell, who urged Nixon to proceed with the bombing and the mining. They assured Nixon that his actions would not kill the summit.[48]

When he went on the air on May 8 to announce the mining of North Vietnamese waters and the continuance of air and naval strikes against North Vietnam, Nixon also included a peace proposal with a cease-fire in place that did not demand the withdrawal of North Vietnamese troops. At the same time as he was escalating the war, Nixon kept on the table the May 31, 1971, U.S. proposal for a cease-fire in place. As Nixon acknowledged in his memoirs, this peace proposal became the reference point for the terms of the final settlement in January 1973.[49]

Nixon advised Thieu of his plans to mine Haiphong Harbor in a message delivered by Ambassador Bunker on May 9. There was no prior consultation. Nixon assumed Thieu's concurrence for "a new course of action designed to bring this war to an end." Nixon's message was:

In my speech, I propose to announce that our two governments have decided that North Vietnamese aggression must be met by action to interdict the delivery of supplies to North Viet-Nam. I will announce that I have ordered the mining of the entrances to North Vietnamese ports and have directed U.S. forces to prevent the seaborne delivery of supplies to North Viet-Nam within its claimed territorial waters. Rail and other transportation means will also be interdicted.

The foregoing actions will continue until the following conditions are met: the implementation of an internationally supervised cease-fire throughout Indochina and the release of prisoners of war.

In my speech I will state that when the foregoing conditions have been met, we will stop all acts of force throughout Indo-China and U.S. forces will be withdrawn from South Viet-Nam within four months.

As we are both aware, Mr. President, neither your country nor mine has ever sought to impose a military defeat on Hanoi. We have always sought to end the conflict through negotiations in a way which would leave the people of South Viet-Nam the opportunity to decide their own future free from outside coercion or interference. In taking the steps I am announcing tonight, a negotiated settlement remains our preferred course; but Hanoi has posed us with absolutely unacceptable preconditions and their military challenge to you and your allies leaves no choice but to respond in the fashion we are.

I am fully confident that the measures I am announcing tonight will be welcomed by your people and Armed Forces as an earnest of our determination to help them defend themselves and as an opportunity to turn back decisively the invasion launched by Hanoi's forces on March 30. It is important that these measures in defense of your country be seen as having been taken in consultation with you and in conjunction with your own efforts of self-defense. I am sure, therefore, that you will agree with my intention to associate your government with the measures I propose to announce.

Permit me to say, however, in the spirit of friendship and frankness that has always characterized our relationship, it is my view that in the last analysis the U.S. air and seapower are only contributing and not decisive factors in the battle now raging in your country. The decisive element will be the performance of the people and armed forces of the Republic of Viet-Nam in resisting the challenge they now face.

I, therefore, want to take this occasion to urge that you and your people use the opportunity offered by the steps I am announcing tonight to redouble your efforts against the North Vietnamese invaders, to regain the initiative against their regular forces and to recover population and territory which has been temporarily lost to their control. It will be hard to explain to the United States people, after I have taken these steps, if the RVNAF does not perform more aggressively and the people of South Viet-Nam are not mobilized for the emergency.

We will be watching developments on the ground in South Viet-Nam in the days and weeks ahead with the deepest interest and concern and I am confident that under your determined leadership the heroic people of your country will prevail over Hanoi's aggression.

Thieu welcomed the news of the mining of Haiphong Harbor and the continued air attacks on the North. In fact, he was so elated by the message from Nixon that he failed to understand the fine shading of Nixon's new peace proposal. Thieu assumed that the American proposal for a cease-fire was only the starting point for a final, comprehensive peace settlement that would bring mutual withdrawal.

In the Vietnamese translation of Nixon's letter, Thieu wrote "eight points" in the margin next to Nixon's sentence insisting that his conditions be met before the bombing stopped. Thieu assumed Nixon was still referring to the eight points of his January 25 peace plan that included ambiguous language on mutual withdrawal. The United States called for "withdrawal of outside forces from Indochina." Thieu still hoped that he could prevail on the United States to agree not to change the joint Saigon-Washington position on mutual withdrawal. Although the language had been softened, it was still open to interpretation, and Thieu was determined to strengthen it so that a final settlement would not leave North Vietnamese troops in the South. In fact, the U.S. position had changed. The United States was ready to accept a cease-fire in place, drop mutual withdrawal, and not maintain a residual force of American troops in South Vietnam as it had done in Europe and Korea.

The excitement and reactions generated by the mining of Haiphong and the renewed bombing of the North took precedence over detailed interpretation of Nixon's peace proposal in his speech.[50] They obscured the major shift in the American position that had formed the basis for Kissinger's secret Vietnam negotiations with Brezhnev in Moscow.

Richard Nixon's strategy was to complement negotiations with the strengthening of South Vietnam through Vietnamization. In theory, the two tracks would be parallel and complement each other. In practice, they competed with and undercut each other. To Saigon, Vietnamization was the key to survival and reaching the capability for self-defense against the North. The more Vietnamization took hold, the less willing Thieu was to negotiate with the North and accept a coalition with the Provisional Revolutionary Government. For Hanoi, there was no incentive to make concessions in the negotiations as long as American withdrawals were being accelerated as part of Vietnamization. The U.S. policy softened domestic political pressures to end the war, but was counterproductive. The policies of Vietnamization and negotiation neutralized each other instead of enhancing the goals both policies sought.

4

Threats of Assassination

DESPITE THE MINING of Haiphong and the bombing of targets in Hanoi, Leonid Brezhnev decided to go ahead with the summit with Richard Nixon. Brezhnev was more concerned with a strategic arms agreement and trade with the United States than he was with North Vietnam's war in the South, and he wanted to counter the impact of Nixon's dramatic trip to China.[1] At the summit, which took place from May 22 to June 1, there were four separate meetings on Vietnam, including a brutally frank evening session at Brezhnev's dacha where Kosygin, Podgorny, and Brezhnev all strongly criticized the United States and its support for President Thieu. He was characterized by Kosygin as the "so-called President in South Vietnam . . . who had not been chosen by anyone." Nixon retorted by asking, "Who chose the President of North Vietnam?"

"The entire people," Kosygin replied. Nixon told him to continue.[2] When Kosygin finished his attack, Podgorny launched into another. Nixon defended his actions in mining Haiphong and told the Soviet leaders that since the North Vietnamese offensive began "30,000 South Vietnamese civilians, men women and children, have been killed by the North Vietnamese using Soviet equipment." They listened intently but made no attempt to respond before adjourning for a lavish dinner accompanied by much joking, laughing, and storytelling—"as if the acrimonious session downstairs had never happened."[3]

Kissinger also met with Foreign Minister Gromyko on May 25. The Russian position was that they could live with the existing situation, which implied acceptance of American bombing of the North, support for Saigon, and the presence of American forces in the South until a settlement was reached. Kissinger indicated that American bombing of North Vietnam did not necessarily have to continue until all the POW's had been returned. This was contrary to his speech two weeks earlier in which he had announced that the bombing and mining would continue until American prisoners were returned.

Kissinger also told Gromyko that the United States was prepared to accept a three-part electoral commission in South Vietnam that would include the Saigon government, the Viet Cong, and the neutralists. Until then, the United States secret proposal had spoken only of an independent body to organize and run "a presidential election." Thieu opposed a tripartite body because he saw it as giving legitimacy to the Provisional Revolutionary Government and evolving into a coalition government. Moscow agreed to pass the word along to Hanoi.

For Hung in Washington, there was a continuing effort to convince supporters of President Thieu that the North Vietnamese offensive could be repulsed. Hung carried Thieu's request for M-48 tanks, TOW anti-tank missiles, 175mm artillery, and the support for two reserve divisions to Warren Nutter at the Pentagon. Hung also met regularly with Dr. Edward E. Elson, chaplain for the U.S. Senate. Reverend Elson, a prominent Presbyterian leader, had visited Vietnam in 1967 as a member of a presidential delegation to observe the Vietnamese presidential election and was favorably impressed. Hung and Reverend Elson would meet in the Senate dining room to discuss how to help senators "better understand American interests in Vietnam." Hung sensed that there was still a chance for continuing military support, but if South Vietnam's forces could not halt the North Vietnamese Easter offensive, the Americans would lose faith in South Vietnam and lessen their support.

After the Moscow Summit, Kissinger set off for Beijing to brief Zhou Enlai on his meetings in Moscow and enlist Chinese support for a Vietnam settlement. On June 6, Le Duc Tho announced he would agree to further secret talks with Kissinger if the United States presented new proposals to end the war and the Paris Talks were resumed. (The official Paris Talks at the International Conference Center on Avenue Kléber had been suspended by the United States on March 26 because the Communists refused to negotiate seriously.) While Kissinger was meeting with Zhou on June 16, Nikolai Podgorny, a high-ranking Politburo member, was in Hanoi reporting on the Moscow Summit to the North Vietnamese. Kissinger urged Zhou to prevail on Hanoi to ease back on its demands. The secret record of the meetings includes summaries of the philosophical conversations between Kissinger and Zhou. The trouble with the North Vietnamese, Kissinger told Zhou, was that they were too greedy and wanted everything at once. They were afraid of the process of history. He asked Zhou why Hanoi was so afraid of history and why it couldn't see the whole process as two separate stages. The first step, according to Kissinger, would be the American disengagement. History would then run its course in Vietnam. Kissinger complained to Zhou that the North Vietnamese were asking the United States to overthrow a friend—something the United States would not do. Kissinger was trying hard to engage the Chinese to play a mediating role with Hanoi.

In his conversations with Zhou, Kissinger tried to play down the importance of Vietnam to American foreign policy. Instead, he spoke of the global strategic balance, the Soviet threat, and the mutuality of American and Chinese interests in Asia.[4]

No sooner had Kissinger returned from China and briefed the President than Nixon decided to send General Haig to Saigon to brief Thieu on the Moscow Summit and Kissinger's trip to Beijing. Talking points for Haig to deliver to President Thieu were drafted by Kissinger and Winston Lord. Kissinger did not, of course, make any mention in the talking points for Haig of his efforts to get Zhou to intercede with Hanoi.

When he arrived in Saigon, Haig did not discuss the U.S. shift in position to accept a standstill cease-fire that would leave the North Vietnamese with their troops in the South. Rather, he described the new U.S. negotiating proposal, which had grown out of Nixon's May 9 speech and which Kissinger would present to Le Duc Tho on July 19. The plan called for a cease-fire, the return of POW's, a four-month U.S. withdrawal, and Thieu's resignation before a new presidential election. As Haig explained it to Thieu: "The United States had been attempting to combine the firm measures taken on the military front with a demonstration of reasonableness on the negotiating front."[5]

Thieu told Haig that Hanoi did not feel under pressure to negotiate and would not settle unless it could obtain a coalition government. His concept of a cease-fire was different from Kissinger's. He believed that the outstanding issues had to be negotiated first and then a cease-fire implemented. A cease-fire without prior agreement would only lead to violations and would be difficult, if not impossible, to supervise. Kissinger, in his memoirs, says that Thieu "was subtly rejecting what we had been offering with his concurrence since October 7, 1970, and what the President had reaffirmed as late as May 8."[6] Thieu insists he never accepted the idea of North Vietnamese troops remaining in the South. A close examination of the record of President Nixon's press conference statements and Kissinger's comments at news conferences and in background sessions for the press, at the time the speeches were made, all indicate that mutual withdrawal was still the public American goal.[7] Only after the Paris Agreement was signed did Kissinger acknowledge that the changes in wording of President Nixon's statements on mutual withdrawal had signaled a change in the U.S. position.

While Kissinger was pressing for a political settlement, both the North and the South Vietnamese were still awaiting the resolution of the military struggle on the battlefield. When Hung had met with Thieu in April, the President told him that the Communists were trying to achieve a decisive military victory so they could enter the final negotiations in a dominant position. Hung wrote to Thieu in late June advising him that American public opinion was being influenced by press coverage of the Vietnam War, which clearly conveyed the message that South Vietnam was being defeated by the North. "It seems to me that the American perception is that there is going to be another Dien Bien Phu,* and South Vietnam is a lost cause,"

---

* The French were defeated at Dien Bien Phu in May 1954, and consequently forced to withdraw from Vietnam.

wrote Hung. He urged on Thieu the importance of a decisive battlefield victory to reverse the trend; otherwise, he cautioned, American support for the war would continue to decline.

Kissinger met with Le Duc Tho in Paris on July 19, for six and a half hours. He was aware that Thieu had complained that any cease-fire had to be linked to the withdrawal of all North Vietnamese forces within three months. Kissinger decided not to pursue this major disagreement with Thieu in his talks with Le Duc Tho, "since it seemed irrelevant to the deadlocked negotiations."[8] On August 1, Kissinger and Le Duc Tho met for eight hours in Paris, their longest session. The North Vietnamese began to make concessions and suggested speeding up the timetable of the negotiations.[9] Another meeting was held on August 14; Bunker reported to Thieu that "the other side said nothing new, merely reviewing their positions."[10] Bunker's brief single-page report to Thieu insisted that the meeting "produced no new developments." Yet, in his memoirs, Kissinger quotes a long memo to Nixon on the same day explaining how in the recent Paris negotiations "we have gotten closer to a negotiated settlement than ever before; our negotiating record is becoming impeccable, and we still have a chance to make an honorable peace."[11]

On August 17, Henry Kissinger, accompanied by his Vietnam negotiating team, visited Saigon to confer with President Thieu on Kissinger's forthcoming negotiations with Le Duc Tho in Paris on September 15. Kissinger's team was chosen for loyalty, stamina, and expertise. His Vietnam expert was John Negroponte, a handsome young Foreign Service Officer out of Yale (class of 1960), who had learned Vietnamese and had six years experience in Saigon and at the public Paris Talks before coming to the National Security Council staff in 1970. The inner team consisted of Winston Lord, then thirty-four, a bright, eager, but self-effacing foreign policy generalist with a special interest in China through his marriage to Bette Bao, the daughter of a former Chinese Nationalist government official. He met her when they were students at the Fletcher School of Law and Diplomacy at Tufts University in Boston. At first, Winston Lord was best known as the son of Mary Lord, a wealthy Republican National Committee woman who was one of the first women to represent the United States at the United Nations. But he quickly established his own reputation as an able and devoted acolyte of Kissinger, ever resilient, smiling, fast and clear with a draft position paper or joint communiqué. Lord and Peter Rodman, then only twenty-four, were like faithful samurai—some said watchdogs—for Kissinger. Rodman, a Harvard Law School graduate, joined Kissinger in 1969. He served as an administrative assistant, combining talents as researcher, organizer, and writer. Rodman carried the black bag with top secret materials, and dutifully saw to it that Kissinger was supplied with his cables and orange juice in the morning. Together with a devoted group of secretaries that included Julie Pineau, Irene Derus, Laura Simkis, and Wilma Hall, they made a formidable team.

The meetings with Thieu did not go well. Saigon was filled with rumors that Kissinger had come to impose peace. Thieu was feeling strong as a result of the successful counteroffensive of his forces under the command of General Truong, who had defeated the invading troops over the summer with the help of American airpower. General Truong was about to retake Quang Tri, thus returning the military balance to the position it had been in before the Easter invasion. Half of the North Vietnamese invasion force, some 75,000 men, were killed or wounded. Thieu's success in the counteroffensive, Ambassador Bunker told Kissinger, would make him reluctant to enter into negotiations with Hanoi. Thieu seemed, according to Bunker, "genuinely afraid of peace." [12]

Kissinger and Thieu spoke past each other. As Kissinger wrote in his memoirs:

> The dialogue between Saigon and Washington thus developed like a Greek tragedy in which each side in pursuit of its own necessities produces what it most dreads. For in essence both sides were right. Thieu was a patriot and a highly intelligent man. He had seen his country through a searing war with ability and dedication. He did not deserve the opprobrium American opponents of the war heaped on him as an outlet for their frustration and as an alibi for the surrender they wanted to force on their government. But the imperatives on him were almost diametrically opposite of ours. [13]

Thieu was adamantly opposed to Kissinger's suggestion that Hanoi's proposal for a coalition government should be dealt with through a three-part Committee of Reconciliation. While Kissinger saw this as burying the issue of a coalition, Thieu saw it as legitimizing the Communist claim for the Provisional Revolutionary Government to participate in the government of the South on an equal basis. Kissinger understood that for Thieu "to accept the potential legitimacy of those seeking to subvert it [the South] was to undermine the psychological basis of his rule. Yet their acceptance in some form was inherent in even the attenuated compromise proposal. Thieu's domestic imperatives imposed intransigence. We could sustain our support for him only by a show of conciliation. Our goal was honor; we could (as the phrase went) run a risk for peace. But Thieu's problem was survival; he and his people would be left indefinitely after we departed; he had no margin for error." [14]

During their meeting in Saigon, Thieu asked Kissinger what had happened to Saigon's point insisting on mutual withdrawal in Thieu's memorandum of April 13, 1972. "We informed you we didn't agree to a change in our position on mutual withdrawal," explained Thieu.

Referring to his meeting in Moscow seeking Soviet support to influence Hanoi, Kissinger replied: "Mr. President, I could not get the Russians to accept your position."

"We want it restated as our joint position," insisted Thieu.

"We'll try, but we don't know if they will accept it," replied Kissinger. [15]

For Thieu, the Kissinger visit was disconcerting. It was again apparent that the American position on mutual withdrawal had softened. Thieu sensed that Kissinger was working behind his back with the North Vietnamese and he was determined to get a reading on how far the negotiations would go in Paris. He was equally determined not to give way on a coalition government. "What we really wanted was not negotiations by proxy, but a chance to negotiate directly with the North Vietnamese," Thieu recalled. "We were prepared to pursue the war with American help." [16]

During their meeting Kissinger raised the idea of a South Vietnamese raid against the North to draw northern troops back from the South. At that point Thieu did not take Kissinger seriously. When Operation Lam Son was proposed in 1971, Thieu had suggested that the South Vietnamese land troops in North Vietnam around the supply base in Vinh, one hundred miles north of the demilitarized zone. That way, he had argued with the Americans, the North Vietnamese would not be able to concentrate their forces around Tchepone and the diversionary attack by South Vietnamese troops would weaken the ability of the North Vietnamese to counter the thrust against their Laos supply center. The Americans rejected the idea and Thieu realized that American public opinion would not permit Nixon to back a South Vietnamese attack against the North on its own territory.

When Kissinger raised the idea with Thieu during his August 1972 visit, Thieu could not imagine Kissinger was serious. As Nha explained: "When Kissinger broached the subject of an attack on North Vietnam, we saw it as a kind of lollipop treatment, you know, tossing us a lollipop to sweeten the situation; but we never paid serious attention. It was a kind of joke to us."

In the same meeting the South Vietnamese made clear their objections to the U.S. proposal for a Committee of National Reconciliation. Kissinger pressed hard, saying, "I'm going to talk to Le Duc Tho again in Paris. This is the position you will agree to." [17] The Vietnamese appeared to be accommodating, and Kissinger left Saigon on August 19 "with a false sense of having reached a meeting of the minds." Messages were to be exchanged through Ambassador Bunker on remaining disagreements.

Nixon was nominated for a second term by the Republican Convention in Miami on August 22, and Vietnam loomed as a major issue in the campaign. There were nearly four weeks until the Paris meeting; but Thieu did not respond to Ambassador Bunker's efforts to obtain a meeting with him. Nor did he respond to a memorandum from Kissinger before Bunker flew to Honolulu for a review of the bidding with Kissinger and President Nixon on August 31.

In Honolulu, Bunker—according to Kissinger—stressed to the President that "he thought we were on the right course." Kissinger told Bunker that "we counted on him to tell us if we went too far; he was our conscience. 'We have not sacrificed all these years in order to sell out now,' I told him. 'If you think this is unreasonable, we'll change it. And we'll pay whatever price we have to.' Bunker reaffirmed his view that our policy was sound; it was indeed the only one possible."

Thieu's refusal to see Bunker was a matter of concern to Kissinger because Thieu's digging in his heels slowed down negotiations with the North Vietnamese. As a result of the discussions with Bunker in Honolulu, Kissinger drafted a presidential letter for Bunker to carry back to Saigon. The letter was signed by Nixon on August 31, and delivered to Thieu on September 6, the day after Bunker returned to Saigon.[18]

In the letter, Nixon overlooked Thieu's slight of Bunker and Kissinger, saying only, "I was most pleased to receive from Ambassador Bunker in Hawaii a full and current report on your views with respect to the ongoing peace negotiations, on which our two governments have recently had a number of detailed exchanges." Nixon advised Thieu that the United States had made a number of adjustments in its position and that Bunker "will give you our thinking in detail. You can be certain that he speaks for me. The letter continued:

At this delicate moment in the negotiations, let me assure you once again, personally and emphatically, of the bedrock of the U.S. position: The United States has not persevered all this way, at the sacrifice of many American lives, to reverse course in the last few months of 1972. We will not do now what we have refused to do in the preceding three and a half years. The American people know that the United States cannot purchase peace or honor or redeem its sacrifices at the price of deserting a brave ally. This I cannot do and will never do.

Our essential task now is to work closely together, on the basis of complete frankness and trust, as we have done so successfully throughout these years. Our objective is a common and mutual one. I have instructed Ambassador Bunker to maintain the closest contact with you, to insure meticulous and thorough consultations with you at every stage. I believe our new proposal reflects unmistakably that we have offered every legitimate concession for a fair political process. If the other side rejects these proposals, it will be proven to even the most skeptical that the obstacle to a settlement is not one leader, but their insistence on being handed at the conference table what they can win neither at the ballot box nor on the battlefield. If they accept our proposal they must accept your Government as a negotiating partner, and you will be fully protected by being present in each forum.

Finally, Mr. President, I want to express to you again the American people's admiration for the courage and performance of the people and armed forces of South Vietnam in their successful defense against the North Vietnamese invasion, and for your sterling leadership. The courage and unity of your people is the ultimate guarantee of their freedom. But for us to succeed on this last leg of a long journey, we must trust each other fully. We must not hand the enemy through our discord what we have prevented through our unity.

With my best personal regards.

Sincerely
[s] Richard Nixon

Nixon's effort to reassure Thieu, "personally and emphatically," that the United States would never dishonor the loss of so many American lives by deserting a brave ally made a deep impression on him. Here was Nixon reiterating the investment theory: America had spent too many lives to cut and run. The American position at the conference table had been underwritten with American blood. Despite his distrust of Kissinger, Thieu, unaware that Kissinger had written the letter for Nixon, believed the American President would back his view on how to deal with the Communists. Nixon was at his conciliatory best, praising Thieu and offering him support, urging unity and trust.

After Thieu read the letter and discussed the American proposals, he gave Bunker Saigon's counterproposals to Kissinger's plan presented during his August 17 visit. Bunker cabled Washington that Thieu left him with the impression that he would go along, and Kissinger congratulated Bunker on the "encouraging" results. In reality, Thieu was merely fending Bunker off. He remained firm in his decision not to allow the Communists a foothold in the South through recognition of the National Liberation Front. Thieu stuck to his position that there was no legitimate Third Force in the South, but only a political front established and maintained by Hanoi. There were legitimate philosophers, poets, lawyers, and doctors who opposed him, Thieu agreed, but the NLF and its successor the PRG were the creations of Hanoi and remained under its control. Recognition would only mean giving political power to the Communists, power they had not won on the battlefield. Those who belonged to the opposition fared badly because Thieu believed that they had been coopted by the Communists. Some political opposition leaders such as Truong Dinh Dzu were harassed and jailed while others joined the Communists and fled to the jungle. Because of the close-knit family structure of the Vietnamese, many families had relatives in the North and there was secret contact between them. President Thieu's daughter had as her friend and guest at her wedding the daughter of the Provisional Revolutionary Government's justice minister, Truong Nhu Tang. His family remained in Saigon while he was in the jungle, and Mrs. Thieu sponsored his daughter Loan's education in the United States.[19]

Thieu complained to Hung that "first the North Vietnamese are concerned with how to rid Vietnam of Americans; they wanted to give the Americans an opportunity for a peace settlement and let them withdraw without losing face. Then they wanted a coalition government, to insure that the U.S. could not return to wage war against the North. The North Vietnamese are only a thousand kilometers from us, but the United States is ten thousand miles away."[20]

On September 13, Thieu rejected the American proposal for the composition of the Committee of National Reconciliation, "not because the committee bothered him, but because he was not ready for a cease-fire," Kissinger argued in his memoirs.[21] The Palace records show that Kissinger told only half of the story. He failed to mention that the American proposal gave the NLF equal status with Saigon by providing for "three components of the Committee of Nation Reconciliation to be of equal proportion." Thieu made a counterproposal on September 9, for the committee to be composed of "representatives of all the political, religious forces and tendencies in South Vietnam, including the NLF." The NLF would only be one of the political forces, not a dominant one on a par with the Saigon government.

Kissinger's true feelings about Thieu rise to the surface in his memoirs when he notes that

> insolence is the armor of the weak; it is a device to induce courage in the face of one's own panic. But that is more clear to me now than it was then. In September 1972 a second Vietnamese party—our own ally—had managed to generate in me that impotent rage by which the Vietnamese have always tormented physically stronger opponents. After a month of exchanges Thieu had dug in on a point so peripheral to the final result that we would never be able to justify our people breaking up a negotiation over it. If we accepted Thieu's conduct, all coordinated diplomacy would vanish; we would have reached the condition that our domestic critics had accused us of permitting: Thieu would have an absolute veto over our policy.[22]

Kissinger finally won Nixon's "far from enthusiastic" approval to proceed without Thieu's acceptance of the revised American position.[23]

On September 15, three days before the deadline set by President Thieu, South Vietnamese forces under the command of General Ngo Quang Truong recaptured Quang Tri, the only provincial capital taken by the North Vietnamese during the spring offensive. On the same day Kissinger met with Le Duc Tho in Paris and was "convinced that Le Duc Tho was well on the way to separating the military and political issues as we wanted. Hanoi, having come this far, would sooner or later table its rock bottom position."[24] In fact, it was Hanoi which proposed a new ten-point plan and the American proposal was never discussed. In their proposal, the North Vietnamese called for the establishment of a "Provisional Government of National Concord" of three equal segments, to be "the central government for the whole of South Vietnam." This "Government" was later changed to a "Council" with similar functions.

In his memoirs, Kissinger turns to hindsight and says it would have been wiser to have accepted Thieu's wording on how the Council of Reconciliation should be composed because it would "perhaps have reduced Thieu's mistrust, though given our different perspectives nothing could have prevented the final blowup. In the negotiation, it made no difference."[25]

Thieu saw himself caught in another American election trap. As his own military situation improved, the Americans would press him to negotiate. His strategy was to win a military victory over the North Vietnamese by recovering lost territory and forcing them to withdraw. The Americans sought only to achieve a cease-fire and withdraw American forces in exchange for political negotiations. In 1968, Thieu had held out long enough to prevent the Paris negotiations from starting before the election took place; now he would try again to prevent the Americans from making military and political concessions. It seemed to Thieu that the Americans did not understand the nature of the North Vietnamese threat and commitment. Hanoi's sense of time was different from Washington's; the Communists were prepared to fight on with no end in sight as long as they received supplies from the Soviet Union and China. A negotiated settlement could not resolve the test of strength and will that still had not been fought out on the battlefield. Thieu sensed that Kissinger was more anxious for peace than Nixon. He, too, watched the American public opinion polls and saw there was growing public support for Nixon's handling of the war while his lead was growing over McGovern. For Thieu, this was not the time for the Americans to make fatal concessions, especially while the South Vietnamese were doing well on the battlefield. Nixon also was inclined to wait until after the election and then bring about a conclusion by a drastic escalation. Kissinger however preferred to attempt to settle before the election on November 7.[26]

When Ambassador Bunker called for an appointment with Thieu on September 16, to report on Kissinger's meeting with Le Duc Tho in Paris, he was given Thieu's reply to Nixon's August 31 letter. The response expressed agreement with all of President Nixon's general points and then went on to warn that no further concessions should be made. "The Communists should not be encouraged to apply a more ingenious and less expensive method to take over countries through so-called negotiated and political peace solutions," wrote Thieu. "Therefore to continue to make concessions to the Communists in a very illogical way serves only to encourage them in being more stubborn in their position and their pursuit of aggression."[27] The next day Bunker met with Thieu, who told him that either the North Vietnamese were trying to reach an agreement in principle before the election or else they were uncertain about the American strategy. In a speech in Hue, Thieu declared: "No one has a right to negotiate for or accept any solution" except the people of South Vietnam. Kissinger again tried to get Thieu on board by sending Bunker a long message on September 23:

> It is also important that Thieu understand that in the sensitive period facing us, his discernible attitude on the negotiations could have a major influence on Hanoi's strategy. If Thieu is genuinely worried that we might settle prematurely, he must understand that the appearance of differences between Washington and Saigon could have the practical consequence of influencing Hanoi toward a rapid settlement in the secret talks so as to exploit what they might perceive as a split between the U.S. and the GVN and the resulting political disarray in Saigon. This would disrupt the carefully measured pace we are attempting to maintain. Our strategy at this point is to force further movement in Hanoi's position and maintain the appearance of constructive activity in Paris while continuing to apply maximum military pressure. Therefore it is essential that Thieu stay close to us so that we demonstrate solidarity to Hanoi.[28]

On September 26 and 27, Kissinger met with Le Duc Tho in the former home of the French Cubist painter Fernand Léger, at 108 Avenue de General

Leclerc in the suburb of Gif-sur-Yvette, fifteen miles southwest of Paris. The whitewashed stucco cottage with green shutters and orange-tiled roof had been given by Léger to the French Communist Party, which made it available to the North Vietnamese. In the main room of the house, Léger's striking paintings were hung around the green baize-covered table where the talks took place. The mood of the negotiations improved and the North Vietnamese made concessions on a cease-fire in all of Indochina. The quality of the food served during the luncheon break also improved, with the Communists offering caviar, shrimp, *banh phong tom* (shrimp chips), and *cha gio* (spring rolls) with white wine and sherry.

Kissinger was elated when he returned to Washington to report to Nixon. Among the proposals to be considered was a Communist suggestion that there be no election for President of South Vietnam but only elections for a Constituent Assembly. Kissinger recommended that this might be acceptable as it would remove the need for Thieu's resignation. He also suggested that "we might ask the proposed Committee of National Reconciliation to review the constitution one year after a peace agreement for consistency with its terms. This seemed to me the safest course since Saigon would have an absolute veto in this body." [29] Kissinger failed to realize that Le Duc Tho's proposal was a not too carefully veiled effort to destroy the foundation of South Vietnamese democracy—the constitution and presidential elections. There are no presidential elections in the Communist system and their only elections are on the level of a Constituent Assembly, which appoints the government. Democracy with the popular election of the highest officials would have been eliminated.

When Thieu learned of this development, he was concerned that Kissinger would make such a concession, and he gave Bunker a memorandum on September 26 warning of his government's objections. If Kissinger persisted in going beyond Saigon's agreed-upon position, then "we shall be obliged to clarify and defend publicly our views on this subject." [30] (See Appendix B.)

Kissinger's next meeting with the North Vietnamese was scheduled for October 8, and General Haig was dispatched to Saigon to discuss the contingencies that might arise in the Paris meeting. Thieu met with Haig for two hours and forty minutes on October 2, and was polite. Their meeting on October 3 was canceled by Thieu. Then, on October 4, in an unexpected and extraordinary session, Thieu confronted Haig with his entire National Security Council and bitterly attacked almost all aspects of the American proposal; at times Thieu was in tears in his anger and frustration. Thieu railed against Kissinger, who he said did not "deign" to consider Saigon's views in his negotiations. Haig described Nixon's domestic situation. If the Communists made a reasonable offer and Nixon refused to act on it, then the Communists would be able to put the blame on Thieu for blocking peace, Haig explained.

Before Haig departed Thieu gave him a memorandum summing up the South Vietnamese position so that Kissinger would be aware of it before his next crucial meeting with Le Duc Tho in Paris. Thieu urged the United States to "avoid giving to the other side the impression that we need to have a certain arrangement within a given frame of time" and to be informed if the U.S. government "has developed a new concept for a peace settlement . . ." (See Appendix C for text of memorandum.)

In his memoirs, Nixon says, "I sympathized with Thieu's position." An estimated 120,000 North Vietnamese troops had crossed the DMZ into the South during the Easter invasion on March 31, and they were still in South Vietnam.

Nixon writes that Thieu was

> naturally skeptical of any plan that would lead to an American withdrawal without requiring a corresponding North Vietnamese withdrawal. I shared his view that the Communists' motives were entirely cynical. I knew, as he did, that they would observe the agreement only so long and so far as South Vietnam's strength and American readiness forced them to do so. But I felt that if we could negotiate an agreement on our terms, those conditions could be met. I sent Thieu a personal message:—"I give you my firm assurance that there will be no settlement arrived at, the provisions of which have not been discussed personally with you well beforehand." Knowing his penchant for headstrong action, however, I reminded him of the dangers inherent in stirring up his domestic situation as well as our own.[31]

Nixon's diary mentions only "the danger inherent in stirring up his own domestic relations as well as our own," but in his letter to Thieu, Nixon was more explicit. He openly threatened Thieu with a coup or worse if he did not accept the terms Kissinger had worked out. On October 6, Bunker delivered Nixon's personal message to President Thieu. Here was Nixon once again simultaneously threatening and promising, trying to reassure Thieu, but also warning him that he faced forcible removal from power unless he cooperated. The dangers of Thieu's position were explained by references to the coup against Ngo Dinh Diem in 1963 and considerations of removing him in 1968 when he refused to cooperate with President Lyndon Johnson's peace initiative. There could be no mistaking the message: Cooperate, or else the atmosphere would be created leading to his elimination as president. The message from Nixon read as follows:

> I have discussed with General Haig the outcome of his meetings with you and your associates in Saigon. There is no doubt that there are serious disagreements between us, but it should be clearly understood that these disagreements are tactical in character and involve no basic difference as to the objectives we both seek—the preservation of a non-communist structure in South Viet-Nam which we have so patiently built together and which your heroic leadership has preserved against the most difficult trials. Therefore, I give you my firm assurance that there will be no settlement arrived at, the provisions of which have not been discussed personally with you well beforehand. This applies specifically to the next round of talks in Paris. In these talks, Dr. Kissinger will

explore what concrete security guarantees the other side is willing to give us as the basis for further discussions on the political point which might be undertaken following consultations with you. In this context I would urge you to take every measure to avoid the development of an atmosphere which could lead to events similar to those which we abhorred in 1963 and which I personally opposed so vehemently in 1968. For this same reason, I would hope that you would also avoid taking precautionary measures against developments arising from these talks which, I assure you, would never arise without full, timely and complete consultations between us.

At the same time, however, we cannot be sure at any point in the process that the enemy will not for propaganda or other reasons make public the details of the secret talks. U.S. tactics thus far have been designed to take account of this contingency. General Haig informed me that you would be writing to me in the near future. I look forward to receiving this communication and hope that you will have had an opportunity to consider the foregoing before completing that message.

President Richard M. Nixon.

For Thieu, the message was infuriating. He had now experienced enough of Kissinger's consultations to realize that their agendas were on a collision course. With the election as a deadline, the Americans were rushing toward their goal—a peace agreement.[32] But Thieu would only accept a role for the National Liberation Front (which had changed its name to the Provisional Revolutionary Government on June 10, 1969) in the Saigon government if the North Vietnamese troops left the South.

Assassination was the nightmare that Nguyen Van Thieu had lived with ever since the coup against Ngo Dinh Diem in November 1963. At the time, Thieu was commander of the 5th Division stationed at Bien Hoa, fifteen miles from Saigon. He was called to Saigon by General Duong Van Minh, former Chief of Staff of the Army, who had been given the powerless title of Special Adviser and asked to take part in the coup. Thieu had already been approached by Do Mau, Diem's military security chief, to join a coup group but had refused. With Big Minh, it was different. Thieu had served as Minh's deputy before being given command of the 5th Division and he was close to Minh. Thieu told Minh that he did not see anything to be gained from a coup unless certain conditions were met. Foremost in Thieu's mind was "the need to increase U.S. military and economic aid to fight the Communists." Second, Thieu insisted that the fight against the Communists continue. There could be no coalition or neutralist government. Third, he urged that a military government be formed to carry out the administration of the country. Fourth, he demanded that Diem and his brother, Ngo Dinh Nhu, not be killed. "Minh and the generals agreed to the first two points, but would not accept the formation of a military government and were vague on not killing Diem."[33]

Diem had become desperate to free himself of American domination— so desperate that he sought to negotiate on his own with the North Vietnam-

ese. He was to establish a pattern that was repeated with only slight variations by his successors. The idea of direct negotiations between North and
South Vietnam was to prove inimical to both Washington and Hanoi, but in
1963 Hanoi was still open to considering them. To explore the possibilities,
Diem and Nhu called in Mieczslaw Maneil, the head of the Polish delegation
to the International Control Commission, and asked him to approach Hanoi
through the French ambassador Roger Lalouette.

The North Vietnamese agreed to a meeting between Ngo Dinh Nhu and
Hanoi's representatives. The encounter took place while Nhu was ostensibly on a hunting trip in the central highlands. Nhu was accompanied only
by his most trusted aide, Cao Xuan Vy, director of the Republican Youth.
The two men took off in a jeep, supposedly to track wild boar and deer, but
instead they drove toward the coast and met with the North Vietnamese in
Khanh Hoa Province. Nhu proposed that the North and South resume
postal service and economic relations as a first step toward gradual peaceful
unification. He also proposed that the railroad line between Hanoi and Saigon be reopened. Nhu offered to send his wife and children to Hanoi on the
first train as evidence of his and Diem's good faith. His overtures to Hanoi
were known to Saigon's top generals, to whom he later bragged about them.
General Tran Van Don recalled a dinner where Nhu had been drinking
heavily. In a flurry of drunken bravado, Nhu boasted: "The North Vietnamese only negotiated with one person in the South and that's me."[34]

Nhu also let the Americans know he was in contact with the North. In
the fall of 1963, as relations with the United States deteriorated, Nhu invited
Lieutenant Colonel Lucien Conein to visit him at the Palace for "intermi-
nable cups of tea and an endless monologue" during the course of which
Nhu told Conein that he was "dealing with the North Vietnamese." Conein
was fascinated with Nhu, who he described as "an intelligent son of a bitch.
I think he was trying to scare us. He wanted the United States to believe
that he could negotiate with the North and that he had an alternative to us
because things were not going right."[35]

When Nhu leaked word that he had been talking to the North to the
American press, it produced the effect he desired. The State Department
was furious. Nhu had overreached himself.[36] The Americans decided that
he must step down. Diem was told to remove or curb his brother. On August
24, 1963, a cable of instructions was sent to Ambassador Henry Cabot
Lodge in Saigon advising him that if Diem refused to remove Nhu, "we are
prepared to accept the obvious implication that we can no longer support
Diem. You may also tell appropriate military commanders we will give them
direct support in any interim period of breakdown of central government
mechanism."[37]

Diem and Nhu made other efforts to come to terms with the North as
their relations with the United States deteriorated. They hoped to reach a
definitive agreement with Hanoi by the end of 1963. Tran Van Dinh, who
was serving in the Vietnamese Embassy in Washington, was called to Saigon in October for meetings with Diem and Nhu. Dinh, who was consul

general in Rangoon from 1958 to 1961, had been in contact with the North Vietnamese in Burma. He was known to the North Vietnamese from his days in the Viet Minh in Central Vietnam and Laos. Dinh recalled that Diem was filled with bitterness against the Americans. He instructed Dinh to negotiate a cease-fire with Hanoi and to agree to the departure of all U.S. forces and the acceptance of National Liberation Front representatives in his government, as well as an election—possibly within a year—in which the NLF could participate.[38] Dinh was scheduled to meet the North Vietnamese in New Delhi early in November 1963, but the coup aborted his mission.

Before the coup took place, Thieu recalled, "the Americans had created the conditions for the army to revolt. There were shortages of fuel, ammunition, and medical supplies. Our feeling was that the Americans had turned against Diem, but they would support the military with a new civilian government once Diem was ousted. American military aid was a constant sword of Damocles over our head. Every time the Americans wanted something, they would exert pressure on us by withholding or offering military aid."

As the time for the coup approached, General Minh became concerned that Diem would learn of the plot, and suggested Diem be assassinated by a sniper as he drove to Ton San Nhut Airport, Thieu recalled. In an angry confrontation with Minh, Thieu argued against the plan. "Assassination is not a *coup d'état*. It is not the army's job to do that. We must explain to the people what we do. We are the noblemen. We are not assassins or murderers."[39]

The day before the coup, there were still doubts among the generals. General Tran Thien Khiem, Chief of Staff of the Joint General Staff, came to the headquarters of General Ton That Dinh, the Military Region III and Saigon commander, who was trusted by Diem and Nhu. Khiem tried to persuade him to drop the plans for the coup. "We should go to see the President, ask him for forgiveness, and try to defend him," Khiem said with tears in his eyes. Dinh replied: "It's too late. It was you who signed the order to move the troops."[40]

Later in the day Dinh was visited by General Paul Harkins, the commander of the U.S. Military Assistance Command in Vietnam, and General Duong Van Minh. Both men urged Dinh not to proceed. Harkins, who was now acting on his own initiative, had opposed the coup within the embassy councils and in his messages to Washington.

"You generals drew up the plans and I carried them out. It is too late to retract," Dinh told Minh. At that point Minh said, "Okay, okay, we will continue."[41]

Sensing the possibility of danger, Diem and Nhu had prepared their own plan to stage an elaborate phony coup code-named "Bravo I." Dinh was supposed to arrest the generals who moved against Diem and Nhu; but Dinh betrayed them. He used the plan to move the forces loyal to Diem out of Saigon and those of the plotting generals into the city. The 5th Division under Thieu was ostensibly sent into the field to clear Viet Cong from the area between Tay Ninh and Thu Dau Mot, fifteen miles from Saigon. When Thieu's forces reached Thu Dau Mot, they diverted to Saigon.

On the night of the coup, Thieu's assignment was to secure the presidential Palace. His wife, hoping to prevent him, put sleeping pills in his coffee, but he awoke anyway and although groggy he arrived late to storm the Palace.[42] Diem and Nhu had already fled to seek refuge in Cholon, the Chinese suburb of Saigon, at the home of a Chinese merchant, Ma Tuyen, on Doc Phu Thoai Street. The villa had been prepared with an emergency communications system and one of the phones was linked to the Palace telephone system so that when Diem talked to the generals later in the night, they did not realize he was not in the Palace. The Palace Guard, unaware that their leader had left, continued to fight through the night.

In the early hours of the morning of November 1, Thieu ordered a fullscale assault on the Palace. One of Diem's military aides who had been ordered to defend the Palace phoned General Khiem to advise him that Diem and Nhu had left the Palace and asked him to halt the attack. Khiem ordered him to surrender, but he and his troops hesitated because they had no orders to surrender. Thieu's troops captured the Palace before dawn.[43] Finding that Diem and Nhu had fled, they helped themselves to the Palace antiques, Nhu's Scotch whiskey, and his wife's lingerie. Outraged, Thieu beat the soldiers with his leather swagger stick to restore order. At 8:30 a.m. Thieu returned to the Joint General Staff (JGS) headquarters where the coup was being run.

Diem and Nhu, having spent the night in Ma Tuyen's house, arose at five as the sky was getting light and joined together to say their prayers. They ate a simple breakfast of steamed rice buns with pork filling, small meat dumplings, and coffee. Diem, who came to Cholon disguised as a Catholic priest, was now dressed in a business suit. At 6:45 a.m. he called General Khiem at the JGS headquarters to tell him his whereabouts and ask for transportation to bring them to the headquarters to discuss the transfer of power. Khiem wanted to go personally for Diem, but General Minh stopped him, saying that he had ordered General Xuan, Colonel Quan, Colonel Lam, Major Nghia, and Captain Nhung to pick them up. Ma Tuyen ordered a small car to drive the brothers to the nearby Cha Tam Catholic Church in Cholon, where they agreed to surrender to the generals and be escorted back to the JGS headquarters.[44]

When Thieu arrived at the headquarters from the Palace, he saw the armored personnel carrier that had carried Diem and Nhu back from Cholon in the courtyard. He ordered the driver to open the back door. On the bloody metal floor were the bodies of Diem and Nhu, punctured with bullet and knife wounds.[45] Thieu was sickened and shocked. He took off his hat and bowed before the bodies.[46] "If I had found the President and his brother in the Palace, I would have taken them to the JGS headquarters in an open jeep. Nobody would dare to kill them in the open," he remarked later.

The vision of Diem and Nhu lying on the floor of the M-113 haunted

Thieu. He always feared assassination instigated or supported by the Americans. The overthrow of Diem and Nhu and their murder was proof to Thieu that if the Americans were displeased with a Vietnamese leader, they would eliminate him violently. While there had been disagreement among the generals over whether or not to kill Diem and Nhu, there had not been a specific plan drawn up to get them safely out of the country. According to Lucien Conein, the generals had planned to take Diem and Nhu to the government hunting lodge in Pleiku until a plane could be arranged to take them out of the country.[47]

In a conversation with Diem at 4:30 p.m. on November 1, 1963, Ambassador Lodge told Diem he was worried about his physical safety and had received a report "that those in charge of the current activity offer you and your brother safe-conduct out of the country if you resign. Had you heard this?"

"No," replied Diem. "You have my phone number."

"Yes. If I can do anything for your physical safety, please call me," Lodge said.[48]

Because of Diem and Nhu's negotiating skills and Diem's ability to escape from previous coup efforts, the generals feared that unless they eliminated both men there would be no way to move ahead with a new civilian government. In the summer of 1961 when the talk of a coup against Diem and Nhu was rising, Schecter's Vietnamese sources in Saigon indicated that the only way to have a successful coup against Diem would be to kill him, otherwise he would worm his way back into power through his political skills. In all previous coup attempts, Diem had stalled and talked his way out of surrendering until he regained control with troops loyal to him. Now his elite unit of the Palace Guard was prepared to mount an attack on the coup leaders in the JGS headquarters, but Diem felt confident enough to negotiate with the generals on the afternoon of November 1, and halted the attack. "If you fight, troops on both sides will die. Better to kill the Communists. If we fight, we fight the Communists. Save the bullets for the Communists. I shall wait for the generals to see what they want. Then the government will institute reforms accordingly," Diem told the deputy commander of the guards.[49]

The Generals had decided there was no longer any room to compromise with Diem and they had the support of the Americans for a coup. Who gave the order to kill Diem remains in dispute, but General Tran Van Don, a key plotter against Diem, insists it was General Minh. When he heard Diem and Nhu had been killed General Don rushed to General Khiem's office where Big Minh was supposed to be waiting for Diem to arrive. "Why are they dead?" asked Don. In a "haughty and proud tone of voice" Minh answered: "And what does it matter that they are dead?" At that moment General Xuan, the security chief who had been responsible for escorting the deposed brothers to the JGS headquarters, burst into the room. Unaware of Don's presence, General Xuan turned to Big Minh, saluted and said in military fashion, *"mission accomplie"* (mission accomplished).[50]

After the coup General Don was instrumental in promoting Thieu to the rank of general. A handsome, French-educated officer, Don was known for his military skills and as the *Galant Général* for his attraction to women. Don had served as military aide to former Emperor Bao Dai, and he was a master intriguer with ties in all camps. Thieu respected his opinions and his ability to make the Republic of Vietnam's case to American and French leaders.

Thieu saw the coup as an object lesson in what could happen to Vietnamese officers when they took orders from the Americans and tried to please them. The coup was also a bitter lesson to Thieu on the importance of loyalty among his own officer class. Critics of Thieu in Saigon insisted that it was on the basis of his loyalty to Diem during the coup that Thieu chose General Cao Van Vien to be the head of the Joint General Staff. Vien was an officer in the elite airborne unit at the time of the coup, and he refused to join the plot against Diem. According to General Ton That Dinh, a key leader of the coup against Diem, General Minh ordered that Vien be eliminated, but Dinh saved him by insisting that Vien would not oppose the coup. Vien was held under arrest at the JGS headquarters when he refused to join in the coup against Diem. Vien, whose wife often played mahjong with General Ton That Dinh, had agreed to have Diem and Nhu take refuge in their home. When the call came from the Palace, Mrs. Vien said that her husband had been arrested and her house was being watched. Diem and Nhu then fled to Cholon.

Although he was a brilliant paratrooper in the field, Vien was a mediocre staff officer, without imagination. He remained as Thieu's Chief of the General Staff for eight years, from 1967 until he fled from Saigon a day before the surrender on the grounds that there was a plot to assassinate him.

Thieu's private fears of assassination were expressed to Hung in their talks in London in 1976. The assassination of Diem made a deep impression on Thieu's perception of the Americans and how he came to believe they really operated. Despite his working relationship with the Americans and his personal friendship with some American CIA agents in Saigon, such as Stuart E. Methven, Thieu remained essentially aloof and isolated from the Americans. He rarely socialized with the American ambassador, engaging only in correct and formal relations.

Thieu was a very traditional Asian leader, who saw American behavior in Confucian terms. His role models were Chiang Kai-shek and South Korean President Park Chung Hee—the only men whose pictures he had framed on his office wall. He was in essence a military man, trained by the French and the Americans, with little interest or skill in conceiving or playing diplomatic games with the North Vietnamese. He saw negotiations as a losing battle. Thieu believed that if he displeased the Americans enough, he would be eliminated by them—either by an assassin or by his own generals encouraged by the Americans. He never realized that the American public's repugnance and shock after the assassination of Diem created a restraint against repetition of such behavior. Though he never showed his inner fear, Thieu often worried that the Americans were arranging for his elimination, especially in 1968 when he openly opposed President Johnson's peace initiative. When he left the presidential Palace for the drive to the National Assembly on Tu Do Street, Thieu was concerned that the CIA might be planning to eliminate him and blame it on the Viet Cong. He knew that his offices were bugged by the Americans and lived in a state of concern for his life. "I only relax when I'm on the tennis court," he told Hung. "The moment I put the racket down, the specter of a coup returns to me."

When Thieu was reminded by Nixon, in his letter of October 6, 1972, of the "events similar to those which we abhorred in 1963," his mind flashed back to the M-113 armored personnel carrier with the slain bodies of Diem and Nhu. And when Nixon mentioned, in the same letter, the "events which I personally opposed vehemently in 1968," Thieu was convinced that there was an American plot to eliminate him after the 1968 American presidential election. In his resignation speech on April 21, 1975, Thieu reminded the Vietnamese people: "You must remember that in 1968 the American pressure was not small . . . I told you in those days that, if you listened to these political schemes of the Americans, you would be lost. Now you are going to find out what I meant in those days in 1968."

In fact, Thieu's fear of a coup before Nixon's inauguration may not have been groundless. According to an account by William Buckley cited in Seymour M. Hersh's *The Price of Power,* there was an alarming report by Henry Kissinger to Nixon via Buckley shortly after the 1968 election: "Nixon should be told that it is probably an objective of [Clark] Clifford to dispose of Thieu before Nixon is inaugurated." Kissinger added: "If Thieu meets the same fate as Diem, the word will go out to the nations of the world that it may be dangerous to be America's enemy, but to be America's friend is fatal." Buckley called Frank Shakespeare, who promptly arranged with John Mitchell for him to meet Kissinger; from this developed Kissinger's appointment as Assistant to the President for National Security Affairs.[51] Another account, which was published in *Survey* magazine (London) in 1980 by Edward J. Rosek, who had close ties to the Nixon camp—and is also cited by Hersh—disclosed that in mid-1971, "Buckley told friends in the Pentagon that Kissinger claimed in a telephone call to Buckley to have heard that the Johnson administration was planning to assassinate Thieu." Buckley however insists this is incorrect: "there was no talk of assassination."[52]

Robert Komer, who was Deputy for Civil Operations and Revolutionary Development Support (CORDS) at the time, recalled that "a few memos may have been written suggesting that Thieu be removed, but they did not surface."[53] Clark Clifford said he had "no independent information" of plans to oust Thieu. "The U.S. feeling was that was not our province. We wanted to disengage, not exert more control and influence. We wanted them to take over their own war," explained Clifford. "It was clear to me that Thieu was not interested in ending the war and we had a clear parting of the ways. We wanted to get out and he didn't want us to get out. Out of that came a conspiracy to slow the process of peace," Clifford added.[54]

If Nixon and Kissinger saved Thieu in 1968, by 1969 they were being presented with options by the National Security Council (NSC) staff to consider forcibly removing him from power. On October 21, 1969, NSC staffers Roger Morris and Anthony Lake wrote a memorandum to Kissinger arguing that Vietnamization was doomed and ultimately would become unilateral withdrawal. They urged Kissinger to give in to the North Vietnamese on major points and offer a "new caretaker government in Saigon, acceptable to both sides," to oversee a new election in the South. The Communists would be assured of a major role in the transitional government. Morris and Lake added: "We must be prepared to exert means of imposing the settlement over Saigon's opposition. The stakes would warrant steps we have not contemplated since 1963." In an interview with Seymour Hersh, Morris confirmed that the allusion was to the assassination of South Vietnam President Ngo Dinh Diem. Morris said: "I told Tony [Lake] that we have to make it plain to Henry that we have to be willing to knock off Thieu."[55]

As his relations with Kissinger and Nixon worsened, Thieu made one decision that seemed out of character for an austere military man. On January 18, 1973, he spent the day at the Independence Palace in religious ceremonies and festivities for the marriage of his daughter, Le Thuy, to Nguyen Tan Trieu, the son of the chairman of Air Vietnam. Thieu was getting his family affairs in order if he should be removed from the scene. Ngo Dinh Nhu, Diem's brother, had called his family together in October 1963 when he feared an American coup. Nhu told his eldest son Ngo Dinh Trac, then fifteen, that he must be prepared to lead the family if something happened to him.[56]

Thieu believed that the assassination of Diem and Nhu was a mistake that cost South Vietnam dearly in terms of morale and military and economic progress. "There was no policy and no leadership after the coup," said Thieu. "I went back to my division to fight the Communists." An example of the mistakes made by the military was abandonment of the strategic hamlet program by General Minh, who dropped the program without any research or study simply because it had been associated with Diem and Nhu. For similar reasons Minh dropped the Republican Youth program. "General Giap applauded when he heard what had been done," said Thieu. "The coup and elimination of the strategic hamlet program created two years of chaos in South Vietnam during which the Viet Cong had time to build their strength. By 1965 we were on our knees and the country needed an infusion of American troops to prevent it from going to the Communists. Ho Chi Minh made a big mistake in 1965 by not agreeing to negotiate with the United States. The United States would have accepted a coalition government then, but the North Vietnamese refused to go to the conference table. They thought the United States was a paper tiger and would not respond to the military challenge."[57]

Diem's death set in motion a series of coups and countercoups that ceased with the presidential election of 1967 and a balancing of power within the military between Thieu and Nguyen Cao Ky, who was elected vice president. From then until the end in 1975, the generals ruled the country; rumors and threats of a *coup d'état* were part of the operating style in Saigon. Plotting and counterplotting undercut the unity of the leadership and weakened Saigon's position in the United States. Democracy was secondary to the military officers' own power relationships. Democratic institutions such as the Senate, the National Assembly, and the Supreme Court possessed little power and remained more cosmetic than effectively functioning bodies. The concept of democracy was seen as an American institution that had taken two hundred years to develop and had little relevance in the Confucian context of Vietnamese values and personal relationships. Family loyalties and relationships took precedence over the law and public institutions.

Along with American support it was Thieu's ability to divide his generals and rule, to juggle his officers in the provinces and to shift their commands, that contributed to keeping him in power. The Americans would make recommendations for or against officers. The snappy-looking English- or French-speaking officers rose to the top, but they were not necessarily the best. The rules of professional behavior had given way to personal loyalty. The Americans, by supporting the coup against Diem, had shown that the institutions they were trying to encourage could not stand the strain of wartime.

Thieu had to deal with the Americans, his own control over the military, the government, and the war against the North Vietnamese. His own values were molded in very traditional ways. He saw himself having to please the Americans while forging solutions to the problems of a rigid Confucian society. In the midst of a war that demanded national discipline and unity, Thieu turned to those he knew were loyal. That became the key criterion. As a result, he surrounded himself with a number of uncritical yes-men whose wives abused their husbands' prerogatives of office in order to become rich. Thieu had to retain his own power while trying to move forward. Often he stood still and avoided or delayed making decisions to prevent a conflict that would have undercut his own power.

Every year on November 1, the day that Diem and Nhu had been overthrown and murdered, Vietnam's National Day was celebrated publicly as a national holiday, over which Thieu presided. Publicly, the nation was celebrating the overthrow of Diem and reviling his memory. Privately, Thieu and his wife held a memorial mass for President Diem in the Palace chapel and prayed for the repose of his soul. The mass was conducted by Thieu's private chaplain, who asked its intention. "May his soul soon come to Heaven and may he pray for us in this difficult time," Thieu replied. Thieu was comforting Diem in the other world of his ancestors—praying both for Diem and for himself.

5

Kissinger's Design

AT 1700 HOURS on October 17, 1972, President Nguyen Van Thieu ordered the Joint General Staff to bring to Saigon, immediately, a ten-page set of documents captured in the underground bunker of a Viet Cong district commissar in Quang Tin Province. In a series of rapidly coordinated moves, the documents were flown from the field by helicopter and light plane to Danang. By midnight they were on President Thieu's desk. He read them as soon as they arrived—and realized that Communist cadres in an isolated province of Central Vietnam knew more about the details of the Paris Talks than he did.

Entitled "General Instructions for a Cease-Fire," they contained what appeared to be the draft text of the agreement being negotiated by Henry Kissinger and Le Duc Tho in Paris, and revealed the fundamental concessions made by Kissinger. President Thieu had not been shown the draft agreement, nor had he been advised of it in detail by Kissinger.[1] Yet in a remote province south of Danang, Communist cadres and troops were studying the documents and preparing for operations based on them. They contained the North Vietnamese strategy and tactics to maintain their forces in the South after a cease-fire was proclaimed.

The documents indicated that the Americans had agreed to allow North Vietnamese troops to remain in the South after the cease-fire. There would be a total and complete American withdrawal, with no residual forces. Kissinger had agreed to allow the North Vietnamese access to the South through the demilitarized zone, thus assuring resupply of their forces. There was a provision for a National Council of Reconciliation and Concord that would undercut the authority of the Saigon government. Thieu considered this to be a coalition in disguise. After reading the captured documents, he said: "I knew for the first time what was being negotiated over my head. The Americans told me the negotiations were still going on and that nothing was fixed, but the other side already had all the information."[2]

Not only did the documents contain what turned out to be an accurate description of the Paris Agreement, they also prescribed a three-phase implementation plan for the Viet Cong to take the initiative and violate the letter and spirit of the agreement.

Phase I: The pre-cease-fire, preparatory phase called for cadres to study and memorize the provisions and learn how to interpret them to their advantage. Cadres were instructed to be prepared to present the terms of the agreement to the public or to debate them with adversaries. Propaganda teams were to be organized to interpret the agreement. All sewing machines were to be requisitioned for the manufacture of NLF flags, which would be planted on cease-fire day in every house, every hamlet, and on every hill. The North Vietnamese would thus demonstrate their ubiquitous presence to whatever international control body was in place. Major Communist units, meanwhile, were to conduct attacks in order to pin down Saigon forces. Communist regional forces and the local militia, broken down into small elements, were to penetrate every hamlet and every populated area, block every important axis of communication, and stay in place until international representatives arrived.

Phase II: Implementation centered on the cease-fire day. Three days before the cease-fire, all Communist units were to push military attacks to secure land and population as part of the campaign. The plan called for holding on to newly gained territory and flying the NLF flags over it. Demonstrations were planned to demand that the Saigon government implement the cease-fire and return soldiers to their families. The demonstrations would insist on the exercise of rights of freedom, movement, meeting, and the abrogation of military service and a curfew. Armed propaganda units were to push agitation actions by explaining the agreement, exhorting ARVN soldiers to stop fighting, go on leave, or visit their home villages and renounce military service.

Phase III: In the post-cease-fire, or consolidation phase, all the gains achieved were to be held and consolidated. New actions would depend on the results of the first two phases, but the objective was to press on toward dismantling the Thieu government while keeping up a propaganda effort to enhance Communist prestige and to demand the implementation and observance of the Paris Agreement.

Thieu was shocked by the news. Before he had even been informed in detail of the final negotiations or been shown a text of the agreement, the Communists were already utilizing it on the operational level and preparing to circumvent its conditions. His worst fears, that a secret deal had been made, began to materialize. Only two weeks earlier, on October 4, Thieu had given a memorandum to General Haig in Saigon, reminding him of the basic negotiating principles that had been agreed upon. Thieu stressed that, "if the U.S. Government has developed a new concept for a peace settlement, the GVN will greatly appreciate the necessary information."[3] Yet Nixon's October 6 letter to Thieu had assured him nothing would arise from the talks "without full, timely and complete consultation between us."

The pieces suddenly began to fit together. Thieu had been warned by his ambassador in Paris, Pham Dang Lam, that the Americans and Le Duc Tho were rumored to be reaching an agreement after lengthy meetings. The October 6 letter from Nixon had puzzled him. Why the timing and the specific nature of the threat "to avoid the development of an atmosphere which could lead to events similar to those we abhorred in 1963 and which I personally opposed so vehemently in 1968"? On October 14, Bunker gave Thieu a short pro forma letter of a page and a half on the contents of Kissinger's meetings with Le Duc Tho in Paris from October 8 to 11. There was no mention of a breakthrough.[4]

Now he could see Kissinger's design: It was a replay of 1968, a rush to a settlement before the American election. Kissinger was coming to Saigon with an agreement reached in the October meetings in Paris. Contrary to Nixon's promise, there had been no meaningful consultations with Thieu on the final points of that agreement. Never had Thieu been shown the text or asked to comment in detail on any part of the final draft.

In anger and sadness, Thieu called in Vice President Tran Van Huong, Prime Minister Tran Thien Khiem, Chairman of the Joint General Staff Cao Van Vien, and Hoang Duc Nha, to discuss the American betrayal and how to prepare for Kissinger's visit.

The American actions were devastating to the South Vietnamese. After more than one million casualties—5 percent of the population—the South Vietnamese armed forces had assumed the initiative and were fighting well on the battlefield against the North Vietnamese; they were prepared to maintain their position of strength. Yet after a litany of promises of "no secret deals," "nothing behind the back of our allies," and "full consultations," Kissinger was coming with a proposal that made fatal concessions to Hanoi.

Nixon's instructions to Kissinger before he departed for Saigon were to treat the meetings with Thieu as a "poker game" in which Kissinger should hold back the "trump card" until the last trick. "Thus I should show the political portion of the agreement to Thieu immediately. I should imply that Hanoi was asking for more than it actually was," Kissinger explained.[5]

The next morning, October 18, Kissinger arrived at the Independence Palace with a full retinue of Secret Service men, the accompaniment for a head of state rather than a presidential emissary. Thieu was not impressed. To show his pique, he kept Kissinger and his entourage waiting for fifteen minutes in the Palace reception room in full view of the correspondents and photographers who had gathered to record the arrival. When Kissinger was received by Thieu, there was no cordiality. Thieu remained aloof and cold.

Before leaving Washington for Paris and Saigon, Henry Kissinger had drafted a letter dated October 16, 1972, to President Thieu for Richard Nixon. In it, the President laid forth his views on the negotiations in Paris, which he said "now appear to be reaching a final stage." The letter was presented to Thieu by Kissinger as soon as they met. It was meant to set the stage for the meeting and to assure Thieu that Kissinger had Nixon's full support. It read:

> As you know, throughout the four years of my Administration the United States has stood firmly behind your Government and its people in our support for their valiant struggle to resist aggression and preserve their right to determine their own political future.
>
> The military measures we have taken and the Vietnamization program, the dramatic steps that we took in 1970 against the Cambodian sanctuaries, the operations in Laos in 1971 and the measures against North Vietnam just this past May have fully attested to the steadfastness of our support. I need not emphasize that many of these measures were as unpopular to many in the U.S. as they were necessary.
>
> At the negotiating table we have always held firmly to the principle that we would never negotiate with North Vietnam a solution which predetermined the political outcome of the conflict. We have consistently adhered to positions that would preserve the elected government and assure the free people of Vietnam the opportunity to determine their future.
>
> Until very recently the North Vietnamese negotiators have held firmly to their long established position that any settlement of the war would have to include your resignation and the dismantlement of the Government of the Republic of Vietnam and its institutions.
>
> It now seems, however, that the combination of the perseverance and heroism of your Government and its fighting forces, the measures taken by the United States on the 8th of May, 1972, and our firmness at the conference table have caused a fundamental shift in Hanoi. In the course of Dr. Kissinger's recent meetings with the North Vietnamese negotiators in Paris, it has become progressively more evident that Hanoi's leadership is prepared to agree to a ceasefire prior to a resolution of the political problem in South Vietnam. This is indeed an important reverse in doctrine and must represent a decision for them which cannot have been taken lightly. They know the weakness of their own political forces in the South and therefore the risks involved in reaching an agreement that does not meet their political objectives must indeed for them be great.
>
> The consequence of this change in strategy has resulted in a situation wherein we and Hanoi's negotiators have reached essential agreement on a text which provides for a cessation of hostilities, the withdrawal of remaining allied forces, the exchange of prisoners of war, and the continued existence of your Government and its institutions after the ceasefire takes effect. In addition to the document itself a number of private assurances have been obtained designed to meet the security concerns of your country and whose implementation we consider an essential part of this agreement.
>
> Dr. Kissinger will explain to you in the fullest detail the provisions of the proposed agreement which he carries with him and I will therefore not provide further elaboration in this message. I do, however, want you to know that I believe we have no reasonable alternative but to accept this agreement. It represents major movement by the other side, and it is my firm conviction that its implementation will leave you and your people with the ability to defend yourselves and decide the political destiny of South Vietnam.
>
> As far as I am concerned, the most important provision of this agreement,

aside from its military features, is that your Government, its armed forces and its political institutions, will remain intact after the ceasefire has been observed. In the period following the cessation of hostilities you can be completely assured that we will continue to provide your Government with the fullest support, including continued economic aid and whatever military assistance is consistent with the ceasefire provisions of this government.

I recognize that after all these years of war a settlement will present an enormous challenge to your leadership and your people. We all recognize that the conflict will now move into a different form, a form of political struggle as opposed to open military confrontation; but I am of the firm conviction that with wisdom and perseverance your Government and the people of South Vietnam will meet this new challenge. You will have my absolute support in this endeavor and I want you to know it is my firm belief that in this new phase your continued leadership of the destiny of South Vietnam is indispensable.

Finally, I must say that, just as we have taken risks in war, I believe we must take risks in peace. Our intention is to abide faithfully by the terms of the agreements and understandings reached with Hanoi, and I know this will be the attitude of your government as well. We expect reciprocity and have made this unmistakably clear both to them and their major allies. I can assure you that we will view any breach of faith on their part with the utmost gravity; and it would have the most serious consequences.

Allow me to take this occasion to renew my sentiments of highest personal regard and admiration for you and your comrades in arms.

Sincerely
[s]Richard Nixon

Underneath his signature, Richard Nixon had written in by hand: "Dr. Kissinger, General Haig and I have discussed this proposal at great length. I am personally convinced it is the best we will be able to get and it meets my *absolute* condition that the GVN must survive as a free country. Dr. Kissinger's comments have my total backing."

Thieu read the letter but made no comment. Then he asked Kissinger to meet with his National Security Council in the Situation Room connected to his office.[6] Kissinger requested thirty minutes to describe the agreement.

Kissinger emphasized the political parts of the agreement he believed were advantageous to the Republic of Vietnam. The United States, he pledged, would maintain its air bases in Thailand and keep the Seventh Fleet off the coast to deter any attack by the North Vietnamese. Kissinger promised that economic and military aid would continue to South Vietnam. Meanwhile, the United States believed that secret understandings with the Soviet Union and the People's Republic of China would drastically reduce the supply of war material to North Vietnam and permit the United States to withdraw its troops and recover its prisoners with honor. This was a good time to arrive at an agreement with the Communists because, after all, the Republic of Vietnam had an army of more than one million men and controlled 85 percent of its nineteen million population. The Republic of Vietnam, he was confident, would develop and prosper in the postwar period.

Kissinger did not go into the details of what remained to be resolved with Hanoi, nor did he inform President Thieu of the timetable he had agreed upon with the North Vietnamese—to initial the agreement in Hanoi on October 24.[7]

Only when he had finished did Kissinger hand a single copy of the text of the agreement, in English, to President Thieu. Thieu motioned to Nha, sitting at the far end of the long, highly polished mahogany table, to join him. Nha stood behind Thieu and read over his shoulder as Kissinger presented the terms of the agreement. "This is not what we expected, so let's use some *banalité* and have time to think about it," Nha whispered to Thieu. Thieu smoked one of his thin Schimmelpennick cigars and watched Kissinger carefully.

As Nha recalled, "It was a shock to me. All of our points and counterpoints were washed out. I knew the treaty by heart, like my first love. This was very different. This was tantamount to surrender. I was very shocked, but I was careful not to display it."

Thieu was shocked, too, but he was determined not to show any emotion. Later, he told aides he was so furious with what Kissinger had done that "I wanted to punch Kissinger in the mouth." Instead, he stifled his anger and asked Kissinger for a Vietnamese-language copy of the text. Kissinger did not have one, but said he would find one in the files. Thieu thanked Kissinger for his "good presentation," and added, "Let me have time to think about this. We'll reconvene at five p.m." In the meantime, he promised to study the English-language text carefully.

The meeting ended on a friendly note and Kissinger was encouraged. Thieu immediately directed Nha to analyze the entire plan by 3:00 p.m. so they could discuss it before the five o'clock meeting. As Nha describes it, "I made copies and asked Foreign Minister Lam, Nguyen Phu Duc, and Ambassador Phuong to join me for lunch at La Cave Restaurant. When we sat down, I said, 'What do you think?'

"They said, 'This is not so bad. We expected worse.'

" 'What do you mean, it's not so bad? Have you read it carefully?' "

Nha had noticed that there was no provision for the removal of North Vietnamese troops, and he saw difficulties with providing for the replacement of used or destroyed equipment from the way the agreement was worded. He also spotted a reference to three Indochinese states, Vietnam, Laos, and Cambodia. As far as the North Vietnamese were concerned, the Democratic Republic of Vietnam was the legitimate government of Vietnam. The Republic of Vietnam, the fourth state, with its capital in Saigon, did not exist as a legitimate government.

"Did you see the National Council of Reconciliation? I'm going to ask them what the hell they mean by National Reconciliation Council. This is in English. I want to see the Vietnamese text," said Nha.[8]

Although he did not have the Vietnamese text, Nha analyzed the English-language version and reported to a meeting of the National Security Council in the Palace at 3:00 p.m. as ordered. They decided on five major points that needed clarification. Then, in a strategy session with Nha before Kissinger arrived, Thieu decided to question Kissinger on his major concerns, ask for a Vietnamese-language copy of the text, and insist on a working group to discuss the details before he met with Kissinger again.

At five o'clock Kissinger and Bunker returned to the Palace to meet with Thieu and Nha. Kissinger appeared to be in "an ebullient mood." Thieu was polite but insisted on asking questions in Vietnamese and having Nha serve as interpreter to keep the meeting on a stiff, formal level. Thieu told Kissinger, "We have made a cursory analysis and we would like to ask for a few points of clarification and then have more time to study the text in English and Vietnamese." Then Thieu added, "By the way, what are these three Indochinese states that are referred to?" Kissinger, without skipping a beat, replied, "Ah, that must be a typographical error."[9]

The English draft spoke of the "three nations of Indochina"—referring to Laos, Cambodia, and one Vietnam. Thieu would not accept such a formulation. There were four countries and two of them were the Democratic Republic of Vietnam (the North) and the Republic of Vietnam (the South). This had been sanctioned by the Geneva Conference of 1954 and was not about to be changed, Thieu insisted. The National Liberation Front, which had changed its name to the Provisional Revolutionary Government, could not be permitted to claim it represented the Vietnamese state south of the 17th parallel.

Kissinger insisted that the reference to "three nations of Indochina" was inadvertent and a typographical error, even though the reference to three nations appeared more than once in the agreement and was both written out and given with the numeral 3.

Thieu was also especially concerned with the definition of the National Council. Several times in the text it was referred to as an "administrative" structure. In Vietnamese, the terms for "administrative structure" (*co cau hanh chanh*) and "governmental structure" (*co cau chanh guyen*) are very close, and the meaning could easily be confused as a coalition in disguise.

The Council would have no governmental powers, Kissinger explained, but would only serve to carry out what had been agreed upon by the parties. It was not a coalition. "It is a miserable little council. It has no power. It is only a consultative body," Kissinger insisted.

What would happen to the North Vietnamese troops in the South when the Paris Agreement was signed?

There would be no more infiltration of troops from the North, and the South Vietnamese armed forces, 1.1 million strong, should have nothing to fear from the presence of 140,000 North Vietnamese troops, Kissinger replied.

Asked why there was no specific reference to withdrawal of the North Vietnamese troops, he explained, "Well, as you know, we discussed that with the North Vietnamese and they didn't accept, so we didn't think that we should put it in so as not to poison the atmosphere."

What upset Thieu most in Kissinger's presentation, recalls Nha, was his insistence that "the agreement was the greatest thing that could have been achieved and a collapse of the North Vietnamese position." Nha remembers Kissinger saying, " 'Le Duc Tho came to me and told me this is the worst concession he has to make, but for the sake of peace he has to give this to me, and he was crying.'

"To make the assertion that the Communists cried set us on our guard. Communists don't cry," remarked Nha. "Either Kissinger was naive or he thought we were stupid."

At that point Thieu proposed a meeting on the working-group level with Foreign Minister Tran Van Lam the next morning to discuss the agreement in more detail. Kissinger agreed.

Following the meeting with Thieu and Nha, Kissinger and Bunker met with Thieu, Chairman of the South Vietnamese Joint General Staff Cao Van Vien, and General Creighton Abrams, the head of the American Military Assistance Command Vietnam (MACV). They discussed the rapid build-up of supplies for Saigon before the cease-fire in a program called Enhance Plus. The equipment would arrive before the agreement was signed and then would be replaced on a one-for-one basis by the United States under the terms of the agreement.

Before examining the actual proposal that Kissinger brought from Paris, it is critical to explore his differences in approach with President Nixon. Kissinger was scheduled to be in Hanoi to initial the agreement on October 24. The emphasis by Kissinger was on negotiation. He believed the window of opportunity would remain open until the election. Afterwards it would be more costly in political and in military terms to achieve a cease-fire.

A presidential election is the end of a political cycle and a time for renewal. Acceptance of the political concessions to end the war and start anew would be easier if carried out before Nixon's second term. Kissinger's personal style was coming under increasing criticism in the White House and Haldeman was orchestrating a campaign to keep Kissinger in his place and stress the primacy of President Nixon's role in the negotiations. Haldeman was concerned that Kissinger was detracting from the image of the President's control of foreign policy decisions and downplaying Nixon. Kissinger was very sensitive to this criticism and his own role in the second term. He hoped to increase his influence and Nixon's dependence on him with a settlement before the election.

Kissinger had his own agenda for the second term, which included expanded detente with the Soviet Union and normalization of relations with the People's Republic of China. Vietnam was a drag on his long-range goals —as long as Vietnam remained an issue, it would be difficult to move ahead.

Kissinger saw himself approaching a historic moment. "Statesmen must act *as if* their intuition was already experience, as if their aspiration was truth," he wrote in *A World Restored,* his study of Metternich.[10] It was to become a guiding personal principle when he sat in the corner office of the West Wing of the White House. In his interview with the Italian journalist Oriana Fallaci, Kissinger explained that his strength came from acting on his own. "The main point arises from the fact that I've always acted alone," he said. "Americans like that immensely. Americans like the cowboy who leads the wagon train riding ahead alone on his horse, the cowboy who rides all alone into the town, the village, with his horse and nothing else. Maybe even without a pistol, since he doesn't shoot. He acts, that's all, by being in the right place at the right time. In short, a Western." [11]

Being alone was part of Kissinger's style, but he also worked hard to ingratiate himself with those who might oppose him. He was determined to lead the American wagon out of Vietnam because until it had departed he could not move ahead with his grand design for detente, strategic arms control, and a new world equilibrium of power.

At a lunch with Kissinger and a small group of editors from *Time* and *Fortune* held in Washington, D.C. on September 29, 1972, Schecter was struck by Kissinger's rejection of both the North and South Vietnamese. "Our problem with the Vietnamese," said Kissinger, "is that one of them [North or South] always thinks he's winning, and generosity is not one of their attributes." Then he rated Thieu and Le Duc Tho as both being very Vietnamese in their thinking and behavior—it was a pox on both North and South Vietnam. For the first time Kissinger was referring to them both in the same way, a definite hint that the United States was distancing itself from Thieu and seeking a military withdrawal from the South, leaving the political resolution up to the Vietnamese. "The war has essentially run its course," Kissinger went on. "Nobody can win. There is no American interest except to get out with a sense of dignity." Then he added, "Le Duc Tho is a fanatic who has no sense of domestic normality toward which to move." This remark proved to be prophetic and was to be Kissinger's deepest insight into the North Vietnamese leader.

The Vietnamese were different, insisted Kissinger, "their minds work differently than ours." Dr. Eric Wulff, head of the Psychiatric Division at the University of Freiburg in West Germany, who established a psychiatric program at the University of Hue, believes that the Vietnamese mind establishes reality in mythical situations. Kissinger said Wulff had told him that for Vietnamese, real-life situations do not correspond to perceived reality but to a set of myths. "The main problem is to find out which myths the Vietnamese are relating to in a given situation." Kissinger needed to find out what the South Vietnamese accepted as reality, because for the United States the reality was that the war must end.

The mood and tone were clear. The United States had done what it could in Vietnam; now it was time to disengage with honor. "The Vietnamese were a difficult, stubborn, and suspicious people," Kissinger explained. The only problem for Hanoi was "when to settle—before the election or after." On the question of timing, Kissinger insisted that "the President is not pushing me. He has never urged me to speed up the timetable."

At another point in the lunch Kissinger said that ideally the solution would be to reach agreement with the North Vietnamese before the election, but not announce the results until after the voting was over. This was too much for Hedley Donovan, editor in chief of Time, Inc., a great Kissinger admirer. He firmly lectured Kissinger on the importance of integrity in the electoral process and how it would be damaging to have a settlement reached because of the election. Kissinger reluctantly agreed.[12]

Then Kissinger went off to Paris to press for a settlement before the election in hopes of regaining his own position in the White House by contributing to Nixon's election victory. Kissinger feared he might be overtaken by events and the flow of Nixon's plans for the second term. He knew that Nixon planned to replace Secretary of State William Rogers with Ambassador to West Germany Kenneth Rush, whom Nixon admired for his role in the 1971 Berlin negotiations.[13]

Nixon had a timetable that was based on his political strength, while Kissinger had a timetable based on his personal and intellectual ambitions. Both men spoke of peace with honor and the importance of ending the war honorably. In his January 1969 article in *Foreign Affairs* on the Vietnam negotiations, Kissinger wrote: "However we got into Vietnam, whatever the judgments of our actions, ending the war honorably is essential for the peace of the world."

Kissinger's definition of honor was to suffer heavily, however. Kissinger was concerned about a cease-fire with honor, a "decent interval" during which South Vietnam could prove its ability to survive with American aid or collapse. Nixon never publicly adopted this view. He spoke only of "winning the peace," which suggested continued support for South Vietnam. Kissinger was appealing to a different constituency than his President. He was concerned that his friends in the academic world would see him adopting the role of a toady to Nixon's hard-line political views, an intellectual wet-nurse, the despised Court Jew among the Germanic White House staff. Kissinger had a flair for elegant language and high-minded rhetoric. With his liberal friends and most of the White House press corps, he played the secret good guy amidst the Nixon black hats. Kissinger worked hard to distance himself from the Nixon team. This infuriated H. R. (Bob) Haldeman, for one, who expected Kissinger, like other staffers, to be subject to his discipline as chief of staff. To the Nixon loyalists it appeared that Kissinger worried about his own image more than the President's, which brought him under fire from Haldeman in the White House.

Kissinger had worked for Nelson Rockefeller in his presidential primary campaign in 1968 and had been on the Rockefeller payroll since the mid-1950s. While still working for Rockefeller, before Nixon was nominated in 1968, Kissinger was quoted as saying, "Richard Nixon is the most dangerous of all the men running to have as president."[14]

For Kissinger, Nixon was a stranger—cold, impersonal, and basically uninteresting as a human being.* With Nixon, Kissinger was the fawning

---

* That is how Kissinger described him in private sessions with Schecter when the latter was covering the Nixon White House for *Time*.

courtier, always careful never to openly oppose the President. He used several techniques to win approval from Nixon. In most cases the substance of the issues was secondary in importance to Kissinger's own control over the issue through Nixon's support. On occasion Kissinger would ask others to take a position that he knew would be in opposition to the President's views just to weaken their position with Nixon. He would even falsify his position so that he might discredit his opponents.

A classic example occurred in May 1972, when Nixon decided to mine Haiphong. Secretary of State William Rogers was called back from Europe for the meeting of the National Security Council. Kissinger called Under Secretary for Political Affairs U. Alexis Johnson and told him he was trying to persuade the President against the mining. Kissinger said he believed the odds for the chances of a summit with Moscow were 95 to 5 against. He claimed the mining was the brainchild of John Mitchell and John Connally, and "we would have to rely on Secretary Rogers to sway the President's mind at the NSC meeting scheduled for Monday morning. Laird could not do it because 'he was always on every side of every problem.' " [15]

When Rogers and Johnson met, the Secretary of State said he doubted that Kissinger was against the mining. Johnson talked with Kissinger again, and he confirmed to Johnson that he opposed the mining, and according to Johnson, acted depressed about the way the President was heading. Again, Kissinger urged Johnson to convince Secretary Rogers to speak up against the mining at the NSC meeting. "Henry said he did not intend to himself because he did not want to oppose the President in an open meeting," recalls Johnson. [16]

In his own memoirs, Kissinger recounts how he agreed with the mining of Haiphong and obtained Connally's support. At the NSC meeting Rogers did not take a firm position and Kissinger reports that he was "ambiguous." He had evidently succeeded in neutralizing Rogers. [17] He had been devious with the Secretary of State and the highest-ranking career Foreign Service Officer.

During the election campaign of 1972 Kissinger's relations with Nixon grew strained, especially as the White House staff, led by Haldeman, sought to keep Kissinger in line. The relationship deteriorated as the Vietnam negotiations proceeded. Kissinger was working for a political solution that would disengage the United States from Vietnam and bring American prisoners back. His emphasis was on negotiations and getting out, while Nixon spoke of the need to "win the peace." In his study on the Vietnam negotiations, Allan Goodman quotes a member of Kissinger's negotiating team on Kissinger's goal: a negotiated settlement "that Hanoi would sign to return the prisoners of war and to end the U.S. involvement." Nixon "believed that the only way to end the war by negotiation was to prove to Hanoi and Saigon that Saigon can win it." [18]

The South Vietnamese certainly did not believe that Kissinger was negotiating a "decent interval" for them. Nixon's letters to Thieu gave him a sense of support from the President and a feeling of personal rapport.

Nixon had begun with his personal commitment to mutual withdrawal to Thieu at Midway. Later, in 1969 during his brief visit to Saigon, he told Thieu: "We have gone as far now as we can or should go in opening the door to peace, and now it is time for the other side to respond."

Nixon emphasized Vietnamization and American support. He backed his words with action. The build-up of Saigon's armed forces went on without interruption. The invasion of Cambodia in May of 1970, the secret bombing of the North in 1971, and the operation against the North Vietnamese supply center at Tchepone in Laos in 1971 all increased Saigon's chances for survival. In Thieu's eyes, Nixon was committed to the survival of the Saigon government. Yet there were two contradictory lines in American policy: Vietnamization and negotiations.

As mentioned in an earlier chapter, Vietnamization, based on the withdrawal of American troops and the strengthening of the Saigon government's military prowess, was supposed to complement negotiations. Actually, the two worked in opposition, with negotiations undercutting Vietnamization. In his Foreign Policy Report to Congress in 1970, the President stated:

> Vietnamization is not a substitute for negotiations, but a spur to negotiations. In strengthening the capability of the Government and people of South Vietnam to defend themselves we provide Hanoi with an authentic incentive to negotiate seriously now. Confronted by Vietnamization, Hanoi's alternative to a reasonable settlement is to continue its costly sacrifices while its bargaining power diminishes.[19]

In theory, Nixon and Kissinger walked together, but if they were moving toward the same goal, they often stressed taking different paths to that end.[20] Nixon placed his emphasis on Vietnamization, Kissinger on negotiations. "I had great hope for negotiations," Kissinger wrote in his memoirs. Nixon did not: "No wonder that Nixon, always skeptical of negotiations, bombarded me with missives on my round-the-world trip to toughen up our stance in Paris and bring matters to a head," Kissinger complained.[21]

Contrary to Kissinger's belief that he could convince Hanoi to compromise, Nixon viewed the negotiations as an extension of Hanoi's struggle for a Communist victory. Kissinger saw the negotiations in a traditional diplomatic format and the North Vietnamese as players who would respond to diplomatic pressures from Beijing and Moscow. Although he often spoke of Hanoi's ideological tenacity and fanaticism, Kissinger discounted these factors when it was convenient to do so as a means to achieve his immediate political ends. Nixon placed less stress on negotiations and more emphasis on military power. In his report to Congress on U.S. Foreign Policy in 1972, Nixon said: "The North Vietnamese view negotiations as an alternative route to victory, not a compromise with opponents. For them negotiations are a continuation of a military struggle by other means, rather than an effort to bridge the gap between positions."[22]

The President viewed Vietnamization as an alternative that was not dependent on Hanoi. When he called on "the great Silent Majority of Americans" for support on November 3, 1969, Nixon explained that he needed their help to search "for a just peace through a negotiated settlement, if possible, or through continued implementation of our plan for Vietnamization, if necessary. A plan in which we will withdraw all of our forces from Vietnam on a schedule in accordance with our program as the South Vietnamese become strong enough to defend their freedom."

Nixon said his peace plan would "end the war and serve the cause of peace, not just in Vietnam but in the Pacific and the world."[23] In his personal letter to Thieu on the eve of his trip to China, Nixon repeated this theme of supporting Vietnam's desire for direct negotiations and its growing ability to defend itself.

In contrast to Nixon, Kissinger was less optimistic about Vietnamization, considering the program primarily as an incentive for Hanoi to negotiate. Kissinger understood that Vietnamization, as conceived and pushed by Defense Secretary Melvin Laird, was an "elegant bugout," in the words of the late Stewart Alsop. Laird was primarily concerned about the domestic impact of the Vietnam War and what the draft was doing to spur the antiwar movement. His plan was to remove American troops as quickly as possible and commit the President by announcing the schedule as far in advance as possible. Kissinger saw this as weakening his negotiating position and he engaged in bitter infighting with Laird for Nixon's favor.

In his memoirs, Nixon says that as Vietnamization succeeded, the negotiations became bogged down. "The stronger Saigon appeared, Henry believed, the less likelihood there would be that Hanoi would sign the agreement," a Kissinger aide said.[24]

If Nixon viewed Vietnamization as a means to provide Saigon with the maximum amount of time to develop its self-defense capability, Kissinger saw it as a way to prevent Thieu from criticizing America. Vietnamization was a means "to assuring that when an agreement was at hand, Saigon would have little ground on which to argue that it was premature."[25] Kissinger's goal was an agreement before election day at any price because he feared the negotiating moment could not be recaptured after Nixon took office for a second term.

In his critique of the mistakes of the Johnson administration, Kissinger argued that "our diplomacy and our strategy were conducted in isolation from each other."[26] This was an error Kissinger and Nixon were certain they could avoid; but the secret negotiations in Paris bore little relation to the Vietnamization being planned and executed in the Pentagon. Kissinger also argued that Johnson, by offering to negotiate "unconditionally, at any moment, anywhere" with Hanoi, "left the timing of negotiations to the other side." Kissinger was soon to close the window of timing on himself as the 1972 election deadline approached. He ceded the other side an advantage that could only be overcome by force or prolonged negotiations.

Kissinger, ever the advocate of negotiation over confrontation, thought that Vietnamization would provide an incentive for the North Vietnamese to negotiate. The American build-up of the South would force the North to make compromises at the bargaining table and serve to speed up the negotiations. "We needed a strategy that made continuation of the war seem less attractive to Hanoi than a settlement," he explained in his memoirs.[27] But he failed to realize that Hanoi had only one primary goal: the unilateral withdrawal of American troops from the South.

Fear is a more powerful factor in the Asian calculation than inducements and incentives. Hanoi's greatest fear was a permanent American presence in the South. For the North Vietnamese, the Americans were the historical successors to the Mongol invaders of the thirteenth century and the French in the twentieth century. In 1969, when Nixon announced the withdrawal of 25,000 American troops, Ho Chi Minh decreed "a total, complete unconditional withdrawal."[28] In his *Testament* before he died, Ho wrote:

> Our mountains will always be, our rivers will
> always be, our people will always be;
> The American invaders defeated, we will rebuild
> our land ten times more beautiful.
> No matter what difficulties and hardships lie ahead,
> our people are sure of total victory.
> The U.S. imperialists will certainly have to quit.[29]

There was to be no compromise on the total withdrawal of American forces from Vietnam. For two years Kissinger focused on mutual withdrawal as the key. This was to become the point that made the major difference in the negotiations and demoralized South Vietnam. From the North Vietnamese point of view, Vietnamization hardened its negotiating position. The more Vietnamization progressed, the more Hanoi feared its ability to implement its goals in the South. This fear of Vietnamization was echoed in Hanoi's propaganda from 1969 onward. In 1971, "To frustrate the Vietnamization Plan" became Hanoi's top priority. Rather than accept the American plan at face value—America would withdraw as the South Vietnamese improved their capability—Hanoi interpreted Vietnamization as scheme for keeping South Vietnam in the American orbit forever.

Kissinger believed in 1968, before he took office, that since Hanoi was "unable to force American withdrawal, it must negotiate about it."[30] When the first contingent of 25,000 American troops was withdrawn in 1969 under Vietnamization, Kissinger thought that Hanoi had been given an incentive to negotiate the withdrawal of its own troops. In his first secret meeting in Paris, he told Xuan Thuy that "the U.S. had made a series of significant, unreciprocated gestures: We had stopped sending reinforcements. We had announced the unilateral withdrawal of 25,000 men and we had promised further withdrawals." It was then Hanoi's turn to respond, thought Kissinger.[31] As Vietnamization became caught up in the domestic American political process, Defense Secretary Melvin Laird pressed his own agenda and timetable for extricating America from Vietnam. The North Vietnamese realized that American withdrawal would take place whether or not they made concessions.

In fact, the longer they held out, the fewer American troops they would have to face. The more American troops that were withdrawn, the less incentive there was for Hanoi to negotiate. As America deescalated, the Communists' demands escalated.

For the South Vietnamese, Vietnamization was to provide the means for developing a capable self-defense. When that point was reached, Saigon would be more determined to resist Communist domination and thus less willing to compromise its independence in negotiations with the North. The more South Vietnam progressed with Vietnamization, the less it wanted to accept a coalition government with the National Liberation Front.

From an operational viewpoint, Vietnamization, as summarized by Nixon, included two components. First was the strengthening of the armed forces of South Vietnam in numbers, equipment, leadership, combat skills, and overall capability. Second was the extension of the pacification program in the South—an effort to secure rural villages and market towns and prevent the Viet Cong from controlling the countryside.

Responding to Nixon, President Thieu launched a campaign for *Ba Tu*, or Three Selves: self-recovery, self-powering, and self-sustaining. General mobilization was decreed to increase the numbers in the ARVN to 1.1 million men. American equipment had been quickly flown in; nearly a million M-16 rifles were finally distributed to South Vietnamese troops, replacing outdated M-1s and Garrand rifles that were no match for the AK-47s supplied to the North Vietnamese by the Soviet Union. The United States also provided 12,000 M-60 machine guns, and 40,000 M-79 grenade launchers. In 1969 the leadership program produced 100,000 civilian and military graduates; more than 1,000 people, including pilots, went to the United States each year to receive advanced training. By 1970, Thieu was able to announce that South Vietnam was officially "crossing over into the postwar era." [32] Combat skills and South Vietnam's overall capability improved substantially by 1971 although 80 percent of the American troops had left.

Pacification, the other component of Vietnamization, also moved forward in the form of the Phoenix Program under the direction of CIA and William E. Colby. Between 1969 and 1971, according to Colby, the Phoenix Program reduced the insurgency by 67,000, of whom 21,000 were killed in those years. The others either returned to their villages or were considered prisoners. Under the Phoenix Program the villagers were provided with weapons and trained to root out the local Viet Cong apparatus, and to stop them from moving from one village to another. [33] Regional Forces (RF) of 300,000 and the Popular Forces (PF) of 250,000 were armed by the U.S. By 1970, 80 percent of these forces had received automatic weapons. In his U.S. Foreign Policy Report to Congress early in 1971, President Nixon said:

> In mid-1969 the indicators showed roughly 40 percent of the rural population under South Vietnamese control. Fifty percent under the influence of both

sides, and ten percent under the control of the other side. Recently these proportions were respectively 65 percent, 30 percent and 5 percent. When South Vietnam's urban population of six million, all under government control, is added to the over seven million rural population in that category roughly eighty percent of the total population of South Vietnam is controlled by the Government.[34]

Under the terms of the Paris Agreement, at the precise moment that the South had taken the initiative and was prevailing, there was to be a cease-fire in place that allowed the North Vietnamese to remain in the South. They were not to be regrouped in well-demarcated areas but were free to remain like "spots on a leopard" wherever they had established a position. The South Vietnamese called it a "leopard skin" cease-fire. Most difficult for the government was the problem of the peasants; they had been given weapons and trained for four years to kill the Viet Cong. Now they were going to be told to accept their presence and permit them to move freely throughout the countryside. South Vietnamese who had been trained to defend themselves against the Communists now would be told to accept them in their midst. A bitter joke went the rounds: "Before, we went into the jungle to hunt down the wild beasts. Now, we have to take them into our arms and sleep with them."[35]

Thieu likened the American insistence that he accept North Vietnamese troops in the South to forcing the head of a household to accept a thief he had just caught red-handed in his bedroom. He told the story of a man who called the police to arrest a thief. When the police came, they could not get the thief out of the house. So the chief policeman put his gun back in the holster and told the man, 'He's not that bad. Why don't you try to learn how to live with him? After awhile he may get homesick and go back to his family.' After a while, of course, the man was afraid that the thief would jump into bed and rape the wife."[36]

On Friday morning, October 20, at 10:00 a.m., Kissinger met with members of Thieu's National Security Council at the official residence of Foreign Minister Tran Van Lam on Hong Thap Tu Street. By then the Vietnamese had had a chance to study the text in their own language. John Negroponte of Kissinger's staff had delivered the text to Nha at the Palace the previous evening and the Vietnamese team worked late into the night analyzing the documents in English and Vietnamese. The Vietnamese text fully confirmed their fears.

Kissinger had accepted the Vietnamese-language draft with all the Communists' terminology, and it differed sharply from the English-language text. The North Vietnamese had indeed used the words for "government structure" to describe the National Council, and American forces were described in a derogatory term (*quan my*) that meant "American pirates." Another section in the Vietnamese text called on the Americans and their "vassals" to withdraw.

Before the meeting began, around a long blackwood dinner table with a linen cloth, Foreign Minister Lam, a Catholic, said a prayer: "Dear Lord, bless those of us who are here to work for peace." Nha was amused and restless. As soon as Lam finished his prayer, he asked to have "twenty-three preliminary points clarified by Kissinger." Kissinger and Nha sparred heavily until Kissinger conceded that the Vietnamese-language problems would be raised with the North Vietnamese. Of the twenty-three points, Nha recalls that Kissinger considered eight worthy of clarification. Nha insisted on having all the points clarified. The meeting broke at lunchtime and Nha hurried to the Palace to consult Thieu. Kissinger was scheduled to meet Thieu at the Palace at 5:00 p.m.

Thieu was in his quarters lunching on boiled chicken and he asked Nha to join him. "I don't have time for lunch. This is very serious," said Nha. "What is it?" asked Thieu. Nha ran down the list of differences with Kissinger. "I could see as I went on down the list that he was losing his appetite," said Nha. Nha urged Thieu to take more time to study the agreement. "Please cancel the five o'clock meeting, Mr. President," he suggested. "Well," replied Thieu, "we already made a promise."

Nha reminded Thieu of the incoming reports from the corps headquarters that enemy troops were massing in line with the instructions in the captured documents. If Thieu went ahead and initialed the agreement, he could expect an enemy offensive across the country prior to the signing in Paris, Nha warned. It had all been worked out over the previous month with Kissinger in Paris. "We should convene all the province chiefs in Saigon tomorrow and I'll use that as an excuse to Kissinger." Thieu decided not to tell Kissinger about the captured documents because he wanted to see what Kissinger would say about the terms he had reached with the North Vietnamese and did not want to give him a chance to comment on the North Vietnamese documents or suggest they were part of a disinformation campaign. If he confronted Kissinger with the captured documents, Thieu felt it would only aggravate tensions further.[37]

At 4:30 p.m. Nha called Ambassador Bunker and told him the meeting with Thieu would have to be canceled. "I'm very sorry, some unexpected developments have occurred, enemy troop concentrations. We are calling all of the province chiefs and corps commanders home for a meeting."

"When can we reschedule the meeting tomorrow?" asked Bunker, still not displaying any anger.

"I'm going to have to apprise you of that later," said Nha.

Bunker asked to speak with Thieu, but was told, "I'm sorry, the President has imposed a total communications blackout. He doesn't want to take any phone calls. I'll have to get back to you when I get word from him that he can see you."

Nha then left the Palace to brief members of the National Security Council on the morning meeting with Kissinger and their concerns with "the loopholes we found." The members of the Council agreed with the points that had been raised, as they usually did after Thieu had made up his mind.

While at the home of Vice President Huong, Nha received a call from Bunker, who asked, "Can we go and see the President now? We are ready to leave the Embassy."

"The Palace is not ready and we have other plans. You cannot see him. I'd hate for you to leap into your limousine and be turned back at the gate because I have already been given instructions that the President is not going to see anybody this afternoon," said Nha.

"Oh, you cannot do that," sputtered the now enraged ambassador, who had been subjected to Kissinger's rising fury. Kissinger grabbed the phone: "This is Dr. Kissinger."

"How are you?" asked Nha.

"Why can't we have a meeting with the President?" demanded Kissinger.

"As I explained to the Ambassador, I'm sorry, the President cannot see you now. He will see you tomorrow," replied Nha.

"I am the Special Envoy of the President of the United States of America. You know I cannot be treated as an errand boy," said Kissinger.

"We never considered you an errand boy, but if that's what you think you are, there's nothing I can do about it," Nha responded.

"I demand to see the President."

"May I remind you again what I just told you? I'm sorry."

Kissinger gave the phone back to Bunker, who told Nha, "You better get back to me."[38]

Kissinger now had a new problem he wanted to talk about with Thieu. The North Vietnamese real intentions to consider the Council of Reconciliation and Concord as a coalition were confirmed in the text of *Newsweek* correspondent Arnaud de Borchgrave's exclusive interview with North Vietnamese Premier Pham Van Dong. De Borchgrave had flown from Hanoi to Vientiane with his story and arrived on Friday afternoon. To make his deadline, he asked the American ambassador, G. McMurtie Godley, to transmit his copy via embassy channels to New York. In exchange he gave the ambassador a copy of his on-the-record interview with Pham Van Dong as well as the off-the-record portions. Within two hours Kissinger was reading the copy in Saigon.

In the interview, Pham Van Dong was asked about Thieu's role in a three-sided coalition. "Thieu has been overtaken by events. And events are now following their own course," Dong said. After the cease-fire there would be two armies and two administrations in the South, "and given that new situation they will have to work out their own arrangements for a three-sided coalition of transition and defuse the situation in the wake of the American withdrawal." Kissinger was furious with the North Vietnamese. A coalition was not what he believed he had negotiated in Paris.[39]

After filing his Hanoi material, de Borchgrave flew to Saigon and called on General Tran Van Don to help arrange an interview with Thieu. "It would be astonishing if Thieu agreed to sign the agreement that Pham Van Dong disclosed to me as it stood when I interviewed him on October 18," de Borchgrave told Don.[40] Don called Nha to ask for an interview on de

Borchgrave's behalf. He also told Nha of the Pham Van Dong interview, but he did not have the text for Nha.

When Kissinger called the Palace on Friday afternoon asking to see Thieu, he had decided to show Thieu the interview text and explain that it was not what he had negotiated in Paris. On the phone with Nha he had said only that there had been "a new development and I must speak to the President." Nha held firm and insisted on Kissinger waiting.

Kissinger and Bunker met with Thieu and Nha at 10:00 a.m. the following morning, Saturday, October 21, for two hours at the Palace. During Saturday's meeting, however, Kissinger did not raise the de Borchgrave interview. Nha and Thieu did not know that Kissinger had the text. Thieu reviewed the results of the Friday meeting with Foreign Minister Lam and the National Security Council. Of the twenty-three changes Nha had requested, Kissinger insisted that sixteen were probably manageable, but seven remained and raised "impossible demands." [41] The major points were the presence of North Vietnamese troops in the South and the status of the National Council of Reconciliation and Concord as a governmental body. To boost Kissinger, Nixon had sent him a letter which he carefully arranged to have delivered while the meeting with Thieu was in progress. "Mr. President, may I read you the telegram from President Nixon?" asked Kissinger.

Nixon urged Thieu to sign the agreement and threatened him with the cut-off of aid if he did not go along.

> Were you to find the agreement to be unacceptable at this point and the other side were to reveal the extraordinary limits to which it has gone in meeting demands put upon them, it is my judgment that your decision would have the most serious effects upon my ability to continue to provide support for you and for the government of South Vietnam. [42]

Kissinger handed the message to Thieu, who did not bother to read it but just smiled. Nha took a copy of the message, read it, returned it to Bunker, and said, "Thank you." No progress was made, but Kissinger left still encouraged that Thieu would accept the agreement. Another meeting was set for Sunday morning at 8:00 a.m.

At six o'clock on Sunday, Nha was awakened by a call from Washington reporting on the details of the de Borchgrave interview with Pham Van Dong. Nha copied down the text and rushed to see Thieu before their meeting with Kissinger and Bunker. When he read the text of the interview, Thieu was outraged. He had told Kissinger repeatedly that Hanoi considered the Council a coalition with real powers and now he had the proof. The North Vietnamese were insisting on the right of the National Liberation Front to have its own administration in the South, backed by its forces and the remaining North Vietnamese troops. The "leopard spot" cease-fire would provide the basis for a rival administration, Thieu had told Kissinger. The Council would be the structure to carry out the strategy. Now there was public evidence to back him. [43]

Thieu decided not to confront Kissinger with the Pham Van Dong interview, but to see if he would raise it himself. "We played cat and mouse with Kissinger," recalled Nha, "and waited to see what he would say. He never brought it up."[44] At the end of an inconclusive forty-five-minute meeting, Thieu told Kissinger that he could not sign the Accords as they existed. Kissinger, however, felt that Thieu was seeking a way to accommodate him, and left the meeting heartened. He cabled Nixon optimistically: "I think we have made a breakthrough." As Kissinger flew to Phnom Penh, Bunker followed up and advised the White House that both he and Kissinger left the meeting with Thieu encouraged. Bunker suggested that the North Vietnamese efforts to seize as much land as possible before the cease-fire were a failure.[45]

During the day Thieu met with his cabinet and assured them that he would not accept the coalition that Pham Van Dong proposed as part of "a prefabricated package" brought by Kissinger. At this point Thieu was convinced that Kissinger had been duped by the North Vietnamese. He had the North Vietnamese operational orders for a land grab during the cease-fire period in hand, hard evidence that Hanoi had no intention of observing the spirit of the agreement before it was scheduled to be signed on October 31. How could Kissinger have done all that behind his back?

In Washington, Hung read the text of Pham Van Dong's *Newsweek* interview, which confirmed his fears that the Americans were about to make an unfavorable settlement with the North Vietnamese based on a coalition government in the South. Over the preceding summer, as the military fortunes of the South had improved and the North had appeared more willing to negotiate, Hung had renewed his efforts to press for direct contact between North and South through trade. At that point it was still unclear how the negotiations between Kissinger and Le Duc Tho would proceed, and Hung, in desperation, believed a trade agreement could be an alternative to American negotiations with the North. At a minimum, such a forthcoming initiative would improve South Vietnam's image in the eyes of the world.

On September 24, 1972, *The Washington Post* had published Hung's article, "The Vietnams As Partners in Trade," in its Outlook section. In it he stressed the importance of trade between North and South as an important element of the negotiations, with considerable appeal to the North— "The resumption of economic cooperation between the two Vietnams must be seriously considered in the current negotiation." He had followed up with a letter to Thieu urging the president to revive the trade option before Kissinger arrived in Saigon. Hung assumed, as did Thieu, that there was still room to negotiate if Saigon was permitted by the U.S. to negotiate directly with Hanoi. He thought his idea would at least provide a positive initiative from the Vietnamese side, rather than continued opposition to the American design for peace.

While Kissinger was in Phnom Penh to meet with Cambodian leader Lon Nol, American officials were traveling in Southeast Asia advising government leaders in Thailand, South Korea, and Laos that the South Vietnamese had agreed to sign the Accords. In Saigon the word was being spread by American officials, under Kissinger's instructions, that Thieu would sign. Nha met with Bunker and angrily told him: "This is no way to treat an ally."

In his meeting with Lon Nol, Kissinger behaved as if President Thieu had fully endorsed the Accords. Lon Nol smiled and ordered champagne: "Peace is at last coming. We are going to drink to it and to compliment Dr. Kissinger on his mission."[46] Kissinger returned from Phnom Penh, only 130 miles away, in time to meet with Thieu again at five o'clock on Sunday, October 22. Thieu and Nha had conferred after their morning meeting with Kissinger and agreed not to change their position. "Thieu said we would insist on Kissinger getting back to the other side and clarifying our concerns in a new formal draft. That was to be our position and there was no fall-back," recalled Nha.[47]

This was the decisive meeting between the four men—Kissinger, accompanied by Bunker, and Thieu, with Nha at his side. Kissinger had gained Lon Nol's concurrence for his plans and returned to Saigon "excited at the prospect of success." He was greeted by Thieu telling him through Nha, who interpreted from Vietnamese into English, "I do not appreciate the fact that your people are going around town telling everybody that I signed. I have not signed anything. I do not object to peace, but I have not gotten any satisfactory answers from you and I am not going to sign." Thieu then repeated his three main objections: the continued presence of North Vietnamese troops in the South, the potential for a coalition government growing out of the National Council of Reconciliation and Concord, and the failure to establish the Demilitarized Zone (DMZ) as a secure border. The North Vietnamese kept insisting that there was no separation between North and South, but that they were one country. Under this reasoning, North Vietnamese troops were not invading the South and did not have to return to the North or leave the South. For Thieu, recognition of the DMZ as a border between North and South was critical to his argument that North Vietnamese troops had to be withdrawn from the South and return to their own country.

Kissinger became enraged and told Thieu that he had succeeded in Beijing, Moscow, and Paris, and now Thieu had become "the obstacle to peace." "If you do not sign, we're going to go on our own," he threatened.

Nothing was barred. Thieu charged that Kissinger had "connived" with the Soviet Union and China to sell out South Vietnam. "I was surprised and outraged," Thieu recalled. "The American administration was not an honorable ally. They did not have my agreement beforehand. The Americans betrayed us. We were doomed to failure, but we could not do otherwise [and not sign the agreement]. Can you imagine? Kissinger told me the Russians told him the North Vietnamese would not accept mutual withdrawal and the United States just went along with that. What could South Vietnam do?"[48]

Thieu would have no part in Kissinger's deal because he could see nothing but disaster on the horizon. All his smoldering resentment now rose to the surface and he told Kissinger:

> Ever since the U.S. asked me to resign and bargained with me on the time of my resignation, had I not been a soldier I would have resigned. Because I see that those whom I regard as friends have failed me. However great the personal humiliation for me I shall continue to fight. My greatest satisfaction will be when I can sign a peace agreement. I have not told anyone that the Americans asked me to resign, since they would share my humiliation, but have made it appear voluntary on my part.[49]

Kissinger, determined not to give way, did not concede anything, but replied:

> I admire the courage, dedication and heroism which have characterized your speech. However, as an American I can only deeply resent your suggestion that we have connived with the Soviets and Chinese. How can you conceive this possible when the President on May 8 risked his whole political future to come to your assistance? When we talked with the Soviets and Chinese, it was to pressure them to exert pressure on Hanoi. We genuinely believed that the proposed agreement preserved South Vietnam's freedom—our principles have been the same as yours and we have defended them. You have only one problem. President Nixon has many. Your conviction that we have undermined you will be understood by no American, least of all by President Nixon.
>
> As to specifics: we have not recognized the right of North Vietnam to be in the South. We have used the language of the Geneva Accords, since we thought this was the best way to work out a practical solution. Had we wanted to sell you out, there would have been many easier ways by which we could have accomplished this.[50]

Kissinger's hurt pride and vexation at having his integrity challenged did not have any impact on Thieu. Kissinger alternated between anger and charm, but to no effect. Nha shortened Thieu's answers in English, which angered Kissinger further.[51] "Why does your president play the role of a martyr? He does not have the stuff of a martyr."

Thieu laughed and answered in Vietnamese. Nha translated the reply: "I am not trying to be a martyr. I am a nationalist and I am trying to be a very pragmatic man who is trying to get answers to valid points."

As he perceived what was being presented to him, Thieu grew angrier, but he suppressed his rage by turning his back on Kissinger and staring at a giant map of Vietnam on the wall of the Situation Room where they were meeting. As Thieu recalled his feelings and thoughts: "It was the duty of America to fight for its allies, not to be an *avocat du diable* [devil's advocate]. Kissinger had come not as a comrade in arms, but to advocate the North Vietnamese cause. He gave me the impression that he was a representative of Hanoi, not of America. He was not on my side but on the side of Le Duc Tho and advocated his position. He was pleading for the North

Vietnamese. That's the strange thing. Why was an American comrade in arms pleading for the enemy? I didn't understand for whom he was working. Was it for us or for the North Vietnamese? The proper thing would have been for Dr. Kissinger to come to Saigon and to work together with us from the very beginning, mapping our strategy and supporting each other." [52]

Thieu felt he understood the North Vietnamese better than the Americans and that Kissinger had either been tricked by Le Duc Tho or had made a secret deal with him. He tried to explain to Kissinger that he was not an obstacle to peace, but that the Accords were "a matter of life or death for my country." But as Thieu hardened, Kissinger's anger flared, and he told Thieu: "I'm not going to come back to South Vietnam. This is the greatest diplomatic failure of my career." [53] Angrily Thieu asked Kissinger: "Why are you rushing to get the Nobel prize?" [54]

In his frustration Kissinger turned his back to Nha and Bunker continued the conversation. "Well, is that your final position not to sign, Mr. President?" asked Bunker, now angry too.

"Yes, that is my final position. I will not sign and I would like you to convey my position to Mr. Nixon," said Thieu. "Please go back to Washington and tell President Nixon I need answers."

Kissinger, determined not to let his massive efforts collapse, asked Thieu for a final meeting before his departure on Monday morning, October 23.

"What for?" asked Thieu.

"The press still thinks we have a solution at hand, so let us have a short meeting and make sure that the consultation between allies is taking place," replied Kissinger.

"Well, if that is of some help to you, fine, we'll have a short meeting tomorrow, five minutes," said Thieu.

The following morning at 8:00 a.m. when they met it was clear that Thieu was not going to change his mind. He gave Kissinger a letter for Nixon outlining his objections to the Accords, repeating that he wanted to sign a peace agreement, but only under the right terms at the right time. Before he left, Kissinger asked Thieu: "Please, let's agree between ourselves not to reveal to the press anything that went on. Let it appear as if we had a constructive meeting." Kissinger shook hands with Thieu and left hurriedly without shaking hands with Nha.

At Tan Son Nhut Airport Kissinger saw newsmen and photographers lined up behind a barrier fifty-yards from his plane. He stopped briefly. "Was it a good trip?" a reporter asked.

"Yes," he replied.

"Was it productive?"

"Yes, it always is when I come here."

"Are you coming back?"

Kissinger did not answer. He just flashed his diplomatic smile. [55]

Thieu told Nha to issue a statement describing "four days of constructive talks leading to a peace settlement." Then the president convened his

National Security Council and in cold, unemotional terms summarized the areas of disagreement in the final meetings with Kissinger and Bunker. "We are not going to sign unless we get some qualifications," said Thieu. After the meeting Thieu and Nha met alone in his private apartment in the Palace. "What are we going to do now?" asked Nha. "This is when the action gets tough. I bet the moment Kissinger gets back to Washington he's going to muster the press and tell them that we are the obstacle to peace. He's going to portray us in a very unfavorable light, so let's preempt that."

"How are we going to preempt that?" asked Thieu. "If we talk about what we discussed, then we will be violating our agreement with him."

Nha suggested that Thieu go on television and discuss Hanoi's newest peace plan, which had been broadcast three weeks earlier, and refer to that rather than to the points in the draft agreement. " 'Since the points are essentially similar to what Kissinger brought, we can attack the Communist plan and imply that is what we discussed with Kissinger.' It was a clever subterfuge," recalled Nha. "We would use Kissinger's technique against him, as we say, *Gay ong dap lung ong,* hit his back with his own stick." [56]

6

Peace Out of Hand

A T PRESIDENT NIXON'S INSISTENCE, Henry Kissinger returned to Washington from Saigon on October 23 after warning Thieu "in anguish" that if the war continued at its present scale for another six months, the Congress would cut off funds to South Vietnam."[1] Kissinger had failed. Instead of arriving in Hanoi in triumph with President Thieu's approval of the draft agreement, he was forced to return home empty-handed, in a state of distress and deep concern for the fate of the negotiations and his own future. With only two weeks to the election, Nixon cautioned Kissinger that too hasty an agreement, without Thieu's support, would be a political liability. Nixon wanted to deal with Vietnam after the election.

Thieu could not possibly believe that the agreement Kissinger had brought from Paris was, as Nixon had written him, an agreement "that meets my absolute condition that the government of South Vietnam must survive as a free country."

In the captured documents that Thieu read, but never discussed with Kissinger, the North Vietnamese had declared complete victory over the Americans and South Vietnamese.[2] Their interpretation was totally opposite to what Nixon had written and Kissinger had explained. Thieu realized that the North Vietnamese planned to violate the agreement before it took effect, which would lead to the continued presence of North Vietnamese troops in the South. The agreement would be used to provide the power to back up a coalition government to be formed with the Thieu government.

Thieu was prepared for the worst. He had been through the American election campaign of 1968, and believed that the longer he held out the better off he would be. Nixon appeared certain to beat McGovern. With a major victory behind him, Nixon would be more likely to carry out the promises in his letters and be under less pressure to settle on Hanoi's terms. Thieu's struggle to avoid being swept up in the floodtide of the final weeks of the American election campaign was also good politics for him. By opposing an American-dictated settlement, he gained broad popular support in Saigon.

But his people knew he could not hold out indefinitely. If he refused to cooperate, the Americans would cut off aid, remove Thieu forcibly, or go it alone without him.[3]

The way the United States had conducted the peace negotiations hurt the prestige of the Republic of Vietnam. Kissinger had violated the cardinal rule he himself had laid down on how to carry on negotiations with the Vietnamese. In the *Foreign Affairs* article of January 1969, written before he was appointed Assistant for National Security Affairs but published after he took office, Kissinger wrote:

> To survive, the Vietnamese have had to learn to calculate—almost instinctively —the real balance of forces. If negotiations give the impression of being camouflaged surrender, there will be nothing left to negotiate. Support for the side which seems to be losing will collapse. Thus, all the parties are aware—Hanoi explicitly, for it does not view war and negotiation as separate processes; we in a more complicated bureaucratic manner—that the *way* negotiations are carried out is almost as important as *what* is negotiated. The choreography of how one enters negotiations, what is settled first and in what manner is inseparable from the substance of the issues.[4]

Kissinger's negotiating style had made Thieu appear little more than an American puppet, and diminished his stature by negotiating on his behalf without meaningful consultations. The unilateral cessation of bombings, the American initiatives or concessions in the negotiating process, arising out of the secret talks, were major sources of concern and anxiety for the South Vietnamese people. Thieu was rarely asked to take part in the planning stage for developing American positions; from time to time he was presented with a North Vietnamese secret proposal and an American counterproposal. He could then comment and list his objections, but most often he was still ignored.

Thieu's views on relying on an American negotiator were summed up in a TOP SECRET/SENSITIVE memorandum from President Thieu to Kissinger dated September 26, 1972, and presented to Ambassador Bunker that day. The memo read in part:

> On the fundamentals of a negotiated settlement of the Vietnam conflict, especially on the political aspects of it, it is the considered view of the GVN [government of Vietnam] that an honorable settlement could be achieved only if parallel to the Vietnamization of the war there is also the *Vietnamization of peace*. In other words, the other side should be brought to accept that the protagonist in the settlement is the GVN, and that it *should negotiate directly with the GVN for a negotiated solution*.
>
> We believe that by conducting the 1968 "exploratory" talks without the participation of the GVN, the USG [United States Government] lent itself to the description of the role which Communist propaganda has portrayed for many years, namely that the US is an aggressor in both South and North Viet-Nam, and that the GVN is only a "pupet" [sic] creature of the US, put to materialize US "neo-colonialism."

The "exploratory" Paris talks which began in March 1968, in which the GVN was excluded, has placed the USG, in our view, in an awkward position and allowed Hanoi to take continuously the offensive in portraying the US as the "aggressor."

Instead of having to answer on its aggression of GVN, Hanoi has been able to revert [sic] the roles, and assumes for itself the role of an "heroic" victim of "US aggression." As a result of this Hanoi has systematically refused the principle of reciprocity in the deescalation of the war, because to be consistent with itself Hanoi said the U.S. "aggressor" has no right to ask for reciprocity, a phraseology which corresponds to our statements that "aggression should not be rewarded."[5]

In Saigon it was a sore point that while the United States spoke for the Republic of Vietnam, the Soviet Union did not negotiate on behalf of North Vietnam. The Russians, instead, built up their client, advocating its interests and stressing its "independence." "In all international meetings the Communist side always played up the role of the Viet Cong, while the United States did little to support Saigon," complained former Foreign Minister Vuong Van Bac. Since South Vietnam could not negotiate directly with North Vietnam for its own survival, South Vietnamese diplomats found it difficult to be taken seriously. In Saigon there was a joke that the open meetings between North and South Vietnam at the French Foreign Ministry's International Conference Center on Avenue Kléber in Paris were "a soap opera" compared to the secret talks that Kissinger carried on with Le Duc Tho at Gif-sur-Yvette.

"Each U.S. concession at the negotiating table resulted in a fever in South Vietnam and in those circumstances how could anyone explain the whole truth to a perplexed population?" noted Major General Nguyen Duy Hinh in his study *Vietnamization and the Cease-Fire*. "The initiative displayed by the U.S. effectively blurred the cause of the RVN and worked to the advantage of Communist propaganda." Hinh acknowledged that while the great majority of the South Vietnamese population did not like communism, "at the same time, they felt heart-broken when realizing that the nationalist cause was not strong enough to instill the confidence which was necessary for continued sacrifices and continued struggling. And so, on the political and psychological front, the RVN found itself in a precarious and disadvantageous position."[6]

For Kissinger, the problem was to keep both the North and South Vietnamese in line. Privately, he compared them to tigers balanced on stools in a cage, with himself as the animal trainer, cracking the whip to force the recalcitrant beasts to go through their paces. "When one is in place, the other jumps off. If it was only the U.S. and the North Vietnamese, it would be easier to reach agreement," he remarked.[7] Kissinger elegantly states the case against his own behavior, then proceeds to rationalize his actions:

Ideally, perhaps we should have given him [Thieu] more time to prepare for what was coming. But speed also greatly improved the terms, and personal respect for him aside, I do not believe that a more deliberate schedule and earlier consultations would have altered his conduct. That was the stuff of tragedy, not a trifling error in human calculation. At that point both sides, on courses they had to take, were doomed to collision. The logic of Thieu's position required a posture of defiant intransigence to prove that Washington and Hanoi could not decide his fate—just as Hanoi's procedure with us, forcing the pace, was partly designed to demonstrate that he was our puppet. Whatever we did, Thieu would have maneuvered to gain time and found a way to confront us, as indeed he had confronted Haig and me on previous visits.[8]

Thieu denies this, and insists the core of the problem was that Kissinger never treated him as an ally. Thieu's suspicions of Kissinger began at Midway: "At Midway, when I saw the way the chairs were placed and the way I was called to the press conference without advance notice, I said to myself, 'These small things are not done by the President of a great nation. This is not a presidential thing to do. You should treat another president sympathetically.' I thought it came from Kissinger, not from Nixon or the Navy captain. Ever since those tricks I observed that he [Kissinger] was not an honest man."[9]

Thieu could not accept a situation in which Kissinger was making the negotiating policy with the North Vietnamese on his own and then getting Nixon's concurrence. He had understood Nixon at Midway to mean that there would be serious consultations before negotiations with the North Vietnamese took place. "If he [Kissinger] had met with me before the negotiations, and America and Vietnam acted as one to deal with Hanoi, I would have trusted him. I suspected him when he said that he had President Nixon's agreement. In principle, I must believe him, but I would request the signature of Nixon on a letter to confirm the most important points. Two, three, or five days later a letter comes. I am a careful man. I suspect that Kissinger did things first and then reported to President Nixon later. I have the feeling that he answered on behalf of Nixon because he wanted to be the architect. I wanted to know the real opinion of the U.S. President for grave decisions. Often I asked myself who Kissinger was working for."[10]

Thieu now began a series of speeches and meetings with political leaders to criticize and release portions of the draft agreement. Saigon newspapers carried his reaction to the draft agreement. The stories charged that the North Vietnamese were demanding a cease-fire to strengthen their forces and form a coalition government; after being a member of a three-segment government for six months, they would "resume the war with a deadly blow."[11]

Thieu also went on radio and television on October 24 to calm the rumors that had spread, and invite the public's backing. When Ambassador Bunker heard of Thieu's plans, he called the Palace and asked to speak with him. Nha answered and told Bunker that Thieu was not available. "The President just wants to tell the nation what went on over the last four days, but as we promised, we are not going to reveal the details of anything we talked about," he told Bunker.

In his two-hour talk, Thieu rejected any form of a coalition and the presence of 300,000 North Vietnamese troops in South Vietnam.[12] He proposed that Saigon and Hanoi negotiate directly to settle military problems and that Saigon and the Provisional Revolutionary Government negotiate a political settlement. In the event of a cease-fire, Thieu urged the population to "make preparations so . . . we will not be in a disadvantageous position. Therefore, we have planned measures to win over people and protect our land, wipe out enemy forces and ensure safety along communication lines . . . as well as security in the villages and hamlets. . . . I have also ordered that all Communist schemes to sow disturbances and foment uprising must be nipped in the bud and the Communist infrastructure must be wiped out quickly and mercilessly. . . ."[13]

Kissinger in an effort to sell the agreement in Saigon changed tactics; he attempted to reassure the people around Thieu that U.S. support for Saigon remained strong. Kissinger cabled instructions for the embassy in Saigon to generate acceptance of the agreement by promising continued American support. General Tran Van Don, then chairman of the Foreign Affairs Committee of the National Assembly, recalls that the Deputy Chief of Mission, Charles Whitehouse, met with him and said: "This agreement has its good side. It must be signed. It is only a piece of paper and will change nothing. You'll see!"[14] Prime Minister Tran Thien Khiem and Foreign Minister Tran Van Lam were contacted by Whitehouse and Deputy Assistant Secretary of State William H. Sullivan with suggestions that it would be best not to defy the Americans nor to totally reject their proposals. On a lower level embassy staffers went out among their Vietnamese contacts to sell the agreement. The guidance they received from Kissinger stated that the cease-fire could be enforced and the North Vietnamese troops in the South would gradually wither away. They would either get homesick, fall prey to malaria, athlete's foot, or dysentery, or desert to the South Vietnamese side.[15] There was an explanation to appeal to everyone. The military men were told the agreement was only a piece of paper and what really counted was President Nixon's willingness to back South Vietnam with military force. Kissinger told Saigon's Ambassador to the Court of St. James, Vuong Van Bac, that the agreement provided a legal basis for the United States to support South Vietnam which had not existed until then. Bac was Thieu's legal expert at the Paris Talks in addition to his ambassadorial duties in Europe. "Thus far the U.S. support for South Vietnam," Kissinger insisted, "has been based on only political declarations of presidents from Eisenhower on; as such there is no legal foundation for us to argue with Congress for more aid to Vietnam." Now we need a legal document to ask Congress for continued assistance." Bac thought that Kissinger's argument sounded plausible, and he noted that Kissinger "could be a very brilliant lawyer."[16]

Nixon and Kissinger feared that the North Vietnamese, believing Kissinger's trip to Saigon was baiting a trap for them, would reveal their version of the Paris Talks. At a crucial point in the negotiations Kissinger noted that "the North Vietnamese are more afraid of being tricked than of being defeated."[17] At 5:30 a.m. on October 26, Kissinger was awakened with the news that Radio Hanoi was broadcasting a full, detailed account of the agreement in Vietnamese, French, and English. He conferred with Nixon at 7:00 a.m. in the White House, and they agreed that Kissinger would give a press conference at ten o'clock that morning.

Kissinger's October 26 press conference in the White House Briefing Room was a strange event—the first time he was permitted by Nixon to appear on the record before television cameras. It appeared that he and Nixon were caught by surprise and were responding to the North Vietnamese with little time for preparation. That was part of the White House design. In reality, they had been expecting the North Vietnamese to bolt, and had devised the tactics to deal with such a situation. As early as October 6, in his personal letter to Thieu, Nixon had warned of just such an eventuality (". . . we cannot be sure at any point in the process that the enemy will not for propaganda or other reasons make public the details of the talks. U.S. tactics thus far have been designed to take account of this contingency").

The Briefing Room was jammed with reporters, confused and skeptical. Kissinger was calm and professorial as he spoke in his heavy German accent. He appeared full of outer confidence, promising to explain where the talks stood procedurally, the substance of the negotiations, and "where do we go from here."

Kissinger was at his deceptive best announcing, "We believe that peace is at hand. We believe that an agreement is in sight, based on the May 8 proposal of the President and some adaptation of our January 25 proposal which is just to all parties." In fact, he was proceeding with desperate optimism. Only the relatively less important issues remained to be settled, he insisted.

Reporters raised the question of why the same settlement could not have been achieved four years earlier. Indeed, it was the first question asked of Kissinger, who replied: "There was no possibility of achieving this agreement four years ago because the other side consistently refused to discuss the separation of the political and military issues, because it always insisted that it had to settle the political issues with us, and that we had to predetermine the future of South Vietnam in a negotiation with North Vietnam."[18]

After watching the press conference, Hung was shocked at Kissinger's arrogance and defiance of the world in insisting that his concessions were a victory for the United States. Nobody challenged him. Immediately after the press conference Hung dispatched a memo to Thieu analyzing the terms of the agreement as announced by Radio Hanoi. He told Thieu Kissinger's claims were outrageous. From the South Vietnamese point of view, the political future of South Vietnam had been predetermined. There was no significant difference between the terms of the draft agreement and what the Communists demanded in the ten-point peace program they had presented to the Nixon administration on May 8, 1969. Hanoi succeeded in having all of its demands satisfied, in some cases with more specificity than originally demanded. Article Two of the draft agreement was a case in point since it established a sixty-day deadline for withdrawal. (See Appendix F for a comparison of Hanoi's ten points and the final agreement.)

President Thieu, after studying the Hanoi broadcast and the Kissinger briefing, wrote directly to Nixon complaining bitterly of the way Kissinger had performed. He also took issue with the timetable Kissinger had established with the Communists without consulting him. Kissinger had said only one more negotiating session of three or four days was needed with the North Vietnamese, while Thieu had insisted that no deadline be set.[19] This appeal by Thieu, intended to divide Nixon and Kissinger and point out to Nixon that Kissinger had exceeded his instructions, did not work. Kissinger drafted the reply to Thieu's letter. He was not about to let the South Vietnamese president undercut his position any more than Bob Haldeman and John Ehrlichman, Nixon's key aides—who feared that Kissinger's peace efforts would weaken Nixon's right-wing support in the Republican Party—had already done in the White House.

Thieu's letter and the accompanying "Memorandum Re: Radio Hanoi's Broadcast on October 26, 1972 and Dr. Kissinger's Press Briefing on October 26, 1972" had been drafted for Thieu by Nha. Kissinger was clearly outraged by the tone of the memo and determined not to let the crack between himself and Nixon widen or be exploited further by Thieu. The detailed reply, written on October 29, was delivered by Ambassador Bunker on October 31 and read:

Dear Mr. President:

I have just completed a careful reading of the October 28, 1972 memorandum entitled "Memorandum Re: Radio Hanoi's Broadcast on October 26, 1972 and Dr. Kissinger's Press Briefing on October 26, 1972." As I have informed you, Dr. Kissinger has spoken and continues to speak on my behalf. There has not been nor will there be any distinction between his views and mine. As I wrote to you in my letter of October 16, "Dr. Kissinger's comments have my total backing."

With specific reference to the points raised in this memorandum, we are astonished to be asked to comment on claims emanating from Radio Hanoi. Dr. Kissinger gave a full and detailed explanation of the ad referendum character of his discussions with the representatives of the Democratic Republic of Vietnam. Therefore, the Government of South Vietnam should not ask itself why theoretical planning dates were given to the DRV; it is patently obvious that they were ad referendum since none of these dates have been carried out.

With respect to your concerns about my messages of October 20 and October 22 to the Prime Minister of the Democratic Republic of Vietnam, you will recall that Dr. Kissinger specifically referred to the content of these messages during his discussions with you in Saigon. These messages essentially concerned three matters concerning Laos and Cambodia. With respect to South Vietnam, we informed Hanoi that we rejected any claim regarding your resignation and insisted on the replacement and prisoner provisions which you have seen. With respect to Laos and Cambodia, we demanded assurances with respect to ending the conflict in these countries. Dr. Kissinger, in the presence of

Ambassador Bunker, told you that in their replies the North Vietnamese yielded on all these points. I consider that you were fully informed.

Concerning the current status of the draft agreement, Dr. Kissinger has made a solemn commitment to you to obtain the maximum number of changes reflecting the views expressed to him during his visit to Saigon. With respect to the inclusion of reference to the "three" countries of Indochina, Dr. Kissinger explained to you that the use of "three" was simply inadvertent and we would demand of the North Vietnamese to have it deleted from the present text.

With respect to the National Council, Dr. Kissinger made amply clear in his press conference, as he did in his talks with you, that it has no governmental functions. All American and foreign observers have seen its real meaning—a face-saving device for the communists to cover their collapse on their demands for a coalition government and your resignation. It is therefore incomprehensible to me why your government has chosen to portray the Council as a structure which encompasses governmental functions. This constant reiteration by your officials of misleading comments may bring about what we have struggled so hard to avoid.

Our position continues to be that we can live with an "administrative structure" which in English clearly implies advisory functions and not governmental ones, but that we reject the North Vietnamese translation which would imply that the structure is endowed with governmental powers and functions. This is precisely what Dr. Kissinger meant when he referred to language problems in his press conference. This is what we will clarify when we meet the North Vietnamese next. We chose the phrase linguistic ambiguity to give everybody a face-saving way out. You and I know what is involved.

Dr. Kissinger's press conference was conducted on my detailed instructions. He was doing his utmost to prevent you from being portrayed as the obstacle to peace with the inevitable cutoff by Congress of U.S. funds to the Government of South Vietnam and the creation of unmanageable impediments to continued U.S. support for you and your Government. Constant criticism from Saigon can only undercut this effort. We will continue our efforts to present a united front, but they cannot succeed without the cooperation of your associates.

Beyond these specific points I cannot fail to call to your attention the dangerous course which your government is now pursuing. You know my firm commitment to the people of South Vietnam and to you personally. As Dr. Kissinger and Ambassador Bunker have informed you, I would like to underline this commitment by meeting with you within one or two weeks after the signing of this agreement. It is my conviction that the future depends on the unity which exists between us and on the degree to which we can make clear our unequivocal support to do what is necessary in the days ahead to ensure that the provisions of a peace settlement are strictly enforced. Just as our unity has been the essential aspect of the success we have enjoyed thus far in the conduct of hostilities, it will also be the best guarantee of future success in a situation where the struggle continues within a more political framework. If the evident drift towards disagreement between the two of us continues, however, the essential base for U.S. support for you and your Government will be destroyed. In this respect the comments of your Foreign Minister that the U.S. is negotiating a surrender are as damaging as they are unfair and improper.

You can be assured that my decisions as to the final character of a peace settlement are in no way influenced by the election in the United States, and you should harbor no illusions that my policy with respect to the desirability of achieving an early peace will change after the election. I have taken this opportunity to comment on the memorandum of October 28 so that there can be no doubts in Saigon with respect to the objectives sought by me and my Government.

I urge you again, Mr. President, to maintain the essential unity which has characterized our relations over these past four years and which has proven to be the essential ingredient in the success we have achieved thus far. Disunity will strip me of the ability to maintain the essential base of support which your Government and your people must have in the days ahead, and which I am determined to provide. Willingness to cooperate will mean that we will achieve peace on the basis of what I consider to be a workable agreement—especially with the amendments which we are certain to obtain. From this basis, we can move with confidence and unity to achieve our mutual objectives of peace and unity for the Heroic people of South Vietnam.

Sincerely
[s] Richard Nixon

This letter marks a sharp departure in tone and substance from the earlier ones. Kissinger, who had drafted the letter, was deeply angered with Thieu, and there was a harsh, threatening, almost desperate tone. The plea for unity is mentioned seven times. No longer is there talk of mutual trust, but a hardheaded quid pro quo: no agreement, no aid. Between the lines there was concern that Thieu would continue his attacks to the point that they would hurt Nixon at the polls and cut into what appeared to be his mounting election victory. In 1968 candidate Nixon had urged Thieu not to go to Paris for negotiations with the North Vietnamese. Four years later he was forcing on Thieu the reverse course of action. It was clear to the South Vietnamese that Humphrey, Nixon, and Kissinger all operated from the same motive— their own political ambitions and interest, which no longer coincided with the Republic of Vietnam's interests.

The reference to the coalition was Kissinger's way of insisting on trying to finesse the issue and make it disappear. The letter spoke of language problems in the text, a euphemism for defining the powers and functions of a National Council. In his interview with Arnaud de Borchgrave of *Newsweek,* Pham Van Dong was precise and plain spoken, never referring to the Council, but to the three Vietnamese sides—Saigon, Hanoi, and the PRG— working out their own arrangements for a "coalition of transition." Thieu used the interview as evidence of North Vietnam's real intentions in the South. Both the North and the South agreed that Kissinger had produced the formula for a coalition government; but Kissinger insisted that the National Council would only be an advisory body with no legal or juridical powers. "Just a miserable little council," as Kissinger had called it.

Thieu did not accept such fine distinctions. He saw the Council giving a real role to the Provisional Revolutionary Government. Even with a veto power—because all decisions had to be unanimous—Thieu believed South

Vietnam would be at a disadvantage. To the Vietnamese way of thinking, if Saigon vetoed proposals from Hanoi and the PRG, this would reflect badly on Thieu and his government. They would be accused of being obstructionist and their credibility would be diminished.

Thieu refused to face the weakness of his own political and military base. From the American viewpoint, Thieu had been unable to use America's massive support over seven years to strengthen his own position in relation to the North.

There was no public hint of Nixon's letter to Thieu. Instead, Kissinger moved swiftly to repair the damage caused by Hanoi's disclosure of the terms of the agreement. For weeks Kissinger had been saying privately that he hoped to have an agreement before the election, although it had been pointed out to him that linking the signing of an agreement to the election deadline smacked of cheapening the election process and would have an adverse effect. Kissinger, however, was less concerned about such impressions than he was about tying down an agreement and forcing it through to a conclusion. He sensed that after the election was won, Nixon would be more difficult to deal with and would increase his demands on the North Vietnamese.

Without Thieu's agreement, the President could be accused of selling out an ally. Thieu was not unaware of Nixon's dilemma and that Nixon needed his signature to avoid being accused of a sell-out. "What he [Kissinger] and the U.S. government exactly wanted was to withdraw as fast as possible, to secure the release of U.S. prisoners. They said they wanted an honorable solution, but really they wanted to wash their hands of the whole business and scuttle and run. But while they were washing their hands and scuttling, they did not want to be accused by the Vietnamese and the world of abandoning us. That was their difficulty," said Thieu.[20] He decided to stand fast.

When he traveled out of Washington to campaign, Nixon utilized the Kissinger press conference for his own purposes, indicating that the talks were still on track and that he was confident that "we shall succeed in achieving our objective, which is peace with honor, and not peace with surrender, in Vietnam. There are still differences to be worked out. I believe they can and will be worked out."[21]

Nixon was determined not to let Vietnam overwhelm his campaign. By asserting his control of the situation, he indicated that he would work out the differences. Indeed, he had forced the North Vietnamese to make concessions in the negotiations. Both Nixon and Kissinger carefully avoided discussing the substance of the negotiations with Hanoi and the real differences between Washington and Hanoi. But it was clear from Pham Van Dong's interview with de Borchgrave that North Vietnam had no intention of going along with a National Council of Reconciliation playing a mere advisory role. Nixon had no illusions about Hanoi's intentions. In his diary, he noted: "Some of the intelligence indicates that they instructed their cadres the moment a cease-fire is announced to kill all of the opponents in the areas they control. This would be a murderous bloodbath, and it's something that we have to consider as we press Thieu to accept what is without question a reasonable political settlement but which must also be justified on security grounds." [22]

Both Thieu and Hung believe that Kissinger and Nixon made a strategic error when they sought to end the war through secret negotiations. Not only did the secret talks undercut South Vietnam and devalue Thieu's position, but they put the United States in the position of negotiating behind the back of its ally. Kissinger's personal prestige became attached to the success or failure of the talks and he was trapped with no way to disengage without paying a heavy personal price. This became clear when he returned from Saigon after Nixon refused him permission to make the "final leg" of the journey—the trip to Hanoi to work out the final details and initial the agreement on October 24. Despite the secret nature of the talks, the reality of the negotiations was determined by military conditions in the field in Vietnam and political conditions in Washington. After Hanoi's March invasion was repulsed and it became clear that Nixon would be reelected, Hanoi decided to negotiate seriously. By then Kissinger had failed to separate the military and political elements of the negotiations. For Hanoi and Saigon the central issue was who controlled the South, and military control could not be separated from political control. For three years Kissinger had floundered through the negotiations, gradually giving way to the North Vietnamese demands not to separate the military and political elements of the negotiations.

From the start of the negotiations Hanoi had had two specific goals: withdrawal of U.S. forces from South Vietnam, and a coalition government in Saigon as the means for taking control of the South. The first goal, withdrawal of American forces, was the most critical element of Hanoi's strategy. This was confirmed by the North Vietnamese after the fall of Saigon. Nguyen Co Thach, now foreign minister of Vietnam, said to journalist Seymour Hersh: "I must tell you this: the most important thing was the American withdrawal. Second is that they allow all our troops to stay in South Vietnam." [23]

On the basis of their experience with the French, the North Vietnamese insisted on the highest "quality" of withdrawal. Although never spelled out in public, in private the North Vietnamese, through their contacts with South Vietnamese in Paris, indicated that the American withdrawal must comprise four elements: to be unilateral, prompt, complete, and permanent. Gradually, step by step, the United States conceded on all four counts.

At first the United States began with "the unshakable principle" of mutual withdrawal of American and North Vietnamese forces from the South, spelled out clearly by Nixon on May 8, 1969. For two years the United States held firmly to this position. Then on May 31, 1971, Kissinger presented a new plan that for the first time dropped the American demand for mutual withdrawal in return for a North Vietnamese pledge not to infil-

trate new forces into South Vietnam, Laos, and Cambodia. This was a
complete abandonment of the American position. Mutual withdrawal had
been dropped. Kissinger had conducted a series of studies indicating that
the continued presence of North Vietnamese troops in the South, without
continued outside resupply and support, would be manageable for Saigon.
It was on this basis that he urged Nixon to change the American position.[24]

In Thieu's opinion and that of his cabinet and the Joint General Staff,
Kissinger had made a serious initial tactical error by focusing the negotiations on the withdrawal itself instead of making withdrawal of troops a
precondition for negotiations.

For Thieu, the 17th parallel was the boundary between North and South
Vietnam, two separate states. Yet it seemed that Kissinger had accepted
the North Vietnamese claim that Vietnam was one country and that there
were only three countries in Indochina: Vietnam, Cambodia, and Laos.
When Thieu pointed this out to Kissinger, he said that the mistake was
"simply inadvertent" and he would have it removed from the next version
of the text.

The agony of being an unequal ally struck Thieu and his cabinet deeply.
Kissinger's virtuoso performance left them with a sense of fury and helplessness at his distortions of the record. There were very deep and substantive disagreements between Washington and Saigon over the terms of the
agreement, yet Kissinger stood before the world and called them "certain
ambiguities," "linguistic problems," and "technical problems." The longest part of the road had been traversed, said Kissinger, "and what stands in
the way of an agreement now are issues that are relatively less important
than those that already have been settled." There is a Vietnamese saying
often cited in reference to Kissinger and his style: *ca vu lap mieng em,*
literally, a full breast fills the baby's mouth. Kissinger was able to stifle the
anguish of the South Vietnamese with promises and elegant phrases. His
tone suggested that the agreement was a triumph for the United States and
Saigon, and that it was the North Vietnamese who had made the concessions.

Kissinger was manipulating the American press and few had taken the
time to analyze the changes in the American position. On the question of
withdrawal, the United States had shifted from mutual withdrawal to unilateral U.S. withdrawal; from a nine-month withdrawal schedule to six
months, then to three, and finally to sixty days, completely washing its
hands of the political developments, which had been orchestrated by Hanoi
and would no longer be left to the South Vietnamese parties to resolve.

When Pham Van Dong confirmed to Kissinger that indeed the National
Council of Reconciliation and Concord (NCRC) was a coalition, as Thieu
had warned him, Kissinger continued to deny that he had misread the terms.
Thieu could not understand how Kissinger could keep on saying it was not
a formula for a coalition when both Saigon and Hanoi insisted it was. According to the text of the draft agreement released by Radio Hanoi, which
Kissinger agreed was correct, all the functions vested in the Council were

the exact functions of a provisional coalition government proposed by the North Vietnamese on May 9, 1969.

Thieu wondered what was next for South Vietnam. He remembered that in 1968 Nixon had urged him not to go to Paris and to boycott the negotiations with Hanoi. But once he had been elected, Nixon joined with Johnson in urging him to go to Paris. Thieu sensed that Nixon's pleas for unity meant there would be new pressures on him once the election was over.

7

Nixon's Second Term

THE DAY AFTER the massive victory at the polls which returned him to the presidency for a second term, Richard Nixon wrote another long letter to Nguyen Van Thieu reopening the dialogue on the draft agreement to end the war. The letter was to be delivered to Saigon by General Alexander Haig, who would make the President's intentions clear and win Thieu's cooperation. Kissinger was furious and frustrated with Thieu's denunciation of the draft agreement as a "surrender." Thieu for his part had lost patience with Kissinger and believed that the National Security Advisor was operating on his own agenda which had been worked out with the North Vietnamese. Thieu wanted to deal directly with Nixon. He mounted a campaign, through Nha, in the Saigon press alleging that Kissinger had not accurately informed Nixon of Thieu's views. Kissinger knew better than to return to Saigon; Nixon chose Haig to both placate and brace Thieu. Nixon respected Haig's toughness as a military man and played him skillfully against Kissinger. Haig could be counted on to follow orders and not come up with any agenda except one to advance him in rank. He was a good judge of character and seemed to understand Thieu. In October, when interviewed for a *Time* cover, Haig described Thieu as "complicated, competent and shrewd. He likes to work with a very small group and he is suspicious. He is extremely conscious of his survival and yet he has a flexible mind. The pattern of his behavior is to be ahead on most issues involved in the negotiations. He is a good political operator and he is a patriot. Thieu is not necessarily loved in Saigon, but he is respected by his own bureaucrats. I see no alternative to him in the short term."[1]

Haig arrived in Saigon on November 10, and immediately went to the Palace to present Nixon's letter, which had once again been drafted by Kissinger. Haig was the ideal emissary. His craggy features, military bearing, and serious tone put Thieu at ease. Haig had served in Vietnam as a battalion commander in 1966–67 and was decorated for bravery in action by both the U.S. Army and the Vietnamese government for his combat role. Thieu respected him as a military man and was comfortable in his presence.

Haig knew the military situation in Vietnam firsthand and Thieu sensed from their conversations that Haig was more sympathetic to his cause than Kissinger. Yet Thieu had no illusions; Haig was a messenger with no power of his own, although he did have influence with President Nixon. Haig showed a firmness to his personal style that was impressive at first, but began to wear thin as he delivered his instructions in a way that became bland and unconvincing the longer he spoke, as if he lacked conviction.

The President, Haig told Thieu, was determined to proceed with an agreement, but he was also anxious to meet Saigon's objections. The thrust of Haig's presentation was that Thieu should take the political and psychological initiative and move ahead to rebuild South Vietnam and consolidate his power. The reward for cooperation would be a meeting with Nixon. Haig stressed that Congress was losing patience with Saigon. Although Nixon had won by a landslide, the Senate was even more dovish than before the election. If there was not a settlement before Congress returned in January, and Thieu became an obstacle to peace, the Senate would cut off funds for South Vietnam.[2]

Haig was accompanied by Ambassador Bunker, and Nha sat in on the meeting at Thieu's request. Thieu and Nha had gone over a "game plan" of what Haig might bring and the alternatives he could present. At a critical point during the meeting Thieu indicated that he would not accept the Paris Accords without further modifications. Haig bristled; his eyes narrowed and he drew in his breath. Then very quietly he told Thieu that unless he went along with the Accords the United States would be forced "to take brutal action." Although unused to such blunt threats, Bunker registered no emotion except to raise his eyebrows. Thieu and Nha, although they had anticipated a threat from Haig, both laughed loudly to ease their embarrassment. Neither asked for a clarification of Haig's threat and Haig appeared uneasy when Thieu refused either to answer him or to pursue the subject.[3]

The President's letter, as Thieu expected, was firmer, even harsher than those Nixon had written before the election; but while he threatened, Nixon also promised. It read in part:

Dear Mr. President:
I must first of all express my deep disappointment over what I consider to be a dangerous drift in the relationship between our two countries, a tendency which can only undercut our mutual objectives and benefit the enemy. Your continuing distortions of the agreement and attacks upon it were unfair and self-defeating. These have persisted despite our numerous representations, including my October 29 letter to you. They have been disconcerting and highly embarrassing to me.

In my previous communications, and in the presentations of Dr. Kissinger and Ambassador Bunker, we have repeatedly explained why we consider the draft agreement to be sound; we continue to believe that it reflects major concessions by the other side, protects the independence of South Vietnam, and leaves the political future to the South Vietnamese people themselves. You are fully informed as well about the massive resupply movement that is underway to strengthen your forces before a ceasefire. I have repeatedly given firm guarantees against the possibility that the agreement is violated. I have offered to meet with you soon after the agreement is signed to symbolize our continuing support. I will not recount here the numerous arguments, explanations, and undertakings that have been made. They all remain valid. In the light of the record, the charges by some of your associates are becoming more and more incomprehensible. . . .

It seems to me you have two essential choices. You could use the public support your recent actions have mobilized to claim the military victory the agreement reflects and to work in unity with your strongest ally to bring about a political victory for which the conditions exist. You could take the political and psychological initiative by hailing the settlement and carrying out its provisions in a positive fashion. In this case I repeat my invitation to meet with you shortly after the signature of the agreement, in order to underline our continued close cooperation.

The other alternative would be for you to pursue what appears to be your present course. In my view this would play into the hands of the enemy and would have extremely grave consequences for both our peoples and it would be a disaster for yours.

Mr. President, I would like you to tell General Haig if we can confidentially proceed on this basis. We are at the point where I need to know unambiguously whether you will join us in the effort General Haig is going to outline or whether we must contemplate alternative courses of action which I believe would be detrimental to the interest of both of our countries.

I hope that you and your government are prepared to cooperate with us. There is a great deal of preparatory work that needs to be done and we believe joint US-GVN task forces should begin working together so that we will be in the best possible position to implement the settlement.

It is my firm conviction that your people, your armed forces, and you have achieved a major victory which the draft agreement would ratify. It is my intention to build on these accomplishments. I would like to work with you and your government in my second term to defend freedom in South Vietnam—in peacetime as we have worked during my first term to defend it in conflict.

In four years you and I have been close personal and military allies. Our alliance has brought us to a position where the enemy is agreeing to conditions which any objective observer said were impossible four years ago. Our alliance and its achievements have been based on mutual trust. If you will give me continued trust, together we shall succeed.

Sincerely
[s] Richard Nixon

After Haig left the Palace, Thieu reread the letter and noted on the top: "Read to the National Security Council and the task force to work on the points underlined." He scratched three big question marks in the left margin next to the underlined words "distortions of the agreement and attacks upon it are unfair and self-defeating."[4]

Thieu was dismayed by the change in Nixon's tone when he began by speaking of "a dangerous drift in the relationship." Thieu was neither intimidated nor convinced by the "two essential choices" presented to him. He decided it was his turn to take part in the negotiations, and that if Kissinger was to remain as the negotiator he would have to press Saigon's demands. Thieu had received word from Hung that there was dissension in the White House staff and Kissinger was being isolated. (There were hints of a rift in the press and Haldeman's wife had complained about Kissinger's behavior on the Vietnam negotiations to a Vietnamese friend of Hung.[5]) There was a strong reaction against the Kissinger peace plan by military leaders such as Admiral Thomas Moorer, chairman of the Joint Chiefs of Staff, and General Westmoreland, then Chief of Staff of the Army. Conservatives such as Warren Nutter, Assistant Secretary of Defense for International Security Affairs, opposed Kissinger's plan, on which there had been no interagency discussion inside the Nixon administration.

Thieu was convinced that if he persisted in getting across his message of the fatal nature of the agreement to South Vietnam, Nixon would understand and insist on revisions in the Paris Agreement. Thieu simply did not believe that Nixon was serious when he said that "you have achieved a major victory which the draft agreement would ratify." He preferred to interpret the letter in accordance with his own views. Thus, Thieu emphasized Nixon's promise of "firm guarantees against the possibility that the agreement is violated." "Guarantees" became the operational word for Thieu and his own National Security Council. They outlined a series of demands for guarantees on the key issues of the presence of North Vietnamese troops in the South and their return to the North: respect for the demilitarized zone, and the effectiveness of the international machinery to supervise the cease-fire.

Thieu's National Security Council met with Haig and Ambassador Bunker on November 11 and rejected the American suggestion that priorities be established. Thieu gave Haig a letter reiterating his demands and seeking specific understandings on the key issues of the presence of North Vietnamese troops in the South and the policing of the cease-fire.

With no place to turn but to Nixon, Thieu persisted in clinging to the positive parts of Nixon's letter. In the letter Nixon had spoken of his desire "to work with you and your government in my second term to defend freedom in South Vietnam—in peacetime as we have worked during my first term to defend it in conflict." Thieu pondered how to win Haig's support for the military correctness of his position. He told him: "You, General Haig, are a general. I am a general. Have you ever seen any peace accord in the history of the world in which the invaders had been permitted to stay in the territories they had invaded?" I asked him: "Would you permit Russian troops to stay in the United States and say that you had reached a peace accord with Russia?"[6]

Haig, said Thieu, could give no reply. "How could he—it was so illogical, how could he reply?" Thieu saw Haig, the military man, as less theoretical and therefore less naive than Kissinger when it came to dealing with the Communists. Thieu feared that Kissinger was being duped by the North Vietnamese, and tried to win Haig to his side. Thieu knew that Nixon, too, wanted America out of Vietnam because of public pressure and his own desire to move ahead in the second term, but not at the price of abandoning South Vietnam. This was not so much because of any Nixon commitment to Thieu or South Vietnam, but because of America's prestige and credibility as a world power.

Haig returned to Washington bringing a written reply from Thieu and convinced that Thieu would come along in the end. He reported to Nixon on November 12: "We are now dealing with a razor's edge situation. Thieu has firmly laid his prestige on the line with his entire government and I believe if we take a totally unreasonable stance with him, we may force him to commit political suicide. I am not sure that this would serve our best interests and therefore recommend the scarier approach of trying to work this problem with Thieu right up to the wire."[7]

Nixon agreed with Haig's analysis "that the price of keeping Thieu aboard is of course risky but I do not believe unacceptable at this juncture." December 8 was set as the deadline for an agreement in Paris. If Thieu could not be convinced to come along by then, Nixon decided that he would reach a separate agreement.[8] The President now adopted a more moderate tone. On November 14, he sent Thieu a reply in the diplomatic pouch and cabled the text to Saigon for Bunker to deliver on the evening of December 15. The letter aimed at uniting the United States and Saigon before the negotiations resumed in Paris between Kissinger and Le Duc Tho on November 20. It read in part:

Dear Mr. President:
. . . I understand from your letter and from General Haig's personal report that your principal remaining concern with respect to the draft agreement is the status of North Vietnamese forces now in South Viet-Nam. As General Haig explained to you, it is our intention to deal with this problem first by seeking to insert a reference to respect for the demilitarized zone in the proposed agreement and, second, by proposing a clause which provides for the reduction and demobilization of forces on both sides in South Viet-Nam on a one-to-one basis and to have demobilized personnel return to their homes. . . .

I will not repeat here all that I said to you in my letter of November 8, but I do wish to reaffirm its essential content and stress again my determination to work towards an early agreement along the lines of the schedule which General Haig explained to you. I must explain in all frankness that while we will do our very best to secure the changes in the agreement which General Haig discussed with you and those additional ones which Ambassador Bunker will bring you, we cannot expect to secure them all. For example, it is unrealistic to assume that we will be able to secure the absolute assurances which you would hope to have on the troop issue.

But far more important than what we say in the agreement on this issue is what we do in the event the enemy renews its aggression. You have my absolute assurance that if Hanoi fails to abide by the terms of this agreement it is my intention to take swift and severe retaliatory action.

I believe the existing agreement to be an essentially sound one which should become even more so if we succeed in obtaining some of the changes we have discussed. Our best assurance of success is to move into this new situation with confidence and cooperation. . . .

Above all we must bear in mind what will really maintain the agreement. It is not any particular clause in the agreement but our joint willingness to maintain its clauses. I repeat my personal assurances to you that the United States will react very strongly and rapidly to any violation of the agreement. But in order to do this effectively it is essential that I have public support and that your government does not emerge as the obstacle to a peace which American public opinion now universally desires. It is for this reason that I am pressing for the acceptance of an agreement which I am convinced is honorable and fair and which can be made essentially secure by our joint determination.

Mrs. Nixon joins me in extending our warmest personal regards to Madame Thieu and to you. We look forward to seeing you again at our home in California once the just peace we have both fought for so long is finally achieved.

Sincerely
[s] Richard Nixon

Nixon here replied to three of Thieu's major worries: the North Vietnamese troop presence in the South, the supervisory mechanism, and North Vietnamese violations of the agreement. He reassured Thieu that the supervisory mechanism for the cease-fire "in itself is in no measure as important as our own firm determination to see to it that the agreement works and our vigilance with respect to the prospect of its violation." Thieu took this commitment very seriously.

On the continued presence of the North Vietnamese troops in the South, Nixon and Kissinger no longer argued that they would simply "wither away," but now stressed the importance of Vietnamese and American actions to enforce the cease-fire. Nixon encouraged Thieu by stressing: "But far more important than what we say in the agreement on this issue is what we do in the event the enemy renews its aggression. You have my absolute assurance that if Hanoi fails to abide by the terms of this agreement it is my intention to take swift and severe retaliatory action." In case of violations of the agreement, Nixon repeated "my personal assurances to you that the United States will react very strongly and rapidly to any violation of the agreement."

Thieu underlined this sentence, penciled a frame around it and, in the margin, struck two heavy emphasis marks and a big asterisk. The letter closed for the first time on a personal and friendly note, with the President looking forward to meeting Thieu and his wife "at our home in California."

Thieu was impressed with the improved tone of this letter, but he remained uneasy. He needed specific provisions in the agreement, guarantees that would bind the North Vietnamese in terms that would be publicly spelled out. Nixon's personal promises were reassuring, but Thieu could not make them public. Hung and other of his advisers in Saigon urged him to specify that Nixon should give unambiguous guarantees to accompany the agreement. Thieu sensed that the Americans wanted to leave Vietnam behind once their prisoners were released. How could he pin down the Americans and underscore for Nixon that Kissinger had let the North Vietnamese dominate the negotiations?

On November 18, two days before the talks were to resume in Paris, Thieu called in Ambassador Bunker and handed him a memorandum with sixty-nine suggested modifications to the agreement. There was an objection in nearly every clause to impress on Nixon that Kissinger had been careless, duped, or had given in to the North Vietnamese.

At the same time Thieu proposed to send his foreign affairs adviser, Nguyen Phu Duc, to Washington to explain the need for the changes. Thieu, aware that Kissinger was on his way to Paris to meet Le Duc Tho, hoped that he could have his emissary meet with Nixon, rather than Kissinger, but with the more sympathetic Haig in attendance.

Kissinger however considered Thieu's suggestion to send an emissary "a slap at me and another blatant stalling tactic because there was no way an emissary could arrive before I had to leave." Careful to guard against an end run and retain control of the negotiations, Kissinger insisted to Nixon that he be present for the meeting. According to Kissinger, Nixon sent "an icy Presidential letter warning again that these changes could not possibly all be achieved and refusing to receive an emissary until the next round of negotiations with Hanoi had been completed."[9]

In fact, the letter was quite conciliatory. Twice Nixon reassured Thieu that he had given specific instructions to Kissinger to seek "to the maximum extent possible" to incorporate Thieu's proposals in the agreement.

The November 18 letter to President Thieu read:

Dear Mr. President:
I have read with great attention the November 18 memorandum from the Government of the Republic of Vietnam. I am sure you recognize the enormous difficulties posed to us by another set of extensive changes following the many proposed changes we have already discussed. Nevertheless, I shall instruct Dr. Kissinger to seek to the maximum extent possible to incorporate your proposals. I must point out to you, however, first that the express reference to North Vietnamese troops in the South have the disadvantage of legitimizing any force that may remain and, secondly, as we have repeatedly pointed out are clearly unobtainable. Also, it is impossible at this point to change the composition of the International Control Group. As for the other changes, Dr. Kissinger will brief your Ambassador at the end of each day as to what progress is being made.
My instructions to Dr. Kissinger are to press to the maximum extent possible to incorporate your proposals. I must point out, however, that I am not prepared to scuttle the agreement or to go along with an accumulation of proposals which will have that practical consequence. It may therefore not be possible to get all the changes.
As for the proposal to send an emissary to Washington, I believe that after two visits by Dr. Kissinger and three by General Haig, three personal letters from me and numerous exchanges through Ambassador Bunker as well as my personal reading of all your communications, we have all of the suggestions

that you have made fully in mind for this phase of the negotiations. I would therefore think that the best occasion for a meeting of your emissary with me would be immediately after the Paris phase when we have a new set of issues to consider jointly. I therefore suggest if you select Mr. Duc as your emissary that he return to Washington on Dr. Kissinger's aircraft immediately upon the conclusion of the next Paris round. If, on the other hand, you prefer that Foreign Minister Lam serve as your emissary, I recommend that he proceed to Paris immediately and take part in the discussions which will follow each day's session and then return to Washington with Dr. Kissinger for a meeting with me.

I again urge you to join us in the course that I am determined to follow. I must once more impress upon you the enormous danger of losing public support in the United States with all the risks for continuing our joint effort. We will, of course, be in close touch after the completion of the negotiations in Paris.

Sincerely
[s] Richard Nixon

Thieu was disappointed that Nixon would not receive his emissary while Kissinger was in Paris. He decided to send Nguyen Phu Duc to Paris to observe the meetings and prepare to go to Washington after the sessions were over. On the second page of Nixon's letter, Thieu wrote instructions for Duc to go to Paris *on time* and bring along the documents that would make Thieu's case.

In his diary, Nixon mused about the prospects for a successful conclusion to the negotiations and expressed concern over the effect Kissinger was having on Thieu. Nixon made up his mind to go ahead without Thieu if the latter did not accept the agreement, but he also wanted to rein in Kissinger: "As I told Henry when he began to rumble around to the effect that we have a very good record in this instance, I said, Henry, we're not concerned about being right on the record. What we are concerned about is to save South Vietnam and that's why we had to temporize with Thieu as much as we did, because our interest is in getting South Vietnam to survive and Thieu at present seems to be the only leader who could lead them in that direction." [10]

Kissinger arrived in Paris on November 19, and held his first meeting with Le Duc Tho on Monday, November 20, at Léger's house in Gif-sur-Yvette. The South Vietnamese assembled their own task force to follow the negotiations. The three Vietnamese ambassadors to Washington, London, and to the Paris Talks were all on hand. Duc and Nha were dispatched to Paris. They were to assist the ambassadors and draft a letter to Nixon to be delivered by Duc after the sessions ended with the North Vietnamese. Nha asked President Thieu to sign his name in different places on five blank pieces of official stationery embossed with the gold presidential seal. That way, when the final copy of the letter was typed, Thieu's signature would appear in the proper place on the stationery and it would not be evident that the letter had not been signed in Saigon. Nha also took the presidential seal with him. "Boy, this is dangerous," he joked with Thieu.

"What do you mean?" asked Thieu.

"Well, I can type, 'I hereby resign and abdicate in favor of my cousin Hoang Duc Nha.'"

"You have some imagination," Thieu said, smiling.[11]

Thieu also requested General Tran Van Don, chairman of the Defense Committee of the National Assembly, to proceed to Paris and invite Hung there to serve with him as a consultant to the delegation. Don was well known in the Vietnamese community in Paris and had close high-level contacts with officials in the French Foreign Ministry. Thieu wanted Hung in Paris to work with Don and follow developments, especially on the fine points of the agreement.

Nha served as Thieu's crisis manager, always ready with a scenario or game plan to deal with a new situation. But Thieu had little in-depth staff work, especially the kind of textual analysis Hung produced. Hung, with his American education, had been trained to write theses, to document, to analyze and distinguish nuances of meaning. Thus, Thieu and Nha welcomed Hung's detailed studies of the North Vietnamese positions and his ability to compare them to earlier demands.

Hung took advantage of the Thanksgiving holidays to leave Howard University and fly to Paris. But before he left, he met with Warren Nutter at the Trader Vic's restaurant in the Capital Hilton Hotel to get a fix on the administration's thinking in light of the Kissinger press conference. Nutter was upset.

"I'm really confused. I don't know what is going on any more. Kissinger has kept it all to himself," Nutter said, "but I can assure you South Vietnam still has a lot of sympathy from many people in the government." Nutter told Hung that he was leaving the Nixon administration in the second term because he felt his effectiveness in the Pentagon had ended and he could help more outside the administration. He complained bitterly about the way Kissinger dominated policy decisions and excluded others from the process. Nutter recalled that from the very beginning of the Nixon administration, in 1969, Kissinger had a preconceived view of the Saigon government as weak and ineffective, and showed no faith in it. Nutter said that in his appraisal of the two regimes, Kissinger's analysis concluded that a Spartan police state like North Vietnam was better organized than the South and could control its population with uniformity and no sign of dissent. Nutter explained that he never felt Kissinger had any respect for South Vietnam. "How can you negotiate effectively for what you don't believe in? I'm not so sure Kissinger really has feelings for American democracy and the importance of the openness of American democracy," Nutter added. Hung was surprised by these comments. "How can a brilliant Harvard professor not understand democracy?" asked Hung." "No, he understands the theory of democracy better than you, or even me, but to have a commitment to the democratic process and to love it is a different thing," explained Nutter.[12]

On the overnight flight to Paris, Hung drank black coffee and chewed ginseng root to stay awake while he wrote a memorandum to Thieu. Worried and exhausted, he wrote emotionally: "Mr. President, I want you to know that you are in my thoughts and prayers in this hour of agony. I pray that you will be steadfast in defending the interests of Vietnam." Having studied the agreement closely, Hung believed as did Thieu that it contained the seeds for South Vietnam's destruction. He pointed out how the demands of the United States for the North Vietnamese to withdraw their troops from the South had weakened in various stages of the negotiations until the United States capitulated to Hanoi's demands for an in-place cease-fire with no regroupment of forces or provisions for removal of Hanoi's forces.

When he arrived in Paris, Hung unexpectedly met Nha at Orly Airport. Nha, too, was pale and bedraggled after the long flight from Saigon. They talked with sadness about Kissinger's "sellout" of their position and the need to get this message to President Nixon through a direct appeal.

8

The Christmas Bombing

OVER DRINKS at the modest Monceau Hotel on the Left Bank of the Seine, Nha told Hung of President Thieu's attempts to get to see President Nixon himself. Nixon had turned Thieu down but agreed to see Thieu's emissary, Nguyen Phu Duc, in Washington after the Paris negotiating round was over. President Thieu did not want to accept an agreement before he had a chance to make his case directly to Nixon. Thieu was convinced that Kissinger had not reported the full details and meaning of the agreement honestly and accurately to President Nixon.

Thieu was disappointed and concerned that Nixon wanted to put off a personal meeting with him until after the Paris Accords had been signed. "I asked to meet Nixon to explain our position loud and clear in the United States and gain support. I also wanted to see if there were other alternatives before us, because I doubted what Kissinger had reported to Nixon. I wanted to see what lies he was telling and what he was not telling. I wanted to see Nixon before the Paris Agreements were signed to explain to him what I felt the agreements would really do to us. Nixon did not like my idea. As President, how could he meet with me and tell me face to face that it was a good agreement and I had to sign it?" commented Thieu.[1]

Thieu believed the agreement ran counter to the promises Nixon made in his letters, especially when Nixon said that it met his "absolute conditions" for the survival of an independent South Vietnam. In Saigon, the local press, with encouragement from the Palace, began to refer to the Paris Agreement as "a sellout", a "death warrant", and "a surrender agreement."

After the initial November 20 meeting with Le Duc Tho, Kissinger was encouraged that agreement might be reached; but the progress quickly evaporated and the negotiations were stalemated by North Vietnamese intransigence. Kissinger and Nixon had expected that the North Vietnamese would view Nixon's victory as an incentive to settle the outstanding issues and come to terms before a tougher Nixon began the second term in January. Instead, the North Vietnamese brooded about being tricked by the Americans. They thought they had a deal to initial in Hanoi on October 24, and sign in Paris on October 31. When Thieu balked and Kissinger returned to Washington, the North Vietnamese believed they were being double-crossed. They thought Nixon was taking back what had been agreed upon and was trying to change the terms of the agreement.[2]

Kissinger, who had been interpreting the agreement loosely, now found himself with detailed South Vietnamese demands to improve and tighten the terms. Kissinger put forward Thieu's minimum demands, carefully noting they were not his own. Then he put forward Nixon's minimum demands so that the North Vietnamese would be sure to see the differences between the two.[3] Nixon had adopted Thieu's demand that the demilitarized zone (DMZ) between the North and South be respected and recognized as the dividing line between North and South. As Kissinger explained later, "We wanted some reference in the agreement, however vague, however allusive, however indirect that would make clear that the two parts of Vietnam would live in peace with each other and that neither side would impose its solution on the other by force."[4] But the North Vietnamese refused to meet the South Vietnamese demands or Nixon's requests for changes as put forward by Kissinger. By November 23, Thanksgiving Day, it was apparent that Le Duc Tho was digging in and would not yield to Kissinger on the changes he demanded. He insisted that Kissinger had already agreed to the draft treaty in October. Why should it be changed now?

The South Vietnamese also were angry with Kissinger. Both Hung and General Don heard that Kissinger was very friendly to the North Vietnamese and had brought them presents. Kissinger presented Le Duc Tho with picture books of Harvard to prepare him to take up Kissinger's flattering suggestion that he teach a seminar in Marxism-Leninism there after the agreement was signed. His deputy, Xuan Thuy, received a Steuben glass horse's head because he was said to like horse racing. Kissinger used the presents to create an atmosphere of cordiality and dampen speculation that the talks might not be succeeding.

Within the Vietnamese community in Paris, rumors spread that Kissinger had begun to socialize with the North Vietnamese and was eating lavish meals which the North Vietnamese prepared as the talks reached the final stages. Hung heard that both the North Vietnamese and Kissinger were upset with his article analyzing the agreement, which appeared in the November 20 *International Herald Tribune*. Entitled "Settling the War on Hanoi's Terms" it showed how the North Vietnamese had used Kissinger to accept their basic demands. After carefully comparing the ten points originally put forward by the National Liberation Front in the May 8, 1969, proposal and the Radio Hanoi version of the Paris Accords, Hung concluded that the NLF's original ten points were contained in the draft agreement. He argued that "the contention that Hanoi has dropped two demands—one on 'coalition government' and another on 'veto over the personality of the existing government'—is highly questionable."[5]

Kissinger was anxious to wrap up the talks for a December 22 deadline that would bring American prisoners of war home for Christmas. He agreed to hold regular briefings with the South Vietnamese in Paris after his meetings with Le Duc Tho. The three South Vietnamese ambassadors—Pham Dang Lam, the head of the delegation in Paris; Vuong Van Bac from London; and Tran Kim Phuong from Washington—left the South Vietnamese delegation's modest offices on the Avenue Raymond Pointcaré in the eighth *arrondissement* and drove to the residence of the American ambassador in Paris at 41 Faubourg Saint-Honoré, a former Rothschild mansion with an elegant garden. Each night at about nine, after dinner, Kissinger or General Haig briefed them on the day's talks with the North Vietnamese.

Kissinger was businesslike and correct. He explained where the meeting with the North Vietnamese took place and, in general terms, what was discussed. On one occasion he could not resist asking the South Vietnamese why they needed three ambassadors in Paris. "Do you really need three ambassadors to look after me or, perhaps, it is to look after each other?" he asked. The Vietnamese ambassadors felt he stressed peripheral technical matters and avoided the central issues. Kissinger would "go round and round in circles and pick out unimportant details, such as how we would sign, and dwell on that and the protocol and supervisory mechanisms; but he remained ambiguous about the key issues of the presence of North Vietnamese troops in the South and the formation of a coalition." Kissinger kept insisting that the presence of the North Vietnamese regular units in the South was "manageable." He tried to win Ambassador Lam to his side by saying, "Vietnam has no friends in Washington but me."[6]

The Vietnamese ambassadors found General Haig to be more direct and straightforward. At times Haig was moody and let his annoyance show. When the North Vietnamese began to withdraw the concessions they had made, Haig blamed the South Vietnamese for not being more flexible. "Our problem," recalled Ambassador Phuong, "was whether the Americans were really presenting our objections to Hanoi. We would ask the Americans to do this and that and they would say, 'We already did that and the North Vietnamese did not accept.' How were we to know if an objection had really been raised? The Americans always said in their communiqués that we played a leading role in the negotiations, but that was just not so. The negotiations were monitored badly by us, but we had no way to check on what the Americans were doing."[7]

Lam, the South Vietnamese delegation head, said that he learned more about the inner workings of the meetings from his sources throughout the Vietnamese community in Paris. The network of family ties and loyalties was stronger than political ideology. In the steamy Vietnamese restaurants and in the sidewalk cafés around the Place Maubert Mutualité on the Left Bank, where the Vietnamese community mingled, the word was out that the North Vietnamese were hardening their position.

The Vietnamese fascination with Paris grew from their love-hate relationship with the French under colonial rule. Paris was the key to wealth and power in Vietnam, and the glorious romantic center of French culture.

The French Romantic poets appealed to the Vietnamese—Hung remembers reading Verlaine and memorizing one of his poems: *Il pleure dans mon coeur comme il pleut sur la ville* ("There is weeping in my heart like the rain falling on the city"). The atmosphere of Paris has been an endless source of inspiration for Vietnamese poets and song writers. A Vietnamese song recounts the sad farewell of a young couple under the yellow lights and baroque grillwork of the Gare de Lyon. The Luxembourg Gardens, where golden leaves fall on the shoulders of a white marble statue, is a popular place for Vietnamese students to meet to discuss law, political science—and love. A French education in the capital guaranteed social status in the upper class and a well-paid job at home.

The French education stressed the liberal arts, law, and philosophy; there was little emphasis on engineering, physics, and the technical sciences. Pharmacy and medicine were the favored sciences for Vietnamese. "Like the French, the Vietnamese would cherish a famous sonata above a new invention," former Foreign Minister Bac explained. The French left a legacy of the concept of law and a parliamentary system, but it was never really allowed to take root.

The French ruled Vietnam for more than eighty years by keeping the country divided into three separate units: Tonkin in the North, Annam in the Center, and Cochin China in the South. Each had its own legal and administrative system, which helped the French to reenforce the geographic and cultural differences between North, Center, and South. This decision bred regional differences and loyalties that later plagued the Republic of Vietnam with a pervasive divisiveness.

The poor Vietnamese students settled on the Left Bank in the small, cheap hotels and student apartments on the narrow streets near the Sorbonne. They gathered at inexpensive restaurants like Le Maubert off the Place Maubert on the Rue de la Montagne Sainte-Geneviève. Small and darkly lit, Le Maubert offered meal tickets at bargain prices to Vietnamese students. The restaurant was subsidized by the North Vietnamese government as part of its propaganda efforts to win supporters against the Thieu government and the United States. A gathering place for gossip and rumors, Le Maubert offered cheap noodles and North Vietnamese propaganda leaflets.

During the days of the Paris negotiations, the Vietnamese community in Paris was divided between North and South. The old church, renamed the Maubert Mutualité, off the Place Maubert, was the site for rallies and meetings by both sides. The meetings would often be scheduled back to back and the supporters of North and South would shout at each other in the street, waving banners and fists; frequently fights broke out.

Hung stayed at the Hôtel Studia, 51 Boulevard Saint-Germain, in the heart of the Sorbonne University district, so he could make contact with young Vietnamese. He had a small room on the fifth floor with a balcony overlooking the plane trees below and a fine view of the gray slate rooftops with their terracotta chimneys. The owner of the hotel had relatives working for both the North and South and proved an excellent conduit for rumors. Hung laughed when the hotel owner told him about one of his relatives, an official in the North Vietnamese delegation. The official said that when he returned to Hanoi he had to turn in his shoes, carefully polished, so they could be passed on to the next delegate to Paris.

Hung spent his days in Paris gathering opinions and rumors. He picked up isolated facts and vignettes that could be compared with friends at lunch and dinner to build up a mosaic of the talks between the Americans and the North Vietnamese.

Hung and General Don had lunch every other day with Ambassador Pham Dang Lam at the Pieds de Cochon restaurant in Les Halles. Lam habitually ordered a dozen *oursins,* raw sea urchins, and a glass of white wine "to restore my energy to deal with Kissinger." Lam told Hung and Don: "I really do not know what is going on at Gif-sur-Yvette except through the Vietnamese community."

The South Vietnamese community in Paris, recalled Hung, began to wonder if Kissinger had changed sides; there was a bitter joke that he had become part of the North Vietnamese delegation. The South Vietnamese were frustrated and desperate. Control of their lives was beyond their reach. Kissinger was making a match they despised, yet they were helpless to resist without being disinherited and losing the American Mandate of Heaven.

By November 24, after four days of meetings, Kissinger cabled Nixon suggesting two options: Break off the meetings and resume the bombing, or settle with the changes that had been agreed upon. "I had, of course, no way of knowing whether Hanoi would accept this; I was certain Saigon would refuse. It was symptomatic of the wary relationship between Nixon and me that I offered no recommendation between the two options," Kissinger explained in his memoirs.[8]

Nguyen Phu Duc, President Thieu's personal representative to the Paris Talks, arrived from Saigon on November 24, with no new instructions. Duc was an elegant, fastidious bachelor of forty from a wealthy family. His colleagues remember him as refusing to drive in Washington, and walking to the embassy from his home with a rolled umbrella everyday. After earning a law degree from Harvard University, he entered the diplomatic service. Duc served in the embassy in Washington, where he was first secretary in charge of political affairs, then returned to Saigon in the mid-1960s. When Thieu became chairman of the Military Council in 1966, he began meeting with foreign visitors and played a role as a foreign policy decision maker. Duc was assigned to him as an aide. Then, when Thieu moved up to the presidency, he took Duc with him to the Palace as his foreign affairs adviser. Duc was a careful and precise analyst, expert at picking up fine points and elaborating them or demanding explanations.

Unlike Kissinger, Duc had only limited power and served primarily as a dogged, loyal staff man. Cautious in offering advice, Duc had no grand conceptual overview of foreign policy.[9] He was content to play the part of a senior aide in the Palace; Thieu relied on him and trusted him, but he never gave him major responsibilities.

Thieu was working hard to convince Nixon either to press the North Vietnamese to accept his demands or else to stalemate the talks. From cable intercepts and the behavior of Duc and the South Vietnamese ambassadors in Paris, it was clear to Kissinger that Thieu was in "a deliberate stalling pattern." [10] On November 23, Nixon sent a message to Thieu labeled TOP SECRET/SENSITIVE for delivery by Ambassador Bunker. It laid all the festering problems in the open:

Dear Mr. President:

I am increasingly dismayed and apprehensive over the press campaign emanating from Saigon. There are allegations that my associates are not informing me accurately of your views and that you have therefore dispatched a special emissary to Washington to accomplish this task. The unfounded attacks on the draft agreement have continued with increasing frequency.

In addition, I am struck by the dilatory tactics which we are experiencing from your side in Paris. It is evident that your representatives there have been unable to obtain with sufficient timeliness the answers to questions which we must have if we are adequately to represent your views during the negotiations including the Protocols related to the draft agreement which were provided to your Government in Saigon some two weeks ago.

As I told you in my letters of November 8, 14, and 18, I will proceed promptly to a final solution if an acceptable final agreement is arrived at in Paris this week. Given my clear messages and those conveyed by my representatives these past several weeks, any further delay from your side can only be interpreted as an effort to scuttle the agreement. This would have a disastrous effect on our ability to continue to support you and your Government.

I look forward to seeing your emissary in Washington as soon as the Paris sessions have been concluded, but in the interim I must urge you this one last time not to put ourselves irrevocably at odds. If the current course continues and you fail to join us in concluding a satisfactory agreement with Hanoi, you must understand that I will proceed at whatever the cost.

Sincerely
[s]Richard Nixon

On Saturday, November 25, Kissinger met again with Le Duc Tho and it was apparent that a deadlock had developed. The talks were recessed until December 4. The South Vietnamese were delighted. In Hanoi, the Communist Party newspaper *Nhan Dan*, in an editorial signed by "Commentator," the pen name for the Politburo, asked if Kissinger's actions in Paris were "a demand that the whole problem be considered all over again? Is this a trick to prolong the talks in hopes of covering up the acts of intensification and prolongation of the war and continuing to pursue an evasive military victory?" [11]

Kissinger returned to Washington. Nguyen Phu Duc was huddled with his team in Paris preparing a twenty-five page letter from Thieu to Nixon in an effort to circumvent Kissinger and win Nixon's sympathy. The letter was drafted by Nha, Duc, and the ambassadors to Washington, London, and Paris with background memos from Hung. They were hopeful Nixon would change his mind and not go ahead with the agreement.

Duc and Ambassador Phuong were accompanied to the Oval Office by Kissinger on November 29 to present "an extremely long, eloquent letter from Thieu to Nixon." In it, Thieu recounted the concessions extracted from Saigon over the years with the promise that no other sacrifice would be demanded. This promise, said the letter, had been broken. Thieu raised the possibility of an appeal to world opinion if his "just" demands were not met.[12] In his memoirs, Kissinger noted that "Thieu had a point, of course; the tragedy was that what Thieu considered intolerable pressure by us had been regarded by our critics as crass intransigence. We had to navigate in this gulf; to adopt Thieu's view at this late hour would have guaranteed the collapse of all remaining support at home."[13] Kissinger failed to mention that at the time he was encouraging a negative view of Thieu in his meetings to background the press.

Nixon was determined to convince Thieu that the agreement had to be concluded without further delay and that there were no differences between him and Kissinger. "We thought that if I made a brutally tough presentation to Duc, that would succeed in bringing home to Thieu the precariousness of his position and the danger of being left on his own. I said that it was not a question of lacking sympathy for Saigon's predicament; but we had to face the reality of the situation. If we did not end the war by concluding a settlement at the next Paris session, then when Congress returned in January it would end the war by cutting off the appropriations."[14]

Nixon was relentless, explaining that there could be no other course than the one the United States was following. The President said the National Council of Reconciliation could not be described as a coalition government because it was an organization operated by unanimity in an advisory role, was selected jointly, and had few specified functions. There could be no turning back and Saigon's attitude would not determine the outcome of the negotiations, though it would affect the ability of the United States to provide aid after the Accords were signed and to enforce the agreement.

Duc stuck to his instructions; he listened carefully and insisted he had no desire for a confrontation. Nixon, his mind made up, then suggested that Kissinger and Duc meet to work out a "practical solution." Duc had two more meetings with Kissinger and one more with Nixon. The President told Duc that he was confident the United States would be capable of detecting North Vietnamese infiltration into the South. Then Nixon discussed contingency plans that he had worked out with the Joint Chiefs of Staff in case the North Vietnamese violated the agreements. Again, Nixon warned Duc that if the agreement failed, Congress would probably cut off funds by mid-January.[15]

For the first time, Nixon and Kissinger outlined for Duc a U.S. contingency plan to keep North Vietnamese targeting information updated even after the cease-fire. There would be a communications network established connecting the U.S. Seventh Air Force base at Nakorn Phanom in Thailand (known as NKP in military slang) with Saigon and the four regional military headquarters in South Vietnam. The South Vietnamese commanders would be in direct telephone contact with the U.S. Seventh Air Force commander, General John W. Vogt, at the base in Thailand, and targets would be updated weekly.

This secret plan had a major impact in reassuring President Thieu that the American commitment to enforce the agreements was real. Thieu was told that from NKP, tactical aircraft would be flown to attack North Vietnam and B-52 raids would be coordinated if the North Vietnamese violated the agreement.[16]

Over and over in his letters, and again in his meeting with Duc, Nixon insisted that his promise of the U.S. willingness to enforce the agreement and retaliate swiftly and forcefully in case of North Vietnamese violations was more important than the agreement itself. The direct link-up to Nakorn Phanom was a tangible guarantee for Thieu and he counted on it being implemented.

Returning to the embassy off Sheridan Circle after his meeting with Nixon, Duc told Nha that he and Phuong had the impression Nixon was surprised by the contents of the letter they presented to him. Although Nixon had not changed his position, the Vietnamese believed they had gained Nixon's personal attention to their concerns, had put Kissinger on the defensive, and bought more time before the Accords were signed. They had, in effect, forced Nixon to choose between Hanoi and Saigon.

Duc returned to Saigon to report on his meetings; still, there was no response from Thieu. Nixon turned to Kissinger and said he believed that Thieu was playing "chicken" and that the United States probably had no choice except to turn on him.[17]

The talks resumed in Paris on December 4, and it quickly became obvious that the North Vietnamese were holding back; an agreement would be hard to reach. At an "open hearted" private discussion between Kissinger and Le Duc Tho, the North Vietnamese special adviser accused the United States of trying to strengthen the "puppet administration" of Saigon. For every concession that he made, Le Duc Tho withdrew two. The North Vietnamese feared that the agreement had unraveled and they doubted American sincerity. Kissinger cabled Moscow and urged the Soviet Union to influence Hanoi; the Russians counseled Washington to have patience. Vice President Agnew was on hold in Washington awaiting word from Paris to proceed to Saigon and discuss the final agreement with President Thieu. Kissinger still pressed for a December 22 deadline.

On December 7, Kissinger and Le Duc Tho met again for four hours and Kissinger sensed that the prospects for an agreement were fading. Whatever those pressures and his own personal demands, Kissinger reported to Nixon realistically and presciently:

It is now obvious as the result of our additional exploration of Hanoi's intentions that they have not in any way abandoned their objectives or ambitions with respect to South Vietnam. What they have done is decide to modify their strategy by moving from conventional and mainforce warfare to a political and insurgency strategy within the framework of the draft agreement.

Thus, we can anticipate no lasting peace in the wake of a consummated agreement, but merely a shift in Hanoi's *modus operandi*. We will probably have little chance of maintaining the agreement without evident hair-trigger U.S. readiness, which may in fact be challenged at any time, to enforce its provisions. Thus, we are now down to my original question: is it better to continue to fight on by scuttling the agreement now, or be forced to react later, vindicated by the violation of a solemnly entered agreement?[18]

Kissinger recommended that the United States proceed with an agreement, and Nixon concurred, saying he preferred almost any agreement to a recess. He directed Kissinger to seek "some" improvement over the October draft.[19] In his private analysis to Nixon, which bore no relation to what he was telling the South Vietnamese ambassadors, Kissinger was in agreement with Thieu's assessment of North Vietnamese motives and intentions. Yet he continued to press Thieu to sign the Paris Accords. Under Nixon's orders he returned to the negotiations with Le Duc Tho to reach an agreement. Nixon set a deadline of Inauguration Day, January 20, 1973, for signing the agreement with Hanoi.[20] The President wanted to enter his second term in peace.

In the December round Kissinger described two options. Under Option One, the United States would agree to an immediate settlement on the best terms it could negotiate. Under Option Two, the United States would break with Thieu and continue the bombing until the North Vietnamese agreed to return American POWs in exchange for complete American withdrawal. Nixon first favored Option One, then had second thoughts and told Kissinger in a follow-up cable that he could interrupt the talks on the pretext of giving the negotiators an opportunity to consult their principals. Kissinger then threatened Le Duc Tho with "actions as strong as the ones of May 8" —when Nixon had bombed Hanoi and mined Haiphong.[21] Still Thieu balked.

During these ten crucial days of negotiations the most difficult issue was the status of the demilitarized zone separating North and South Vietnam. Thieu insisted that the DMZ be recognized as a boundary between North and South Vietnam, thus formalizing the separation of the two countries and denying North Vietnam's claim that North and South were one country. To the North Vietnamese, the DMZ was a temporary separation line; to Thieu, it was an international boundary that could not be crossed or violated. Thieu feared most that North Vietnam, not recognizing the sanctity of the DMZ, would move its army into the South to join with forces already there and mount a full-scale attack to conquer the South. Le Duc Tho stubbornly refused to seal off the DMZ and insisted on the right to move civilian and military forces through the DMZ.[22]

On December 14, Le Duc Tho said he had to return to Hanoi to obtain the approval of the Politburo on the DMZ issue.[23] On December 15, Kissinger flew back to Washington in a black mood. Before he left Orly Airport he told Ambassador Phuong, who had come to see him off, "I am going to do something drastic." Phuong arrived in Saigon on December 16, and briefed Thieu. It appeared as if Thieu had won a tactical victory.

On his return, Kissinger met in the Oval Office with Nixon and Haig, both of whom had become dubious about concluding the negotiations as a result of Thieu's appeals and the North Vietnamese intransigence.

Haig's role was complex and difficult to pin down. Thieu found him a keen analyst of the situation, who agreed with him on the danger to South Vietnam if the DMZ was not respected. Haig wore two hats: as the general who had served in Vietnam and was about to become Chief of Staff of the Army, and as Nixon's special envoy to Thieu. "When he is a general, Haig thinks like me," said Thieu. "When he is a special envoy of President Nixon, he does the job of a special envoy."[24]

In the White House on December 14, Haig favored B-52 attacks north of the 20th parallel, on the grounds that only a massive shock could bring Hanoi back to the conference table. Kissinger argued that the only options were a massive bombing of the North or "letting matters drift into another round of inconclusive negotiations, prolonged warfare, bitter national division, and mounting casualties. There were no other options."[25]

Kissinger's two options did not match Saigon's perceptions. According to Nha, "Kissinger had two choices: either to do something drastic in Saigon or to bomb North Vietnam." The South Vietnamese anticipated a coup against Thieu from the time Nixon established the date of his inauguration, January 20, 1973, as the deadline for signing the Paris Agreement.

On December 16, Kissinger held a press conference in Washington, and publicly signaled to both Hanoi and Saigon that Nixon was determined to proceed with an agreement. In his remarks, he told the South Vietnamese: "With respect to Saigon, we have sympathy and compassion for the anguish of their people and for the concerns of their government. But if we can get an agreement that the President considers just we will proceed with it." To Hanoi, he said: "Our basic objective was stated in the press conference of October 26. We want an end to the war that is something more than an armistice. We want to move from hostility to normalization and from normalization to cooperation. But we will not make a settlement which is a disguised form of continued warfare and which brings about by indirection what we have always said we will not tolerate."

In the question period Kissinger was asked if the situation had gone "back to square one?" "No," replied Kissinger. "We have an agreement that is ninety-nine percent completed as far as the text of the agreement is concerned." This was a classic Kissinger deception to avoid the truth without directly telling a lie. Kissinger simply dodged defining the remaining "1 percent": the crucial issue of the DMZ. Asked what the remaining 1 percent was, he replied: "Well, you know, I have found I get into trouble when I give figures, so let me not insist on one percent. It is an agreement that is substantially completed, but I cannot go into that. But that alone is not a problem. The problem is as I have described it in my presentation."[26]

On December 17, Nixon ordered Operation Linebacker II, for B-52 raids to recommence over North Vietnam and again mine Haiphong Harbor. Within twenty-four hours 129 B-52s in three waves attacked military targets in the Hanoi area while F-111 bombers struck at MiG airfields nearby.

At the same time he was exerting military pressure on the North Vietnamese, Nixon was writing "the strongest letter I had yet written to Thieu." The December 17 letter was dictated by Nixon directly and entrusted to General Haig to deliver personally to President Thieu in Saigon. Nixon considered sending Vice President Agnew, Defense Secretary Melvin Laird, and former Treasury Secretary John Connally to Saigon, but in the end decided that "Haig is still the one to carry the message to Garcia."[27] Haig cabled ahead asking for a meeting with Thieu alone, not with his National Security Council. Thieu insisted on having Nha present at the meeting, so Bunker accompanied Haig.[28] Haig was to advise Thieu of the bombing of North Vietnam and gain his promise to sign the Accords.

In his letter to Thieu, Nixon wrote:

> General Haig's mission now represents my final effort to point out to you the necessity for joint action and to convey my irrevocable intention to proceed, preferably with your cooperation but, if necessary, alone. . . . I have asked General Haig to obtain your answer to this absolutely final offer on my part for us to work together in seeking a settlement along the lines I have approved or to go our separate ways. Let me emphasize in conclusion that General Haig is not coming to Saigon for the purpose of negotiating with you. The time has come for us to present a united front in negotiating with our enemies, and you must decide now whether you desire to continue our alliance or whether you want me to seek a settlement with the enemy which serves U.S. interests alone.

He added, "I am convinced that your refusal to join us would be an invitation to disaster—to the loss of all that we together have fought for over the past decade. It would be inexcusable above all because we will have lost a just and honorable alternative."

Thieu read the letter twice, then looked up at Haig. There was no mistaking the message: Haig was "not coming to Saigon for the purpose of negotiating with you," but "to obtain your answer to this absolutely final offer on my part." Thieu said it was obvious he was being asked to sign an agreement for continued American support, not an agreement for peace. Haig replied that as a soldier and as someone completely familiar with Communist treachery, he agreed with Thieu's assessment.[29]

Despite Nixon's assurances, Thieu felt that the Paris Accords as they had been drawn left him vulnerable to North Vietnamese infiltration and continued fighting. He foresaw a period of warfare and political jockeying for power that would undermine the stability of the Saigon regime and lead to its disintegration. The Communists would use the Accords to change their strategy to a "war in peace" strategy, a continued fever strong enough to weaken the South but not openly virulent enough to justify renewed American bombing or intervention.

Thieu prepared a letter for Haig to take back to Washington with him, still defying Nixon's "absolutely final offer." In it he expressed his deep concerns about the continuing presence of North Vietnamese troops in the South and asked for American guarantees. Thieu was so angry with Haig's failure to act on his pleas and warnings of the North Vietnamese intentions that he sealed his reply to Nixon, a rebuff to Haig to indicate his black mood, since he knew that Haig would have to open the sealed envelope and cable its contents to Washington. Normally, the letters from Thieu were delivered unsealed to Haig for immediate transmission from the code room of the American Embassy. Thieu was underscoring Haig's role as an emissary, despite their intellectual agreement. In his letter, Thieu did not flatly say he would refuse to sign the agreement. He was still struggling for more time and more favorable terms.[30] When he returned to Washington, Haig reported to Nixon that Thieu seemed almost desperate.

The bombing that began on December 18 occurred during the Christmas recess of Congress and thus there was no immediate formal reaction from a vacant Capital Hill. Nixon was in Key Biscayne, Florida, isolated in his hideaway on the bay side of the key, determined to continue the bombing despite outraged reaction at home and around the world.

When Hung heard the news, he was elated and thought his prayers had been answered. Suddenly, it seemed as if the meeting with Duc in the White House had been successful in bringing the South Vietnamese case to Nixon, who would now force the North Vietnamese to withdraw from the South. Christmas is a time of joy for Vietnamese Catholics, and Hung and his family celebrated with the traditional duck soup in their apartment in Arlington. For a brief moment it seemed as if the United States was determined to turn the tide of the war in Saigon's favor.

The only halt in the bombing was on Christmas Day. Over the course of the bombing, which ended on December 30, the United States lost thirty aircraft, including fifteen B-52s, all downed by surface-to-air (SAM) missiles. It was the first time that the North Vietnamese had succeeded in downing so many B-52s. After three days of bombing, six B-52s were lost in one night. The head of the Strategic Air Command, General John C. Meyer, called General Vogt in Thailand and said: "God, we've got to do something. These guys are getting to us with missiles. We have got to do something." Vogt and Meyer agreed that the problem was the North Vietnamese ability to assemble the missiles. They were coming in on lighters, loaded offshore from Soviet ships at anchor. Then the missiles were trucked to a small assembly plant in southeast Hanoi during the day and taken to the SAM sites for firing that night when the B-52s attacked. "All of our electronic capability couldn't screen those B-52s from these missiles. They were burning through and were homing on the bombers," said Vogt.[31]

General Meyer tried to get authority from Washington to hit the SAM assembly plant. "The only thing we can do is hit this missile assembly plant and destroy it so they can't fire the missiles at me," Meyer told Vogt. Authority was denied because the missile assembly plant was located in a densely populated area and the B-52s would be making their raids from high altitude in bad weather. There would be high civilian casualties and no certainty the plant would be hit. Finally Vogt was given permission to attack with F-4s, which were more accurate, and the assembly plant was destroyed. By the end of the bombing the SAM firings had decreased and there were reports that the North Vietnamese had exhausted their supply of SAM missiles and were badly demoralized. Hanoi's major sources of power were inoperable and the North Vietnamese reported 1,318 civilian casualties.[32]

Nixon hunkered down and bore the brunt of the criticism for the renewal of the bombing. He was convinced that a show of force was necessary to make the North Vietnamese settle. The mood was black in Washington, filled with uncertainty and concern that the peace process had been destroyed. David Broder, writing in *The Washington Post,* recalled a breakfast with Henry Kissinger in the early days of Nixon's first term when Kissinger said: "Vietnam may be one of these tragic issues that destroys everyone who touches it."

Around the White House the press corps was being called "the gloom and doom brigade," and there was continued sniping at Kissinger by White House staffers close to Chief of Staff Bob Haldeman. The President was "hanging tough" and his staff were assigned to project an image of certainty and determination. "When things are tough, he's calm and sure," his press secretary Ron Ziegler whispered in confidence to reporters, reminding them that everybody had wrongly predicted that the mining of Haiphong and the bombing of Hanoi in May would cause the Soviet Union to cancel the summit meeting.

Reports from North Vietnamese who came south after the war indicated that morale dropped sharply as a result of the bombing and that Hanoi was running out of SAM missiles to attack the B-52s. Former Finance Minister Chau Kim Nhan, a southerner in the Thieu cabinet, was told by refugees that NLF members said if the bombing had continued even for another week, Hanoi would have been on its knees and there could have been major changes in the peace agreement. Refugees later confirmed this account. Some even said their relatives in the North told them that they were preparing white flags to surrender, believing that the tide of the war had turned against the North.[33] General John Vogt described the bombings as "a very substantial victory," which forced the North Vietnamese to the conference table. Vogt said, "Kissinger himself told me, after his first visit to Hanoi following Linebacker II operations, that these people were on their knees and eager for a settlement."[34] In fact, the bombing did have a major impact on the North Vietnamese attitude toward the timing of the agreement.

At the same time as the bombing resumed on December 18, Kissinger cabled Hanoi complaining that its government was "deliberately and frivolously delaying the talks." He suggested a date for resuming them. While the bombing continued, Kissinger again suggested, on December 22, that the talks be resumed on January 3, 1973. If Hanoi agreed to the meeting, the United States would stop the bombing on December 31 for the duration of the negotiations. On December 26, after one of the biggest B-52 raids, Hanoi agreed to meet on January 8 in Paris, "in a serious negotiating attitude . . . to settle the remaining questions with the U.S. side." Inside the White House and throughout the Nixon administration, nobody except General Alexander Haig urged Nixon to continue the bombing. "Had we had the national will and the concensus here at home to go on with the bombing," commented Haig, "there is no question in my mind that we could have established terms which would have included the withdrawal of the North Vietnamese forces from the South. I think we could have insisted on that." Haig said he was the only one of Nixon's advisers to urge the bombing be continued. "During that very difficult period the outrage here in the United States grew to such proportions that every single adviser of the President except Al Haig, everyone including those robust fellows who had always been clearheaded advocates of strong action when it was called for, all of them were calling the President daily, hourly, and telling him to terminate the bombing. And it was backed up by legislative assessments that as the Congress reconvened there would have been legislative restrictions which would have been national suicide from the standpoint of ever negotiating a settlement." [35]

It was apparent that once Congress returned, Nixon would face strong and concerted opposition to the bombing. On January 6, Nixon met with Kissinger at Camp David to discuss the negotiating strategy for Paris. The President was not prepared to resume the bombing again. In his diary, he noted that once the negotiations resumed, "Henry, of course, is going to continue to play the hard line, indicating that I might resort to the resumption of the bombing in the Hanoi area, even though I have told him that as far as our internal planning is concerned we cannot consider this to be a viable option." [36]

At the same time as he was preparing to settle with Hanoi, Nixon continued his efforts to persuade Thieu to go along. He had used the bombing to convince both Hanoi and Saigon that the time to settle had arrived. He wrote again to Thieu on January 5.

Dear Mr. President:
This will acknowledge your letter of December 20, 1972.
    There is nothing substantial that I can add to my many previous messages, including my December 17 letter, which clearly stated my opinions and intentions. With respect to the question of North Vietnamese troops, we will again present your views to the Communists as we have done vigorously at every other opportunity. The result is certain to be once more the rejection of your position. We have explained to you repeatedly why we believe the problem of North Vietnamese troops is manageable under the agreement, and I see no reason to repeat all the arguments.
    We will proceed next week in Paris along the lines that General Haig

explained to you. Accordingly, if the North Vietnamese meet our concerns on the two outstanding issues in the agreement concerning the DMZ and the method of signing, and if we can arrange acceptable supervisory machinery, we will proceed to conclude an agreement. The gravest consequences would then arise if your government chose to reject the agreement and split off from the United States. As I said in my December 17 letter, I am convinced that your refusal to join us would be an invitation to disaster—to the loss of all that we together have fought for over the past decade. It would be inexcusable above all because we will have lost a just and honorable alternative.

As we enter this new round of talks, I hope that our countries will show a united front. It is imperative for our common objectives that your government take no further actions that complicate our task and would make more difficult the acceptance of the settlement by all parties. We will keep you informed of the negotiations in Paris through daily briefings of Ambassador Lam.

I can only repeat what I have so often said: The best guarantee for the survival of South Vietnam is the unity of our two countries which would be gravely jeopardized if you persist in your present course. The actions of our Congress since its return have clearly borne out the many warnings we have made.

Should you decide, as I trust you will, to go with us, you have my assurance of continued assistance in the post-settlement period and that we will respond with full force should the settlement be violated by North Vietnam. So once more I conclude with an appeal to you to close ranks with us.

Sincerely
[s] Richard Nixon

Nixon promised to present Saigon's views on the question of North Vietnamese troops in the South; but he predicted that "the result is certain to be once more the rejection of your position." He insisted that the problem of North Vietnamese troops was "manageable under the agreement." There were only two outstanding issues to be resolved: the DMZ and the method of signing. If these could be resolved, the United States would conclude an agreement with or without Thieu. Again Nixon repeated his pattern of threats and promises. If Thieu did not go along, his refusal "would be an invitation to disaster." If he accepted a "united front," all would go well; if not, Congress would cut off aid. Should Thieu sign, he was promised Nixon's "assurance of continued assistance in the post-settlement period and that we will respond with full force should the settlement be violated by North Vietnam."

The South Vietnamese accepted Nixon's promise of guarantees with the utmost seriousness. After the Christmas bombing, they believed that Nixon was ready and willing to use B-52s to enforce the Paris Agreement. Hung recalled how impressed South Vietnamese officials were with Nixon's pledge. "Full force" meant B-52 raids over the North. "There was no other definition or interpretation for us. 'Full force' could not mean the use of nuclear weapons when applied to North Vietnam, it was B-52s," Hung recalls Foreign Minister Tran Van Lam saying. "Full force means actions

similar to the May [Linebacker I] and Christmas [Linebacker II] bombing."
Often, the vice president and the prime minister referred to Nixon's pledge
as being made at the height of his presidential power because of his landslide
election to a second term—the greatest mandate since Eisenhower's election in 1952. Foreign Minister Bac insisted that the Vietnamese had no way
of knowing that Nixon was not prepared to use the bombers again. "The
Christmas bombing was seen as the back-up to Nixon's pledge of 'swift and
severe retaliation' and responding with 'full force' if Hanoi violated the
agreement."[37] The Vietnamese perception was that Nixon was making a
commitment on behalf of the American government and people. "It is a
matter between the United States and the Republic of Vietnam, not a commitment by Mr. Nixon and Mr. Thieu as individuals," Vice President Tran
Van Huong remarked after being shown Nixon's January 5 letter by President Thieu.

Thieu was still unhappy with the terms of the agreement but he took
heart in Nixon's guarantees. For Thieu, there was no choice. He told his
cabinet: "The United States leaves us without any alternative except that if
we sign, aid will continue and there is a pledge of retaliation if the agreements are violated. Otherwise they will leave us alone. Kissinger treats both
Vietnams as adversaries. He considers himself as an outsider in these negotiations and does not distinguish between South Vietnam, as an ally, and
North Vietnam, as an enemy. The Americans let the war become their war;
when they liked the war, they carried it forward. When they want to stop it,
they impose on both sides to stop it. When the Americans wanted to enter,
we had no choice, and now when they are ready to leave we have no
choice." After the Christmas bombing Thieu told his National Security
Council with bitter, black humor: "If Kissinger had the power to bomb the
Independence Palace to force me to sign the agreement, he would not hesitate to do so."[38]

9

The Real Agreement

AFTER THE CHRISTMAS BOMBING, Kissinger and Le Duc Tho met for four and a half hours in Paris on January 8, 1973; it was apparent that Hanoi was ready to settle. Le Duc Tho accepted Kissinger's proposed compromise on the language for the demilitarized zone and the signing of the Accords. The North Vietnamese essentially accepted the same agreement they had backed away from in November. There was no change in the terms of the cease-fire in place which permitted North Vietnamese troops to remain in the South. John Negroponte, Kissinger's Vietnam expert, argued that the Christmas bombing had created a new military and strategic reality; the United States should press Hanoi for better terms, especially on the vital issue of removing North Vietnamese troops from the South. Negroponte urged Kissinger not to rush the negotiations and to take advantage of the new situation. But Kissinger told him that Nixon had set January 20 as the deadline for the agreement. Nixon wanted to enter his second term with the war behind him. As Negroponte expressed it privately to friends: "We bombed the North Vietnamese into accepting our concession." [1]

In Washington, Hung was overcome with a sense of helplessness. All the momentum was toward a signing of the agreement in Paris and permitting the North Vietnamese troops to stay in the South. Hung organized demonstrations in front of the White House with a small group of Vietnamese, including his family, who carried posters demanding "Don't Sell Out Vietnam" and "Bring the North Vietnamese Troops Home Too!" There was no response from conservatives who traditionally had been friends of Saigon. Whenever Hung passed the Old Executive Office Building, where he thought Kissinger's office was located, his anger rose against the man he believed was selling out his country. Hung was tortured by Kissinger's heavy German accent on television and the way he said "We," using the imperial we, speaking on behalf of America and South Vietnam. When Kissinger said Thieu had agreed to the presence of North Vietnamese troops in the South, Hung was outraged. He felt a pressing need to counter Kissinger, and prepared an analysis of all the American proposals which showed that the United States had insisted on mutual withdrawal of American and North Vietnamese forces from the South. Hung went to visit Congressman John R. Rarick, a conservative Republican from Louisiana, who published Hung's analysis of the presence of North Vietnamese troops in the South in the Congressional Record. Hung tried to publish his views in *The Washington Post,* but was told he had just had one article in the weekend Outlook section and it was too soon for another.[2]

Hung visited Congressman Clement Zablocki (D.-Wis.), chairman of the House Foreign Affairs Committee, and sought his aid. Hung told Zablocki of his desperation, and said that "Nixon and Kissinger are lying about bringing peace with honor to South Vietnam. I am powerless to bring this point of view to the American public." They discussed Hung's *Washington Post* article, "Settling the War on Hanoi's Terms," and Zablocki said he was sympathetic; Hung had made good points. But when Hung asked him for help, Zablocki said, "Most Americans regard the Vietnam experience as a mistake." Hung replied, "It was not really a mistake. You set out in South Vietnam to contain Red China in the 1950s and 1960s and you did. Assuming that you now think it was a mistake, you don't make a mistake and run away. You have to accept the consequences for that mistake. You don't make a girl pregnant and then run away." Zablocki did not reply directly. He laughed and promised to mention Hung's concern for the presence of North Vietnamese troops in the South to his colleagues. Hung was appalled that there was nobody to put across the South Vietnamese case to the American media.

When he asked Saigon's Ambassador to Washington Tran Kim Phuong to place his article as a paid advertisement in major newspapers, or take out ads to explain Saigon's position, he was told that there were no funds available. Unlike the China Lobby and the Korean Lobby, there was nobody in Washington to speak up for Saigon. Hung had been impressed by the pictures of major political figures on the walls of Mrs. Chennault's elegant suite at the Watergate. They showed her with Nixon, LBJ, JFK, Kissinger, Attorney General John Mitchell, Speaker of the House Tip O'-Neill, and other men of power. Thieu had nobody to play that game for him and now it was too late. Hung was seized with bitterness and frustration as he listened to Kissinger insisting that Thieu had agreed to accept the North Vietnamese presence in the South, and not demand their withdrawal.[3] It was too late. Nixon was determined to have Thieu sign the agreement.

On January 14, the day before all bombing and mining of North Vietnam was stopped for an indefinite period, Nixon wrote to Thieu. He ordered General Haig to Saigon to deliver the letter and obtain Thieu's agreement. Before Haig left, Nixon told Kissinger he was determined to get Thieu on board. "Brutality is nothing," Nixon said to Kissinger. "You have never seen it if this son of a bitch doesn't go along, believe me."[4]

On the morning of January 16, Haig met with Thieu at the Independence Palace and presented a letter from Nixon threatening to sign the Paris Agreement on January 27, "if necessary, alone." Nixon warned that

> I have therefore irrevocably decided to proceed to initial the Agreement on January 23, 1973, and to sign it on January 27, 1973, in Paris. I will do so, if necessary, alone. In that case I shall have to explain publicly that your government obstructs peace. The result will be an inevitable and immediate termination of U.S. economic and military assistance which cannot be forestalled by a change of personnel in your government. I hope, however, that after all our two countries have shared and suffered together in conflict, we will stay together to preserve peace and reap its benefits.
>
> To this end I want to repeat to you the assurances that I have already conveyed. At the time of signing the agreement I will make emphatically clear that the United States recognizes your government as the only legal government of South Vietnam; that we do not recognize the right of any foreign troops to be present on South Vietnamese territory; that we will react strongly in the event the agreement is violated. Finally, I want to emphasize my continued commitment to the freedom and progress of the Republic of Vietnam. It is my firm intention to continue full economic and military aid.[5]

Here was Nixon telling Thieu that in principle the United States did not accept the right of North Vietnamese troops to remain in the South but in practice they would be staying because the United States had not negotiated their withdrawal as part of the agreement except in the vaguest terms calling for the removal of all "outside forces." To Hanoi, its troops were not "outside forces" because Article One of the agreement said, in effect, that Vietnam was one country.[6] Nixon was in a characteristic duality of threats and promises with Thieu: A cut-off of economic aid if he refused to sign; a promise not to recognize the right of foreign troops to remain in the South and to "react strongly in the event the agreement is violated." Thieu also took careful note of the phrasing that the result "cannot be forestalled by a change of personnel in your government." In the political dictionary of U.S.-Vietnam relations, "a change of personnel" was the euphemism for overthrow of the government. In 1963, preparations for the *coup d'état* against President Diem were in full swing when President Kennedy used an interview on September 2 with Walter Cronkite on the CBS Evening News to indicate the need for "personnel changes."

> *Mr. Cronkite:* "Do you think this government has time to regain the support of the people?"
> *President Kennedy:* "I do. With changes in policy and perhaps with personnel, I think it can. If it doesn't make those changes, I would think that the chances of winning it would not be very good."[7]

Thieu was concerned that he might be in line for similar treatment. He called a meeting of his National Security Council to discuss the January 14 letter from Nixon and alternative courses of action. As Thieu went around the Situation Room soliciting opinions, according to Nha, the view was: "Well, if that is what the Americans want, I think we should sign it." They praised Thieu's bravery. Prime Minister Khiem said: "Whatever you decide, Mr. President, we will support you." The JGS chairman, General Vien, repeated his standard line: "The military awaits your orders, Mr. President." The men Thieu had chosen to lead the country with him deferred to him. They lacked imagination, vision, or the courage openly to challenge him. This was one of the rare occasions when Thieu may have wondered why he should have chosen such men to hold key positions in his government. "There were a variety of CYA [cover your ass] answers, but nobody was prepared to offer a suggestion on what to do," recalls Nha. "Everybody was caving in."

When his turn came, Nha said, "We still have some time, let's keep fighting." He offered the Vietnamese proverb, *"con nuoc con tat"* ("As long as there is a drop of water left, scoop it up"). The image is of Vietnamese peasants scooping water from a river by hand, bucket by bucket, to irrigate their fields under the hot sun. Nha suggested another letter seeking further clarifications and guarantees. Thieu directed him to prepare one for Nixon.[8]

Ever since the October encounter with Kissinger in Saigon, Thieu had received advice from many quarters in Saigon to shift from demanding the removal of the North Vietnamese troops to seeking U.S. guarantees of the peace in Vietnam. Despite the firmness of Nixon's letter, his dire threats, and the demand for an answer by the evening of January 17, Thieu did not yield. Instead of giving his answer to Haig the next day, he sent a sealed reply to Nixon asking for another round of changes. Haig returned to the embassy immediately, opened the letter, which he described as "brittle and uncompromising," and transmitted it to the White House.

There would be no more delays. Nixon and Kissinger replied immediately in a letter dated January 17, which Haig and Bunker delivered to Thieu. Nixon was determined to prevail; but yet again he sought to reassure Thieu while warning of dire consequences if he did not sign:

Dear President Thieu:
　　I have received your letter of January 17, 1973, and I have studied it with the greatest care.
　　I must repeat what I have said to you in my previous communications: The freedom and independence of the Republic of Vietnam remains a paramount objective of American foreign policy. I have been dedicated to this goal all my political life, and during the past four years I have risked many grave domestic and international consequences in its pursuit. It is precisely in order to safeguard our mutual objectives that I have decided irrevocably on my present course. I am firmly convinced that the alternative to signing the present Agreement is a total cutoff of funds to assist your country. We will therefore proceed to initial the Agreement General Haig has brought you on January 23, 1973 and sign it on January 27, 1973. Thus we have only one decision before us: whether or not to continue in peacetime the close partnership that has served us so well in war. . . .

In addition to strengthening the Agreement itself, as my January 14 letter pointed out, your overall political and security position has been bolstered in many ways in preparation for a ceasefire. . . .

. . . As I have told you on many occasions, the key issue is no longer particular nuances in the Agreement but rather the postwar cooperation of our two countries and the need for continued U.S. support. It is precisely for this support that I have been fighting. Your rejection of the Agreement would irretrievably destroy our ability to assist you. Congress and public opinion would force my hand. It is time, therefore, to join together at last and protect our mutual interests through close cooperation and unity.

As General Haig has told you, I am prepared to send Vice President Agnew to Saigon in order to plan with you our postwar relationship. He would leave Washington on January 28, the day after the Agreement is signed, and during his visit he would publicly reaffirm the guarantees I have expressed to you. Let me state these assurances once again in this letter:

—First, we recognize your Government as the sole legitimate Government of South Vietnam.

—Secondly, we do not recognize the right of foreign troops to remain on South Vietnamese soil.

—Thirdly, the U.S. will react vigorously to violations of the Agreement.

In addition I remain prepared to meet with you personally three or four weeks later in San Clemente, California, at which time we could publicly reaffirm once again our joint cooperation and U.S. guarantees.

Against this background I hope that you will now join us in signing the Agreement. Because of the gravity of the situation and the consequences for the future, I have instructed General Haig to return to Saigon Saturday morning January 20, 1973. This is the latest possible occasion for us to have your final position so that I will know whether we will be proceeding together with you. The schedule is final and cannot be changed in any way. Dr. Kissinger will initial the Agreement in Paris on January 23; I will make a brief address to the American people that evening; and the formal signing will take place on January 27, 1973. If you refuse to join us, the responsibility for the consequences rests with the Government of Vietnam. . . .

Let me close by saying that I respect the intensity with which you are defending the interests of your country. I recognize that the Agreement is not an ideal one, but it is the best possible one that can be obtained under present circumstances, and I have explained why these circumstances require a settlement now.

It seems to me that you have two essential choices: to continue a course, which would be dramatic but shortsighted, of seeking to block the Agreement; or to use the Agreement constructively as a means of establishing a new basis for American–South Vietnamese relations. I need not tell you how strongly I hope that you will choose what I am firmly convinced to be the only possible path to secure our mutual objectives.

> Sincerely
> [s] Richard Nixon

Thieu read the long letter carefully, tallying the threats and promises to reach a bottom line on the American commitment. He was pleased to see that Nixon had clearly stated that "the freedom and independence of the Republic of Vietnam remains a paramount objective of American foreign policy." With American troop strength reduced from more than half a million to only 23,000 (on December 1, 1972), Thieu sought reassurance of the American commitment. There it was. Nixon promised that "the U.S. will react vigorously to violations of the Agreement." Nixon said the United States recognized Thieu's government "as the sole legitimate Government of South Vietnam" and did not recognize "the right of foreign troops to remain on South Vietnamese soil." Nixon's letter told Thieu that in the U.S. global strategy, Vietnam still loomed large. At the same time Nixon's threats were more specific. A "total cutoff of funds" meant that the operational, working-level American aid funds would end. No more rice, counterpart funds, or the wherewithal to keep South Vietnam afloat. Thieu recalled the first time he had faced an American "cutoff." He was commander of the 5th Division in Bien Hoa in 1963 when the Americans stopped the shipment of fuel and ammunition, severely affecting his division. At the time Thieu saw the American move as a signal of displeasure with Ngo Dinh Diem and decided to join the coup against Diem. The irony of his present predicament was not lost on him.[9]

Yet still Thieu refused to sign; he told Bunker he wanted to think about Nixon's letter. Bunker and Haig felt Thieu was stalling until Inauguration Day, January 20. Nixon also estimated that his inauguration for a second term would be the final deadline for Thieu.[10]

Thieu realized the strong wording of the January 17 letter was an ultimatum, but before giving his answer, he went ahead with the wedding of his daughter in the Palace. It seemed an unlikely time to hold a wedding in the Independence Palace, but for Thieu it meant putting his own life in order and assuring the continuity of his name. On January 19, his gentle daughter Tuan Anh was married to Nguyen Tan Trieu, the son of the chairman of Air Vietnam, in a lengthy ceremony and festivities that kept Thieu unavailable for meetings that day with Ambassador Bunker. The Vietnamese ceremony was held in the Palace, then the family went to the Notre Dame Basilica for the formal Catholic ceremony. Just before they left, Nha was called to the phone to speak with Ambassador Bunker, who said that he needed to see the president because "we need to have an answer." Nha says he told Bunker he was "being very inconsiderate. 'This is a most important day for the President. Can't you wait until the ceremony is over?' Here was the man marrying his only daughter and he couldn't even have a few hours of peace. I said, 'I'll get back to you.'" After the ceremony, Nha told Thieu that Bunker had called. The president was annoyed and said, "Haven't they even got the manners to see that this is a very important day in my life?"

Thieu saw Bunker alone that evening for thirty minutes with nobody to take notes. In private with Thieu, Bunker was more effective than with Nha and others present. When Thieu emerged, he told Nha, "They are pressuring me again but he has given me some more assurances." Bunker had made an eloquent case for Thieu "providing President Nixon with the basis for supporting him with Congress." Bunker had reiterated all of Nixon's promises in the letter and assured Thieu that they would be fulfilled if only he went along with the Paris Agreement.[11]

After the meeting with Bunker, Thieu asked Nha to join him for dinner alone in the Palace. In a reflective mood, Thieu said, "The Americans really leave me no choice—either sign or they will cut off aid. On the other hand we have obtained an absolute guarantee from Nixon to defend the country. I am going to agree to sign and hold him to his word."

"Can you really trust Nixon?" asked Nha.

"He is a man of honor. I am going to trust him," replied Thieu. Then they drafted a final effort to pin Nixon down on the question of North Vietnamese troops leaving the South.

When Haig returned to Saigon on January 20, after stopping in Seoul and Bangkok, Thieu still refused to sign. Yet again he gave Haig a letter to Nixon addressing the danger of permitting North Vietnamese forces to remain in the South. Thieu asked that the wording of the agreement be changed to refer to North Vietnamese troops, not merely foreign troops leaving the South. Haig sought to assure Thieu that it was understood that there would have to be troop withdrawals but that it was too late to change the agreement and his request would stall the talks. Thieu insisted that the letter be sent to Nixon, who replied the same day. Bunker delivered the letter. Nixon tried to reassure Thieu on the presence of the North Vietnamese in the South, writing: "While there is no specific provision in the text, there are so many collateral clauses with an impact on this question that the continued presence of North Vietnamese troops could only be based on illegal acts and the introduction of new forces could only be done in violation of the Agreement."

Nixon cited a string of clauses scattered through the agreement that he said should be interpreted to mean that the presence of North Vietnamese troops in the South was illegal. Reflecting on the moment, Thieu recalled, "To the Communists, even if you put everything clearly on white paper with black ink, word by word, you are still not sure of their compliance; now Nixon was telling me that I could count on the hidden meaning of words here and there in the agreement."[12] The Vietnamese found Nixon's interpretation intriguing but confusing. Words had little meaning to the Communists except as they interpreted them. They were sticking firmly to Article One of the agreement, which said the United States respected the unity and territorial integrity of Vietnam. To them, this meant North and South were one country and the North Vietnamese troops rightly belonged in the South. It was too late in the day to argue the point any longer.

Thieu's mood now was desperate, hanging on to the last possible moment, which was Nixon's inauguration on January 20. At a forty-five-minute-meeting on the same day Thieu told his advisers that the moment had come to make a decision. Everybody remained silent. "Convene the National Security Council tonight. I want to apprise them of the situation," Thieu ordered. Under Nixon's schedule, Foreign Minister Tran Van Lam was to go to Paris the following day. At the meeting the members of the Council all appeared eager to be agreeable with Thieu; they praised Thieu personally, but nobody said that he should go along with Nixon. Instead of getting suggestions or analyses of the situation, he "had his feathers smoothed," as Nha described the comments.

Thieu assembled his National Security Council and told them the issue now was whether he should become an instant hero by turning down the settlement at once or become a statesman by signing the agreement and saving his country later. While still deeply dissatisfied with the terms permitting North Vietnamese troops in the South, Thieu felt that Nixon was becoming more specific in expressing the guarantees the United States would make to South Vietnam. He knew "there was no way we could pull the Americans back by the tail and force them to stay in the war."[13] Yet he felt that once Nixon gave his word, he would stick by his commitments.

The higher a man's place in Vietnamese society, the greater his honor and his duty to uphold this honor. An American President should behave as well. In the Confucian tradition honor is directly related to trust. *Chu tin,* or trust, is the highest of qualities, equated only with loyalty on the scale of values. Thieu saw himself and Nixon in this kind of Confucian relationship. Nixon as the head of the world's greatest superpower was conferring on Thieu a Mandate of Heaven to rule; but at the same time he gave Thieu a solemn commitment based on trust and loyalty. Every schoolboy in Vietnam learns the Confucian maxim that the words of an honorable person are "like a spike driven into a post," *nhu danh dong cot.* They cannot be removed.

While Thieu was deeply concerned about his Republic's survival and self-interest, his framework for viewing the world was essentially Confucian, despite his conversion to Catholicism. He carried within him a blend of values derived from his family, whose religious traditions mingled with a rich respect for Confucian customs.

In dealing with people, Thieu described the importance of the Chinese way of keeping one's word once a pledge is made. When buying a house from a Chinese, a man's word is his bond. If he accepts a price, he keeps it even if the bid is raised the following day. "The Vietnamese love to do business with the Chinese because they keep their word. If a Chinese agrees to sell his house to me for $150,000, he would take out a dirty piece of paper from his pocket and write down $150,000. No witnesses, lawyers, or Notary Public are necessary. The next day if somebody offers him $200,000 for the house, he would say, 'No, I have agreed to an offer of $150,000.' You don't have to make any promise, but once you do, you have to keep it to uphold your honor." In his negotiations with Nixon, Thieu believed that he had gotten a commitment, not only in general terms, but in very specific terms, that the United States would uphold. In all his letters, Nixon repeated the U.S. commitments and elaborated on them. Thieu collected Nixon's letters in a file and referred to them in their totality. For Thieu, the letters formed the context and the continuity of the overall U.S.–Vietnamese relationship.

They were Nixon's pledge, and Thieu hoped that the Confucian maxim: "A gentleman only speaks once" (*Quan tu nhat ngon*) would apply to the American President.

Sacrifices referred to by Nixon, the blood shed by Americans and Vietnamese, would not be allowed to come to naught. His pledge stirred Thieu's own sense of honor and helped convince him that Nixon might not merely be trying to "scuttle and run." He had to believe the American President because he had no place else to turn. His dogged resistance to signing had won a concession on the DMZ, prompted Nixon to state his guarantees in simple, straightforward language, and to promise to make them public once the agreement was signed. Thieu felt that after the American President made these commitments public, they could never be withdrawn. As the Confucian saying goes, "Once a word flies from your mouth, four galloping horses cannot catch it" (*nhat ngon chu xuat tu ma nan truy*).[14]

Thieu kept the letters from Nixon hidden in his bedroom and protected them zealously. For him they were like a crown, a symbol of authority, his formal link to American power and a personal commitment, leader to leader, given by the President of the United States.

Thieu envisioned the American President ruling in the same way that he ruled in Vietnam. The U.S. President was the supreme leader. Even if he was elected by the people, rather than being given a Mandate from Heaven, he was responsible for all decisions and policies, the commander-in-chief. Thieu had heard of the separation of powers between the legislative, executive, and judicial branches of government, but, like most Vietnamese, and Europeans, he did not fully understand how the system worked in practice and why it should be that way. In Vietnam, the ruler had a Mandate from Heaven as well as from the people. If the mandate came for elections, it could be withdrawn and the ruler deposed, but the president could not be overruled by the National Assembly and the courts. There was no tradition in Saigon of an opposition or checks and balances. With checks and balances nothing would ever be accomplished in a country at war, which had only a ten-year tradition of democracy. The separation of powers, checks and balances, to Thieu meant paralysis of government in Vietnam. He was counting on Nixon to be the commander-in-chief.

In his January 20 letter, Nixon again gave Thieu a final ultimatum. He insisted on an answer by 1200 Washington time, January 21, 1973. Nixon told Thieu he planned to meet with congressional leaders on Sunday evening, January 21, to inform them of the course of action being taken. "If you cannot give me a positive answer," he told Thieu he would authorize Kissinger "to initial the agreements without the concurrence of your government." "In that case, even if you should decide to join us later, the possibility of continued Congressional assistance will be severely reduced," explained Nixon.

Again, the letter was a skillful combination of threats and promises. This time Senators Barry Goldwater (R.-Ariz.) and John Stennis (D.-Miss.), two long-time loyal supporters of South Vietnam, were enlisted by the

White House to warn publicly that if Thieu blocked the agreement, aid would be cut. In his memorandums to Thieu, Hung had cited Senator Goldwater as the most ardent support of South Vietnam. Hung had told Thieu how he had assisted Warren Nutter in advising Goldwater on Vietnam policy during the 1963 presidential campaign. For Nixon to use Goldwater in the letter as evidence that support against Thieu was building up in Congress had a strong influence on Thieu. He realized that even his staunchest supporters had deserted him.

Finally Thieu relented. On January 21 he called in Ambassador Bunker and told him, "I have done my best. I have done all that I can do for my country." Nixon in his memoirs pays tribute to Thieu's courage, saying, "even though his conduct had been almost unbearably frustrating, I had to admire his spirit." [15] Nixon had missed the inaugural deadline and could not say he was entering the second term in peacetime, but the end was near. He could leave Vietnam behind and devote his second term to continued development of the new relationship with the People's Republic of China. In the Middle East he would seek to move from "uneasy truce" to real peace. Nixon's new foreign policy priorities would stress a second round of nuclear arms limitation talks, mutual force reductions in Central Europe, and a European Security Conference. The domestic rancor and divisions over Vietnam would be gone. There was no sign of Watergate on the horizon.

On January 22, Nixon wrote to President Thieu praising "the tenacity and courage with which you are defending the interests of your people in our common objective to preserve their freedom and independence." All was well. Nixon said he would tell Congress that Thieu was concurring and promised a letter affirming the guarantees Thieu had asked for in writing. The United States, said Nixon, would accept Thieu's language on the illegality of North Vietnamese troops remaining in the South. Nixon would go on television January 23 and affirm the "essential unity" of the United States and South Vietnam while pointing out that South Vietnam's foreign minister, Tran Van Lam, "personally participated in the final phase of the negotiations." For Lam, who was never consulted on anything but technical details, the claim was ludicrous; but appearances were important. Nixon noted that "Dr. Kissinger will consult closely, and visibly associate himself with your Foreign Minister while they are in Paris."

A light rain fell in the gray cold when at 12:45 p.m. Tuesday, January 23, after a final round of wrangling over the numbering of pages and the comparing of texts, Kissinger and Le Duc Tho initialed the Paris Agreement and the protocols in thirty-six places at the International Conference Center of the Hotel Majestic on Avenue Kléber. Kissinger signed with his distinctive H and K linked together, while his North Vietnamese counterpart signed Tho in English letters. Kissinger used a series of black felt-tipped pens and gave one to every member of his staff. Le Duc Tho gave his pen to Kissinger "to remind the U.S. side to correctly implement the agreements." [16] Both Kissinger and Le Duc Tho made conciliatory speeches. The war was officially over. In the final session Le Duc Tho had raised the issue of American reparations and Kissinger insisted that they depended on observance of the agreement and congressional approval. Le Duc Tho told Kissinger American planes could fly to Hanoi to pick up the American prisoners of war.

The formal signing on January 27 left both sides ready to press their advantages as the cease-fire went into effect. There was no real expectation of peace, but only of a temporary lull in the fighting and the beginning of a new stage of the struggle. As Kissinger explained to Schecter in an interview just before the signing, "To get an iron-clad, crystal-clear agreement, we would have had to fight for another year or two. We need patience, wisdom, and generosity, all of which are not in excessive supply in Vietnam." A North Vietnamese official in Paris said: "We will stick by the agreement, but compared to 1954, we're staying down south." To the South Vietnamese, the four years of fighting from 1969 to 1973 accomplished nothing in the sense of the final results of the negotiations. The terms of the Paris Agreement remained essentially the same as those proposed by the Communists in May 1969. (See appendix F for detailed comparisons.)

When all the agreements were signed, the view in the White House was that the prolonged negotiations had strengthened Thieu's position. There had been time for him to build domestic support and establish his own position by not crumbling under American pressure. Militarily, South Vietnam was in a favorable position, and American intelligence estimates at the time of the cease-fire in January were that "the Communists do not pose a major military threat in the South and are not in a position to seize large chunks of territory that will be particularly significant before or after a ceasefire."[17]

For most Vietnamese, the cease-fire meant a new phase of warfare and a return to terrorism and political subversion. For President Thieu and his government, the real agreement in Paris was not what had been signed on separate sheets of paper with North Vietnam and the Provisional Revolutionary Government, but the private promises Nixon had made in his letters to Thieu ever since December 1971. Thieu studied the letters and assessed his position in terms of what the American commitment would really be once Americans prisoners were returned and all its troops withdrawn. Unlike the end of the Korean War, when 60,000 American troops remained, South Vietnam would be on its own. The vast influx of supplies sent to Saigon under the Enhance and Enhance Plus scheme was for Thieu a demonstration for political purposes that had no real military effect because most of the equipment was old and needed to be replaced. It had been sent to Saigon to avoid the cease-fire deadline which would prohibit the influx of new military aid. Yet the fact that it had been sent at all gave the public impression that Thieu was well prepared to face the North Vietnamese and did not need more aid.

Thieu saw the aid for what it was, an incentive for him to sign the Paris

Accords. His ambassadors in Paris had reported that Kissinger told them several times: "We have given you one billion dollars worth of arms. You will either conclude the agreement or be cut off from U.S. assistance."[18] To Thieu, Enhance Plus only increased his dependency on the United States since most of the equipment needed American maintenance support and logistics to be serviceable. Much of the equipment, such as F-5A and C-123 aircraft, was old and not operational. It was there so it could be replaced after the cease-fire. Unless the United States came up with spare parts and the funds to keep the vast flood of supplies in operation, Enhance Plus would be little more than an empty gesture.[19]

The highest American military officer in Vietnam, General John E. Murray, head of the Defense Attaché Office (DAO), called the Enhance and Enhance Plus program "a fallacy." Altogether, about $750 million worth of equipment was "pushed" into South Vietnam to make up for battle losses sustained in the Easter 1972 offensive and to add to the "counters" in the one-for-one cease-fire agreement.

Murray said, "There is a persistent fallacy about the wealth of equipment that was turned over to the RVNAF. Not that a great deal was not turned over, but much of what was turned over was battle damaged, or otherwise damaged, worn out—or nearly so—or obsolete. Much that was turned over as excess was in fact extraordinarily demanding in excess requirements for maintenance." While the turnover of equipment "glutted the RVNAF system," Murray added, one ought "to note well that these were major end items—not operational and sorely needed spare parts which the war had exhausted." The special tools that went with major items such as jacks and lug wrenches for vehicles were missing and "requisitions for direct delivery of these shortages to ARVN were subsequently cancelled. ARVN was left holding the bag."[20]

In his letters and in his private conversations with Thieu and his senior aides, Nixon stressed that the Paris Agreement would be implemented by the United States together with South Vietnam. That was the real Paris Agreement. In Thieu's mind the United States had made a series of binding commitments.

In public, Kissinger repeatedly insisted that the elaborate international control mechanism set up under the agreement was crucial to its successful implementation. In addition, an international conference of twelve countries convened in Paris following the cease-fire to guarantee "the ending of the war and the maintenance of peace in Vietnam." After the conference an "Act" to this effect was signed on March 2, 1973, carrying the signatures of these countries, including the Soviet Union, the People's Republic of China, France, the United Kingdom, and the United States.[21]

In reality, neither the International Commission for Control and Supervision (ICCS) nor the nations that signed the Act were to effectively enforce the peace. It was to be enforced solely by the United States. Nixon had written Thieu in his November 14, 1972, letter: "In any event, what we both must recognize is that the supervisory mechanism in itself is in no measure as important as our own firm determination to see to it that the Agreement works and our vigilance with respect to the prospect of its violations.''

From President Nixon on down, the Americans kept assuring Thieu that ''far more important than what we say in the agreement on this issue is what we do in the event the enemy renews its aggression.'' Thieu counted on the United States to be the final supervisor and enforcer of the peace.

10

San Clemente and Watergate

VICE PRESIDENT SPIRO AGNEW visited Saigon briefly after the signing of the Paris Accords to keep a promise President Nixon had made; but he only kept part of the pledge. In his January 17 letter to Thieu, Nixon had assured him that Agnew would come to Saigon and publicly reaffirm the guarantees made secretly in the letter. First, Nixon guaranteed that the United States would recognize Thieu's government as the sole legitimate government of South Vietnam. Second, Nixon declared that the United States did not recognize the right of foreign troops to remain in South Vietnam; and third, but most important, "the United States will react vigorously to violations of the agreement." There was also the pledge of continued military and economic aid.

In his arrival statement at Tan Son Nhut Airport on January 30, 1973, Agnew reaffirmed American support for South Vietnam, but he carefully avoided any mention of how the United States would react in the event of renewed North Vietnamese aggression against the South. Agnew spoke fulsomely of the American commitment to Vietnam and heaped personal praise on President Thieu; but neither publicly nor privately did the Vice President refer to U.S. concerns with or responses to a renewal of hostilities by the North. Agnew's talking points and statements had been carefully prepared by Kissinger and his staff to keep him from making a public commitment to resume bombing in case of North Vietnamese violations of the cease-fire. In fact the North Vietnamese violations of the cease-fire by infiltrating men and supplies into South Vietnam through the Ho Chi Minh Trail began within a week of the signing of the agreement, and reconnaissance photos along with messages of urgent concern were being sent to Washington by U.S. Seventh Air Force Commander General John Vogt, based in Nakorn Phanom, Thailand.[1]

"When Mr. Agnew arrived, he only talked about two commitments, and he failed to mention the third one: he ignored the one dealing with U.S. interference, reaction, and vigorous retaliation. I became doubtful about the U.S. commitments at that point," Thieu said later.[2] Thieu was anxious to see Nixon in person and have him confirm in public the guarantees stated in the letters. He knew he had to try to build American support for continued aid now that the Accords had been signed. John Negroponte, Kissinger's Vietnam expert, accompanied the Vice President to Saigon. In a quiet moment he took Nha aside and told him: "I have to tell you I'm sorry for everything we did in October. We know we cannot pressure you and now we are going to do our best to live up to what was promised." [3]

After South Vietnam signed the Paris Agreement, Hung wrote Thieu a long memorandum pointing out the importance of favorable American opinion to Vietnam. Hung stressed the need to win sympathy from the American news media, and warned that "support for South Vietnam is vanishing." An information office in Washington to disseminate materials on South Vietnam and present the Saigon story was urgently needed. He told Thieu that to many people in America the Viet Cong and the Provisional Revolutionary Government in the South were seen as a genuine southern movement, not a puppet front manipulated by Hanoi. To most Americans, Hung explained, South Vietnam was facing a civil war, not a foreign invasion, and a coalition was viewed as a fair way to resolve the differences between the two opposing sides. "If the Democrats and the Republicans form a coalition on an issue dividing America, that would be good for the nation, but in Vietnam a coalition is a death sentence for us, yet most Americans do not understand this." Hung reminded Thieu that Ho Chi Minh, who had died in 1969, was still regarded in America as a Nationalist leader in the postwar liberation struggle, not as a Communist leader whose goal was to conquer all of Indochina and then subvert Thailand and Malaysia. He was trying to impress on Thieu the American perception of Vietnam as a potential Titoist state. Ho had been compared to Yugoslavia's Marshal Josef Broz Tito as an independent Communist leader. There was still speculation even after Ho's death that North Vietnam could become an independent Asian Communist power balancing its self-interest between the Soviet Union and China.

"American public opinion is based on the power of the people, and public opinion can change policy. Unlike Vietnam, the opinion of the American people influences policy. We cannot let public misperception of the situation in Vietnam continue or we will be finished," Hung warned.

Thieu ordered Nha to respond to Hung immediately and gave him approval to proceed with organizing an information office in Washington. Hung was to select the staff, find a suitable office, and run it with the rank of deputy ambassador. Hung went ahead, planning a full agenda of seminars with scholars, dialogues with the press, and debates with critics of South Vietnam. He selected offices in Roslyn, Virginia, overlooking the Potomac River and the Lincoln Memorial.

Hung's plan called for engaging the press and the academic community on major issues affecting Vietnam, such as the origins of the revolution, the meaning of coalition in Vietnam, and the presence of North Vietnamese forces in the South. His top priority was to challenge the anti-war groups spreading the line that Vietnam was engaged in a civil war and that the Viet

Cong was an indigenous southern movement independent from North Vietnam. Nha said Thieu would be coming to America soon to meet with President Nixon and Hung would then have an opportunity to see Thieu personally.

Thieu's real reward for signing the Paris Agreement was the promise of a trip to San Clemente three or four weeks after the cease-fire, "so," as Nixon said, "we could publicly reaffirm once again our joint cooperation and U.S. guarantees." The timetable slipped and Thieu was not invited to the United States until April 3. Thieu issued instructions to his embassy to treat his visit to America with the utmost severity and solemnity. There were to be no gaffes; mistakes would not be tolerated. He dispatched an advance team to Washington to plan the visit to San Clemente and Washington. Air Vietnam was ordered to charter a Pan American Boeing 707 and paint a Vietnamese flag on the body to foster an image of sovereignty and dignity.

To Hung, it seemed strange that Thieu was going to San Clemente instead of Washington to see Nixon. Heads of state come to Washington first during a state visit, but Thieu was most concerned with meeting Nixon. When Ambassador Bunker suggested making the visit to San Clemente an official one, Thieu declined the offer. As the head of state of the Republic of Vietnam, he was determined that his visit to American would be a full-fledged state visit, not a summit, a private visit, or an official visit.

The protocol for a state visit is the most elaborate. The facilities at the Western White House in San Clemente did not come anywhere near those of the White House in Washington, D.C.—Thieu could not be received in San Clemente in the same elegant style as at the White House. Nevertheless, Ambassador Phuong negotiated for Thieu to receive the protocol treatment for a state visit at the Western White House. A full Marine honor guard would welcome him on the lawn. Nixon's dinner for Thieu at his home, Casa Pacifica, overlooking the Pacific Ocean, was to be billed as a state dinner, even though there would only be twelve people in attendance. Thieu was told there was no more room at the dinner table. The Vietnamese wanted to give their return dinner at the Century Plaza Hotel in Los Angeles, but they were told that it could not be held there because of security considerations. In reality, as Kissinger notes in his memoirs, there were doubts that "we could generate a representative guest list and fear of hostile demonstrations."[4]

As the visit drew near, Nixon's involvement in Watergate deepened. Washington was totally preoccupied with the revelations of high-level administration involvement in a cover-up of the burglary attempt at Democratic National Committee offices in the Watergate. On March 29, Nixon made the decision to waive executive privilege for Watergate testimony.

That night the President gave a television address welcoming home the last group of American POWs. For the first time in twelve years there were no American combat forces in Vietnam. The issue of the more than 2,000 Americans missing in action, however, was still to be resolved.[5] At the same time, Nixon warned Hanoi about its breaches of the Indochina cease-fire, but made no mention of American retaliation.

The next day, before Nixon departed for San Clemente, press secretary Ziegler announced that members of the White House staff would cooperate fully if called before the grand jury investigation of Watergate.

Thieu's visit was like the stop frame in a film, a sudden interlude to examine a brief moment before proceeding to the main events. The passions unleashed by the Vietnam War had still not abated and seemed to be exacerbated by Watergate. Thieu's visit was an embarrassment for Nixon. In his memoirs Nixon dismisses the San Clemente visit in only eight lines, noting Thieu's concern with the blatant lack of good faith demonstrated by the Communists in their violations of the Paris Accords. He wrote, "I fully shared his concern, and I reassured him that we would not tolerate any actions that actually threatened South Vietnam. He was grateful for my reassurances, but I knew that he must be concerned about the effect the domestic drain of Watergate would have on my ability to act forcefully abroad." [6]

The arrival ceremony was held inside the isolated presidential compound on the shore of the Pacific. Security was easy to maintain since the President's Spanish-style home, with its white stucco walls and terracotta tiled roof, was hidden from the main highway and could be reached only by a carefully guarded access road.

Two hours after Thieu landed, Ziegler and Haldeman told Nha there might be no joint communiqué. When Nha relayed this to Thieu, he was furious. "That is unheard of. Is that how they treat allies? Tell them I am ready to go back to Saigon and get our plane ready to return." Kissinger was advised of the fracas and quickly reassured Nha that a mistake had been made. There would be a joint communiqué. Nha realized that Kissinger wanted to make the visit a success and conveyed this to Thieu.

At the end of the first day Nixon gave a cocktail party around the swimming pool of Casa Pacifica. The pool was set in a flagstoned patio, with a low retaining wall planted with geraniums and impatiens. Steps led to a practice putting green below the pool, a gift from the local chamber of commerce to Nixon. As the guests gathered on the lawn, Kissinger spotted Nha and took him aside to chat. After greeting Nha, Kissinger's smile disappeared and he looked straight at him. Then he said, "The past is behind us. I realize now that I moved too fast and that October was a mistake." Nha was astounded at Kissinger's words after their bitter encounters in Saigon. "I could make a lot of money if I released your admission of a mistake in October to the press right now," Nha replied, grinning. He and Kissinger laughed heartily. "I know you wouldn't do that sort of thing," said Kissinger. [7]

Kissinger seemed to have changed; all the hostility, anger, and frustration of the October meetings in Saigon were gone. Thieu had signed the Accords and now Kissinger wanted the meeting to go well for Nixon and for Thieu. In the "decent interval" Thieu should be given an opportunity to survive.

At the reception, Thieu and Secretary of State William Rogers were chatting when Kissinger came up to them. Rogers joked: "Now that the Agreements have been signed, Henry can kiss another famous woman in Paris, Madame Binh." Rogers was referring to Madame Nguyen Thi Binh, the dour foreign minister of the Provisional Revolutionary Government, whom Thieu abhorred. Kissinger was offended and turned his back on Rogers.[8]

At dinner Thieu found the thick steak Nixon offered hard to digest, but he suffered through it so as not to offend his host. When he was told that there was criticism of Nixon for treating him to steak at a time when meat prices were soaring, Thieu complained privately to his staff afterwards about the meal and mentioned a preference for fish, Nha told Thieu the advance team had not been consulted on the menus or the food he preferred. Nixon had just put a price freeze on meat and there was black humor about what an expensive meal Thieu had been served despite his own tastes. Once again the Americans were doing it their way. It was a small point but it rankled Thieu.

In their private talks Nixon repeated the pledges he had made in his letters to Thieu and promised that "the U.S. will meet all contingencies in case the Agreement is grossly violated." He also told Thieu, according to former Ambassador Bui Diem, who was at San Clemente, "You can count on us." The joint public communiqué emphasized economic development and U.S. economic aid while threatening a "vigorous reaction" to any blatant cease-fire violations. Nixon would not make public the pledge of his January 5 letter to "respond with full force" to North Vietnamese violations of the agreement or "to take swift and severe retaliatory action," as he had pledged in his November 14, 1972, letter.

Thieu did not fully appreciate the impact of Watergate because he believed the issues facing Nixon to be essentially trivial and he did not percieve that Nixon could be driven from office. Thieu was concerned, but still confident. "Of course he did confirm his pledges to me privately, and there was the communiqué. But Nixon seemed preoccupied and absent-minded during our meetings. On the one hand I still believed that as President of the United States Nixon had the power to pledge U.S. support and had the ability to implement his pledges with airpower. That was the minimum thing I asked and the easiest thing for Nixon to do as President. The War Powers Act and the bombing prohibition came after San Clemente. If it had come before, I would have questioned the U.S. pledges. I asked the minimum from the United States, just a vigorous response, not nuclear weapons on Hanoi. It was a possible action for the President to take."[9]

The high point of the visit to San Clemente was a reception for Thieu hosted by California Governor Ronald Reagan at the Beverly Wilshire Hotel in Los Angeles. Thieu had received Reagan lavishly when he visited Saigon as governor of California and presented him with an ivory elephant tusk. He joked with him that he hoped the Republicans would be riding high, although later he said he had no expectation Reagan would become President. Nixon and Kissinger were vague and skittish, but Reagan was warm and direct. "I could sense his sincerity and compassion for South Vietnam," Thieu re-called.

At the dinner, Zsa Zsa Gabor and John Wayne were the stars. Wayne took an immediate liking to Thieu and sought to put him at ease in spite of the anti-war demonstrations going on outside the hotel entrance. "You know what I am going to do with those demonstrators, Mr. President?" Wayne asked. Then he acted as if he were lifting two demonstrators in his giant hands and knocking their heads together. "I am going to pick them up and drag them away like they do in the movies," said Wayne to much laughter.[10]

After his private meeting with Nixon, Thieu told his closest aide: "I got the assurances. We're going to get economic aid. We're going to get military assistance and they will react strongly if the North Vietnamese violate the cease-fire." Nha and Thieu argued over whether the Americans would really intervene again with troops and airpower. Nha pointed to the ugly mood in Congress and the prospect of congressional restrictions on bomb-ing. "It is one thing to say and another thing to do," explained Nha. "They have got no legal ground to come back." Thieu did not agree. After his talk with Nixon he said, "The United States will fly out of Thailand and really pound the Communists."[11]

Despite the private promises and the outward air of unity, there was the disturbing matter of the joint communiqué. "We had to fight every inch of the way on the joint communiqué," said Nha. John Holdridge of the National Security Council staff and H. R. Haldeman tried to get the South Vietnamese to concede the specifics of the economic assistance program. They argued that the President could not commit Congress in advance to economic aid. But the South Vietnamese were adamant and insisted that the language reflect President Nixon's promises. Finally, minutes before the deadline to release advance copies to the press, the Americans gave in.

When it was time for Thieu to go to Washington, Nixon accompanied him to the helicopter pad overlooking the ocean. "Nixon's mind seemed someplace else when we said goodbye," Thieu recalled. "As soon as my helicopter took off, Nixon turned his back on me and rushed into his office. I couldn't help but remember our meeting in Saigon in 1969, a month after our meeting at Midway. There were long and ceremonious farewells."[12]

Aboard his plane for the flight to Washington, Thieu was pleased with the visit; his mood was further brightened when chief of protocol Henry Cato served champagne and offered him a birthday cake.[13] Thieu was greeted in Washington by Vice President Agnew—Kissinger noted that "there was little about the visit of which we could be proud." Only one cabinet member, the Secretary of Labor, had been willing to join Agnew for the arrival ceremony, and most senior members of the administration had found an excuse to be out of town. "It was a shaming experience," con-cluded Kissinger.[14]

Thieu stayed at Blair House with his delegation. The embassy did give a lavish reception in his honor at the Washington Hilton, complete with a large ice sculpture shaped like a fountain with colored lights. Hung was briefed on the economic discussions in San Clemente by Finance Minister Ha Xuan Trung. Thieu had brought a series of studies and economic models with him showing how South Vietnam would put its economy and governmental structure in order by economic planning, tax reforms, export incentives, and employment policies. By 1980, the projection was to reduce U.S. economic aid to a minimum level of $100 million a year. Hung was encouraged by the projections and wondered if the meetings in San Clemente had really broken new ground. He was eager to see Thieu and find out firsthand what really happened with Nixon.

In the receiving line at a reception for Thieu at the Vietnamese Embassy, the president greeted Hung warmly and said he would call him to arrange a meeting. Hung waited and waited but there was no phone call. On the last day of the visit Hung had still not heard from Thieu. At midnight he gave up, figuring the president must be too busy to see him since he was leaving in the morning.

The next morning Hung went jogging on the high-school track near his house in Arlington on 31st Street. At seven-thirty, after breakfast, he left the house to take his daughter to her babysitter. When he got to the car, he realized he had forgotten the keys and returned to the apartment for them. As he walked through the door, the phone rang. It was Thieu's military aide. "The President wants to see you at seven-forty-five at Blair House."

"I had only fifteen minutes to get to Blair House in heavy traffic. I left my daughter with the babysitter and rushed to Blair House just in time for the meeting," says Hung.

He was escorted to the second floor, where Thieu was seated in a French provincial chair in front of the fireplace sipping tea. He appeared calm and resigned. Hung had not been alone with Thieu since the battle to change the Paris Agreement had been lost. He was a field captain who had fought a small part of the campaign in Washington. Together they would assess the results on American intentions and the future of South Vietnam. It was an emotional moment for Hung. Thieu had still not approved the funds for the public relations effort in Washington. The Ministry of Information, the Foreign Ministry, and the Prime Minister's Office had all fought over who would control the new information office in Washington. As was his usual practice when faced with a difficult decision that might alienate the loser, Thieu took everything into consideration but postponed any action.

Thieu thanked Hung for his help in dealing with American officials and praised his memoranda explaining American attitudes. He asked Hung if he had read the communiqué and Hung nodded. Thieu shook his head with resignation, indicating he had hoped for more specific economic and military commitments. "It is the time for economic Vietnamization," he said.

"What is the future for us?" Hung asked.

"We are going to have a very difficult time but it is not hopeless." Hung was intrigued but did not press; he had expected Thieu to be in a desperate mood in private.

"What can you do to join hands with us?" Thieu asked.

"Mr. President, the Washington front is critical to us in the years ahead. I can see two situations: Either the Communists will force you into a coalition to implement the Paris Agreement, or they will find some excuse to attack again on the ground that you are violating the agreement; but this time there will be no American troops in Vietnam. In either case American public opinion is essential for continued American support, which is wavering. The American people are very sensitive to accusations against our government, especially in the case of political prisoners and the Tiger Cages.* We have never really dealt with those charges properly."

Thieu explained that the so-called Tiger Cages on Con Son Island were built by the French half a century ago and were only kept for hard-core criminals. "When you go to Vietnam," Thieu said "why don't you go there and see for yourself and compare what you see with the American anti-war movement's accusations? Con Son Island is not only for hard-core Viet Cong terrorists; it is the prison for hardened criminals with long term or life sentences. Except for those in isolation, the prisoners do manual work on the island and are allowed out of their cells during the day."

Hung said he would go when he had the chance, but the immediate problem was answering charges that they were jailing the political opposition.[15]

Thieu complained that the anti-war movement in America had confused Communist agents and Viet Cong saboteurs with political prisoners. "We just don't jail people because they oppose the government. You know we have emergency detention of suspected Viet Cong agents. We are at war. We cannot let terrorists run loose. They are prisoners of war."

Hung knew the problem; it had been the most difficult to discuss with students challenging him on the campuses. He had talked with Vietnamese government officials who acknowledged that under the Phoenix Program to destroy the Communist cadres in the villages, officials at the local level were overly zealous and many innocent people were killed or jailed.[16] The North Vietnamese raised the issue of political prisoners as part of their propaganda campaign to undermine Thieu. In December 1971 the magazine *Vietnam Courier,* published in Hanoi, asserted that there were more than 200,000 South Vietnamese patriots who were dying a slow death. After the Paris Accords were signed in 1973, the editor of the paper, Nguyen Khac Vien, alleged in an interview in Paris that there were 300,000 political

* The so-called Tiger Cages of Con Son Island, a former French penal colony, were built by the French in 1941 as punishment cells. They were still being used as isolation cells for Viet Cong hard-core prisoners and convicted criminals when they were visited in 1970 by Congressmen William Anderson and Augustus Hawkin, accompanied by staff aide Thomas Harkin and Don Luce of the World Council of Churches. Harkin, now the junior Democratic senator from Iowa, photographed the Tiger Cages. His pictures, published in the July 17, 1970, issue of *LIFE* magazine, were one of the lasting images of the war. It was alleged that the prisoners in the cells were shackled to a bar unable to move their legs and were paralyzed. In a detailed analysis of the Tiger Cages, Guenter Lewy writes: "As to the claimed paralysis, there is evidence to indicate that this condition was simulated by hard-core communist prisoners as part of a propaganda scheme." *America in Vietnam,* pp. 296–298.

prisoners in the South.[17] In Saigon Father Chan Tin, "a left-wing Catholic priest who operated somewhere in the hazy boundary zone between the overt dissident movement and the revolutionary underground," alleged that there were 202,000 political prisoners. Arnold R. Isaacs, a severe critic of the Thieu regime, noted that "though the figure of 200,000 prisoners was never verified by any meaningful investigations, it was nonetheless parroted by Amnesty International and other well meaning human rights and antiwar groups in the U.S. and Europe."[18]

Hung told Thieu that the North Vietnamese were incredibly clever in creating an issue that was such an anathema to American values of human rights and democratic liberties. For Hung and Thieu, the Viet Cong were not a political opposition party; they were an arm of the North Vietnamese Communists. In December 1960, when the North Vietnamese created the National Liberation Front in the South, they succeeded in making it appear to be a genuine indigenous southern movement. It included lawyers, doctors, and intellectuals who opposed President Diem, and later, Thieu. They naively believed they were part of a united popular non-Communist front, a Third Force; in fact, they were completely under Hanoi's domination. (When the North Vietnamese took over the South, the Provisional Revolutionary Government, successor to the NLF, was abandoned within six months.)

Hung told Thieu that although he understood that the NLF was controlled from Hanoi, the perception in America was that it was a legitimate political opposition group. Therefore when a Viet Cong was arrested, he became a political prisoner in the eyes of the world. To the Republic of Vietnam, which outlawed the Communist Party in its constitution, a Viet Cong was a criminal. For Hung, who had lived through the tactics of the Viet Minh in his boyhood in the North, it was the same scenario being replayed in the South. On the world stage, the political-prisoner issue was the North Vietnamese cutting edge to discredit Thieu as a repressive dictator.

The Tiger Cages were ingrained in the Vietnamese memory of colonialism. Con Son Island as a prison for Vietnamese revolutionaries fighting the French was the theme of a song Hung's mother had sung in 1945 when the Viet Minh took power. The verses spoke of prisoners being taken in chains to Con Son by ship. They gaze with longing at the birds flying overhead and dream of them heading for land and freedom. The prisoners ask the birds to bring the people the message of the revolution.

Hung realized that in the post-cease-fire period the North Vietnamese would vigorously exploit the political-prisoner issue. He outlined for Thieu his plans to answer these charges through an information office in Washington, but he needed funding to get started.

"Maybe you could do that from Saigon and help out with the economic reconstruction of the country," suggested Thieu.

Hung was caught unprepared and with mixed feelings. Returning to Saigon would mean he would have to leave his family in Washington and go back alone. At that moment Thieu's military aide entered to remind Thieu of his press breakfast and impending departure. "I have to go to Europe from Washington, but as soon as I return to Saigon I will call you back for consultations and we will discuss this further," he said.

When Hung returned to his car, parked illegally on Pennsylvania Avenue, he was pleasantly surprised to find that it had not been towed away or ticketed for a violation. He considered it a good omen of his meeting with Thieu. For the first time in months Hung felt relieved. Thieu's confidence fed his spirits. Instead of the desperation he had expected, Thieu conveyed a calm strength that inspired Hung. "If he is not desperate, why should I be?" thought Hung.

In the Blair House dining room over scrambled eggs and bacon, Thieu held a deep background meeting for Washington columnists, bureau chiefs, and diplomatic correspondents. The ground rules were no direct quotations attributable to President Thieu. The writers could describe Thieu's thinking. His message was clear: As long as North Vietnamese forces in Laos and Cambodia continued to violate the cease-fire and refused to withdraw, the United States should continue to bomb them. Dressed in a light gray suit with white shirt and striped silk tie, Thieu was formal yet calm. He said his own army was "strong enough to contain the remaining Communist forces within South Vietnam. If the United States prevents new supplies from coming from North Vietnam into the South, Saigon will take care of the rest." He would not ask for U.S. troops or airpower to stem a Communist offensive within South Vietnam, but he expected the United States "to continue bombing in Laos and Cambodia if North Vietnamese supplies continue to pour into Vietnam for an offensive." He could handle the situation within his own country, but could not counter the Communist build-up in Laos and Cambodia without American airpower. Thieu was careful not to commit President Nixon to any action. In answer to questions, he stressed that he and Nixon had not reached any understanding on what circumstances would be required for the United States to bomb again in either South or North Vietnam.

Thieu placed his emphasis on American economic support. From the level of more than $1 billion in 1975, aid would be gradually reduced to $100 million in 1980. He spoke optimistically of his plans for economic self-sufficiency and reducing economic aid completely after 1980. When the conversation turned to the specifics of long-term economic development, beyond normal budgetary support, however, Thieu seemed vague. It became apparent that he had not received any firm commitments from Nixon or the World Bank.

The impression Thieu tried to create for the newsmen was that South Vietnam was stronger than the Communists and that the Communists were stalling in the talks between the two sides in Paris. Thieu said he would like to hold elections in South Vietnam within two or three months, but the Communists refused to discuss the details in Paris. With continued American economic support, Thieu indicated he would not have to share power with the Communists. The North Vietnamese were consolidating their positions in Laos and Cambodia now that American forces had departed from South Vietnam.

It was an effective performance. Thieu gave no ground. He was not considering sharing power with the Provisional Revolutionary Government of the Viet Cong or beginning a political process to broaden the base of his government. Asked about the role of the Soviet Union and China, he left that to the United States. "Kissinger said he had an understanding," Thieu replied when pressed. His own understanding from Kissinger was that China and the Soviet Union would not encourage the North Vietnamese to pursue their objectives in the South and would not provide them with weapons. "We have no carrots and we have no sticks," Thieu explained. "The United States has some leverage on the Russians and the Chinese, some carrots and some sticks." He took an uncompromising view of the North Vietnamese as the most doctrinaire Communists in the world, "more Russian than the Russians, more Chinese than the Chinese, and more Communist than the Communists." It was up to the United States to enforce the Paris Accords with its power and influence. The United States must force the Communists to respect the agreement. "Only you have leverage. If we send troops there, the whole agreement will be broken," he stressed. His survival depended on continued American economic aid and U.S. bombing in Laos and Cambodia to protect his borders against infiltration.[19]

What Thieu didn't tell the press was that at Nixon's request he had agreed to keep secret the American contingency plan for updating the targeting of North Vietnamese supply bases by the U.S. Seventh Air Force at Nakorn Panom in Thailand. General John Vogt, commander of the Seventh Air Force, received permission from the Joint Chiefs of Staff to visit the Vietnamese corps commanders and, as he reported, "some of the things I saw I didn't like." Vogt found that the Ho Chi Minh Trail "was being used in an ever-increasing rate. . . . After we had left and stopped our military activity in Laos and all bombing on the Ho Chi Minh Trail, they were jamming the trail with vehicle convoys numbering three hundred vehicles or more. I sent all these reconnaissance photos back with urgent messages of concern and, of course, received no answers, because at this point everybody in Washington didn't want to have to face up to the possibility of resuming bombing again."

General Vogt reported the violations through channels, "and the next thing you know I was told by our American ambassador I was no longer permitted to visit the corps commanders." Vogt says that in the summer of 1973, Graham Martin told him, "I don't think the presence of a four-star general, who has been leading the bombing campaign, is conducive to the proper settlement of the postwar situation in Vietnam and that, henceforth, you will not be permitted back in the country except with my express permission." Vogt continued to fly the Vietnamese generals to his Thailand headquarters to update the targeting details and "to reassure them that I was still there, and that our plans were current for the resumption of the bombing if and when it was necessary."[20]

Thieu was beginning to realize that his support in America was fading as a result of war weariness and the preoccupation with Watergate. Deep within, however, Thieu still felt that no matter how public opinion lined up against Nixon, the American President could find a way to make the system bend to his will.

Thieu always felt—as he told Hung privately—that he expected Nixon to come through and keep his promises. The record of five presidents had been for America to keep its word. Even after the October 15, 1969, Vietnam Moratorium, when more than half a million people gathered to protest the war, Nixon had gone ahead with the invasion of Cambodia in April and May 1970. In spite of the Cooper–Church amendment in January 1971, which prohibited the use of funds for "the introduction of U.S. ground combat troops into Cambodia, or to provide American advisors," Nixon authorized American air cover for the Lam Son operation against North Vietnamese supply centers in Laos. At the risk of his summit with Brezhnev, Nixon had mined Haiphong and prevailed. The Christmas bombing of North Vietnam had aroused strong press opposition throughout the world, yet Nixon had persisted until the North Vietnamese agreed to return to Paris and negotiate. The Vietnamese perception was that the President, as commander-in-chief, could still take decisive military action, despite congressional and public opposition, if the situation warranted the use of American airpower and troops. In private, Thieu had faith in Nixon, as did the members of his cabinet and general staff.

Thieu's perception was not the reality in Washington, however. With the American POWs home, Vietnam was dropping fast on the list of foreign policy priorities. The nation wanted to leave the nightmare of the war behind and have Vietnam fade away. Deputy Assistant Secretary of State William Sullivan summed up the administration's view when he said, only partially in jest, "Our hope is that Indochina will return to the obscurity that it so richly deserves."

In the evening, after Thieu departed, Hung celebrated with his family at the same Chinese restaurant where Kissinger had Peking duck before his trip to China.

San Clemente was a way station for Thieu in his fall from the center of American attention. Kissinger was preoccupied with his "Year of Europe" and new moves for peace in the Middle East. In the second term Kissinger was determined to restore the equilibrium of the great powers which had been disturbed by Vietnam.[21] In an interview with Marvin Kalb on CBS on February 1, 1973, Kissinger explained the Nixon administration's strategy for the second term:

Now, what this administration has attempted to do is not so much to play a complicated nineteenth century game of balance of power, but to try to eliminate those hostilities that were vestiges of a particular perception at the end of the war and to deal with the root fact of the contemporary situation—that we and the Soviet Union, and we and the Chinese, are ideological adversaries, but we are bound together by one basic fact: that none of us can survive a nuclear war and therefore it is in our mutual interest to try to reduce those hostilities that are bureaucratic vestiges or that simply are not rooted in overwhelming national concerns.[22]

On the way home, Thieu stopped in Rome to see the Pope, who advised him in a private audience to try to reach a reconciliation with the Provisional Revolutionary Government. Thieu was taken aback; he had expected Pope John to criticize the Communists because of the persecution of the Church in the North. Pope John's predecessor, Pope Paul VI, had told Nixon that the Communists murdered Christians and suppressed religion after they took power in North Vietnam in 1954. In his memoirs, Nixon recalled that, "with emotion in his voice he [Pope Paul] agreed that America should continue to hold the line against the Communists in South Vietnam."[23]

The new Pope, John, was more liberal and less sympathetic to South Vietnam. He urged Thieu to try to accommodate to the Viet Cong, referring to the fighting in the South as a civil war, and stressed the importance of meeting with the Provisional Revolutionary Government, whose foreign minister, Mrs. Nguyen Thi Binh, had also visited with the Pope as part of her campaign to win support. Now it seemed to Thieu that even his Church was turning against him and had fallen under the influence of the Communist propaganda campaign.[24]

11

Coming Home

THIEU RETURNED to Saigon for a hero's welcome at Tan Son Nhut Airport at the end of April 1973, after stops in Europe and Taiwan to gather support. In the middle of May, Hung received a call from the embassy inviting him to return to Saigon for consultations with the president. As soon as school ended, Hung flew to Saigon for the first time on a first-class ticket. He stopped in Paris to see his eldest brother, Father Joseph Phong, a scholar at the French National Research Center. Phong was the head of family since the death of Hung's father in 1954. In the Vietnamese tradition he had to be consulted on major decisions such as education, marriage, career choices, and financial matters.[1]

Phong took Hung to an early morning church service for inspiration. Hung knelt for an hour before the altar of a small Catholic church in the Paris suburb of Ivry-sur-Seine while his brother conducted mass in Latin. Hung told his brother of his conflict in returning to Saigon. His American wife and two children had to remain in Washington because his daughter Christine had asthma which required advanced medical care. His children suffered from allergies and his wife Catherine was concerned that Saigon did not have the facilities to handle their problems. Phong told Hung that even if he had to make a personal sacrifice, he should go to work for the government in Saigon.

Hung looked up to his older brother. In September 1945, as a seminary student, Phong had made the speech on behalf of Catholics supporting the revolution at the National Cathedral in Hanoi. Ho Chi Minh and his cabinet came to the church to celebrate independence from France and listened to Phong's impassioned praise for the "righteousness of independence and what it means to the Catholic Church." Looking directly at Ho, he said: "We Catholics join the whole population in supporting the nationalist struggle against colonialism which is being vigorously pursued." Within a few months the Communists had turned against the Church and dissolved the seminary where he was studying. Father Phong fled to the countryside and did not come back until 1949, when the French retook Hanoi. In 1952 he went to France to study for his doctorate and never returned to Vietnam.

They reminisced about another brother, Nguyen Huu Chinh, an early supporter of the Viet Minh. After the August 1945 revolution Chinh, president of the student body of a prominent Catholic school, led the students in a demonstration in front of the provincial archdiocese in Thanh Hoa, demanding the Belgian archbishop and French priests "return the Vietnamese church to the Vietnamese." He was expelled from the school to the great disappointment of their father. In 1946 the Communists began to confiscate church lands, carry out "land reform" and arrest nationalist leaders. The veil of Nationalist unity against the French was torn away and Communist discipline took hold. In 1949, Chinh fled from Thanh Hoa Province in North Vietnam with his cousin Tran Kim Tuyen in a sampan. They were trying to reach Hanoi, which the French had reoccupied, when their boat was swamped by a typhoon. They succeeded in swimming to shore, only to see a Viet Minh patrol in the distance. The two men dug frantically in the sand and managed to cover themselves, with only their nostrils above the sand to breathe. The patrol passed without noticing them. With help from Hung's family they bought another boat and rowed to the South China Sea where a French ship took them to Hanoi. Tuyen, a tiny man, with intense eyes and great ability, became the head of Ngo Dinh Diem's secret intelligence organization.[2]

Chinh, a teacher of French literature, moved to Hue and then to Saigon in 1952. When Diem took power, he was appointed Deputy Minister of Education. He served until 1963 when Diem was overthrown. Then Chinh fled to Paris and, with Hung's financial support of $100 a month, he received a Ph.D. in political science at the Sorbonne in 1971. He returned to Saigon in 1972 when Thieu reappointed him Deputy Minister of Education.

Back in the ministry, Chinh complained to an old friend that corruption had spread to the education system. Admissions to public *lycées* and colleges were subject to bribes, as were scholarships to study abroad. Not only did students obtain much-coveted foreign degrees but they avoided the draft and the battlefield. Chinh tried to break the bribery pattern by setting up a system to examine all the applications for study abroad in one committee that would meet once a month. All the applications were to be sealed and opened before the committee. Awards would be on the basis of merit, not family ties or pay-offs. The new reformed system worked well for three months. One day, the ministry's secretary general was absent and Chinh went to his office for a document he needed. Chinh could not find what he was looking for; instead, he noticed a thick folder jammed with nearly one hundred applications to study abroad, all approved directly by the secretary general. None had ever been brought to the committee and it was clear the secretary general was conducting a lucrative business in awarding permissions to study overseas. Chinh brought the file to the minister and demanded that he fire the secretary general for taking bribes. The minister smiled and said: "When you have a seat on the couch, lift up your feet, fold your legs under you, and don't look down. Let the rats run underneath you." Chinh was devastated. Chinh died when he suffered a severe attack of the flu in the fall of 1972.

Saigon seemed less frenzied when Hung arrived in May 1973. The airport was calm; there were no planes taking off and landing to carry on the war as on his previous trips. There were no artillery flashes in the night sky. The mood was one of relief and resignation—relief that the cease-fire had taken hold, resignation to the rumors that the Viet Cong were going to establish their headquarters at Tan Son Nhut. The newspapers carried pictures of the Viet Cong setting up their offices at the airport and reported that they had begun to drive around the city unchallenged. This was the first time that the people of Saigon had actually seen the Viet Cong since the Tet Offensive in 1968. Then the Viet Cong came out into the open with their AK-47 automatic rifles, shooting wildy in the streets, burning houses, and trying to rally the people against the Thieu government. Despite their attack on the American Embassy that made headlines in 1968, they had failed. The general uprising the Communists called for never developed. The people of Saigon, especially the native southerners who had never experienced Communist rule, were shocked by the Tet Offensive. They rapidly developed a fear of the Viet Cong and remained loyal to the Thieu government. The Viet Cong presence again in the midst of the city made Hung's mother ask him if the Viet Cong had come to take over the city now that the Americans had left.

To celebrate Hung's return home, his mother made a family feast. She cooked the plumpest of the six chickens she was feeding, after carefully boiling the chicken's blood for Hung and serving it to him on a small plate. The blood, boiled with Chinese herbs and ginseng root, was to provide strength. She also produced two bottles of Haig and Haig pinch bottle whiskey which she had saved, a gift from an American who rented rooms in their house. "We are not going to have this any more," she said, "now that the Americans are gone." The Vietnamese mistress of the American came to visit his mother often to ask if he would return.

Hung's mother talked of the family history and her regrets at not being able to leave her children more money, but their father had died in Saigon and everything he owned, including the family's hundreds of acres of land, remained in North Vietnam. They discussed the possibility of Hung's permanent return to Saigon. She suggested it might be safer to make periodic trips to consult in Saigon rather than to accept a permanent government position. Everyone in Saigon lived with the fear of random Communist rocket attacks at night. There was no control over the situation. The absence of American troops on the streets and in the bars made the city seem as it was in 1954 when Hung had first come to Saigon from Hanoi. Calm and dignity had returned, but the fear remained.

The day after his return, Hung sent Thieu a note, but received no reply from his office for three weeks. While he was waiting, Hung spent most of his time with Nguyen Van Ngan, Thieu's special assistant for political affairs. A former Viet Minh cadre, Ngan was an intense and shrewd political operator in charge of liaison with the National Assembly. He was the prime mover in organizing the Democracy Party, which Thieu established with American support to counter the Communists' ideological message. In Ngan's office, he and Hung compared the Democracy Party to Ngo Diem's *Can Lao Nhan Vi Dang,* Personalist Labor Party, and its philosophy of Personalism. They agreed the message was too esoteric and never had a broad appeal. Thieu was trying to develop a political ideology that would take root in the South and have more appeal than the Viet Cong promise to take land and wealth from the rich and give it to the poor. The Democracy Party was a means for Thieu to administer power and to mobilize the people to fight the Communists on a political level, but it never developed a widespread party organization with broad popular support. In the face of North Vietnamese political subversion, the Democracy Party never reached the masses. Instead, it remained a symbol and became the conduit for patronage and political pay-offs. Money was contributed on the expectation of favors, the most lucrative of which were import licenses, financed by precious foreign exchange. Jobs such as province chief, district chief, manager of a public enterprise, director of customs, and police chief of the fifth district in Cholon, where the rich Chinese merchants lived, could be arranged through the Prime Minister's Office or the Democracy Party.

Later, Hung often overheard conversations between Thieu and Ngan on how to deal with corruption in the provinces. Ngan told Hung about his talks with Thieu, in which the president instructed his deputy to fire district and province chiefs. Thieu had given Ngan power to take draconian action to eliminate corruption. Ngan did fire some district chiefs and what Vietnamese called the "small fish." The most basic of abuses continued to worsen because the armed forces and civil servants were so poorly paid. They had to supplement their income to survive. Second Lieutenants in the army received only $1.00 a day while major generals got $2.00. The military increased their pay with deals and private enterprise: real estate, hotel ventures, restaurants and bars for generals' wives; trade in fish and vegetables for the private's wife. The stealing and sale of government supplies and gasoline was common practice. One of the most pernicious acts of corruption was the system of "flower soldiers" and "ghost soldiers." Flower soldiers paid their superiors so they did not have to be present for duty or serve in action against the enemy; ghost soldiers remained on the payroll after they were killed in action or transferred—their senior officers pocketing the pay.

These were heady days as Hung learned the Palace routine. He watched Ngan's efforts to build the Democracy Party, *Dang Dan Chu,* and was impressed with Ngan's efforts to eliminate corruption. Ngan tried to persuade Hung to join the party, saying, "We need highly motivated, new people to run this country." Together they would persuade the president to change the leadership. They faced new conditions after the cease-fire, with a drastically reduced American presence. No longer could they rely on the Americans to plan and provide.

At the same time Hoang Duc Nha was pressing Thieu to remove Prime

Minister Khiem and General Vien, chairman of the Joint General Staff, because they were ineffectual. But Thieu was reluctant to act. Khiem and Vien were both loyal, and firing them would undercut his own power base. Nha complained bitterly to Thieu that the government was seized by a "neo-mandarin mentality" that prevented initiative and action.

Tran Van Khiem was a sullen, bespectacled Southerner of medium height who looked and acted more like a mid-level business executive than a five star general, the rank he still held as Prime Minister. Khiem remained in the background, avoided controversy and direct responsibility. He defered to Thieu while providing him with the necessary political support. In return Khiem was handed big blocks of patronage to dispense and his ambitious wife's business ventures prospered.

Cao Van Vien was also a southerner and a serious Buddhist. He had the lean strong features of a paratrooper who had distinguished himself in battle. Vien never acquired the administrative and managerial skills to transform the Joint General Staff into a coherent organization to replace the American Military Assistance Command. As conditions worsened he shunned responsibility and often went off to meditate on top of a tower in his backyard.

Nha urged Thieu to clean house: "We either have to dynamite the whole bloody house, or we have to replace the bad bricks one by one, painstakingly. Let's dynamite the whole house and rebuild it. Unless we do that now, it will never get rebuilt in time."[3] Thieu listened carefully to Nha but did not act.

Ngan believed the Democracy Party would play a key role in building a new generation of officials. As he explained to Hung, "The South needs a political organization strong enough to face the Communists in the North. American democracy is a vague term nobody understands, so let's make a Democracy Party that can propagate appeals for democratic institutions in a popular way that people can understand."

Hung was enthusiastic and said: "Let's confucianize democracy. Let's tell the people they have power. There is a saying in the village that customs are important, *phep vua thua le lang,* the power of the emperor stops at the village gate. By emphasizing the importance of local rule and participation, we can build democracy. The southerners who never had really bitter experiences under Viet Minh occupation do not see the same threat as we do, who experienced their rule in the North." "You are a professor and a good theoretician. You should join us," Ngan urged Hung. Hung protested that he was a technocrat, not a politician, but after several meetings Ngan began to convince him.

Now that he had returned to Saigon to work for Thieu, he would need to be part of the political apparatus and have a power base, Hung figured. He decided to join. He would relate American democracy to the Vietnamese experience. After so many years in America he understood how democracy worked; now he had to combine it with Vietnamese tradition. Hung told Ngan of his first experience in politics as a student in 1955. Hung's older

brother Chinh was working for Diem. In 1955 a referendum was held between Diem and Bao Dai, the former emperor who held the title of chief of
state. Hung was sent to villages north of Saigon to organize Catholic refugees from the North to vote for Diem. The first task was to convince the
villagers to participate in the election. To attract them, Hung borrowed two
documentary films on American agriculture and American life from the U.S.
Information Service. Then he borrowed his sister's gift money from Tet, the
new lunar New Year holiday, and rented a small generator. The village,
thirty-five-miles north of Saigon, had never had sound movies before and
there was no electric light. Hung's generator lit up three big floodlights and
his portable loudspeaker was a sensation. People gathered round as he
promised them entertainment, then told them, "By the way, before I show
the movie, let me tell you that a tremendous thing is going to happen in this
village. We are going to elect the President, *tong thong,* to replace Emperor
Bao Dai."* The peasants were startled at his message. An old woman said
very respectfully to Hung, who was then only twenty years old, "Sir, what
does President mean?"

To the villagers, Bao Dai was still emperor. When Hung told them that
tong thong, President, was a new title for the person to govern Vietnam,
similar to Emperor Bao Dai, they were shocked. The old woman looked at
Hung in amazement and said: "What, me choose the Emperor? If you look
at the Emperor, your head will be chopped off!"

"I spent the rest of my time trying to explain to the people that we
came from North Vietnam to escape the Communists and we were in a new
era of liberty and freedom," said Hung. "Now under Ngo Dinh Diem we
had the right to select the new person to govern called the President. In a
simple way I explained the difference between the new days and the old
days. In the old days we wrongly believed that the power of the Emperor
came from Heaven. The Emperor had a *thien menh,* or Mandate from
Heaven, which was the basis for his rule. In the new days the power comes
from each of us. Therefore, we can select the king." The old lady shook her
head and fled. The rest of the crowd of more than five hundred people stayed
to watch the movies. "It was my first practical lesson in democracy and I
worried that nobody understood what I was talking about. The concept was
new to me, too. I read Jean-Jacques Rousseau's *Social Contract,* but I could
not use such words in the village. 'What we are going to choose,' I told the
villagers, 'is whether we will return to North Vietnam or stay here in the
South with a new life and a new liberty.'

"I am going to show the movie very soon. Before I do, please let me
know who wants to stay in the South and vote for Ngo Dinh Diem. Please
raise your hands with me." Hung had learned this technique as a boy in the
North. When the Communists held agitation and propaganda meetings, the
cadres would raise their hands to stimulate the crowd. Hung had lined up
the village church guardians and altar boys to raise their hands and shout

* At that time Bao Dai was no longer emperor but head of state, a title he took when the French
returned to Vietnam in 1949–50.

"Yes" when he raised his hand. A few followed his example and soon everybody joined in, saying they wanted to remain in the South and vote for Diem. Then he showed the movies. "The election between Diem and Bao Dai turned out to be an election between Diem and Ho Chi Minh," recalled Hung. For the villagers, Hung's appeals identified Diem with remaining in the South and with the bounty of America shown in the movies: Louisiana rice, Idaho potatoes, Kansas pigs and chickens, Texas cattle. Diem, whose ballot was colored red, the symbol of good luck, won by an overwhelming margin over Bao Dai, whose ballot was green, the color of misfortune.[4]

As he looked for ways to make democracy meaningful, Hung argued that the North Vietnamese Communists had a big advantage. They explained that Communism meant getting rid of the rich landlords and capitalists who exploited the poor. To take land from the rich and give it to the poor is easy for everybody to understand. Hung wondered how to make democracy attractive in the Vietnamese context. How could he suddenly explain that power comes from the bottom up, from the consent of the governed to the ruler on top? He thought of what in American democracy would be appealing to Vietnamese in terms of their own tradition. The idea of power coming from a social contract, as in Rousseau, was alien to Vietnam. Perhaps, Hung thought, the idea of everybody being equal under the law would have an appeal for Vietnamese. It would be compatible with Buddhist and Catholic teachings that all men are brothers.

They would have to change old ways and enforce a new one: nobody could violate the law. Traditionally in Vietnam, influence on the law could be purchased or exerted through privilege. One had only to mention the name of a superior for such influence to work. When one of Hung's nieces was stopped by a policeman for speeding, she mentioned his name and was released. One of Thieu's favorite stories, when he was alone having a Scotch with his inner cabinet, was about the beautiful woman who was stopped for speeding and said she was on her way to the Palace for lunch with the president. She never arrived. "You guys have all the fun while I only get the bad reputation," Thieu joked.

One Sunday afternoon after he had been named to the cabinet, Hung drove in a private car with his family to the countryside. With his security escort behind him, he came to a toll bridge. They were stopped to pay 50 piastres. Hung's escort came to the toll collector and asked him why he had stopped the car. "I am collecting tolls for the government," said the man. "This is the government," said the security guard, pointing to Hung. "That's him. That's him." The toll collector saluted and offered to let Hung pass; but Hung paid the toll. Only when they had returned home could Hung convince his guards that they had not lost face, that "everybody must pay tolls, everybody is equal under the law." The guards were impressed. A thousand years under Chinese dominion and eighty years under the French had accustomed Vietnamese to paying tribute and granting privilege, the mentality of oppression.

Democracy stressed the importance of rights, but Hung thought it more important to talk about the duties of citizens. The concept of duty to the family and to the ruler, of son to father and wife to husband, of father to children, is the keystone of Vietnamese values, which stem from the Confucian tradition.

Rights are an alien concept to Vietnamese. The Vietnamese were surprised when Americans were so moved by John Kennedy's inaugural speech: "Ask not what your country can do for you, but what you can do for your country." To Hung it meant, do not ask about your rights, but think of your duty to your country. That is the normal standard in Asian countries.

Ngan liked Hung's ideas and promised him a bright future in the party. There had been no time for political work and organization since the days of Ngo Dinh Diem, but now in the period of cease-fire a viable ideology had to be framed in the South to counter the Communists. Hung filled out the party forms in what seemed to him a serious and thoughtful procedure. Ngan said Thieu was busy and in a grim mood, but he would prevail on him to hold a ceremony admitting Hung to the Democracy Party.

Finally Ngan brought Hung to Thieu's office, where the flag of the Democracy Party, yellow with a red star, stood ready on his desk for the ceremony. Thieu apologized for not meeting Hung sooner. Hung thought it strange that even before his consultations with Thieu he was being signed up as a member of the president's political party. Clearly, he was not going to be hired merely as a technocrat. Ngan asked Hung to stand at attention and ended the pleasantries. "Mr. Chairman," said Ngan, "I would like to start the swearing-in ceremony."

Hung stood to attention in front of Thieu. Ngan, in a solemn voice, then said: "Mr. Chairman, I have the honor to present to you the candidacy of Comrade Nguyen Tien Hung for admission to our party." Thieu asked Hung if he would pledge his loyalty to the country and the party. Would he vow to fight against communism and read an oath of fealty to the Democracy Party? Hung assented. "I officially accept you into the party," said Thieu.

Right after the ceremony Hoang Duc Nha came into the office to report the latest news from Paris. Thieu looked grim on hearing the problems the Vietnamese ambassador was having with Kissinger. Saigon and Washington were still fighting over the terms of a Paris Communiqué that would supplement the January Accords. Military and political survival were Thieu's top priority; despite constant prodding from the Americans to reduce corruption, it was a secondary problem for Thieu.

Since the end of May it had become evident that there were difficulties in Paris with Kissinger. Nha now derisively called Kissinger "the Jewish Doctor," with anti-Semitic overtones portraying him as a stereotyped schemer. Hung had also met frequently with Nha, who was then Commissioner of Information. When he sat in Nha's office on the third floor of the Palace, he overheard conversations between Nha and the South Vietnamese ambassador in Paris discussing Kissinger's return to Paris to work out the implementation of the Paris Accords. Suspicion was in the air.

On June 5, Thieu called Hung to his office for a working session to discuss his role in the government. The difference from his earlier optimistic mood at Blair House was striking; he seemed worried and preoccupied. When Hung reviewed the plan for an information office in Washington, Thieu said, "We'll deal with the information office later. I need an economist. Since you are not familiar with the political scene in Saigon, it would be best if you started as my Special Assistant for Economic Reconstruction."

Thieu said he was aware of Hung's discussions with Ngan on the need to build a strong political appeal for the nation. Hung felt a strong sense of mission and told Thieu it would be a great honor for him to serve the country. But he asked for a few days to discuss the offer with his family before giving his final acceptance. His family in Saigon advised him not to return to Vietnam. His brother-in-law told him: "If you are in America, maybe when the time comes you can save us. If you are here, we might end up saving you." Hung struggled with his decision and arrived at two hypotheses: Either the country still had a chance to survive and he must do what he could to strengthen that chance, or the country had one or two years before the end and it would be his last chance to serve. In either case, it would be a rare opportunity to work close to the president and play a role in shaping policy.

In two days Hung returned to the Palace and told Thieu he would take the job with only one reservation, that he return to America first to work out the financial arrangements for his family. Thieu agreed and signed the decree appointing Hung a special assistant to the president.

Thieu invited Hung for tea that evening and told him he was impressed with his patriotism and his ideas to improve the economy. It was heady talk for a young economics professor. Hung was to be ranked as an ambassador for his trip to Washington and back to Vietnam. In Washington, Hung asked his family's consent to return to Vietnam. In his new job his salary would be the equivalent of $250 per month, which left him nothing extra to send them. The family would have to give up their five-bedroom house in Arlington and dig into their savings to supplement his wife's income from her job at the International Monetary Fund. She would move in with Hung's brother, Nguyen Huu Tri, and live in a single room with the children in a low-income apartment in Lee Gardens, Arlington. Hung was afraid to take their young daughter to Saigon because the humid climate would worsen her asthma. In Washington, frequent visits to Children's Hospital were part of the family routine. In 1972 Christine's condition had been so bad that Hung asked their doctor to try red ginseng treatment as a possible cure and it had a positive effect.*

If things went badly in Saigon, it would be easier for Hung to survive on his own, not burdened by the family. Hung, who had been granted tenure

---

* Dr. William A. Howard, chairman of the board of Children's Hospital, was fascinated with the results from the Korean root, which has strong medicinal properties; later he did research and wrote an article on the effects of red Korean ginseng in the treatment of asthma.

at Howard, persuaded his dean to grant him a leave of absence. He told the children that it was very important for their father to go to Saigon to help their people. The children—Christine, six, and Daniel, three—found his words difficult to understand, but Hung decided he must return to Saigon.

Leaving the family behind was painful, but becoming a special assistant to President Thieu had its rewards. The embassy in Washington welcomed him. No longer did he have to see a third secretary in the basement to apply for a passport extension. Ambassador Phuong hosted an elaborate farewell party for Hung at the elegant Vietnamese Embassy on R Street. A chauffered black Mercedes replaced his 1959 Volkswagen Beetle, whose rear fenders had rusted away. Hung made the rounds of the State Department, the Agency for International Development, and the Pentagon in his new role before returning to Saigon in mid-August.

He was given an office in the Gia Long Palace adjacent to the Independence Palace. His office had once been occupied by Ngo Dinh Nhu and Thieu, when the latter was chairman of the Military Council in 1965. Hung had a choice of offices and was advised by his friends to take a small one in the Independence Palace closer to Thieu. Hung, however, liked the style of the old French-built palace with its blackwood and lacquer furniture and its giant antique blue-and-white-porcelain vases, many with bullet hole scars from the attack on the Palace when Diem was overthrown. The teakwood desk, which used to belong to a French governor, was so heavy it took twelve soldiers to carry it.

Hung met with Thieu, who described his job as that of coordinating reconstruction aid and overall economic and financial policy. Hung would recommend policy options for Thieu. Hung explained the system of the American President's Council of Economic Advisors, and Thieu authorized him to work toward establishing such a council. Hung's first priority was to cope with the terrible unemployment problem created by the departure of the Americans; two million people, 30 percent of the labor force, were out of work. All the people working directly for Americans, or receiving money from the Americans, especially women and children, had lost their incomes. During the war the city of Saigon, with a normal population of 500,000, exploded to four million. Once they settled in, Saigon people refused to return to the countryside even when faced with unemployment. Hung saw a $100 bill for the first time in his life in 1971 on his first trip back to Saigon from the United States. On the streets of Saigon $100 bills were the favored means of money exchange; Americans used them to pay their mistresses and their rent. Half a million Americans were each spending $400 to $500 a year in the city for drinks, women, cleaning, meals, entertainment, tailoring, and haircuts. Then, suddenly, all the dollars vanished. As an economist, Hung could see the danger to the economy of the multiplier effect as dollars disappeared. Every American dollar lost in expenditures meant several dollars lost in income to the local population.

Agricultural schemes, to absorb the unemployed without heavy spending of capital, were started to generate jobs and reduce Saigon's transient population. "Land to the tiller" was the slogan. The emphasis was on reconstructing agriculture to make the country self-sufficient without great expenditures of capital. However, as soon as a plan was put into action, the Communists started to mine the roads vital to the rice-distribution system and created disturbances in the areas where rice production was highest. To prevent rice from reaching Saigon, they mined roads and carried out sniper attacks on truck drivers. Their aim was to isolate the Saigon market. Prices soared because of a shortage of rice in the autumn of 1973. In the decent interval most of the government's time was spent trying to supply rice to the soldiers and the urban population.

Hung got his first taste of how the bureaucracy worked when he appointed to his staff Cung Tien, a high-school classmate who had studied economics in Australia and England. Cung was also a composer of note, and had translated foreign novels into Vietnamese. He was rejected by the Presidential Security Office on the grounds that he had "Communist leanings and was a Communist sympathizer." Hung appealed directly to Thieu, who overruled the Security Office. Hung investigated further and found that his friend had been rejected because he had translated Alexander Solzhenitsyn's *A Day in the Life of Ivan Denisovich* from English into Vietnamese. This story of a prisoner in a Soviet labor camp is a moving testimonial to the power of the human spirit against communism, but the Security Office was only concerned about a book in Russian by an author who still lived in the Soviet Union. (Solzhenitsyn was deported from the Soviet Union in 1974.) The head of Palace Security, General Dang Van Quang, was to remember his defeat by Hung and thereafter often attempted to discredit Hung in front of Thieu by calling him "the American professor," with the emphasis on American, implying that Hung was on the CIA payroll. It was ironic because Thieu knew that Quang was the prime informant in the Independence Palace for the CIA.[5]

Hung began to take part in the Palace staff meetings. He soon realized that economic problems, while pressing, had a lower priority than military violations of the cease-fire by the North Vietnamese. A great deal of effort was expended trying to involve Kissinger in making changes in the Paris Agreement.

Hung met with Nha and Ngan to send memos directly to Thieu with three different priorities: very urgent, urgent, and nonurgent. If it was very urgent, Thieu would deal with it within twenty-four hours; if it was urgent, within three to four days; and if it was not urgent, within two weeks.

Every Wednesday there was a cabinet meeting with the prime minister in charge that lasted for the whole day. During the two years that Hung attended cabinet meetings, not a single one was devoted entirely to discussing defense strategy even though Khiem was concurrently Minister of Defense. It was a strange atmosphere. The ministers spent their time discussing administrative matters of the paper and cement companies, where to build a Hyatt and Hilton hotel, or how to improve tourism. There was no sense of urgency and no effort to develop a national strategy for survival. The prime minister and the chairman of the Joint General Staff had grown accustomed to letting the Americans plan and execute for them and they were loathe to take the initiative because they thrived on inaction.

Thieu often spoke privately of replacing them but he found it difficult to make the move. Thieu feared that he would lose his power base in the South and he was loyal to those he felt would not betray him.

Prime Minister Khiem always wore a dark blue suit with a blue shirt and red tie because his wife's favorite astrologer said it was a lucky combination for him. In the Palace it was a joke that Khiem had even painted his official Mercedes blue for good luck. Khiem was smooth, but was criticized by many in and out of government for giving his wife too much power. He was in charge of the cabinet and kept a low public profile, working carefully and discreetly behind the scenes. He was favored by the Americans because of his willingness to accept American suggestions. A favorite Khiem command was: "Check it with the Americans." Thieu found it difficult to fire Khiem because he was a loyal senior general, a southerner, and a Buddhist, all of which balanced well with Thieu, who was Catholic and from Central Vietnam. But at one point Thieu was so exasperated with Khiem he pleaded with General Tran Van Don: "Please go and see Khiem and ask him to work a little harder."[6]

Khiem's powers in dispensing personnel appointments conflicted with those of Ngan and the Democracy Party. By the end of 1974, Thieu fired Ngan. There were rumors that he was planning a coup and had started to move against "the big fish," the dishonest businessmen, black market dealers, and generals who permitted their wives to take bribes. Thieu knew their corruption was undermining morale, but he felt trapped into keeping them, choosing loyalty over integrity. Thieu also asked his cousin Nha to resign. Nha was under heavy pressure from Khiem, and the other neo-mandarins he had so long criticized. They saw Nha as a flashy upstart trying to snatch power and insisted that he step down from the cabinet. Reluctantly, Thieu gave in.

To expedite decision making, Thieu activated the Council of Ministers' meeting, which he presided over every two weeks. Hung briefed Thieu on economic policies and prepared the agenda for the meeting. The most pressing problem was how to maintain one million men under arms at a time when income was contracting in the economy and foreign aid declining drastically. The country was faced with a terrible dilemma: The army needed a large number of soldiers which the economy could no longer support. South Vietnam had to increase production quickly to compensate for the loss of American external resources, funds, and supplies no longer brought in by American troops. At the same time the "leopard spots" inhabited by North Vietnamese troops demanded an increase in armed forces. The North Vietnamese leopard spots exerted heavy pressures on the economic front because no area was secure enough to undertake economic reconstruction, especially in the Mekong Delta.

The Joint General Staff insisted on keeping the armed forces intact while the Economics, Finance, and Planning ministries tried to reduce the size of the armed forces as a way to increase production and reduce the drain on the budget. They argued that the "big tail" of the armed forces, the support troops, should be reduced. The American Army had a five-to-one ratio of support troops to fighting men. The South Vietnamese army should have even fewer support troops, they insisted. Thieu was caught in the middle. JGS Chief General Vien was critical of the economists, who he said were naive. If there are no fighting forces, there is no country, Vien argued. Hung's staff drew a huge production possibility curve on white paper the size of a double bed sheet, that showed the trade-offs between different combinations of defense and development spending. Hung demonstrated that it would make economic sense to reduce the size of the army. Thieu was being forced to choose between guns and rice. Within weeks the president quietly agreed to demobilize 100,000 troops without any public announcement.

Thieu asked his staff to study trade-offs between increasing production and maintaining security. Could the army be utilized to produce food? General Don was sent to Israel to study how armed *Kibbutzim* produced food. The concept was good, but it would be difficult to apply in Vietnam. Under the cease-fire terms, 300,000 North Vietnamese were spread over the country and, combined with the Viet Cong, were paralyzing the distribution system by conducting a "war in peace" policy to undermine the Thieu government.

The leopard spots were multiplying in size and numbers, soon to disrupt the activities of the entire government. The long-promised American response to the North Vietnamese violations of the cease-fire in the South was nowhere in sight. In fact, the Communist build-up in Laos and Cambodia continued unabated.

12

Fatal Concessions

THE PARIS ACCORDS was a charade; barely a month after it was signed in March and April 1973, North Vietnamese violations of the cease-fire multiplied, including the build-up of a surface-to-air missile complex south of the demilitarized zone. The North Vietnamese were playing for time to continue their infiltration of the South before the rainy season made the roads unusable. Personnel and war supplies were coming through Laos, Cambodia, and across the DMZ. The Defense Department estimated that by the fall of 1973, the North Vietnamese would be at least as strong in the South as they had been before the start of the 1972 offensive.

A series of notes was sent to Hanoi by Kissinger warning that if infiltration continued and led to military action by Hanoi, the consequences "would be most grave." The Washington Special Action Group (WSAG), an interagency policy-making group on the assistant secretary level, met in the Situation Room of the White House to study the problem. It recommended bombing of the trails in Laos after the third group of American POWs was released, and possible bombing of the DMZ to force adherence to the cease-fire. Kissinger sought to convince Nixon that bombing was necessary and that "the future of the Paris Agreement indeed depended on action now to enforce it."[1] Ambassador Tran Kim Phuong was invited to the Pentagon in March by General Haig, then Vice Chief of Staff of the Army, and told that the bombing would resume as soon as the order was given. "When will the order come?" asked Phuong. "Soon," replied Haig. But it never came.

Nixon had become obsessed and distracted by Watergate, writing in his memoirs, "I needed desperately to get my mind on other things. We were faced with the possibility of having to resume bombing in Laos as retaliation for the failure of the North Vietnamese to abide by the ceasefire provisions of the Paris peace agreement."[2] But he would not make a decision to resume the bombing. Watergate replaced Vietnam in the press, dominating the headlines and the President's news conferences. "The Watergate venom came from estrangement over Vietnam," believes General Alexander Haig.[3]

Nixon was almost totally preoccupied. As Kissinger noted, "it was a different Nixon. He approached the problems of the violations in a curiously desultory fashion. He drifted. He did not home in on the decision in the single-minded, almost possessed manner that was his hallmark. The rhetoric might be there, but accompanied this time with excuses for inaction. In retrospect, we know that by March, Watergate was boiling."[4]

During this period Kissinger sent NSC staffer Sven Kramer to Saigon to assess the degree of North Vietnamese violations and determine if the situation warranted resumed American intervention. In a meeting with Kramer, Hoang Duc Nha, who was still serving as an unofficial adviser to Thieu, asked him: "Really? You mean you are going to bring back the bombers?" "Yes," replied Kramer. Nha rushed to bring the news to Thieu and reassure him.[5]

The reality was different. On April 17, Kissinger suggested to the WSAG that it continue its planning and await a clear-cut provocation from Hanoi. "I did not see," recalled Kissinger, "how I could urge Nixon to put his diminishing prestige behind the new prolonged bombing campaign that the situation required and that his own hesitations made necessary. By the end of April our strategy for Vietnam was in tatters."[6]

The North Vietnamese continued their build-up before the rainy season made travel difficult. They replied to the American protests against their violations with the suggestion that it might be time for private talks in Paris. Thieu was told about the messages from Hanoi during his visit to San Clemente in early April, but only after he left did Kissinger reply to Le Duc Tho and agree to a Paris meeting. Another strong U.S. warning was coupled with a proposal for a meeting between Kissinger and Le Duc Tho in the first week of May. Thieu was not informed of the message to the North Vietnamese.

By mid-April, 35,000 fresh North Vietnamese troops had entered South Vietnam or nearby sanctuaries in Laos and Cambodia. The total increase in combat personnel and supplies was greater than before the 1972 Easter offensive. Nixon still did not act to renew the bombing. "We had decided to bomb. We had picked out targets on the Ho Chi Minh Trail and at Vinh. It was a turkey shoot. The roads were jammed with trucks carrying supplies into the South. Nixon did not want to bomb while the North Vietnamese still held American prisoners. He wanted to wait until the prisoners were out. We planned one month of bombing from the middle of April. Then we would meet with Le Duc Tho in May. We wanted to show our determination to uphold the Accords with a show of force the North Vietnamese would understand. We were deadly serious about enforcing the Agreement, but Watergate interfered. John Dean went to the prosecutor and that was the end of the plan to bomb. Nixon's influence had declined to the point where he could not act on the bombing," Kissinger recalled.[7] The North Vietnamese accepted a meeting in Paris for any day after May 15, and the 17th was agreed upon. Saigon was again not advised of Kissinger's plans.

Ever since the last U.S. troops departed from Saigon in March 1973, the attitude had strengthened in Washington that Saigon was on its own. The Vietnamese were beginning to sense that, too. General Ngo Quang Truong recalled waving farewell to General Fred Weyand, the last head of the U.S. Military Assistance Command, and realizing that "up to now we had been talking about American withdrawal in theory, now we were really on our own. No longer could we call in American air support for our operations."[8] The sense of uncertainty was accelerating.

The question constantly being asked in the Independence Palace and Saigon's political circles was, "What will be America's next move?" Kissinger's trip to Hanoi in February had made Thieu uneasy. Kissinger had gone to seek implementation of the Paris Accord, withdrawal of North Vietnamese forces from Laos and Cambodia, and to discuss American economic grant aid to "heal the wounds of war." The aid would be contingent on North Vietnam adhering to the Paris Accords and congressional approval. The idea of American economic aid to the North was acceptable to Thieu if North Vietnam did not attack the South.[9] Now Kissinger was returning to Paris. Whenever he traveled, Thieu sensed trouble. North Vietnamese troop movements and attacks on the seaport of Sa Huynh, near the DMZ, had been reported to the highest levels of the American government, yet there was no American response. Near the Cambodian border the North Vietnamese overran the district town of Hong Ngu in March. Both incidents were deliberately played down because Nixon did not have the political power to punish North Vietnam. The lull glossed over the potential danger of the new North Vietnamese buildup and came as a relief to the people of Saigon.

The Americans seemed to be adopting a wait-and-see policy. In the cafés there was a relaxation of tension. The curfew hour of midnight was only lightly enforced and the nightclubs reopened.

Sitting on the deck of the My Canh floating restaurant on the bank of the Saigon River after an exacting day in the Palace, Hung liked to relax. He ordered frog legs with garlic sauce and 33-brand beer. The river flowed by peacefully and the night sights and sounds no longer included artillery fire or tracer bullets searing the sky. The voices of Chinese and Vietnamese parties on the boat mingled with the sound of bells on food carts on the dock and the smells of broiled squid, jasmine flowers, and fresh-pressed sugar cane juice. The raucous sounds of peace blared from transistor radios: Vietnamese opera, and American pop hits translated into Vietnamese.

Radio Saigon interpreted the Paris Agreement to stress the independence of the Republic of Vietnam and the requirement that the North respect the DMZ. Mention of cease-fire violations always reported ARVN troops repelling the North Vietnamese. On the surface, all seemed well. The Voice of America still spoke of peace with honor in its daily broadcasts. There was no fighting in or around Saigon. The streets were quiet. No longer were American troops to be seen riding by in trucks and jeeps.

Only a day before Kissinger arrived in Paris, Ambassador Bunker informed President Thieu of the American plans to meet with the North Vietnamese and negotiate for the strict implementation of the Paris Accords. Thieu complained to Bunker that the American promises at San Clemente had not been kept—"You promised to retaliate, but now you tell me to renegotiate." Bunker said that the meeting was only to improve the implementation of the cease-fire. If this was the case, Thieu wondered why Kissinger's presence was necessary. Couldn't a lesser official like Deputy Assistant Secretary of State for East Asian and Pacific Affairs William Sullivan carry out the task? Whenever Kissinger was involved, South Vietnam had come out badly. Now it appeared he was going back to Le Duc Tho to make additional concessions. Thieu and Nha wondered if perhaps Kissinger had gotten the North Vietnamese to agree to sign in January with a promise that outstanding or unresolved matters could be renegotiated in the spring. How could America negotiate with North Vietnam without any military cards in its hand? For Thieu, the original Paris Agreement was bad enough; now he decided to resist further concessions as strongly as possible. He authorized a spokesman to say, "We are not going to yield one more inch." [10]

Kissinger was in Paris from May 17 to June 13, ostensibly to meet with Le Duc Tho and bring about a strict schedule of adherence to the cease-fire and end the fighting in South Vietnam and Cambodia. Actually, he was to preside over a final and fatal set of political and military concessions that would undermine the ability of South Vietnam to survive. At this point it also seemed as if Kissinger was most concerned with his own survival. Realizing that he had no arrows left to fire from the military quiver because of President Nixon's political vulnerability, Kissinger returned to Paris seeking a cease-fire in Cambodia and a papering over of the differences between Hanoi and Saigon.

Le Duc Tho, however, was an astute reader of the American press and knew that Nixon was not about to resume the war. He had only to read *The New York Times* or listen to Kissinger on American television to realize that the President was crippled. On April 8, James Reston wrote in his *Times* column that Nixon had no intention of resuming the war. "He merely wants to talk about it." In his press conference on March 15, Nixon used mild language when asked about cease-fire violations, saying they "could lead to serious consequences—we do not believe it will; we hope it will not." Then he added: "I would only suggest that based on my actions over the past four years, the North Vietnamese should not lightly disregard such expressions of concern when they are made with regard to a violation." The joint communiqué issued with Thieu at San Clemente had said: "Actions which would threaten the basis of the Agreement would call for appropriately vigorous reactions." Kissinger, in private, had promised Thieu at San Clemente that "if Hanoi's lack of good faith in the agreement could be demonstrated," there would be "massive and brutal" American retaliation. [11] In public Kissinger had backed away from any mention of the use of force and reinvolvement of American military power. There was no public mention of the secret commitment to Thieu to use "full force." Rather, in a lengthy interview on television with Marvin Kalb, when Kissinger was asked about the possibility of the United States having to use military power again, he replied: "Marvin, we did not end this war in order to look for an excuse to reenter it. But it would be irresponsible for us, at this moment, to give a precise checklist to potential aggressors as to what they can or cannot safely do." [12]

Kissinger's strategy of secret diplomacy, with its shifting and contradictory sets of promises to both sides, was about to unravel because it was no longer backed up by the use or credible threat of the use of force. In the context of American democracy Kissinger had overreached himself. With Nixon under heavy pressure from Watergate, the foreign policy establishment had turned to Kissinger and relied on him to separate American prestige and international commitments from the domestic turmoil. As long as he did not reenter the Vietnam War, he would have no restraints placed on him; but he was without power to enforce the peace.

In a conversation with Warren Nutter about Kissinger's strategy before he returned to Vietnam in May 1973, Hung was told that ultimately secret diplomacy does not work. Foreign policy, if it is to be credible, must be translated into American military or economic power to back up threats and promises. Agreements must be translated either into military aid or action or into economic aid or investment. The implementation of secret diplomacy must become public, and at that point, unless the Congress and public have been prepared and accept the policies, they will be rejected at great cost to the nation. It is necessary to build a base of public support for foreign policy actions, not merely to push them through and hope that they can be sustained by continued secret agreements.

American foreign policy is indeed a public policy because any secret or covert actions must eventually be approved in the open by Congress and the American voters. In background meetings with reporters, Kissinger spoke of the need to make agreements with the North Vietnamese self-enforcing. The offer of major American economic aid to North Vietnam was supposed to serve that function.

The failure of Kissinger's strategy was demonstrated in the final negotiations with Le Duc Tho in Paris in May and June 1973. Two sets of problems were involved. Kissinger believed that secret negotiations between himself and the North Vietnamese were the only way to end the war. When they faltered, Kissinger's strong ego led him to continue to negotiate in this style even though his chances for success were marginal.

Kissinger locked himself into the secret talks and had to end up with something tangible, no matter how slim or weak, especially when the negotiations were carried on for nearly four years at a heavy cost in the loss of men and materials and a mounting number of prisoners of war. He was trapped: either he must prove that secret negotiations worked and were the correct way, or he lost prestige and power. He had to produce an agreement or an accord, otherwise he would be held accountable for the cost involved. Kissinger could not afford to be wrong, even though he was playing with a hand now seriously weakened by Watergate and the strong public desire not to resume the war. When, within a year after the secret talks started, he found that it was impossible to get the North Vietnamese to move out of the South on the basis of mutual withdrawal, the most substantive and important issue in the negotiations was abandoned. The United States continued the secret talks without publicly admitting that it had conceded this point. Only when the time came to make the text of the agreement public was mutual withdrawal dropped and replaced with clauses allowing South Vietnam to interpret the presence of the North Vietnamese in the South as being illegal. Only after Kissinger had negotiated with the North Vietnamese on his own was Thieu told that the North would not accept mutual withdrawal.

Once again Kissinger was to meet with Le Duc Tho. The American strategy was to bomb for a month before the talks began but Watergate intervened and there was no U.S. response to the North Vietnamese cease-fire violations. As a result Kissinger was in an untenable position. "Going to Paris in May was a disaster which showed our weakness because it wasn't our strategy. Our strategy was to bomb for a month. We figured if Le Duc Tho comes after being bombed it is a sign of weakness. If he doesn't come we will continue bombing. We wanted to repeat the experience of January. Under those conditions a new agreement would have had some significance. Then, having proposed a meeting we couldn't cancel it on the ground that we didn't bomb, since he didn't know that was our strategy, So we were stuck with a meeting that we didn't want anymore."

Kissinger believes that had the U.S. bombed before the Paris meeting "we would have met a different Le Duc Tho then because either he would have cancelled the meeting and said, "I won't come until you stop.";' in which case we wouldn't have stopped, or he would have come, which would have already been a sign of weakness. Under those conditions getting new conditions would have been meaningful. But as it was I was there naked and he kept reading me documents about our weakness. On the other hand given our weak position at home I could not have the thing fail. This was our problem in May." [13] Kissinger had no room to manoeuver. Nixon was being held hostage to Watergate and was unable to act against the North Vietnamese violations of the ceasefire.

Hung recalled that when the news of Kissinger's trip to Paris was announced, he was bombarded with questions. " 'Why is the Doctor going to see Le Duc Tho again? What has happened to the Paris Agreement? What is Kissinger up to?' "

Kissinger needed a document to make it appear that all was well in Vietnam—and he was held hostage to Le Duc Tho's signature. All along Kissinger believed that there could be a basis for negotiating. He insisted that "even in Vietnam there must be some realities that transcend the parochial concerns of the contestants and that a point must be reached where a balance is so clearly established that if we can make generous and farseeing proposals . . . a solution may be possible." With the absence of Nixon's power, the balance was broken. Since he could not change Hanoi's behavior, Kissinger forced his ally, South Vietnam, to change its behavior. [14] South

Vietnam was not strong enough to force the North to change its behavior or to resist U.S. pressures.

Gradually the relationship between Washington and Saigon worsened. Thieu did not see negotiations as the way to end the war. He was prepared to continue fighting with American support or to maintain an armed truce and consolidate the economic and political structure of the South. He did not envision sharing power with the Provisional Revolutionary Government as long as the North Vietnamese troops remained in the South. Kissinger sought a process of accommodation and power sharing whereas Thieu sought to prevent that from taking place. Allan Goodman, in his perceptive study of American negotiating behavior, quotes a key Kissinger aide as saying, "What had to be created was a way of talking to the North Vietnamese where we could try out various formulations for an agreement without them having to risk losing face in front of their people or their allies. Henry was profoundly disappointed when the North Vietnamese appeared to be using the secret talks for many of the same advantages they sought in the Paris talks: to probe to discover how far the Americans would go in making concessions to the North Vietnamese position." [15]

By the time the Paris Agreement was signed, the Congress and public had lost faith in Nixon and Kissinger's ability to fulfill their promises in Vietnam. In January 1973 Nixon had been working to solve the Vietnam problem for four years and the results that he achieved were not seen as being any better than he could have gotten four years earlier. During those four years 20,000 American soldiers were killed in Vietnam and 13,000 wounded; more than 107,000 South Vietnamese soldiers were killed and 307,000 wounded.

Peace with honor was the Nixon–Kissinger goal, and the Paris Agreement was placed in that context by them. To maintain American and South Vietnamese honor demanded American use of force against North Vietnam to gain adherence to the agreement. In his memoirs, Kissinger notes: "All too soon, the leaders of North Vietnam showed that the ceasefire was merely a tactic, a way station toward their objective of taking the whole of Indochina by force. Before the ink was dry on the Paris Agreement they began to dishonor their solemn obligation: in truth they never gave up the war. . . . During March it . . . became apparent that the ceasefire was a barely disguised cover for moving men and weapons into position for another offensive." [16] This should not have come as a surprise to Kissinger after his arduous negotiations with Le Duc Tho and his understanding of Hanoi's goals, which he often reported privately to Nixon. Kissinger had the latest intelligence reports from the South Vietnamese and President Thieu's frequent warnings to President Nixon that the North Vietnamese would violate the agreement.

The final negotiations between Washington and Saigon proved even more difficult than those between Hanoi and Washington. This time the exchanges between Thieu and Nixon were more bitter than in January. There were no holds barred. The American prisoners had been returned and

Kissinger wanted to be done with Vietnam. There was no stomach for a prolonged set of negotiations or a renewal of the bombing. Kissinger and Nixon were determined to bring Thieu along. Kissinger's priority in Paris was to bring about a cease-fire in Cambodia.

The North Vietnamese strategy in Paris was to strengthen the position of the Viet Cong in the South, to move toward a coalition government, and to obtain access to the South through the demilitarized zone. The Communists had achieved the goal of placing their army in the South, but they still had to build an administration and establish a capital. The presence of North Vietnamese and Viet Cong troops in undemarcated areas of the South, the leopard spots on the map, worked to their advantage. Unlike 1954, when the Viet Minh had had to regroup in designated areas, the Communists this time had no restraints placed on them.

The meetings in Paris alternated between the North Vietnamese site, Léger's villa at Gif-sur-Yvette, and the home of an American businessman astride the golf course at St. Nom La Bretèche that had been lent to the American delegation. They were long and tedious because each point in the agreement and the protocols was discussed, along with violations and methods of achieving compliance.

The North Vietnamese pressed for a return of all political prisoners in the South and now brazenly demanded a guaranteed political role for the Provisional Revolutionary Government in the communiqué being negotiated with Kissinger.

On May 21, Nixon wrote to Thieu, sending Deputy Assistant Secretary of State William Sullivan to Saigon to deliver the letter personally and bring Thieu a copy of the new draft communiqué. Nixon told Thieu: "In our correspondence before the Paris Agreement, and when we met in San Clemente, I emphasized my determination to stand by your country and to see the agreement enforced. This is the effort in which we are now engaged."

Kissinger was in Paris, said Nixon, "in order to negotiate with the North Vietnamese an improved implementation of the ceasefire agreement." This time Nixon did not speak of the use of force against North Vietnam, but complained about the behavior of the Saigon delegation in Paris and warned Thieu not to back away from his commitment to the Paris Accords. The U.S. President gave no hint that he was wounded by Watergate when he wrote: "I need hardly emphasize the importance of this enterprise in the present climate of American public opinion. As you know, I have publicly pressed for the strict implementation of the agreement and have both American prestige and American willingness to engage itself behind me. It would never be understood in America if the negotiations failed as a result of avoidable obstacles."

He threatened Thieu openly on the need to sign the agreement if he wanted economic aid to continue:

> I want to reiterate that our only desire is to strengthen the agreement and to reaffirm our solidarity with you. I cannot believe that you will put me into the position of having to explain to the American people a reason for the break-

down of negotiations, which would lead to an immediate cut-off of funds for
Laos and Cambodia and ultimately for Vietnam.

When we talked together at San Clemente, I told you of the growing
difficulties in obtaining adequate aid levels from the Congress. Nevertheless, I
told you I would exert every effort to secure not only an aid level adequate for
your immediate needs, but also enough additional growth to give an added
momentum to the economic growth your just announced program should put in
motion. This effort to secure additional economic aid for Vietnam has been
going well. It has clearly been given first priority. But I must frankly caution
you that I can think of nothing that would so surely wreck this effort as to have
even the appearance of disagreement between us just at this moment in time. I
am certain you will keep this consideration very much in mind as you reflect
on the contents of this message.

Thieu, however, refused to accept or sign the new communiqué drafted
in Paris and aimed at clarifying and strengthening the implementation of the
January Accords. He replied to Nixon that a series of changes would be
needed before he would sign. Most onerous to Thieu was Kissinger's
concession to Le Duc Tho on the right of military movement across the
demilitarized zone. In Thieu's opinion, during the final January negotiations
after the Christmas bombing Hanoi made only one major concession: no
military movement across the DMZ. Now, only four months later, Kissinger
was back in Paris and ready to give it away. To Thieu, the DMZ was
sacrosanct because it provided the semblance of a frontier between North
and South Vietnam and established a boundary between the two countries,
thus debunking North Vietnam's claim that there was only one, not two
Vietnams.

After the initialing of the Paris Accords on January 24, 1973, Kissinger
had returned to Washington and held a press conference. In a statement, to
please Thieu, Kissinger declared that the provisions "make it clear that
military movement across the demilitarized zone is in all circumstances prohibited." Now the North Vietnamese insisted on moving military equipment
across the DMZ. Thieu laughed bitterly and asked his advisers: "How can the
tanks move across the DMZ without drivers and troops to maintain them?"

In the Independence Palace, Thieu and his key advisers smelled a secret deal between Kissinger and Le Duc Tho. (In fact, Kissinger had promised Le Duc Tho that American reconnaissance flights over North Vietnam
would be suspended and all American technicians withdrawn from South
Vietnam within a year if Hanoi accepted the January Paris Agreement.)[17]

The international telephones to Paris were located in only a few rooms
of the Palace and connections were so bad that shouting was often the only
means of communication. Everybody in nearby offices knew the delegation's instructions and the problems developing in the negotiations. Hung
could hear Nha hollering, as if that would somehow force his instructions to
be followed. There were no secrets on the French telephone system, which
was condemned as inferior to the American with curses by Nha, as he told
the Paris delegation head, Ambassador Pham Dang Lam, to "hold the line."

Thieu could not understand why Kissinger was giving in on the DMZ.

He told Hung that he felt it had to be part of a package deal that had been arranged in advance between Kissinger and Le Duc Tho. With American troops gone, there was a mood of suspicion and every American action was studied for ulterior motives. Kissinger's animosity toward the South Vietnamese and his own arrogance rankled Thieu and his key aides. The rumor spread that Kissinger, who had been concentrating his efforts on a Middle East settlement, was trying to cut aid to South Vietnam so that aid to Israel could be increased.

Thieu still did not believe that the Communists were likely to attack in strength during 1973. He told his cabinet in May that the Communists would have the best advantage if they waited until near the end of Nixon's term to launch their offensive. Thieu believed they would not move sooner for fear that President Nixon would intervene in the defense of South Vietnam.[18]

In his meeting with Thieu, William Sullivan sought to reassure him of the terms Kissinger had negotiated in the communiqué. A major point Sullivan argued was that establishment of the National Council of Reconciliation and Concord would be put off "into the indefinite future." The joint two-party military commission to supervise the cease-fire would be removed from populated areas. But Thieu was unimpressed and stuck to his reservations.

Nixon wrote to him again on May 30. This message was delivered by Deputy Chief of Mission Charles S. Whitehouse, the American chargé d'affaires. Nixon again asked Thieu to sign the communiqué. This time he told Thieu that he had instructed Kissinger to seek agreement to "a number of the proposals you have made," but that if the changes were not accepted by the North Vietnamese, Thieu should sign because the document was "helpful" to South Vietnam and "useful to both our governments." Nixon warned Thieu that unless he signed, there would be an aid cut-off. The letter said in part:

> However, given the circumstances of its [the communiqué's] negotiation, I believe it is the best we can obtain and that it contains nothing which could remotely occasion adverse effects for your Government. It will be enormously helpful to me to have the communique issued with the signature of your representative alongside that of Dr. Kissinger. We need an action of this kind if I am to be able to obtain from the Congress the sort of legislative cooperation which will be required to carry out the programs of peace and stability which you and I discussed in San Clemente.
>
> Consequently, I seek your assurance that you will accept the text of the communique as it emerges from our negotiations with the North Vietnamese and that you will designate a representative to meet with the other three parties in Paris June 7 in order to sign the document on June 8.
>
> Sincerely,
[s] Richard M. Nixon

It was sign-or-else. If Thieu did not sign, there would be no long-term economic aid program for Vietnam. Congress was to be Nixon's club over Thieu.

Still Thieu refused to sign. He wrote to Nixon on June 2 giving renewed objections and requesting a copy of the latest version of the draft agreement. Nixon replied on June 5 by cable, and the message was delivered by Chargé d'Affaires Charles Whitehouse. Once again Nixon tried to reassure Thieu that Kissinger would seek the changes he had requested:

Dear Mr. President:
Thank you very much for your letter of June 2 in which you express the concern of your Government about two elements of the draft communique which Dr. Kissinger and Le Duc Tho are negotiating in Paris. The first has to do with your desire to have a specific reference to the electoral process in the communique. The second has to do with the communist effort to give geographical substance to their political pretensions by describing their "territory" and locating their "capital."
With particular respect to your two elements of concern, you will note that we have included a sentence on elections, and we have made the territorial question much vaguer that in the previous draft. The mention of Loc Ninh was not eliminated, because your own representatives to the Two Party Joint Military Commission included it in the text of their press announcement on May 16. However, its mention has been subordinated in the text to the issue of the Two Party Joint Military Commission, and it has been separated from the mention of Hanoi in order to avoid any suggestion of parallelism as a capital city.
In view of these changes, I would appreciate receiving your assurance that a representative of your Government will join Dr. Kissinger on June 7 and 8 in Paris to sign the joint communique in the format which has been agreed between our two governments.

Sincerely,
[s] Richard M. Nixon

Thieu marked up Nixon's letter with a series of question marks and reviewed a draft of the communiqué. In the margin, he wrote: "too favorable to the Communists," and, "why repeating only whatever is favorable to the Communists with nothing for South Vietnam in exchange?" What the Communists had failed to gain in terms of the principles of the Paris Agreement they were seeking in the fine-print details of the communiqué. They could now cross the DMZ and station their troops along the dividing line of the zones separating North and South Vietnamese troops in the villages. Thieu objected to the status accorded the North Vietnamese in the communiqué, especially the fact that they would be permitted to come to Saigon to live. References to the election were vaguer in the new document. There was no provision for a cut-off of North Vietnamese infiltration into the South through Laos and Cambodia.

After reviewing the draft, which was supposed to be signed in Paris on June 8, Thieu wrote to Nixon on June 6, saying: "We are the victims of aggression. The Communist aggressors have systematically violated the Agreements. However, while they suffer no 'violent reactions' from our side, as they have been warned, they now want to enjoy unilaterally all the gains from the Communiqué.''

Both Nixon and Kissinger were infuriated by Thieu's demands and delaying tactics. Nixon's reply sent the same day, June 6, again stressed that there could be no further changes made in the communiqué.

Dear Mr. President:

I was astounded to receive your letter of June 6 which seems to suggest that you will refuse to instruct your representative in Paris to sign the joint communique which Dr. Kissinger has negotiated with Le Duc Tho. As I made clear to you in my letter of June 5, the text of the Communique is final and is not subject to further revisions.

It is therefore absolutely unrealistic to suggest, as you do in your letter, that a great number of paragraphs in the text be reopened and that further efforts be made to change the language. I would like to remind you that every change you have previously requested has been included in one form or another. Moreover, the suggestions which you have made do not reflect certain fundamental facts which have been explained to members of your staff.

Similarly, your expressed preference for Le Duc Tho's wording of the prohibition of introduction of military personnel and war material into South Vietnam ignores the fact that this wording makes no provision for the legitimate replacement of war material in accordance with Article 7 of the Agreement. Had we accepted it you would have been cut off from any U.S. military assistance.

I feel I must tell you, Mr. President, that we are now at a point where the text must be viewed as final. The decision you must make is to instruct your representatives in Paris to join with Dr. Kissinger in signing the Communique as it currently exists, despite the minor misgivings which you express, or else to refuse to sign, to scuttle the Agreement, and to face the inevitably disastrous consequences for Congressional support. Phrased in these stark terms, which are my honest appraisal of the situation, the choice seems obvious to me. We have been through too much together to have our whole common enterprise collapse in this way on these points. I count on your broad understanding of your own interests and of ours to give me your urgent positive answer no later than noon Saigon time on June 7.

Sincerely,
[s]Richard Nixon

Again Nixon was threatening the cut-off of aid by Congress, a prospect that was very real. But his letter had no effect on Thieu, who continued to resist signing the communiqué and replied once more with his objections. At the same time Nha briefed editors in Saigon of Thieu's objections to the Paris negotiations being carried out by Kissinger. On June 7, the same day he received Thieu's letter, Nixon replied, determined to proceed without Thieu.

Dear Mr. President:

Before I actually received your letter of June 7, before I could even consider a response to the points you raised in it, and while my negotiators in Paris were preparing for a session with the North Vietnamese, I was dismayed to learn that your Government had announced in Saigon that you would refuse to be a signatory to the document under discussion between Dr. Kissinger and Le Duc Tho.

On reading your letter, I was further troubled that you should accuse me of "undue haste" in these negotiations. The facts are that we consulted with you in April concerning our intentions. We briefed your representatives daily in Paris during our talks in May, we sent Ambassador Sullivan to Saigon to consult with you while the talks were in suspense, and we have been in almost daily correspondence with you since their resumption. All your views were taken into account and we have achieved the best consideration of them which was possible in the document which any objective observer will readily recognize as being favorable to your interests.

However, by your actions, you have left me no choice as to the manner in which we must now proceed. I have instructed Dr. Kissinger to propose to Le Duc Tho that the two of them should sign the text of the communique as it now stands and that we and the North Vietnamese should issue a public appeal to the two South Vietnamese parties to carry out its terms. If Le Duc Tho refuses to do this, we will of course end our Paris talks in failure, which will involve the issuance of the aborted document, the record of our negotiations, and the record of our consultations with you.

If Le Duc Tho agrees to our proposal (and I assume he will), this will mean that the entire world will look immediately to you to issue the ceasefire order and to take the other measures stipulated in the communique. It will mean that all your actions will be scrutinized, not as voluntary steps being taken because you wish peace, but rather as concessions which you appear to be making with reluctance. It is a totally unfavorable posture you have chosen for yourself and your government.

I regret also to inform you that your action has thwarted any realistic prospect we might have had for an agreement on Cambodia. The position you have chosen for yourself deprives the North Vietnamese of any possible motive to achieve an understanding with us on this key issue.

It is impossible for me to calculate the consequences which your action will have on public and Congressional opinion in the United States. These consequences will certainly be negative for you and it is quite likely that they will be disastrous. That fact is a cause of most serious regret to me and it saddens me to contemplate that the enterprise in which we have shared so much should seem doomed to collapse in this manner.

Please let me have your answer to this letter by 8:00 a.m. Paris time June 8, so that we can act in accordance with your decision.

Sincerely,
[s] Richard Nixon

On the cable he received from Chargé d'Affaires Whitehouse, Thieu underlined the sentence saying South Vietnam would not sign the communiqué and wrote: "Who? If necessary, we must make a correction. We should not let the news media destroy our position." (To put pressure on Kissinger, Nha had spread the word to Vietnamese newsmen that Thieu would not sign.) When Nixon threatened to make a public explanation if the

negotiations failed, Thieu noted in the margin that "we must prepare ourselves very carefully for this eventuality."

In his answer to Nixon on June 8, Thieu still held out, telling Nixon
that he favored a formula whereby the United States and North Vietnam
would approve the communiqué and call on the government of Vietnam and
the Provisional Revolutionary Government to carry out its provisions.
Nixon rushed back a reply telling Thieu he would have to sign because the
North Vietnamese rejected the two-party document. Nixon explained:

> If they [the negotiations] fail, there will be an inevitable confrontation between
> you and me in which I shall have to disavow your reasons for refusing to sign
> and in which I shall have to state publicly that you have blocked the achieve-
> ment of progress in the search for peace. In your letter you mention a public
> explanation of your position. You should keep in mind that it will be in the
> context of attacking a draft to which we have agreed. Unlike October, we will
> oppose and not back your position.
>
> You should keep in mind that Senate and House conferees will be voting
> on Monday on an absolute prohibition of funds for military operations in or
> over Cambodia and Laos. The impact on your country of an immediate cessa-
> tion of our air operations in Cambodia, and the inevitable subsequent extension
> of such a prohibition to all of Indochina should be apparent to you. Failure to
> sign will thus lead to a sequence of events which can only become disastrous
> for you and your government. In the context of American opinion, everything
> which subsequently goes wrong in Indochina will be blamed on the GVN,
> no matter what its cause. Hanoi will demand that we force you to sign the
> communique. Congress and much of our press will join. There is a high
> probability that the Congress will block all funds for economic or military
> assistance to your government until you sign the communique. Therefore, I
> must reiterate, in the most insistent way, that we need your government's
> signature on the communique if we are to avert a disaster for you and your
> government—and for everything we have sought to achieve in ten years of
> common effort.
>
> I will need your reply to this message, agreeing to that signature, in time
> for me to instruct our negotiators in Paris how to proceed by 0700 Paris time
> June 9. . . .
>
> . . . I ask you to consider in formulating your answer to this letter, whether
> you really feel that a rejection of that course for the reasons you have advanced
> is worth giving total satisfaction to all those who have opposed everything we
> worked together to achieve in our common endeavors, and for which so many
> thousands of our countrymen have already given their lives.
>
> Sincerely,
> [s] Richard Nixon

Thieu read this letter carefully, underlining the parts he disagreed with.
On Chargé d'Affaires Whitehouse's accompanying letter of transmittal
Thieu wrote in English: "Unbalanced and unjust." In heavy black pencil he
commented: "America has left South Vietnam with no choice. Accept the
best provisions and do not say no flatly." In the margin next to Nixon's

words—"I shall have to disavow your reasons for refusing to sign and in which I shall have to state publicly that you have blocked the achievement of progress in the search for peace"—Thieu wrote, "Why??" with two large question marks. When Nixon said that the draft had been agreed upon, and that this time the United States would oppose, not back, the GVN's position, Thieu wrote in English, "agree between who and who?" In Vietnamese, he added: "In October when did the U.S. back the GVN's position?"

Whitehouse also told Foreign Minister Tran Van Lam on behalf of President Nixon: "I was asked to bring to your attention that there is no longer a question of textual changes or other modifications in the Communiqué and the choices which confront us are those outlined in President Nixon's letter." The hectic schedule was accelerated by the twelve-hour time difference between Saigon and Washington. Thieu could write to Nixon at the end of the day in Saigon and Nixon would receive the letter that same morning when he arrived in his office and reply the same day. His answer would arrive at midnight or later Saigon time or at dawn. Whitehouse was in close touch with Foreign Minister Lam, who received the letters on behalf of Thieu. Whitehouse would track him down at home, on the tennis court, or in a restaurant to keep the chain from breaking. The coded messages were sent directly to Whitehouse with no distribution in the embassy. Thieu's answers would be encoded and sent directly to the White House on a back-channel communications link, so that the existence of the letters was known only to those directly involved in the correspondence.

Thieu notified Whitehouse that he would meet with his National Security Council early in the morning on June 9 to reply to Nixon's letter. Whitehouse immediately advised Washington that Thieu would hold another meeting before answering. Nixon rushed another message to Saigon to convince Thieu to sign. The message was delivered by Whitehouse just before the meeting convened in the Palace Situation Room. This time Nixon's letter appealed to Thieu's sense of realism and warned him that he had to sign whether or not he wanted to.

Dear Mr. President:
        I wish you to know that I appreciate the fact that the choice which has been placed before you as a result of developments in our negotiations with the North Vietnamese entails a difficult decision for you. I understand you will be meeting with your advisors on the morning of June 9 to face this decision. As you enter that meeting, there are several considerations I feel I should bring to your attention.
        The first consideration concerns all those various matters which I have raised with you in our earlier communications as they affect public and congressional opinion in the United States. I repeat, once again, that no matter how strongly you or your advisors feel about some of the matters which trouble you, they cannot compare in magnitude with the problems which will beset you by your refusal to sign the communique. The mood in our country is such that I can predict that the consequences of that refusal will be disastrous.

The second consideration, which I want to convey to you in total confidence, is that we have an arrangement concerning Laos which will involve the withdrawal of North Vietnamese forces from that country over a period of sixty days beginning July 1. We feel this is of paramount importance to you and should not be lightly dismissed as one of the elements which will be lost if this communique is not signed.

Finally, I want to inform you that we are engaged in a complex three-cornered negotiation on Cambodia. We have made some progress in this effort and we hope to be able to exploit it further in order to forestall some of the shortsighted steps which our Congress is prepared to take with respect to that country. We will need some time for that purpose and this communique will buy it for us.

Mr. President, these are the thoughts which I wish to impart to you on this fateful morning in our relations. I hope they will prove of value to you in your deliberations.

Sincerely,
[s] Richard Nixon

Thieu replied again insisting that changes be made in the communiqué before he would sign it. On June 10, Chargé d'Affairs Whitehouse returned to the Independence Palace with Nixon's answer:

Dear Mr. President:

In your letter of June 9, you informed me that you could instruct your representative to sign the communique which has been agreed upon in Paris if certain changes were made in the text. In order to meet your desires, I instructed our negotiators to propose these changes to the North Vietnamese. They were rejected in a long and acrimonious session. . . .

In previous correspondence, I have told you in the frankest possible terms of the disastrous consequences which will result not only for you but also your Lao and Cambodian neighbors if the talks collapse. In order to avoid those consequences, we have arranged a forty-eight hour delay during which Dr. Kissinger will be returning to Washington for consultations. At my instructions Dr. Kissinger agreed to return to Paris on Tuesday to sign the communique. We are now at the point where no further delay is possible.

During this same period, you will have an opportunity to reconsider your position. In this reconsideration, I trust you will reflect upon all those factors which I have previously cited, as well as a number of other factors which I wish to call to your attention in this letter.

There is, for example, the factor of the restraints which we hope to impose upon Chinese and Soviet supplies of equipment to North Vietnam. These restraints can be effective only so long as you and we are clearly seen to be following a common policy and to share the same evaluation of events. If we are split by a public confrontation, the opportunity to insure the restraints will vanish.

In a similar way, our ability to sustain international support for your position, even in such matters as obtaining satisfactory membership in the International Control Commission, will be weakened. The economic assistance group which we have been trying to mobilize among friendly nations to aid you in your economic program is also jeopardized.

All these results will flow from the fact that your government refuses to accept language in a communique which neither adds to nor detracts from arrangements which you accepted in the January 27 Agreement, indeed which in its major provisions is drawn from that document.

I emphatically reject the arguments your Government has advanced to suggest that the communique represents a "form of disaster" for you. I consider this an unwarranted slur on negotiations conducted under my direction and incorporating many of your suggestions. If repeated publicly, I would have to rebut such an outrageous charge in strong terms.

The choice, therefore, remains up to you. Either you choose the collapse of all that we have constructed over a document whose primary significance is the split it threatens between us, or you instruct your representative to join in signature of the communique on Tuesday, June 12. I trust you will not treat this choice lightly or doubt the impact your action will have on our relationship. We have agreed to inform the North Vietnamese of your decision on Monday June 11. I trust it will be one that denies Hanoi the great victory an open split between us would bring.

Sincerely,
[s] Richard Nixon

In the margin, Thieu noted that the order of actions he believed should be followed. He could see that the steps were being reversed in the communiqué to the advantage of the North Vietnamese. He wrote: "must be: a serious ceasefire, troops remain in their positions, then delineation of areas of control. Why are these steps skipped over?"

In his reply to Nixon on June 12, Thieu complained that the communiqué Kissinger had negotiated would in effect produce "two territories under two governments in South Vietnam." He harked back to Nixon's earlier pledge that the United States would recognize only the GVN as the legitimate government in South Vietnam. The communiqué, he argued, would give the North Vietnamese and the Provisional Revolutionary Government a separate administration in the South.

Nixon and Kissinger made a final attempt to press Thieu's objections with the North Vietnamese, and Nixon wrote to him on June 13:

Dear Mr. President:

Your letter of June 12 came as a sharp and very painful blow to our friendship and mutual confidence, and to our common interests. In the light of the sacrifices we have made and the risks we have run in your behalf it seemed inconceivable that you would respond in such negative fashion. I cannot hide from you the strain on our relationship caused by the fact that you would totally ignore the offer of assurances I was prepared to make if you signed the Communique in its current form.

Nevertheless, because the consequences of failure of the negotiations risk making a mockery of so much heroism and suffering, I instructed Dr. Kissinger once again to delay his initialling of the text and to seek some satisfaction of your "minimum" conditions, even though I do not consider them of sufficient intrinsic merit to justify the risks you have pressed me to take or the attitude you have adopted toward my Government.

Then, Nixon reported on the "long and bitter session with Le Duc Tho in Paris today," and how Kissinger had failed to obtain any change in the paragraph concerning the location of the two-party joint military commission teams. However, he said that Kissinger had been successful in obtaining a significant change in the paragraph concerning the South Vietnamese people's right to self-determination. This was the end, Nixon told Thieu:

Mr. President, this is frankly more than I thought we could achieve on your behalf. But, in order to accomplish this, I have had to give my personal word to the North Vietnamese, that this is the last change we will seek. If you refuse to accept these results and continue to decline to instruct your representative to sign the Communique, you will have repudiated my entire policy of constant support for you, your Government and your country.

If you choose this course, Mr. President, you will have determined the future of my administration's policy with respect to Viet-Nam. I will be forced to follow American Congressional and public opinion by supporting only marginal humanitarian necessities with respect to your people and will be able, with justice, to forego all the hard decisions and tasks which would have been involved in the military and economic programs we discussed in San Clemente. Needless to say, it will be the end of our effort elsewhere in Indochina. I will regard such a choice as being directed at my personal judgment and my personal commitments.

This has ceased to be a matter between negotiators, or lawyers, or experts. This is now a matter directly between the two of us. The choice is yours. Please give me a positive, unequivocal answer before 0100 Washington time June 13 so that I can confirm my instructions to our negotiators. I have ordered Dr. Kissinger to sign, together with Dr. Vien,* at 1600 Paris time June 13 and to return to Washington that same evening. Prior to that time, he must initial the text with Le Duc Tho and our staffs must prepare the documents. Please understand that I will regard any qualifications, requests for further changes, delays, or other deviations from a simple affirmative agreement as a direct and deliberate decision to end the existing relationship between the U.S. and the GVN.

Dr. Kissinger has been instructed to return to Washington by tomorrow evening. No further delay or evasion for whatever reason is acceptable. I expect that your representative in Paris will be adequately instructed by the morning of June 13 Paris time.

Sincerely,
[s] Richard Nixon

Thieu was angered by the harshness of Nixon's words and his insistence that any further delays would be taken "as a direct and deliberate

* Dr. Nguyen Luu Vien was the chief adviser to the South Vietnamese delegation to the Paris Talks.

decision to end the existing relationship between the U.S. and the GVN.'' He could not imagine their relationship ending over the Paris Communiqué, yet he finally realized that he had to sign. Before he gave the order to the delegation in Paris to join in the signing ceremony, however, he wrote a bitter note to himself in the margin of Nixon's letter: "This is outrageous! This is what you say; not what I say or the people of South Vietnam or the American people say.''

Thieu understood that the last American diplomatic concessions had been made by weakening the sanctity of the demilitarized zone as a border between the two states. The isolation of South Vietnam was growing in the face of massive North Vietnamese violations of the Paris Accords.

On May 10, 1973, the House voted 219 to 188 to stop the U.S. bombing of Cambodia. Nixon vetoed the bill. Publicly, presidential counsellor Melvin Laird said that Nixon would veto every bill that came to him with an immediate Cambodia bombing cut-off provision. Privately, Laird sent Nixon a memo warning him that he would be overridden by Congress.

The Senate broadened the bombing ban to include Laos and added it to every piece of legislation that the President would have a hard time vetoing. Senate Democratic Majority Leader Mike Mansfield vowed that the Senate would attach the amendment to every piece of legislation "over and over again." "If the President doesn't want to stop the bombing but does want to stop the government, that's his business," said Mansfield angrily.[19] By June 29, the House of Representatives passed an amendment tacked on to a supplemental appropriations bill that barred U.S. combat activities not only over Cambodia and Laos but over North and South Vietnam as well.

In an effort to compromise, Nixon agreed to an August 15 cut-off of the Cambodian bombing instead of an immediate halt. The administration's position in the debate was represented by House Republican leader Gerald Ford. Nixon was in San Clemente with Kissinger, Haig, and Laird.

As Ford recalled: "On the night before the Cambodia vote, I wrote down three points I was going to make. Number one, Nixon would accept August 15 as a bombing deadline. Number two, the ban on U.S. military activities would apply to all of Southeast Asia. And number three, the president would veto any legislative deadline earlier than August 15." Ford read the points to two members of the White House Staff and a legislative aide from the Pentagon. Again, early the next morning Ford read the points to the aides "because I wanted specific reconfirmation. I had the feeling that they didn't quite understand the significance of the words 'all of Southeast Asia' but I had written it down on a piece of paper which is now in my scrapbook."[20]

As soon as Ford made his speech on the House floor, White House lobbyist Max Friedersdorf and the Pentagon's chief legislative aide John O. Marsh called Ford off the floor and said: "Oh, Jerry, you can't say Southeast Asia, you've got to limit it to Cambodia." Ford replied: "I have said it on the floor, you confirmed it and reconfirmed it and there's no way to go back on it. Sorry, that's it, period." The aides argued with Ford and insisted. "It can't be that way." "I'm sorry," repeated Ford.

As the debate continued over whether Ford had actually talked to the President about what he would accept, a call was put through to Nixon in San Clemente and he called Ford back. Ford took the call in the booth number 3 of the Republican cloakroom off the House floor. He talked to Nixon for about ten minutes and read him the three points he had made on the House floor. According to Ford, Nixon said, "That's fine." Then Ford went back on the floor and reconfirmed what he had previously said, telling the House that the President approved.

"Five minutes later or so I got a call from Al Haig. He said, 'Oh, you can't do that. The president won't accept it.' I said, 'Al, it's done. That's it. I'm sorry but there's no way I can erase what I said. It is my understanding that this is what the president approved in his conversation with me." Ford recalled Haig's disappointment and quoted him as saying, "I was sitting in the room with the president when you talked to the president. What you have said was apparently not what the president understood you to have said." Ford replied: "I'm sorry, Al, but that's the way it has to be." Shortly afterwards, Mel Laird called and said, "Everything's okay. Don't worry about it." [21] Haig was appalled. He believes that Laird and Ford conspired to change the wording because of their "total preoccupation with domestic policy. . . . The mischief involved in that piece of legislation defies description," said Haig. After the vote setting August 15 for the cut-off date, Haig told Nixon, "We've lost Southeast Asia, Mr. President."

"Al, I'm afraid you're right," replied Nixon.[22]

13

Standing Alone

T HE SENSE OF ISOLATION grew in Saigon after the June 1973 Paris
Communiqué was signed. Thieu was still reluctant to make major
personnel changes, so he compromised and signed an executive order
announcing the Administrative Revolution, *cach mang hanh chinh,* to make
every government employee conscious of the struggle with the Communists.
His objective was nothing less than to rid the government of its passive,
buck-passing *fonctionnaire* mentality inherited from the French. He sought
to improve morale, change the government's image, and bring it closer to
the people. Thieu's goal was to turn the *fonctionnaires* into revolutionaries
in both appearance and spirit. Ties and coats were declared a symbol of
Western formality and aloofness from the people; they were to be replaced
with functional bush jackets like the one with four big pockets that Thieu
wore every day to his office. Air conditioning was restricted as an unnecessary luxury, part of an effort to cut back on the use of electricity and reduce
oil imports. Thieu's tennis court was no longer lit at night.

In theory, the usual safe course, to "refer the matter to superior authority," would be replaced by individual initiative and action. (Prime Minister Khiem, however, continued to refer all administrative matters to Thieu
for action instead of making decisions himself.)[1] In practice, ministers were
to have more contact with local governments. The traditional isolation between the rural countryside and the capital would be broken.

The instrument for the revolution was the cadre training program at
Vung Tau or Cap St. Jacques, two hours drive from Saigon on the South
China Sea. For the first time there was a nationwide Vietnamese-run campaign to revolutionize the administrative machinery without American or
French advisers. Thieu called his military commanders and province chiefs
to the Palace to meet with the cabinet for a series of day-long discussions
concerning the conditions of the cease-fire. He conducted a dialogue between the central government and local leaders. Cabinet members raised
nationwide policy issues and province chiefs outlined problems they faced.

Each meeting began with Thieu explaining the Communist strategy in the new post-cease-fire phase. His overall theme: The agreement was a respite for the Communists before mounting a major attack against the South. Until the attack came, the Communists would combine economic, political, and diplomatic struggle to weaken the government in the South. Economically, they would cause disturbances to isolate the cities and cut off the food supply. Militarily, they would initiate attacks to tie down the army. Diplomatically, they would roam the world pleading their case, seeking recognition for the Provisional Revolutionary Government and pressing for the formation of a coalition government in the South.

Key government ministers outlined how to deal with these challenges. Hung discussed the economic problems confronting Vietnam in the new phase and advocated concentration of government resources to develop "security pockets" to counter the leopard spots of the North Vietnamese. He asked the province chiefs to explain to the people the economic impact of the American withdrawal, otherwise they would blame the government for the sudden lack of resources. The press was already calling the government's efforts to raise taxes "pointing the sword at the people." Hung used simple language to explain the economic effects of contraction. Wives of soldiers could no longer sell cleaning services or hawk cigarettes to American soldiers around their camps. Every dollar removed from the economy meant the loss of jobs. He outlined the reconstruction plan, which focused on agriculture as the outlet to absorb the unemployed and increase national production. There were plans to dredge canals, which would absorb thousands of workers and bring an increase in food production by irrigating new lands. The problem was to find secure areas where there were no North Vietnamese units or major Viet Cong pockets of strength. The impact of the leopard spots began to be felt strongly because the North Vietnamese were scattered throughout the country and were a barrier to comprehensive, integrated economic development. Hung, for example, found it difficult to obtain raw sugar cane for the national sugar company mill in Phan Rang Province. The peasants were prevented from delivering the cane to the mill by the Viet Cong. There were similar examples: rice could not be moved from the Mekong Delta on Highway 4 to Saigon; tea and coffee production in the central highlands was prevented from moving down Highway 19; while Highway 20 from Dalat to Saigon was mined to prevent shipments of fruit and vegetables reaching the Saigon market.

Faced with American aid cuts after the Paris Accords in early 1973, the South Vietnamese government began a campaign to diversify the sources of economic aid. Saigon turned to France. Relations had been severed under Prime Minister Nguyen Cao Ky in 1966; Thieu now attempted to improve them. The French sent Jean-Marie Mérillon to Saigon, the first French ambassador in seven years, and offered a long-term, low-interest reconstruction loan as a gesture of goodwill and improved relations. Because of his experience at the International Monetary Fund, Hung was called on to lead the delegation and show the French the high technical capability of young Vietnamese who were American and French-trained at the Sorbonne,

MIT, and Harvard. In August 1973 Hung led a delegation of seven young technicians with advanced degrees, all newly returned to Saigon from abroad, to Paris to seek aid. They had been handpicked by Hung to convey a clean, competent image to the French; each one was a recent graduate who had never been corrupted.

Hung quickly realized that the French foreign aid mechanism was much more complicated than the American aid system. Under the French system, every franc in aid from the French treasury must be accompanied by an equivalent loan from private French banks. On first hearing, that sounds reasonable because it involves the private sector, but on the operational level it is very difficult for the country receiving aid. The French are proud of the fact that they contribute 1 percent of their gross national product for foreign aid, in accordance with the United Nations goal set for industrialized countries. One of the problems with French aid is that while money from the French treasury is provided on concessionary terms of low interest over a long term, the funds from the private banks are on conventional terms at market rates over a short term. On close scrutiny, Hung found the terms less attractive than they appeared on the surface. French aid also is tied to buying of French products. The private bankers, with the exercise of their influence, eventually become the ultimate executors of the aid program.

Hung met with Finance Ministry officials and after a week of difficult negotiations the French agreed to 130 million francs in aid, about $30 million. Hung wanted to focus the entire program on agriculture to sustain Thieu's "land to the tiller" program. He needed dredging equipment for canals and irrigation facilities, but the French bankers pushed color televisions and telephones on him. They urged him to buy unneeded thermal electric plants, a color television transmission system, and suggested the importation of fancy French bicycles. Their strongest recommendation and the one they pressed hardest was for Hung to buy French telephone equipment. At one meeting Hung said: "Gentlemen, the Saigon telephone system is more advanced than the French system in some of the *quartiers* in Paris. The old ceramic receiver broke at my hotel the other day, but in Saigon we have plastic phones." The French were trying hard to develop their own industries through their economic aid.

The bankers took turns inviting Hung to Maxim's and the Tour d'Argent for dinner, but he refused to go alone, insisting on taking the whole delegation. He agreed to accept the French hospitality only after all the details of the projects had been agreed upon. The bankers found one of Hung's French classmates at the University of Virginia and he called on Hung at the Claridge Hotel on the Champs-Elysées. His friend suggested dinner and a round of Paris nightclubs "to meet some nice girls" afterwards. "You and I saw a lot of beautiful girls in America," recalled Hung, "but it is not the time for me to see them here."

Hung asked the Vietnamese ambassador to host a reception for the French officials and bankers. Among those invited was former Foreign Minister Maurice Schumann, who was representing a private-sector bank. How-

ever, at the party Hung ignored him because of his sympathy for North
Vietnam and the Viet Cong during the Paris Talks. In the end Hung could
not come to terms with the French on how the money should be spent and
it was agreed the discussions would continue in Saigon.[2]

The practical lesson of foreign aid was that every country has its own
pet projects aimed at strengthening its domestic industries and its position
in the international market. Japan pressed for sales of hydroelectric plants;
aid funds were tied strictly to the purchase of Japanese goods. Over the
years Hung's predecessors had permitted the importation of more than one
million Honda motorbikes, making Saigon known to the world as Honda-
ville. Now the Japanese wanted to use part of their aid to finance "commercial imports"—a euphemism for spare parts for the motorbikes. To
diversify aid and find the funds to solve the critical shortages in Saigon was
proving impossible without American help.

When Hung returned to Saigon, the Administrative Revolution was in
full swing. Every high government official below the rank of minister was
required to attend the training camp for three months. Everybody had to
wear black pajamas and go barefoot like the Viet Cong. On weekends Hung
took his turn eating rice and dry fish and drinking water from a tin cup,
squatting on the grass, like the Viet Cong, at an indoctrination session. The
evenings were spent discussing how to counter Communist tactics in the
villages. One of the suggestions was for a cabinet committee to visit the
provinces and try to resolve problems on the spot. All the officials slept on
hard bunk beds in the camp.

At the beginning, the officials felt humiliated and resented the program.
Gradually they seemed to accept its importance, but their dependency on
the Americans, who had replaced the Mandarin system and the French
colonial mentality, was hard to break. Still, after meetings, Prime Minister
Tran Thien Khiem would say, "Check with the Americans." Hung wondered whom to check with—Ambassador Martin, the CIA station chief, or
the AID director. Hung found it strange that the mentality of dependency
still prevailed.

When the Joint Chiefs of Staff and military intelligence officers briefed
the president on the military situation, they used American terminology to
define the status of forces as "friendly force situation" or "enemy situation." One day Hung asked at a cabinet meeting, "Why do we say 'friendly
forces?' We have no more American or allied troops here." His colleague
replied: "That is the way they have been doing it for the last ten years and
it remains that way in their minds." After the Paris Agreement the mentality
did not change. Hung asked for a change because it reflected badly on the
Vietnamese sense of independence; it made them sound as if they were still
dependent on American and allied forces. But the old terminology remained. General Cao Van Vien even used this terminology in 1982 throughout his book, *The Final Collapse,* on the fall of South Vietnam.

Dependency was an addiction that devoured the Vietnamese body politic. With the Americans gone, Saigon was forced to go cold turkey, and the withdrawal symptoms were painful both physically and psychologically. The American advisers with the Vietnamese army were gone. The American, Korean, and Australian bases were abandoned; "they were like ghost towns," recalled Hung. The comforting presence of American jeeps and trucks and troops on leave in Saigon was gone. There was no place else to turn except inward; but the continuing conditions of instability in the countryside made it impossible to carry out the programs for agricultural development. At the same time the cutback in American military and economic aid prevented Thieu from rebuilding his armed forces with enough reserve depth to counter the North Vietnamese resupply and offensive to come. At the time of the Paris Agreement and the June Communiqué it was the judgment of American military experts that the South Vietnamese armed forces, with continued military aid, were capable of countering a major Communist attack. Major General Charles J. Timmes, an adviser to the South Vietnamese army since the early 1960s and a CIA contact with the Joint General Staff, after his retirement from the Army, concluded: "Despite repeated serious Communist violations of the cease-fire agreement, the South Vietnamese armed forces were capable of containing and turning back the NVA division-sized attacks in 1973 and division and corps-sized attacks in 1974."[3]

Kissinger's private view was that the South Vietnamese needed a "decent interval" of about two years after the Paris Agreement so that the United States would not be blamed if Saigon fell to the Communists. On January 24, 1973, the day after the initialing of the Paris Accords, John Ehrlichman, then counsel to the President, asked Kissinger how long South Vietnam could survive under the terms of the agreement. "I think," said Kissinger, "that if they are lucky, they can hold out for a year and a half."[4] In his state of the world report to the Congress in May of 1973, President Nixon insisted that "the military outcome was not clear-cut and therefore the political future was yet to be determined." The report, written by Kissinger and his staff and signed by Nixon, noted that the South Vietnamese "have every opportunity to demonstrate their inherent strength." The report was full of promises that the United States would remain a "steadfast friend" and would supply economic aid for the South to recover from the ravages of war.

In the same report Nixon raised the prospect of substantial economic aid to North Vietnam, if Congress approved, and Hanoi pursued its objectives peacefully. The President's report spoke of "allowing the historical trends of the region to assert themselves." Here was Kissinger sending a not too heavily coded message between the lines to both the Chinese and the North Vietnamese, suggesting, as he had in his private talks with the Chinese, that time favored Hanoi, and that if they followed a course of peaceful development they might prevail and be assisted by the United States in the form of economic aid.

Instead of developing the inherent strengths of South Vietnam—its rich agricultural lands, natural resources, and ambitious, easily trainable labor force—the withdrawal of the U.S. troops led to the disintegration of the country. The fragile, constantly violated cease-fire did not permit normal economic development under peacetime conditions.

There were two major factors: military and economic. In his role as Minister for National Planning and Economic Development, Hung was deeply involved in the interaction between the two. The ministry was responsible for coordination of all government development planning and projects, the budget, credit and foreign aid, and supervision of all publicly owned sectors of the economy including the sugar monopoly, cement, paper, and glass. In its review capacity the ministry carried out many of the same functions as the U.S. Office of Management and Budget (OMB).

Shortly after he took office, Hung walked to an outdoor café, the Thanh The (High Reputation) Restaurant, on the street near the central market for lunch. He sat down and inhaled the rich aromas of boiling shrimp paste, stewed goat, French filter coffee, and tangy fresh coriander. The restaurant was crowded and noisy under the aluminum roof covering the sidewalk. The food was fresh and tasty. Hung ordered a bowl of shrimp noodle soup, *suong,* and French bread, with a cold beer.

On the street six or seven young boys with wooden shoeshine boxes squabbled over who would shine his shoes. Until the cease-fire they had shined shoes at American military facilities. Four girls came by vending packages of cigarettes: Bastos, the French cigarettes, or 555, the British brand. Each insisted her brand was best. Soldiers on crutches or wheeled platforms, their legs amputated, would move past the tables begging for piastres. The scene struck Hung hard and he reached out to give the crippled veterans his bread and a few piastres. But the more he gave, the more they gathered around.

The number of people increased each day as they realized his timing for lunch. Every day the same people were there and brought their friends. "Soon it became impossible to eat. The woes of our economy paraded before me. The picture of these people stayed in my mind and motivated me to work," said Hung. One day when a Dutch delegation told Hung that he did not need more aid because "you are getting lots of money from the Americans," he invited them to lunch. After seeing the veterans, cigarette girls and shoeshine boys, they were chastened.

Normally lunchtime was from 12:30 p.m. to 2:00 p.m. with time for a nap afterwards. The heat and humidity of Saigon made the early afternoon hours difficult to work in, but Thieu had eliminated the long lunch hour to save gasoline and increase productivity as part of the Administrative Revolution. The picture of the veterans and the cripples sustained Hung in his work. Customers at the restaurant got used to the beggars, but Hung was so upset by the scene that for weeks he ate lunch at his desk in the office.

In the summer of 1973 there was not much leeway in the South's economy to cope with the problems of unemployment brought on by the cease-fire. Agriculture and manpower were the key resources that had to be utilized and put to work. Then came the oil price hike after the Yom Kippur War in the fall of 1973. The piastre had to be devalued almost monthly to reflect its declining value. During the war years imports of more than $800 million a year found their way into the economy; in addition a full range of consumer goods from the network of American Post Exchanges (PXs) that spread across the country formed the basis for a flourishing black market. Then in 1973 imports were cut in half and the government revenues declined sharply, since import taxes were a major source of revenues. There was no way to make up the loss of funds. Income taxes were never effectively collected and revenues dropped as unemployment rose. The meager salaries of the soldiers, instead of increasing, dropped as a result of inflation. Rice was still being imported and its price rose with the inflation. A typical soldier earned 20,000 piastres or less than $30 per month, while a 100-pound bag of rice cost 14,000 piastres or $20 in the summer of 1973. After buying a bag of rice that would last less than a month for a family of five, there was little left over to pay for rent, other food, and medicine. When the Americans were there, a soldier's wife or children could supplement the family income by selling cigarettes, shining shoes, or finding cleaning jobs with the Americans. Soldiers were allowed to bring their families with them to the military camps. Soldiers had to pay for their meals if they ate at the mess; by eating with their families they saved money, and being with their families was psychological compensation for the hardships of war. There was no money to establish a system of dependent allowances or housing allowances for families of soldiers as in the American armed services. In the end the price of allowing families to accompany soldiers in the field was to prove higher than the cost of inflation.

One friend of Hung's was a training officer in a military camp at Thu Duc, outside Saigon. He was charged with raising morale of the troops, but all he had to eat was a stick of *nam xoi,* sticky rice pressed together in the form of a bread. He would divide the rice into thirds and eat a portion for each meal with a little salt and water. Morale eroded steadily from 1973 to 1974.

The defense burden increased as the North Vietnamese maintained the pressure through their policy of "war in peace," selective guerrilla-style attacks aimed at undermining the Thieu government. The Communists kidnapped ninety workers from the Michelin Rubber Plantation to cripple a major source of foreign exchange earnings; they mortared refugee camps to break morale and spread rumors that the wells in a village were poisoned by the government as they sought to move peasants to areas they controlled.[5] It was difficult to adopt an economic policy for peacetime because of the continued needs of security. Demobilization was not possible, but economic resources did not permit the government to maintain an army of 1.1 million men under arms.

The debate continued in the cabinet between the priorities of defense and the inability of the government to sustain more than a one-million-man army. Hung argued for a small, unannounced cutback of nonessential elements of the Regional and Popular Forces. "Actually, we do not have to make a drastic choice," explained Hung. He recommended a gradual demobilization that would absorb the men into agriculture in the countryside rather than add them to the unemployed in Saigon. Thieu smoked a Schimmelpennick cigar and nodded his head in agreement.

In October 1973 the army began to turn some troops into production teams that contributed to the economy by cultivating the land along the perimeters of their outposts and raising pigs and chickens. Six months later Thieu advised the cabinet that he had demobilized 100,000 men in the Regional Forces and moved them back to their homes to cultivate the land. The slogan was "*tay sung tay cay*" ("One hand on the gun, one hand on the plow").

By the end of 1973 economic development plans became irrelevant as the level of attacks by the North Vietnamese increased and intelligence reports indicated that the North Vietnamese were involved in a massive build-up along the DMZ and the Cambodian border. Hanoi was completing a complex petroleum pipeline system along the Ho Chi Minh Trail to supply its tanks and trucks for an offensive.

The one bright spot in the economic picture was oil. When the world prices for oil jumped in October 1973, Thieu turned his attention to developing South Vietnam's offshore oil potential. America and foreign companies bid for offshore concessions at the end of 1973, and by October 1974 Pecten Viet-Nam, a subsidiary of Shell Oil Co., announced that a test well had produced oil at a test rate of 1,514 barrels a day. A five-year program was envisioned for commercial development. Oil was expected to provide financial relief and bring the government an income of at least $1 billion a year. The psychological impact was stunning. Pictures of Pecten's Pioneer Oil Well appeared on Vietnamese television and reports of bidding by fifteen foreign oil companies gave Vietnamese the idea that they possessed a major world resource that would eliminate their dependency on oil imports and America. Vietnam could make decisions on its own without consulting the Americans and the burden of dependency would be lifted.

The Americans were coming back for the oil. There was a new investment theory. Before, the Americans had invested blood and military equipment in Vietnam; now they were committing substantial amounts of dollars for oil exploration and development. In a cabinet meeting, Hung's colleagues said: "Before, America was looking for strategic profits in the region. Now this will be converted into monetary profits. Perhaps this is the way to secure the American commitment."

Hung took the opportunity to discuss the differences between the American and Vietnamese way of doing business. "The Americans are always conscious of profits and are willing to abandon an investment that is not paying its way," he cautioned. To his Vietnamese colleagues, watching the Americans pour billions of dollars into South Vietnam, it seemed that the Americans had carefully calculated how to protect their investment and that the cost of the investment had risen so high that there was no way to abandon it. Hung tried to explain the American mentality by warning that there is no sentiment or loyalty attached to investments. He used the example of a noodle (*pho*) shopkeeper, who maintains his family business whether or not it makes money. The shop is passed down from father to son and will remain in the family as part of the patrimony that is handed on from generation to generation. If it is profitable, the son will be happy. If it is incurring losses, the son will continue the business because it is a part of the family structure. Profits are not the primary consideration of business success in Vietnam. Unlike the Vietnamese, Hung explained, Americans consider profit the primary criterion for the value and worth of a business. An American running a gas station, even if it was passed on from his father, would sell it if it lost money continually. The average life of a small business in America is five years, Hung told his colleagues. "The Americans do not believe in the traditional Confucian saying: '*trong nghia khinh tai*' ('Look up to loyalty, look down on profits').[6] Everything is measured in money. I remember when my roommate at the University of Virginia came back from a date with a Sweet Briar girl and I asked him if he had a good time; he sighed and said, 'She was a million-dollar baby.' "

The longer he stayed in Saigon, however, the more convinced Hung became of the Vietnamese view that the Americans would not permit the loss of South Vietnam. The sheer physical weight of the American commitment seemed to be relentless and permanent, even after the withdrawal of American troops. American honor and prestige were at stake. "It is in our absolute interest that you survive in freedom. We are not going to withdraw politically from South Vietnam even though we will withdraw militarily," Henry Kissinger told Thieu's ambassadors in Paris.[7] Now private American investment was coming into the South. Perhaps the American motto, "In for a penny, in for a pound," was correct. Hung wondered if he was wrong and the investment theory was still valid. His compatriots, working side by side with the Americans in wartime, may have had a better knowledge of American intentions in Vietnam than he did, even after all his years in the United States.[8]

After the oil discovery, Hilton and Hyatt hotels made proposals to build a convention center complex in Saigon. The American companies wanted to buy the site of the prime minister's office near the Palace. Selling the prime minister's office was equivalent to selling the Old Executive Office Building next to the White House to Hilton or Hyatt for a hotel. In the cabinet there were jokes that the Americans were free to do anything. Thieu said: "Let the Americans come in. Make things easy for them, no taxes, give them concessions on land. Let them come in."

One day on a helicopter trip with Thieu to an oil rig in the South China Sea to observe the exploratory drilling, Hung asked the American pilot if he thought there was oil in South Vietnam. "I am not a technical expert," replied the pilot, "but I have flown offshore for twenty years. Wherever I have flown where there were large quantities of big shrimp in the waters there was also oil present.'' Shrimp abounded in the freshwater rivers of the South as well as offshore in the South China Sea. At the end of 1974, Hung was approached by an oil company with a plan to drill for oil in Can Tho Province. The oil executives asked Hung to convince the government to let them commence immediately without the formality of competitive bidding. They agreed to pay $15 million on signing the contract and to share the oil revenues fifty-fifty with the government. Hung outlined the proposal in a memo to Thieu, who was fascinated. The president approved the idea and said to proceed as rapidly as possible.

From the time the bidding began in July 1973, oil fever spread through the economy. Military commanders told their soldiers in the field that their suffering would not be endless and that South Vietnam would become rich, like a Middle Eastern country, once its oil reserves were developed. At Wednesday cabinet meetings during the lunch break oil exploration was the favorite topic. It was the new tonic, an antidote to dependency, the cure for the depression of having to rely on handouts. Hung cautioned that the presence of oil and American investment would be a major irritant for the North Vietnamese. A year later, in the summer of 1974, during the height of Watergate, Hung visited Washington and was warned by Agency for International Development officials to tell President Thieu not to complain too loudly and frequently about North Vietnamese violations of the cease-fire because his protests would deter foreign investors from proceeding with their projects in the South. It was a deadly dilemma. The military urged him to expose the North Vietnamese violations while the economists and State Department and AID officials warned him not to chase away the investors.

Ellsworth Bunker left Saigon in May 1973, and Graham Martin, his replacement, arrived in early July. Martin's reputation as American Ambassador in Thailand (1963–67) preceded him. He was tough, action-oriented, and close to Richard Nixon. Nixon had known Martin in the 1950s when Martin was chief of staff for Under Secretary of State Douglas Dillon and Nixon was Vice President. In 1967, Nixon made a trip to Japan and Southeast Asia as a lawyer representing Pepsi Cola; he was preparing for the 1968 presidential race. Martin was his host in Thailand and they spent long hours discussing developments in Indochina. Nixon respected Martin as a seasoned career diplomat, cut from a different mold than the traditional Foreign Service Officers for whom Nixon had no respect. His appointment to succeed Bunker was announced when Nixon met Thieu at San Clemente. Martin joined Kissinger in Paris for the final round of negotiations with Le Duc Tho leading to the signing of the communiqué in June. "I refused to go to the signing,'' Martin recalled. "Which was worse, the substance [of the communiqué] or the fact that Kissinger was negotiating for the South Vietnamese without them?''[9]

In Saigon the name Martin is associated with a brand of French coffee and Thieu gave Martin the codename "Mr. Coffee.'' He would use the name only with close associates and within the Palace. "What do you know about Mr. Coffee?" Thieu asked Hung. They would probably get along well, Hung explained, because Martin was an older man who came from North Carolina. Hung had started his teaching career at North Carolina Wesleyan College in Rocky Mount, and he had many stories to tell. Hung suspected that Martin would be a Bunker type, correct but a messenger and less supportive than Bunker, playing a purely diplomatic role. Hung soon discovered that Martin was completely different from what he anticipated. Martin was an activist who spoke of mobilizing various aid schemes for Vietnam. He promised to talk to the press and back the aid plans by personally lobbying for them on Capitol Hill. He asked Hung about his background and was delighted to find out that he had studied at the University of Virginia under James Schlesinger, who was then Secretary of Defense, and that he had taught in North Carolina. Martin was fascinated to learn that Hung had been in the Newman Club, a Catholic study organization, with Teddy Kennedy when he was a law student at the University of Virginia in 1958.

"Do you know what Senator Kennedy is doing for your country?" Martin asked Hung at their first meeting.

"Of course, Mr. Ambassador," replied Hung. "First his brother moved against President Diem; now he is undermining us by leading the fight for military and economic aid cuts."

Later in the year Hung invited Martin to dinner at La Paix Restaurant on Dinh Tien Hoang Street, where they feasted on Nha Trang oysters and leg of lamb. When Kennedy's name came up, Hung reminded the ambassador that he knew Kennedy at the University of Virginia and both had been members of the Newman Club.

Kennedy had started the aid slide by deducting $266 million used the previous year from the current budget. "He probably does not realize what will happen to the Catholics in South Vietnam if the Communists take over," said Hung.

"I'm not so sure," said Martin.

Hung recalled Kennedy's reputation as a playboy in Charlottesville and said his real fear was that Kennedy would become President. "That will never happen," insisted Martin. "The American people are not that stupid."

In the summer of 1973, after the arrival of Graham Martin, it appeared that American promises would be kept. In July, Hung returned to Washington to appraise the aid situation and get an overview of where Saigon stood with the White House, Congress, AID, the Defense Department, the International Monetary Fund, and the World Bank. His mentor Warren Nutter, who had returned to academic life at the University of Virginia after serving as Assistant Secretary of Defense for International Security Affairs, urged Hung to meet with Melvin Laird at the White House. Laird, the architect of Vietnamization, was counsellor to the President, and had been called in to help Nixon as Watergate worsened. Nutter and Hung were hopeful that Laird would serve as a counterforce to Kissinger in the White House. If

Kissinger was urging Nixon to resume bombing of the North Vietnamese because of their violations of the cease-fire, it was not apparent to the South Vietnamese, and they looked on Kissinger as their enemy within the White House.

Vietnamization created great ambivalence in Vietnam. While ostensibly a program to build the Vietnamese army, in practice it was to become, in the late Stewart Alsop's phrase, a plan for "an elegant bugout" of the United States from Vietnam. Having followed Laird closely during the first Nixon administration, Hung was acutely aware that Laird was primarily concerned with bringing American troops out of Saigon as fast as possible. He had shown little interest in the problems of South Vietnam and was preoccupied with the domestic political impact of the war and what it was doing to the nation and the Republican Party.

Hung was accompanied by Nutter when they visited the smiling, affable Laird in his office in the West Wing of the White House. The most impressive thing about Laird was his high forehead, which indicated high intelligence to Hung. Laird's type of forehead, both long and wide, was what the Vietnamese looked for in a wise man with finely tuned political maneuvering skills. In Asian terms, Laird looked the role of the Mandarin wiseman, with verbal skills and political agility. It all showed on his forehead.

Nutter told Hung that Laird was skillful at avoiding confrontation and maneuvered around an issue to get his way. Hung appealed to Laird to continue Vietnamization, phase two, the economic development of the South, while continuing support for the military. By Vietnamizing the economy, South Vietnam would be less dependent on the United States, Hung explained. "Of course, of course," replied Laird. At first Hung got a sense of confidence from Laird and a feeling as he spoke that there would be no problems with military and economic aid to continue the Vietnamization process.

But the longer they talked, the more surprised Hung became at Laird's lack of knowledge of what was actually happening in Vietnam. Laird listened carefully and expressed sympathy with Vietnam's problems, but he was difficult to pin down on aid requirements and what he would recommend to follow through on Vietnamization. Hung was pressing for the funds and equipment to establish two reserve divisions to augment Saigon's thirteen divisions.

Laird stuck to generalities, speaking of the bravery of the South Vietnamese and how they could handle the North. Despite his apparant sympathy, it seemed clear that the withdrawal of American troops from Vietnam had been Laird's primary goal and there was really nothing left to bargain over. Now they were completely out; without any American residual force in Vietnam, Hung had no bargaining leverage except in emotional terms.

Laird had been well briefed on Hung and recalled that Hung had been a student of James Schlesinger's at the University of Virginia. Laird praised Schlesinger and said he would be of help to Saigon in the modernization of the army, adroitly shifting the burden to his successor as Secretary of Defense. After the meeting, Hung asked Nutter if Laird would really be as helpful as he had promised. Nutter smiled and told Hung: "You are learning."

Before leaving for Washington, Hung, in his capacity as special assistant to the President of the Republic of Vietnam, had officially requested a meeting with Schlesinger. He was ambivalent in his feelings about Schlesinger. At the University of Virginia he had found Schlesinger's imperious attitude formidable, and interpreted his professor's gruff impatience as a dislike for Asians. He did not consider Schlesinger a friend of South Vietnam; yet compared to Kissinger, Schlesinger was less devious and more open-minded and honest.

As he was driven to the Pentagon by an embassy chauffeur, Hung recalled that back in 1958 Hung and his Japanese friend Yoshio Hara were the only two Asian students in the venerable Department of Economics at the University of Virginia. Hung and Hara, both feeling lost, violated regulations to cook rice together in their room and share their wonder, homesickness, and difficulty in adjusting to America. One hot July afternoon Hara returned to their room crestfallen. Schlesinger had told him that it would be difficult for him to obtain a Ph.D. at Virginia. "Why? What were his reasons?" asked Hung. "Well," replied Hara, "Schlesinger told me, 'A master's degree is good enough for you guys.'" Hung was deeply upset, not only for his friend, but for himself. If a master's degree was good enough for a Japanese, what about a Vietnamese? He would also be precluded from getting a Ph.D. Hung was having difficulty with Schlesinger's course in monetary economics and he had gone to see Warren Nutter, who was also teaching in the department at the time. Nutter, who disliked Schlesinger, told Hung not to worry, he was doing fine, and encouraged him to continue his studies. Hung stayed up studying until 3:00 a.m. for weeks, determined to pass Schlesinger's course with the B grade necessary to continue graduate studies. The exam paper with his grade arrived with a B and three minus signs on it. He had passed.

Hung also remembered election evening, 1960, when the economics graduate students had been invited to the Schlesingers' home to watch the returns. Schlesinger's attractive, red-headed wife Rachel prepared dinner for everybody, and there was drinking, cheering, and groaning as the returns came in. When it finally became apparent that Kennedy would win, Hung was downcast; he was shocked to find that Schlesinger seemed pleased that Kennedy would beat Nixon. In 1974 Hung wondered what kind of loyalty Schlesinger had to Nixon.

As his Mercedes pulled up in front of the Mall Entrance to the Pentagon, Hung was determined to change the professor-student relationship with Schlesinger. He reviewed how he would make his arguments, speaking slowly and carefully—the way Schlesinger had done in his lectures, never referring to notes and walking around the class room to hold his students' attention. "It seems to me perfectly clear," Schlesinger would say, and then pause to puff on his pipe, his shirt tail hanging out from the back of his pants. "Let me attempt to indicate to you," was another of his favorite expressions. Hung remembered them well, along with each accompanying gesture of superior wisdom being passed down; the remembered pain of the long class hours returned vividly. Again he was to sit before Schlesinger, now no longer as a student but as a high official in a friendly government dependent on America for its survival. Schlesinger would again be making decisions that would influence his life.

Hung was kept waiting for ten minutes and he told General Wickham, Schlesinger's military aide, that in the future he expected to be informed if the appointment would not be kept on time. Schlesinger got up from his desk to greet Hung. It was as if nothing had changed; he was in shirt sleeves, his tie open and the shirt tail hanging out in back, his pipe clenched between his teeth. His hair had become gray and he looked much older than his forty-three years. "Let me indicate to you what the situation appears to be" —and he paused to puff on his pipe several times before pronouncing, "Fluid." It was uncanny. The style and the mannerisms were the same as in the classroom as Schlesinger pontificated to an astonished Hung. He told Schlesinger that Laird said he would be very supportive of Vietnam. "Of course, of course," replied Schlesinger, who asked Hung about his new responsibilities.

"My job is to assist the President in reconstructing the economy, which requires not only physical reconstruction but the supporting monetary and fiscal measures," explained Hung, speaking slowly and deliberately to gain dignity. "In carrying out the monetary measures, I hope I will be able to apply some of your lessons such as to establish realistic interest and exchange rates."

"That seems to be appropriate," said Schlesinger with a smile.

Hung realized that despite his efforts he was back talking as if he was a student. Schlesinger's shell was difficult to crack. "It seems to me quite clear that your responsibility is"—Schlesinger paused to ponder and puff his pipe before he added—"very taxing."

Hung explained that part of his job was to assist the president in the area of military aid. He made the point that the Enhance Plus Program, the resupply of Saigon's military hardware before the cease-fire, had turned out to be more show than substance because it contained a lot of equipment that was not suitable for use by the South Vietnamese armed forces. For example, the old F-5A aircraft with cracked wings were not suitable for use and were borrowed from Taiwan. The South Vietnamese were anxious to receive 75 F-5E's that were already in the pipeline. He asked for help in expediting production and delivery. Hung also requested increased training of South Vietnamese pilots.

"Now that the North Vietnamese troops are all over the country that makes economic reconstruction and defense extremely difficult for us," explained Hung. He discussed congressional efforts to cut off the bombing in Cambodia and the rising opposition to the war in Congress. Schlesinger was sympathetic. "I'm sure your people are able to handle the situation quite well, but if a crisis really arises I am quite certain that the President will go to the Congress and to the American people to ask for support for your country," said Schlesinger. Hung expressed his gratitude and promised to convey the message to President Thieu.

Hung reminded Schlesinger that he was the only Secretary of Defense in the Nixon administration who had not visited Vietnam. Schlesinger said a visit was a possibility and Hung promised a red-carpet welcome in Saigon.

Hung also met with Robert Hill, Assistant Secretary of Defense for International Security Affairs, Senator Ted Kennedy, Congressmen Otto Passman of the House Appropriations Committee, and Clement Zablocki of the House Committee on International Relations. From the Nixon administration officials came the message that, although it would be difficult, the administration would try its best to help South Vietnam and in the end adequate aid would be forthcoming. On the Hill, the story was different. Congress was less sympathetic to Vietnam; military aid would be difficult to come by but economic aid would be possible for a few more years. Hung also had a meeting with Anna Chennault, who told him: "Don't worry about Kissinger, he will soon be on the decline."

When he returned to Saigon, Hung was convinced that Schlesinger could be an ally of Vietnam. As a result of his meeting he had changed his mind about Schlesinger's indifference to Vietnam. His initial fears, left over from college days, that Schlesinger favored Kennedy over Nixon and that he was vainly imperious, gave way to a realization that Schlesinger could be the force in the administration to counter Kissinger. With his knowledge of the military situation Schlesinger could provide the necessary support to sustain the South Vietnamese military defense. Hung urged Thieu to issue a formal invitation to Schlesinger to visit Saigon. Hung planned not only to have Schlesinger visit the areas where there were North Vietnamese violations of the cease-fire, but to take Thieu's helicopter to spend a day on Hon Yen, Swallow Island in the South China Sea, where thousands of swallows make their nests on the limestone cliffs. The swallows' nests are joined with their saliva and are a considered a great delicacy in Chinese and Vietnamese cuisine. The island is a panorama of blue sea, white sand beaches, and gray cliffs with darting, golden swallows; it would be an ideal outing for Schlesinger, whose hobby was bird watching.

Hung consulted with Eric Von Marbod, Principal Deputy Assistant Secretary of Defense for International Security Affairs, who was handling logistics support for South Vietnam. Von Marbod was first introduced to Hung by Nutter and he had been sympathetic to South Vietnam's problems. Hung had met with him often when he had come to see Nutter. Now Von Marbod was close to Schlesinger. Hung drafted a letter from Thieu to Schlesinger thanking him for his "noble and sustained effort on behalf of the United States Government commitment to the integrity and military, political and economic stability of Vietnam."

Hung urged Thieu to send the letter, but Thieu was reluctant for fear of offending Kissinger. Instead, he asked Hung to send a message to Schlesinger through Von Marbod, thanking Schlesinger and promising to invite the Secretary formally a week before he was ready to come to Saigon. Thieu did not want a formal invitation to be rejected and he did not realize that given the nature of Washington politics his invitation to Schlesinger would have strengthened the Secretary's hand against Kissinger. With only a verbal invitation, it would be more difficult for Schlesinger to overcome Kissinger's opposition to anybody else in the government playing a major role in Vietnam policy.

Von Marbod reported back to Hung that Schlesinger accepted Thieu's invitation and planned to come in 1974. However, any time Hung offered a tentative date, the Secretary's visit had to be postponed. Thieu believed that Kissinger was responsible for delaying the visit. After the third postponement Hung told Thieu: "Ever since Agnew came, I guess Washington does not want any high-level government officials to associate with us." Thieu did not reply, but picked up one of his thin cigars and puffed on it, his mouth set in a grim smirk as if to say: "See, I told you we should not send a formal invitation."

On August 30, 1973, Thieu called a meeting of the National Supreme Guidance Council at the Independence Palace. His analysis was that the Communists would weaken the South by disrupting economic reconstruction and mounting a "generalized offensive," but not a "general offensive," attacking everywhere on a small scale, not grand enough to attract American retaliation. "They will await a time approaching the American elections in 1976 to stage a large-scale attack. A major offensive in an American election year is a certainty," said Thieu, recalling the Communist attacks in 1964, Tet in 1968, and the spring of 1972; therefore 1976 was certain to be a year for a major attack.

Still, an ominous pattern was building. Visits by senior American officials to Saigon declined sharply. The congressional campaign to halt the bombing in Cambodia was successful and went into force on August 15, 1973. Senator Kennedy accelerated his efforts to cut military and economic aid. A feeling of unease was growing in Saigon, as Watergate revelations continued to weaken Nixon. Nobody would focus on Vietnam's needs since the departure of American troops. On August 3, Nixon wrote to the Speaker of the House and the Senate Majority Leader to comment on the congressional end to bombing in Cambodia on August 15:

> I can only hope that the North Vietnamese will not draw the erroneous conclusion from this congressional action that they are free to launch a military offensive in other areas in Indochina. North Vietnam would be making a very dangerous error if it mistook the cessation of bombing in Cambodia for an invitation to fresh aggression or further violations of the Paris Agreements. The American people would respond to such aggression with appropriate action.

During a luncheon meeting of the Vietnamese cabinet, a minister asked Hung, "Why did Mr. Nixon say, 'I can only hope that the North Vietnamese will not draw erroneous conclusions'? What does he mean by 'only hope'? That is really something. It looks like Nixon is writing the letter to Saigon, not to the Congress. That letter doesn't mean anything in American terms. He says the American people will respond, but what about him as President and his secret pledges? Why isn't he responding?''

When Hung began to take part in top-level meetings, "It became apparent that our armed forces were facing a morale crisis as American aid began to decline." In analyzing the 1.1 million men under arms, it turned out that the majority were territorial forces made up of Regional and Popular Forces. "I always had the impression we had 400,000 to 500,000 fighting men. But it turned out that our main combat forces were only thirteen divisions, about 150,000 men, and of these an estimated 20,000 were flower soldiers—men who were listed on the roles but who did not exist in the ranks and whose pay was taken by the company or division commander. If the air force of 62,000 and the navy of 39,000 were included, then we were operating on a ratio of one to five: one combat soldier for every five in a supporting role, an exact copy of the American Army. The others provided local security, logistic support, communications, intelligence, medical, artillery, and construction support. Our army had an enormous logistics 'tail,' and this was a structural weakness that was accentuated during the post-cease-fire period," Hung explained.

"The total of 130,000 combat troops was shockingly small compared to the 230,000 main force fighting troops the North Vietnamese had under arms. Even to this day I am certain that most of our people and the rest of the world still think that South Vietnam had a 1.1 million man army. In an accounting sense this was true, but not in terms of real fighting capability. More than half were territorial forces, comprised of Regional Forces (RF) and Popular Forces (PF) whose training and objectives were to provide local security: guarding bridges, keeping roads open and clear, guarding administrative buildings and patrolling the villages at night. They were confined to static security missions to protect the rural population and were capable of repelling Communist guerrilla activities. They were not organized or equipped to face a full-fledged North Vietnamese combat division equipped with Soviet tanks."

The South Vietnamese armed forces were primarily defensive in nature, a structure that arose out of the separation of missions between the Vietnamese and Americans during the early years of American intervention. This was followed by the policy of Vietnamization beginning in 1969, which followed the organizational structure of the American armed forces and emphasized equipping the Vietnamese army with modern weapons.

When the first American Marines landed at Danang in March 1965, they were assigned only the task of providing security for the Danang airfield. As more troops were requested by the field commander, General William Westmoreland, and approved by Washington, a controversy arose as to their role. Should they be deployed against the North Vietnamese or confined to providing security in the coastal enclaves and cities such as Danang, Pleiku, Kontum, and Darlac? The enclave strategy, advanced by General Maxwell

Taylor, then Ambassador to Saigon, maintained that restricting the American forces to defense of coastal enclaves would limit the American involvement and keep casualties down. At the same time it would be a demonstration of the American resolve to stay the course.

The theory was refined in 1966 by General James Gavin, who argued that if the United States were to secure all of South Vietnam far more forces than those already deployed would be required, along with increased bombing of North Vietnam. Such large-scale American intervention, Gavin maintained, would bring the Chinese Communists into the war. Gavin recommended that the U.S. forces defend a limited number of coastal enclaves and that the United States cease bombing the North and seek a negotiated solution.[10]

Had it been followed, the enclave strategy might have benefitted Vietnam greatly. The ARVN would have been pushed to pursue the North Vietnamese in the highlands and along the DMZ and thus to have become the primary fighting force in the early years of the war. Among those who supported the enclave theory was Assistant Secretary of State for Far Eastern Affairs William Bundy. The South Vietnamese favored this theory, too, and General Tran Van Don, who had just been replaced as Chief of Staff of the Army, urged the strategy, along with General Cao Van Vien.

But the American military favored deployment of American troops in direct combat with the North Vietnamese and the Viet Cong. The deployment strategy was advocated by General Westmoreland and supported by General Earl Wheeler, chairman of the Joint Chiefs of Staff, and by General Harold Johnson, Chief of Staff of the Army. They maintained that to be effective, American soldiers had to be where the enemy was. As General Westmoreland, who was appointed Commander United States Military Assistance Command Vietnam (COMUSMACV) in 1964, put it: "Intrinsic in my proposal was that American troops would be used in offensive operations. Whereas I saw the commitment as strategically defensive, aimed primarily at forestalling South Vietnamese defeat, the adage that a good offense is the best defense was as applicable in Vietnam as it has been elsewhere throughout history."[11]

To resolve the issue, a meeting was held in Honolulu on April 20, 1965, to decide on the level and nature of American troop deployment in Vietnam. On the civilian side those attending were Defense Secretary McNamara; John McNaughton, Assistant Secretary for International Security Affairs; and William Bundy, Assistant Secretary of State for East Asian and Pacific Affairs. On the military side were Ambassador Taylor, General Westmoreland, General Wheeler, and Admiral Sharp, Commander in Chief of the Pacific. The group recommended to President Johnson that a total of 82,000 American troops be sent to Vietnam, to be based in coastal defense positions. Less than two months later, however, on June 13, following serious setbacks for the ARVN forces in the central highlands, General Westmoreland sent Washington a dramatic request for authority to deploy American troops in the central plateau region to defend Pleiku and Kontum. A week later, on June 20, President Johnson approved the request. William Bundy sent a message to Ambassador Taylor in Saigon informing him of Westmoreland's new authority to deploy troops in combat "in any situation in which the use of such troops is required by an appropriate GVN commander, and when, in COMUSMACV's judgment their use is necessary to strengthen the relative position of the GVN forces."

Bundy's message relayed a fateful decision with far-reaching implications for the course of the war and American commitments to Vietnam. The immediate effect of the decision was adverse American public opinion resulting from mounting American casualties. The decision also gave General Westmoreland total authority to deploy U.S. troops in combat action in Vietnam. The "search and destroy" strategy was born from that authority. American troops undertook the active fighting of the war, searching out large Communist units and attacking to destroy them. This strategy reduced the Vietnamese armed forces to a secondary role of providing security and dealing with the Viet Cong on a local level. There was a clear separation of missions: the Americans were to fight the Communist main force units in the highlands, while the Vietnamese were to provide territorial security in the populated enclaves along the coast and in the delta. The Americans would soon joke that their mission was to search and destroy while the South Vietnamese mission was to search and avoid.

The search and destroy strategy relied heavily on the mobility of helicopters and fire support from artillery and American bombers. The South Vietnamese units, which from time to time joined the battles with their American counterparts, were greatly impressed. Vietnamese generals and soldiers quickly learned to evoke three magic phrases: helicopters, close air support, and artillery.

By specifying that the American troops were to respond to the GVN commander's requests to strengthen their relative positions, Bundy's message had the effect of accelerating the dependence mentality of the Vietnamese. It encouraged GVN commanders to call for American support to bail them out in case of need.

This pattern of dependency developed rapidly and lasted throughout the war; at the end it proved impossible to break. The separation of missions strategy and the decision not to have a joint American-Vietnamese command had the effect of reducing the ARVN to a static security role. The ARVN did not have a chance to develop a dynamic offensive capability prior to the withdrawal of American forces; by then it was too late. Whatever experience the Vietnamese gained in combat was based on the American experience, which relied on mobility, close air support, and virtually unlimited firepower. When this was eliminated with the withdrawal of American forces, the Vietnamese were left without a combat strategy or the means to implement it.

The program of Vietnamization begun in 1969 aimed at extricating American ground forces from South Vietnam while building up South Vietnamese forces and providing the country with what President Nixon described as "a reasonable chance for survival." Until the Nixon administration, the awkward word used was "de-Americanization" of the war. Defense Secretary Melvin Laird was the primary proponent of Vietnamization, and he popularized the term in March 1969 when he spoke of Vietnamizing the war through a program of "modernizing the forces of the South Vietnamese on a realistic basis." [12]

President Thieu did not like the word "Vietnamization." He felt it was demeaning and indicated that it had been an American, not a Vietnamese war. Thieu felt it connoted that the Vietnamese had been mercenaries and were not fighting their own war. In the 1950s the French had used the term *vietnamisation* to refer to their efforts to strengthen the Saigon government, but the term was rejected and later replaced by "modernization." On November 15, 1973, President Thieu publicly urged the Vietnamese media to avoid using the term because he felt it gave credence to North Vietnamese charges that the United States was turning the fighting over to "puppet mercenary troops." Thieu felt the terms should have been "modernization" or "arming the Vietnamese forces"; but "Vietnamization" had already taken hold. [13]

Thieu and his officials believed that Vietnamization started too late. In meetings of the National Security Council the view was expressed that if Vietnamization had started in 1965, the Vietnamese could have taken advantage of the American shield to develop their armed forces to take over the burden of defending themselves when the Americans began to leave in 1969. The reality was that when Vietnamization began in 1969, the speed of American withdrawal was so fast that in little more than a year the Vietnamese armed forces had to be trained and equipped to take over the major role the Americans had played. "The program of Vietnamization was carried on with as much sense as if by making nine women pregnant you can produce a baby in one month," said Eric von Marbod. Just as signs of progress were beginning to be seen, the Communists mounted the 1972 spring offensive and destroyed the momentum.

Despite the flood of nearly one billion dollars' worth of equipment and weapons into South Vietnam with the Enhance and Enhance Plus programs late in 1972, the United States never gave South Vietnam the logistical capability to supply its armed forces. The logistics function was never transferred to the Vietnamese but remained in the hands of the American Defense Attaché's Office in Saigon. These complex functions included storage of supplies, repairs, distribution, inventory controls, and, above all, management and maintenance of equipment. Aircraft maintainance was a major problem, as was radar.

During the American presence these functions were performed by the American military command with the help of private contractors. When the Americans left, the private contractors left too. Page Communications, a subsidiary of Northrop Corp., maintained the radar systems and overall communications. In the summer of 1974 when conditions became critical,

Hung sought to get Page to maintain the radar and airports, but there was a shortage of funds to pay them. As a result key radar networks in the highlands and along the coast and on navy ships were out of commission.

In the summer of 1974 Hung visited a destroyer that outwardly appeared in good condition, but the commander told him he had been requisitioning radar parts for six months and that the ship had no working radar. "We are just a floating sampan. There are limited shells for the guns, a shortage of fuel and no radar," said Pham Gia Luat, commander of the coastal defenses for Military Region IV. "The morale of the troops is so low and their rations so poor that in pursuing the Viet Cong boats, we approached Cambodian villages along the coast and I closed my eyes while my men herded cows aboard our ship to supplement our rations," said Luat.

The net effect of Vietnamization was to increase Saigon's dependence on American supplies rather than minimizing it and making South Vietnam more self-sufficient. South Vietnam had no capability to produce its own guns or ammunition. Hung once asked Thieu why there was no factory for M-16 ammunition in South Vietnam. The Americans insisted it was cheaper to ship ammunition from America, Thieu explained. Self-sufficiency always was overridden by "cost effectiveness." It was cheaper to bring in M-16 rifle bullets and 105mm howitzer ammunition than try to manufacture them in South Vietnam.

In 1974 the Vietnamese army had 127,000 different "line items" that were supplied by the United States, while the air force had 192,000 items and the navy 62,000. The unseemly haste of Vietnamization accented the shortcomings in the U.S. system for supplying the South Vietnamese armed forces, which always found themselves lagging behind the North Vietnamese in armament modernization. The case in point was the AK-47 assault rifle, which was standard issue to North Vietnamese troops. Only in 1968, after three years of being inferior in firepower, did ARVN infantry units receive the M-16 rifle, equal to the AK-47 in performance. The same lag occurred with M-48 tanks and self-propelled 175mm artillery pieces, which were supplied to ARVN forces only after the North Vietnamese had successfully deployed T-54 tanks and 130mm guns. TOW anti-tank missiles were supplied only after the enemy had successfully deployed tanks. "The enemy, therefore, always caught us by surprise as a result of this lagging modernization," explained General Nguyen Duy Hinh, commander of the 3rd Infantry Division.[14]

Senior officers on the Joint General Staff sought to activate two additional combat divisions. While the South Vietnamese had no mobile reserves, the enemy had as many as seven reserve divisions that could be committed from the North. A senior JGS officer reported: "From 1969 on, the United States had been asked many times to support the activation of additional combat divisions in South Vietnam but had 'never satisfied' these requests." MACV turned down these requests on the grounds that the costs would be too high, arguing instead that it was better for the Vietnamese to build up the less costly Regional and Popular Forces.[15] The real reason was the initial American concept of the separation of missions: the Americans would fight the North Vietnamese main force units, while the Vietnamese task was primarily to provide territorial security for pacification. When the Americans left, the Vietnamese army had only two reserve divisions, both of which were tied down in the north to defend the DMZ and the I Corps.

Hung first raised the importance of creating two new reserve divisions after being briefed by Thieu in April 1972. He met with Nutter and other Defense Department officials in Washington, but the answer, while American troops were in Vietnam, was always "You don't need them." Once the Americans were gone, the answer was "Too costly." Yet these were the divisions Thieu said he needed to give him an offensive mobility and capability against the North Vietnamese.

Vietnamization also created a structural problem in that it failed to replace the mechanism that had been the powerful Military Assistance Command Vietnam (MACV) with 6,681 officers and men at its height in 1972. MACV was an elaborate intelligence-gathering, planning, and logistics center that was the brain for command, control, and coordination of all military operations. The fully staffed and computerized MACV disappeared after the Paris Agreements. MACV was replaced by the Defense Attaché Office, which coordinated aid requests. The Vietnamese Joint General Staff was supposed to assume all the MACV functions, but it remained passive and failed to adjust to the new reality. With little experience in planning, the JGS behaved as if the Americans were still running the war; operational responsibility rested entirely with the four regional military commanders and there was no effective planning at the top. Instead of changing the structure of the armed forces to compensate for the American withdrawal, the JGS simply failed to act.

In the summer of 1973 Hung visited CINCPAC headquarters in Hawaii and was briefed by Admiral Noel Gaylor, the Pacific commander. With his American-trained background, Hung was impressed by the briefing boards and maps in the Situation Room showing the current organization and status of forces in Vietnam. Gaylor pointed to giant wall maps with details of North Vietnamese bases and concentrations of troops in North and South Vietnam. Hung noted that the Americans were up to date and Gaylor indicated that they were still closely following North Vietnamese activities.

"I had a lot of respect for our own JGS because I assumed that they would have a similar system to keep track of the enemy and coordinate forces for daily operations with our field commanders," said Hung. He himself had avoided any involvement in the military planning process or military matters, naively assuming that the generals were moving toward self-sufficiency in the same way he was working on the economy; but in fact each Vietnamese corps commander was an island unto himself and Thieu often communicated directly with them. There was no effective centralized war-planning machinery in the Ministry of Defense. When the Americans withdrew from the Marine base at Khe Sanh near the Laos border in 1968, it was a carefully coordinated operation. Operation Lam Son, which was carried out by the Vietnamese in 1971, was based on a plan provided by the Americans.

Hung, at first, was impressed by General Vien, who had appeared honest, patriotic, devoted, and loyal to President Diem in the 1960s, at the end even risking his life. He looked strong and had command bearing. All along it appeared that Vien and his staff were in full control. Whenever Hung saw the barbed wire blocking the road to Cong Ly Street to allow General Vien's jeep to pass along with his security forces, his morale was boosted. The jeeps were left under the tall tamarind trees in the park in front of the Palace. Hung had confidence that the chiefs were discussing high military matters which were beyond the competence of an economics professor or minister. Toward the end of 1974 and in 1975, when Hung attended military planning meetings to take notes for Thieu, however, he realized that General Vien was vague in his answers to the president and was not in control of the situation.

Vien, in his memoirs, says that the decisions were made by Thieu and that the role of the Joint General Staff was primarily advisory.[16] Hung noted that decisions were made casually without planning and backup, and he grew concerned. Thieu would always ask Vien: "What do you think, *dai tuong* [General]?" Vien would simply nod his head in agreement.[17]

For a while in 1973 there was genuine hope that the ARVN would be able to absorb the traumas of Vietnamization; and until the summer of 1974, it did carry out the defense of the South well. A major factor in the success of the ARVN during this period was the continuation of American aid and the bombing of North Vietnamese supply bases in Cambodia until the cut-off in August 1973. During 1973 there were three major attacks by the North Vietnamese, aimed at securing entry points into South Vietnam as part of establishing an elaborate logistical support system for a full-scale invasion of the South. In each of these battles the South Vietnamese divisions fought well and repulsed the northern attack.[18] The prevailing view was that division by division the South Vietnamese army, with adequate firepower and mobility, was capable of containing its enemy counterparts. If the North Vietnamese did not violate the Paris Agreement by mounting a large-scale offensive, then Saigon would prevail. But the threat of U.S. intervention was critical to deterring a North Vietnamese invasion.

14

Promises to Keep

ON DECEMBER 19, 1973, General John Murray, head of the Defense Attaché Office in Saigon, received a message from the Defense Department informing him that Congress was about to sharply cut military aid funds for Indochina for the remaining six months of fiscal year 1974, ending June 30, 1974. Murray was asked to recommend programs that could be cut to adjust to the new lower spending limit. In the meantime, Headquarters, Department of the Army, not waiting for Congress to act, peremptorily cut off all operational and maintenance funds for Vietnam for the rest of the fiscal year. The arbitrary move was a bureaucratic effort to beat the system by using the Vietnamese funds for other purposes before the cuts were made.[1] When General Murray found out about the cut, he informed Ambassador Graham Martin, and appealed to him to tell the South Vietnamese. Murray wanted to warn them so they could conserve supplies until more money was made available. But Martin refused, telling Murray not to pass on the information because it would be too unsettling politically.[2]

On December 26, Ambassador Martin appealed directly to the White House for support to restore funds. Congress had cut the funds for the year to $900 million. Martin insisted that the original ceiling of $1,126,000,000 be restored and an additional $494.4 million be added, for a total of $1.62 billion, "to reasonably discharge our commitments." It was a vintage Martin message, carefully worded, filled with the history of American commitments and promises, along with detailed examples of where funds were needed.[3]

While Washington juggled the figures, Murray, early in January 1974 began to warn the Vietnamese of the need to conserve supplies, especially ammunition. He held a series of conferences with General Cao Van Vien, chairman of the Joint General Staff, and Lieutenant General Dong Van Khuyen, commanding general of the Central Logistics Command. Murray did not go into detail about the problems ahead for the remainder of the fiscal year, but he got the message across. Up until then General Murray had been telling the Vietnamese, "You are going to get what we promised." They would receive the one-for-one replacement of equipment under the Paris Accords. "No one ever told me or President Thieu or General Vien that we were running out of money. It was painful to have to go back on our word," said Murray. On February 13, General Vien ordered restrictions on all types of weapons. With a four-month time lag between ordering and shipping, the supply line dried up by April 1974 and "the system was never to recover."[4]

There was a growing list of critical shortages, including ammunition, medical supplies, and funds for the subsistence of South Vietnamese troops. Infantrymen, accustomed to carrying six hand grenades into battle, were issued only two. Mortar and artillery rounds for defense of outposts were limited to four rounds a day and all harassing fire was halted to save ammunition. More than half of all armored vehicles were out of operation and 20 percent of all aircraft were grounded. The use of firepower to save lives, the American way of fighting, was being eliminated, and by the spring of 1974 the Vietnamese realized that "Vietnamese blood is being used as a substitute for American ammunition."[5] The casualty rate increased drastically so that by the end of June, during a period of increasing North Vietnamese violations of the cease-fire, there were already 19,000 dead for the year and more than 70,000 wounded. As a result of supply reductions military hospitals did not have enough medicine or bandages. In many cases bandages were washed and reused.

The American congressional debate and the reduction of funds coupled with the actual reduction of ammunition and supplies had a drastic and immediate impact on morale. The Viet Cong stepped up their propaganda and tried to prove to the local troops and people that the GVN forces no longer had enough ammunition to defend themselves. The Communists would mount probing attacks long enough for the villagers to see that the ARVN forces were short of ammunition. The Viet Cong agitation and propaganda units would spread the word in the marketplace that the village well had been poisoned and ARVN officers and the United States were leaving. Then, after a dramatic display of their own firepower, the Viet Cong agents, who infiltrated into the families of the soldiers living around the camps, would urge the wives of the local troops to abandon their posts.[6] The Viet Cong also used astrologers and monks to predict natural calamities which foreshadowed the fall of South Vietnam.

In his memoirs, General Cao Van Vien concludes:

> Thus the South Vietnamese soldier of 1974–1975 marched into combat with the deep concern that his ammunition might not be replenished as fast as it was consumed and that, if wounded, he might have to wait much longer for evacuation. The time of abundant supplies and fast helilifts had gone. . . . To reduce that aid so drastically and so abruptly ended any chance of success and generated panic among the people and armed forces of South Vietnam while encouraging the Communists to accelerate their drive to conquer by force.[7]

The year 1974 was fateful in deciding the outcome of the war. By the end of 1973, Thieu realized that the American Congress had lost its taste for the war. The promises that were made to induce him to sign the Paris Agreements and the June Communiqué were proving hard to redeem.

In April as the supply problem worsened, Thieu, with the encouragement of Ambassador Martin, urged General Cao Van Vien to visit Defense Secretary James Schlesinger and seek his help in providing more military aid for Vietnam. Ambassador Martin had told Thieu that the San Clemente promises were still good and that Thieu should make his case directly to gain Schlesinger's support. Thieu imagined that Vien would be well received in the Pentagon because of his long association with the American generals. Vien, who had no experience in the American aid appropriation process and procurement, called on General Murray to help him. Together they prepared a list of equipment—for 105 and 115mm howitzers, ammunition, communications equipment—and funds that were needed to maintain the South Vietnamese army as a viable fighting force. Then Murray forwarded the request to see Schlesinger along with the "wish list."

Back came a cable from Schlesinger's military aide, Brigadier General John Wickham, requesting guidance for the Defense Secretary on how to respond to the Vietnamese request. A seasoned bureacrat as well as a soldier, Murray saw his opportunity to convince the Vietnamese that Ambassador Martin was being unrealistic in urging President Thieu to ask for more American aid. He promptly sent a cable to Washington suggesting that Schlesinger tell General Vien that the Vietnamese had been making good progress in the war against the North Vietnamese, but there would be no new arms forthcoming because of growing congressional restraints on military aid for Vietnam. Murray felt he understood the situation better than Martin, and he thought this would be the best way to convince the Vietnamese of how dire the prospects were for more aid, despite the duplicity involved.

When Murray arrived at the Defense Department with General Vien, he saw General Wickham briefly and was told his guidance cable had been presented to the Secretary on 3 by 5 file cards. General Vien first made his appeal to General Creighton Abrams, the Army Chief of Staff, who said the problem was not in the Pentagon but on Capitol Hill with Congress. Then Vien was taken to see Schlesinger, where he explained the needs of the South Vietnamese armed forces before the Defense Secretary and thirty senior officers, including members of the Joint Chiefs of Staff.

Schlesinger leaned back in his chair, puffed heavily on his pipe, and proceeded to make the points that General Murray had drafted for him. He heartily assured Vien of his full support, but explained that the final decision was up to Congress. After the meeting as they left his office, Schlesinger asked Murray, "How did I do?" "Fine, Mr. Secretary," replied General Murray.

Back at their motel General Vien was disturbed. He confided to General Murray that he "couldn't understand what Secretary Schlesinger was saying. He spoke so quickly and now I must report immediately to President Thieu." Murray reached into his pocket for a copy of the guidance he had sent to Schlesinger and proceeded to brief General Vien, who gratefully took it all down to brief Thieu in Saigon.[8]

Schlesinger did promise to try to help with Congress, but it soon became apparent that there was a new reality in Washington. If it accollished nothing else, the visit of General Vien established how things had changed.

In Saigon Graham Martin kept reassuring Thieu that U.S. aid was difficult to obtain but in the end everything would work out as promised. Thieu was growing suspicious and sent his own people to Washington to test the waters. Hung was ordered to assess the economic and military aid situation. When he arrived at Dulles Airport, he was anxious to meet with General Vien and find out how his appeal had been received. Thieu had instructed him to work with Vien and follow up on Capitol Hill. As he stepped into the terminal, Hung saw a group of Vietnamese Embassy officials. He thought they had come to greet him. Then he noticed General Vien. His first thought was that Vien too had come to meet him. "I'm glad to see you here," said Hung. "I was going to call you as soon as I got to the Embassy."

"I'm leaving now," said Vien. Hung, surprised, pulled Vien to one side to talk with him privately. "Are you really going? Can't you stay?" he asked.

"I've done my job. I have to return. I briefed them. Schlesinger and General Abrams assured me of their full support. The only thing is that they are worried about Congress."

Hung was bewildered. He would need General Vien to help present the case to the Congress; but Vien, who thought he only had to deal with the Pentagon, was leaving.

"Good luck to you," said Vien as he headed for his plane.

Hung was assigned to appeal to Senator Edward Kennedy, the leader of the movement to cut aid to Vietnam. Kennedy held the view that President Nixon had "failed to redirect or change the basic character and purpose of our aid and policies toward the countries of Indochina." He insisted that U.S. aid was being used to prolong the fighting, instead of lessening violence. Kennedy argued that "in the absence of any meaningful efforts to carry out the political goals of the ceasefire agreement [the formation of the National Council of Reconciliation and Concord and the holding of free, internationally supervised general elections], the purposes of the massive expenditures in South Vietnam are not . . . to help war victims, postwar reconstruction and development but to buy still more time for the Thieu government to keep Saigon's war economy afloat."[9]

On May 6, the Senate voted 43 to 38 to adopt a Kennedy amendment to a Defense Department supplemental appropriations bill barring the use of funds to be spent in, for, or on behalf of any country in Southeast Asia. With great reluctance, because of Kennedy's opposition to Thieu and the war in South Vietnam, Hung went to see Kennedy on May 15 in his Senate office. He was received by Jerry Tinker, a Kennedy aide who explained that

Kennedy was very busy. Tinker listened sympathetically while Hung told of North Vietnamese violations of the Paris Agreement and South Vietnam's pressing economic and military needs. Finally, Hung met briefly with the senator, who recalled their student days and was interested in Hung's new role as Minister for Economic Reconstruction. Kennedy was short on time and seemed distracted as Hung appealed for his support and warned of the fate Vietnamese Catholics would face if the Communists took over.

Kennedy was wearing a conservatively cut dark blue suit and was obviously overweight. Hung could not get over how much older he looked since their days at the University of Virginia. His hair was turning gray. Kennedy then said he had to leave. But Hung felt he had not told his story properly and pleaded to accompany the senator to his next appointment so he could continue. As they walked through the marble corridors of the Senate Office Building, Hung could not help but feel like a beggar approaching a rich man; but he steeled himself to explain that South Vietnam needed both economic and military aid. Kennedy towered over Hung and strode rapidly to his appointment. Hung kept the pace, explaining: "Military aid is not increasing the fighting; it is preventing the North Vietnamese from attacking our people and committing acts of terrorism."

Kennedy remained firm. He told Hung he liked him personally, but added: "I don't think you can count on Congress for military aid. I have a lot of sympathy for your people and I'll try to see what I can do with humanitarian aid." Hung finally appealed to Kennedy as a fellow Catholic. "Senator, please think about the Catholics and what will happen to them under the Communists." Kennedy stopped and asked: "What about the Catholics?" "If you look carefully, Senator, you will see the history of the Vietnam War shows that whenever the Communists take over, the Catholics are first on the list for persecution. I am a Vietnamese Catholic and I know firsthand." Kennedy, however, insisted that "military aid will not solve the problem." Hung felt dejected and desperate as he left Kennedy at the door of the Senate Committee Room.

During his visit Hung also met at the Pentagon with Eric Von Marbod, Comptroller of the Pentagon and Principal Deputy Secretary of Defense for International Security Affairs. In the summer of 1973, Von Marbod, the most experienced and respected logistics expert in the Pentagon, was assigned to determine the military needs of South Vietnam. Defense Secretary Schlesinger gave him the job after the Senate Armed Services Committee complained that there were so many claims for aid coming from Saigon that the picture was confused. Von Marbod, husky and red headed, was sympathetic to Hung. His open manner instilled confidence.

Alone with Von Marbod in his office in the E-Ring of the Pentagon, Hung asked for a frank and detailed picture of military aid for 1974. "We are confused by the cuts and the back charges. We need to know what we can count on," Hung pleaded.

"I'm sorry to tell you this but in the Pentagon books there is only $625 million or maybe even as little as $500 million, not the official figure of $1.1

billion that is being discussed publicly by Congress and in the press," said Von Marbod.

Then he tore out a piece of paper from a steno notebook and wrote:

Vietnam–Laos	$ 1.126 billion
Laos only	110
Back charges	266 *(for spending in previous years)*
F-5E Program	125
Balance	$ 625 million *(possibly only $500 million after deducting costs for shipping and running the Defense Attaché Office [DAO] in Saigon).*

Hung was shocked by the figures. "What are we going to do? There is nothing left?" he asked.

Von Marbod explained that there was not much that could be done; the allocations had been made. Hung said he understood the $266 million had to be paid back because Congress had demanded it before agreeing to further spending. He asked if the $125 million for the F-5E program could be shifted to more essential needs. "No," explained Von Marbod, "it was committed a long time ago and it can't be changed." Hung had never heard that in Saigon and wondered who in the Vietnamese military had made the decision, or if they had ever been consulted. In 1973 military aid had totaled $2.2 billion. Von Marbod said he was not giving up and told Hung to urge Schlesinger to lobby harder for Vietnam with Congress because "Kissinger is hopeless."

When he returned to Saigon, Hung immediately reported to President Thieu. It was painful for Hung to have to show the president Von Marbod's analysis of the cut in military aid funds. Instead of good news, Hung had to explain that the dollar cuts meant that the fighting capability of the South Vietnamese armed forces had been reduced by 60 percent. After hearing Hung's analysis, Thieu was silent and resigned. He pressed his lips together, clenched his hands behind his back, and walked out of the room to his apartment.

Alone in the Situation Room, Hung saw on the table a handsome red plastic binder with Thieu's portrait on the cover. It was an analysis of military aid levels worked out by General Murray and submitted to Thieu by the Joint General Staff. There were four levels of aid and four lines of defense. If aid was at the $1.4 billion level, the populated centers of all four military regions could be held. If aid dropped to $1.1 billion, then Military Region I would have to be written off. If aid dropped to $900 million, there would be no opportunity to maintain Military Regions I and II or to counter a North Vietnamese offensive. At $750 million, only selected areas of the country could be defended and it would be impossible to get the North Vietnamese to negotiate seriously. If aid dropped to $600 million, the GVN would be hardpressed to hold onto Saigon and the Mekong Delta. Murray concluded in the report: "You can roughly equate the loss of funds to the loss of real estate." (see Appendix E: Defense Attaché Office Analysis Fiscal Year 1975 Funding Impacts on Republic of Vietnam Military Assistance Funding Program.)

Thieu was so upset that he wanted to make public the true picture of American military aid to Vietnam, but he faced a deadly dilemma. To make his distress public would accelerate the already falling morale of his generals and troops; not to make his concerns known would enable Congress to cut aid further. By making his problems public Thieu would also be weakening his own domestic political strength, which was based largely on his ability to deal successfully with the Americans.

The war had cost $25 billion a year to fight from 1967 to 1970 at the height of the American commitment. During 1970 and 1971 this had been reduced to $12 billion. Now, with American troops gone, the South Vietnamese were being forced to carry on their own defense with as little as $500 million in effective military aid.

In addition to the military aid reductions, Congress continued the demoralization process by imposing severe restrictions on the use of economic aid. Under heavy pressure from anti-war groups, led by the Indochina Resources Center,[10] Congress imposed a ban on economic aid funds being used to pay the salaries of soldiers. In Vietnam, where the troops pay a part of their wages for their meals, this had a devastating effect on morale. Until then, up to 75 percent of the government budget deficit had been financed by aid counterpart funds. Counterpart funds was the money generated from the sale of imports financed by U.S. economic aid. As aid decreased and counterpart funds were forbidden to be used to finance the defense budget, there was a panic. Only with the help of sympathetic American officials in Saigon was a scheme developed to accommodate the legislation. Domestic taxes would be used to finance the defense budget and the counterpart funds would go for nondefense items in the budget. Later in the summer Congress further restricted the use of counterpart funds so they could not be used to pay for the national police's salaries. Food aid was no longer provided as a grant but became a long-term loan. On July 11, 1974, Senator Kennedy called for a 50 percent cut in economic aid, from $943 million to $475 million.

A few days later at a cabinet meeting Prime Minister Khiem, reacting to the economic crisis, directed the cabinet to cooperate with Ambassador Martin in his efforts to lobby for a five-year economic aid commitment for South Vietnam. Thieu had presented the plan at San Clemente with the goal of reducing economic aid to $100 million by 1980. Nixon had been enthusiastic and promised his support, but nothing materialized; Vietnam had also become a casualty of Watergate.

Hung met frequently with Thieu during this period to review the latest possibilities for aid. At the end of a long day, over drinks in the Palace, Thieu expressed his growing frustration with the lack of aid funds and supplies. "This is incredible. First the Americans told me at Midway to agree to the withdrawal of a few thousand troops and I would still have half a

million Americans left to fight with me. Then, when they withdrew more
troops, they said, 'Don't worry, we are strengthening you to make up for
the American divisions that are being withdrawn.' When the pace of withdrawal speeded up in 1972, they told me, 'Don't worry, you'll still have
residual forces and we are making up for the withdrawals with an increase
in air support for your ground troops.' Then after there was total withdrawal
and no more air support, they told me, 'We will give you a substantial
increase in military aid to make up for all that. Don't forget the Seventh
Fleet and the air bases in Thailand to protect you in case of an eventuality.'
Now you are telling me American aid is cut by sixty percent. Where does
that leave us?'' [11]

Hung told Thieu there was not much that could be done. Searching his
memory for a bright spot, Hung recalled that funds for the seventy-five
F-5Es had been obligated from the 1974 budget, but the planes had not been
delivered. Thieu was surprised to hear this. Hung suggested he might go to
America to expedite the delivery of the planes.

Hung was back in Washington again in the last week of July to expedite
the shipment of the F-5Es and to review the economic aid situation. He was
to work with AID to seek additional funds for 1974 imports and reconstruction. He was also directed to assess the military aid situation and appraise
Nixon's status in view of Watergate.

Hung arrived amid the throes of the campaign to impeach Nixon. He
made the rounds of the Defense Department on steamy days, so hot they
reminded him of Saigon. The atmosphere was bleak, unlike anything he had
ever experienced in America. Nixon faced removal from office and Congress had no time or inclination to deal with any other issue, let alone aid
for South Vietnam. Vice President Agnew was gone. Gerald Ford, the new
Vice President, remained an unknown quantity to the South Vietnamese.
There was no aid vote for Vietnam and money came only from a continuing
resolution from the previous year's level of $395 million. A continuing res-
olution meant vague uncertainty in the American commitment.

There was no place to turn within the government, so with high expectations, Hung sought help from Robert McNamara, President of the World
Bank. In public, McNamara had disassociated himself from Vietnam, but
Hung felt that in private, as the man who was responsible for the build-up
of more than 500,000 American troops in Vietnam and escalation of the war,
he would have a high degree of sympathy for the problems of South Vietnam. In his huge office on the twelfth floor of the World Bank, McNamara
greeted Hung with a broad smile and a penetrating stare. Hung had seen
him on television, in and out of Vietnam, the enthusiastic cheerleader for
fighting the war with his cost analysis, quantitative approach. Under Mc-
Namara, defoliation with the use of Agent Orange had been approved and
the Phoenix Program to decimate the Viet Cong had begun. Under Mc-
Namara, the use of body counts of enemy dead and statistics of captured
weapons quantified the American success.

"I expected a candid meeting with McNamara, but instead he was very

remote, businesslike, and asked, 'Mr. Minister, what can we do for you?'
He never asked about Vietnam and its problems,'' said Hung. Since Hung
realized McNamara's sensitivity about the war, he explained how Saigon
needed financing for agricultural projects to rebuild the war-torn economy.

McNamara was noncommittal and complained how difficult it was for
him to get Congress to increase funds for the World Bank. ''I want to help
your country, but until Congress votes on funding for the International
Development Association there will be no action on Vietnam,'' he said.
Hung then appealed to McNamara as a professional economist on the
grounds that Vietnam was one of the oldest members of the World Bank
and had never borrowed any money before. ''When the Americans were in
Vietnam, we had plenty of money,'' said Hung. ''The first hundred-dollar
bill I ever saw was in Saigon.'' McNamara did not smile.

Hung continued to outline South Vietnam's agricultural needs. Mc-
Namara replied: ''Yes, agriculture fascinates me. We are doing important
work with Miracle rice.'' He picked up samples imbedded in crystal from
his huge coffee table and showed them to Hung.

''Yes, Mr. President, agriculture also fascinates me, and my people are
looking to the World Bank to help us now because they think of this institution not as the World Bank but as the Bank for Reconstruction and Development. As far as I am concerned, my country is the only one in the
world where postwar reconstruction is taking place,'' said Hung. Again
McNamara shifted the conversation back to how South Vietnam had rich
agricultural resources and was experimenting with Miracle rice. He picked
up the rice samples and reiterated, ''This is IR-3 Miracle rice.'' At that point
Hung's patience evaporated. ''Thank you, but I have seen the more advanced IR-8 Miracle rice in Vietnam,'' said Hung. With that he rose to say
goodbye, realizing that there was no way to gain McNamara's interest or
cooperation.

As he waited for the elevator, Hung wondered how McNamara could
be so insensitive to the very problems of Vietnam that his own policies had
created. How could such a man with so much responsibility in Vietnam—
which he mispronounced as *vit nam* or lying duck, in Vietnamese, so that
the Vietnamese snickered whenever they heard him—be so aloof?[12] Hung
was saddened. It was in McNamara's power to have the World Bank play
an active role in rebuilding an economy ravaged by the war for which he
had been one of the main policy makers. Yet despite South Vietnam's strong
credit record and economic potential, McNamara had remained distant and
withdrawn.

Before returning to Saigon, Hung stopped to see Von Marbod at the
Pentagon to check on the delivery of the seventy-five F-5Es ordered for
South Vietnam ''Eric, you already took $125 million out of our 1974 budget.
Where are the planes?'' asked Hung. The money, explained Von Marbod,
was being held in reserve. It took time to produce the aircraft and assemble
them in the Philippines before delivery to Saigon.

''Both Taiwan and Iran have also ordered F-5Es and they may have a priority over you for delivery." Hung was shocked. The cease-fire had broken down and the planes were badly needed, not only to make up for the loss of American airpower but as a morale booster. Hung insisted that Von Marbod arrange for him to meet Thomas Jones, chairman of Northrop Corp., at his office in Century City in Los Angeles.

Von Marbod was surprised that a Vietnamese was trying to get directly involved in the American procurement process, but after Hung's plea he made the appointment. On his way back to Saigon, Hung visited Jones and urged speedy delivery of the F-5Es. He explained that the lack of firepower was causing high casualties. Jones said Northrop was producing on schedule, "but there are other clients and I will have to look into your request." Hung asked for three squadrons—thirty-six aircraft—by Christmas 1974.

"Why do you need them by Christmas?" asked Jones.

"It looks like 1975 is going to be a tough year for us. We would like these planes to fly over Saigon on New Year's Day to lift people's morale," answered Hung.

He promised Jones that since he understood the American system, he would enlist President Thieu, if necessary, to ask the Pentagon to make the disbursement of funds to Northrop as soon as the planes were delivered.

With that said, Jones looked at Hung pleasantly and promised: "I will try to do my best for you and your country."

To avoid any misunderstanding, Hung then said: "Mr. Chairman, when the planes are received, we will invite you to Saigon for a celebration. As for my part, you can give me a bottle of Coca-Cola to toast with. I will be more than happy."

Jones gave Hung a plastic model of the F-5E for President Thieu, who was delighted to receive it and placed the fighter behind his desk in the Situation Room next to his red alert phone.

The early delivery of the F-5Es was the only bright spot on the horizon. On his return to Saigon early in August, Hung reported to Thieu that Nixon was about to be impeached or forced to resign. In either case he would be politically impotent until the end came. The atmosphere in Washington was rancorous and Americans could focus on nothing but Watergate. To isolate American foreign policy from the effects of the domestic upheaval, Kissinger seemed to have been given a waiver of immunity from any involvement in the scandal and allowed to concentrate on foreign policy. In these final days he was becoming, in effect, the President for foreign policy.

Ford still remained unfathomable. His conservative Republican credentials and his support for Vietnam could be helpful, if he wanted to help. If he ascended to the presidency he would be in a better position than Nixon. While Congress gave him a honeymoon there might be a dramatic change in American attitudes to Vietnam. Thieu listened carefully as Hung explained that although Vietnamese think of a honeymoon as lasting for one week, the Americans used the term figuratively to describe the President's relationship with Congress that might last for one hundred days or longer if the President was effective. Although Mrs. Chennault predicted that Kissinger would soon be gone, Hung warned Thieu that Kissinger's strength was growing and he would be retained by Ford as Secretary of State. Ford's reliance on Kissinger would not be helpful to Saigon's cause.

On August 9, 1974, President Thieu sat alone in his office at the Independence Palace, closing his eyes, biting his lips and grinding his right fist into the palm of his left hand. The news of Richard Nixon's resignation that day had left him in a state of high tension when Hung saw him. Nixon's resignation compounded Thieu's dilemma. The cutback in American aid funds forced him to face the prospect of reducing the size of his country and giving up half of it to North Vietnam. Rather than face the idea of retreat, Thieu began to use the word "redeployment."

As the result of an analysis prepared before his retirement by the American Defense Attaché, General John Murray, and the Joint General Staff, Thieu was considering the drastic alternative of ceding the central part of South Vietnam to the North and consolidating South Vietnam's territory along a line that would include Saigon and the rich Mekong River Delta to the south, what had been drawn as Cochin China on pre-World War II French maps. The rich bottomlands of Vietnam could be consolidated and defended.

Just four days before his resignation, Nixon signed into law an aid ceiling of $1 billion for Vietnam, reduced from the $1.6 billion originally requested. Not only was aid reduced, but the way it was to be allocated made it equivalent to only about one third of what it had been the previous year. For Nixon, this was a massive defeat inflicted on him by a vengeful Congress. In his prostrate political condition there was nothing he could do to keep his promises to Thieu.

In an effort to maintain morale and political stability, Thieu suggested to Hung to put a good face on the situation and not publicly display any pessimism about future American support. Privately, Thieu realized that something had to give. He could not support armed forces of 1.1 million with that small an amount of aid. He was searching for a way to give up territory without critically damaging the national defense and the economy. Thieu had ordered the Joint General Staff to analyze the effects of possible cuts in military aid on the fighting ability of the armed forces. Privately, he was assessing their ability to hold the four military regions of South Vietnam.

Aware of Thieu's concern, Hung prepared an economic analysis of the impact of the loss of Military Regions I and II, with the exception of the key coastal cities. His conclusions paralleled those of General Murray presented to Thieu by the JGS.

Hung concluded that the loss of most of Military Regions I and II would not drastically change the economic profile of the nation. The total population under government control would shrink by about six million, or less than 30 percent; of these at least one to two million could be moved South to the delta to escape Communist control. There would be a net loss of four

million people. The report did not assess the political impact such a redeployment would cause, nor what would happen to morale when four million
people were, in effect, surrendered to the Communists.

On the positive side, there were more than one million acres of arable
land to be developed in the delta to resettle refugees from the central highlands and the coastal plain. Gross national product would be reduced by
less than 20 percent, and most of the loss would be in the areas of animal
husbandry and forestry. The mining industry would suffer a 65 percent
decline from the loss of coal, but manufacturing activities would decline by
only an estimated 7 percent. A realistic appraisal of the military aid picture,
as well as the economic factors, appeared to support a draconian decision
to reduce the size of South Vietnam. Thieu appeared to be ready to give
way on one of his Four No's and concede territory to North Vietnam.

In staff meetings Thieu began to talk about "each strategy for each aid
level." He never explicitly explained his plan to reduce the size of the
country, but Hung began to sense that he was considering a major decision.

To Hung, the choice was inescapable. He had gone over the studies,
which were clear, precise, and concise,[13] fitting the pattern that Thieu demanded from his subordinates. It was clear that a reduced 1975 aid program
could support only a truncated South Vietnam. Thieu surprised his aides
one morning by crudely describing a strategy of *dau be dit to*, literally, small
head, big ass—later to be more elegantly translated into English as "light at
the top, heavy at the bottom."

The idea of truncating South Vietnam was not new. Back in 1961,
President Ngo Dinh Diem had warned President Kennedy of similar results
unless sufficient American aid was forthcoming for two new divisions.
"Failing this," Diem wrote to Kennedy, "we would have no recourse but
to withdraw our forces southward from the demilitarized zone and sacrifice
progressively greater areas of our country to the communists."[14]

Thieu was reflecting on how to drop or modify the Four No's policy,
the keystone of his opposition to the Communists—no territorial concessions, no coalition, no recognition of the Communist Party, and no neutralization of South Vietnam. One evening, alone with Thieu, Hung discussed
the Four No's. Hung was curious to see if Thieu was prepared to compromise in view of the pressures being exerted on them. "Never mention the
word 'coalition' in public," Thieu told Hung. "With the Communists you
have to act tough. You have to raise your price just as they do. Then, when
compromise comes, you can lower your price." Thieu explained to Hung
that "there are various combinations of the Four No's, perhaps eighty percent of one and sixty percent of another. At some point there will be a
compromise that is less than one hundred percent of each. I never said we
had to press for one hundred percent of each 'No.' " It was clear to Hung
that Thieu was considering a "redeployment strategy" or "truncation,"
retreating south and narrowing the defense line to what amounted to halving
the first No, on territorial concessions.

Nixon's resignation compounded the uncertainty Thieu faced. He feared that the new President, Ford, might disassociate himself from Nixon's promises and void Nixon's pledges to retaliate against North Vietnamese truce violations. There would be no way out of abandoning the central highlands and the coastal plain. Thieu remained in seclusion in his office.

Unexpectedly, on August 10, Thieu received a message from President Ford delivered by Chargé d'Affaires Wolf Lehmann. The letter read:

Dear Mr. President:

As I assume the office of President of the United States, one of my first thoughts concerns the savage attacks your armed forces are now successfully resisting with such courage and bravery. I do not think I really need to inform you that American foreign policy has always been marked by its essential continuity and its essential bipartisan nature. This is even more true today and the existing commitments this nation has made in the past are still valid and will be fully honored in my administration.

These reassurances are particularly relevant to the Republic of Vietnam. We have traveled a long and hard road together. I have listened to Ambassador Martin's report on the remarkable progress the Republic of Vietnam has made under your leadership. In the period since the signing of the Paris Agreements, I have been heartened by his report of your personal determination to continue the improvement of your governmental processes to insure that our aid and the increasing aid we confidently expect from other donor countries can be rapidly and effectively utilized to bring the South Vietnamese economy to a self-sustaining level in the next few years. As the professional efficiency, the high morale, and the combat effectiveness of the armed forces of the Republic of Vietnam become increasingly evident to the leaders of the Democratic Republic of Vietnam in Hanoi, it is my earnest hope they will agree to return to participation in the mechanisms set up by the Paris Agreements and begin to seriously work out with you modalities for the full and complete implementation of the Paris Agreements which I know is your desire.

I know you must be concerned by the initial steps taken by the Congress on the current fiscal year appropriations for both economic and military assistance to the Republic of Vietnam. Our legislative process is a complicated one and it is not yet completed. Although it may take a little time I do want to reassure you of my confidence that in the end our support will be adequate on both counts.

In these important endeavors I shall look to Dr. Kissinger, whom I have asked to remain as Secretary of State, for guidance and support. He has my fullest confidence, as does Ambassador Martin.

Sincerely yours,
[s] Gerald R. Ford

To Thieu's delight, the new President had reiterated that America's existing commitments to Vietnam "are still valid and will be fully honored in my administration." Thieu was elated that Ford said: "These reassurances are particularly relevant to the Republic of Vietnam." It seemed that Ford meant what he said. The mandate from Washington had been renewed once again. Ford promised adequate military and economic aid, despite the initial setbacks. There was a smile on the president's face such as Hung had not seen for a long time, and an abrupt change for the better in his mood. At that time Hung had not been shown the file of Nixon letters and did not know of the written American commitments. For Thieu, this letter was proof of the continuity of American policy, and he took it to mean that Ford, who had been handpicked by Nixon as his successor, would carry out the pledges made by Nixon.

After a cabinet meeting Hung was invited to have a drink with Thieu; they sipped Black Label Scotch together and discussed the future. Thieu seemed confident that Ford could be counted on to support Saigon's cause and validate Nixon's promises. Traditionally, Congress gives a new President a honeymoon for six months, Hung explained. Thieu hoped Vietnamese aid would be one of the wedding gifts. To send the message to Washington, Thieu issued an official government statement on August 10 referring to Watergate as "internal matters of the United States. . . . The Government of the Republic of Vietnam is fully confident that the Government and people of the United States of America will continue the policy which has been pursued by five U.S. presidents and endorsed by the two major political parties of the U.S. and maintain their cooperation with the government and people of Vietnam so that a just peace in South Vietnam based on the Paris Agreement could be achieved."[15] Thieu stopped talking about "redeployment" and the plan to truncate South Vietnam was put on hold.

In his final meeting with the Vietnamese generals before his departure on August 16, General Murray counseled them about the dwindling prospects of military aid and urged them to think seriously of shortening their defense lines, concentrating their remaining troops and ammunition on the defense of more populated enclaves along the coastal areas. Murray did not know of the Ford letter; neither did Congress.

Only a few days after Ford's reassuring letter to Thieu, Congress appropriated just $700 million of the $1 billion authorized ceiling for Indochina that had been signed by Nixon. Thieu was deeply upset and confused. Congress, it seemed, was divorcing the President before the honeymoon began. Hung had invited Warren Nutter to Saigon to provide advice and try to win support in Washington. Nutter joined Thieu and Hung at a breakfast meeting on August 23 in the Independence Palace. Thieu expressed deep concern with the reduced aid level. "A few days ago it was a billion dollars, now it is cut to $700 million. What am I going to do with that aid?" asked Thieu. "This is like giving me twelve dollars and telling me to fly first class from Saigon to Tokyo."

Nutter, a long-time supporter of Thieu, was upset. He found it difficult to explain the congressional action and hoped it could be reversed. "Our Congress sometimes behaves in a very irresponsible way," he told Thieu. "The Indochina Resource Center is trying its best to destroy your country." He promised Thieu that on his return to Washington he would make an effort to call the President's attention to the critical situation in Saigon.

"Nobody at the high levels of our government is paying any attention to Vietnam any more," explained Nutter sadly. Thieu was so absorbed in what Nutter had to say that he neglected his noodle soup.

When he returned to Washington, Nutter wrote to John O. Marsh counsellor to President Ford, urging support for South Vietnam. Nutter insisted that South Vietnam was viable if only it could remain militarily secure from main force North Vietnamese attacks; but declining U.S. support was taking a psychological as well as a physical toll. Nutter told Marsh:

> I have never seen Thieu or his military leaders in deeper gloom, and that mood is bound to spread in the form of crumbling morale, particularly if the North keeps up its relentless pressure. The waning congressional support and consequent deteriorating prospects for security are largely responsible, I believe, for the outbreak of public demonstrations seen in recent weeks. Political and economic stability is being undermined, and things could fall apart if trends are not reversed. If a choice must be made, military assistance comes first, ahead of economic aid, because all else hinges on countering the military threat. Perhaps the need for aid will go on, as critics assert, but we should take one day at a time.
>
> To abandon South Vietnam to the dangers of destruction and massacre for the sake of a half billion dollars or so would do more than sear the American conscience. It would deal a crushing blow to our still mighty, if weakened, influence in world affairs.[16]

The military aid cut to $700 million and the economic aid cut from $800 to $400 million forced Saigon to reconsider its entire position and brought into question the nature of the American commitment as far as the Vietnamese were concerned.

In the meantime, Ford moved to reassure Thieu by dispatching a presidential delegation to Saigon, headed by Deputy Secretary of Defense William Clements, a Texas oil company executive who joined the government as a tough-talking, hardline supporter of the Vietnam War.

Clements carried the bravado and self-assurance of a powerful Texan, and his easygoing, informal style appealed to the Vietnamese. He promised Thieu that a major effort would be made by the administration to find military aid funds. "Don't worry. We will make a major effort in the Congress. I am convinced Congress will provide the money," said Clements.[17] There was no sense of a crisis. Clements had been sent out to reassure Thieu. He did it by discussing new strategies to raise supplemental aid funds in Congress and to request higher aid in the future to make up for the funds that had been cut in the final days of Nixon's administration. Clements's sincere manner was seductive. He made it all sound possible.

Thieu listened carefully and nodded with what one member of the delegation characterized as "a pervasive skepticism." He seemed very beset and deeply concerned about the ability of the U.S. to deliver, but the only thing he could do was to listen to the American reassurances and hope they would come to fruition."[18]

In front of the Vietnamese, the American delegation discussed the question of timing to request new military aid funds and how to juggle the development loan funds to meet current needs. They talked about asking Congress for an immediate $300 million military aid supplement. Ever optimistic, Ambassador Martin assured Thieu that "the door to aid is not closed" and "our procedures are not exhausted." Martin derided the "fiscal whores" in the Pentagon and on Capitol Hill who would not appropriate money for Vietnam and prevented funds from being used to support the Saigon government. Clements promised immediate action on his return to Washington.

Neither the military nor the aid situation improved in September and Vietnamese casualties rose. The North Vietnamese began to shell Hue and took the high ground dominating National Route 1 in Military Region I, forcing a major counterattack to regain the territory. In the other three military regions the North Vietnamese continued to probe and overextend the ARVN forces.[19] Thieu grew more concerned and nervous. There was no response from Washington and he asked to meet directly with Ford. In an effort to make his case, he dispatched Foreign Minister Vuong Van Bac to Washington with a letter requesting the meeting with Ford and a clarification of American aid policy.

Bac, a handsome, self-assured lawyer who fled from the North in 1954, had been named foreign minister on November 8, 1973, replacing Tran Van Lam, who became President of the Vietnamese Senate. Bac spoke excellent English, having spent nine months in Washington in 1956 during the Eisenhower administration with an office in the Old Executive Office Building learning how the American government works.[20] He served as Ambassador to London and took part in the Paris Talks as an adviser to the Vietnamese delegation in 1968 and again in 1972. Bac had first met Kissinger at a breakfast in Saigon in 1965, when Kissinger was a professor at Harvard and Philip Habib was Political Officer in the embassy in Saigon. They had worked together over the years. Bac was thus at ease as Kissinger, in a dress suit, accompanied him and Ambassador Phuong to the Oval Office to meet Ford.

Ford was wearing a blue-checked sport coat and slacks for the meeting, which lasted thirty minutes. Bac presented the letter from Thieu and went over the points verbally. He assured Ford of South Vietnam's willingness to negotiate with the North Vietnamese if the terms of the Paris Agreements were adhered to. Bac passed over Watergate and Nixon's resignation by referring to them as "internal American matters into which we do not want to interject ourselves; but the fact remains the events have an effect on public opinion in Vietnam and the morale of our troops. We want to be sure that the changing of personnel will have no effect on the assistance provided by the United States in the defense of our liberty."

Ford was friendly and went out of his way to praise Kissinger in front of Bac and Phuong, explaining how he would be relying heavily on Kissinger during his term of office. "You can be sure that we will always act as a good friend and partner of South Vietnam," said the President.[21] They discussed compliance with the Paris Agreements and ways to deal with the North Vietnamese violations. Although Ford avoided making any specific commitments other than general expression of continued support, Bac was impressed with his positive declaration of "partnership" with South Vietnam.

On Capitol Hill, Bac encountered "hostility and many reservations." Congressmen urged him to reach an accommodation with the Viet Cong. Senator Adlai Stevenson III (D.-Ill.) told Bac to urge Thieu to step down. After that, if the North Vietnamese still continued to attack, then the United States would intervene. "Senator, our constitutional government is the only semblance of legitimacy and stability we have left. If we give that up we are finished," Bac explained.[22]

Inside the administration there were still promises of support. Bac was told that even if it was difficult to win congressional approval, in the end it would be worked out favorably to South Vietnam. When he went to the Pentagon, Defense Secretary James Schlesinger told him: "I will be at your side in any parliamentary situation." "I remember the phrase he used, 'parliamentary situation,' because it was such an unusual way to say he would support us in appealing to Congress for more aid." recalled Bac.

"I was reassured," Bac went on. "We believed in the promise of the President, but we were not familiar with the intricacies of the appropriation and authorization process for aid. We believed that the presidential promises in the letters predated the congressional restraints. The U.S. had a solemn obligation made to the Republic of Vietnam at the time of the signing of the Paris Accord."[23]

On October 24, President Ford wrote secretly to Thieu, again insisting that there had been no change in American policy toward Vietnam under his administration. He gave Thieu "my firm assurance that this administration will make every effort to provide the assistance you need." But the letter was tepid in tone and denied Thieu a personal meeting. It had a stale, pro forma ring to it. Ford wrote:

Dear Mr. President:

I very much appreciated meeting with Foreign Minister Bac and receiving from him your letter of September 19.

American policy towards Vietnam remains unchanged under this Administration. We continue strongly to support your government's efforts to defend and to promote the independence and well-being of the South Vietnamese people. We also remain confident in the courage, determination and skill of the South Vietnamese people and armed forces.

I fully understand and share your concern about the current situation in the Republic of Vietnam, particularly the growing Communist military threat which you now face. I am also well aware of the critical necessity of American military and economic aid for your country. I give you my firm assurance that this Administration will continue to make every effort to provide the assistance you need.

Although I would welcome the opportunity to meet with you to discuss ways and means to achieve a genuine and lasting peace in South Vietnam, prior commitments preclude such a meeting at this time. But I hope that such a meeting can be arranged in the future.

I agree with you that it is essential that my government clearly indicate its support for your government and for the full implementation of the Paris Agreements. I believe my public statement of October 9, my meeting with Foreign Minister Bac and Deputy Defense Secretary Clements' visit to Saigon all clearly demonstrate that we are standing firm in our commitments to you. We have also conveyed to other powers having an interest in Vietnam that we continue to support your government and that we favor a complete implementation of the Paris Agreements. I shall take advantage of other occasions to show my support for your government and for the peace that we achieved together.

Our countries have been through many difficult times together. It appears likely that we shall face other difficulties in the future. I am confident, however, that these problems can be overcome if we work together to meet them with strength and determination.

With best wishes for you and the valiant people of the Republic of Vietnam.

Sincerely,
[s] Gerald R. Ford

This time Thieu was deeply distressed. There seemed no place for him to turn, yet he realized that American aid was dwindling. He would have to adopt a radical strategy if he was to break the bonds of total dependency on the United States.

15

Twilight of the Republic

"I N OCTOBER 1974, as the late autumn weather began to turn cold, we military cadres were reminded of the campaign season ahead," wrote Van Tien Dung, Chief of Staff of the Vietnam People's Army, in his memoir *Our Great Spring Victory*. The driving force behind Hanoi's final decision to launch the 1975 invasion, Dung admitted, was the observation that "Nguyen Van Thieu had to call on his troops to switch to 'a poor man's war.'" Dung was fully aware of the reduction in American military aid to Saigon and its impact on the fighting capabilities of the ARVN. As Dung noted: "The decrease in American aid had made it impossible for Saigon troops to carry out their combat and force development plans." Dung, whose intelligence agents had provided access to secret internal South Vietnamese assessments prepared by the Joint General Staff and Hung, correctly estimated that South Vietnamese fighting capability had fallen by nearly 60 percent in firepower because of the shortage of bombs and shells; mobility dropped by 50 percent because of the shortage of aircraft, vehicles, and fuel.[1]

After the congressional aid cut in August 1974, Communist violations surged. Thieu began to speak publicly about the dangers ahead, but there was no response from Washington, which officially rejected the view that a large-scale enemy offensive would take place in 1975. Inside the Palace Thieu demanded a complete review of the aid situation. The JGS was ordered to accurately appraise the current fighting capability of the ARVN in terms of troops and actual supplies of ammunition in the field. Ammunition supplies had reached a dangerously low level and there was concern that if used at intensive combat rates the "supply system could get perilous overnight."[2]

Thieu insisted there was to be no more theoretical estimating based on requests or supplies in the pipeline. This was to be a hard, bottom-line inventory of how many artillery pieces, how many tons of shells, and how many helicopters were available. Hung was ordered to present a report on the pattern, the structure, and the level of past, current, and future eco-

246

nomic and military aid in actual dollar terms. The conclusion of his report: The effective aid level for fiscal year 1975 was only about one third of the average annual aid from 1970 to 1973. "Military aid, and therefore our fighting capability, has been reduced by 60 percent and economic aid by 66 percent," Hung wrote. In his memoirs, Dung used exactly the same figures as in Hung's report to Thieu, including the term "fiscal year," a concept that was strange even to the South Vietnamese generals who worked side by side with the Americans for years, let alone to a Communist general— unless he had the actual documents to quote from.

The findings on the aid situation and its impact on the fighting capability of each of the military branches were incorporated into an intelligence briefing on the anticipated North Vietnamese offensive in 1975. This classified report was utilized to warn the Ford administration and Congress of the inevitable fall of South Vietnam unless the United States increased military aid. The document, dated January 9, 1975, was translated into English and used by JGS Chairman General Vien to brief U.S. officials and members of Congress who visited Saigon. Vien presented in detail the North Vietnamese violations of the cease-fire and their heavy build-up of men and equipment in the South since the cease-fire. Then he listed the "numerous indicators of enemy preparations for large-scale attacks in 1975." Along with revamping their command structure and activating new divisions, the Communists were redeploying divisions into the South and preparing to move their strategic reserve to the South. The possibilities for an intensified war in 1975 were apparent. Either NVA forces would try to speed up deteriorating conditions by a general attack, or they would continue the high level of truce violations "while readying themselves for seizing what they call a 'strategic opportunity' to launch a big offensive of the type seen in 1972." [3]

Contrary to popular belief, Saigon and Washington were not caught by surprise when the 1975 spring offensive was launched. A series of captured directives issued by the Central Office for South Vietnam (COSVN), the Communist command headquarters, had clearly spelled out the enemy strategy and its evolution.

In the wake of the cease-fire the Communists had adopted a "half war, half peace" course of action. This was followed in April 1973 by a "peace in war" strategy; then, beginning in October 1973, an "attack in peace" directive was put into force. By January 1975, in the first issue of the year, an editorial in the North Vietnamese Communist Party journal *Hoc Tap* indicated that the 23rd Plenum of the Central Committee of the Lao Dong (Communist) Party had been held and implied that a general offensive would be conducted in South Vietnam. Resolution 23 ordered an all-out attack. [4]

Even before the 23rd Communist Party Plenum, captured intelligence documents and prisoner interrogrations pointed to an offensive in 1975. At a secret meeting in the Independence Palace on December 6, 1974, to appraise the year-end military situation it was concluded that 1975 would mark the launching of a general North Vietnamese offensive at approximately the level of the 1972 Easter offensive. The projection was for the North Vietnamese to increase the momentum of their attack to coincide with the October 1975 Vietnamese presidential elections and continue into 1976 to influence the U.S. presidential election, the same way Hanoi tried to have an effect on the U.S. 1968 and 1972 elections.

The warning to Washington was direct and specific: An offensive was about to begin and the central highlands would be the first objective.

President Thieu, through Ambassador Martin, wrote to President Ford and set forth his estimate of North Vietnamese intentions. At the same time he had General Vien give his briefing to the American Defense Attaché, General Homer Smith, and all ranking Americans who visited Saigon. General Tran Van Don, then deputy prime minister, made a trip to Washington in the winter of 1974. He met with Deputy Defense Secretary William Clements and tried to impress upon him the danger of an impending Communist offensive. Don recalls Clements telling him, "Don't worry. There will not be an offensive. Besides, we are here."[5]

At the end of December 1974, after the loss of Phuoc Long seventy-five miles northeast of Saigon near the Cambodian border, Hung had a chance to warn American officials, including Defense Secretary James Schlesinger, of the impending offensive. Phuoc Long was the first provincal capital to be lost to North Vietnamese regular forces. It was a clear-cut violation of the cease-fire. Hung returned to Washington to rally support for increased aid and to assess the prospects for the coming year. Only Eric Von Marbod took any interest in Hung's predictions of a coming offensive and promised to brief Schlesinger. The warnings were ignored. The official U.S. response was always that no large-scale offensive would take place in 1975.

What the Vietnamese took as American disbelief in a North Vietnamese offensive was actually a growing consensus within the Ford administration, particularly among those advisers Ford had brought with him to the White House, that politically the Congress and the American public would not support reinvolvement in the war through increased military aid and a resumption of bombing.[6] Although the stalwarts such as Ambassador Martin and Deputy Defense Secretary Clements kept reassuring the Vietnamese, sentiment had turned against "Nixon's" war. When he resigned, the will to fight the war went with him. Invariably, Hung was advised by State Department and Agency for International Development (AID) officials to counsel Thieu against publicly warning of the Communist threat because it would have an adverse effect on American investment in Vietnam. They said talk of a North Vietnamese invasion would frighten away potential investors with badly needed foreign exchange to replace American aid money. Plans to build the twenty-two-story, 550-room Hyatt Regency Hotel with a convention center on the Saigon waterfront, at a cost of $15.5 million, would be canceled. Hung thought the arguments unreal and told his American counterparts: "If there is no military aid, there will be no country and no tourists. Military aid at this point is more important than economic aid."

As a result of Washington playing down the threat from Hanoi, rumors began to circulate among Vietnamese officials that the Americans had decided to make a deal on Vietnam with the Soviet Union and China. When the time came for Saigon to collapse, "the death watch should be short to minimize the adverse consequences for the U.S. on the international scene."[7]

On January 2, 1975, President Thieu chaired an emergency meeting in the Situation Room at the Independence Palace. With all the top military men present, Thieu decided not to reinforce Phuoc Long or to try to retake the city. The cost would be too high; there were no replacement aircraft and no reserve troops. If reserve units were committed to Phuoc Long, they would have to be taken from other more critical regions where intelligence reports indicated the North Vietnamese were preparing for the 1975 offensive. For the Communists, Phuoc Long was not merely the gain of a poor provincial capital. As General Vien noted: "What they gained psychologically and politically was more important. It was their first big step toward total military conquest, boldly taken yet apparently without fear of any reaction from the United States. What more encouragement could the Communists have asked for?"[8]

As late as January 14, 1975 after the loss of Phuoc Long, Defense Secretary James Schlesinger still downplayed the North Vietnamese intentions. In a news conference following the attack, Schlesinger said:

> Now the situation in South Vietnam appears to be that the North Vietnamese are not likely to launch a massive, country-wide offensive. What they are attempting to do is to weaken the control that the South Vietnamese regime has over the country, in particular to reverse the processes of pacifications that have been eminently successful to date. So what we can expect over the course of the next few months is a number of high points on the part of the North Vietnamese. I am not at this time anticipating a major, country-wide offensive of the type of 1972.[9]

Asked on what he based his estimate that Hanoi would not launch a large-scale offensive in 1975, Schlesinger replied: "On what we take to be the movement of their forces."[10]

Hung was shocked. During his visit to Washington he had been shown aerial reconnaissance pictures of the North Vietnamese build-up with newly supplied Soviet weapons. He had shown the pictures to Thieu on his return to Saigon. Thieu shook his head in dismay.

Schlesinger's comments came as a personal blow. Hung had looked up to Schlesinger as his professor and a friend. "I had personally explained the situation to him in December 1974 and asked Eric Von Marbod to follow up. In my conversations with Schlesinger I always felt that he was sympathetic to Vietnam and had an integrity that Kissinger lacked. I could not imagine that Schlesinger did not know of the intelligence foreshadowing the North Vietnamese attack plans," said Hung. Schlesinger's remarks were analyzed and discussed within the Saigon government. There was only one conclusion: the senior levels of the American administration had made a decision to play down the North Vietnamese violations of the cease-fire. "It appeared to us that the Ford administration had decided to abandon South Vietnam, that the end of the decent interval had come." said Hung. "To us it looked as though the United States did not want it to appear that it was not helping its ally, because this would have an adverse impact on America's image as a great military power. Rather, the impression was being created, falsely, that we could not cope with the normal level of North Vietnamese attacks."

Schlesinger's intention was to try and restrain Hanoi by hinting at the resumption of bombing. In reply to a question at his press conference Schlesinger noted: "I think that the North Vietnamese continue to have an abiding respect for American power, that they do not discount American power, and that they are reluctant to take those steps that they fear might conceivably lead to a reintroduction of American power." [11]

It was to no avail. Reading Schlesinger's comments in Hanoi, General Dung and the Politboro could only be heartened. The American lack of response was a major influence in convincing the North Vietnamese to proceed. Commenting on the American reaction to the fall of Phuoc Long, the first province to be captured, Dung wrote:

> At first the United States belligerently sent the nuclear aircraft carrier Enterprise with a special task force from the Seventh Fleet steaming from the Philippines toward the coast of Vietnam, and put the third Marine division in Okinawa on alert. Pentagon hawks threatened to resume bombing the North. But in the end, U.S. Secretary of Defense Schlesinger had to pass over the "Phuoc Long business" and announced that "This is not yet an all out offensive by North Vietnam." He turned a cold shoulder to Thieu's heart-rending cries. United States Ambassador Martin in Saigon told Thieu, "We have no authorization to give you American support at this time." By now the U.S. position had weakened; they could no longer do whatever they pleased. [12]

Schlesinger's remarks were made even as Hanoi's reserve forces—the 312th, 316th, 341st, and 308th divisions—were on their way to the South. Movement of the Communist troops could be observed in broad daylight along the two corridors leading to the South, the Ho Chi Minh Trail through Laos, and the Truong-Son corridor, a 600-mile-long route from the DMZ to Tay Ninh Province.

Thieu was alarmed by the Defense Secretary's apparent effort to play down the attack on Phuoc Long. A "delphic pronouncement," a member of the Pentagon press corps described it at the time. Thieu decided to write directly to President Ford. On January 24 and 25, he warned of the enemy's activities and intentions and appealed for prompt military aid to uphold the Paris Agreement. Thieu also proposed resuming negotiations with the North Vietnamese.

There was no longer any question of scaring off potential American investors. In Saigon, talks were still going on with representatives of the Hilton and Hyatt hotel chains to build convention centers and tourist complexes. Major international oil companies were bidding for rights to drill offshore in South Vietnam's territorial waters. But all would be lost unless there was enough military aid to halt a Communist offensive.

Hung urged Thieu to go public with the secret promises contained in the Nixon and Ford letters in a series of interviews for American television, but Thieu was still unwilling to give the Americans a pretext to say that he had violated their secret understandings. Despite the Schlesinger comments he still hoped to salvage the situation. On January 28, the day President Ford requested a $300 million supplemental appropriation for military aid for Vietnam, Thieu gave a lengthy interview to *The Washington Post* correspondent in Saigon, Philip A. McCombs.

In the hour-long interview, Thieu made no mention of the Nixon and Ford letters or of their promises. He appealed to Congress for "the minimum of $300 million in emergency military aid." When asked if he felt betrayed by the Americans, Thieu replied: "Not yet, I am very confident that the U.S., which has never lost any war, which has never failed to help any people who would like to preserve their independence," would support the Saigon government. Thieu noted that since the cease-fire agreement 149,000 Vietnamese had died and 1.4 million had been made homeless.

Around the same time Thieu also turned privately to General Alexander Haig, who had become the commander of North Atlantic Treaty Organization forces in Europe. Thieu sent Nguyen Phu Duc, who had left the Palace and become Ambassador to Belgium, to see Haig. During their meeting, Duc, who knew Haig well from their bitter sessions in Saigon, reviewed the deteriorating situation. He told Haig: "President Thieu has asked me to ask you only one question. If you knew then what you know now, would you have asked us to sign the Paris Accord?" Haig was deeply moved by the meeting and returned to Washington in February to request a meeting with President Ford. He was so upset by the failure of the United States to respond to the North Vietnamese violations that he considered resigning. Haig saw Ford alone and told him: "Mr. President, in view of the blatant North Vietnamese violations of the Paris Accords, you have got to take a stand on resuming the bombing, even if the Congress overrules you." Ford replied: "Al, I can't. The country is fed up with the war." Haig persisted and urged Ford to reconsider for the sake of the country and his own political future as a presidential candidate. "You've got to roll up your sleeves like Harry Truman did and take a principled stand. If you do, you'll be elected President. If you don't, you'll never be returned to the White House. You must show your leadership now, before it is too late." [13]

In an effort to assess President Ford's request for a $300 million aid supplemental, the Senate and House of Representatives formed a bipartisan group to fly to Vietnam. Two members of the group, Senator Dewey F. Bartlett (R.-Okl.) and Congressman Paul McCloskey (R.-Cal.), arrived in Saigon on February 24, three days in advance of the main party. Others in the delegation included Representatives William V. Chappell (D.-Fla.), Donald N. Fraser (D.-Minn.), Bella Abzug (D.-N.Y.), Millicent Fenwick (R.-N.J.), John P. Murtha (D.-Pa.), and John J. Flynt (D.-Ga.). They were accompanied by Philip C. Habib, Assistant Secretary of State for East Asian and Pacific Affairs; Eric Von Marbod, Deputy Assistant Secretary of Defense; and a dozen staff members and escorts.

President Ford's letter replying to President Thieu arrived on February 26, the day before the main group landed in Saigon. Ford reassured Thieu that the United States would "continue to press for the full implementation" of the Paris Agreement. "We strongly support your effort to resume negotiations, and we will make every effort to provide the assistance that is so necessary to your struggle until peace comes," said Ford. His tone was careful and restrained.

> Your thoughtful letters of January 24 and 25 come at a time when Viet-Nam is very much on my mind and on the minds of other people here and throughout the world. I share your concern about North Viet-Nam's failure to observe the most fundamental provisions of the Paris Agreement and about the heightened level of North Vietnamese military pressure. I wish to assure you that this Government will continue to press for the implementation of this Agreement.
>
> Once again the South Vietnamese people and Armed Forces are effectively demonstrating their determination to resist Hanoi's attacks. Despite your existing limitations on ammunition and other supplies, I was particularly impressed by the performance of your forces at the Phuoc Long province capital and at Ba Den mountain, where they were overwhelmed by greatly superior numbers after being cut off from resupply and reinforcement.
>
> Even though your offers to reinstitute negotiations have been rejected thus far, they clearly demonstrate that it is the Communist side—not the Republic of Viet-Nam—which is prolonging the war. We continue to believe that implementation of the Paris Agreement, with direct negotiations between the Vietnamese parties, is the quickest, most effective way to end the bloodshed in Viet-Nam. But I remain hopeful that if we persevere we will yet reach our objective of a fair peace, a lasting peace and a peace which is consistent with the will of the South Vietnamese people—justifying the sacrifices of the Vietnamese and American peoples.
>
> Sincerely,
> Gerald R. Ford

Thieu realized that Congress now played the key role, and Ambassador Martin stressed to him the importance of convincing the congressional delegation to approve the $300 million supplemental which now became a magic talisman for American support. After billions in aid, the fate of the South seemed to hinge on the supplemental. Having captured Phuoc Long, the North Vietnamese were regrouping their forces and awaiting a possible American response to their blatant violation of the cease-fire. Since there had been no American bombing, the new aid request by President Ford would be a litmus test of American intentions.

During the war, congressmen had come and gone almost unnoticed. It was the President who made the decisions and with whom Thieu had to deal. Now the Congress, not the President, seemed to hold the power. The chairman of the Joint General Staff, General Vien, spoke to his generals and the cabinet of "the sword of Damocles held over our heads by the American Congress." Until that moment, General Vien referred to the American B-52 bombers as the Damocles sword held over the North Vietnamese. The Vietnamese people, both in the North and the South, watched the American congressional group's actions and statements with hope and fear.

Hanoi looked to the delegation with hope, Saigon with fear. Hanoi's expectation was that the Americans would cut off support to the South. Saigon's fear was that the delegation might, by words or gestures, send a signal that would encourage the North Vietnamese to carry out the second phase of the offensive that had begun with the seizure of Phuoc Long.

Since he came to Saigon in 1973, Hung could not recall any other single event that occupied so much of the attention of the entire government machinery and personnel. There were a series of agonizing meetings over how to treat the delegation. Thieu even thought of the human dimension: how to cope with Congresswoman Bella Abzug. He assigned handsome Foreign Minister Bac to pay personal attention to her. "Bac, you are *séduisant* [seductive]," said Thieu, as the cabinet laughed. "You must take care of Mrs. Abzug."

Two schools of thought emerged. One argued that the South Vietnamese should permit the delegation to go anywhere, including prisons that held political prisoners, and meet anyone, including the Viet Cong. The other group argued that the government should minimize the contacts of the delegation and make it concentrate on the military and economic situation, not the problems of political dissent. They urged that delegation members be taken to the battle areas where they could meet with top military commanders and be briefed on the gravity of the situation.

Hung supported the view that a well-planned, organized, and controlled visit would most benefit Saigon. To allow the delegation to roam freely would confuse the issues Saigon faced. But President Thieu decided the Americans could do whatever they wanted and "see whomever they were pleased to see."

The South Vietnamese leaders were tense about how to handle the delegation. They feared a negative reaction would mean the end of aid to Vietnam, yet the ground rules of total access were bound to uncover the worst of Saigon's political problems. Hung knew Thieu's sensitivity to criticism and his impatience with those who underestimated the Communist threat to Vietnam, so he was concerned as to how the president would handle the direct clashes that were anticipated with the members of the delegation. It was to be Saigon's last chance. Once the delegation returned to Washington, it would set the line on Vietnam. There would be no second or third chances. Hung knew how far the mood in Washington was shifting away from involvement in Vietnam and he knew the North Vietnamese

were watching closely to assess the congressional reaction. Rejection of
Thieu and his government would be a signal that American aid was ended
and Hanoi could move against the South at will.

Saigon's morale would be demolished if it were rejected by the American Congress. Up to now, Thieu had had to deal with tough-minded, politically astute American presidents who made difficult demands but kept their
word. Suddenly he was faced with an undisciplined, unruly, and unfriendly
group of congressmen and women whose whim would decide the fate of
South Vietnam.

What made it all the worse was that the North Vietnamese offensive
had begun. "I'm not going to beg them," Thieu told Hung. He was determined to be dignified and not lose his temper. "We've got to find out if there
is anything left in the Vietnamese-American relationship, or if it has hit the
bottom." Thieu repeated the phrase *can tau rao mang* at several meetings;
literally, it refers to animals who "lick the last grain of food and suck the
last drop of water from the trough." Thieu was trying to decide whether or
not he should go public with the file of letters from Nixon and Ford, the
secret American commitment to continue support for South Vietnam. To do
so would mean publicly accusing the United States of betrayal. As an American-trained professor, familiar with the American sense of fair play, Hung
counseled Thieu to release the text of the letters and make a public appeal
to the American people. Others close to Thieu, such as Foreign Minister
Bac and Tran Van Lam, president of the Senate, advised him to maintain a
more cautious posture; the two countries had come too far together for too
long and there was still hope. Thieu agreed. His choice was "not yet." He
would make efforts to reach Ford through private channels and through
direct letters.

The government of Vietnam wanted to go to any lengths of hospitality
to please the congressional delegation. A full schedule of briefings and arrangements for them to visit all parts of the country, including military
bases, political prisoners, even the "Tiger Cages" on Con Son Island were
arranged; but all to no avail. On the day of their arrival several members of
the delegation went off on their own to find opposition political leaders,
Communist sympathizers, and the press corps to obtain evidence of corruption and the dictatorial powers of Thieu's government. Bella Abzug, Don
Fraser, and Paul McCloskey spent much of their time contacting opposition
leaders and interviewing prisoners in Saigon jails. They met with the Viet
Cong representatives stationed at Tan Son Nhut Airport to discuss the
oppressive Saigon government and how it violated the Paris Agreements.

Prior to their arrival, the South Vietnamese had hoped that the American delegation would attempt to determine the extent of the impending
Communist threat of invasion and how best to respond. Instead, their energies were focused on proving the oppressive and corrupt nature of Thieu's
regime. Abzug and Fraser were particularly undiplomatic and openly hostile
to the Vietnamese in Saigon. So was McCloskey, until Hung introduced him
to a winsome young woman member of the National Assembly who spoke

English and explained the problems of living under the threat of a Communist takeover. At the prime minister's reception, Abzug clearly showed her contempt for the Republic of Vietnam by refusing to raise her glass of champagne to toast the Vietnamese officials when everyone else did. Foreign Minister Bac did his best to win Mrs. Abzug's sympathy with his smile and favorable comments about American labor unions. "I ran out of topics to attract her interest very quickly," recalled Bac.[14] Mrs. Abzug considered herself an expert on Vietnam. She had visited Laos on a previous visit and showed no interest in anything the Saigon government or U.S. officials had to offer.[15]

The issue of political prisoners was still a major liability for Thieu. The congressional group demanded the release of eighteen journalists who had been arrested by the government for openly advocating a coalition government in their articles and defying the government censorship. Representative McCloskey and Senator Bartlett demanded to see the arrested journalists and made headlines when they reported that one of the prisoners, a nineteen-year-old girl, told McCloskey: "They beat us very much." When the congressmen asked Thieu about the journalists, he defended the government's actions. Later Thieu ordered their release, but he never reversed the impressions caused by the stories of arrests and beatings of the journalists. The delegation continued to investigate the charges that Viet Cong agents were still being arrested following the Paris Accord. One of the cases raised with Thieu was that of Huynh Tan Mam, president of the Vietnam National Student Union. Supposedly a pacifist and neutralist, Huynh Tan Mam led demonstrations against the Thieu government and American involvement in the war. The congressmen demanded his release and Thieu acceded. On May 1, 1975, one day after the fall of Saigon, Huynh Tan Mam appeared on television praising the North Vietnamese and was honored and rewarded for his services to the Communist cause.[16]

The American Embassy estimated that the South Vietnamese were holding 35,000 prisoners of all types in 1973. In Chi Hoa Prison, the largest in Saigon, the embassy estimated that there were 7,911 prisoners. (After the fall of Saigon 7,000 prisoners were freed from Chi Hoa Prison.) The leader of the campaign to free political prisoners was Father Chan Tin, a left-wing Catholic priest from Central Vietnam. American newsmen and visitors to Saigon reported Father Chan Tin "to be a man deeply concerned with human suffering"; the Indochina Resources Center portrayed Chan Tin as a hero and brought his charges to Congress as proof of Thieu's repression. After the fall of Saigon it was revealed that Chan Tin and several other Catholic priests had been part of the Viet Cong underground. According to Tiziano Terzani, a leftist European journalist who witnessed the fall of Saigon and stayed on in the aftermath, the priests "presented themselves as exponents of the Third Force, but in reality they were part of an operation whose purpose was to back up the struggle of the National Liberation Front."[17]

It was a new situation. The delegation's activities, their words and actions, were monitored in full detail by the Saigon government, the press, and the Communist intelligence operatives. The congressional delegation would be both judge and jury. The promises of Nixon and Ford seemed to have little relevance.

After their trips to the provinces facing attack, the delegation met with President Thieu at the Independence Palace for a review. Hung was at Thieu's side to take notes and assist him with his English. The working session turned into a hostile interrogation of Thieu. The thrust of the questions was: Why had South Vietnam violated the cease-fire? There were no questions about the Communist violations of the Paris Agreement. The entire burden was on Thieu. "You imposed conditions on the North Vietnamese to implement the Paris Agreement. You required North Vietnamese withdrawal as a condition for the talks. How long do you need economic and military aid?" Hung was shocked by the hostility. There was no longer a sense of shared purpose between allies. In his notes of the meeting, Hung recorded a congressman's warning: "We think that aid depends on a number of elements, such as the release of the political prisoners, the establishment of the Third Force, and liberty for journalists. What have you done on all these issues? We are very much concerned."

There was little discussion of the reality of the North Vietnamese military build-up. Asked when the general offensive would begin, Thieu replied bluntly: "It all depends on whether or not they [the North Vietnamese] have an opportunity. They said that 1975 gives them an excellent opportunity because the balance of forces has shifted in their favor. They are waiting for more aid cuts in Washington and political developments in South Vietnam."

As Hung listened to the questions of the congressional delegation, he enumerated to himself Thieu's successes and failures. Thieu's outstanding accomplishments were land reform, the "land to the tiller" program, and pacification of the countryside, which had been succeeding until the North Vietnamese cease-fire violations increased in intensity in the summer of 1974.[18] The territory lost to the Communists in the Easter offensive of 1972 had been retaken. Even after the American troops departed in 1973, he had held the line against the North Vietnamese efforts to expand their control in the Mekong Delta and the territory near the Cambodian border. As long as American aid was forthcoming, the ARVN forces held their own. Thieu could stand up to the Americans and he had fought against signing the Paris Accords with courage and tenacity. The Vietnamese people respected this.

What kind of a dictator was Thieu? In Saigon there were twenty-two newspapers, many of them openly critical of Thieu. In the midst of the war dissent was being tolerated. Thieu was painted as corrupt. The population criticized him for tolerating corruption and permitting his family to benefit from his position, but that was the Vietnamese way. Hung knew how frustrated Thieu was with the extent of corruption.

Obsessed by Diem's fate, loyalty was a primary criterion for Thieu. He tolerated corruption in the government and among his province chiefs in exchange for their steadfast support, arguing that their replacements would be no more honest. Profiteering from authority was an age-old system and he did not believe he could change it in the middle of the war. Better that his subordinates be loyal and work hard than that they be clean. The Vietnamese people still accepted the common practice: the bottom paid homage to the top. Until the nineteenth century, Vietnam and the other vassal states of Asia had to pay tribute (*Trieu Cong*) to the Emperor in Beijing.

When the French first came to Vietnam, they were surprised to find that during the Tet holidays it was part of the tradition for parents to offer money to the village teachers to provide *l'huile pour la lampe* (oil for the lamp). The teachers were paid so poorly that they depended on their annual gifts to survive. Bribing of government officials, both French and Vietnamese, was a common practice. Corruption was predictable; it eased the way, and one knew who and how much to pay for favors. In wartime Vietnam corruption became unpredictable, there were no limits, and the system suffered. As Guenter Lewy has noted in *America in Vietnam:* "Graft and bribery soon went beyond reasonable limits and became exposed to public view: ostentatious high living demonstrated a lack of style. In this new situation the fact that government officials used and subverted the war effort for personal enrichment began to alienate and embitter the population and corruption became a significant deterrent to victory." [19]

Corruption became a political weapon used against the Thieu government by anti-war groups and the North Vietnamese at a time when the country's survival was at stake. The failure to build institutions to establish accountability and the inability to control the vast influx of American dollars and equipment were a casualty of the war. Thieu's priority was survival— he tolerated corruption in order to prosecute the fight against the North. Although he realized that corruption was hurting his political image and his ability to project South Vietnam as an independent, thriving democracy, his top priority was fighting the war. Only when corruption became so blatant and unpredictable that it involved the obvious selling of equipment to the enemy or impinged on the survival of a province did Thieu act. In the fall of 1973 he instituted a series of administrative reforms that included the removal of three of his four corps commanders and several district and province chiefs on charges of corruption; but by that time the dam had burst and the deteriorating military situation forced other priorities.

As Hung became more comfortable with Thieu, and the situation worsened, they had discussed how to deal with the problem of corruption. "The Americans have not helped us." Thieu complained. "The PX system has flooded our country with radios, television sets, refrigerators, air conditioners, Bourbon whiskey, and menthol cigarettes. They come from the Americans."

Vietnamese who worked at the sprawling Long Binh logistics complex, near Bien Hoa, told Hung that pilfering was common. Vietnamese trash-disposal trucks loaded with appliances stolen by American personnel passed through the front gate with the connivance of American Military Policemen.

An MP would tell his Vietnamese girlfriend from a nearby bar what time he would be on duty to let the trash truck go through. They all shared the profits.

There was a black market for dollars despite the military payment currency used to prevent abuses of the system. Many of the best and brightest American journalists added thousands of dollars to their paychecks by putting in expense accounts at the official exchange rate, then changing money on the black market to pay their cable bills with black market currency.

Commercial imports financed by U.S. aid during the war came to between $700 and $800 million a year. All nonessential items—cosmetics, motorcycles, cars, and consumer goods—entered with import licenses under a quota which "became a license to steal," recalled Hung. Licenses were sold for what the market would pay, and the Minister of the Economy became known as the Minister of Ten Percent for his commission. In wartime there were no restraints and enforcement was virtually impossible. The effect was to create an atmosphere of corruption and vested interests.

In the post-cease-fire period the artificial prosperity of American aid dried up, replaced by a new psychology of impoverishment that created both resentment and bewilderment. The staggering rise in gasoline prices after the Arab oil embargo in 1973, coupled with a decline in foreign aid, forced a change in Saigon's lifestyle. Honda drivers found themselves out of gas and back to bicycles. Gas for fishermen and farmers was also in short supply. The withdrawal symptoms from American aid were painful.

Hung suggested to Thieu that he consider replacing corrupt province chiefs with dedicated new young men. Thieu sighed and likened his problem to that of the archbishop who sent a young priest to a parish straight from the seminary. Before going forth, the priest swore to be faithful to the Church and set a good example. Within six months the archbishop received reports that the young priest was lazy and flirted with women parishioners. The priest was recalled and protested his innocence. "You have been given the wrong report. They are evil people there who are trying to undermine the Church," the young priest said in his defense. The archbishop sent him back to the parish; another six months passed and the same reports began to arrive. "If he replaced him with another priest, the same tales would be told within six months, "Thieu said.

"Hung, give me the name of anyone you want to be province chief, guarantee his behavior, and I will appoint him immediately." Hung was astonished. He had not come to Thieu with the idea in mind of naming candidates for province chief, and he had none to offer. Thieu smiled and explained: "Our priority now is survival. I will deal with the corruption issue later. In the next term I hope we can pursue the problem of corruption vigorously. Prepare a cadre that can take over."

In October 1974 Thieu was considering making Hung deputy prime minister in charge of economic affairs. After deliberating, he asked Hung if he had enough people to replace the old guard. "Right now I don't, Mr. President," replied Hung, "but in a year or so I can recruit enough young technocrats who are being trained abroad to take charge." Thieu told Hung to "use ministry funds to prepare these people and after the elections in 1975 you will have complete authority to take over the economic sphere."

Thieu's strength, Hung believed, was his uncompromising anti-Communist stand and his skill in facing up to Kissinger, Haig, and Nixon. Thieu did not accept Kissinger's style of negotiations with North Vietnam, an approach that he thought would turn the Republic of Vietnam into a Communist state or give the Viet Cong political legitimacy. He firmly held that his refusal to join the peace talks in 1968 prevented the formation of a coalition government which would have meant a Communist takeover. For seven years he had held the country together and staved off defeat.

His greatest failure was his suspicious nature, which had become indelibly stamped on his personality the day he saw Ngo Dinh Diem and his brother Nhu sprawled in their blood on the metal floor of an armored personnel carrier in the courtyard of the Joint General Staff headquarters. Thieu's suspicions denied him the services of competent people, adequate staff work, consultation, and coordination. In the end his secretive nature confused his generals about his true intentions. Thieu did not share his fallback goals with those around him until it was too late to rally his own forces and the time to develop sound operational plans had passed.

Once, in a private moment, Hung asked Thieu why he was so suspicious. Thieu flared up, and said: "That's my problem, not your problem." In fact Thieu had good reason to be suspicious. Hung recalled Thieu asking for an extra copy of his speech one day before addressing the National Assembly. "There is already a copy of your speech on the podium and one for the file," answered Hung. Thieu insisted on another copy to be carried with him in his breast pocket. Hung ran to his office to fetch it. Later, Thieu told him that he wanted another copy of the speech just in case somebody stole the copy on the podium. "How could that possibly happen?" Hung asked. "It's very easy. In all the excitement of setting up the microphones and getting ready for the speech, someone in the audience may pretend to be going to the men's room, walk by the podium, and take the speech away," explained Thieu. "Shall I call for Hung to bring me another copy when I am on TV before the nation and the world after being solemnly announced as the President of the Republic?" Thieu could see the look of skepticism on Hung's face so he explained: "Well, it happened to me twice. My opponents must have great respect for me because I took the speech from my pocket and carried on. In Vietnamese politics you have to be careful even with a period or a comma."

Thieu consulted infrequently with his own generals and top staff members. It was never done in a systematic, organized manner. He brooded and worried, and he rarely gave direct orders. Instead, he often suggested or intimated what should be done. Foreign Minister Bac recalled that Thieu "rarely gave a direct clear-cut order. Rather, he would make an imprecise suggestion such as, 'anh lieu lay ma lam' ['Calculate carefully and handle it yourself']. When you left the meeting, you were never sure if Thieu was

firmly behind the decision or not.''[20] It was Thieu's way of creating denia-
bility if the plan went wrong. He took only the chairman of the Joint General
Staff, the prime minister, and his chief of security—the venal, disliked
General Quang—into his confidence on military matters. He did not usually
include his military corps commanders in the planning stages, but only
called them in to announce his decisions. Thieu's reputation among the
urban, educated Vietnamese was that he excluded the best young military
commanders because he feared their competition and, more important, because he was ever watchful for a *coup d'état* against him. (The rural population was less critical of him because of his land reform program.) He
retained General Vien as chairman of the JGS and General Khiem as prime
minister for eight years because he needed their support to remain in power.
Of all the generals, they had appeared most loyal to President Diem, and
Thieu believed they were the least likely to mount a coup against him. Thieu
was president in name but his legitimacy depended on his retaining the
support of the generals; the presidential letters were his weapon to demonstrate that he, better than any of them, could deal with the Americans.

As much as Thieu thought he understood Nixon as a politician, however, he could not fathom Watergate and what, to the Vietnamese, seemed
to be trivial charges against the American President. Watergate was often
discussed among Thieu's inner staff and Hung recalled a discussion after
Nixon resigned. Vice President Huong asked, ''Why wasn't there a Le Lai
to save President Nixon?'' He was referring to the famous story of Emperor
Le Loi, who led a revolt against the Chinese in 1418 and ousted them from
Vietnam. In a critical battle he was surrounded by Chinese troops and there
appeared no way to escape. One of his retainers, Le Lai, who looked like
Le Loi, pleaded to exchange his uniform for the emperor's gown and sword
to outwit the Chinese. The Chinese captured the double, Le Lai, but Emperor Le Loi escaped to fight another day. The Vietnamese cited this example of loyalty and wondered why no member of Nixon's staff stepped
forward to take the blame for Watergate, serve a prison term, and then
return to public life, having protected the President. ''If there was only one
Le Lai in the White House, Nixon would have been saved and perhaps
Vietnam too,'' said one of the senior staff members. ''I'm not even sure
there is any Le Lai left in Vietnam,'' joked Thieu. ''Nowadays if Le Loi
gave his gown and sword to Le Lai, he would sit on the throne and take
power for himself,'' he mused.[21]

As Hung watched the congressional meeting come to an end, it was
clear to him that there was little hope of receiving the magic $300 million.
Mrs. Fenwick lit her pipe and puffed continually through the meeting, to the
amazement of the Vietnamese, who had never seen a woman smoking a
pipe in the Palace. There was no sign of rapport with the congressional
group, and after they left the Vietnamese felt dispirited and humiliated.
''Representatives of the U.S. Congress turned their back on us,'' said a
cabinet minister. Congressman Flynt had a split in the rear seam of his

trousers and his underwear was showing. Von Marbod was so angry with the performance of the delegation that he did not tell Congressman Flynt how ludicrous he looked.

Next day, early in the morning, Thieu called Hung on the phone. His voice was loud and full of anger. "These arrogant people came over here with no respect or even politeness for the host country, their ally," he said bitterly. "Prepare a statement for me to make at the dinner reception." Thieu added that it must be clear that "the way to give is more important than what is given."

Late in the evening of March 1, President Thieu gave a lavish state dinner in honor of the visiting Americans who were to leave the next day. Vietnamese and French delicacies graced with French wines were served. Thieu, pensive and distracted, tried his best to appear calm and confident. The guests were on time, in spite of the rumor that some of them would boycott the dinner. They showed no visible emotions. With the exception of Senator Bartlett and Representative Flynt, the heads of the delegation, who appeared to be seriously concerned for the fate of Vietnam, all the other members of the group seemed indifferent to the plight of the country.

Mrs. Abzug was sitting across the table from Hung. Sensing great tension between her and President Thieu, Hung tried to be gracious and put her at ease. It was almost a monologue; Hung recalled his experiences in America and his visit to Brooklyn where he had enjoyed wonderful Chinese food in Flatbush. Mrs. Abzug was unmoved, and barely listened to him. She could hardly wait for the evening to end and her impatience was obvious.

To restore his calm, Thieu had a few glasses of wine and rose to deliver his remarks. With firmness, he told the guests:

> During the past two decades, the people of South Vietnam have been told time and again by five U.S. presidents, belonging to both parties of America, all of them supported by successive legislatures of the U.S., that the United States is determined to provide them with adequate assistance as long as they are willing to resist communist aggression to preserve their freedom. That solemn commitment had been [sic] renewed at the time of the signing of the Paris Agreement. The issue boils down to a simple question, Are the commitments made by the U.S. to be of any value? Is the word of the U.S. to be trusted? That is the message I want you to convey to the 94th Congress of the United States.

Then, no longer able to contain his bitter feelings toward his guests, Thieu departed from the text to add: "May I compliment these genuine friends for their sound vision, and may I recall here the meaningful saying: 'The gift is important, but the manner in which it is given is even more important.'

Hung was not sure whether Thieu's words reached Abzug, who seemed half asleep throughout the speech, her chin falling to her bosom, her eyes closing. Thieu chose not to look at her and turned to Millicent Fenwick, who he thought was a friend. The mood was tense and solemn. A strong wind ripped through the open glass doors of the state dining room. It blew out the tall candles in the silver candelabra, scattering wax over the tables and flapping the long, white lace curtains like flags of surrender. "A bad sign," Hung whispered to Philip Habib, who was sitting on his right. Habib nodded in agreement.

The March dinner was the last state function of the Republic of Vietnam, the last official banquet at the Independence Palace, and President Thieu's last formal dinner to entertain foreign dignitaries in his ten years in office. In every sense it was also the last grand gesture of Vietnam to mark the end of two decades of American sponsorship of the Republic of Vietnam.

16

The Last Enclave

AT 0200 HOURS on March 10, 1975, the North Vietnamese attacked
Ban Me Thuot in the central highlands. Ever since the war against
the French the Vietnamese generals—North and South—had believed that "who controls Ban Me Thuot controls the South." The North
Vietnamese succeeded in surprising the defenders of the small market town
for French rubber, coffee, and tea plantations, and gained an advantage
which they never ceded. Ban Me Thuot, 150 air miles north-northeast of
Saigon, is carved from the red earth and jungle that borders on the Annamite
Chain of mountains separating the central highlands from Laos. A cluster of
shops, run by Chinese, line the main road that passes through the center of
the town. Ban Me Thuot is colorful and exotic because the local mountain
tribesmen, in loincloths, and their bare-breasted wives and daughters, wan-
der through the red dirt streets on their way to trade in the outdoor market.
The *montagnards,* as they were called by the French, or *moi,* savages, by
the Vietnamese, come mostly from the Rhade and Jarai tribes and are ra-
cially different from the Vietnamese. There are an estimated 700,000 *montagnards* in the highlands bordering Laos and the Ho Chi Minh Trail. In
their historical sweep south, the Vietnamese conquered the *montagnards;*
the relationship has always been an antagonistic one between conqueror
and conquered. The mountain people live in wooden long houses on stilts
to avoid the mud, and survive by slash and burn type agriculture. They
believe in animist spirits that are propitiated by animal sacrifices and ceremonies that include imbibing strong rice wine, flavored with scorpions,
through long bamboo straws. Relations between the Vietnamese and the
montagnards improved in the 1960s when the Central Intelligence Agency
and later the U.S. Army Special Forces sent in teams to organize and arm
the *montagnards* and win their support against the North Vietnamese. The
Americans provided medical care, rifles, and food supplies for the tribesmen, and acted as a buffer between them and the Vietnamese, who began
calling them "Compatriots of the Highlands." Tensions still smoldered be-
neath the surface even when the *montagnards* were recruited as part of the

Vietnamese army Regional Forces.[1] When the Americans left in 1973, conditions deteriorated. The Vietnamese neglected the tribespeople and the shortages of supplies deepened traditional animosities.

The commander of Military Region II, Major General Pham Van Phu, had been warned of a North Vietnamese attack on Ban Me Thuot by the Joint General Staff and his own intelligence officers, but he refused to move substantial reinforcements to strengthen his position. General Phu believed the reports were a North Vietnamese effort to divert him from the defense of Pleiku, where his headquarters were located.[2] The entire 23rd Division was deployed in the Pleiku area, leaving the defense of Ban Me Thuot to an ARVN Ranger group, provincial Regional Force and Popular Force units composed mostly of *montagnards*.[3] General Phu remained in Pleiku, ninety-four miles to the north (see map). He was quickly isolated and never able to mobilize his 23rd Division to regain the initiative. His badly planned and poorly executed efforts turned "redeployment" of his troops into a rout that never stopped until the fall of Saigon.

For months, since the cutback of American aid in the summer of 1974, President Thieu had been considering the necessity of redeploying his forces to compensate for the reduction in funds. On March 11, following initial reports of a Communist success at Ban Me Thuot, Thieu called in his three closest military advisers, Prime Minister Tran Van Khiem, General Cao Van Vien, and Lieutenant General Dang Van Quang, his Assistant for Military Security, for breakfast at the Palace. Thieu chose the open but inaccessible hallway with high white walls on the third floor of the Independence Palace for his private meetings with senior aides. He believed this area of the Palace was free of electronic bugs; if not, the background roar of the motorcycles on the street below would dominate the tape recording.

After food had been served and the three generals were alone with Thieu, he placed a small-scale map of South Vietnam on the table and reviewed the military situation. Without emotion Thieu outlined a drastic new strategy: "Given our present strength and capabilities, we certainly cannot hold and defend all the territory we want. We have to redeploy our forces in such a way as to hold and defend only those populated and flourishing areas which are really the most important."[4]

With a sweeping motion of his hand, Thieu drew on the map the lines of defense for the areas he considered essential: all of Military Region III, Military Region IV, and their offshore territorial waters where successful test oil wells had been drilled. This included the Mekong Delta, the most densely populated and agriculturally productive region of the country, south from Saigon through the Mekong Delta to the Camau peninsula.

The coastal provinces of Military Regions I and II would be held as firmly as possible, depending on remaining capabilities. Thieu sketched a series of phase lines across MR-I at different locations on the coastline from north to south, and told his advisers that within its capabilities South Vietnam could successfully hold enough of its national territory to survive and prosper as a nation. Above all, Thieu cautioned, nobody was to tell the Americans of his plans.

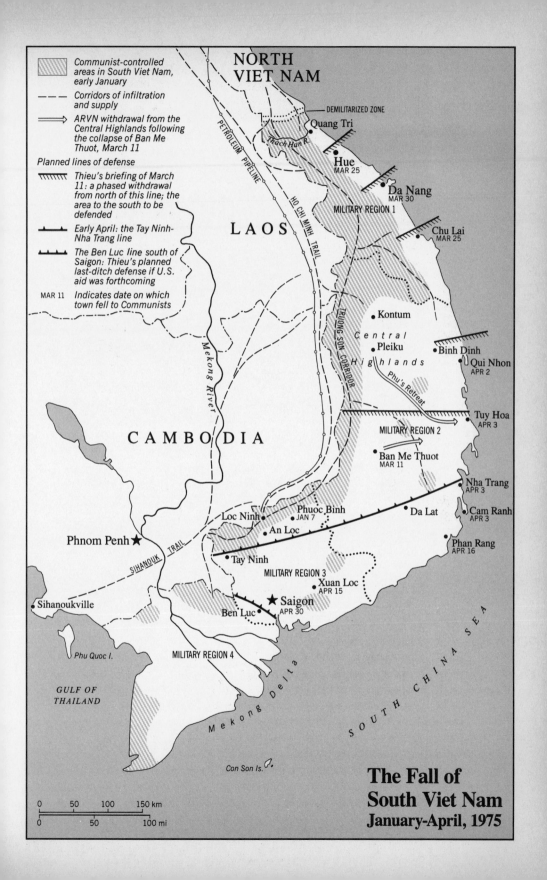

Communist-controlled areas in South Viet Nam, early January

Corridors of infiltration and supply

ARVN withdrawal from the Central Highlands following the collapse of Ban Me Thuot, March 11

Planned lines of defense

Thieu's briefing of March 11: a phased withdrawal from north of this line; the area to the south to be defended

Early April: the Tay Ninh-Nha Trang line

The Ben Luc line south of Saigon: Thieu's planned last-ditch defense if U.S. aid was forthcoming

MAR 11 Indicates date on which town fell to Communists

NORTH VIET NAM

DEMILITARIZED ZONE

Quang Tri

Thach Han R.

Hue
MAR 25

Da Nang
MAR 30

MILITARY REGION 1

Chu Lai
MAR 25

LAOS

Central

Kontum

Pleiku

Highlands

Binh Dinh

Qui Nhon
APR 2

Phu's Retreat

Tuy Hoa
APR 3

MILITARY REGION 2

Ban Me Thuot
MAR 11

Nha Trang
APR 3

CAMBODIA

Phuoc Binh
JAN 7

Loc Ninh

Da Lat

Cam Ranh
APR 3

An Loc

Phnom Penh ★

Phan Rang
APR 16

Tay Ninh

MILITARY REGION 3

Xuan Loc
APR 15

Sihanoukville

Ben Luc

Saigon ★
APR 30

Phu Quoc I.

MILITARY REGION 4

MILITARY REGION 4

Mekong Delta

GULF OF THAILAND

SOUTH CHINA SEA

Con Son Is.

The Fall of South Viet Nam
January-April, 1975

0   50   100   150 km
0   50   100 mi

This was a radical departure in strategy. Until that moment Thieu had never openly conceded the idea of giving up territory to North Vietnam. The strategy of *dau be, dit to*—lighten the top, keep the bottom, as he called it—meant leaving behind six million people, assuming all of MR-I and II were lost. In theory, truncating the country sounded logical, given the dire developments resulting from the increased North Vietnamese military strength, which improved with massive Soviet aid after the cease-fire.[5] In practice, it would be a political and logistical nightmare.

The "bottom" was the rich Mekong River Delta, wet and fertile, with three crops of rice a year in the best areas, which supplied rice, fish, and fruit for 75 percent of the population of South Vietnam. The "top" had traditionally been an economic deficit area and political liability because of easy infiltration from the North. The idea of the delta as an independent South Vietnam made theoretical sense. But how to accomplish such a mammoth task in the midst of a deteriorating military situation?

Thieu's radical strategy did not evoke any debate among those present. General Vien, the senior military officer present, voiced the opinion that "this redeployment was indeed necessary, and I had embraced such an idea for a long time. But so far I had kept it to myself and considered it an improper proposal." Vien noted that the truncation conflicted with the prevailing national policy, and "if I had made such a suggestion, it could well have been interpreted as an indication of defeatism." Vien, always careful not to upset Thieu, adds in his memoirs: "Besides, it looked to me like a decision that precluded any unfavorable comment. After all, as commander in chief, it was the president's perogative and responsibility to dictate the conduct of the war. He must have known exactly what he was doing."[6] Nothing was done by the JGS to prepare plans to implement the new strategy outlined by Thieu.

The first problem at hand was how to deal with the loss of Ban Me Thout. Thieu called for a meeting with General Pham Van Phu, the Region II Corps commander, at Pleiku. Phu had been in the Vietnamese army set up by the French in 1954 and was captured with the French at Dien Bien Phu. He spent several years in a Viet Minh prison where he suffered from tuberculosis. The experience left him with an abiding fear of being captured again. Thieu knew him well because they had risen through the ranks together, and when Thieu took power he advanced Phu's career.

When Vice President Tran Van Huong insisted on replacing the II Corps commander, Lieutenant General Tran Van Toan, a capable and experienced commander, because of charges of corruption in December 1974, Thieu reluctantly named Phu as the II Corps commander. Phu was not a favorite of Vien, who refused to meet with Phu before he took over his new command. Vien's aide was instructed to tell Phu that "if he does a good job, General Vien will come and visit him."[7]

Thieu wanted to review the situation with Phu and try to save Ban Me Thuot; he set the meeting with Phu for Friday, March 14, and told Phu to come without his American adviser. Phu advised Thieu that Pleiku was unsafe for a meeting so they chose Cam Ranh Bay instead. Ban Me Thuot was almost totally under Communist control and all efforts to reoccupy it had failed.

The meeting took place in a building erected for the 1966 visit of President Lyndon B. Johnson to Cam Ranh. Thieu was accompanied by the same three advisers he had met with at the Palace on March 11. Phu briefed them on the status of forces in II Corps; he reported that all of the major roads had been interdicted by the North Vietnamese forces and traffic was halted. Reinforcements could not be moved by road. Thieu asked if it was possible for General Phu to retake Ban Me Thuot. Phu did not give a definitive answer. He asked for more troops and helicopters, but was told there were no reserve forces to commit.[8] Of the VNAF's four hundred helicopters, some two hundred had been shot down by newly arrived Soviet Strella anti-aircraft missiles or were inoperative because of a lack of spare parts.

Thieu ordered Phu to withdraw his troops from Pleiku and Kontum and redeploy them to retake Ban Me Thuot. In French, Thieu commanded the JGS, *"Suivre et surveiller"* (Follow and supervise) the withdrawal. Then Thieu explained his new strategy to truncate the South and sketched on a map the areas he expected General Phu to hold. The II Corps was to redeploy its forces as rapidly as possible to reoccupy Ban Me Thuot at all costs. Pleiku and Kontum were to be abandoned; the troops were to form in convoys and proceed to Tuy Hoa on the coast, where they would regroup for the campaign to retake Ban Me Thuot.[9]

Thieu's rationale for retaking Ban Me Thuot was based on three premises. First, if Ban Me Thuot were retaken, it would be easier to recapture Kontum and Pleiku. Ban Me Thuot was to be a blocking point against a North Vietnamese thrust to the coast and down to Saigon. It was the center for the shortest north-south route and dominated the area, controlling access to Laos and the seacoast. Thieu looked to the example of the French Colonel Vanuxem, who held Vinh-Yen in January 1951 in order to thwart a Viet Minh attack on Hanoi.[10] Thieu also took as an example the Americans' strategy in Normandy to consolidate their beachhead as the key to forming a base from which to move on to victory.[11]

Second, Thieu wanted the 23rd Division to destroy Hanoi's powerful 320th Division, which was holding Ban Me Thuot. The 320th Division was a main force unit on which Hanoi relied heavily. If the 320th could be crippled, the North Vietnamese offensive would be halted, Thieu believed. "In 1972, the reason we were successful in recapturing Quang Tri was General Truong's ability to meet and destroy Hanoi's main force units. Dealing with the Viet Cong querrilla forces was less important than being able to destroy Hanoi's crack divisions," recalled Thieu.

Third, Thieu believed it was necessary to save the men in the 6th, 22nd, and 23rd divisions, some of the ARVN's best troops, by withdrawing them from isolated, vulnerable positions in the highlands. If he did not regroup his forces, he believed "they would be decimated because of a lack of reserves to support them and the inability of the air force to resupply them and to provide close-in fire support.'' By consolidating them for an attack to retake Ban Me Thuot, Thieu could then decide whether to move against Kontum and Pleiku or to deploy his forces to assist General Truong in MR-I. Thieu did not realize that he had been overtaken by events.[12]

The North Vietnamese already dominated all the major routes. Therefore, General Phu said he would use Interprovincial Route LTL-7B, a narrow, poor-quality road that was neglected and out of use. The only thing to commend it was the element of surprise. Bridges were out along the route and Phu would need river-crossing facilities. The journey would be over 160 miles of unknown and hazardous road through jungles and mountains.

Instead of asking Phu to come to Saigon to devise and coordinate a strategy for withdrawal with the JGS, General Vien merely warned Phu of the dangers of such a movement and how the North Vietnamese had decimated French elite units, including the famous Group Mobile 100 in June 1954 when the French withdrew along the same route.[13] Phu made only one more request. He asked that the commander of the Ranger Forces in MR-II, Colonel Phan Van Tat, be promoted to brigadier general. Thieu agreed, and when Phu returned to Pleiku, the newly named Brigadier General Tat was placed in command of the forces to be redeployed. Phu withdrew from Pleiku by helicopter to set up his new headquarters in Nha Trang, leaving General Tat, his officers and men to fend for themselves.

There was little planning and no coordination. To try to preserve security, Thieu insisted that the retreat be carried out with secrecy so that the Regional and Popular Forces in the area, comprised of *montagnards,* were not informed before the withdrawal began.

As soon as the first two hundred truck troop convoy departed from Pleiku on March 16, the word spread that the city was being abandoned. When the *montagnards* found out that the Vietnamese were leaving without them, they turned their guns on the retreating regular troops. The population, including large numbers of ARVN dependents, fled from the city, jamming the road with every means of transportation on which they carried their possessions and followed on foot. After two days the exodus was halted at the Ea Pa River because engineers had not completed a pontoon bridge across by March 16, its scheduled completion date. The troops and civilian dependents massed along the riverbank were a sitting target for the North Vietnamese 320th Division's mortars and artillery. During the night the first North Vietnamese attacks began. From then on, the column had to fight its way for the remaining one hundred miles to the coast. When air support was called in to back up the government troops, the bombs accidentally landed on their own troops, causing heavy casualties. It took until the night of March 27 for the first vehicles of the column to reach Tuy Hoa on the coast. From a military point of view the redeployment had turned into a rout and was ''a complete failure.'' The entire column, seven regiments and one armored brigade, withdrawn from Kontum and Pleiku were destroyed as fighting units, and it was impossible to move to retake Ban Me Thuot.[14]

The Americans did not find out about the redeployment strategy of President Thieu until March 17, when a CIA agent in Thieu's cabinet provided the first insights into what Thieu meant by "small head, big bottom." [15]

The debacle culminated the charade that passed for the command system of the Joint General Staff. The South Vietnamese had a weak logistics system and virtually no effective organization for planning and coordination. During the years of direct American involvement combat operations were undertaken by the Military Assistance Command Vietnam (MACV), which planned, coordinated, and supplied the American and Vietnamese troops in the field.[16] There was never a joint command between the Americans and Vietnamese.[17] The four Vietnamese corps commanders had both military and administrative control of their areas and, while the Americans were present, had little to do with battle planning and actual combat.[18] They were primarily concerned with static defense.

When the Americans departed, they did not leave behind a logistic capability and the JGS was unprepared to create one or step into a decision-making role. General Vien considered his role as primarily advisory.[19] There was no central direction at the JGS. The corps commander would call General Vien, who would suggest calling President Thieu. Then Thieu would call Vien, and Vien would get back to the commander in the field. "Sometimes it took me between one to two hours to reach the chairman of the JGS," lamented General Truong.[20] The JGS seemed to be oblivious of the crisis and refused to take responsibility. When Eric Von Marbod called the JGS at 4:30 p.m. on April 1, after the fall of Danang, there was no response. General Vien and his staff had left for the day.[21]

While MR-II was crumbling, the situation in MR-I was also disintegrating. On March 13, Thieu summoned Lieutenant General Ngo Quang Truong, the MR-I commander, to Saigon to discuss his new strategy.

During the meeting in the Independence Palace, Thieu told General Truong and the MR-III commander, General Nguyen Van Toan, who was also present, that "Up until now I have asked you to do the impossible." Thieu then gave his own analysis of the situation and the crisis he faced in obtaining military aid from the United States. For the first time Thieu admitted to his generals that he did not hold out much hope of American bombing if South Vietnam was faced with an all-out offensive by North Vietnam. Thus, concluded Thieu, there was nothing else to do under the circumstances but to change strategy. Thieu explained his plan to redeploy forces and truncate the country. Even if the jungle and mountainous areas of the country were lost to the Communists, it would be better than living with them in a coalition government.

At the meeting Thieu told General Truong to abandon Hue and to withdraw his troops down the coast to Danang. In his mind Thieu was seeking the last enclave, a beachhead along the coast that could serve as a landing area for American troops, if the Americans decided to return and assist South Vietnam to counter the North Vietnamese invasion.[22] At the time he did not explain this hope to Truong or his other generals. He only told Truong to withdraw from Hue and move to Danang. It was not Thieu's style to confide his hopes even to his closest advisers.

Thieu needed a general reserve, what he called a "strike force," to make his truncation plan work. For this purpose he wanted to withdraw the Airborne division and the Marine division from MR-I to Saigon and other critical areas, "if the situation permitted without endangering the Corps defense posture." Thieu did not explain to General Truong his intention to withdraw the Marine division. Truong only learned of it afterwards at a luncheon meeting with Prime Minister Khiem. At the luncheon Truong said he had heard a rumor that Saigon planned to withdraw the Marine division from his command. Khiem, in his quiet, understated manner, said: "Well, it's true." After a moment of silence, he added: "The reason you know about it is our third bureau [intelligence in the JGS] has leaked it out." Truong was amazed; he could hardly believe that even though he was commander of MR-I he had not been informed of the president and prime minister's real intentions.[23] Thieu's decision to withdraw these elite divisions from the Northern front gave rise to rumors that he feared a *coup d'état* in Saigon and had brought back the troops to protect himself.

Truong flew back to MR-I headquarters in Danang thinking hard about what Thieu had told him. As Truong worked with his staff to develop a plan to carry out the president's orders, the number of refugees descending on Danang reached 500,000 and continued to increase. The rumor was spreading among the soldiers' families that a deal had been made with North Vietnam and the central highlands would be abandoned. The soldiers grew concerned about the safety of their dependents, who were traveling with them, and discipline broke down. The morale-boosting factor of having families live with the troops in the field suddenly turned into a nightmare. There was no way to get the families out except as part of the retreating troop columns. The retreat from Pleiku and Kontum triggered the worst fears of an already wary population.

The BBC reported the details of the retreat fully and predicted that the Communists would reach the outskirts of Saigon within two to three weeks because National Route 14 from Ban Me Thuot was open to the North Vietnamese. On the Voice of America (VOA) came reports that the House Democratic Caucus on March 12 voted 189–49 against additional military aid for South Vietnam and Cambodia. On March 13, the Senate Democratic Caucus followed suit, voting 34–6 against any additional military aid in fiscal 1975. The word, carried by VOA, spread quickly among the troops, who had been told that American aid was coming. "The vote against more military aid was like a kick in the groin, deep and painful," recalled Hung.

Hung was besieged by requests for supplies of food, medicine, and temporary housing materials. Order was breaking down and there was need for a strong, decisive policy from the central government. He requested a meeting with President Thieu and suggested that his trusted cousin Hoang Duc Nha, who under heavy pressure from political enemies had resigned as

Commissioner of Information, be sent to Danang to play a direct role in dealing with the refugee problem. Thieu said what was needed was a logistics expert like JGS Chief of Staff General Dong Van Khuyen. "But Khuyen is in Tokyo now," explained Hung. Khuyen had gone to Japan to assist his father, who was being treated for cancer. Nobody had advised him not to leave or cabled him to return. As Chief of Staff of the JGS, Khuyen was the man who held the key to the available supplies for the South Vietnamese armed forces and the only person who really knew how to handle the supply system developed by the Americans. (Khuyen finally arrived after the fall of Danang and broke into tears, never having been told that he was needed.)

Thieu decided to send the whole cabinet, led by Prime Minister Khiem, to Danang. On the morning of March 18 they gathered in the VIP room at Tan Son Nhut Airfield. Hung met Buu Vien, minister in the prime minister's office, in the men's room. "Have you heard anything about the highlands?" he asked Hung.

"No," replied Hung.

"I heard that our troops are moving out of Pleiku and Kontum and it's a mess up there," said Buu Vien. That was the first time Hung learned of the actual redeployment.

In Danang before the meeting on the refugee problems, General Truong took Prime Minister Khiem aside for a briefing on the military situation and his plan for withdrawal. Khiem still held the rank of a five-star general and Thieu respected his opinion. Truong warned that a coordinated North Vietnamese attack against Hue and Danang was imminent; it was growing difficult to control the exodus of refugees who were flooding the roads and stalling military traffic. The prime minister was shocked at the mood of panic and ordered Truong to return to Saigon the following day to confer with the president.

The meeting on the refugee problem laid forth the staggering extent of the disaster. Khiem promised to return to Saigon to work out solutions. But the on-the-spot decision making Thieu had asked for never took place. Khiem did little to coordinate transportation and failed to provide for food, water, or supplies. He refused to get directly involved and passed the problems onto others. Nothing was done to ease the conditions and disorder broke out in Danang. After he returned to Saigon, Khiem's response was to send money to Danang to assist the refugees. The central government in Saigon failed miserably to provide assistance for its own people.

The same evening he returned to Saigon, Khiem met with Thieu and told him that it would be difficult to hold both Hue and Danang: "It is better to abandon one of them."[24] Vice President Huong had also told Thieu that "it is too costly to keep both Hue and Danang." At 11:00 a.m. on March 19, with the vice president in attendance, General Truong was back in Saigon to present his plan for troop withdrawals. The presence of the vice president was unusual since until then Thieu had included only Prime Minister Khiem, General Vien, and General Quang when discussing military matters. He was going to need the added support of the vice president to persuade Truong to give up Hue. The meeting centered on the cost and difficulty of holding on to both Hue and Danang. Truong presented a contingency plan with two options.

The first option assumed that National Route 1, the main highway along the coastal plain, was open. In that case the troops would move south from Hue to Danang and north from Chu Lai to Danang (see map, p. 265). The other choice assumed the highway had been cut by the North Vietnamese and could not be used. Then there would have to be three enclaves, Hue, Danang, and Chu Lai, with all troops withdrawing to the three coastal cities to make their stand.

"Mr. President," said General Truong, "we have only one choice. We had better act before it is too late." That choice, he argued, was to defend Hue, Chu Lai, and Danang by taking advantage of the fortifications in the cities, particularly those in the hills around Hue. Hue and Chu Lai were to serve as recovery and assembling stations for the troops, who would be sealifted to Danang in the final stage of the redeployment. Danang would become a stronghold to be defended by four divisions and four Ranger groups, all the troops left in MR-I.

Truong told the meeting that with Route 1, the major north-south highway, cut, a fight to reopen it would put his men at a tactical disadvantage. It would be better to hold in the three enclaves, consolidate, and then move the forces to Danang by sea. By moving back toward Hue and Chu Lai, the enemy would be engaged, and Truong's forces would be in a better position to fight than if they moved out exposed onto Route 1. Finally, Thieu, according to Truong, reluctantly agreed to his plan, saying, "Even though history might judge me an imbecile, because of the circumstances we are in and my love for the country, I will go along." Truong felt he could hold Hue and was ready to return to Danang resolved to fight a historic battle.[25] President Thieu accompanied General Truong to the door and told him: "I shall wait until your arrival in Danang to make my radio speech on the defense of Hue."

As soon as he landed in Danang, Truong received a call from his deputy in Hue, General Lam Quang Thi, reporting that the North Vietnamese were shelling his command post with 130mm artillery and had begun to cross the forward defense line at the Thach Han River (see map, p. 265). Alarmed, General Truong called Saigon to report to General Vien and ask for authority to deploy the 1st Airborne Brigade. As usual, Vien told Truong to call President Thieu. Truong repeated his story to Thieu and asked him to hold off his radio speech "for the time being because Hue may be indefensible." At that point Thieu cautioned Truong that both the prime minister and the vice president were opposed to trying to hold both Hue and Danang. President Thieu said that Vice President Huong, whom he called "the venerable old man [cu]," had said that "to hold Hue would be too costly. If you hold Hue, you will lose thirty thousand troops."[26] Truong was familiar with this pattern of the president giving generalized orders and expecting his generals to decide on the details of carrying them out. Truong understood that to hold Hue would be difficult, but he felt the alternative was total chaos.

The Independence Palace in Saigon, 1968.

Hung and Thieu in the Independence Palace, 1973.

Nixon and Mao Zedong in Beijing, February 1972.

Kissinger and Zhou Enlai in Beijing, February 1972.

Left: *Nixon and LBJ meet in the White House after the November 1968 election.*

Below: *Nixon and Mrs. Anna Chennault (left) during the 1968 campaign.*

Above: *Ngo Dinh Diem on the floor of the armored personnel carrier after he was slain on November 2, 1963. The killing of Diem changed the image of the United States among the leaders of southeast Asia.*

Right: *Vice President Hubert Humphrey congratulates Thieu at his inauguration as President in 1967, as Vice President Nguyen Cao Ky looks on.*

Facing page
Top left: *President Thieu and Ambassador Bunker in Saigon after Thieu's reelection in 1971.*

Top right: *Thieu and Nixon on Midway, June 1969, announce the first American troop withdrawals from Vietnam.*

Bottom: *President Thieu addresses troops who took part in Operation Lam Son 719, March 1971.*

*South Vietnamese armored vehicles heading for
the Laotian border during Operation Lam Son 719.*

Above: *Kissinger (right) talks with Special Advisor Le Duc Tho in Paris through an interpreter while Xuan Thuy (left) looks on.*

Left: *Hoang Duc Nha greets Henry Kissinger on his arrival at the Independence Palace, October 1972.*

From the left: *Winston Lord, Peter Rodman and John Negroponte, the Kissinger inner team enroute to Paris for talks with the North Vietnamese.*

Kissinger announces peace is at hand, October 26, 1972. Left to right: Alexander Haig, William Sullivan, Kissinger and Press Secretary Ron Ziegler.

Special Envoy Nguyen Phu Duc meets President Nixon in the Oval Office to discuss the Paris peace talks, November 29, 1972. Schecter is reporter in the middle directly behind Duc.

*North Vietnamese and U.S. delegations meet
outside Paris in 1972 to discuss the Paris Accords.
Le Duc Tho is on left pointing his finger.* From
the right: *Winston Lord, Kissinger, William
Sullivan, Peter Rodman and Irene Derus.*

Above: *Henry Kissinger and Le Duc Tho initial the Paris Accords, January 1973.*

Right: *Secretary of State William Rogers and Foreign Minister Tran Van Lam toast the signing of the Paris Accords and a cease-fire, January 27, 1973.*

Left: *President Thieu in traditional mandarin robe and black turban at a ceremony honoring the founding of the ancient Vietnamese kingdom.*

Bottom: *Henry Kissinger meeting in Hanoi with North Vietnamese Premier Pham Dong (center), February 1973.*

Tran Van Lam

Duong Van Minh

Tran Van Huong

General Tran Van Don

General Ngo Quang Truong

Vuong Van Bac

Warren Nutter

Melvin Laird

James R. Schlesinger

General Alexander Haig

Graham Martin

General John Vogt

House Minority Leader Gerald Ford with President Thieu at a Congressional reception, April 5, 1973, joined by Vice President Spiro Agnew and House Speaker Carl Albert.

Hung, Minister of Economic Development and Planning, at his desk, 1973.

Hung (left) addresses the diplomatic corps in the Independence Palace as Supreme Court Justice Tran Van Linh, President of the Senate Tran Van Lam, President Thieu, Speaker of the National Assembly Nguyen Ba Can and Prime Minister Tran Thien Khiem listen.

*Military cemetery at Bien Hoa, January 1974. In the year
after the cease-fire, 12,000 South Vietnamese were killed.*

*President Nixon welcomes home Vietnam POWs
at the State Department auditorium.*

Above: *President Nixon greets President Thieu at San Clemente, April 1973.*

Left: *California Governor Ronald Reagan and Nancy Reagan (right) host a dinner for President and Mrs. Thieu at the Beverly Wilshire Hotel in Los Angeles, April 1973.*

Right: *Vietnamese National Assembly member Truong Thi Bich Diep smiles at Congressman Pete McCloskey while Congresswoman Bella Abzug looks on. Febuary 1975.*

Below: *Hung (left), Ambassador Martin, President Thieu meet with an American Congressman in Thieu's office (1975).*

*The Weyand Mission meets in President Thieu's
office, March 31, 1975. Left to right: George
Carver, General Homer Smith, Eric Von Marbod,
General Fred Weyand, Ambassador Graham
Martin, President Thieu, Vice President Huong,
Prime Minister Khiem, General Cao Van Vien,
and Hung.*

Right: *Refugees fleeing from Ban Me Thuot, April 1975.*

Below: *South Vietnamese soldiers at Xuan Loc, April 9, 1975.*

Aerial view of Tan Son Nhut airfield, April 1975.

*President Ford and
General Fred Weyand at
Palm Springs, April 1975.*

*Henry Kissinger, President
Ford and Eric Von Marbod
at Palm Springs.*

*President Ford addressing
Congress on April 9, 1975.
Vice President Nelson
Rockefeller and House
Speaker Carl Albert look on.*

Above: *Kissinger, Ford,
Schlesinger, Clements,
Rockefeller (hidden), and
General Brown in the Roosevelt
Room, April 28, 1975,
contemplating the fall of Saigon.*

Left: *Vietnamese refugees
aboard the USS* Blue Ridge *after
the fall of Saigon.*

Henry Kissinger, Ron Nessen and Brent Scowcroft enroute to the Executive Office Building to announce the evacuation from Vietnam on April 30, 1975. (Secret Service Agent is behind Kissinger and Nessen.)

North Vietnamese tank outside the Independence Palace, after the surrender of South Vietnam, April 30, 1975.

Despite Thieu's reservations, Truong arose the next day, March 20, determined to proceed with the plan for three enclaves he had proposed and for which he thought he had received approval in Saigon. He flew to his forward command post, eighteen miles north of Hue, to discuss the defense of Hue with his troop commanders. President Thieu, he told them, had ordered that Hue, the former imperial capital and symbol of control of Central Vietnam, must be held "at all costs." Despite the loss the previous night of Quang Tri, morale and discipline were good and the bulk of the Marine division had been withdrawn to Danang. Truong was now optimistic that he could hold Hue and carry out the redeployment as ordered.

Truong also stopped in Hue and inspected the disposition of his troops for defense of the city. At 1330 hours he joined the thousands who paused to listen to President Thieu on the radio order the defense of the city at all costs. The president had publicly committed his prestige to saving Hue and Truong left believing it would be possible to hold the enemy back.

When he returned to his headquarters in Danang at 7:30 p.m., Truong was handed secret cable number 2238 signed by General Vien, chairman of the JGS, transmitting President Thieu's instructions to follow a completely different set of orders from the message he had publicly given to the country in his address over the radio. Hue was not to be defended. After Truong had left, Thieu, influenced by Prime Minister Khiem and Vice President Huong, had decided against an all-out defense of Hue.

The message transmitted by Vien said, "Because of the inability to simultaneously defend all three enclaves, the I Corps commander is free, depending on the situation and enemy pressure, to redeploy his forces for the defense of Danang only."[27] The Airborne brigade, on hand as a reserve unit and confidence-building factor because of its well-proven fighting record, was ordered to proceed to Saigon.[28]

Truong was so shocked that he asked one of his aides to read the cable because he could not believe its contents. Then Truong called General Vien for clarification, but was told only that he should talk with President Thieu.[29] Truong turned on his radio. Radio Saigon was still broadcasting the president's speech pledging to hold Hue "at all costs." Nobody in the president's office had bothered to inform Radio Saigon officials that the signals had been changed. Lack of coordination and control from the government and the JGS compounded the confusion.

General Truong was devastated. Earlier in the day he had personally staked his reputation on the defense of Hue after meeting with the city's elders and government officials. He had primed his troops for battle with the North Vietnamese. Now the orders were countermanded by the president who had personally agreed to the city's defense. Truong felt confused and betrayed. Under operating procedure he was required to acknowledge the receipt of the cable and advise the JGS that he understood its contents and would execute the instructions. Truong sent a written message to General Vien: "In reference to your 2238 I would like to express my reservations and am uncertain whether I can carry it out. Please find a replacement for me." The next day Truong received a reply from Vien: "The situation is very critical. Try to do your best." Truong had won his reputation as an officer who followed orders; now he would be loyal to the president. There was no timetable in the orders and Truong was not getting any assistance from Saigon, which had nothing left to offer. It seemed as if he were being told to do the best he could without additional help; his orders now were to accomplish a successful withdrawal to Danang. The president and the JGS were leaving their very limited options open and placing the full burden on General Truong.

The JGS seemed to vanish in the critical moment. Orders were improvised based on the rapidly crumbling tactical and strategic situation. There were no contingency plans and no procedures to execute a systematic withdrawal. According to the CIA station chief in Saigon, Thomas Polgar, "There was no Vietnamese general with experience in major unit warfare." [30]

In reviewing the events after the war, Thieu told Hung that he had initially decided to hold Hue because General Truong had told him and his advisers that there was no other option: the route for withdrawal, National Route 1, had been blocked. When Truong called from Danang to report on the rapid pace of the North Vietnamese advance and to ask Thieu to delay his radio address, Thieu began to lose confidence that Hue could be held. Thieu found the advice of Prime Minister Khiem and Vice President Huong credible. Then he received a report that elements of the 1st Division, the key unit defending Hue, had withdrawn secretly without the permission or knowledge of General Truong. "When I learned about the withdrawal, I called General Vien to ask why. Vien told me that he had not received any report of such movement. I then called General Truong, who told me: 'They have already left. I cannot call them back.' " At that point Thieu felt Hue had become indefensible. "Who advised General Diem [commander of the 1st Division] to withdraw? I don't know." said Thieu. [31]

The deteriorating tactical situation, compounded by the sudden and drastic reduction in American aid, forced Thieu to adopt the strategy he had been contemplating for nearly a year. Thieu believed that the territory to be defended by South Vietnam's armed forces had to be reduced in size, yet he still hoped to retain Danang as a final enclave. In recalling the decision, Thieu said that he wanted to keep Danang because "from a military viewpoint it was tenable," and "holding Danang would keep the beach open for a Normandy-type American landing to relieve our forces. I did not want to give the Americans a pretext to say that if they wanted to land troops again, there was no place for them to come ashore." [32]

At the time Thieu never confided this idea of an American rescue landing to his civilian advisers, but Hung recalls that in several meetings at the Independence Palace Thieu spoke about Danang as "the last enclave." In one meeting he said: "Even if all the enclaves in MR-I and MR-II have to be abandoned, Danang must be defended at all costs." The second-largest city in the republic, Danang has a fine natural harbor. It was on Danang's white sand beaches that the first American Marine combat units landed in

March 1965 to be welcomed by schoolgirls with flowers. During the period of American presence, the port was developed for both military and commercial use. The airfield was one of the best in Vietnam. Danang was a logical place to house the headquarters for Military Region I. In Thieu's mind, Danang was critical to control of the coastal plain. Thieu was still imagining another American armada landing at Danang to come to the rescue of his country.

Danang fell on Easter Sunday, March 30. In a Lutheran church in Arlington, Virginia, Secretary of Defense James Schlesinger wept for South Vietnam. He had been told by then Deputy Director of the CIA Vernon Walters that the South Vietnamese Ambassador to Washington had said: "On us the night is descending beyond which there is no dawn." As Schlesinger recalled: "I had in mind Churchill's description of the collapse of France in World War II. It was a disaster of that type, though not of the same magnitude. I don't blame the Vietnamese for holding out little shreds of hope. I sympathized with them. I grieved for them," said Schlesinger.[33]

For the American military, Danang was no longer of strategic importance. The only American military option to stop the North Vietnamese was tactical nuclear weapons, Schlesinger explained to President Gerald Ford, who would not consider their use. South Vietnam was on its own. President Ford decided that the United States would not intervene militarily.[34] There was no rescue fleet of amphibious landing craft and supply ships on the horizon as there had been ten years earlier. The fleet this time was a motley collection of twenty Japanese, Vietnamese, and American cargo ships and tugboats. The three American ships, the *Transcolorado,* the *USS Miller,* and the *Pioneer Contender,* arrived to carry off survivors from the last enclave. One of the passengers was General Truong, who was forced in the end to swim from Danang for his life.

17

The Final Appeal

A T FIRST HUNG THOUGHT he was dreaming that the telephone was
ringing. It was dark when he awoke, turned on the pink lamp on
his night table, and looked at the clock: 6:00 a.m. on March 20.
The air conditioning was still rumbling, shutting out the street noises and
creating a dulling pattern of sound that had helped him to drift into sleep.
The windows were shuttered and the curtains drawn in the bedroom of his
villa at 623 Phan Thanh Gian, across the street from St. Paul's Hospital.
Hung was exhausted. He reached out to flick a switch shifting the phone to
the quarters behind the main house where his security guard would answer.

For the past week Hung had been working past midnight, going from
one round of meetings to another, desperately trying to organize and coordinate a plan to feed, house, and extricate more than 500,000 refugees who
had descended on Danang, nearly tripling its population. Hung was part of
the ministerial team ordered to come up with a solution for the refugees who
were flooding the roads and creating chaos in the coastal cities as they fled
the Communist offensive. The focus was on Danang since Ban Me Thuot,
Kontum, and Pleiku had fallen to the North Vietnamese. Hue, Danang, Tam
Ky, and Quang Ngai were under attack. The combination of civilian refugees and military dependents had created insufferable conditions. Morale
was falling and control weakening.

As he drifted back to sleep, there was a heavy knock on the bedroom
door. "Mr. Minister, the President wants to talk to you," Hung's security
guard announced. Half asleep, Hung thought something terrible had happened. The president had never called him so early in the morning. He
picked up the phone and listened nervously. The president's aide repeated
the message: Thieu wanted to speak with him. To gauge the president's
mood, Hung asked the aide what phone he was speaking from. "Number
9404," came the reply, the number in Thieu's bedroom. Hung thought Thieu
must be in a very bad mood to be calling so early from his room. "Could
you come and see me at eight?" Thieu asked. "We can talk over breakfast."

Hung sensed the urgency in Thieu's voice and realized he was being called on to play a new role in the crisis. They would meet in the third-floor hallway which Thieu believed was immune to bugging by the CIA.

When Hung arrived, Thieu's personal doctor was giving him an injection. "Are you sick, Mr. President?" he asked.

"No, I just need an extra dose of vitamins whenever I have to deal with the Communists and the Americans at the same time," replied Thieu. Hung laughed, but the doctor did not smile and carefully injected the vial of vitamins into the president's arm.

At the table, set for two, a white-coated waiter served them Vietnamese breakfast: *pho,* rice noodles and beef broth with thin slices of beef garnished with fresh coriander, and *banh cuon,* rice crêpes with chopped pork and mushroom filling. When the waiter had moved out of hearing range, the president said: "I think that within the next few days, the situation will become grave very quickly." He sketched out the order of battle: five of the seven North Vietnamese reserve divisions had arrived in the South. Together with the fourteen infantry divisions already in the South, the enemy now had nineteen well-equipped divisions with nearly one thousand tanks and artillery. They had achieved predominance in the balance of forces and firepower on every battlefield. After pausing to allow Hung to take notes, Thieu continued: "Yesterday [March 19] the Communists' tanks crossed the Thach Han River to occupy Quang Tri and they have begun to shell Hue."

Hung had heard rumors that the retreat from Pleiku and Kontum had become a disaster and that the local *montagnard* forces had turned their guns on the Vietnamese troops. When the Agence France Presse bureau chief in Saigon, Paul Leandri, reported that *montagnard* troops had rebelled against the South Vietnamese, he was called to the national police headquarters for questioning. After being held for several hours, Leandri walked out of the station and refused to stop when ordered to by the police. Shots were fired to stop his car; one of them hit Leandri and killed him. Hung was depressed when he heard the news. Not only was the retreat turning into a disaster but it seemed that the old Vietnamese saying, *"hoa vo don chi,"* ("One misfortune follows another"), was coming true. The shooting of the French correspondent reinforced the worst images of a repressive Thieu government.

The military dependents fleeing with their husbands had slowed down the columns; only half of the trucks and troops reached the coast. The refugees were continuing to pour into Danang. Nobody wanted to be left behind because the North Vietnamese had buried alive and executed 2,800 people in Hue in 1968 when they held the city briefly during the Tet Offensive.[1]

Thieu did not mention the battle for the central highlands, nor did he tell Hung of his meetings with his military advisers to work out the defense of Hue and Danang. The president compartmentalized his relationships with his key aides, rarely communicating his inner thoughts or strategy. He preferred to keep his people guessing and trying to anticipate his wishes.

As Hung ate his noodles, Thieu took out a pen and began to write. As if to convince himself, he read out the three phrases he had written:

> Interest of the country;
> Personal interest;
> Political position.

Hung understood immediately that Thieu was making a political calculation to arrive at a new course of action. Next to "Interest of the country" Thieu wrote, "1." He marked a "ϕ" (phi, the Greek symbol for no) twice for the next two lines, "Personal interest" and "Political position." Then he looked up and said, "The survival of the nation demands that we go for broke [*phai xa lang*], therefore we must confront the United States to say yes or no on military aid. We cannot wait any longer. Soon it will be too late. Assuming there is no other consideration than the survival of the country, what should I do right now so that the U.S. cannot use the argument of a fait accompli as a pretext to tell me: 'Sorry, it is too late to intervene'?" The last sentence he said in English.

Ever since Kissinger came to Saigon in October 1972 to present Thieu the draft of the Paris Agreement arrived at with the North Vietnamese without his approval, Thieu had been haunted by the fear of being presented with another accomplished fact by the Americans. Kissinger's trip to Paris in June of 1973 had resulted in one more fait accompli, the signing of the Paris Communiqué. Now Kissinger was traveling again, this time in the Middle East. He had just been to Saudi Arabia. Who knew what was next? Another deal with Le Duc Tho in Paris . . . a *coup d'état* in Saigon?

Sensing his desperate mood, Hung urged Thieu to make public the presidential letters he had received from Nixon and Ford. He should appeal over President Ford's head to the Congress and the American people for one last act of help in the form of military and economic aid. At the current aid level the South would run out of ammunition and supplies by June of 1975, only ninety days away. With an infusion of aid, Saigon would be in a position to stabilize the front. Above all, a positive attitude in Washington was desperately needed to bolster morale. The first priority was to halt the North Vietnamese offensive with an immediate cease-fire either by military or diplomatic means.

Hung suggested buying network time for a television speech by Thieu to the American people revealing the secret American promises. Thieu was loathe to break his own promise of secrecy with the American presidents. He feared it would create a backlash and allow the Americans to say he could no longer be trusted. The idea of breaking the bond of loyalty was repugnant to Thieu and he was dubious of the practical effects of going public with the file of secret letters. To overcome this objection, Hung suggested that Thieu give an interview to ABC correspondent Frank Mariano. Hung would prime Mariano to ask Thieu about secret American pledges and Thieu could take advantage of the interview to bring them all out while still appearing not to have initiated the question. It would appear natural, as if the interviewer had pressed the question, rather than a deliberate revelation to the public of the American presidential promises.

The main points for the president to make in the interview, suggested Hung, were that when Thieu agreed to Vietnamization and the Paris Agreement he received a firm and continuing American commitment from President Nixon in the name of the United States. The commitment was nothing less than to come to the aid of South Vietnam in the event of a North Vietnamese offensive. This commitment was reiterated by President Ford and now the time had come for the United States to honor its promises. Thieu listened carefully, then suggested they meet again to discuss the idea. Thieu still did not think this was the moment to go public. "I do not want the Americans to have a pretext to point a finger at me," he said.

Hung felt that Thieu would have to take a drastic course of action, perhaps another division of the country along the lines of the president's plan to reduce the Republic of Vietnam to Saigon and the Mekong Delta. Or, there was always some form of a coalition government with the Communists to be faced. "Coalition" was a forbidden word in front of Thieu; no one in the government could muster the courage to discuss it directly with him. But now with conditions so bad, Hung decided to raise it, and asked whether the president had considered concessions on a coalition as a negotiating position. Thieu declined to discuss the matter. He simply did not answer Hung and sat silently, reflecting. It was his way to ignore issues he did not want to face or could not deal with.

Thieu told Hung what he wanted to do first was to send an SOS message to President Ford. "I still think Ford can do something to help us if he really understands the situation," said Thieu. He instructed Hung to draft a "dramatic and specific message requesting American help," but indicated that he was also considering other options.

Together they went over a list of what the American President could do at that moment to save Vietnam from defeat. The options included: public denunciation of North Vietnam's invasion; a powerful declaration of American support for South Vietnam; or the United States could reconvene the Paris Conference, demand an immediate cease-fire, provide military aid, intervene directly, and bomb the North Vietnamese invasion forces that were out in the open.

Thieu and Hung had their doubts whether Ford would act, but they had a strong case and felt there was no other alternative. When Hung expressed reservations, Thieu said: "Look, Hung, if you owe me money, all I can do is ask you to pay your debt. The burden is on you. That's how I feel about Ford. All we can do is try to get him to redeem Nixon's and his pledges."

Under the circumstances it was too late to make any of the political and economic measures effective, Thieu concluded, unless the United States intervened with airpower. From a military viewpoint, American bombing runs over Communist targets within South Vietnam would be opportune. For the first time in the history of the Indochina war the North

Vietnamese regular army was completely exposed, their trucks openly traveling bumper to bumper along the highways of South Vietnam in broad
daylight. The North Vietnamese troop positions were clearly visible and
their forces highly concentrated, rendering them especially vulnerable to air
attack. They had good anti-aircraft defenses, but high-flying American B-
52s could remain out of their range. The South Vietnamese air force, already
crippled by shortages of spare parts, ammunition, and fuel, was no match
for the North Vietnamese SAM (surface-to-air missiles) and Strella air-
defense batteries supplied by the Soviet Union.

Hanoi had shifted from a guerrilla warfare strategy of "attack in peace"
to open full-scale conventional warfare. Now the United States would have
to respond as it had promised; somehow the B-52s would have to be called
in to help stem the offensive and bolster the South Vietnamese troops as
they had done in 1972. The breakfast ended and Thieu ordered Hung to join
a group of experts to study the question of congressional restrictions on the
President. Were Ford's hands really tied, or could he take action to keep
Nixon's and his own promises?

After a day of wrestling with the powers of the American President,
Thieu's team of experts—including his foreign minister Vuong Van Bac, a
prominent lawyer, and Hung—concluded that it was still within the power
of President Ford to order a quick bombing attack within South Vietnam.
Indeed, the group argued, there was an obligation on the part of the U.S.
President to do so. For the Vietnamese, raised in the Confucian tradition,
there is no clear-cut division between law and moral principle. "For us the
law and morality are closely linked and we do not see the law predominating
over moral commitments," explained Bac.[2] Hung summarized and presented the argument to Thieu:

—As a signator, prime mover, and principal author of the Paris Agreement, the United States had an obligation to sustain it. President Nixon,
Kissinger, and the American ambassadors repeated over and over that the
real agreement was between the United States and South Vietnam. They all
promised that the United States would enforce the agreement.

—There were specific written American commitments from President
Nixon, clearly expressed in several letters, then reaffirmed by President
Ford, to retaliate with "full force" in case of violations of the Paris Agree-
ment.

—These assurances had never been secretly or publicly canceled; on
the contrary, there was a specific renewal by President Ford when he took
office.

—The War Powers Act of November 1973, which came after the June
1973 bombing ban, still left the President of the United States with unilateral
authority to commit American troops anywhere in the world for sixty to
ninety days to defend American lives. At the moment some 6,000 American
lives were being threatened throughout South Vietnam, especially in Hue
and Danang. The Americans were Foreign Service officers, AID officials,
technicians, defense attachés, and their dependents.

—Whatever actions the U.S. Congress took on Vietnam, including aid cuts, the June 1973 bombing ban, and the War Powers Act, it did so without prior knowledge of the President's written assurances to Saigon. Nixon's pledges were made before the Congressional restraints and therefore should remain valid.

It was therefore possible, his experts told Thieu, for President Ford to come before Congress to present the administration's commitments to Vietnam and to request authority to provide airpower for a final show of force, with whatever conditions Congress wanted to impose, including the eventual cut-off of aid. The alternative would be for President Ford to act on his own authority and then report to Congress, as required by the War Powers Act. Ford had freedom of action as commander-in-chief for sixty days; Saigon only needed two weeks of B-52 bombing to destroy the North Vietnamese invasion force.

To buttress their case, the experts cited the press conference of Defense Secretary Schlesinger on November 30, 1974. "The war powers legislation passed by the Congress may make it possible for President Nixon to order new bombing in Indochina in the event of a new North Vietnamese offensive in South Vietnam. . . .", said Schlesinger. The President has the power as the commander-in-chief to commit American forces in self-defense of Americans. Under the War Powers Act, which was passed on November 30, 1974, by overriding President Nixon's veto, the President is required to consult with Congress in advance of any military action he may take and report in detail within forty-eight hours. In case of emergency action under conditions of grave threat, the bill restricts the unauthorized use of armed forces to a period no longer than sixty days. By the end of that period the President is required to terminate military action unless the Congress explicitly authorizes its continuation. Within the sixty-day period, the Congress would have the authority to require termination of military action by concurrent resolution of the House and Senate, a legislative method that is immune to presidential veto.[3]

The Congress refused to accept the interpretation of Schlesinger and State Department officials. Senator Frank Church (D.-Ida.) declared: "To resume bombing or any other act of war in Indochina without first obtaining the consent of Congress would violate the law and constitute a presumptive case for impeachment."[4]

There remains unresolved the question of congressional intentions in passing the War Powers Act. Was it meant to punish President Nixon for Watergate? Was it aimed at the war in Indochina, or, as congressmen both conservative and liberal insisted, to deal with "future undeclared or 'Presidential' wars, not the hostilities in Indochina"?[5] Nixon and Ford both identified the War Powers Act as "contributing to the collapse of U.S. supported governments in the Indochina peninsula."[6] President Ford has conceded that while he appeared to comply with the requirements of the act, he never believed himself bound by it.[7]

Thieu chose to accept his experts' interpretation that the War Powers

Act would not prevent President Ford from using B-52s against the North Vietnamese invasion. Following this line of argument, Thieu told Hung to be specific in his draft of the letter to President Ford and to "ask for a short period of B-52 bombing," about two weeks, to stabilize the front and buy time for the ARVN to regroup.

As the military situation deteriorated, Hung noticed that Thieu appeared ready to accept almost any conditions, including division of the country and stepping down from the presidency, if only he would obtain American intervention against the North's offensive.

Thieu was concerned with developing the most effective approach to the Americans and realized that he would have to deal with the Congress as well as the White House. On March 22, he called a strategy meeting with the chairman of the Senate, former Foreign Minister Tran Van Lam, and the chairman of the National Assembly, Nguyen Ba Can. Foreign Minister Bac and Hung were also present. Tran Van Lam, who had met American congressional leaders and Vice President Nelson Rockefeller in February when he sought aid increases in Washington, suggested letters to Speaker of the House Carl Albert and to Rockefeller in his role as president of the Senate.

Thieu agreed and interjected that Ambassador Martin had visited him earlier in the day and advised him to "work quietly" with President Ford. Martin told Thieu that there was a tendency in the United States to identify the Vietnam situation with Cambodia, which at that point was a desperate, lost cause. Martin also advised Thieu that Saigon should not press for the $300 million in supplemental military aid. The implication was that the $300 million would not be granted and had become irrelevant—more drastic measures were necessary. The Congress would soon begin its Easter recess so no aid request would come up for immediate action. Most important, said Thieu, Martin had told him that, "in the meantime, we will work together quietly."

The question, said Thieu, is "have we reached the bottom yet in our relationship with the United States? Is it the moment to cry out publicly?" The consensus of the group, except for Hung, was that the moment for last resorts had not yet come. Vietnam must not accuse the United States publicly, but in private the case for aid had to be pressed as hard as possible so that the Americans could not say it was too late to be of use.

Thieu had just seen an article by Millicent Fenwick (R.-NJ) on the Op-Ed page of the March 12 *New York Times* strongly urging that no more aid be sent to Cambodia or South Vietnam. It had upset him because Mrs. Fenwick seemed like one of the most reasonable and responsible members of the congressional delegation that had visited Saigon. In direct prose Mrs. Fenwick wrote:

> In the case of both Cambodia and Vietnam, I think we must face the fact that military aid sent from America will not succeed. It will only delay the development of any kind of stable situation—whatever form that takes—that will at

least stop the horrible suffering of war. We have no alternative. Those who sent arms to North Vietnam and the Khmer Rouge may well continue to do so for the next thirty years. The citizens of the United States will not. It is not only that we feel we have many problems at home that need attention. It is also a feeling that we should not be in the business of maintaining endless and futile wars.

"What about the American people? How will we reach them? Should it be me or the leaders of our National Assembly to make the case to the American people?" asked Thieu.

"It should be done confidentially, not publicly," Foreign Minister Bac suggested. "We do not want to be accused of interfering in the internal affairs of the United States."

"But the American people must have the opportunity to hear us tell the truth," retorted Thieu. "The only question is in what form."

Bac reminded Thieu of the precedent set by Madame Nguyen Thi Binh, foreign minister of the Provisional Revolutionary Government, who wrote to the Congress on behalf of the Viet Cong and urged Congress to repudiate the Nixon administration's policies. Her letter stirred a strong reaction against the Vietnamese Communists for her presumption in interfering in the internal American legislative process.

"That woman was an enemy of the United States; we are friends," countered Thieu. "Besides, we are not asking the Congress to repudiate the administration, we are only reminding it of the solemn obligations made by two presidents."

Senate president Tran Van Lam was asked to write to the U.S. Senate and House leaders. The normally calm, genial Lam, who never showed emotion and who always prayed for divine guidance, rose to recount the promises he had been given repeatedly by Kissinger in Paris. Lam was then foreign minister and had signed the Paris Accords. It was Kissinger's constant assurances and pledges, he told the meeting, that would form the basis for his letter. "It's incredible. How can a giant nation like the United States behave like this?" Then, with deep feeling, but in his usual pedantic manner, he listed the five promises Kissinger had given him "time after time in Paris." Lam was both moving and pathetic. First, he said that Kissinger had told him it was agreed that fifteen days after the signing of the agreements the North Vietnamese would stop crossing from Laos into South Vietnam, thus ending the North Vietnamese build-up in the South. This had been systematically and blatantly violated.

Second, Kissinger had assured Lam that Russia and China would use their influence on North Vietnam to assure compliance with the Paris Agreements.

Third, if there were violations of the agreements, the United States would respond vigorously and with full force against the North Vietnamese. In private Kissinger had promised that the United States would implement the one-by-one replacement of military equipment permitted in the Accords.

As part of this promise Kissinger said the United States would provide adequate military aid for the self-defense of South Vietnam and the exercise of self-determination. In addition both Kissinger and Nixon had promised economic aid for reconstruction. "The Paris Agreement," Kissinger had said to Lam and the South Vietnamese delegation in Paris on several occasions, "is only a piece of paper. What counts is the power of the American President to back it up. If you sign the agreement, you have the power of the American President behind you." In search of that power, Hung and the Vietnamese congressmen now went to work on the letters. This was the first and only time the Vietnamese Congress appealed directly to President Ford and the American Congress. The letters were dispatched via the American Embassy but they were never answered. To this day Hung still wonders if the letters were ever delivered. (See Appendix J for full text of the letters.)

There had been many conflicting orders from Washington during the war, and there had been contradictions between different branches of the U.S. government. The final days of South Vietnam brought yet another confusing contradiction. At the moment when the U.S. Congress sent a clear public message that it was ending all military and economic aid to Saigon, President Ford sent a private message to President Thieu promising adequate military aid and assuring Thieu of America's resolve to stand behind the Republic of Vietnam.

On March 22, Ambassador Phuong in Washington transmitted a letter from President Ford to President Thieu which arrived on the morning of March 23, Saigon time. It was to be Ford's last direct communication with Thieu. In it, Ford tried to boost Thieu's morale, but he was very imprecise about what actions he would take. This was the first and only letter to be sent to Thieu through the Vietnamese ambassador in Washington.[8] It was coded by the embassy and decoded in Saigon and contains several mispellings and missing words. The letter reads:

Dear President Thieu:

The current North Vietnamese offensive against your country is profoundly disturbing and personally anguishing. It is my view that Hanoi's attack represents nothing less than an abrogation by force of the Paris Agreement.

This turn of events bears the most severe consequences for both our nations. For you and your countrymen it is a time of supreme sacrifice which will determine the very fate of your nation. I am confident that under your leadership the armed forces and people of the RVN will continue their tenacious defense against this new agression [sic]. I am equally confident that given additional external support you will prevail in your struggle for self determination.

As for the United States the issue is no less critical.

By the[ir] action, Hanoi is again seeking to undermine all that we have fought to achieve at enormous cost over the past ten years. Concurrently at stake is American resolve to support a friend who is being attacked by heavily armed forces in total violation of a solemn international agreement.

I, for my part, am determined that American [sic] shall stand firmly [behind] the RVN at this crucial hour. With a view to honoring the responsibilities of the U.S. in this situation I am following developments with the closest attention and am consulting on an urgent basis with my advisors on actions which the situation may require and the law permit. With regard to the provision of adequate military assistance to your armed forces you can be sure that I shall send [sic] every effort to meet your material needs on the battlefield.

In closing I wish to repeat my continued high respect for your resolve and for the constancy and courage of your people.

Sincerely signed GR R. Ford"

Hung was handed a copy of the letter underlined by President Thieu. The first time he read it, he found it vague and noncommittal; but as he read it again and took careful note of Thieu's underlining, he took heart. Thieu had underscored "American resolve to support a friend," "America shall stand firmly [behind] the RVN at this crucial hour," "honoring the responsibilities of the U.S. in this situation," "actions which the situation may require and the law permit," "provision of adequate military assistance to your armed forces," and "I shall send [sic] every effort to meet your material needs on the battlefield." The language echoed Ford's first letter to Thieu on August 10, 1974, in which he had said that "the existing commitments this nation has made in the past are still valid and will be fully honored by my administration."

Hung's hopes rose as he drafted the reply to Ford; but the new phrase "and the law permit" gnawed at his optimism. Ford, for the first time, was signaling his difficulties with Congress. It certainly was not a letter in the forceful, determined style of Nixon, but the language of Ford's condemnation of Hanoi's invasion as "a total violation of a solemn international agreement" resembled Nixon's message to Thieu prior to his mining Haiphong in 1972. If Thieu was taking heart from the verbal commitments of the American President, so would Hung. In the end, somehow, someway, America would come to the rescue of its ally. It always had done so in the past. In despair one clings to illusions.

For the next twenty-four hours in Thieu's office in the Palace and in his bedroom at home Hung labored over drafts of the letters to President Ford and congressional leaders. While Hung was working on the letters, Thieu's military aide arrived at his residence with a black looseleaf binder sealed in a heavy envelope. Thieu had sent Hung the full file of presidential letters. Hung was instructed to use them for reference in writing Thieu's letter. Hung had seen some individual copies of Nixon's letters, but never all of them in carefully numbered sequence. Now he read them through, one after the other, late into the night, and was amazed at how they fit together as a whole. The pattern of American promises was clearly spelled out and Nixon's pledges were reiterated by Ford. If only he had had the file earlier, Hung believed he could have used the letters effectively in helping South Vietnam. There could have been a quiet but direct confrontation with Kissinger on the promises and insistence that Congress be told. "If the Congress knew of the presidential promises right after the Paris Agreement, when there was still some sympathy for South Vietnam, an appeal for military aid on the basis of American fairness might have prevailed," Hung felt.

In 1973 and 1974, when his American friend Eric Von Marbod asked if he had any evidence of Kissinger's promises to Thieu, Hung thought he might be seeking information to supply to Schlesinger in his bureaucratic wars with Kissinger; but he had nothing on paper to show him. The letters then would have made a big difference. Hung kept the file under his pillow that night.

In the draft letter to Ford, Hung wrote in detail of the rapidly deteriorating military situation. The goal of the letter was to convince Ford of the urgency for action, since there seemed to be no appreciation of the crisis in Washington. Senior American officials kept saying there was no general offensive and refused publicly to build support for Saigon.

To prove his points, Hung outlined the military situation in each of the four regions, listing the numbers and locations of the North Vietnamese divisions in a detailed, professional manner. As Hung wrote, the battlefield crumbled. By the time he finished one draft, it had been overtaken by events and become obsolete and he had to begin another.

After receipt of Ford's letter, Thieu decided to go all out for American support. He instructed Hung not to make a detailed military report to Ford but to get right to the point of Saigon's dire situation. "Cut out all generalized appeals and be specific, ask for B-52 raids and prompt military assistance," Thieu directed. The final draft submitted to Thieu on the evening of March 24 read: "Dear Mr. President: By the time this letter reaches you, the city of Hue will have been left undefended, and very possibly, Saigon itself is being threatened. . . ." The next morning, March 25, Hue was abandoned. Thieu removed the sentence and said, "Let's get to the point." Now it read:

Dear Mr. President:

Thank you for your letter of March 22, 1975.

As I am writing to you, the military situation in South Vietnam is very grave and is growing worse by the hour.

The serious disequilibrium in the balance of forces in favor of the North Vietnamese as well as their strategic advantage accumulated over the past two years, have led to the present critical situation, especially in MR II, as you already know. Heavy pressures are being exerted on all the rest of our national territory and Saigon itself is threatened.

It has become evident that it would be extremely difficult for us to contain the advance of the communist forces to hold the line in order to push back the invaders without drastic and prompt measures on your part to redress the balance of forces.

Hanoi's intention to use the Paris Agreement for a military takeover of South Vietnam was well known to us at the very time of negotiating the Paris Agreement. You may recall that we signed it, not because we naively believed in the enemy's good will, but because we trusted in America's solemn commitment to safeguard the peace in Vietnam.

Firm pledge was then given to us that the United States would retaliate swiftly and vigorously to any violation of the Agreement by the enemy.

We consider those pledges the most important guarantee of the Paris Agreement. We know that the pledge is most crucial to our survival.

Mr. President,

At this crucial hour when the fate of free South Vietnam is at stake and when peace is severely threatened, I hereby solemnly request that the Government of the United States of America live up to its pledge.

Specifically, I earnestly request that you take the two following necessary actions:

To order a brief but intensive B-52 air strike against the enemy's concentrations of forces and logistic bases within South Vietnam, and

To urgently provide us with necessary means to contain and repel the offensive.

Only with these two actions can we stop the enemy from tearing off the last remnants of the Paris Agreement.

Mr. President,

Once again, I wish to appeal to you, to the credibility of American foreign policy, and especially to the conscience of America.

I am heartened that upon assuming the Presidency, you were prompt to renew to us the assurance of the continuity of American foreign policy and the validity of its existing commitments. I am grateful for your determination to honor these commitments in full in your administration. As you so rightly noted, these assurances are particularly relevant to the Republic of Vietnam.

Generations of South Vietnamese who will be living free from the horror of North Vietnamese domination will be indebted to your prompt actions and to the steadfastness of the great people of America.

Sincerely,
[s] Nguyen Van Thieu
President of the Republic of Vietnam

It was the first time that Thieu had asked for B-52 raids in writing—an indication of his desperate need to find a means to halt the North Vietnamese momentum. In his draft, Hung wrote: "It has become evident that we can no longer resist the communist offensive . . . without drastic measures on your part to redress the balance of forces." Thieu changed this to: "It has become evident that it would be extremely difficult for us to contain the advance of the communist forces . . . without drastic and prompt measures. . . ." He was careful not to make the situation appear hopeless, and to urge "prompt" measures from Ford lest it be thought too late for help.

Thieu called a military meeting in his office at 9:30 a.m. on March 25. There was a deadly silence in the Situation Room as the group gathered. The red dots showing the North Vietnamese position on the huge wall maps had multiplied like fever spots blighting the landscape. In addition to the regular group of Thieu, Prime Minister Khiem, JGS chairman Vien, and

General Quang, Thieu asked Vice President Huong, General Khuyen (the logistics expert and deputy chief of the JGS), Foreign Minister Bac, and Hung to attend the military review.

As the briefing started, Thieu picked up the phone and called General Truong in Danang. Those in the room heard Thieu ask Truong, "Can you still hold Hue?" Thieu then repeated the answer out loud: " 'If there is an order, I will.' "

"How long can you hold?" asked Thieu.

" 'One day or two days,' " replied Truong, as Thieu repeated his answers to the group.

"If you cannot hold, you have got to decide immediately. Once you have decided [to abandon Hue], you must execute the plan quickly," said Thieu.

Thieu did not repeat any more of the conversation but hung up, saying, "Truong is very depressed." Thieu said the word "depressed" in English.

After consulting with General Vien, Thieu directed him to send a message to General Truong issuing three orders: First, the formal abandonment of Hue. Second, as rapid a deployment as possible of his forces to Danang. Third, to hold Danang at all costs. Thieu sighed. "We counted on three enclaves but now there is only one left in Danang." Everybody looked pale and tired. There was no longer any question of holding Hue.

Hung could hardly believe what he had just heard. He assumed the Joint General Staff military had prepared a series of contingency plans and was well organized, with a full range of options for redeployment. Was that all there was, only a few commands over the phone with no ability to follow through? It was all so vague and imprecise. Hung looked at Foreign Minister Bac, who also did not usually sit in on military meetings. He was pale and appeared shocked. This was the first time they had seen the JGS head in action and it was devastating to realize that there were no real plans. The silence that followed the conversation underscored their helplessness. Hung felt weak and physically ill.

Finally, Thieu resumed the meeting. The rest of the time was devoted to reorganizing the regional troops into main force regular army units to replace the troops that had been lost. The plan was to create two more divisions. North Vietnam had already moved twenty divisions into the South to fight against only thirteen in the ARVN. The North Vietnamese forces had the mobility to attack in strength while the South Vietnamese troops were needed for static defense throughout the four military regions. There were no reserves available to counter a North Vietnamese force massed for an offensive.

After the meeting, Hung stayed behind to get Thieu's final instructions on the letter to Ford. Thieu reached into his desk and handed Hung the letter with his penciled-in corrections in blue. Hung then rushed the letter to the cabinet director, Colonel Vo Van Cam, saying, "This is top priority. Have it typed immediately and invite the American ambassador here so the President can give it to him as soon as possible." Chargé d'Affaires Wolfgang Lehmann, sitting in for Graham Martin who was in America, received the letter from Thieu and sent it to the White House through the direct embassy back-channel link. The last appeal had been made. Saigon could only await the American response.

18

The Weyand Mission

WHEN PRESIDENT FORD received Thieu's letter, his answer was to send General Frederick C. Weyand, the U.S. Army Chief of Staff and the last senior American commander in Vietnam, to Saigon on March 28 to assess the situation.[1] Ford still did not seem aware of how desperate the situation was in South Vietnam. As Ford wrote in his memoirs, "Everyone knew the problems in South Vietnam were serious, but no one seemed to know just how critical they were. We needed on-the-spot assessment of the situation. I asked Weyand to fly to Saigon as soon as possible, spend a week there, and bring back a full report."[2]

The South Vietnamese were cheered by the news of the Weyand mission. He might be the *deus ex machina* they desperately needed to recommend B-52 strikes and immediate military aid. Weyand was an old Vietnam hand, a friend, a defender of the country, who had served there for a total of ten years. Tall and raw-boned, with a thinning hairline on his forehead, Weyand had the command, bearing, and poise that inspired confidence among the Vietnamese. He rose from division commander to Commander Military Assistance Command Vietnam, replacing General Creighton Abrams in June 1972. Thieu hoped that Weyand, who left Vietnam in March 1973 with the last American troops, had some influence on Congress and the President. Unlike the congressional delegations, Weyand and his team would assess the military situation and Saigon's needs and not go off on political tangents. If there was anybody who would recommend the renewal of B-52 raids and immediate military aid, it would be Weyand.

Hung was pleased to learn that Eric Von Marbod would accompany Weyand. Ever since he had been given the file of presidential letters by Thieu, Hung had begun to suspect that President Ford had not seen all of Nixon's letters. How else to explain Ford's promise to Thieu: "the existing commitments this nation has made in the past are still valid and will be fully honored in my administration"? Since they had not been honored, Hung speculated that Kissinger had not shown the full file of Nixon's letters to Ford, and had only briefed the President the way he briefed Thieu on his negotiations with the North Vietnamese in Paris, vaguely and without the real substance of the commitments. (After he left office, Ford acknowledged that while he was aware of Nixon's letters to Thieu, he had not reviewed all the correspondence when he took office and signed his first letter to Thieu.)[3]

In his letter to Ford, Thieu only referred to the American commitments in general terms. Hung wondered if Ford knew of them in detail. He considered attaching Nixon's January 5 letter, promising to use "full force" against North Vietnamese violations of the cease-fire, for Ford to see, but then thought that it might be considered undiplomatic and would create a backlash since it would go through Kissinger before being sent to President Ford. Hung ruled out this idea and thought instead to bring copies of the Nixon letters to Ford through his counsellor John Marsh, with whom Hung had a working relationship. But this would require a trip to Washington and time was becoming desperately short. Ford was on vacation in Palm Springs and it might be hard to reach him. Hung decided to consult with Von Marbod, who knew the workings of the American government better than anybody Hung had ever met. Von Marbod was a friend who had helped in the past; perhaps he would have the answer. Hung called him in Washington and asked him to get in contact as soon as he arrived in Saigon with Weyand.

Recognizing Thieu's suspicious nature, Hung was determined to raise his concerns with Thieu before Weyand arrived. The Americans always reiterated to Thieu, "Keep it secret, keep it secret," especially the letters. (No sooner had Kissinger delivered the draft of the Paris Accords to Thieu than he pleaded with him to keep it secret. Thieu explained stiffly that he had to show it to the members of his National Security Council.) Still, Thieu did not want to do anything to shock the Americans.

Hung summoned his courage to approach the president at breakfast the morning before Weyand arrived. Early in the morning, before the full weight of the day's problems preoccupied him, Thieu was more receptive to new ideas. Hung confided his thoughts that perhaps President Ford had not seen the full continuity of promises in Nixon's letters. Hung knew Thieu did not want to jar the Americans, but it was important to test his hypothesis. Hung had to broach the subject with Thieu, even if he became angry.

Hung knew how Thieu coveted the letters, yet if there was ever a time to use them it was now. Although Ford was still talking vaguely about standing behind the Republic of Vietnam and honoring the responsibilities of the United States, no substantive aid was being sent and there was no response against the North Vietnamese invasion. Instead, the Americans seemed to be downplaying the strength and goals of the North Vietnamese invasion force. Hung asked Thieu if Ford was fully aware of the extent of Nixon's pledges, saying, "Ford doesn't seem to care. He is going off on vacation to Palm Springs while we are dying. When is he going to respond?" Hung was trying to lead Thieu into seriously considering releasing the letters.

At first, Thieu did not react but looked at Hung pensively, assessing his question, not rejecting its implications. Hung rushed to fill the gap in the conversation.

"Well, Mr. President, you may think I am naive politically, but somehow I suspect Mr. Ford does not know much about what Mr. Nixon wrote you.''

"What do you mean?'' asked Thieu. "How can the President of the United States not know about the letters? He renewed the commitment to me.''

"That is precisely the point. Maybe Ford did not know the full extent of Nixon's specific commitments,'' said Hung.

"Why?'' Thieu asked.

"Maybe Kissinger didn't brief him,'' Hung replied.

That clinched Hung's argument with Thieu. He distrusted Kissinger so completely that he believed Kissinger had withheld from Nixon his private concessions to the North Vietnamese in Paris and had never shown Ford the complete record of Nixon's letters.

Thieu did not want to make the Nixon and Ford letters public, yet he felt the need to drive home to the American public and President that commitments had been made by Nixon in the name of the American people and the government of the United States of America. Hung hoped that once Ford was shown the Nixon promises, the new President would be moved to action on behalf of South Vietnam. Hung asked Thieu to let him try to find a way to make the Nixon letters known to Ford without making them public and thus creating a break of trust with Ford.

"Be careful,'' Thieu told Hung. "Don't let the Americans find a pretext for accusing me.'' Thieu's response to Hung, as he sipped his aromatic lotus flower tea at the breakfast table, echoed his answers to Hung in the past. Even though he had decided on a course of action, he was keeping his options open, allowing Hung to proceed on his own so that Thieu could deny Hung's actions if necessary.

Hung was not concerned that his plan would create a backlash. The situation was desperate. How else, after all the repeated promises, could there not be any American response with B-52 bombing or military aid? The Vietnamese could only imagine that the new U.S. President did not understand the full depth of American presidential promises of support after the Paris Accords were signed.

For Thieu, the Nixon promise to "react vigorously'' and "with full force'' to any North Vietnamese violations of the Paris Accords was still uppermost in his mind. Ford's letter on his first day in office had reiterated support for the Nixon pledges. Now, Thieu would try to redeem those pledges in any way he could short of openly breaking with the American President.

General Weyand and his team, which included Von Marbod and the CIA's top Vietnam experts, Theodore Shackley and George Carver, arrived in Saigon on March 28 with the mission of assuring President Thieu of President Ford's "steadfast support'' and examining the "options and actions open to the United States to assist the South Vietnamese.''[4] The night they arrived, Von Marbod called Hung from the American Embassy and arranged to come directly to his house for a beer and briefing.

Von Marbod was tense and concerned. His usual outgoing energy and bluff manner were shrouded by a mood of pessimism. Hung had heard on the Voice of America that Ford was on the way to Palm Springs for Easter vacation and he asked Von Marbod if there were any meetings going on in Washington to discuss the fall of Hue and the pressures on Danang. He was hoping to get a hint of how Thieu's appeal to Ford had been received. But Von Marbod sidestepped a direct answer, saying only, "You know the President sent General Weyand to see what you need from us to help you."

"The situation in Danang is critical," said Hung, "and we are concerned that Saigon may be threatened."

"I am concerned for the security of your family," replied Von Marbod. "I think you ought to send your mother out."

"I have created a shelter in my house for my mother with rice and water," explained Hung.

Hung then took him to see a pile of sandbags in a room off the kitchen. "Looks pretty good. Good stuff, unless there is a direct hit," said Von Marbod, shaking his head gloomily.

"I want to prepare," said Hung, "because the Viet Cong are getting closer. They have even appeared on the road to Vung Tau." On a previous trip Hung had taken Von Marbod to Vung Tau, sixty-five miles southeast of Saigon on the South China Sea. The white sand beaches and blue water made for a perfect resort. Von Marbod recalled their picnic lunch of clams roasted over a charcoal fire on the water's edge. "I don't know when we will have clams again in Vung Tau," he said sadly.

"The situation is growing more desperate by the hour and we need your help immediately," Hung stressed.

"Yes, you sure do. You sure do. The best thing to do now is to declare that the North Vietnamese violations have invalidated the Paris Accords and declare Article Seven void," said Von Marbod. Hung was encouraged to hear that since he knew Article Seven prohibited the introduction of troops, armaments, munitions, and war materials into South Vietnam. If it was declared invalid, there would be no legal restraint on the full-scale resumption of American aid to Saigon, limited to one-for-one replacements under the Paris Accords.

Encouraged, Hung asked directly if he had heard anything in Washington about Thieu's SOS letter of March 25, and whether he was coming in response to that letter. "What letter?" replied Von Marbod, who had not seen or heard of Thieu's appeal.

As they discussed the details of the letter and Thieu's specific request for B-52 raids, Von Marbod explained that "It is very difficult now."

"Well, they promised us," said Hung.

"Who promised you?" asked Von Marbod, curious at what Hung was suggesting.

Hung poured them a *bam ba,* 33-brand beer. He realized then that Von Marbod did not know anything about the exchange of presidential letters.

"I don't know if you or Jim Schlesinger know it or not, but there was a very serious commitment to President Thieu from President Nixon, which was then confirmed by President Ford.''

At first, Von Marbod thought Hung was referring to the public statements of the American presidents and the American commitment in general. He tried to console Hung by explaining that Americans meant well, but there was a rising tide of opposition to the war in the press, on the college campuses, and in the Congress.

"Eric, I am not talking about the overall commitment of America to Vietnam, I am talking about specific written commitments from President Nixon to President Thieu," said Hung.

"What are you talking about, Gregg?" asked Von Marbod. "Did Nixon really make secret promises to Thieu?"

"Before I answer, I want to ask you a few questions. How important is Weyand? Was he sent here by Ford or Schlesinger? To whom is he going to report when he gets back to Washington?"

"He's very important. He was sent by President Ford and he is going to report to the President. This is a presidential mission; but why are you asking me?"

"Well, Eric, remember you used to ask me whether I had notes on Kissinger's talks with Thieu and the promises he made because Schlesinger was interested in them? I said I didn't know then, but now I have something to show you."

Alone with Von Marbod in the dining room Hung opened his burgundy leather attaché case and handed him a copy of Nixon's October 16, 1972, letter to Thieu. Nixon had promised that "we will view any breach of faith on their part with the utmost gravity; and it would have the most serious consequences." In his own handwriting at the bottom on the page Nixon had added: his absolute condition "that the GVN must survive as a free country."

Von Marbod was astounded and read the letter over several times. Then he grimaced. Hung imagined he was wondering what Nixon had meant by "the most serious consequences." "It reads like Nixon really wrote this," said Von Marbod finally.

"Yes, he did," replied Hung. "What do you think he means by 'serious consequences'?"

"It's obvious," replied Von Marbod.

"Let me show you something else," offered Hung, as he pulled out Nixon's November 8, 1972, letter. Hung was sitting across the table from Von Marbod with his brief case at his side on the floor, hidden from Von Marbod's view, so he had no idea how many letters Hung would come up with. By providing the letters one at a time Hung hoped to gauge Von Marbod's reactions and get an indication of how Nixon's promises would be viewed by American officials. Hung had no way of knowing how important the letters would be considered by Americans. He knew how Thieu prized the letters and thought of them as his mandate from Washington, but since they had not been made public it was difficult for Hung to assess their full meaning and impact in the American political context.

Hung pointed to a sentence he had underlined in which Nixon said: "I have repeatedly given firm guarantees against the possibility that the agreement is violated."

Von Marbod frowned, contracting his bushy red eyebrows as he stared at the letter. "This is hard to believe," he said. "Why have you been hiding these letters?"

Hung thought that perhaps he was right in speculating that Ford had not seen all the Nixon letters to Thieu. Here was Von Marbod, the Pentagon's key man on Vietnam, and he had not even heard of the correspondence between Nixon and Thieu, nor had his boss, James Schlesinger, the Defense Secretary.

"Do you think President Ford knows about these letters?" asked Hung.

"I don't know. I'm not so sure," replied Von Marbod.

"What about this?" asked Hung as he slowly read out Nixon's words from Nixon's November 14 letter: "You have my absolute assurance that if Hanoi fails to abide by the terms of this agreement it is my intention to take swift and severe retaliatory action."

"Let me see," said Von Marbod excitedly. He reached forward to take the letter, but Hung would not give it to him.

"Wait a minute," Hung said, "Let me read you some more. 'I repeat my personal assurances to you that the United States will react very strongly and rapidly to any violation of the Agreement.' "

Hung handed the letter to Von Marbod, who read it over carefully. He finished his beer and said: "Gregg, I want to spend more time with you but I think I better see Weyand right away. Can I bring these letters with me?"

"Suppose I give you copies of some of the letters. Do you think that you can do me and Vietnam a great favor by finding some way, perhaps through General Weyand, to give them to President Ford? We don't believe that President Ford has seen them," said Hung.

Von Marbod's immediate reaction was anger that Hung had not shown him the letters sooner. "After all we've been through, how could you have kept these letters secret from me?" he asked in a hurt tone. "Don't you trust me? For God's sakes, Gregg, I can handle this. You don't have to tell me its secret." Then Von Marbod said, "If you had revealed them sooner, we could have taken advantage of the promises to obtain more aid for South Vietnam."

It was too difficult for Hung to explain to his friend how he had gotten Thieu to agree to let him make the letters available, and how he had argued with Thieu over the importance of using the letters to try to rally support for more aid.

"If only we could get copies of the letters to President Ford through General Weyand, then he would realize what we are counting on" said Hung. "Look, Eric, you know my asking you for help is to convey the content of these letters to President Ford on my own assumption that he is not aware of them. We have to proceed very cautiously. Before you take the letters, I want you to find out if Weyand is sympathetic to Vietnam and willing to convey the letters to President Ford. Is he able to do that for us?

The best thing is for me to write down these key sentences and you discuss the letters with Weyand and let me know his reaction. These are delicate, secret letters, and unless you can get them directly to President Ford, I will go to Washington myself and try to present them to him.''

Von Marbod thought for a moment, then said: "Maybe that's good." He promised he would give Hung an answer before he left Saigon. Hung wrote out excerpts from the Nixon promises and Von Marbod pocketed them as he drove off into the muggy night past the fluorescent lights of St. Paul's Hospital.

Eric Von Marbod had been coming to Saigon since 1973, but he had never seen the situation so bad. General Weyand was off visiting the corps commanders to assess the military situation while Von Marbod met with his sources, and the CIA members of the team were working their networks. They were all getting the same message: Only American intervention in the form of B-52 bombing would halt the enemy advance and "stabilize the front," the code words the ARVN military men used for B-52 bombing. A massive infusion of military aid was needed immediately if a total collapse was to be prevented. As things stood, ammunition supplies would be exhausted by June 30, and there was nothing on the way. To Von Marbod, the American commitment was a moral obligation of national honor that had to be sustained. He believed that the Vietnamization process had not worked because it did not really serve the needs of South Vietnam. Rather, it was a program whose very name, Vietnamization, carried a paternalistic and arrogant ring. The program had moved too quickly, and now that the Americans had gone, the South Vietnamese found themselves with equipment but no logistics system. "Vietnamization was like getting nine women pregnant in order to have a baby in one month," Von Marbod had said.

Saigon was dependent on the Americans for the technical expertise to service the equipment. The South Vietnamese inherited a mentality of warfare based on unlimited supplies of ammunition, total helicopter mobility, and on-demand, close-in air support from fighters and bombers as well as scheduled B-52 raids. The political process had never been Vietnamized; Henry Kissinger was still in charge of the negotiations with the North Vietnamese, who refused to deal with the Thieu government. Von Marbod believed that the least the United States could do, now that it had gotten its prisoners back and withdrawn its combat forces, was to give Saigon a last chance for survival. Decency and American character warranted nothing less.

That night Hung waited for Von Marbod at home, delaying his dinner until his friend arrived. It was nearly ten o'clock, the curfew hour, when a grim-faced Von Marbod came in, the sweat shining through his fatigues, dust on the M-16 rifle he was carrying. He was just back from a field trip with Weyand.

"Any news?" asked Hung.

"General Truong is in grave trouble in Danang. We are trying to save the remaining troops. It's total chaos up there."

"I know," Hung said sadly.

At the table over fish soup, roast duck, and beer, Von Marbod said he had spent the whole day traveling with Weyand. "I have some news for you. Weyand was very surprised and impressed by my briefing on the letters, and he agrees with you that President Ford may not be aware of the full extent of the letters. Nothing was said to him by the President about the letters prior to his coming here. You must give me the letters right away. Weyand will try to see Ford privately." [5]

Hung took out copies of the three letters he had shown Von Marbod. Then he said, "Here's another one, Eric," and added a fourth, dated January 5, 1973, in which Nixon wrote: "you have my assurance of continued assistance in the post settlement period and that we will respond with full force should the settlement be violated by North Vietnam."

"I'll be dammed," said Von Marbod as he read the letter. "I've got to see Weyand immediately." They agreed on a code for a telephone call from America after Weyand presented the letters to Ford. Because it was after the curfew hour Hung had his jeep full of security guards, with M-16 rifles, accompany Von Marbod back to the DAO quarters at Tan Son Nhut; the guards were for the letters as well as his friend.

On the morning of April 1, Saigon's population awoke to hear on the radio that American weapons were to be delivered to Tan Son Nhut Airport momentarily. At noon, the government television station showed new 105mm howitzers, sixteen in all, being unloaded from a giant C-5 military transport in the glaring sun. The guns harked back to earlier days and the unending flow of American aid. The news helped to quiet rumors of an impending *coup d'état* against Thieu. In reality the ARVN needed ammunition for the guns in the field more desperately than it needed new guns in Saigon. The arrival of the howitzers was more of a morale booster than of real military significance. Their presence deceptively demonstrated that American still cared and that, perhaps, General Weyand could really help Vietnam again.

Fred Weyand had an easy manner, despite his four stars. He was sympathetic to the needs of the South Vietnamese. He listened to their pleas and offered encouragement. Alone, one on one, the generals had told him the only thing that would halt the North Vietnamese advance was B-52 bombing. Then the ARVN would have the breathing time and space to regroup and hold against the North Vietnamese onslaught. Without American help, a respite would be impossible.

On April 3, the day before Weyand was scheduled to leave, a meeting with President Thieu was scheduled in the Situation Room at the Independence Palace. The night before, Thieu asked Hung to prepare a summary of important quotations from the Nixon and Ford letters for him to use at the meeting with Weyand.

"Mr. President, I have already summarized the letters and General Weyand already has some of the most important ones," said Hung.

"When did you see him?" asked Thieu.

"I didn't see him. I went through a friend in the delegation. He was very surprised and so was Weyand. They think that Ford does not know of the full extent of the Nixon promises to you. They understand the delicacy of the situation and will handle it carefully and with full discretion." Hung explained about his meetings with Von Marbod, giving the president a summary of the quotes from the letters he had provided. "I shall take the whole responsibility for the letters and you may blame me or even fire me if and when the U.S. protests," said Hung.

The following day, April 3, Thieu was in a foul mood. Prime Minister Khiem had just resigned, bringing down the cabinet with him. The stolid prime minister who had contributed little to activating the government in its hour of need had decided that Thieu was in serious trouble because of the fall of the highlands and Danang. As soon as he left the government, Khiem began shipping his possessions to Taipei and Paris.[6] Coup rumors were in the air. To make matters worse the VOA carried a report that President Ford, still on vacation, had finally spoken with newsmen to criticize President Thieu for his hasty decision to withdraw from the highlands. Ford admitted that the evacuation of the 6,000 Americans still in Vietnam was under consideration. Hung was in anguish over the internal strife within the government. How could Prime Minister Khiem resign at such a moment? He knew his action would undercut Thieu and yet he was leaving with the entire cabinet.

The bad news mounted. Hung received reports from the JGS intelligence officers and from friends in the police that the Communists had infiltrated assassination teams with silencers on their guns into the hordes of undisciplined troops and refugees that were falling back into Saigon. He called Thieu and asked to see him before the Weyand meeting.

Hung told Thieu of the reports of the assassination teams and said: "Mr. President, I feel strongly that there is a need for a twenty-four-hour-a-day curfew right now to prevent the teams from moving into the city." Thieu agreed and ordered the curfew to begin that evening and last for twenty-four hours.

The meeting with Weyand was scheduled for the Situation Room at 5:00 p.m. The two sides gathered around the mahogany table marked off with freshly lettered nameplates. They exchanged forced pleasantries and smiles as TV cameramen entered for a "photo opportunity" of the Weyand team and the top Vietnamese officials. But the mood quickly became somber when the press left.[7] Ambassador Martin asked the Americans on Weyand's team to brief President Thieu individually on their findings and assessments.

First, Martin called on Theodore (Ted) Shackley, former CIA station chief in Saigon (1968–72), who had been promoted to head of the Agency's Asian Division. Shackley, an intense, experienced operator, had been station chief in Laos, where he often had disagreements with Martin, who was ambassador in neighboring Thailand. Martin complained that Shackley had wanted to involve Americans based in Thailand in operations in Laos and Martin felt strongly that the American role should be limited.[8]

Shackley sat at the far end of the mahogany table. For him the meeting was a culmination of the American effort in Vietnam. It would "confirm the situation on the ground and determine what could be done to save something or set up a program to pull the plug." Shackley still saw a possibility for the Vietnamese to help themselves and build support in Washington. He had conferred earlier with Thieu on the military situation and now he looked at Vietnam in terms of how it should be viewed by the outside world. "There is a need for your government to address itself to the refugee problem and make it apparent to the people of Vietnam and the world that the government cares for them and that the problem is being well handled," said Shackley. "The refugee problem can be used to generate sympathy for Vietnam."

Next, he discussed information. "There is a need to present to the American public that this is a clear-cut North Vietnamese invasion and there are not simply more Viet Cong coming out of the woods." The American public's perception was still that there was a civil war in the South, he explained. The refugees had voted with their feet and were expressing their fear of the Communists by fleeing south. The government must stress the importance of assistance it received to help the refugees. This would make it easier to generate more support. There was a need for the government to dispel the "rumors" circulating about the truncation of the country, abandonment of South Vietnam, and a superpower deal to carve up the country. As Shackley droned on, Hung could see grave disappointment on the faces of the Vietnamese. They hardly expected such a rambling discourse at this critical moment. They knew the problems. They were waiting for the Americans to solve them.

Hung put his pen down and gave Shackley a long look, hoping he would get the point and allow the meeting to proceed to a discussion of military aid and a resumption of the bombing. Martin then called on the CIA's George Carver, who pressed the same themes and stressed the need for more information to reach the American people. "The invasion story has not been told well and we have not been able to turn around the arguments criticizing the GVN," he said. Carver cited the World Council of Churches, which opposed the war and was critical of Thieu, as an example. "We should invite them here to see for themselves the suffering caused by the North Vietnamese invasion," he urged. The South Vietnamese should use its propaganda machine, including leaflets and radio, to focus on the newly infiltrated North Vietnamese soldiers who were far away from home. They should try to weaken the morale of the North Vietnamese. Unbelievable, Hung thought to himself, as he looked at Carver and sighed.

Martin could sense the Vietnamese growing restless so he continued around the table, skipping the Defense Attaché, General Homer Smith. He called on Von Marbod, who explained that the South Vietnamese air force was flying too high in order to avoid enemy aircraft fire and was dropping bombs on its own troops. There had to be better coordination between the army and the air force to save Military Region III, which included Saigon.

Ambassador Martin slipped Von Marbod a note on which he had written: "You talk too much."

In the first positive note of the meeting, Von Marbod said that restrictions on ammunition could be lifted by the Saigon government. Martin seized the moment to follow up. As always, Ambassador Martin was optimistic. He considered the renewal of aid as a given, and asked Von Marbod, "Assuming aid is appropriated, how long will it take to get it here?"

"We can have supplies here practically as soon as they are appropriated," Von Marbod replied. "We have them in Okinawa and Korea." He told the Vietnamese it was no longer a time to conserve ammunition: "Now is the time to start to fire and remove all restrictions on ammunition for the morale of the troops. We can provide them with more now."

Carver raised his hand to interrupt with a discourse on how South Vietnam could learn a history lesson from the British Army. What South Vietnam was facing nothing less than a Dunkirk, referring to the crisis facing the British Army before the fall of France in World War II from which Britain had recovered. "It is not quite clear to the American people yet, but it can be made clear," said Carver. Martin then cut him short and called on General Weyand.

Weyand presented a comprehensive but succinct review of the military situation. He was highly critical of two of the generals who lost the highlands, singling out General Phu, the II Corps commander, and General Thuan, who was in charge of the naval training center at Nha Trang. Thuan had left his post before the order to retreat was given. Weyand then promised President Thieu: "We will get you the assistance you need and will explain your needs to Congress."

Now it was the Vietnamese turn. Thieu called on General Vien, chairman of the JGS, to discuss the critical question of how to halt the Communist advance. General Vien appealed to the Americans. "We desperately need to stabilize the front line now." Here was the code word for renewed B-52 bombing. Hung, however, looked for a fall-back, and asked, "Assuming the B-52s are no longer available, what about providing us with heavy bombs such as the Daisy Cutter?"[9] General Vien interjected that Daisy Cutters would be very helpful. Von Marbod promised that "we will deliver a few of them now." Hung wondered why Vien had not sought the bombs earlier.

With Von Marbod's promise to send a few Daisy Cutters, the meeting turned to a tactical discussion of the military situation. Weyand said goodbye to Thieu and promised to report to President Ford immediately on his return to the United States.

After everyone had left, Hung lingered behind to see Thieu. The President looked deflated and sad. The Vietnamese had appealed directly for B-52 raids and the Americans had been noncommittal. This was the moment, said Hung, when the President must appeal directly to the American people for a last act of assistance. Thieu should go on television and read out loud Nixon's secret pledges, but not Ford's letters, so as to save the new President personal embarrassment before Congress. Thieu was still not sure that such a course of action would be wise. The fate of Saigon was in General Weyand's hands. There was little to do but await his report and President Ford's response before making any new waves.

19

Playing to the Congress

AFTER GENERAL WEYAND had promised to seek emergency aid, but before he departed from Saigon, a contradictory signal came from Washington. On April 2, after the loss of Danang, Secretary of Defense James Schlesinger spoke in his news conference of "relatively little major fighting" in Vietnam. In fact the Secretary of Defense was minimizing the crisis. Schlesinger was convinced after the fall of Danang that it was all over and the major concern of the United States would be to safely withdraw the 6,000 Americans who were still there. Before Weyand left for Saigon Schlesinger had cautioned him, "Fred be careful. Don't overpromise. Don't get caught up by the notion that you are going to reverse the tide. It is all coming down." Schlesinger and his Asian expert, Deputy Assistant Secretary of Defense for International Security Affairs Morton Abramowitz, believed the tide had turned against Vietnam and there was no way it could be reversed.[1]

In Saigon, Weyand left the impression that he would recommend increased military aid, but he was noncommittal about the use of American B-52s to halt the North Vietnamese offensive. The South Vietnamese were counting on the bombers to provide a minimum two-week respite for their troops to regroup.

Weyand was in the air on the way to Washington to report to Schlesinger when he received orders to divert, fly to Palm Springs, and report directly to President Ford. Before Kissinger arrived, Weyand managed to have five minutes alone with the President and showed him the letters from Nixon. Then Weyand and Von Marbod met with President Ford and Kissinger in the bedroom of Ford's vacation home while Mrs. Ford and Nancy Kissinger had tea in the living room. Weyand gave the President his report, citing the military justification for renewed B-52 bombing and calling for $722 million in emergency military aid. In a covering Memorandum for the President, Weyand summed up:

The current military situation is critical, and the probability of the survival of South Vietnam as a truncated nation in the southern provinces is marginal at

302

best. The GVN is on the brink of a total military defeat. However, the South is planning to continue to defend with their available resources, and, if allowed respite, will rebuild their capabilities to the extent that the United States support in material will permit. I believe that we owe them that support.

We went to Vietnam in the first place to assist the South Vietnamese people—not to defeat the North Vietnamese. We reached out our hand to the South Vietnamese people, and they took it. Now they need that helping hand more than ever. By every measure we have been able to apply 20,000,000 people have told the world they fear for their lives, they cherish values that are closely allied with those of non-communist systems, they desperately need the opportunity to continue their development of a way of life different from those who now live under North Vietnamese rule.

The present level of U.S. support guarantees GVN defeat. Of the $700 million provided for FY 1975, the remaining $150 million can be used for a short time for a major supply operation; however, if there is to be any real chance of success, an additional $722 million is urgently needed to bring the South Vietnamese to a minimal defense posture to meet the Soviet and PRC supported invasion. Additional U.S. aid is within both the spirit and intent of the Paris Agreement, which remains the practical framework for a peaceful settlement in Vietnam.

The use of U.S. military airpower to reinforce Vietnamese capabilities to blunt the North Vietnamese invasion would offer both a material and psychological assist to GVN and provide a much needed battlefield pause. I recognize, however, the significant legal and political implications which would attend the exercise of this option.

Given the speed at which events are moving, there is one other matter you should consider. For reasons of prudence, the United States should plan now for a mass evacuation of some 6,000 U.S. citizens and tens of thousands of South Vietnamese and Third Country Nationals to whom we have incurred an obligation and owe protection. The lessons of Da Nang indicate that this evacuation would require as a minimum a U.S. task force of a reinforced division supported by tactical air to suppress North Vietnamese artillery and anti-aircraft, as required. At the appropriate time, a public statement of this policy should be made and the North Vietnamese clearly warned "of U.S. intention to use force to safely evacuate personnel." Authority should be obtained to authorize appropriate use of military sanctions against North Vietnam if there is interference with the evacuation.

United States credibility as an ally is at stake in Vietnam. To sustain that credibility we must make a maximum effort to support the South Vietnamese now.

A more detailed analysis is contained in the attached report.

Respectfully,
[s] Fred C. Weyand

(See Appendix J for the full text of the Weyand Report)

In the body of the report, Weyand made the case for $722 million in emergency military aid and B-52 bombing. Weyand stressed that "the actions of the US are vital in restoring confidence."

The action which the US could take which would have the greatest immediate effect on Vietnamese perceptions—North and South—would be the use of US air power to blunt the current NVA offensive. Even if confined to South Vietnam and carried out for only a limited time, such attacks would take a severe toll on the North Vietnamese expeditionary force's manpower and supplies, and have a dramatic morale impact on North Vietnam's invading troops. These attacks would also give Hanoi's leaders pause and raise concerns, which do not now exist, about the risks involved in ignoring a formal agreement made with the United States.

South Vietnamese military leaders at all levels have repeatedly cited the importance of B-52 attacks to the conduct of a successful defense against superior enemy forces and there is sound military justification for such a point of view.

During the meeting with President Ford, according to Von Marbod, Weyand pleaded the case for providing Saigon with a last chance through renewed use of American airpower. But Kissinger objected, telling Ford: "If you do that, the American people will take to the streets again." [2]

After the meeting, Kissinger went to the White House Press Center at Palm Springs to brief the correspondents traveling with the President. He drove to the briefing with Ford's press secretary, Ron Nessen. On the way they discussed the disintegration of South Vietnam. Kissinger commented, "Why don't those people die fast? The worst thing that could happen would be for them to linger on." [3]

In the Briefing Room Kissinger did not discuss Weyand's recommendation to resume bombing, but made the case for consideration of military aid to Vietnam. Kissinger was setting up the Vietnamese for a congressional turndown and was trying to protect Ford. He told the reporters:

Regardless of the probable outcome of the war, I think it is a serious question . . . and I really believe that at this moment, having paid so much in our national unity on this issue, we should conduct this debate, not with an attitude of who is going to pin the blame on whom, but with an attitude that we are facing a great tragedy in which there is involved something of American credibility, something of American honor, something of how we are perceived by other people in the world on which serious people may have different questions but in which, for God's sake, we ought to stop talking as if one side had the monopoly of wisdom, morality and insight. [4]

Ford met again with Weyand, Von Marbod, and Kissinger after Kissinger briefed the press. Then the President flew to the San Francisco International Airport in a rainstorm to welcome the Vietnamese orphans brought to the United States by "Operation Babylift." Ford helped to carry the children from the aircraft to ambulances and buses. For days, while playing golf on vacation, he had been avoiding the press. On one occasion he actually ran away from reporters to avoid commenting on Vietnam. Evening TV news programs showed terrified refugees struggling to flee Danang, the South Vietnamese army in a shambles—and Ford playing golf.

When he read of Ford's visit to the orphans, Hung thought the President might finally have had a change of heart. He searched the American press for indications of Ford's attitude toward the deteriorating conditions in Vietnam, but found nothing. On April 6, on "Face the Nation," Schlesinger again attempted to play down the agonies of Vietnam: "It is plain that the great offensive is a phrase that probably should be in quotation marks. What we had here is a partial collapse of South Vietnamese forces, so that there had been very little major fighting since the battle of Ban Me Thuot, and that was an exception in itself."

At first, Hung could not understand Schlesinger's remarks. Why was the Secretary of Defense saying that the full-fledged, all-out North Vietnamese offensive should be put in quotation marks? Hung quickly realized that by playing down the collapse of the South Vietnamese forces, Schlesinger was abandoning the Saigon government and minimizing the need for continued American involvement. Schlesinger did not believe that South Vietnam was of strategic importance to the United States; its loss would not significantly alter the world military balance.[5] "There is no U.S. strategic interest in Vietnam," he told Von Marbod.[6] When Congress was moving quickly to cut aid and end the war, his views would prove to be lethal, Hung felt.

Schlesinger's comments on "Face the Nation" traveled around the world within hours. They so upset General Homer Smith, chief of the Defense Attaché's Office in Saigon, that he sent a cable contradicting the Secretary. "On the contrary, there is heavy fighting all along the coastal plain and in the foothills from south of Phu Bai to Khanh Duong in Khanh Hao province," said Smith. He enumerated the battles being fought and concluded: "Respectfully recommend that you suggest to the Chairman [of the Joint Chiefs of Staff] that he acquaint the Secretary with these facts so that an accurate representation of what has occurred might be presented to the American people. There is a 'great offensive' underway."[7]

Saigon was awash with rumors of a coup being planned to overthrow Thieu. Hung awaited word by telephone from Von Marbod on Ford's response to Weyand's report. When he went to his office, Hung stationed his sister Kim Loan in his villa to wait for Von Marbod's call.

That day, April 7, a motorcycle drove into the yard of the jungle COSVN headquarters near the Vietnamese-Cambodian border with a tall, lean man wearing a soldier's hard helmet over his gray hair. A black leather satchel was slung from his shoulder. It contained the operations orders Le Duc Tho was carrying from Hanoi for the final assault on Saigon, approved by the Politburo in Hanoi. The Paris negotiator, who would receive the Nobel Peace Prize with Henry Kissinger, was in charge of organizing the Ho Chi Minh Campaign before the final week of April. Hanoi had decided to press for final victory.[8]

There was still no word from Washington on the morning of April 8, but as Hung awoke he heard the sounds of anti-aircraft guns being fired and bombs exploding in what seemed to be the area of the Palace. He waited for word and did not move until he learned Thieu was safe and there was not a

coup. An F-5E pilot, on his own initiative, had attacked the Palace. One of
the bombs destroyed Thieu's breakfast spot on the balcony, but he was in
another part of the Palace and escaped injury. Hung reflected that the calamities were coming together. Ever since the congressional delegation left
at the end of February and it became apparent that American support
was collapsing, there had been a series of defeats and ominous omens. The
rout in the highlands, the fall of Danang, and the aid cutbacks were the
worst.

Then, too, there was the assassination of Saudi Arabia's King Saud al
Faisal on March 25. King Faisal had expressed sympathy and admiration
for the South Vietnamese struggle against communism and offered help. In
early 1975 Faisal had agreed in principle to a loan of several hundred million
dollars. The money would be used to boost the South Vietnamese economy
and allow Thieu to buy fuel and ammunition from whatever sources were
available. An alternative to the loan plan was also raised with Faisal. Under
this scheme Saudi Arabia would guarantee a U.S. military aid loan to South
Vietnam. Hung preferred the guarantee plan because it would eliminate the
uncertainty, and perhaps the impossibility, of buying American ammunition
outside the American market. Furthermore, the whole Vietnamese war machine was Made in U.S.A. It could not possibly be fed with foreign equipment.

"Perhaps it seems weird to connect Saudi oil with Vietnamese survival
in our efforts to find ways to obtain military aid," recalled Hung, "but in
the darkest days of April 1975 it did not seem strange at all. When you are
drowning, you grab for whatever floats."

The South Vietnamese believed that they were doomed. At the moment
when King Faisal's plan was about to materialize, the king was assassinated
by his nephew. President Thieu sent a cable of condolence to the royal
family and urged that the Saudi government continue the late king's plan for
Vietnam. The Saudis replied that they would consider the suggestion and
Thieu sent Foreign Minister Vuong Van Bac to Saudi Arabia. The Vietnamese muttered to themselves that it was their fate to be abandoned.

With the bombing of the Palace, the talk of heavenly omens of doom
and calamities occurring in sequence intensified. As the reality worsened,
people turned to superstition and mythology to explain events.

The next night, April 9, Von Marbod called Hung on the direct Pentagon line to Saigon to report that "by his hand" had been delivered. "By his
hand" was the code words they had agreed upon, indicating that Weyand
had given the copies of the Nixon letters to President Ford. Without mentioning Ford by name, Von Marbod said that "he seemed moved" after
reading the letters. He told Hung, "There is a chance for heavy stuff. I'm
somewhat optimistic now." Hung was not sure whether "heavy stuff"
referred to B-52 raids or the shipment of more Daisy Cutters, but his spirits
were boosted. He could still hope for the possibility of some kind of American bombing response. (During an interview in 1986 Ford read the Nixon
letters again. He still seemed moved, and said, "Well, there is no doubt
these were very categorical commitments.")

In an early draft of the Weyand report, the resumption of bombing had been rejected. The early draft read:

> In Vietnamese perceptions, the most dramatic action that the U.S. could take would be the use of U.S. military power and especially B-52 bombers to blunt the current NVA offensive. Vietnamese military leaders at all levels repeatedly cited the importance of B-52 bomber attacks to the conduct of a successful defense. Not only would they have been militarily significant and perhaps decisive in preventing the capture of Hue, Da Nang, and other major centers, but they would also have had the psychological impact of stiffening the will and resolve of both Vietnamese military and civilian personnel to resist. With all of this in mind, I did not consider the use of selectively limited U.S. military participation for three reasons: First, because I believe that such proposals could in themselves jeopardize Congressional consideration of the important material assistance requirements for the defense of South Vietnam; secondly, because of the potentially devastating effect on South Vietnamese morale of negative Congressional reaction to a request by the President to set aside current Congressional restrictions on the use of U.S. military force in Vietnam; and finally, because such actions would abrogate the Paris Accords, which remain the only framework for a peaceful settlement in Vietnam.

Weyand and Von Marbod, after reading the letters from Nixon to Thieu, insisted on including the military recommendation on the importance of B-52 bombing to halt the North Vietnamese offensive. Shackley and Carver were not shown the letters but they agreed to including the bombing option for the President.[9]

On April 8, in Washington, Senator Henry Jackson (D.-Wash.) charged publicly that "secret agreements" existed between the United States and Vietnam. Jackson said he had been "reliably informed" that the agreements had never been acknowledged and that President Ford had heard about them only recently. Jackson had been briefed on the Nixon letters by Schlesinger, who had received copies of four of them from Von Marbod after his return to Washington. Schlesinger was close to Senator Jackson and had a long working relationship with him and his legislative aide Richard Perle. In response to Jackson's charges, the administration publicly denied that there were any secret agreements. Ford's press secretary Ron Nessen acknowledged that Nixon and Thieu had exchanged private letters, but said, "The public statements made at the time reflected the substance of those private communications."[10]

Henry Kissinger would not comment directly, but he authorized a State Department spokesman to refer reporters to a Kissinger statement which said that the United States had no "legal commitment" to come to Vietnam's aid, but it did have a "moral commitment." There was a flurry of press interest in the Jackson charges but nobody could produce the details of the secret promises.

Schlesinger was upset. He recalled: "I believed Ford was being bamboozled on the letters. I found them quite shocking at the time. I was really disturbed by them, particularly because the administration was in a period of launching an attempt to blame the defeat in South Vietnam on the Congress, which, Lord knows, had its responsibilities. But it sure as hell wasn't going to help the country if we had a great stab-in-the-back argument, particularly given the fact that the letters were floating around, which showed that, to say the least, the Congress had not been fully informed with regard to the nature of our commitments after the departure of our forces from South Vietnam. Congress knew nothing of these letters, when it started bugging out of Vietnam in the summer of 1973." [11]

In the White House there were lengthy meetings among President Ford, Secretary Kissinger, National Security Advisor Brent Scowcroft, and Donald Rumsfeld, President Ford's chief of staff, who was hoping to run as Ford's vice-presidential candidate in 1976. The Ford strategy was to end the war and heal the nation before the 1976 election. Continuing to aid South Vietnam would transfer responsibility to Ford, making it his war instead of Nixon's. Kissinger was less interested in the political posturing of Ford for 1976 than he was in protecting his own and American credibility. He was having problems in his Mideast negotiations because American support for Vietnam was not forthcoming from Congress, thus throwing into question the validity of American promises. Watching the American performance in Vietnam, the Arabs and Israelis were unwilling to sign new acords based on U.S. guarantees. A decision was made not to discuss in detail or reveal the contents of the letters.

President Ford's press secretary Ron Nessen was authorized to acknowledge only that Nixon and Ford had exchanged private letters with Thieu, and to stick to the line that "The public statements made at the time reflected the substance of those private communications." [12] The Senate Foreign Relations Committee also requested copies of the Nixon-Thieu correspondence, but was rebuffed by the President. "I have reviewed the record of the private diplomatic communications," Ford wrote to the Committee. "Since the same policy and intentions contained in these exchanges were declared publicly, there was no secret from the Congress or the American people." [13]

There were only seven Nixon letters to Thieu in the National Security Council files, according to Nessen, who wrote in his memoirs that "In fact, Nixon's private assurances to Thieu seemed to go beyond public statements of support at the time." [14]

Nessen, who had strong feelings against the war from his days in Vietnam as an NBC correspondent, was opposed to any actions that would extend the war. "Why then," he asks, "did the Ford White House fudge on the truth and play word games to avoid revealing the now irrelevant contents of Nixon's letters?"

He answers:

Mostly, to protect the principle of confidentiality, the necessary ability of a president to communicate privately with foreign leaders. But also because the letters could be used as ammunition in any postwar recriminations over who was responsible for losing the war. Thieu and American hawks might claim that Ford failed to carry out Nixon's commitments. Doves in Congress might claim they blocked further aid because Ford never informed them of the secret promises.[15]

Nessen acknowledges that Ford wrote to Thieu, but he fails to mention Ford's August 9, 1974, letter, the day after he took office, renewing the U.S. commitments to South Vietnam made by Nixon and promising that they would be "fully honored in my administration." Ford was presented with the draft of his letter to Thieu by Kissinger, who urged that he sign it to reassure Thieu. At the time, Ford said he "knew of the exchange of letters between Nixon and Thieu but I had not read them." [16] Again on October 24, 1974, Ford reassured Thieu that there had been no change in American policy. Nessen argues that the assurances in Ford's final letters to Thieu "were sharply limited by a clear recognition of congressional restrictions and public opposition." Ford, however, never shared his letters with members of his cabinet or Congress.

Hung hoped that the interest in the letters, hinting at commitments from Nixon to Thieu and South Vietnam, would help to influence Congress to vote for aid to Vietnam. In fact, the reason Senator Jackson wanted the letters revealed was to show that Nixon had made secret commitments to Thieu without consulting with Congress.[17] There was no inclination to vote more aid to Vietnam. Given the mood of Congress, it is unlikely the letters would have swayed many votes. Senator Jackson had been a staunch supporter of the war, but even he had joined the opposition to the war after he decided to seek the Democratic presidential nomination in 1976.

Ford refused to do much work on his Vietnam speech at Palm Springs; at one point Rumsfeld complained about the enticements of golf and parties. "Maybe I'm just going to stop trying to get him to be the kind of president I think he should be," grumbled Rumsfeld, "and let him be the kind of president he wants to be." [18]

On his return to Washington Ford buckled down to his State of the World speech and a decision on how to handle the Weyand report. The basic draft of the speech was prepared by Kissinger and his aides. Ford notes in his memoirs: "Henry Kissinger had urged me to tell the American people that Congress was solely to blame for the debacle in Southeast Asia. In fact, Henry had written a 'go down with the flags flying' speech for me to use. My instinct was that this was not the right approach to take at the time." [19]

On the evening of April 9, a cable from the Vietnamese ambassador in Washington reached President Thieu with a bleak assessment for approval of President Ford's aid request and its reception on the Hill. Ambassador Phuong had no suggestions on what might be done, but told Thieu what he already knew: General Weyand had requested military aid of $722 million, which would "create shock and outcry" from the Congress when it was announced by the President. Such a reaction was a bitter blow. Opposition

had been expected, but it was hoped that because the recommendation came
from Weyand, a professional military man, who stressed America's moral
obligation, there might be a change of heart. Even before Weyand's departure from Saigon, Hung had learned that there would be a recommendation
for $722 million in emergency aid by Weyand, and he had briefed Thieu in
detail on how it would be broken down. "I don't understand the Americans.
How can we expect $722 million when they have already refused to give us
the $300 million supplemental?" lamented Thieu.

Saigon could only wait for Ford's words to Congress and hope for a
favorable response to Thieu's plea. Would Ford tell Congress the truth
about America's moral obligation to Vietnam and the promises Nixon had
made and he had confirmed? Hung was so nervous he could not sleep the
night before the Ford speech. When the speech was broadcast live on the
morning of April 11 in Saigon (the night of April 10 in Washington), Hung
was in his villa hugging his Zenith Transoceanic radio, after putting in new
batteries so he could follow every word carefully and assess Ford's intentions. Had Ford read the letters? How would he respond to them? What
would he say to President Thieu's personal letter to him of March 25, to
which there had been no answer?

First, President Ford explained why the United States had failed to
respond to North Vietnamese violations of the Paris Accords:

> We deprived ourselves by law of the ability to enforce the agreement—thus
> giving North Vietnam assurance that it could violate that agreement with im-
> punity. Next we reduced our economic and arms aid to South Vietnam. Finally,
> we signaled our increasing reluctance to give any support to that nation strug-
> gling for its survival.

Ford then outlined the options on Vietnam. The United States could do
nothing, or, "I could ask Congress for authority to enforce the Paris accords
with our troops and our tanks and our aircraft and our artillery, and to carry
the war to the enemy." Then he put forward two "narrower" options: To
stick with his January request for a $300 million supplemental, or increase
the request for emergency military and humanitarian assistance. Increasing
aid, said Ford, "might enable the South Vietnamese to stem the onrushing
aggression, to stabilize the military situation, permit the chance of a negotiated political settlement between the North and South Vietnamese, and, if
the very worst were to happen, at least allow the orderly evacuation of
American and endangered South Vietnamese to places of safety." [20]

As Hung listened, his heart beat faster. Would Ford mention President
Thieu's letter and request the bombing? Ford cited the Weyand report, but
made no mention of his recommendation for B-52 bombing. He asked for
the $722 million Weyand had recommended and set an April 19 deadline for
Congress to act. It seemed to Hung that Ford was setting up a request and
giving Congress a way to turn him down. He was putting the blame for
Vietnam's fall on Congress's shoulders. Vietnam, in its hour of agony, was

mentioned amidst a bundle of other issues, including the forthcoming visit of the Japanese emperor, the 1974 Trade Act, detente, SALT, energy problems, and ocean resources. Ford read a letter asking for help from the acting president of Cambodia, but there was no mention of President Thieu's letter of appeal to the President, nor did Ford refer to the letters from the Vietnamese National Assembly to the president of the Senate and the Speaker of the House.[21] In the Palace Thieu and his aides were upset and puzzled that there was no response to their letters to the Congress and President Ford. They wondered if the letters ever reached the American Congress or if they had been intercepted by the State Department. Hung joked bitterly with Senate President Lam: "Next time it would be safer if you carried the letter to Capitol Hill yourself." Lam did not smile.

Hung had advised Thieu that if Ford mentioned the President's letter, it would be hopeful. Ford spoke bravely of American intentions. "Let no potential adversary believe that our difficulties or our debates mean a slackening of our national will. We will stand by our friends. We will honor our commitments." The words had a hollow ring. As Brent Scowcroft, Ford's Assistant for National Security Affairs, explained: "Nobody thought we would get the money. It was a way to make it look as if we were still serious about the whole effort. We were primarily concerned with how to get out and disengage."[22]

Thieu planned a radio address for that evening to comment on Ford's expressions of support for South Vietnam; but he could not find any good news to tell the Vietnamese people. Worst of all, Thieu thought, Ford had asked Congress to act on his aid requests "not later than April 19." Why such a self-imposed deadline? If Congress rejected the requests, it would be all over. Thieu asked Hung to follow up on developments in Washington and report to him. Another cable came from Ambassador Phuong giving a bleak assessment of congressional opposition to even an emergency aid request. The day after the President's speech *The New York Times* reported that leading members of Congress "reacted quickly and negatively" to President Ford's request for $722 million in emergency military aid to Vietnam. "It's dead," said Senator Jackson. "I don't know of anyone on the Democratic side who will support it."[23]

To minimize the depressing effect of what was actually happening in Washington, Ambassador Martin intervened to lift Saigon's morale. While Thieu was wondering what to tell his people, Martin volunteered a list of talking points suggesting how to make the best out of Ford's speech. "The President might make these points," wrote Martin, in a memo to Thieu:

1. President Ford spoke as one would expect the leader of a great nation to speak. The Vietnamese people warmly welcomed his understanding words about Vietnam.

2. I call on the Vietnamese armed forces to fight for the defense of their country with renewed valor and courage. Now that President Ford has clearly set forth the realities of the North Vietnamese aggression against South Viet-

nam, our armed forces can be confident that the American people will respond to his call to send South Vietnam war material for defense.

3. After so many years of war, the people of South Vietnam yearn for peace. Last November 21, I said in a speech that the Republic of Vietnam was willing to discuss, and implement without delay, the political solution called for in the Paris Agreement—including setting up the National Council of National Reconciliation and Concord. The Republic of Vietnam has not changed its position. It still asks the other side to join it in talks to implement the political parts of the Paris Agreement.

4. So long as the North Vietnamese Army continues in its naked aggression against South Vietnam, we have no choice but to fight. We will fight until the North Vietnamese accept our invitation to resume talks on securing the right of the South Vietnamese people to self-determination, as provided in the Paris Agreement.

5. I appeal to all South Vietnamese of all political groups and all religions to set aside their individual differences in this time of supreme danger to the nation and unite behind the new government of national union being formed by Prime Minister Nguyen Ba Can. In the present crisis the needs of the nation must take absolute priority over all other concerns.[24]

Hung advised Thieu to ignore Martin. Thieu did not give a speech that night; he found Martin's talking points irrelevant and insulting. So desperate was he by now that he was ready to delegate power to the new cabinet and say publicly that he would be willing to negotiate with the Communists.

Over the past two years, ever since it became apparent that American support was declining, Thieu had tried to free South Vietnam from its image as an American puppet and establish its own identity. His efforts ranged from the ludicrous to a skillful attempt to contact and deal with the Chinese Communists.

In the fall of 1974, Foreign Minister Vuong Van Bac embarked on a campaign to win diplomatic support for the Republic of Vietnam from Morocco, the Ivory Coast, and Saudi Arabia. King Hassan of Morocco and President Felix Houphouet-Boigny of the Ivory Coast were sympathetic, but they reminded Bac that they were under pressure from members of the Organization of African States, such as Algeria, which were totally committed to North Vietnam and the Provisional Revolutionary Government in the South. Thieu began to invite African leaders to Saigon. The foreign minister of Gambia (pop. 400,000) was welcomed with full honors and his visit was a success. Saigon TV commentators spoke of a surge of support for South Vietnam in Africa. The centerpiece of Thieu's campaign was to be President for Life and Keeper of the Seal of the Central African Republic Jean-Bedel Bokassa.

Bokassa had taken power in January 1966. In 1972, when he was made President for Life, he sent a request to President Thieu to find his daughter Martine. In the early 1950s Bokassa had been a sergeant in the Foreign Legion in Vietnam and he had known Thieu, then a rising young officer.

Bokassa had a Vietnamese mistress who had borne him a daughter whom he remembered fondly. A search was made and the girl was found living in a Mekong Delta village. She was delighted to go to Bangui, capital of Bokassa's empire, and claim her place as the emperor's daughter. The Vietnamese press reveled in the story of the peasant girl whose father was a head of state. The Cinderella tale appealed to the romantic Vietnamese soul. But within several months another daughter appeared, this time with a better story about her father the ex-Foreign Legionnaire and identification papers that appeared to be correct. The Vietnamese government was upset and advised Bokassa that apparently a mistake had been made. The President for Life was unconcerned. He told the Vietnamese to send the second girl along; he would adopt them both.

Inviting Bokassa to Saigon was not easy. The Taiwanese ambassador advised the Foreign Ministry that Bokassa had an eye for women and could not be deterred once a woman caught his fancy; he had already exercised his whims during an embarrassing visit to Taiwan. Thieu was determined to proceed with the invitation and the visit was scheduled for the summer of 1975. The problem of Bokassa's roving eye was discussed in a senior staff meeting in the Palace in November 1974 and it was suggested, amidst much laughter, that the receiving line be stacked with hostesses from the best nightclubs in Saigon. Thieu laughed too, and joked that President for Life Bokassa would be greeted by the diplomatic corps, government officials, and the choicest dancing partners in Saigon from Maxim's and the Van Canh nightclubs.

In the autumn of 1974, Bac approached President Thieu suggesting that South Vietnam make a secret approach to the People's Republic of China to urge the Chinese to moderate their support for the North Vietnamese and the Provisional Revolutionary Government in the South. Thieu was prepared to come to terms with the Chinese on offshore oil exploration in disputed waters in the South China Sea and to adopt a foreign policy line that accepted Chinese influence in Southeast Asia.[25]

During his stay in London as ambassador, from 1972 to 1973, Bac became very friendly with a Conservative Member of Parliament. At the end of 1974 the MP was scheduled to visit Beijing as a member of a parliamentary delegation. The MP was approached on behalf of Bac by the South Vietnamese ambassador in London and asked to sound out the Chinese on the possibilities of rapprochement with Saigon. The South Vietnamese hoped to take advantage of the deep suspicion between China and North Vietnam following Nixon's trip to China. The British MP spoke with Deputy Foreign Minister Xiao Quan hua. The Chinese, explained Xiao, were totally committed to the Provisional Revolutionary Government. It was too late to initiate a change in policy toward Saigon, he said. It was clear to Bac that the Chinese were trying to build the PRG into a force that would rule South Vietnam and counter the power and influence of the Hanoi regime. By supporting the PRG, the Chinese expected to retain their influence in Indochina once the Americans departed.[26] The Chinese used every occasion to glorify the PRG. Whenever Madame Nguyen Thi Binh returned from Paris to Hanoi, she was invited to stop in Beijing where she was feted and met with Mao or Zhou Enlai.[27]

The South Vietnamese effort was totally rebuffed. Bac was surprised that the Chinese were so committed to the PRG. He knew that it had no real power base in the South and he believed that the North Vietnamese would not allow the PRG to be independent or even autonomous if they took power. When Bac reported to Thieu on the Chinese rebuff of his overture, Thieu said: "The Chinese are too confident. They are saying to themselves, 'Why should we help you now? We have the whole of Vietnam.' They are confident the North Vietnamese will let the Provisional Revolutionary Government rule the South so there is no reason why they have to share a piece of the cake with Thieu."[28]

The rationale for American involvement in South Vietnam was the Domino Theory and the containment of Communist China. First Ngo Dinh Diem, then his generals, then Thieu and his army were holding the line in Southeast Asia to prevent the Domino effect from coming into play; if South Vietnam fell, it would be the first Chinese Communist domino. The rest of Southeast Asia would follow. Yet ironically, as the end drew near and Thieu sensed he was about to be abandoned because of Nixon's shift in strategy toward China, he turned to the Chinese to contain North Vietnam. In desperation Thieu hoped that the traditional Chinese role of suzerainty in Southeast Asia would dominate Beijing's approach. Thieu was prepared to pay tribute to Beijing rather than be ruled by Hanoi. He believed that the Chinese feared Hanoi's influence in Indochina more than Saigon and might just be willing to step back from the North Vietnamese, whom the Chinese considered their primary rival in Indochina. Thieu's vision was correct, but he moved too late.

At the end of 1974, Thieu authorized former Foreign Minister Tran Van Do to negotiate secretly with the National Liberation Front representative in Paris. Do, a southerner, had the confidence of the PRG representatives whom he had known before the fighting broke out. Do's efforts were not approved by the United States, but they never got beyond the talking stage. Hanoi did not want the PRG to negotiate directly with Saigon for the same reasons that the Americans did not want Saigon to meet directly with the PRG. Both wanted to control the action and the results.

Early in 1975, General Tran Van Don, then a roving ambassador for Thieu and chairman of the Defense Committee in the National Assembly, went to Paris to meet with Nguyen Van Hieu, head of the Provisional Revolutionary Government delegation in Paris. In public Hieu took a tough line, accusing the Thieu government of bad faith and not implementing the Paris Agreement. When they met in private, however, Hieu told General Don, "We are stuck with the North Vietnamese. They are too dangerous to deal with; we want to break ranks with them." Hieu asked Don to talk to Thieu and urged him to get Thieu to bring the PRG into the Saigon government as part of a coalition to fight domination by Hanoi.[29] Most of the

Vietnamese families living in the South had relatives serving with the North Vietnamese or the PRG. They believed that the ties of family and traditional Vietnamese values would make it possible to come to terms in some form of political coalition or alignment of power sharing.

General Don's American contact in Paris was Lee Williams of the Central Intelligence Agency, who reported on Don's meetings. According to Don, Williams discouraged him, saying, "It's not worthwhile." Don reported to Thieu, who was unimpressed and told him to "check with the Americans." Later Don was told that the Americans were not interested in pursuing the PRG proposal.[30] There was no way out alone.

As the situation in Saigon and Washington deteriorated by the hour, Thieu now told Hung to activate a contingency plan called the "Aid Loan Plan" which he had been considering since the summer of 1974. Thieu considered the plan a final gesture to South Vietnam from America. "Vietnam," he told Hung, "has now become an old mistress about to be discarded."

Under the plan, Thieu would approach the U.S. Congress for a military aid loan to be repaid by Saigon. There would be no request for a grant. Saigon would offer its offshore oil revenues as collateral for the loan. The plan, if adopted, would help to dampen the impact of the "open-ended aid" argument. The popular criticism in Congress was that there would be no end to U.S. military aid for Saigon—the more aid, the longer the fighting would continue. In Saigon Thieu believed the last loan would force the armed forces, the government, and the people to face the reality of a last chance. It would also help military planning by providing a degree of certainty about the level and structure of aid. If adopted, the plan would minimize the terrible waiting for year-to-year, even month-to-month, appropriations on aid. The long-drawn-out process of aid legislation had caused confusion and disorder in Saigon ever since the Paris Accords were signed in January 1973. The public aid debate every year was humiliating and weakened morale.

During the first months of 1975 Thieu considered Hung's loan plan, but first he wanted to request a fixed period of military aid rather than a loan. When that did not work, he tested the loan idea on several U.S. legislators visiting Saigon and got a favorable response.

Hung urged Thieu not to be defensive in his discussions about American aid; when asking for the $300 million supplemental he should show confidence in Vietnam's capability to become self-sufficient by 1980. Then Thieu would ask for a three-year loan package as a transition from American-style warfare to true Vietnamization and "a poor man's war." The Americans liked the idea. Ambassador Martin and the Defense Attaché suggested Thieu proceed and develop a more detailed plan. When Thieu met with Senator Sam Nunn (D.-Ga.), an influential member of the Senate Armed Services Committee, he got a favorable response. Nunn even floated the idea in an editorial-page article in *The Washington Post,* arguing that "the transition period is essential because we have encouraged the South Vietnamese to fight an American style war with sophisticated equipment and massive supply. They need time to convert their armed forces to defend their country in their own style, but while converting they must fend off the attack from the North Vietnamese."[31]

Ambassador Martin, in Washington lobbying for aid, made a concerted effort to support the "last chance" plan, suggesting it to President Ford, Henry Kissinger, and whoever in the press would listen. At an editorial lunch at *The Washington Post* he sold the idea and, on March 19, the *Post* carried an editorial calling for "a firm and final decision to help Saigon for three more years and then to accept the results, whatever they may be." If that kind of approach had been made in 1972 and at the time of the Paris Accords, when American troops were being withdrawn, Hung believed there might have been a more realistic chance to win congressional approval.

As Congress moved to close the lid on the aid basket, Thieu accepted Hung's plan and proposed an "aid loan" from Washington. Martin was ready to do whatever he could for Thieu. Hung said everyone in the Vietnamese leadership was impressed with Martin's dedication to save the country. Besides the U.S. stake in Vietnam there were Martin's personal feelings. His adopted son, Glen, a helicopter pilot, had been killed in a crash. Like millions of Americans whose loved ones had served in Vietnam, Martin refused to believe that his son's sacrifice had been in vain. The ambassador's sympathy reminded the Vietnamese of the former French commander, General Jean de Lattre de Tassigny, and his determination to save Indochina after his only son, Lieutenant Bernard de Lattre, was killed there in May 1951 in a battle with the Viet Minh near Hung's family home in Ninh Binh Province. The Viet Minh chopped his head off, tied the body to a water buffalo, and sent it back to his unit.[32]

Thieu's efforts to arrange a military aid loan started on March 5, 1975, at a meeting with Congressman Steven Symms (R.-Ida.). Symms was one of the few conservatives who would still listen to a plea for a loan. Briefed in advance by Martin, he responded positively. "Are you prepared to pay back, say, ten percent of the money appropriated if you strike oil offshore?" asked Symms.

"We have a good oil potential offshore which the United States could have a lien on," replied Thieu. To underscore his commitment, Thieu promised to ask the National Assembly for a specific pledge of oil collateral for the loan. The Vietnamese were projecting an income of $1 billion a year in oil revenues if their offshore drilling program met its projections.

The dreams of oil revenues were part of the myth making and unreality that swept over Saigon as the war effort crumbled. Surely something would happen to come to their rescue. If it did not, then it was fated that South Vietnam should fall. The Vietnamese viewed the events in a larger mythical framework; they were not temporal events that signaled military defeat and political change, but bad cosmic omens representing the coming together of the forces of the universe to punish the Vietnamese people for an historic crime. There is a Vietnamese saying: "*Troi sa dat lo,* the sky falls, the earth splits open.

The heavens were unleashing vengeance on them for destroying the Cham nation, which had flourished in the South from about A.D. 200 until the Vietnamese conquest. For nearly five hundred years, from 982 to 1471, the Vietnamese had warred against the Chams before crushing and annihilating them. Hung heard his colleages and friends recall the fate of the Chams and listened to them wondering about whether they were being faced with cosmic retribution for a collective national guilt as the North Vietnamese pressed ever further to the south.[33]

20

The Last Mission

AFTER PRESIDENT FORD's speech, Thieu pressed his new prime minister, Nguyen Ba Can, to organize a war cabinet of national unity to include opposition leaders, religious groups, and labor leaders. Thieu was anxious for a new cabinet with fresh personalities to rally their supporters behind him. He was gathering forces for a last stand against the Communists, who were grinding down the coast toward Saigon. Can was named prime minister on April 5, to replace Tran Thien Khiem, who had been in office since 1969. Thieu was angry with Khiem for stepping down in a time of crisis and felt personally betrayed. But Khiem had nagged Thieu to allow him to resign, and Thieu was too proud to ask him to stay. The new prime minister was the Speaker of the National Assembly, a smooth southerner, loyal to Thieu, with a reputation as a good compromiser in local political circles although he was unknown to foreigners.[1] Prime Minister Can asked Hung to remain in the new cabinet as Minister of Economic Development and Planning with broader authority in the new government.

On April 11, Can held a series of meetings in his house on Bach Dang Street, near the Saigon River, to recruit the cabinet. Around the long table in his living room Can spoke bravely about organizing Saigon for the eventual North Vietnamese attack and dealing with the mounting refugee problem. The Communists were infiltrating the refugees with terrorist squads, committing acts of sabotage, and assassinating government officials. During a lull in the interviews the new prime minister asked Hung to brief him on the Freedom Loan concept. "Is there any chance?" Can asked.

Hung replied, "You know there is an April 19 deadline. What if the Congress says no, which is very likely? Our priority now is to forestall a negative vote to prevent the destruction of what is left of our morale. We need a counterproposal to take to the American Congress to postpone that no vote."

The cabinet agreed to appear on television to discuss measures to provide food and security for Saigon. It would be an effort to raise morale and assure the population that the government had made preparations to prevent panic.

When they broke for lunch, the prime minister was alone with Hung and complained how difficult it was to reassure the population. "The Americans are building helicopter landing pads on top of their buildings and it is obvious they are getting ready to leave," said Can.

"It is devastating," agreed Hung. "Perhaps you could suggest they do it at night when not so many people would see and it would have less impact on morale."

The prime minister shook his head and said he heard that the Americans were suggesting the evacuation of Vietnamese who worked for them. "If worse comes to worst we should think about evacuating to the offshore islands of Phu Quoc and the nearby islands," said Hung. "Priority should be given to soldiers, police, civil servants and their families—there are at least two million people."

The meetings went on late into the night and resumed over the weekend. On Monday, April 14, the prime minister presented the new cabinet to the president. Throughout the formalities and picture taking, Thieu was solemn and tense. He looked gray and pale, as though drained of his energy and power by the strain of events. The Communists were closing in on Phan Rang Province, Thieu's birthplace. Usually the swearing in of a new cabinet was the occasion for a dinner with the president, but the mood was grim, and Thieu quickly returned to his office after the ceremonies. Hung joined him there and they discussed the worsening situation.

Thieu showed Hung a cable dated April 14, sent from London by Foreign Minister Bac, who had just returned from Saudi Arabia. While in Riyad, Bac had been invited to the palace to meet the new ruler, King Khalid, for his first audience with a foreign statesman. Bac had appealed to King Khalid for "support" and "assistance," the code words for continuing with the late King Faisal's loan offer.

Bac said his mission had been successfully completed and King Khalid "gave me strong assurances about continued support and economic assistance. . . ." Bac's message indicated the new King's willingness to help Saigon with either a direct loan or a guarantee of a U.S. loan to provide military aid, Thieu said.

Thieu expressed his fear to Hung that Congress would turn down the $722 million in aid; a new course of action was needed to stop the vote. It would still take time to realize the Saudi promise. In the meantime, Hung suggested that Thieu activate the "Freedom Loan" plan and move to an offensive posture with the Americans. The Saudi offer should be linked to the loan plan and if necessary the Saudi funds could be offered as collateral. Instead of worrying about a yes or no vote, Hung proposed that the South Vietnamese present a new, reasonable alternative plan to the Americans. "In the anti-Vietnam atmosphere we should go to the Americans and tell them we have not come to beg from them but to borrow," suggested Hung. "We need something immediate to build morale. The only thing I can see for you to do is to activate the loan plan immediately."

Thieu ordered Hung to draft a formal proposal to President Ford for a "three-year Freedom Loan, $1 billion a year for the next three years. Get on the first plane for Washington and be there within twenty-four hours if possible."

Hung's primary mission was to seek postponement of the vote on the $722 million in aid requested by Ford and arrange for the Freedom Loan. "A negative vote would make all the rest of our soldiers lay down their arms," Thieu said. "The Freedom Loan will be a final gesture of support for South Vietnam, before the United States abandons our cause."

Thieu and Hung had no way of knowing that on April 14 in Washington the Senate Foreign Relations Committee, in a rare move, had requested a meeting with President Ford to discuss the situation in Southeast Asia. The last time there had been such a meeting was during Woodrow Wilson's administration. The meeting, attended by the President, Kissinger, Schlesinger, and Scowcroft, was tense. Ford recalled that "the [senators'] message was clear: get out, *fast*." "I will give you large sums for evacuation," New York Republican Jacob Javits said, "but not one nickel for military aid." Idaho Democrat Frank Church saw grave problems, which "could involve us in a very large war" if the United States attempted to evacuate all the South Vietnamese loyal to America. Delaware Democrat Joseph Biden said, "I will vote for any amount for getting the Americans out. I don't want it mixed with getting the Vietnamese out."[2]

At Hung's ministerial office, Dr. Nguyen Manh Hung,* his deputy and most trusted associate, assisted Hung in drafting the letter from President Thieu to President Ford. Before giving his secretary the letter to type, Hung asked her to swear that she would not reveal the contents. Being a good Buddhist, she was unfamiliar with Hung's Catholic references of swearing to God. Instead of repeating the vow, she kept saying "Yes, sir, yes sir," and trembling. Hung finally handed the draft letter to her for typing.

Dear Mr. President:

Events in the last few weeks have led to a new and grave situation in South Vietnam. Although we now have a more defensible border and a more manageable economy, we are faced with a far more numerous and better equipped enemy force. As Communist troops are massing at the doorstep of the delta region, our people and our armed forces are prepared and determined to fight with all our might to protect our territory and preserve our freedom. To do this successfully, we badly need the means to fight with, namely, weapons and ammunition.

I, therefore, am very gratified by your energetic drive to urge the Congress to vote immediately on additional military aid to the Republic of Vietnam. However, since military aid to SVN has become a public issue and inevitably built up some expectation a negative vote by Congress would undoubtedly deal a severe blow to the morale of our troops as we are preparing for the forthcoming epic battle. This we want to avoid.

We deeply appreciate and are grateful for all the sacrifices in terms of blood and treasure endured in the past by the American people to help protect

---

* Nguyen Manh Hung had attended the University of Virginia with Hung, but they were not related.

a free South Vietnam. We fully understand the various political and moral issues confronting the American lawmakers as they are asked to consider military aid to the Republic of Vietnam. If for some reason they find it impossible now to *grant* military aid to SVN, I would propose an alternative situation.

I urge you, Mr. President, to request Congress to provide us a final long-term *loan* of 3 billion U.S. dollars, to be disbursed in 3 years, with a 10 year grace period, at an interest rate to be determined by Congress. Our oil potential and agricultural resources shall be collateral for this loan. This will be called "freedom loan," a loan that would permit us to defend ourselves against the aggressors and give us a reasonable chance to survive as a free country.

We appeal to the conscience and compassion of the American people for the plight of our people, a people that have been your faithful ally in the last twenty turbulent years, a people that have made great sacrifices and suffered tremendously for 2 decades in order to preserve a place to live free. Such a people deserves sympathy and assistance.

In this hour of our greatest need, I ask you, Mr. President, to urge Congress to consider urgently and favorably our request for a freedom loan. This will be the last act of compassion that we, as an ally, ask of the U.S.

> Sincerely,
> Nguyen Van Thieu

Hung's plan was to bring the draft to Washington, where he would make a final check of the feasibility of such a move and cable Thieu to dispatch the letter to President Ford via Ambassador Martin. Hung was authorized by Thieu to spend $20,000 on advertisements in *The New York Times* and *The Washington Post* to explain the Freedom Loan plan and try to gain support for it. He was to get the funds in Washington from the Vietnamese Procurement Office (VINAPO). It was the first and only time Hung asked Thieu for money to spend in America. Since there was no time to go to the Central Bank to obtain American dollars for travel expenses, Hung reached into the bottom of his bedroom drawer and took his last $300.

Late that night, after returning from the Palace, Hung called Ambassador Martin at his residence to brief him on his trip to Washington. It was imperative that Martin know that Thieu wanted to forestall the vote in Congress and activate a campaign for a final $3 billion Freedom Loan. His help was needed; a turndown would totally destroy whatever power Thieu had left. "Do I have any chance?" Hung asked, after explaining the mission.

"You might have a chance," said Martin slowly in his rich Southern accent, but even the smoothness of his manner could not mask that he was noticeably lacking in enthusiasm, thought Hung, as if he were preoccupied with other plans.

"Good luck to you, hurry back," said Martin.

"I'll be back in one week," replied Hung.

"By the way," asked Martin, "is your President going to step down?"

Hung was surprised and wondered why the American ambassador had asked him such a deadly question in a most casual manner at this critical moment. Hung told Martin he did not know what he was talking about, adding, "I do not think this is an appropriate time—in the middle of a crisis —for President Thieu to resign." Hung could not help but notice that this was the first time Martin had referred to "your President." Usually he spoke of "the President" or "President Thieu." Hung immediately wrote a note to Thieu reporting on his disturbing conversation with Martin. Then, exhausted, he took a sleeping pill and turned his air conditioner on full force to drown out the night sounds for a few hours of sleep before his flight to Washington.

Hung was given a formal send-off by his colleagues in the cabinet, who gathered at Tan Son Nhut Airport's VIP lounge to wish him well. It was 1:30 p.m. Saigon time on Wednesday, April 15, but with the twelve-hour time difference it was still early in the morning of the same day in Washington. Hung felt confused, uncertain, and sad. With only two hours notice he had arranged for another minister to take over his duties. He bid farewell to his colleagues at the ramp of the Pan American Boeing 747. Hung realized he had to complete his mission before April 19, the deadline set by President Ford for Congress to say yes or no to his aid request for Vietnam. For days, the BBC and the Voice of America had carried the news that American aid to South Vietnam was to be cut off, and a collapse was expected in a matter of days.

"My bodyguards looked sad. I could see tears in their eyes. I could barely contain my own. It had never occurred to me that the Communists might actually march into Saigon while I was in Washington. I thought that when the end came, there would be negotiations between us and Hanoi, either to divide the country again or to form a coalition government with the Viet Cong. For the Communists to accomplish a military victory over the South would be too damaging to America's credibility. The whole process of America's disengagement had been designed to uphold American honor. We could not comprehend that Ford and Kissinger would permit the eventuality of American humiliation and our own defeat to occur," said Hung. Thieu often mentioned the Vietnamese saying, "*Vuot mat phai ne mui,*" literally, "When you wipe your face, watch out for your nose." The meaning, which every Vietnamese learns in childhood, is simple: When you attack a person, beware of his friends.

"We could not understand," said Hung, "why Ford should have set a deadline for congressional action, unless he hoped to end the agony. With luck and the time difference in my favor I would be in Washington the same day I left Saigon, and I would have only three days before Congress voted. But what was I going to do to convince the Congress to postpone the vote on aid? I sensed that a 'no' vote was inevitable and would be fatal. Whatever was left of morale depended on that vote." Hung realized he would have to make the letters public to win support.

After Hung departed, President Thieu summoned Ambassador Martin to the Palace and asked for his help for Hung's mission. Martin was sympathetic and quickly sent a cable to Kissinger urging a delay in the vote. Martin told Kissinger:

I reported to you Thieu's comment that if it were absolutely clear that the request for military aid—the $722 million supplemental—was to be defeated, it would be highly preferable to find some way to delay the final vote. Although he did not say so, it seems clear that he, as well as everybody else, is unsure of what comes next.

Although he did not confide it to Martin, or to any of his closest associates, Thieu did have a final contingency plan.[3] Thieu believed he could still hold on and resist the Communists in the Mekong Delta if he could be assured of continued American support. He envisioned a last-ditch stand in Saigon, with one division to block the North Vietnamese while the rest of the armed forces and the government retreated to the fourth corps area, which encompassed the fertile Mekong River Delta. This was to be the final contraction of the defense lines to a still viable core center. There Thieu envisioned a front line that was to begin at Ben Luc, south of Saigon (see map). There was no "light at the top" left, so the "big bottom" was the last hope. If Thieu could hold on to the delta, he would retain a majority of the population and the richest agricultural lands with an abundant food supply.

Hung knew of Thieu's concept to contract his forces and try to hold on to the delta, but he also knew there was no way such a strategy could be made to work without an American commitment of military and economic aid. "We were in a pitiful state. I had long been told that the Americans' credo was 'He who pays commands'; now I was to play the part of a cabinet minister turned beggar."

All requisitions, authorizations, liquidations, all possible juggling of Defense Department books had been exhausted. Congress had even banned the use of American-supplied Vietnamese piastres for payment of troops and police. The local currency, generated by imports financed by U.S. aid, was now restricted to humanitarian relief for refugees.

Ever since he had returned to Vietnam in the spring of 1973 to work for Thieu, Hung had been reminded by his colleagues, friends, and politicians that everything in Vietnam—whether it was the election of the president, the promotion of a general, a new tax, or an exchange devaluation—had to have American blessing. A bridge in the Mekong Delta was ironically named the My Thuan Bridge, literally, "Approved by the Americans." Hung never knew whether it was for technical reasons or lack of funds that the bridge was not completed, but it stood as an eyesore. The Vietnamese officials in the Ministry of Public Works soon began to joke that despite its name the Americans never approved the completion of the bridge.

Never before had Hung been so deeply disturbed by Vietnam's dependence on the United States. After stepping aboard the jumbo jetliner, Hung was in a state of misery. "I could only think that I would have to make a dramatic move to convince the Congress that it could not deliver the *coup de grâce* to Vietnam by publicly denying the President's request for aid. My only hope was the file of presidential letters that I carried with me. Despite President's Thieu's reluctance to disclose the contents of the letters, I planned to use them once I arrived in Washington. I believed that only with the letters could I possibly persuade the Congress that it should not and could not casually abandon my country." Hung believed once it became known that there had been presidential promises by both Ford and Nixon, "the essential American quality of fairness would surface." "The Freedom Loan," Thieu had told Hung, "will be a final gesture to an ex-mistress of America." Hung had not discussed revealing the letters with Thieu. He knew that Thieu was reluctant to do so, but Hung felt he could use them privately with members of Congress. He also wanted to preserve Thieu's ability to deny leaking the letters.

Hung realized how difficult it would be to convince Congress that aid to Vietnam was no longer open-ended and that the Freedom Loan would be final. In America, long years earlier, Hung had learned that in any situation there were infinite possibilities; all you had to do was make an effort. He had also learned the American respect for the underdog and those who never said die. Now there were no other options. With $3 billion South Vietnam could continue to exist and the ARVN could secure enough land for the majority of its people to survive until the economy was reconstructed and oil revenues began to flow.

Congress wanted no part of the South Vietnamese military effort, even to aid in defense against a North Vietnamese invasion. The new line was, the more aid the more bloodshed. Still, Hung maintained his hope that Congress might just have a change of heart at the last minute when the letters were made public and the full extent of the presidential promises was revealed.

Hung carried the full file of presidential letters with him in a thin black Samsonite attaché case. When he settled into his giant first-class seat, he sat on the case. The stewardess asked him to put it in the overhead rack, but Hung did not want to part with the letters. Finally, they compromised. Hung put the attaché case on the floor and his feet on top of it.

As the near-empty jet rose from the runway, Hung was overwhelmed. A great dulling pain struck him in the chest and he felt dizzy. He had a sharp premonition that this was the last time he would see his country; that he would never again see his mother, his brothers and sisters. Desperately he looked down on Saigon from the window of the jet. From the air the city was a vision of beauty, enhanced by memories of the past. How could this magnificent city fall to the Communists?

As if to accommodate his mood, the jet circled Saigon twice. Hung looked down on the cathedral in Kennedy Square, where in the summer of 1954 after the fall of Dien Bien Phu, he led a choir of Catholic refugees at high mass to thank God for saving them. It was his first day in Saigon after fleeing from North Vietnam. He remembered how nervous he was in 1955 when he sang a solo in the choir during the high mass for the grand welcome of Cardinal Spellman to Saigon. Cardinal Spellman had been a key supporter of Ngo Dinh Diem and his visit signaled to Vietnamese Catholics that America was truly behind Diem.[4]

There was the Saigon River below, chocolate brown, lined with palm trees, where Hung had spent weekends fishing for catfish and giant shrimp. The Independence Palace flashed in the distance and the agonies of the past three months poured in on him. Then the plane moved past the city over the polluted Cong Ly Canal along the road leading to the airport. According to Hung's reconstruction plan, the canal was about to be dredged. Also high on his list of development projects was a factory to convert Saigon's trash to fertilizer. He could not help but imagine that very soon Saigon would be destroyed by enemy rockets and shells. For the first time in the war a North Vietnamese air attack on Saigon was possible from the newly captured Danang airfield. Saigon had no air-defense system, a fact Hung had only recently discovered.

Hung sifted through his papers and looked at the latest military balance estimates. There were only about 53,000 South Vietnamese troops left, the remnants of six divisions. The North Vietnamese had more than 200,000 troops in the South with twenty-two divisions, including the six reserve divisions they had recently moved in. He stared at the daily briefing for April 12, prepared by General Quang for President Thieu. It was fragmented, lacked any sense of reality, and contained only exaggerated figures that made it appear the South was winning. In the briefing, Quang quoted from Joint General Staff reports. In MR-I, there was an enemy attack on Phan Thiet. "Friendly forces: 9 dead and 20 wounded. Enemy forces: 600 dead." In MR-III, at Long Khanh, the enemy had mounted a tank assault. The results: "Friendly forces: 33 dead, 178 wounded. Enemy forces: 837 dead, 5 captured, and 12 T-54 tanks destroyed." There was no comprehensive overview and no strategic analysis. Quang still used the terms "friendly forces" although the Americans, Koreans, and Australians had long since gone.

The jet moved smoothly out over the South China Sea and Hung began to plan his strategy for Washington in detail. He would approach key congressmen through his personal contacts. He worked with his able colleague Nguyen Ngoc Bich, director of the Vietnam Press, traveling with him, to prepare an appeal to the conscience of America in support of the Freedom Loan. Even as they worked, the trip weighed on him and seemed to take longer than ever before. When he finally fell asleep in the black solitude over the Pacific, Hung dreamed that Saigon was being attacked by the F-5E aircraft he had arranged to purchase from Northrop.

His plane arrived in San Francisco early on the morning of Wednesday, April 16, the same day he left Saigon, because of the twelve-hour time change. Although he had lived in America for fifteen years and had become a part of the suburban Washington lifestyle of cars, fast food, neat lawns, and shopping centers, Hung now felt as if he had entered an alien land. All around him people rushed to catch buses and taxis or board planes, oblivious that Saigon was facing its final agony. Nobody seemed to care how many more days Saigon could last. The war, which had never been declared, but which America had fought for ten years, was now remote and about to end.

Hung had a diplomatic passport and he was escorted through Customs. The customs officer was friendly. "Welcome to the United States, hope you enjoy your stay." Then he asked: "How are things over there? It doesn't look very good, does it?" Hung looked at him and his eyes began to fill with tears. He thanked the customs officer for his courtesy and rushed to find a news stand. The headlines were devastating.

During the time he had been in the air several more provinces had been lost, including Phan Rang, President Thieu's home province, 240 miles north of Saigon. Before he left, there was hope that Phan Rang could be defended for at least another month; it had a large supply of ammunition and a good airfield where a dozen F-5Es were stationed. Only a month earlier Hung had been there to inaugurate a new sugar mill. In spite of the difficulties ahead, Hung had told the farmers they could expect better prices for their next crop. Now, all he could imagine was how the North Vietnamese would use the F-5Es to attack Saigon. They would take their revenge on Thieu by destroying his family burial grounds and the tombs of his ancestors, the ultimate indignity and a curse for eternity.

While waiting for his connection to Washington, Hung bought a small portable radio to listen to the news. After twenty minutes of Elvis Presley and Linda Ronstadt, Hung heard a report on President Ford's meeting with the American Society of Newspaper Editors. Ford had spoken of America's commitments to South Vietnam. It sounded encouraging. "It appears," said Ford, "that they [the Russians] have maintained their commitment. Unfortunately the U.S. did not carry out its commitment." Ford added: "I don't think we can blame the Soviet Union and People's Republic of China. If we had done with our allies what we promised, I think this whole tragedy would have been eliminated."

Then Hung realized Ford had not had a change of heart. Even though he had seen at least four of President Nixon's letters, which Hung had made available through Von Marbod and General Weyand, President Ford had not changed his mind. Ever since Von Marbod had told him Ford had read the letters, Hung thought Ford seemed to show sympathy to Saigon in some of his statements and actions, but this hope disappeared as Hung listened further. Pressed by the editors to elaborate on the nature of the American commitment to Vietnam, Ford quickly replied that there was "no legal commitment, only a moral commitment." He had adopted the Kissinger line.

The news broadcast also mentioned that only about 50,000 Vietnamese refugees would be rescued, pending approval of parole authority for them by Congress. The news made Hung feel even more weary than the long flight across the Pacific. He had never felt so helpless. For the first time he felt that whatever President Ford had been saying to argue the case for military aid for Vietnam was only for the record; there was no real belief, no willingness to rally support behind the words. Perhaps Ford wanted to do nothing more than shift the blame to Congress. Hung had heard that Ford would be running for President in 1976 and his domestic policy aides had told him he had to get the war "off his back" and behind him.⁵ Hung's pulse quickened and he closed his eyes, wondering how many days were left and what would happen if his country collapsed.

Hung was flying to Washington—the center of American power. In Saigon, Washington's image had become arbitrary, mysterious, and fearful to Hung. Despite his years in America, he found it impossible to predict Washington's moods and responses. One day, all requests were honored and the relationship was filled with promises; the next day, there was fickle, cynical rejection and a lack of interest.

Hung's wife Catherine and their children greeted him at Baltimore-Washington International Airport. A Vietnamese Embassy Aide was also on hand to meet Hung. The first question he asked was, "When will Thieu negotiate a coalition?" This upset Hung even more. He was still thinking in terms of a last stand and raising American aid to maintain South Vietnam in a Mekong Delta redoubt south of Saigon. He and Thieu were still clinging to the old Vietnamese farmer's saying: *"Con nuoc con tat"* ("As long as there is a drop of water left, scoop it up"). Hung could sense that the mood had changed drastically in Washington since his last visit in December of 1974. Everyone presumed Saigon was lost. Hung looked at his children, tangible evidence of his own involvement with America. They reminded him of the Vietnamese-American children he had seen along the roadside while traveling to the delta. Hung often thought of these children, fathered by American soldiers, as the legacy of America's involvement with Vietnam and he wondered what would happen to them. "Americans say it was a mistake to get involved in Vietnam. Seeing what I saw in Vietnam, I am now ready to tell the Americans that you don't get a woman pregnant and then run away. You don't get deeply involved with our country, say it was a mistake, and then run away," Hung thought.

In desperation Hung arranged to announce the Freedom Loan plan in a broadcast over the Voice of America that would boost morale in Saigon. It would convince the troops in the field, who listened to the VOA, that there was still a possibility of major American aid.

Hung stayed up most of the night to prepare for the VOA interview and his presentation to Congress; then he went to the VOA studio, where he was met by his friend Le Van. Shortly before he was scheduled to go on the air on the morning of April 18, a news broadcast announced that the Senate Armed Services Committee had voted to reject additional military aid for Vietnam. The House Committee on International Relations had approved legislation giving President Ford limited power to use American military forces to evacuate Americans from Vietnam.

Hung's plans disintegrated. He was overwhelmed by the news over the radio. There was no one to talk to about a Freedom Loan. The Ford administration had decided to call it quits. Henry Kissinger declared: "The Vietnam debate is over. The administration will accept the Congress's verdict without recrimination and vindictiveness." The American concern now was to get its people out. President Ford appointed Dean Brown of the State

Department to head the Evacuation Task Force. On April 17, Kissinger had sent an eyes-only message to Ambassador Martin urging him to speed up the evacuation of Americans from Saigon. The message read:

TO: MARTIN
SENSITIVE
EXCLUSIVELY EYES ONLY
WE HAVE JUST COMPLETED AN INTERAGENCY REVIEW OF THE STATE OF PLAY IN SOUTH VIETNAM. YOU SHOULD KNOW THAT AT THE WSAG MEETING TODAY THERE WAS ALMOST NO SUPPORT FOR THE EVACUATION OF VIETNAMESE, AND FOR THE USE OF AMERICAN FORCE TO HELP PROTECT ANY EVACUATION. THE SENTIMENT OF OUR MILITARY, DOD AND CIA COLLEAGUES WAS TO GET OUT FAST AND NOW.

IN ADDITION, AS I INDICATED IN MY MESSAGE TO YOU LAST NIGHT, THE CONGRESSIONAL SITUATION IS FAST GETTING OUT OF HAND. OUR TASK—YOURS AND MINE—IS TO PREVENT PANIC BOTH IN SAIGON AND WASHINGTON, AND I KNOW THAT YOU RECOGNIZE THIS MORE CLEARLY THAN ALMOST ANYONE IN THE UNITED STATES GOVERNMENT.

I APPRECIATE YOUR INDICATION THAT YOU CAN WILL MEET MY REQUEST THAT WE REDUCE TO APPROXIMATELY 2,000 OFFICIAL AND NON-OFFICIAL AMERICANS BY THE END OF NEXT WEEK, BUT MUST NOW, IN LIGHT OF THE SITUATION, ASK THAT THIS SCHEDULE BE ADVANCED. IT IS ESSENTIAL, DESPITE THE CONCERNS THAT YOU HAVE EXPRESSED AND THAT I ACCEPT, FOR YOU TO SPEED THE MOVEMENT OF AMERICANS OUT OF VIETNAM. WE MUST BE AT OR BELOW 2,000 OFFICIAL AND UNOFFICIAL U.S CITIZENS BY TUESDAY, APRIL 22. I ASK THAT YOU MOVE IMMEDIATELY TO ACCOMPLISH THIS AND ASSURE YOU THAT WE ARE PREPARED TO DO EVERYTHING WE CAN TO GIVE YOU ANY ADDITIONAL ASSISTANCE YOU NEED. YOU WILL BE RECEIVING A FRONT CHANNEL MESSAGE TO THIS EFFECT, PLUS CERTAIN OTHER QUESTIONS AND INSTRUCTIONS IN TANDEM WITH THIS MESSAGE. KISSINGER.

In Saigon, Graham Martin was still not giving up. On the night of April 17 (Saigon time), he cabled Kissinger through his own secret back channel to the White House. The message was so sensitive Martin typed it himself and handed it to the code clerk. Martin laid out a strategy to prevent panic in Saigon and raised in detail the problem of Thieu's future:

. . . IF THERE IS A NEGATIVE VOTE, I HOPE YOU AND THE PRESIDENT WILL CALMLY ANNOUNCE YOU ARE GOING ALL OUT TO WIN THE FIGHT FOR THE FISCAL YEAR 76 APPROPRIATION. AS UNREALISTIC AS THIS MAY SEEM, IT WILL HAVE GREAT EFFECT HERE. . . . THERE IS ONE GREAT AND MOST IMPORTANT CAVEAT. THERE MUST BE NO PANIC IN WASHINGTON. THE ONE THING THAT WOULD SET OFF VIOLENCE WOULD BE A SUDDEN ORDER FOR AMERICAN EVACUATION. . . . THE ONE THING THAT COULD TRIGGER ANGER WITH INCALCULABLE RESULTS WOULD BE TO SEND IN THE MARINES OR HAVE ANY GREAT TALK ABOUT IT.

. . . THE ARVN CAN HOLD THE APPROACHES TO SAIGON FOR QUITE A WHILE, AND I STILL DOUBT THAT HANOI DESIRES A FRONTAL SMASH AT SAIGON, FOR A MULTITUDE OF REASONS. . . . MOST OF THE AMERICANS LIKELY TO

PANIC HAVE ALREADY LEFT AND THE ONES WHO ARE LEFT AFTER WE GET THE
GREAT REMAINDER OUT IN THE NEXT FEW DAYS WILL BE COOL, TOUGH CHAR-
ACTERS.

I REPEAT ONCE AGAIN THE ONE THING THAT ALMOST SURELY WOULD
TRIGGER VERY GREAT ANGER WOULD BE TO SEND IN AMERICAN ARMED FORCES
NOW, EXCEPT A VERY FEW IN THE MOST UNOBTRUSIVE MANNER. THE REAC-
TION, BITS AND PIECES OF WHICH I AM SENDING TO YOU, ALL CONFIRM THIS IS
THE ONE THING WE MUST NOT DO. IT WILL BE UNIVERSALLY INTERPRETED AS
A MOST CALLOUS BETRAYAL, LEAVING THE VIETNAMESE TO THEIR FATE WHILE
WE SEND IN THE MARINES TO MAKE SURE WE GET ALL OF OURS OUT. IT WILL
NOT BE BELIEVED WE CARE A TINKER'S DAMN WHAT HAPPENS TO THEM. AND
FROM THAT DEEP FEELING, THE TINIEST INCIDENT COULD TRIGGER A HELL OF
A MESS. AS IT IS, WE HAVE THE SYMPATHY OF MOST VIETNAMESE, WHO BELIEVE
THE AMERICANS HERE HAVE, TOO, BEEN BETRAYED. ALSO, MANY OF THEM
WANT TO GET OUT. . . . ALL THAT CAN SWITCH IMMEDIATELY IF SOME GOD-
DAMNED FOOL PERSUADES ANY OF YOU IN SENIOR POSITIONS TO SEND IN THE
MARINES UNTIL I SEND FOR THEM. I WILL NOT HESITATE IN THE SLIGHTEST TO
DO SO IF PUBLIC ORDER BEGINS TO CRUMBLE.

Martin was still hopeful that a negotiated settlement with the North
Vietnamese would be the final solution. Before that could happen, he argued, Thieu would have to step down. If there was a negative vote by
Congress on the aid proposal, Martin told Kissinger, "Thieu will be finished." In Saigon, former Ambassador to Washington Bui Diem and General Tran Van Don, who had become Minister of Defense in the new cabinet,
were anxious, said Martin, to get the negotiations with the North Vietnamese under way. Martin said he would meet with Diem and Don. He continued his cable to the White House proposing he be allowed to persuade Thieu
to step down:

I SHALL STILL SAY THAT ANY CHANGE IS THEIR [DIEM AND DON'S] BUSINESS,
BUT THAT IT SEEMS TO ME THAT THE ESSENTIAL PROCESS OF NEGOTIATIONS
CANNOT BE STARTED WITH THIEU IN POWER. I SHALL THEN, UNLESS IN-
STRUCTED TO THE CONTRARY, GO TO THIEU AND TELL HIM THE SAME THING,
MAKING IT ABSOLUTELY CRYSTAL CLEAR THAT I AM SPEAKING ONLY FOR MY-
SELF, THAT I AM SPEAKING AS A FRIEND WHO HAS ALWAYS TOLD HIM THE
WHOLE TRUTH, AND THAT IT IS MY CONCLUSION, ARRIVED AT MOST RELUC-
TANTLY, THAT HIS PLACE IN HISTORY WOULD BE BETTER ASSURED, WITH THE
RECORDING OF ALL THE TRULY SIGNIFICANT THINGS HE HAS ACTUALLY ACCOM-
PLISHED, IF HE DOES NOT, BY STAYING TOO LONG, BE REMEMBERED [SIC] FOR
FAILING TO PERMIT THE ATTEMPT TO BE MADE TO SAVE WHAT IS LEFT OF
VIETNAM AS A REASONABLY FREE STATE. . . . I WILL SAY THAT IT IS MY DIS-
PASSIONATE AND OBJECTIVE CONCLUSION THAT IF HE DOES NOT DO THIS, HIS
GENERALS WILL FORCE HIM TO DEPART. I WOULD SAY THAT IT WOULD SEEM
TO MOST OF THE WORLD A MUCH MORE HONORABLE WAY TO GO, IF HIS DEPAR-
TURE WAS AT HIS OWN VOLITION, TELLING HIS COUNTRY HE DID SO TO PRE-
SERVE THE LEGITIMACY OF THE CONSTITUTION AND THE SUCCESSOR
ADMINISTRATION, WHICH WOULD HELP THEM NEGOTIATE FROM A GREATER
POSITION OF STRENGTH TO PRESERVE A FREE VIETNAM. I WOULD SAY IT WOULD

BE AN ACT WHICH COULD ONLY BE TAKEN BY A MAN OF GREAT COURAGE, WHO PLACED HIS COUNTRY'S INTEREST FIRST AND FOREMOST. I WOULD MAKE IT QUITE CLEAR SEVERAL TIMES THAT I WAS GIVING HIM ONLY MY PERSONAL ASSESSMENT OF THE SITUATION, THAT I HAD NOT BEEN INSTRUCTED TO DO SO EITHER BY THE PRESIDENT OR THE SECRETARY OF STATE WHO, I ASSUMED, WOULD CONTINUE TO SUPPORT THE GOVERNMENT AND PEOPLE OF VIETNAM TO THE BEST OF THEIR ABILITY.

THIS IS BEING PERSONALLY TYPED. THERE WILL BE NO RECORD EXCEPT IN WASHINGTON. I BELIEVE THIEU WILL LISTEN TO ME. I KNOW HE BELIEVES THAT WHAT I SAY IS WHAT I BELIEVE TO BE THE TRUTH, AND HE KNOWS WHAT I HAVE TOLD HIM ALMOST ALWAYS TURNS OUT TO BE RIGHT.

IN THE MEANTIME, IT DOES SEEM TO ME THAT THERE SHOULD BE AT LEAST A SMALL PRICE FOR DÉTENTE, AND PERHAPS SOME WAY COULD BE FOUND TO MAKE THE SOVIET UNION AND CHINA BELIEVE IT WOULD BE TO THEIR ADVANTAGE IN THEIR FUTURE DEALINGS WITH US TO EXERCISE THE MOST MASSIVE RESTRAINT ON HANOI TO BACK AWAY FROM SAIGON AND RESUME THE NEGOTIATING TRACK.

OF ONE THING I AM CERTAIN, DEADLY CERTAIN, IF U.S. ARMED FORCES COME HERE IN FORCE UNDER THE PRESENT CIRCUMSTANCES, THEY WILL BE FIGHTING THE SOUTH VIETNAMESE ON THE WAY OUT. IF WE PLAY IT COOL, I CAN GET OUR PEOPLE OUT ALIVE IN A WAY THAT WILL NOT, REPEAT, NOT ADD A RATHER GHASTLY MISTAKE TO THE THOUSANDS THE AMERICANS HAVE ALREADY MADE IN AND ABOUT VIETNAM. WARM REGARDS. MARTIN.

Kissinger quickly sent a reply to Martin the same day, marked "Secret Sensitive Exclusively Eyes Only Via Martin Channels," telling him:

"I HAVE DISCUSSED YOUR SAIGON 710 WITH THE PRESIDENT. THERE IS NO OBJECTION TO YOUR PROCEEDING AS YOU INDICATE IN PARAGRAPH 9. YOU WILL BE RECEIVING A FULL REPORT ON TODAY'S WSAG WITH FURTHER INSTRUCTIONS ON A VARIETY OF QUESTIONS."

Kissinger and the President had approved Martin telling Thieu he should step down.[6] The Washington Special Action Group, the senior interagency operations team, would deal with the specifics of evacuating American personnel.

For Hung the weekend had arrived and there was nobody to reach for help to rescue Vietnam except his old friend and professor, Warren Nutter. In Saigon, time had run out for President Thieu. On Sunday evening, April 20, Ambassador Martin called on Thieu to review the situation and to suggest candidly that he resign.[7] "I believe that in a few days your generals will come to tell you to step down," he told Thieu.

"If I step down, will military aid come?" Thieu asked.

"I cannot promise you, but there may be a chance," replied Martin.[8]

Before Martin left, Thieu said: "I will do what is best for the country."

Instead of waiting for the generals to come, Thieu preempted them by calling them to the Independence Palace the following day. At the meeting,

Thieu told the generals and a select group of cabinet officials the details of his conversation with Ambassador Martin. He would base his decision on their reaction and whether they now considered him to be an obstacle to peace. "No one said a word," recalled Thieu. At that moment Thieu decided. He said he would resign. Vice President Huong would assume the presidency. General Cao Van Vien walked back to Thieu's office with him, tears in his eyes. "Mr. President," said Vien, "I never imagined that there would be a day like today."

Before Thieu announced his resignation, Kissinger cabled Martin suggesting that he hold up Thieu's resignation so he could take credit for it with the Soviet Union. Kissinger hoped to offer Thieu's resignation at an opportune moment to facilitate the negotiations that were to be resumed between North and South. Martin refused to play the game. He ignored the message from Kissinger. "It just went from the incoming basket to the file with absolutely no action at all," said Martin.[9]

Thieu formally resigned the next day. He appeared before a joint session of the National Assembly and on national television for three hours in an often disjointed, but always intense and heartfelt address which deeply impressed the Vietnamese people. Many said it was his best political address in his eight years in office. He reviewed his efforts to defeat the Communists and heaped scorn on the Americans for deserting South Vietnam. Said Thieu:

> The Americans have asked us to do an impossible thing. I have therefore told them: You have asked us to do something you failed to do with half a million powerful troops and skilled commanders and with nearly $300 billion in expenditures over six long years. If I do not say that you were defeated by the Communists in Vietnam I must modestly say that you did not win either. But you found an honorable way out. And at present, when our army lacks weapons, ammunition, helicopters, aircraft, and B-52s, you ask us to do an impossible thing like filling the ocean up with stones. This is like the case in which you give me only $3 and urge me to go by plane, first class; to rent a room in the hotel for $30 per day; to eat four or five slices of beefsteak and to drink seven or eight glasses of wine per day. This is an impossible absurd thing.
>
> Likewise, you have let our combatants die under the hail of shells. This is an inhumane act by an inhumane ally. This is the reason why, on the day a U.S. congressional delegation came here, I told the congressmen that it was not the problem of $300 million in aid, but it was the question of complying with the U.S. pledge to assist the Vietnamese people in the struggle to protect their independence and freedom and the ideal of freedom for which the Americans fought together with our people here and for which some 50,000 American citizens were sacrificed.
>
> The United States is proud of being an invincible defender of the just cause and the ideal of freedom in this world and will celebrate its 200th anniversary next year. I asked them: Are U.S. statements worthy? Are U.S. commitments still valid? Some $300 million is not a big sum to you. Compared to the amount of money you spent here in ten years, this sum is sufficient for only ten days of fighting. And with this sum, you ask me to score a victory or to check the

Communist aggression—a task which you failed to fulfill in six years with all U.S. forces and with such an amount of money. This is absurd!

After the transfer of presidential power, the new president, Tran Van Huong, called Ambassador Martin to ask him to urge Thieu to leave the country and to arrange for Thieu's departure. Martin agreed. Huong then called Thieu and suggested he leave Saigon to make his own position easier. Otherwise, Huong said, "I will be accused by the Communists of running a Thieu government without Thieu." In order to make Thieu's departure legal, President Huong signed an order appointing Thieu as a Special Emissary from the Republic of Vietnam to Taiwan to pay respects to President Chiang Kai-shek, who had died on April 5.[10]

The arrangements for Thieu's departure were made by CIA station chief Thomas Polgar on the instructions of Ambassador Martin. Thieu told Polgar that he would like to take Prime Minister Khiem and several aides with him to Taiwan. A propellor-driven Air Force DC-6 available for the ambassador's use was flown to Saigon from Thailand on the night of April 25. Polgar and General Charles Timmes, the CIA's liaison with the generals, met Thieu and his party at Khiem's residence in the Joint General Staff Compound outside Tan Son Nhut airfield. Polgar had organized three black sedans—the ambassador's car, the deputy chief of mission's car, and his own; CIA staffers were the drivers.[11] Khiem had arranged to station a trusted officer at the JGS to allow the Americans to enter and exit without incident. Thieu and his party were each permitted one handbag. There was no other luggage.[12] Thieu's wife and children had already left the country and were in London.

While Thieu and his party quietly sipped a farewell drink in Khiem's house, Polgar prepared travel orders, a manifest, and parole papers for the group. Then they quickly boarded the black sedans and drove to the air base past the Vietnamese monument to the American war dead with its inscription: "The Noble Sacrifice of the Allied Soldiers Will Never Be Forgotten." Thieu was seated between Polgar and Timmes, "so that a guard at the gate would see an American face when he looked into the car," explained Polgar. The official American sedans were waved onto the field and drove to the plane standing outside the Air America terminal, where Ambassador Martin was waiting to escort Thieu aboard. Thieu was somber and resigned, but he maintained his dignity and thanked Martin for arranging his departure. Martin said: "It was the least I could do. Goodbye. Good luck."[13] It was done quickly and quietly, without ceremony or any display of emotion.

After Thieu departed, Martin and Polgar went to a cocktail party given by the Polish delegation to the International Commission for Control and Supervision of the Cease-fire to give the appearance that nothing out of the ordinary was going on. Two hours later the President's Office at the Independence Palace announced the departure of Nguyen Van Thieu.

On April 29, Mrs. Anna Chennault visited Taiwan on private business, but she carried a private message to Thieu on behalf of President Ford. Mrs. Chennault had been asked to tell Thieu that it would not be a good time for him to come to the United States because of strong anti-war feelings; it would be better if he went someplace else. His family, however, would be welcome in the United States. Mrs. Chennault asked Thieu where he wanted to live and said efforts would be made to help him leave Taiwan. Thieu smiled bitterly and told her: "It is so easy to be an enemy of the United States, but so difficult to be a friend." [14]

21

The Exodus

THE NEWS OF THIEU'S departure sparked a rumor that he had taken the nation's sixteen tons of gold reserves, valued at $120 million, with him. Actually, the idea of removing the gold from Saigon for safe keeping originated during a meeting in the Palace on April 1, after the fall of Danang. General Vien warned, "The only way now is to use enough firepower to stop the enemy advance and gain a respite. If we do not have B-52s, we need CBUs, [cluster bomb units] promptly." When nobody followed up on Vien's remarks, Hung suggested: "Perhaps we can use our own reserves, whatever is left in gold and foreign exchange, to buy ammunition." There was no further discussion until the regular Wednesday cabinet meeting the following day, April 2. Again Danang and its aftermath were the primary subjects of concern. There were reports that the North Vietnamese had tortured hostesses in bars frequented by American G.I.'s by pulling out their fingernails, and had hammered nails into the heads of captured policemen. Would the police in Saigon stand and fight after hearing of such atrocities?

At that point Hung raised the question of security for the Central Bank, housed in elegant French-built headquarters overlooking the Saigon River. Hung told the cabinet that his concern was based on past North Vietnamese behavior. In his research on North Vietnamese economic planning Hung came across a critique of the August 1945 revolution. One of the admitted mistakes of the Viet Minh was their failure to immediately seize the Institut d'Emissions in Hanoi, the currency-issuing institute and the predecessor of the Central Bank. "I would not be surprised," Hung told the cabinet, "if the Central Bank is a primary target when the North Vietnamese attempt to infiltrate Saigon. This time they will try to seize the gold first. Either we should reinforce the Central Bank with a company of troops or move the gold out of the country to Switzerland or New York." Hung then explained the practice of maintaining gold reserves with the Bank of International Settlements in Geneva or the Federal Reserve Bank in New York. There were no spare troops to guard the bank; they decided to move the gold out.

In the back of Hung's mind was a plan to use the gold to buy arms for a final defense of the South.

The Prime Minister's Office called the Central Bank governor and instructed him to implement the cabinet decision. He immediately called TWA, Pan American, and Lloyd's of London. Two days later the news leaked out to "Radio Catinat," named for the former French street in Saigon where rumors circulated in the cafés. The Saigon elite who sat in the Café Brodard and the Café Givral heard that Thieu was moving the gold out of the country in a final effort to enrich himself after the fall. Nobody believed that the gold was going to the government's account. Once the plan became public, it was difficult to obtain insurance for commercial shipment of the gold. The Central Bank contacted Ambassador Martin and asked for the help of the American Embassy in arranging transportation and insurance. But the State Department moved slowly, and by the time it responded to Martin's request for assistance, Thieu had resigned.

On April 26, the State Department cabled the embassy that insurance for $60,240,000 had been arranged for the gold valued at twice that amount. The gold would have to leave Saigon by 0700 on April 27 for the insurance to remain in force. A plane was on standby at Clark Field in the Philippines to carry the gold, which had already been crated at the bank.

The Vietnamese contact with the embassy was Deputy Prime Minister Nguyen Van Hao, a southerner, known for his naive views on the Communists. Hao believed that he could come to terms with the North Vietnamese. Earlier he had told Hung that if the country fell, he would stay on and "accept the fact that my children will grow up under communism."

Jean-Marie Mérillon, the French Ambassador to Saigon, urged the remnants of the government of South Vietnam to form a coalition with the Provisional Revolutionary Government during the final days. Hao played an active role in the negotiations and he aspired to a leading role in a coalition government. After President Thieu's resignation, Hao warned President Huong that if he permitted the gold to leave Saigon, Huong would be accused of treason. Huong agreed and Hao called the embassy economic counsellor, Daniel Ellerman, and told him the President had decided not to transfer the gold. As Ambassador Martin recalled, "Hao did not want the gold to leave and that was that. He had visions that he could work with those people [the Communists]."[1] The North Vietnamese seized the gold when they entered the city.

Before the fall of Saigon, Hao publicly broadcast that he would not leave the country. Afterwards Hao was well treated by the Communists, who used him as an adviser until they permitted him to depart. (He now lives in Houston, Texas, with his wife and children.) In 1984 former Finance Minister Chau Kim Nhan confronted Hao and asked him why he had prevented the shipment of gold from leaving Saigon. Hao told Nhan, "You know what would have happened to me if I let the gold go."[2]

On April 9, while the political maelstrom was rising in Saigon, the Communists reached Xuan Loc, the capital of Long Khanh Province, thirty-six miles east of Saigon on Highway 1. Before three main force NVA divisions converged on Xuan Loc, the city had a population of 100,000 and was best known for its surrounding rubber plantations. A 4,000-round artillery barrage, one of the heaviest of the war, leveled more than half of the city; then the North Vietnamese attacked but were repulsed. When the NVA struck, the 18th ARVN Division held firm for a last-stand effort. Their commander, General Le Minh Dao, vowed to hold Xuan Loc, saying: "I don't care how many divisions the other side sends against me, I will knock them down."[3]

The city was destroyed, but still the ARVN held and waited for relief by the 1st Airborne Brigade, which had been sent north on Highway 1 from Saigon to open the road to Xuan Loc. The North Vietnamese threw three divisions into the battle, part of the nine divisions advancing on Saigon. Xuan Loc was the chokepoint through which the North Vietnamese would have to pass to reach Saigon and the South Vietnamese were determined to hold. There were 25,000 men committed to the battle. To prevent the South Vietnamese from reinforcing Xuan Loc, the North Vietnamese encircled the city and blockaded a sixteen-kilometer stretch of Route 1. The Vietnamese air force (VNAF) used its fighter bombers and modified C-130 transports to drop 750-pound bombs, lashed to wooden cargo pallets, against enemy positions. After five days of savage hand-to-hand fighting and extensive North Vietnamese losses (800 killed, 300 weapons captured, and 11 T-54 tanks destroyed), the situation stabilized. The ARVN 43rd Regiment was holding east of Xuan Loc.

General Homer Smith, chief of the Defense Attaché's Office (DAO) in Saigon, sent a message to General George S. Brown, chairman of the Joint Chiefs of Staff, on April 13, praising the will and the courage of the RVNAF to fight even though the odds were heavily weighted against them. After reviewing the results of the first five days, General Smith said: "The valor and aggressiveness of GVN troops, especially the Long Khanh Regional Forces, is certainly indicative that these soldiers, adequately equipped and properly led, are man for man vastly superior to their adversaries. The battle for Xuan Loc appears to settle for the time being the question, 'will ARVN fight?' "[4]

On the night of April 15, the North Vietnamese continued their assault of ARVN positions on Route 1, taking heavy casualties. The 1st Airborne, frustrated in its drive toward Xuan Loc from Saigon to relieve the units defending the city, held but could not advance: The 1st Airborne then withdrew through the rubber plantations and the jungle. Despite their valiant showing the ARVN forces were vastly outnumbered. Rather than be surrounded and decimated, they finally withdrew. The South Vietnamese fought "splendidly" but the NVA high command used the battle as a "meat grinder," sacrificing its own units to destroy irreplaceable ARVN forces.[5] Xuan Loc was the last major battle of the war.

On April 21, Eric Von Marbod and General Weyand testified before a Subcommittee of the House of Representatives Committee on Appropriations seeking approval of the still stalled $300 million supplemental for military aid and $170 million in economic aid. Even though Congress had failed to act on the $722 million Weyand had recommended, he and Von Marbod were determined to make a final appeal for funds. General Weyand summed up the situation: "I would say that the options open to the enemy are almost limitless now in military terms. They have the capability within some period of time of overwhelming the South Vietnamese. Now, whether or not they will take that option I am sure will depend upon their perception of the cost to them and the relative advantages and disadvantages of going on with that course of action; and with some modicum of strength on the South Vietnamese side it is quite likely that the North will choose an option less drastic than the one I just mentioned."[6] With more aid, Saigon might hold out long enough so that a negotiated end to the war might still be achieved—either some form of a coalition government, or Thieu's plan to hold Saigon and the delta. Assistant Secretary of State for East Asia and Pacific Affairs Philip C. Habib met privately with committee members and urged support for the appropriation so that "if they go down it is not because we didn't give it to them."[7] When asked what additional funds could be provided, Von Marbod and Weyand said they could not promise anything more than "hopes." The Committee members were hostile for the most part; Representative Clarence Long (D.-Md.) typified the spirit of the hearing when he told Weyand and Von Marbod, "I think most of us would say that we could offer something better than a hope if that money were spent in our district."[8]

That afternoon Secretary of State Henry Kissinger appeared before the Committee and he was asked what commitments were made to South Vietnam at the time the Paris Accords were signed. Kissinger insisted that there had been no secret agreements, saying:

> The commitments that were made to South Vietnam are all on the public record. It was stated publicly, as well as in the discussions that were taking place at the time, that if the South Vietnamese would permit us to withdraw our forces and thereby enable us to return our prisoners, and if they accepted the provisions of the Paris Accords, that under those conditions it was our—the Administration would support—and it was our belief that the Congress would go along, an adequate level of economic assistance.

Kissinger explained that military assistance depended on the level of combat. He insisted he had stated this when he explained the Paris Agreement and it had been reiterated in press conferences by President Nixon and Elliot Richardson, then Secretary of Defense, and himself. Kissinger added: ". . . and there were no other commitments, and they were in the form of a statement of intentions."

Congressman Bill Chappell (D.-Fla.) asked Kissinger if there was any intention to enforce the agreement with North Vietnam in case of its violation. The exchange is revealing:

> *Secretary Kissinger.* When the United States signs an agreement, it is not generally believed that it can be violated with impunity. And therefore, there was a presumption that the United States would make an effort to enforce the agreement and there were statements on the public record that the United States would not look lightly at violations of the agreement.
> All of these statements were made—
> *Mr. Chappell.* What did that mean, Mr. Secretary?
> *Secretary Kissinger.* What it meant was left ambiguous; partly for its impact on Hanoi, because it makes a great deal of difference whether the other side thinks you probably will not, or it knows that by Act of Congress you certainly cannot. It will affect the degree to which it will commit itself.
> So this is the extent of the formal—the word "commitment" is not an exact expression in any event. It is a statement of an intention to maintain the agreement. And one has to say that it cannot be assumed and it should not be assumed in the future that when a nation signs a solemn agreement with the United States that it can then be broken with total impunity; for the future this must remain a very special case due to the particular domestic situation that developed on the issue of Vietnam.
> *Mr. Chappell.* Was the presence of the Air Force in Thailand in any way to be a deterrent to the North Vietnamese not to violate the agreement?
> *Secretary Kissinger.* It was one of the factors, yes.
> *Mr. Chappell.* Was it in any way part of the understanding?
> *Secretary Kissinger.* No, no there was no understanding to that effect.[9]

In fact, it was part of the understanding. Both President Nixon and Secretary Kissinger promised Thieu that the 7th Air Force at Nakorn Phanom would be used to bomb North Vietnamese targets if the Paris Accords were violated. General Vogt's oral history clearly demonstrates that his forces were not only a deterrent, but he expected to mount a full-scale response to North Vietnamese violations. Certainly, the letters from President Nixon to President Thieu were commitments that had not been made public or shared privately with the Congress. Even at the very end, when he came before Congress to request $300 million to stabilize the situation and aid in the evacuation of the Americans, even when he spoke of the need to "urgently reestablish some unity between the Congress and the Executive," Kissinger did not acknowledge the record of secret promises in the letters from Presidents Nixon and Ford.

That night Eric Von Marbod flew to Saigon under orders from Defense Secretary James Schlesinger to save as much equipment as possible from falling into North Vietnamese hands. After the debacle in the central highlands and Danang, the Defense Department was sensitive to congressional criticism that sophisticated equipment would be lost to the North Vietnamese, including the F-5E fighter bombers, which were also the front-line aircraft in Taiwan and Iran. Deputy Assistant Secretary of Defense for International Security Affairs Morton Abramowitz, Schlesinger's Asian expert, had suggested that Von Marbod be sent to Saigon to oversee the operation and Schlesinger agreed. On his way to Saigon Von Marbod stopped in Thailand, where he met with General Kriangsak, Chief of Staff of the Thai Supreme Command, who agreed to permit Vietnamese aircraft to be flown to three Thai air force bases.

When he arrived in Saigon on April 23, Von Marbod met with Ambassador Graham Martin, who expressed his concern that no equipment be removed from the country while the South Vietnamese could continue to use it to fight against the North Vietnamese invasion. Martin was convinced that there would be an orderly evacuation with U.S. Air Force transport planes and that there would be enough time to remove the Vietnamese air force planes. Von Marbod left the embassy to survey the battlefields and make his own assessment of how soon the end might come.

By helicopter he was taken to fly over the Xuan Loc battlefield and the surrounding area where the South Vietnamese troops were fighting the final phase of the battle. He landed to observe conditions on the ground before returning to Saigon. "When I saw a soldier with one leg left still point his rifle at the enemy positions and fire, I was deeply moved," said Von Marbod.

At Tulane University in New Orleans on April 23, President Ford urged the American people to forget the past and look to the future. "America can regain the sense of pride that existed before Viet Nam. But it cannot be achieved by refighting a war that is finished as far as America is concerned." Later that day Von Marbod was briefed on President Ford's Tulane speech and the critical paragraph saying the war was "finished" was read to him. "He raised the white bed sheet. I felt overwhelmed and ashamed," recalled Von Marbod.[10]

In Washington, Hung also listened to the speech and burst into tears. "Was it really the way the war should end? Was it really the America that I cherished and loved that could just casually walk away from the people who had been persuaded to stake their lives and shed so much blood?" Hung asked himself. That evening he wrote a letter to his family. "I am trying very hard to save our beloved family, but if I should fail, then you, my brother-in-law, should consider seriously to take the life of our family members before you take your own if the Communists are going to arrest the family. Even though Catholics are forbidden to take their lives on religious grounds, I have consulted with Monsignor Nott,* who told me that 'if you are absolutely sure that the alternative would be a more painful death, then God will understand such an action.' " Hung wrote his brother-in-law, Hoang Ba, that he had left a new .38-caliber revolver, given to him by Von Marbod, in the drawer of his bedroom dresser with two boxes of cartridges.

* The Reverend Monsignor S. Harold Nott, of St. Agnes Catholic Church, Arlington, Va.

Hung sent the letter with his friend Nguyen Ngoc Bich, director of the Vietnam Press, who returned on April 24 to evacuate his own family.

When Von Marbod reached Saigon, he told his assistant Richard Armitage, who spoke fluent Vietnamese, to arrange for Hung's family to leave the country. Armitage rounded up ten members of the family and brought them by car to Tan Son Nhut Airport. "Don't say a word," he cautioned Hung's eighty-year-old mother, who was astonished to hear the stocky American issuing orders in Vietnamese. There was limited parole authority on the American side, at that point, to permit people to leave legally. The question of how many Vietnamese to accept in the United States was still unresolved.

Thieu had authorized Hung to spend $20,000 from the Vietnamese Procurement Office (VINOPO) in Washington to appeal Vietnam's case before the American people. Hung wanted to print his appeal in *The Washington Post* and *The New York Times*. He called Director Le Van Kim for the money, but he was out of town arranging a shipment of rice. Hung's own $300 was gone and he was living on his family savings. On the morning of the 25th, Kim returned and told Hung he had reported to the FBI that the money had been embezzled from the office. There was no money either for full-page newspaper ads or for expenses.

At noon on April 25 Hung met Warren Nutter in his Arlington apartment to seek his help and advice. They discussed how to appeal for American aid to evacuate a substantial number of Vietnamese. While Nutter was with him, Hung received a phone call from Von Marbod in Saigon: "Gregg, I am here at Tan Son Nhut Airport right now and I have seen your family proceeding toward the plane." Once he got the cars past the Vietnamese military police at the gate, Armitage joined Von Marbod and they put the family aboard a C-141 military transport that flew them to Clark Field in the Philippines.[11] Hung wept with relief.

Hung asked Nutter whether he should call Kissinger or Schlesinger for a private appointment to discuss the letters. Nutter knew it was too late. "They have washed their hands of Vietnam," he said. Distraught, Hung kept calling everyone he knew in Washington throughout the week. He sought Mrs. Chennault's help in getting a plane to Saigon to fly out his staff from the Ministry of Planning and Development. He beseeched Reverend Elson, the Senate chaplain, to appeal to his friends in the Congress to save those Vietnamese who had placed their trust in America. His target was a million Vietnamese, the number rescued by the Americans and the French in 1954 when the country was partitioned.

Hung discussed his plight with Nutter: how to save Vietnamese lives. Nutter suggested that the best and cheapest way was to call a news conference "using some of the letters to back up your appeal." Inside the White House, "Everybody was telling Ford, 'It's all over, get the Americans out.' But President Ford had decided to get out as many Vietnamese as possible and turned his back on the advice to evacuate only Americans. He hung on at great political peril to try to get out as many Vietnamese as possible," explained General Brent Scowcroft, Ford's National Security Advisor.[12] Nutter was concerned with the effect of the letters on Congress at the same time that President Ford was making an effort to gain support for evacuation of Vietnamese. He urged Hung to wait until the moment that the evacuation began; then the letters would have a positive impact in marshalling support.

In Saigon Ambassador Martin still held out the hope of an agreement with the Communists. He sent Kissinger a message advising him that negotiations might still be possible between the Saigon government (GVN) and the Provisional Revolutionary Government (PRG). On April 26, 1975 Kissinger cabled Martin:

YOU HAVE MISUNDERSTOOD MY COMMENTS ABOUT NEGOTIATIONS WITH THE PRG. I WAS NOT SPEAKING OF GVN-PRG TALKS BUT U.S.-PRG TALKS. I WANT ANY U.S. POLITICAL DISCUSSION WITH THE PRG TO TAKE PLACE IN PARIS.

Kissinger did not want the North and South negotiating directly without the United States in control.[13]

On the morning of April 27, Von Marbod flew to Bien Hoa air base, where he found enlisted men, with only a few officers, and the base under sporadic artillery fire. Nothing was being done to fly out the remaining aircraft and there was no plan for the destruction of the logistics facilities which were the best the United States had to offer. They included a full range of precision measuring equipment. There was no sign that the extensive VNAF Air Logistics Command facilities had been destroyed. The material and chemical laboratory, the jet-engine overhaul facilities, the instrument laboratory, liquid oxygen plant, precision measuring equipment lab, and the airborne radio shop were all still intact. Von Marbod returned to Saigon and met with General Dong Van Khuyen, Acting Chief of the JGS. Khuyen had succeeded General Cao Van Vien, who had resigned and fled the country in civilian clothes when he heard rumors that there was a plot to assassinate him. Von Marbod complained to Khuyen that nothing was being done to destroy the equipment at Bien Hoa. Then Von Marbod flew to Tan Son Nhut to meet with Vietnamese air force officers, including the air force commander General Tran Van Minh and Marshal Nguyen Cao Ky. Von Marbod asked them why they were not flying air strikes against the North Vietnamese and what was being done to destroy the equipment at Bien Hoa which was simply being abandoned. He was told that the North Vietnamese were firing heat-seeking Strella missiles at their aircraft and had radar-guided quad-mounted anti-aircraft guns that made it impossible to fly F-5 or A-37 bombing sorties.

Von Marbod discussed evacuation plans with them and suggested storing fuel bladders on Phu Quoc Island, off the southern coast of Vietnam in the Gulf of Thailand, in case an evacuation was to take place. "I briefed them on a plan to use Phu Quoc as a supply and staging base for evacuation of helicopters to Thailand. I told them the decision had to be based on combat imperatives. If they did not use the equipment, they should destroy it in place or relocate it, but not let it fall into the hands of the enemy," recalled Von Marbod.[14]

The following morning Von Marbod met with Ambassador Martin in his embassy office. Martin told him he had been advised by "sources" that they could expect a cease-fire in place. During their meeting Ambassador Martin did not rescind his order prohibiting the removal of operationally ready equipment and cautioned Von Marbod "against initiating actions which could create a morale problem with the RVNAF." Martin told Von Marbod that he expected a cease-fire in place while a coalition government was being formed by General Duong Van Minh, who would succeed President Huong that day. "Eric, why are you risking your life?" Martin asked. "We'll have thirty days here to do things."[15]

The Hungarian and Polish representatives from the International Commission for Control and Supervision of the Cease-fire (ICCS) had told the CIA station chief Thomas Polgar that a truce could be arranged to carry out an orderly evacuation of Americans and some South Vietnamese. They said the North Vietnamese would allow a corridor from Saigon to the South China Sea to move refugees to Vung Tau or some other seaport. They had also hinted that the Communists would accept a truce and a coalition government if Thieu would resign. Parts of this rumor were confirmed by French Ambassador Jean-Marie Mérillon, who was told that the Communists were willing to work out a compromise end to the war once Thieu was out and General Minh was named president. An extensive effort was made by the Communists to create the impression that a compromise end was possible. Even the Viet Cong representative to the four-party Joint Military Commission at Tan Son Nhut, Colonel Vo Dong Giang, hinted at a peaceful arrangement rather than an all-out North Vietnamese assault on Saigon. All these reports conflicted with what the CIA had learned from a reliable agent within the Communists' headquarters, the Central Office for South Vietnam (COSVN). The agent reported on April 8 and confirmed on April 17 that the Communists were devoting all their resources to achieving total victory in 1975 and that there would definitely not be a truce or negotiations, even if Thieu resigned. The plans to attack Saigon were complete.[16]

The French effort to have the war end with a cease-fire and a coalition government was still in full swing with frantic scurrying back and forth between Pierre Brochand, the head of the French Intelligence in Saigon, and the Vietnamese on both sides. General Minh, who took over as president from Huong on April 28, was told that he should order all Americans to leave the country if he hoped to negotiate with the North Vietnamese. In order to show his sincerity, General Minh wrote to Ambassador Martin requesting the evacuation of all American personnel in the Defense Attaché Office "within twenty-four hours beginning April 29, 1975, in order that the question of peace for Viet Nam can be settled early." The letter provided the formal grounds for the American decision to remove all personnel from Vietnam. (See Appendix L for text.)

When he left the embassy around 11:00 a.m. on April 28, Von Marbod took off in an Air America helicopter to survey the fighting. The situation had deteriorated drastically. Von Marbod saw North Vietnamese forces moving forward in the open, bumper to bumper along the roads. An enemy machine-gun nest had been set up at Newport Bridge on the four-lane American-built highway to Bien Hoa from Saigon. An orange fireball and black smoke from a petroleum depot rose into the bright blue morning sky. Flying over Route 15, the road to Vung Tau, Von Marbod's chopper was fired upon. He could see the fighting on the ground, the figures like puppets in a distant shadow play; but when he put down at an aid station behind the battle lines, the violence of the war was immediate and nauseating. He saw soldiers shot through the shoulder and chest, men with stomach wounds and missing limbs. There was no sign of a cease-fire in place and the lines were falling back toward Saigon. Von Marbod was convinced the end was coming quickly and there would be no cease-fire.

Once on the ground, he made the decision to disregard Ambassador Martin. The Bien Hoa airfield was inoperable and there was no possibility of flying out the remaining aircraft. Rick Armitage, Von Marbod's Aide, was on the ground there and only a few enlisted personnel and a handful of officers were left.

Von Marbod had received a North Vietnamese radio intercept at the embassy and he warned Armitage by radio: "Get out as fast as you can. They are moving on Bien Hoa." The F-5Es had been moved to Tan Son Nhut, but the remaining aircraft at Bien Hoa, helicopters, C-130s, and A-1s were destroyed by the North Vietnamese artillery and rocket fire or captured along with the base facilities.

Von Marbod then flew on to Tan Son Nhut airfield. He had been to Bien Hoa over the past three days urging the Vietnamese to remove their planes and destroy the logistics facilities. Now he met again with the VNAF commanders at their headquarters. Marshal Ky joined the meeting as Von Marbod urged the Vietnamese to drop the remaining BLU-82 Daisy Cutters on the advancing North Vietnamese forces. For the first time Von Marbod explained the arrangements he had made in Thailand and persuaded the Vietnamese to fly the F-5Es out.[17]

The Central Political Bureau in Hanoi had cabled the North Vietnamese final plan for a general offensive to seize Saigon on April 22. The plan called for launching "the attack against the enemy from every direction without delay. If we delay, it will not be to our advantage either politically or militarily. To act in time now is to guarantee with the greatest certainty that we will gain total victory."[18] The final Ho Chi Minh Campaign to capture Saigon was launched on April 26. North Vietnamese artillery was scheduled to begin firing on Tan Son Nhut on the outskirts of the city on April 28, and "on April 29 the barrage of attacks on the center of the city would begin."[19]

At 6:20 p.m. on April 28, five A-37 Dragonfly jet aircraft approached Tan Son Nhut airfield at an altitude of 5,000 feet. At the Defense Attaché's

Office, adjacent to the airfield, Von Marbod watched the planes approach and said to a friend: "I thought the Vietnamese air force quit work at 6 p.m.?"

"What squadron are you from? What squadron?" the control tower queried the approaching aircraft.

"American-made planes here," came the reply, as the A-37s made their first bombing run on the main runway, destroying three AC-119 gunships and several C-47s. The attack had been mounted from Phan Rang airfield where the jets were captured. North Vietnamese MiG pilots had been trained to fly them for a single raid on Tan Son Nhut.

After the bombing attack the runways were still usable, despite the litter from the destruction of the Vietnamese air force planes. The evacuation of American personnel and "high risk" Vietnamese who had worked for the Americans continued in C-130 aircraft. Two C-130s each with 180 passengers departed at 8:00 p.m. Ambassador Martin told General Homer Smith, the Defense Attaché, that sixty C-130 flights the following day would be the "maximum practicable" schedule, but that he had agreed to the request of General Minh for all American military personnel to leave the country within twenty-four hours. Martin added that he and twenty members of his staff would remain behind for a day or two "to at least give some dignity to our departure."[20]

At 4:05 a.m. on the morning of April 29, the first North Vietnamese rockets hit Tan Son Nhut, instantly killing two Marines standing guard at a checkpoint just beyond the front gate.[21] Von Marbod was thrown from his cot in the Defense Attaché's compound as the wall of his room collapsed. The toilet was ripped from the floor and water poured across the room. Von Marbod crawled to the toilet and shut the faucet, stopping the flood of water. He escaped with only a heavy ringing in his ears and a hot piece of the 122mm Russian rocket, which had dug a crater in front of the compound, for a souvenir. When the rocket fire ceased, long-range 130mm artillery shells smashed into the runways and flight line. The Vietnamese air force sent up an AC-119 gunship and UH-1 spotter helicopter to destroy the rocket positions. From the edge of the airfield Von Marbod and his assistant, Air Force Colonel Elwood Johnson, watched the staccato orange flashes from the AC-119 firing on the rocket emplacements. "Change your pattern, change your pattern," Colonel Johnson shouted as the AC-119 continued to turn in the same direction. Von Marbod could see the white trail of the Strella missile as it rose to destroy the AC-119 in a ball of fire in the cloud-streaked sky. As the red dawn rose, VNAF pilots rushed to the remaining F-5Es and A-37s and flew them to Thailand. Twenty-three F-5Es and twenty-eight A-37s landed at the three Thai air force bases that Von Marbod had arranged. As they taxied to the end of the runways, American personnel stood ready to paint on new insignia, red, white, and blue American Stars, to replace the insignia of yellow and red stripes of the Republic of Vietnam.[22]

Ambassador Martin was driven to Tan Son Nhut in his bullet-proof limousine shortly after 9:00 a.m. to see for himself if the airfield was no longer operable. He insisted the airlift continue. Martin requested that the Vietnamese Joint General Staff headquarters restore order among the troops roaming the runways. Colonel Le Van Luong, the Intelligence Chief of the Joint General Staff, who was at Tan Son Nhut, made the call. There was no answer at the JGS. Even the switchboard operators had left.[23]

Martin called the White House from General Smith's office to reconfirm approval for his decision that the fixed-wing airlift continue. The White House concurred and Martin insisted the airlift continue if order could be restored.

Martin saw Von Marbod and took him aside to confer alone. Von Marbod insisted that the airfield could not be used because the runways were littered with debris and were still taking fire. Martin was noncommittal, but asked Von Marbod to help with the evacuation of his wife. While they argued, fireballs were rising from the Air America corner of the airfield as incoming shells ignited jet fuel.

An hour passed and still the airplanes could not take off. General Smith called Admiral Gayler, the Pacific commander in chief in Honolulu, and sought his help. Then Smith called Ambassador Martin again and told him it was impossible to continue the C-130 lifts. Martin reluctantly agreed to the helicopter lift, Option IV in the evacuation scenario. Martin called Kissinger at the White House, who asked President Ford to begin the evacuation. At 10:51 a.m. on April 29 Saigon time President Ford gave the order to execute Operation Frequent Wind. The first helicopter did not arrive in Saigon until 2:00 p.m. because the Marines to be used as security forces in Saigon were not aboard the choppers on the aircraft carriers and had to be picked up from their transports before the operation commenced. The Armed Forces radio station in Saigon began playing "I'm dreaming of a White Christmas," the signal that the final evacuation had begun.[24]

More than 6,000 South Vietnamese and 1,373 Americans were evacuated by helicopter in Operation Frequent Wind. Martin did not want to leave until the last Vietnamese and Korean allies had been evacuated from the embassy. He kept asking for more helicopters. Finally at 5:00 a.m. on April 30 he was overruled by Washington and ordered to leave Saigon under orders from the White House transmitted by Admiral Gayler. Gayler had been given the authority to arrest Martin if he refused to obey the final evacuation orders.[25] An estimated 420 people were left behind in the embassy compound when the last helicopter lifted off at 5:30 a.m. Still standing in the parking lot landing zone were Vietnamese, South Korean embassy personnel, General Dai Yong Rhee, who had commanded the 50,000 Korean troops in Vietnam, and other foreign nationals.

In Washington on April 29, Hung heard on the radio that only 50,000 to 70,000 Vietnamese would be rescued, the so-called high risk cases. He was determined to make a last attempt to save more lives, and called Nutter in his office at the American Enterprise Institute (AEI). "The end is near. Any moment now, get ready," said Nutter. "People are fleeing toward the sea and need to be picked up." When the evacuation began, Nutter believed it would be safe to release the letters in an effort to marshal support for those fleeing and increase the numbers who would be accepted in America. Hung went to the AEI offices on 17th Street and with Nutter copied three of President Nixon's letters to President Thieu. Then they walked to the nearby Mayflower Hotel and found it would cost $250 to rent a room for the press conference. Hung had only $200 from the family savings. Nutter chipped in $50.

At noon on April 30, Nutter put out a notice to correspondents on the Associated Press City Wire. "Dr. Nguyen Tien Hung, former Minister of Planning and former Executive Assistant to former South Vietnamese President Thieu, will hold a news conference at 4 p.m. today on the 'nature of secret agreements between former President Nixon and Thieu.' Expected to reveal two letters from Nixon to Thieu."

The press and television reporters gathered in the Mayflower's Pan American Room. They were impatient and told Hung they only wanted copies of the letters. "Gentlemen, this is my place, and you should give me a chance to explain the background of the letters before I hand them over to you. If you don't want to wait for my explanation, you may leave," said Hung, as he tried to bring order to the group. There was grumbling and muttering as Hung proceeded to explain why he was releasing the letters containing President Nixon's promises to support South Vietnam and retaliate against North Vietnamese violations of the Paris Accords. Hung noted that "these assurances were either given explicitly or reiterated after the historical 1972 landslide election victory in which the American people gave their mandate to their leader to go forward in his policy. Thus, to the Vietnamese, the assurances were backed up by the prestige and credibility of the U.S. Presidential Office at the height of its power. If assurances made under those conditions cannot be taken seriously, then what can be?"

Hung quoted from President Nixon's November 14, 1972, letter promising to "react very strongly and rapidly to any violation of the [Paris] agreement." He also revealed President Nixon's January 5, 1973, letter pledging that if South Vietnam signed the Paris Accords, "you have my assurance of continued assistance in the post settlement period and that we will respond with full force should the settlement be violated by the North Vietnamese." He also quoted from, but did not release, Nixon's January 17, 1973, letter, assuring Thieu the United States did not recognize the right of foreign troops to remain on South Vietnamese soil and that "the U.S. will react vigorously to violations of the Agreement."

As the TV cameras recorded his words, Hung appealed to America's sense of justice and fairness. "I believe that, with its vast diplomatic and economic power, America at this hour can still do something humanitarian; that is to save human lives." The letters, explained Hung, were a pledge that had not been redeemed and now the United States could help those who fled from Saigon. The United States should arrange for at least one million more Vietnamese to leave the South—"those who have trusted in America and the American promise."

The newsmen clustered around Hung when he had finished and followed him down the corridor as he left. Murray Marder of *The Washington Post* told Hung he had "a lot of sympathy for you and your people," and offered his assistance. "Please help my people to immigrate to America. The Statue of Liberty reminds us that America is the land of immigrants. Political asylum is in the American tradition and now you must save our people from persecution by the Communists," said Hung.

One journalist, with a black beard, followed Hung and asked him for a copy of the third letter he had mentioned in the press conference but had not released. Hung consulted with Nutter and then declined his request. The journalist listened as Hung talked with Marder and requested help for Vietnamese fleeing from Saigon. Then he told Hung: "Well, sir, let me remind you that the Statue of Liberty faces toward the Atlantic."

Nutter was shocked and embarrassed. He took Hung aside and comforted him: "You did a superb job for your country. A lot of sympathy will be generated and I hope that the number of Vietnamese who are rescued will be substantial."

Von Marbod left Tan Son Nhut on an Air America helicopter at about 11:30 a.m. on April 29 and was flown to the *USS Blue Ridge,* the command ship of Task Force 76 headed by Rear Admiral Donald Whitmire. The *Blue Ridge* had only one landing pad and the storage space for choppers was quickly filled. The crew were forced to push Vietnamese choppers into the sea to allow more to land. Many ditched in the sea and only some survived. Von Marbod landed with two admirals who were taken to see Admiral Whitmire; he turned in his pistol and, exhausted, dirty, and hungry, fell asleep in a passageway. He was awakened by a sailor who told him Admiral Whitmire had a message for him.

In the infrared light of the Operations Center of the *Blue Ridge,* Admiral Whitmire told Von Marbod there was a message from Defense Secretary Schlesinger authorizing him to proceed to the *USS Dubuque* (LDP 8), a landing craft with a helicopter deck and amphibious craft, commanded by Captain R. W. McLain, Jr.

The night before, in a phone call to the Pentagon, Von Marbod had requested an aircraft carrier from Schlesinger to rescue helicopters from the delta that had flown there from Saigon. Von Marbod was to set up a way station in international waters for Vietnamese helicopters trying to reach safety in Thailand from South Vietnam. Rearmed, Von Marbod flew off the *Blue Ridge* into tropical squalls to find the *Dubuque.* After landing once to refuel in his search for the *Dubuque,* his chopper pilot found the ship before night fell over the heavy dark green swells. Von Marbod explained his mission to the captain and they steamed at flank speed to arrive off Phu Quoc Island at first light on the morning of April 30. There the *Dubuque* broadcast radio transmissions advising pilots the course to proceed to Trat, Thailand, the nearest point across the Cambodian border, where they would receive a friendly welcome. The *Dubuque* also received, refueled, and sent on to Thailand any Vietnamese helicopters overloaded with dependents. The airstrip on Phu Quoc was out of fuel and without the *Dubuque* the helicopters could not have reached Thailand. Von Marbod had further arranged with his friend Brigadier General Harry C. Aderholt, the head of the American Military Advisory group in Thailand, to fly a twin-engined U.S. Army L-23 over the area transmitting vectoring instructions for helicopter pilots trying to reach a safe haven in Thailand.

Von Marbod's operation rescued an estimated 2,000 Vietnamese and their dependents and a total of 224 aircraft valued at $233 million. Rick Armitage raised the American flag on thirty-five Vietnamese navy ships valued at $55 million and sailed them to Subic Bay in the Philippines with their crews and families. As the vessels neared port Armitage ordered the Vietnamese to raise the American flag to the masthead. The sailors protested and Armitage calmed them by agreeing to a full ceremony to transfer the ships. The Vietnamese national anthem was played and the crews wept as the Vietnamese flag was lowered. After arranging for the removal of the aircraft to American aircraft carriers off Thailand, Von Marbod flew back to Washington early in May.[26]

In the aftermath, Von Marbod was assigned to be the Pentagon's representative on the Interagency Task Force for Indochina, headed by Julia Vadala Taft, to relocate Vietnamese refugees. As a logistics expert, Von Marbod was called in to find places for Vietnamese refugees to be processed for resettlement. He called on Hung to advise him on the needs of the refugees and together they traveled to Fort Chaffee, Arkansas, Indian Town Gap, Pennsylvania, and Eglin Air Force Base in Florida to establish camps where Vietnamese could begin life anew in America. President Ford led the way to help the refugees. Initially, Americans opposed resettling Vietnamese. A Gallup Poll in early May found 54 percent of all Americans opposed to admitting Vietnamese refugees to live in the United States, and only 36 percent in favor.[27] The House of Representatives rejected President Ford's initial request for $507 million for transportation and care of refugees and he had to mount a full-scale effort to change the mind of Congress. Senator George McGovern, Nixon's Democratic opponent in 1972, said: "I think the Vietnamese are better off in Vietnam, including the orphans."[28] Vietnamese arriving at the camps were greeted with signs that said: "Only Ford wants them," and, "Charity begins at home."

Hung threw himself into the campaign to resettle more than 120,000 Vietnamese. He explained to Vietnamese he met in the camps that the reason they encountered hostility was that they were arriving at a time of high unemployment and that Americans were fearful a mass influx of refugees would deprive them of their jobs and livelihoods.

Hung and Von Marbod met with local officials, the press, and voluntary agency workers to stress the self-reliance and high motivation of the Vietnamese. Hung reminded them that in Vietnam when refugees had come from the North to the South in 1954 the southerners were fearful that the influx would hurt their economy, but in fact the South benefitted and was strengthened. "In five years the Vietnamese will make a contribution to America," Hung predicted. He advised voluntary agency officials to feed the refugees rice, fish sauce, and chicken instead of more expensive hamburger, hot dogs, and beef, which they were not used to and found hard to digest. Hung stressed that the Vietnamese should not be dispersed or there would be a second wave of settlement as they tried to gather together in communities. He urged the camp commanders to avoid the mistakes of the war by doing everything themselves; they should include the Vietnamese in the decision-making process to make the camps run smoothly.

A combination of American goodwill and guilt prevailed. By the end of 1975 more than 120,000 refugees had been resettled. The exodus, which would ultimately lead to more than 500,000 Vietnamese refugees settling in America, had begun.

22

Reflections

THE FINAL OUTCOME of the Vietnam war was quite different from what almost all of those involved might have expected or predicted. The Republic of Vietnam was eliminated. So was the supposedly independent Provisional Revolutionary Government (PRG) and its political organization in the South. As a result of the forced unification of the North and South in the summer of 1975 the National Liberation Front (NLF) and its successor, the PRG, ceased to function and the North assumed total control over the South. Thus ended the myth of the Vietcong and its struggle for independence.[1]

As the late Moshe Dayan put it when he visited Saigon in the 1960s: "North Vietnam will lose the war when it takes over Saigon."[2] North Vietnam has changed the name of Saigon to Ho Chi Minh City. Americans could see for themselves in 1985, in the satellited television programs from Vietnam to celebrate the tenth anniversary of the Vietnamese victory, that after ten years of Communist rule Saigon has deteriorated into a city with a bare subsistence economy run on corruption. The biggest business is selling permission to leave the country. By North Vietnamese admission, there are still some 10,000 people in re-education camps.[3] Refugees estimate the numbers to range from 100,000 to 300,000; and conditions are far worse than the Tiger Cages of Con Son Island. Hung's friends told him, "We ate whatever moved."

In the North the economy continues to flounder. Military expenditures are the largest items in the budget. The armed forces number 1,220,500 in a total population of 59 million, the proportionate equivalent of five million Americans under arms. Vietnam's per capita income of less than $200 is one of the lowest in the world. The North Vietnamese may have won the war, but they are losing the peace.

The great American base at Cam Ranh Bay has been taken over by the Soviet Union. Its surface combat ships, submarines and auxiliary vessels refuel and operate on regular schedules from Cam Ranh, giving the Soviet navy a forward base reach into the Pacific that it has coveted since the days of the Russo-Japanese war in 1904–05 when the Soviet fleet refueled at Cam Ranh Bay enroute to its defeat at Port Arthur in Manchuria. Soviet Bear D and F bombers, based at Cam Ranh and Danang, fly reconnaissance missions over the American Seventh Fleet operating in South East Asian and Pacific waters. TU-16 medium bombers are poised to hit Chinese targets, and MiG-23 tactical strike aircraft from Vietnamese bases provide air coverage for the Soviet fleet in the region. The Soviet Union has established signals intelligence gathering sites to monitor American and Chinese traffic in the region. The Soviet military in Vietnam appears to have a limited role for the defense of the Vietnamese. Its primary purpose is to poise the Russians in a major regional military posture against the Chinese and Americans. North Vietnam, the country that boasted of its independence in the Communist world, has now become subservient to Soviet ambitions in East Asia. Moscow was the biggest winner of the Indochina War.

If the Soviet Union was the winner, the biggest great power loser of the Vietnam War was the People's Republic of China. The irony is that American involvement in the war was undertaken to contain the expansion of Communist China into Southeast Asia; the tactics of the war had been designed to prevent the Chinese from intervening on behalf of the North Vietnamese. The Korean War had left the leading figures of the Johnson administration with an abiding phobia of Chinese intervention in Vietnam because they had misjudged the Chinese intentions in Korea. Secretary of State Dean Rusk had been Assistant Secretary of State for East Asian and Pacific Affairs during the Korean War. An often repeated story in Washington describes Rusk being briefed in detail on Chinese preparations to attack the United Nations Forces across the 38th parallel in Korea in 1950. After listening carefully, Rusk replied: "They wouldn't dare."[4]

The punishing result of this major miscalculation of Chinese motivations carried over into the Vietnam conflict and continued to constrain American actions. Once wrong, twice shy. Those who misjudged the Chinese in Korea expected the same pattern of behavior in Vietnam, although the situation of Korea did not apply to Vietnam.

The threat of Chinese intervention hovered like a dark cloud in the minds of American planners in the Johnson administration.[5] During the bombing of North Vietnam in operation Rolling Thunder, President Johnson approved the targets himself and talked to congressmen in his office about the restraint he was showing. Columnists Rowland Evans and Robert Novak's description of one of these sessions documents the deep concern for Chinese intervention in the war:

> To illustrate his caution, he [Johnson] showed critics the map of North Vietnam and pointed out the targets he had disapproved. As for Communist China, he was watching for every possible sign of reaction. Employing a vivid sexual analogy, the President explained to friends and critics one day that the slow escalation of the air war in the North and the increasing pressure on Ho Chi Minh was seduction, not rape. If China should suddenly react to slow escala-

tion as a woman might react to attempted seduction, by threatening to retaliate (a slap in the face, to continue the metaphor), the United States would have plenty of time to ease off the bombing. On the other hand, if the United States were to unleash an all-out, total assault on the North—rape rather than seduction—there could be no turning back, and Chinese reaction might be instant and total.[6]

Johnson asked Thieu in Manila in October 1966 if he believed the Chinese would intervene. Thieu told him no, the North Vietnamese would not turn to the Chinese because Vietnam had been ruled by China for a thousand years; and if the Hanoi leaders gave up their independence to China they would lose a critical element of their appeal to the North Vietnamese people.[7] Instead, the Hanoi leadership turned for support to Moscow, Beijing's former ally and now a rival for hegemony in Indochina and Central Asia.

When Nixon took office he recognized the change in the Sino-Soviet relationship and tried to exploit tensions between the two powers by opening a political dialogue with the Chinese designed to normalize American relations with China. This strategy became known as "playing the China Card." Because of their fear of the Soviet Union, the Chinese moved to improve relations with the United States at the expense of the North Vietnamese. When Zhou Enlai welcomed Nixon to China in 1972 the People's Republic of China ceased to be a threat in Vietnam. The Chinese continued to support the National Liberation Front and the Provisional Revolutionary Government in the South, as countervailing forces to maintain political tensions between North and South Vietnam after the fall of Saigon, but their proxies were totally eliminated. Mao and Zhou's Vietnam strategy failed.

Then in 1978 the North Vietnamese moved to eliminate Chinese influence in Cambodia by attacking the Chinese-sponsored Khmer Rouge, the Cambodian Communists who came to power in 1975 and committed genocide against their own people, slaughtering more than one million Cambodians. The Khmer Rouge, led by Pol Pot, were forced to flee to the Thai-Cambodian border and fight a guerrilla war supported by China. In February 1980 the Chinese attempted to "teach a lesson" to North Vietnam by attacking across the Sino-Vietnam border, but they were repulsed. Since then the two countries maintain an uneasy truce with periodic outbreaks of shelling and skirmishing. No longer are China and Vietnam "as close as lips and teeth," as Ho Chi Minh was fond of saying.

The Chinese have lost their influence in Laos and Cambodia to the North Vietnamese. The Chinese continue to support Pol Pot, and Prince Norodom Sihanouk, the Cambodian royal heir to the throne ousted from power in a coup in 1970. The two former leaders now are loosely aligned in an effort to free Cambodia from the North Vietnamese, who are still supported by the Soviet Union to the extent of $1.5 to $2 billion per year. The U.S. Congress voted $5 million in 1986 to provide aid for Sihanouk's forces on the Thai-Vietnamese border. The Sihanouk and Pol Pot forces are still recognized by the United Nations as Democratic Kampuchea.

North Vietnam's revolutionary mystique has been badly tarnished and its international support has almost completely disappeared. After annexing South Vietnam, Cambodia and Laos in total violation of the Paris Accord, Hanoi scorned aid offered by the U.S. "to heal the wounds of war." The Democratic Republic of Vietnam today is an economic pariah amidst the booming economies of Southeast Asia. In desperation Hanoi now seeks normalization with the United States by trading on American concern for the 2,436 still missing and unaccounted for American servicemen and 40 civilians. The North Vietnamese periodically produce some remains of Americans in a ghoulish display. American efforts to systematically visit the sites where Americans may be buried have been subjected to political exploitation by the North Vietnamese.[8] The question of whether any Americans remain alive in North Vietnam is still unanswered.

The trauma of the Vietnam war has still to be assimilated into the American experience. Some may ask how President Thieu could believe in the promises of President Nixon and his successor when it was clear that Nixon had been discredited by Watergate and Congress had outlawed the resumption of bombing. It was clear that the American people wanted the Vietnam War to come to an end. Nixon, Kissinger and Haig continue to blame the Congress and Watergate for the failure of the United States to keep its promises to South Vietnam. They downplay the importance of the presidential letters to Thieu and argue that the promises in the letters were made in public statements, thus there was no need to share the letters with Cabinet members, Congressmen or the public.[9] As the record demonstrates, the letters were more detailed and specific in outlining the U.S. commitments to South Vietnam than any public statement made by President Nixon, Henry Kissinger or his other Cabinet members, who had no knowledge of the correspondence.[10] Kissinger, in his memoirs, quotes then Defense Secretary Elliot Richardson as threatening the possibility of resumption of bombing. Richardson was unaware of the letters to Thieu and was never told of them by Kissinger or Nixon. He defended the existing bombing of Cambodia and possible bombing elsewhere "to achieve a ceasefire" as part of the President's authority to end the war, not because of the secret commitments to Thieu. Richardson stayed well away from any public avowal of any commitment whatever to "full force" retaliation against renewed aggression.[11]

The body of letters constituted a consistently reiterated commitment from the elected leaders of the American people to the President of the Republic of Vietnam and was taken by Thieu as a pledge of honor. They constituted a set of promises made on behalf of the American government and people by two Presidents. The letters have never been disclosed in full, and the significance of their existence was minimized by Kissinger in the final days of the Vietnam War. The letters are not merely an abstract set of promises; they were instrumental tools of American diplomacy used to influence and force decisions, create actions and build expectations. As his Palace File, the letters formed the basis for Thieu's belief in the sanctity of American presidential commitments. The letters provide the complete

American strategy for negotiating with the North Vietnamese and with Thieu. As events unfolded, the letters took on greater importance to President Thieu and his associates because they were the one set of promises they had to cling to as a certainty of the American commitment. The failure to honor them constitutes the betrayal of an ally, unrivaled in American history.

The value of the currency of presidential letters has been debased by the breaking of the Nixon-Ford-Kissinger promises to Thieu. Only belatedly, in the final months of the war, do the last two letters of President Ford refer to the need for congressional approval. Never does Nixon speak to Thieu of the need for congressional approval. If the letters had been disclosed as part of the process of consultation with Congress, they could have helped to provide aid funds for South Vietnam back in 1973, when money and arms still mattered. Congress may not have favored the promises, but the substance of the letters would have been openly honored or rejected. After American troops were out of Vietnam and American prisoners returned, Congress and the American people did not want to hear of further obligations to Vietnam. The letters would have made clear the obligations still outstanding, made on behalf of the United States by its President.

If the letters had not been written, Thieu would have held out against signing the Paris Accord. Without the letters to sustain him it would have been apparent that the burden had shifted to Thieu to fend for himself. It would have been apparent to him and to the world that the United States had abandoned Thieu. The weight of the evidence shows that had the United States kept the promises made in writing to Thieu to convince him to sign the Paris Accords, the Republic of South Vietnam could have survived.

Defense Secretary James Schlesinger said that had the letters been made available to him from the time he took office in July 1973 he would have used them in his consultations with Congress on military aid for Vietnam, and would have pointed to the commitments they contained. "We didn't do that, which certainly caused us problems later on," said Schlesinger. "I remember how surprised I was when the letters surfaced, because I felt that they meant a welching by the United States on commitments that had been entered into by the President. However, if you don't know that the commitments have been entered into, you don't know that the country has welched." [12] Melvin Laird asked Kissinger why he was not shown the letters. Laird said Kissinger told him: "It was a deal between Haig and the President." [13]

The letters were never retracted or denied verbally or in writing to the South Vietnamese by any American official. When President Ford took office his first letter to Thieu confirmed his commitment to President Nixon's policies and promises. At every moment until the final two weeks, when Ambassador Graham Martin urged him to resign, President Thieu and his generals were reassured that although American aid would be difficult to obtain it would be forthcoming in the end.

The letters demonstrate the perils of secret diplomacy in an open society and the need for building a consensus on foreign policy. In the letters of The Palace File Nixon, and later Ford, also went counter to the national consensus to get out of Vietnam. Nixon and Kissinger believed for too long that they could control the negotiations with the North Vietnamese and win their compliance with the Paris Accords if they could bring Thieu along to make the necessary concessions. They thought they would be able to enforce the Accord with American air power, but Congress, unaware of Nixon's secret promises, overruled him in the summer of 1973. Nixon, Kissinger and Thieu knew that the Paris Accords was only a piece of paper without American will to enforce it. The American commitment in the letters to force adherence by military "full force" punishment of North Vietnam was the real Accord. This aspect of the letters was always hedged in public statements and never made explicit; nor was it explained privately to the leaders of Congress. Nixon and Kissinger argue that it was Watergate and the accompanying collapse of executive authority imposed by Congress that was responsible for the betrayal of Nixon's promises, reiterated by Ford. The cumulative secretive behavior pattern of Nixon and Kissinger, however, resulted in a loss of faith both in the war and their leadership. When the situation became extremely precarious, Kissinger tried to manipulate the South Vietnamese and the Congress. He hoped to redress the military imbalance he had helped to create by resuming the bombing of North Vietnamese troops infiltrating into the South; but it was too late. The war had been lost in the hearts and minds of most Americans; those who wanted to stand and fight or escalate were outnumbered. A legislated bombing halt and the War Powers Act became the bludgeons Congress used to prevent Nixon from exerting the executive power of the commander-in-chief. He was unable to resume the bombing of North Vietnam and thus had no weapon to force Hanoi to adhere to the cease-fire and the Paris Accords. Watergate, the internal American domestic crisis, emasculated the President's foreign policy powers. As the Watergate scandal grew, Nixon's powers were taken from him. McGeorge Bundy wrote: "What we are left with is contempt for the clear opinion of Congress, and ultimately contempt for democracy itself." [14] To use sustained force for more than a one-time police action the President must have strong public and Congressional support.

The legal status of the letters remains unresolved. Are they anything more than a statement of intentions by the President of the United States? Do they constitute a moral or "legal" commitment of action on behalf of the American government and people by the President? What is needed to enforce the commitments if, unlike a treaty, they are not known to or approved by the Senate? In April 1975 the late Senator Frank Church, co-author of the War Powers Act, said: "Nothing was said to us at that time about any private undertakings by the United States. I do not recall anyone advising the Committee that any understanding, written, tacit or otherwise had been made. We were left with a clear impression that nothing was being kept from us." Senator Jacob K. Javits, referring to the letters, said,

"Whatever you call these documents they should have been provided to the Senate Foreign Relations Committee along with all other materials relating to the Paris Accords." [15]

To the South Vietnamese the letters were a binding American commitment because they were repeated over the course of five years. Thieu often mentioned the continuity of American support for the Republic of Vietnam ever since the Eisenhower presidency in 1954. Nixon misled South Vietnam along the path of the negotiations ("The American people know that the United States cannot purchase peace or honor or redeem its sacrifices at the price of deserting a brave ally, This I cannot do and will never do." Richard Nixon, August 31, 1972). The letters misled Thieu about the goal of American policy in Vietnam, which Nixon said was "to maintain the survival of the Republic of Vietnam and its institutions." Congress was not informed of Kissinger's secret negotiations in Paris for nearly two years, until January 1972. Kissinger was supposed to represent the interests of South Vietnam in Paris. Although Kissinger made it appear that the North Vietnamese had made concessions, in fact it was the U.S. which totally backed down on all major issues. The most important concession was giving up the demand for mutual withdrawal of forces and accepting a cease-fire in place without proceeding further to a comprehensive settlement. The United States agreed to a total removal of American forces within a fixed period of time during which the permanent North Vietnamese presence in the South became legalized. As Kissinger's Vietnam expert John Negroponte put it after the Christmas bombing: "We bombed them into accepting our concessions." [16]

The two most basic promises to Thieu, given verbally and in writing, were flaunted. The United States did not replace equipment lost or destroyed in fighting against North Vietnamese violations of the Paris Accords, nor did it retaliate with "full force," a term used only in the private correspondence and not in public, when North Vietnam flagrantly and systematically violated the Paris Accords.

The failure of the United States to stand by its ally caused friends to become suspicious and adversaries to seek advantage. When Saigon's Foreign Minister Vuong Van Bac visited Saudi Arabia to ask for a loan, he explained to Sheik Yamani that American aid was not forthcoming as promised. Yamani asked him: "How can the president of a corporation sign a document and his successor say, 'I don't know anything about that?' " Clearly, American credibility was badly undercut.

During the nearly four years Kissinger negotiated for an agreement, the bloodshed mounted: 15,000 Americans were killed and 100,000 Americans wounded while hundreds of thousands of Vietnamese lives were lost. In the end he arrived at an agreement that was essentially the same as the one that the Communists presented to him in May 1969. The final indignity was the fixed timetable for American withdrawal within sixty days, a demand the Communists did not make in their original peace offer. Kissinger and Nixon made a fatal strategic error in the conception of their Vietnam strategy: they failed to understand the rigidity and uncompromising nature of North Vietnamese communism and its unwillingness to engage in any give and take on the key issues. By the time Kissinger realized this, two years had passed and he was trapped. The only way out was to force Saigon to make concessions he could not get from Hanoi. First he tried threats and ultimatums; when that failed he gave undeliverable promises to Thieu to get him to sign the Accords. When the bills came due on the flawed Agreement, he was in no position to back up his allies with firepower.

The technique of secret negotiations gave the North Vietnamese two very important advantages. The first was that through their secret contact with Kissinger and his team they could probe the American position and determine how far the Americans would go in the negotiations. Their demand for Thieu to step down was a straw man raised so it could be withdrawn as a concession during a critical stage of the negotiations. That is the way it was played in October 1972: they withdrew the demand that Thieu step down. By then it was irrelevant because a new general election, not for a president, but for a communist style Constituent Assembly would be held. The Americans would be gone and there would be 300,000 North Vietnamese troops in the South.

The second was that secret negotiations gave the North Vietnamese a powerful weapon to divide Saigon and Washington. Hanoi skillfully played on Saigon's suspicion of being sold out. They leaked to the Vietnamese community their negotiations with Kissinger and implied that Thieu was an American puppet. This undercut Thieu's political support and placed him in an inferior position, as a supplicant of the Americans. It gave the North Vietnamese a propaganda advantage by allowing them to point to the United States as "the aggressor." In retrospect Kissinger agreed that the United States should not have negotiated on behalf of South Vietnam. "He [Thieu] was right," said Kissinger, "but that was the way it was being done." Kissinger added: "That was probably a mistake. Although given our domestic situation that is easier said than done." [17]

The secret negotiations precluded the contribution of knowledge and expertise from anyone in the experienced bureaucracy; Kissinger and his inner team held control. The secret process also denied the building of a consensus which is the underlying strength and continuity of democracy. The Paris Accords, signed in January 1973, and the June Communiqué that followed was an executive agreement, not a treaty, as Kissinger suggests. There was no way to criticize or improve the results by submitting it to the Senate for approval. Kissinger and Nixon had acted alone; they never told the American public of their promises, spelled out in the letters, to resume hostilities to defend the Accords.

Kissinger said he preferred to defend Vietnam in the name of a peace agreement and not in the name of a continuing war." [18] The Paris Agreement, which made it appear that peace had come, turned out to be an excuse for Congress to cut aid. The argument was "the more guns the more fighting." Nixon notes that Congress did not refuse to grant aid money, even when it opposed the war, as long as Americans were in Vietnam and had to

be supported. When there were no American troops and no American prisoners in Vietnam, the rationale for American support vanished. Congress
dramatically halted aid and the war was lost. As General John Murray
explained:

> If you want to know about Vietnam, you have to know about war; if you want
> to know about war, you have to know a little bit about arithmetic. At the height
> of American power over there, we had 433 U.S. and allied and combat battal-
> ions; the enemy had 60 (larger) combat regiments. In 1974 when we had pulled
> out, the ARVN had 189 battalions, and the enemy had built up to 110 regiments.
> There was a 40 percent decrease in allied ground firepower. Take away the B-
> 52s, take away the F-4s and take away U.S. naval gunfire—take all that away.
> Then we started to support the South Vietnamese with two percent of the
> money that we had used to support our own U.S. force in Vietnam against a
> lesser enemy. You know what Napoleon said: "God is on the side of the biggest
> battalion . . ." And right about then, God was on the side of the Communists;
> they were bigger, they were stronger. That's why we lost the war.[19]

Former President Nixon notes that "Vietnam was a crucially important
victory in the Soviet Union's war for control of the strategically critical
third world. It was an important victory not so much because it gave the
Soviets dominance over Vietnam but because it left the United States so
crippled psychologically that it was unable to defend its interests in the
developing world, the battleground in the ongoing East-West conflict that is
best characterized as Third World War." As Nixon put it: "Our defeat in
Vietnam sparked a rash of totalitarian conquests around the world as we
retreated into a five year, self-imposed exile."[20]

The United States is still heavily burdened by Vietnam, and the "lessons of Vietnam" are still raised when military aid is requested from Congress for the contras to fight against the Sandanistas in Nicaragua, or to
support the "freedom fighters" in Angola and Afghanistan.

There is one lesson of the Vietnam War that remains unexplored. Contrary to the general belief that arms failed, the record proves that the use of
force can influence diplomatic negotiations. The mining of Haiphong and
Christmas bombing of 1972 forced the North Vietnamese back to the conference table. Had the United States applied similar pressure on North
Vietnam in 1969 it is likely that Hanoi would have been forced to accept
mutual withdrawal of forces from South Vietnam and Thieu would have had
a better chance to defend his country. Thieu never accepted the policy of
gradualism, limited bombing to encourage negotiations, as advocated by
McNamara and adopted by Lyndon Johnson. He expected that Nixon
would keep his word to use "full force" when Hanoi launched its invasion
of South Vietnam after the cease-fire. U.S. airpower could have forced
North Vietnam to withdraw its forces from the South as it did after the 1972
invasion.[21]

Nixon's opening to China was a master stroke, but it had unexpected
consequences. It neutralized the Chinese as an American enemy in the

Vietnam balance of forces, but it increased Soviet influence in Vietnam. After the rapprochement with China the United States wound down its commitment to the war and tried to replace it with negotiations. But the United States soon found itself caught in a contradictory and self-defeating policy of withdrawing and negotiating at the same time. This placed North Vietnam in the advantageous position of having only to wait until the Americans were gone. The North also had the psychological advantage of seeing fulfilled Ho Chi Minh's demand that the Americans must totally withdraw. This boosted their morale for the final thrust against the South and demoralized the Republic of Vietnam.

Thieu's perceptions of the power of American public opinion and the relationship between Congress and the Executive were faulty and primitive. South Vietnam did nothing effective to make its case in America. Thieu continued to rely on Nixon, believing that as in South Vietnam the President could control the public and manipulate it at will.

Internal divisiveness in the South and the lack of a unifying ideology, more than corruption, weakened South Vietnam. Thieu was able to build a government of men based on self-interest, but he was unable to rally his people without continued American support. Thieu had no place else to turn. The loss of American will for the war was instantly communicated to Saigon and added to the dry rot undermining Thieu.

Was there an alternative? If the United States had concentrated on Vietnamization while gradually withdrawing American troops without forcing an Agreement on Saigon, South Vietnam would have been in a stronger position to survive. In 1972 after the Easter invasion, South Vietnam was able to regain the territory it had lost with the help of American air power without American ground troops. The consequences of the Paris Agreement were fatal to South Vietnam. The Agreement legitimized the North Vietnamese position in the South and gave them a decisive strategic advantage. The leopard spots of scattered North Vietnamese troop positions made the country impossible to defend. At the same time the South Vietnamese were in the unenviable position of having to answer North Vietnamese and American congressional charges that they had violated the truce every time they fought the North Vietnamese in their midst. Once the North Vietnamese knew they had immunity from American bombing, they moved their entire army to fight in the South.

Had the secret promises been made public and been part of the public record they would have forced a consideration or a repudiation of the commitments. Either of these actions would have altered the final outcome. The signals Thieu received were false. For Thieu and the South Vietnamese, the real Agreement between the United States and Vietnam was not the Paris Accords, but the continued American support embodied in the presidential letters. Excessive secrecy precluded getting support from American lawmakers or the American people to fulfill the promises in the letters. Nixon's political impotency forced him to break his promises. Because of the continued secrecy that Kissinger maintained when President Ford took office, the

American people still did not know of the promises made in their behalf.
Ford, although inclined to support the struggle for survival being fought by
South Vietnam, realized that he faced an election in 1976 and could not
overcome the American people's antipathy to the war. The American consensus that emerged to end the war, with or without honor, was a tragedy
for South Vietnam; secrecy and deception compounded the shame. The
ultimate success of the American system is that it is based on the advice
and consent of the governed.

Epilogue

PRESIDENT NGUYEN VAN THIEU and Mrs. Thieu live quietly outside London. They have one maid but Mrs. Thieu does most of the cooking. Occasionally the Thieus visit their children in the United States. He is fit and in good health, but keeps a low profile. His first home in London was called "The White House," but he moved when journalists found out where he lived and began to request interviews. He maintains a very private existence around his family. Thieu's fellow general and close associate, Tran Van Don, explains that Vietnamese custom sanctions gift-giving, and over his ten years in power Thieu was able to accumulate, through his wife's jewelry collection, the funds to live on after Saigon fell. Thieu spends his time reading, gardening, and reflecting on his life in Vietnam and the future for his children in America. "I am responsible but not guilty," he told Hung in London in 1976 when he reflected on Vietnam.

Nguyen Tien Hung is a professor of economics at Howard University in Washington, D.C., and a consultant on Asian and African economic development. Hung and his wife Catherine were divorced in 1978 and he married Therese Duong.

Prime Minster Tran Thien Khiem lives in Arlington, Virginia, and still wears blue suits and blue shirts for good luck in his wife's business ventures. He maintains a quiet life style, but lives well and travels periodically to Hong Kong with his wife to visit their children.

General Ngo Quang Truong lives in Springfield, Virginia. He attended Northern Virginia Community College to learn computer programming and works as a systems analyst for the American Railroad Association.

General Cao Van Vien lives in Arlington, Virginia. In 1986 he was elected President of the League of Vietnamese Combat Forces in the United States. His wife runs a cleaning service for government and commercial buildings employing Vietnamese refugees.

Hoang Duc Nha worked for General Electric in New York until 1986 when he moved to Chicago to direct counter trade for a major American corporation.

Foreign Minister Tran Van Lam lives in Australia, where he was once Ambassador, plays golf and travels to the United States to visit his children.

Foreign Minister Vuong Van Bac lives in Paris and is a partner in Mudge Rose Guthrie Alexander & Ferdon, the law firm Richard Nixon was associated with before he became president in 1968.

General Tran Van Don tried unsuccessfully to enter the restaurant business in Washington, D.C. He is now a travel agent and is writing a book on Vietnam with his cousin, General Le Van Kim, who was released after seven years in a North Vietnamese reeducation camp.

Ambassador Ellsworth Bunker died in 1985 and his papers are being collected for publication under the direction of his wife, Carol Laise.

Ambassador Graham Martin retired from the Foreign Service in 1976 and lives in Winston-Salem, North Carolina, where he watches his granddaughters grow, and lays bricks for a backyard patio.

General John Murray retired from the U.S. Army in 1974 and is Special Counsel to American International Underwriters. In 1986 he served on a Pentagon task force to study Americans missing in action in Vietnam and evaluate reports that there are still Americans alive in Vietnam in captivity or being held against their will. He is also a member of a White House Task Force to study the effects of Herbicide Orange on Americans and Vietnamese.

Richard Armitage is Assistant Secretary of Defense for International Security Affairs and is responsible for the MIA negotiations with North Vietnam.

Warren Nutter died of cancer in 1979. The American Enterprise Institute honors his memory with the Nutter Memorial Lectures.

Eric Von Marbod was sent to Iran to oversee American arms sales programs for the Pentagon from 1975 to 1977. He retired from the Pentagon in 1982 and is based in Europe as vice president for an American defense contractor.

General Fred Weyand retired from the U.S. Army in 1976 and lives in Honolulu, Hawaii, where he is on the board of the First Hawaiian Bank and is a trustee of the S. M. Damon estate.

Henry Kissinger is the Chairman and sole owner of Kissinger Associates in New York City, a consulting firm that offers geopolitical economic advice, introductions and international planning to its clients. In January 1980, after reading an interview Thieu gave to the German news magazine *Der Spiegel,* Kissinger wrote to him. The letter, which Thieu made available, was not answered.

Dear Mr. President:

I have just read the interview you gave to *Der Spiegel.* I can understand your bitterness, and indeed sympathize with it. But it is also clear to me that the *Spiegel* interviewers made every effort to create the impression that my book is an attack on you, which is the opposite of the truth.

My book praises you repeatedly for your courage and decency and acknowledges, in essence, that you were right. I am having my British publisher send you a copy of my book so that you may read my account in its entirety. In the meantime, I enclose some of the excerpts that make this clear.

My book attempts to tell, as honestly as I can, the story of the events as they appeared to me. I continue to believe that the balance of forces reflected in the Paris Agreement could have been maintained if Watergate had not destroyed our ability to obtain sufficient aid for South Vietnam from the Congress in 1973 and 1974. Had we known in 1972 what was to come in America, we would not have proceeded as we did. (On the other hand, the effect of Watergate would have been equally, if not more, catastrophic if the war had been continuing and there had been no Paris Agreement.)

I agree with you that the cease-fire terms were harsh. Our tragic dilemma in 1972 was that we had reached the limit of our domestic possibilities. Had we attempted to continue the war, the Congress would have imposed in 1973 what was done later in 1975. If it had been President Nixon's and my intention to betray you, we could have done it in 1969.

You and I had many disagreements, but only over tactics. In view of the outcome, your anger is understandable. However, it would be a pity if those who long advocated our abandonment of South Vietnam were now able to use your bitterness as another weapon against those who tried to save South Vietnam. Ironically, I am under vicious attack these days for my efforts to defend Cambodia in order to ensure the survival of your country.

I do not expect to convince you. I can at least try to assure you of my continuing regret, and respect.

Best Regards,
[s] Henry A. Kissinger

His Excellency
Nguyen Van Thieu
London

Appendix A
Letters, Messages and Proposals of Nixon, Ford, and Thieu

THE PALACE FILE of letters, messages and proposals exchanged among President Richard M. Nixon, President Gerald R. Ford and President Nguyen Van Thieu from December 31, 1971 to March 22, 1975 was maintained by Thieu in his bedroom in the Independence Palace. The file is reproduced as Nguyen Tien Hung carried it from Saigon in 1975. There are 31 numbered letters from President Nixon to Thieu, in which four are duplicates, being the cabled copy of the letter delivered by the American Ambassador to Saigon before the actual letter arrived in the diplomatic pouch. Thieu filed them together but numbered them separately. The duplicate letters are Numbers 4 and 5, dated April 6, 1972; Numbers 10 and 11, dated October 30, 1972; Numbers 13 and 14, dated November 15, 1972, and Numbers 15 and 16, dated November 19, 1972. All are included, since they contain Thieu's handwritten notes and comments. There are four letters numbered 32 through 35 from President Ford to President Thieu. They are also numbered 1 through 4. Also included in the file are five messages addressed to President Thieu and Foreign Minister Tran Van Lam transmitting messages from Nixon and Kissinger on the Paris Accords. There is one letter from Thieu to Nixon in the file dated April 7, 1972. There are two letters known to be missing from the file, since they were not included by Thieu. They are President Nixon's December 17, 1972 and January 14, 1973 letters to Thieu. The letters are referred to by Nixon in his memoirs on page 737 and page 749.

Hung did not imagine he would need copies of President Thieu's letters to Nixon and Ford in his final appeal to the Congress, so he left them behind in the Palace, where they were captured by the North Vietnamese. Some of the letters have been released by them, but Appendix A constitutes the full file Thieu personally guarded and entrusted to Hung.

All the handwritten notes and marks were Thieu's; most of them do not require explanation or annotation. For those that do, explanatory comment is provided with the letter. The quality of the copies that were made by Hung in the Palace is very poor, but they have been reproduced as they are, rather than being reset, in order to preserve the handwritten comments and signatures, and to assure their authenticity.

THE WHITE HOUSE
WASHINGTON

December 31, 1971

Dear Mr. President:

As I prepare for my forthcoming trip to Peking to meet and talk with the leaders of the People's Republic of China, I would like to share with you some thoughts concerning the conversations I expect to have there.

The main purpose of these conversations will be to clarify the positions of our Government and of the Chinese Government on the issues that separate us, and to establish a means for continuing communications. The differences between us are deep and complex and they will not yield to easy solutions. I hope, however, that the conversations in Peking will be a first major step toward easing the long-standing tensions between the People's Republic of China and the United States, a development which would bring lasting benefits for all of Asia and for all the world.

The talks in Peking will focus on bilateral questions between the Chinese and ourselves, of which there are many. Given our differences, the question of formal diplomatic relations will not arise. You may be abso-lutely certain that I will make no agreements in Peking at the expense of other countries or on matters which concern other countries. You should also know that the treaty commitments which the United States has established with other countries will not be affected by my visit to Peking.

Should the question of the Vietnam war arise in Peking, I want to assure you that I will set forth clearly and forcefully the position of the United States and the Republic of Vietnam that the war in Vietnam must be ended through direct negotiations with Hanoi, or, failing that, by the growing ability of the Republic of Vietnam to defend itself against Hanoi's aggression.

- 2 -

I want the Chinese leaders to understand clearly that our two governments stand firmly together on this vital issue.

With respect to my visit to Moscow in May 1972, I wish to make it clear that the United States has no intention of deal-ing over the heads of its friends and allies in any matter where their security interests might be involved. For example, there have been no, and there will be no, bilateral United States-Soviet negotiations on mutual withdrawal of forces from Europe. I hope, however, that some concrete progress might be made, either before or during my Moscow visit, in such bilateral areas as arms control and economic relations.

Please accept my best wishes for the continued success of your economic and military programs as you embark on your second term in office. You can continue to rely on the assistance of the United States in your efforts to bring peace to Vietnam and to build a new prosperity for the Vietnamese people.

Sincerely,

Richard Nixon

His Excellency
Nguyen Van Thieu
President of the Republic of Vietnam
Saigon

Letter 1.   Nixon to Thieu, December 31, 1971 (2 pages).

②

THE WHITE HOUSE
WASHINGTON

March 5, 1972

Dear Mr. President:

Thank you very much for your recent letter which I received shortly before setting out on my trip to China.

I surely agree with your comment that your recent offer to step down from the Presidency prior to a new presidential election which was part of our side's eight-point proposal is an earnest of your desire for peace and that of your government. It was a generous and a statesmanlike offer which can only be regarded as a major move in the search for peace in Indochina. You also comment that, whether or not there can be a signed peace agreement with Hanoi, the ability of the Republic of Vietnam to defend itself is the key to a lasting peace in the area. I want to assure you that I hold the same view.

As you note, the Communist side in Indochina may regard any solution short of their total domination of Indochina as only a strategic pause. This is a possibility against which we must indeed be on guard. In the February 27 communique released in Shanghai, I defined the United States objective in Asia and the world as a peace which is both just and secure -- just to fulfill the aspirations of peoples and

-2-

nations for freedom and progress, and secure to remove the danger of foreign aggression. It is for such a just and secure peace that our two countries have been fighting. You may be certain that I will do all in my power to insure that the enormous sacrifices of the Vietnamese and American peoples do not come to nothing.

My talks with the leaders of the People's Republic of China in Peking were highly useful. Our lengthy and searching discussions concentrated on bilateral issues between the United States and the People's Republic. They removed some misunderstandings between us and launched what I hope will be a continuing dialogue to remove further misunderstandings. Our meetings were marked by honesty, candor, and directness, and there was no attempt to pretend that major differences do not exist. We negotiated nothing behind the backs of friends of the United States; there were no secret deals. In talking with the Chinese we based our position firmly on the principle that the United States stands by its commitments. When our talks touched on Indochina, I set forth the United States position clearly and forcefully, as reflected in the February 27 communique. The Chinese could not have mistaken either our sincere desire for peace or our dedication to the principle of self-determination for the people of South Vietnam.

I have asked Assistant Secretary of State Green, who bears this letter, to inform you more fully of what transpired during my visit to China. He also carries with him my very best wishes for your continuing success in surmounting the.

Letter 2.   Nixon to Thieu, March 5, 1972 (3 pages).

-3-

grave problems that still beset the people and Government of the Republic of Vietnam. You may be confident that you will continue to have the understanding, support, and material assistance of the United States as the people of South Vietnam work to attain security against aggression and to build a just and enduring peace.

Sincerely,

Richard Nixon

His Excellency
Nguyen Van Thieu
President of the Republic
   of Vietnam
Saigon

THE WHITE HOUSE
WASHINGTON

April 5, 1972

Dear President Thieu:

I want you to know that in this moment of great trial for
the Vietnamese people, you have my fullest support as
President of the United States and Commander-in-Chief
of our armed forces.

Hanoi's invasion across the provisional demarcation line
of 1954 is a flagrant and outrageous violation of both the
Geneva Accords of 1954 and the 1968 understandings which
led to the cessation of bombardments and all other acts
involving the use of force by the United States against
North Vietnam.

You can be sure that the United States stands fully behind
the heroic efforts of your people in the defense of their
homeland. I can assure you that in the days and weeks
ahead we will not hesitate to take whatever added military
steps are necessary to support the intense and valiant
struggle in which your country is now engaged. We cannot
allow Hanoi's intensified and blatant aggression to go
unpunished.

Allow me to take this opportunity to express my continuing
and profound admiration for the leadership you are providing
your people in these moments of difficulty and the bravery
they have shown in resisting Hanoi's attacks. I am

-2-

confident that with our assistance you will succeed in overcoming the present threat posed by Hanoi's forces to your
people and that ultimately we will achieve our mutual goal
of a just and lasting peace.

Sincerely,

Richard Nixon

His Excellency
Nguyen Van Thieu
President of the Republic
of Vietnam

Letter 3.   Nixon to Thieu, April 5, 1972 (2 pages).

SECRET

Saigon, Viet-Nam
April 6, 1972

Dear President Thieu:

President Nixon has asked me to transmit to you the following message.

"Dear President Thieu:

I want you to know that in this moment of great trial for the Vietnamese people, you have my fullest support as President of the United States and Commander-in-Chief of our Armed Forces.

Hanoi's invasion across the provisional demarcation line of 1954 is a flagrant and outrageous violation of both the Geneva Accords of 1954 and the 1968 understandings which led to the cessation of bombardments and all other acts involving the use of force by the United States against North Viet-Nam.

You can be sure that the United States stands fully behind the heroic efforts of your people in the defense of their homeland. I can assure you that in the days and weeks ahead we will not hesitate to take whatever added military steps are necessary to support the intense and valiant struggle in which your country is now engaged. We cannot allow Hanoi's intensified and blatant aggression to go unpunished.

Allow me to take this opportunity to express my continuing and profound admiration for the leadership you are providing your people in these moments of difficulty

His Excellency Nguyen Van Thieu
President of the Republic of Viet-Nam
Saigon, Viet-Nam

SECRET

SECRET

-2-

and the bravery they have shown in resisting Hanoi's attacks. I am confident that with our assistance you will succeed in overcoming the present threat posed by Hanoi's forces to your people and that ultimately we will achieve our mutual goal of a just and lasting peace.

Sincerely,

Richard M. Nixon"

With renewed assurances of my highest consideration,

Sincerely,

Ellsworth Bunker
American Ambassador

SECRET

Letter 4.   Nixon to Thieu, April 6, 1972 (2 pages).

April 7, 1972.

NGUYEN VAN THIEU
President of the Republic of Viet-Nam

Dear Mr. President,

I have received your message of April 6, transmitted to me by Ambassador Bunker, and I am very grateful for your prompt response and the assurances of fullest support which, as President of the United States and Commander-in-Chief of the United States Armed Forces, you gave to me at this critical time when the Republic of Viet Nam faces Hanoi's crude invasion.

As Hanoi unabashedly violates the 1954 Geneva Accords and the 1968 tacit agreements which led to the cessation of bombardments of North Viet Nam, it is comforting for us to know that the United States will not hesitate to take whatever added military steps are necessary to support our struggle, and that Hanoi's intensified and blatant aggression cannot be allowed to go unpunished.

Ambassador Bunker and General Abrams have kept me informed on the strategic and tactical measures which have been adopted, as well as others which will be undertaken, relating to the increased participation of the United States Air Force and Navy, in order to stop the Communist aggressors, and to punish them above the demarcation line they have outrageously violated.

It seems to me that the current offensive is the beginning of a supreme effort made by Hanoi before it would decide either to accept a negotiated settlement or to fade away. Therefore it is likely to last throughout this year, which is the electoral year in the United States. It will probably increase in tempo and spread to other Military Regions, aside from Military Region I which is now under very heavy attacks by enemy forces equivalent in strength to five Divisions, using very sophisticated modern weapons including long range artillery, surface to air missiles, tanks, and possibly also MIG planes at a later stage,

2

The Vietnamese Armed Forces and the Vietnamese people are doing their best to repel the aggressors. We have the necessary manpower and the determination to defend our freedom. However, in view of the sophisticated armaments of the Communist aggressors, and of the importance of this supreme test, we greatly need increased and accelerated help from the United States in the modernization and strengthening of the Armed Forces of the Republic of Viet Nam in particular of the Vietnamese Air Force.

I am convinced that, with United States help, we shall successfully meet this great challenge, in a crucial year, to bring about peace in freedom after so many years of arduous struggle and so many common sacrifices made by our two nations in opposing Communist aggression.

To bring about this happy result, I feel that it is most necessary for us to receive full and timely assistance from the United States, for which we are deeply grateful.

Sincerely,

His Excellency Richard M. NIXON
President of the United States of America
The White House, Washington D.C.

This message (*left*) was delivered by Ambassador Ellsworth Bunker. At the bottom, in a longhand that has not survived reproduction, Thieu wrote his instructions to convene a meeting of his National Security Council on May 4, 1972 to discuss the issues of separating political and military issues, North Vietnamese insistence on final withdrawal of the U.S. and "the overthrow of the present regime."

⑤

Message to President Thieu from President Nixon

President Nixon has asked me to convey the following message to you:

At this trying time for you and your brave forces, you can be assured of our continued support for the people of South Viet-Nam in the courageous defense of their homeland. What will ultimately determine the outcome of this struggle is the will and spirit of the South Vietnamese people. Hanoi cannot win unless they break the spirit of the free people of South Viet-Nam.

I am confident that you will continue to provide the inspired leadership which will guarantee the survival of South Viet-Nam as an independent country.

May 3, 1972.

Letter 5.   Nixon to Thieu, May 3, 1972.

Saigon, Viet-Nam
May 9, 1972

Dear Mr. President:

President Nixon has asked me to convey to you the following message.

"Dear Mr. President:

Faced with Hanoi's repeatedly demonstrated intransigence at the conference table and continuing North Vietnamese invasion of your country, I intend to make a speech at 9:00 p.m. Washington time, to announce a new course of action designed to bring this war to an end.

In my speech, I propose to announce that our two governments have decided that North Vietnamese aggression must be met by action to interdict the delivery of supplies to North Viet-Nam. I will announce that I have ordered the mining of the entrances to North Vietnamese ports and have directed U.S. forces to prevent the seaborne delivery of supplies to North Viet-Nam within its claimed territorial waters. Rail and other transportation means will also be interdicted.

All foreign ships in North Vietnamese ports will have three day light periods to leave in safety. Ships staying longer or approaching these ports will be doing so at their own risk.

The foregoing actions will continue until the following conditions are met; the implementation of an internationally supervised cease-fire throughout Indochina and the release of prisoners of war.

In my speech I will state that when the foregoing conditions have been met, we, will stop all acts of force throughout

His Excellency Nguyen Van Thieu
President of the Republic of Viet-Nam
Saigon, Viet-Nam

-2-

Indo-China and U.S. forces will be withdrawn from South Viet-Nam within four months.

As we are both aware, Mr. President, neither your country nor mine has ever sought to impose a military defeat on Hanoi. We have always sought to end the conflict through negotiations in a way which would leave the people of South Viet-Nam the opportunity to decide their own future free from outside coercion or interference. In taking the steps I am announcing tonight, a negotiated settlement remains our preferred course; but Hanoi has posed us with absolutely unacceptable preconditions and their military challenge to you and your allies leaves no choice but to respond in the fashion we are.

I am fully confident that the measures I am announcing tonight will be welcomed by your people and Armed Forces as an earnest of our determination to help them defend themselves and as an opportunity to turn back decisively the invasion launched by Hanoi's forces on March 30. It is important that these measures in defense of your country be seen as having been taken in consultation with you and in conjunction with your own efforts of self-defense. I am sure, therefore, that you will agree with my intention to associate your government with the measures I propose to announce.

Permit me to say, however, in the spirit of friendship and frankness that has always characterized our relationship, it is my view that in the last analysis U.S. air and seapower are only contributing and not decisive factors in the battle now raging in your country. The decisive element will be the performance of the people and armed forces of the Republic of Viet-Nam in resisting the challenge they now face.

I, therefore, want to take this occasion to urge that you and your people use the opportunity offered by the steps I am announcing tonight to redouble your efforts against the North Vietnamese invaders, to regain the initiative against their

Letter 6.   Nixon to Thieu, May 9, 1972 (3 pages).

-3-

irregular forces and to recover population and territory which has been temporarily lost to their control. It will be hard to explain to the United States people, after I have taken these steps, if the RVNAF does not perform _more aggressively and the people of South Viet-Nam are not mobilized for the emergency.

We will be watching developments on the ground in South Viet-Nam in the days and weeks ahead with the deepest interest and concern and I am confident that under your determined leadership the heroic people of your country will prevail over Hanoi's aggression.

With warmest personal regards,

Sincerely,

Richard Nixon"

With renewed assurances of my highest consideration,

Sincerely,

Ellsworth Bunker
American Ambassador

THE WHITE HOUSE
WASHINGTON

August 31, 1972

Dear Mr. President:

I was most pleased to receive from Ambassador Bunker in Hawaii a full and current report on your views with respect to the ongoing peace negotiations, on which our two governments have recently had a number of detailed exchanges. On the basis of the Ambassador's report, we have made a number of adjustments in our substantive and procedural proposals, which the Ambassador will be able to discuss with you. I believe our new drafts represent a constructive peace proposal reflecting our mutual interest in an honorable peace settlement which insures the South Vietnamese people the right to determine their future without an imposed solution or outside interference. The Ambassador will give you our thinking in detail. You can be certain that he speaks for me.

At this delicate moment in the negotiations, let me assure you once again, personally and emphatically, of the bedrock of the U.S. position: The United States has not persevered all this way, at the sacrifice of many American lives, to reverse course in the last few months of 1972. We will not do now what we have refused to do in the preceding three and a half years. The American people know that the United States cannot purchase peace or honor or redeem its sacrifices at the price of deserting a brave ally. This I cannot do and will never do.

Our essential task now is to work closely together, on the basis of complete frankness and trust, as we have done so successfully throughout these years. Our objective is a common and mutual one. I have instructed Ambassador Bunker to maintain the closest contact with you, to insure meticulous and thorough consultation with you at every stage.

- 2 -

I believe our new proposals reflect unmistakeably that we have offered every legitimate concession for a fair political process. If the other side rejects these proposals, it will be proven to even the most skeptical that the obstacle to a settlement is not one leader, but their insistence on being handed at the conference table what they can win neither at the ballot box nor on the battlefield. If they accept our proposal they must accept your Government as a negotiating partner, and you will be fully protected by being present in each forum.

Finally, Mr. President, I want to express to you again the American people's admiration for the courage and performance of the people and armed forces of South Vietnam in their successful defense against the North Vietnamese invasion, and for your sterling leadership. The courage and unity of your people is the ultimate guarantee of their freedom. But for us to succeed on this last leg of a long journey, we must trust each other fully. We must not hand the enemy through our discord what we have prevented through our unity.

With my best personal regards.

Sincerely,

His Excellency
Nguyen Van Thieu
President of the Republic
of Vietnam
Saigon

Letter 7.   Nixon to Thieu, August 31, 1972 (2 pages).

TOP SECRET/SENSITIVE

Saigon, Viet-Nam
October 6, 1972

Dear Mr. President:

I have received a message from President Nixon which he has asked me to convey personally to you.

Personal Message From
President Nixon to President Thieu

I have discussed with General Haig the outcome of his meetings with you and your associates in Saigon. There is no doubt that there are serious disagreements between us, but it should be clearly understood that these disagreements are tactical in character and involve no basic difference as to the objectives we both seek -- the preservation of a non-communist structure in South Viet-Nam which we have so patiently built together and which your heroic leadership has preserved against the most difficult of trials. Therefore, I give you my firm assurance that there will be no settlement arrived at, the provisions of which have not been discussed personally with you well beforehand. This applies specifically to the next round of talks in Paris. In these talks, Dr. Kissinger will explore what concrete security guarantees the other side is willing to give us as the basis for further discussions on the political point which might be undertaken following consultations with you. In this context, I would urge you to take every measure to avoid the development of an atmosphere which could lead to events similar to those which we abhorred in 1963 and which I personally opposed so vehemently in 1968. For this same reason, I would hope that you would also avoid taking precautionary measures against

His Excellency Nguyen Van Thieu
President of the Republic of Viet-Nam
Saigon, Viet-Nam

TOP SECRET/SENSITIVE

TOP SECRET/SENSITIVE   2

developments arising from these talks which, I assure you, would never arise without full, timely and complete consultation between us.

At the same time, however, we cannot be sure at any point in the process that the enemy will not for propaganda or other reasons make public the details of the secret talks. U. S. tactics thus far have been designed to take account of this contingency. General Haig informed me that you would be writing to me in the near future. I look forward to receiving this communication and hope that you will have had an opportunity to consider the foregoing before completing that message.

President Richard M. Nixon

With renewed assurances of my highest consideration,

Sincerely,

Ellsworth Bunker
American Ambassador

TOP SECRET/SENSITIVE

Letter 8.   Nixon to Thieu, October 6, 1972 (2 pages).

THE WHITE HOUSE
WASHINGTON

October 16, 1972

Dear President Thieu:

I have asked Dr. Henry Kissinger to convey to you this personal letter regarding our current negotiations with North Vietnam which now appear to be reaching a final stage.

As you know, throughout the four years of my Administration the United States has stood firmly behind your Government and its people in our support for their valiant struggle to resist aggression and preserve their right to determine their own political future.

The military measures we have taken and the Vietnamization program, the dramatic steps that we took in 1970 against the Cambodian sanctuaries, the operations in Laos in 1971 and the measures against North Vietnam just this past May have fully attested to the steadfastness of our support. I need not emphasize that many of these measures were as unpopular to many in the U.S. as they were necessary.

At the negotiating table we have always held firmly to the principle that we would never negotiate with North Vietnam a solution which predetermined the political outcome of the conflict. We have consistently adhered to positions that would preserve the elected government and assure the free people of Vietnam the opportunity to determine their future.

Until very recently the North Vietnamese negotiators have held firmly to their long-established position that any settlement of the war would have to include your resignation and the dismantlement of the Government of the Republic of Vietnam and its institutions.

2

It now seems, however, that the combination of the perseverance and heroism of your Government and its fighting forces, the measures taken by the United States on the 8th of May, 1972, and our firmness at the conference table have caused a fundamental shift in Hanoi. In the course of Dr. Kissinger's recent meetings with the North Vietnamese negotiators in Paris, it has become progressively more evident that Hanoi's leadership is prepared to agree to a ceasefire prior to the resolution of the political problem in South Vietnam. This is indeed an important reverse in doctrine and must represent a decision for them which cannot have been taken lightly. They know the weakness of their own political forces in the South and therefore the risks involved in reaching an agreement that does not meet their political objectives must indeed for them be great.

The consequence of this change in strategy has resulted in a situation wherein we and Hanoi's negotiators have reached essential agreement on a text which provides for a cessation of hostilities, the withdrawal of remaining allied forces, the exchange of prisoners of war, and the continued existence of your Government and its institutions after the ceasefire takes effect. In addition to the document itself a number of private assurances have been obtained designed to meet the security concerns of your country and whose implementation we consider an essential part of this agreement.

Dr. Kissinger will explain to you in the fullest detail the provisions of the proposed agreement which he carries with him and I will therefore not provide further elaboration in this message. I do, however, want you to know that I believe we have no reasonable alternative but to accept this agreement. It represents major movement by the other side, and it is my firm conviction that its implementation will leave you and your people with the ability to defend yourselves and decide the political destiny of South Vietnam.

As far as I am concerned, the most important provision of this agreement, aside from its military features, is that your Government, its armed forces and its political institutions, will remain intact after the ceasefire has been observed. In the period

Letter 9.   Nixon to Thieu, October 16, 1972 (3 pages).

At the bottom of this letter (*left*), Nixon wrote: "Dr. Kissinger, General Haig and I have discussed this proposal at great length. I am personally convinced it is the best we will be able to get and that it meets my *absolute* condition that the GVN must survive as a free country. Dr. Kissinger's comments have my total backing. RN"

3

following the cessation of hostilities you can be completely assured that we will continue to provide your Government with the fullest support, including continued economic aid and whatever military assistance is consistent with the ceasefire provisions of this government.

I recognize that after all these years of war a settlement will present an enormous challenge to your leadership and your people. We all recognize that the conflict will now move into a different form, a form of political struggle as opposed to open military confrontation; but I am of the firm conviction that with wisdom and perseverance your Government and the people of South Vietnam will meet this new challenge. You will have my absolute support in this endeavor and I want you to know it is my firm belief that in this new phase your continued leadership of the destiny of South Vietnam is indispensable.

Finally, I must say that, just as we have taken risks in war, I believe we must take risks for peace. Our intention is to abide faithfully by the terms of the agreements and understandings reached with Hanoi, and I know this will be the attitude of your government as well. We expect reciprocity and have made this unmistakably clear both to them and their major allies. I can assure you that we will view any breach of faith on their part with the utmost gravity; and it would have the most serious consequences.

Allow me to take this occasion to renew my sentiments of highest personal regard and admiration for you and your comrades in arms.

Sincerely,

Richard Nixon

His Excellency
Nguyen Van Thieu
President of the
Republic of Vietnam
Saigon

THE WHITE HOUSE
WASHINGTON

October 29, 1972

Dear Mr. President:

I have just completed a careful reading of the October 28, 1972 memorandum entitled "Memorandum Re: Radio Hanoi's Broadcast on October 26, 1972 and Dr. Kissinger's Press Briefing on October 26, 1972." As I have informed you, Dr. Kissinger has spoken and continues to speak on my behalf. There has not been nor will there be any distinction between his views and mine. As I wrote to you in my letter of October 16, "Dr. Kissinger's comments have my total backing."

With specific reference to the points raised in this memorandum, we are astonished to be asked to comment on claims emanating from Radio Hanoi. Dr. Kissinger gave a full and detailed explanation of the ad referendum character of his discussions with the representatives of the Democratic Republic of Vietnam. Therefore, the Government of South Vietnam should not ask itself why theoretical planning dates were given to the DRV; it is patently obvious that they were ad referendum since none of these dates have been carried out.

With respect to your concerns about my messages of October 20 and October 22 to the Prime Minister of the Democratic Republic of Vietnam, you will recall that Dr. Kissinger specifically referred to the content of these messages during his discussions with you in Saigon. These messages essentially concerned three matters concerning South Vietnam and two matters concerning Laos and Cambodia. With respect to South Vietnam, we informed Hanoi that we rejected any claim regarding your resignation and insisted on the replacement and prisoner provisions which you have seen. With respect to Laos and Cambodia, we demanded assurances with

2

respect to ending the conflict in these countries. Dr. Kissinger, in the presence of Ambassador Bunker, told you that in their replies the North Vietnamese yielded on all these points. I consider that you were fully informed.

Concerning the current status of the draft agreement, Dr. Kissinger has made a solemn commitment to you to obtain the maximum number of changes reflecting the views expressed to him during his visit to Saigon. With respect to the inclusion of reference to the "three" countries of Indochina, Dr. Kissinger explained to you that the use of "three" was simply inadvertent and we would demand of the North Vietnamese to have it deleted from the present text.

With respect to the National Council, Dr. Kissinger made amply clear in his press conference, as he did in his talks with you, that it has no governmental functions. All American and foreign observers have seen its real meaning -- a face-saving device for the communists to cover their collapse on their demands for a coalition government and your resignation. It is therefore incomprehensible to me why your government has chosen to portray the Council as a structure which encompasses governmental functions. This constant reiteration by your officials of misleading comments may bring about what we have struggled so hard to avoid.

Our position continues to be that we can live with an "administrative structure" which in English clearly implies advisory functions and not governmental ones, but that we reject the North Vietnamese translation which would imply that the structure is endowed with governmental powers and functions. This is precisely what Dr. Kissinger meant when he referred to language problems in his press conference. This is what we will clarify when we meet the North Vietnamese next. We chose the phrase linguistic ambiguity to give everybody a face-saving way out. You and I know what is involved.

Dr. Kissinger's press conference was conducted on my detailed instructions. He was doing his utmost to prevent you from being portrayed as the obstacle to peace with an inevitable cutoff by Congress of U.S. funds to the Government of South Vietnam and the creation of unmanageable impediments to continued U.S. support for you and your Government. Constant criticism from Saigon can only undercut this effort. We will continue our efforts to present a united front, but they cannot succeed without the cooperation of your associates.

Beyond these specific points I cannot fail to call to your attention the dangerous course which your Government is now pursuing. You know my firm commitment to the people of South Vietnam and to you personally. As Dr. Kissinger and Ambassador Bunker have informed you, I would like to underline this commitment by meeting with you, within one or two weeks after the signing of this agreement. It is my conviction that the future depends on the unity which exists between us and on the degree to which we can make clear our unequivocal support to do what is necessary in the days ahead to insure that the provisions of a peace settlement are strictly enforced. Just as our unity has been the essential aspect of the success we have enjoyed thus far in the conduct of hostilities, it will also be the best guarantee of future success in a situation where the struggle continues within a more political framework. If the evident drift towards disagreement between the two of us continues, however, the essential base for U.S. support for you and your Government will be destroyed. In this respect the comments of your Foreign Minister that the U.S. is negotiating a surrender are as damaging as they are unfair and improper.

You can be assured that my decisions as to the final character of a peace settlement are in no way influenced by the election in the United States, and you should harbor no illusions that my policy with respect to the desirability of achieving an early peace will change after the election. I have taken this opportunity to comment on the memorandum of October 28 so that there can be no doubts in Saigon with respect to the objectives sought by me and my Government.

I urge you again, Mr. President, to maintain the essential unity which has characterized our relations over these past

difficult four years and which has proven to be the essential ingredient in the success we have achieved thus far. Disunity will strip me of the ability to maintain the essential base of support which your Government and your people must have in the days ahead, and which I am determined to provide. Willingness to cooperate will mean that we will achieve peace on the basis of what I consider to be a workable agreement -- especially with the amendments which we are certain to obtain. From this basis, we can move with confidence and unity to achieve our mutual objectives of peace and unity for the heroic people of South Vietnam.

Sincerely,

Richard Nixon

His Excellency
Nguyen Van Thieu
President of the Republic
of Vietnam
Saigon

TOP SECRET/SENSITIVE

Saigon, Viet-Nam
October 30, 1972

Given by Bunker
on 10-18 @ 7:14

Dear Mr. President:

I have received the following message from President Nixon which he has asked me to transmit to you.

"Dear Mr. President:

I have just completed a careful reading of the October 28, 1972 Memorandum entitled "Memorandum Re: Radio Hanoi's Broadcast on October 26, 1972 and Dr. Kissinger's Press Briefing on October 26, 1972." As I have informed you, Dr. Kissinger has spoken and continues to speak on my behalf. There has not been nor will there be any distinction between his views and mine. As I wrote to you in my letter of October 16, "Dr. Kissinger's comments have my total backing."

With specific reference to the points raised in this Memorandum, we are astonished to be asked to comment on claims emanating from Radio Hanoi. Dr. Kissinger gave a full and detailed explanation of the ad referendum character of his discussions with the representatives of the Democratic Republic of Viet-Nam. Therefore, the Government of South Viet-Nam should not ask itself why theoretical planning dates were given to the DRV; it is patently obvious that they were ad referendum since none of these dates have been carried out.

With respect to your concerns about my messages of October 20 and October 22 to the Prime Minister of the Democratic Republic of Viet-Nam, you will recall that Dr. Kissinger specifically referred to the content of these messages during his discussions

His Excellency Nguyen Van Thieu
President of the Republic of Viet-Nam
Saigon, Viet-Nam

TOP SECRET/SENSITIVE

TOP SECRET/SENSITIVE

2

with you in Saigon. These messages essentially concerned three matters concerning South Viet-Nam and two matters concerning Laos and Cambodia. With respect to South Viet-Nam, we informed Hanoi that we rejected any claim regarding your resignation and insisted on the replacement and prisoner provisions which you have seen. With respect to Laos and Cambodia, we demanded assurances with respect to ending the conflict in these countries. Dr. Kissinger, in the presence of Ambassador Bunker, told you that in their replies the North Vietnamese yielded on all these points. I consider that you were fully informed.

Concerning the current status of the draft agreement, Dr. Kissinger has made a solemn commitment to you to obtain the maximum number of changes reflecting the views expressed to him during his visit to Saigon. With respect to the inclusion of reference to the "three" countries of Indochina, Dr. Kissinger explained to you that the use of "three" was simply inadvertent and we would drop demand of the North Vietnamese to have it deleted from the present text.

With respect to the National Council, Dr. Kissinger made amply clear in his press conference, as he did in his talks with you, that it has no governmental functions. All American and foreign observers have seen its real meaning -- a face-saving device for the communists to cover their collapse on their demands for a coalition government and your resignation. It is therefore incomprehensible to me why your government has chosen to portray the Council as a structure which encompasses governmental functions. This constant reiteration by your officials of misleading comments may bring about what we have struggled so hard to avoid.

Our position continues to be that we can live with an "administrative structure" which in English clearly implies advisory functions and not governmental ones, but that we reject the North Vietnamese translation which would imply that the structure is endowed with governmental powers and functions. This is precisely what Dr. Kissinger meant when he referred to language problems in his press conference. This is what we will clarify when we meet

TOP SECRET/SENSITIVE

3

the North Vietnamese next. We chose the phrase linguistic ambiguity to give everybody a face-saving way out. You and I know what is involved.

Dr. Kissinger's press conference was conducted on my detailed instructions. He was doing his utmost to prevent you from being portrayed as the obstacle to peace with an inevitable cutoff by Congress of U. S. funds to the Government of South Viet-Nam and the creation of unmanageable impediments to continued U. S. support for you and your Government. Constant criticism from Saigon can only undercut our efforts to present a united front, but they cannot succeed without the cooperation of your associates.

Beyond these specific points I cannot fail to call to your attention the dangerous course your Government is now pursuing. You know my firm commitment to the people of South Viet-Nam and to you personally. As Dr. Kissinger and Ambassador Bunker have informed you I would like to underline this commitment by meeting with you within one or two weeks after the signing of this agreement. It is my conviction that the future depends on the unity which exists between us and on the degree to which we can make clear our unequivocal support to do what is necessary in the days ahead to ensure that the provisions of a peace settlement are strictly enforced. Just as our unity has been the essential aspect of the success we have enjoyed thus far in the conduct of hostilities, it will also be the best guarantee of the future success in a situation where the struggle continues within a more political framework. If the evident drift towards disagreement between the two of us continues, however, the essential basis for U. S. support for you and your Government will be destroyed. In this respect the comments of your Foreign Minister that the U. S. is negotiating a surrender are as damaging as they are unfair and improper.

You can be assured that my decisions as to the final character of a peace settlement are in no way influenced by the election in the United States, and you should harbor no illusions that my policy with respect to the desirability of achieving an early peace will change after the election. I have taken this opportunity to

comment on the Memorandum of October 28 so that there can be no doubts in Saigon with respect to the objectives sought by me and my Government.

I urge you, Mr. President, to maintain the essential unity which has characterized our relations over these past difficult four years and which has proven to be the essential ingredient in the success we have achieved thus far. Disunity will strip me of the ability to maintain the essential base of support which your Government and your people must have in the days ahead, and which I am determined to provide. Willingness to cooperate will mean that we will achieve peace on the basis of what I consider to be a workable agreement -- especially with the amendments which we are certain to obtain. From this basis, we can move with confidence and unity to achieve our mutual objectives of peace and unity for the heroic people of South Viet-Nam.

Sincerely,

Ric... M. Nixon"

With renewed assurances of my highest consideration,

Sincerely,

Ellsworth Bunker
American Ambassador

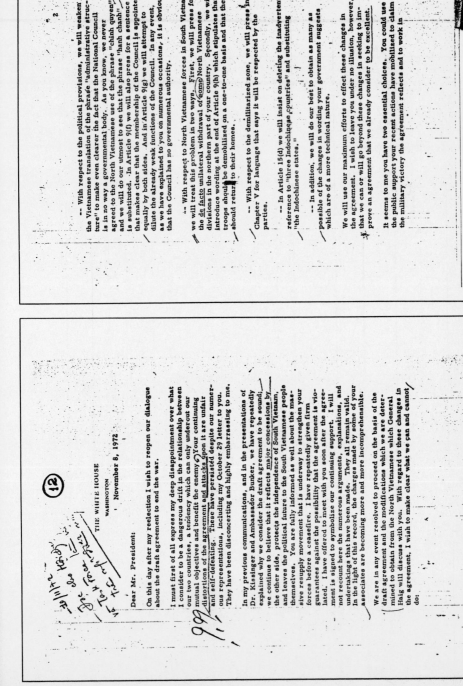

⑫

THE WHITE HOUSE
WASHINGTON

November 8, 1972

Dear Mr. President:

On this day after my reelection I wish to reopen our dialogue about the draft agreement to end the war.

I must first of all express my deep disappointment over what I consider to be a dangerous drift in the relationship between our two countries, a tendency which can only undercut our mutual objectives of the agreement and attacks upon it are unfair distortions of the agreement. These have persisted despite our numerous representations, including my October 29 letter to you. They have been disconcerting and highly embarrassing to me.

In my previous communications, and in the presentations of Dr. Kissinger and Ambassador Bunker, we have repeatedly explained why we consider the draft agreement to be sound; we continue to believe that it reflects major concessions by the other side, protects the independence of South Vietnam, and leaves the political future to the South Vietnamese people themselves. You are fully informed as well about the massive resupply movement that is underway to strengthen your forces before a ceasefire. I have repeatedly given firm guarantees against the possibility that the agreement is violated. I have offered to meet with you soon after the agreement is signed to symbolize our continuing support. I will not recount here the numerous arguments, explanations, and undertakings that have been made. They all remain valid. In the light of this record, the charges made by some of your associates are becoming more and more incomprehensible.

We are in any event resolved to proceed on the basis of the draft agreement and the modifications which we are determined to obtain from the North Vietnamese which General Haig will discuss with you. With regard to these changes in the agreement, I wish to make clear what we can and cannot do:

-- With respect to the political provisions, we will weaken the Vietnamese translation of the phrase "administrative structure" to make even clearer the fact that the National Council is in no way a governmental body. As you know, we never agreed to the North Vietnamese use of the phrase "chinh quyen" and we will do our utmost to see that the phrase "banh chanh" is substituted. In Article 9(f) we will also press for a sentence that makes clear that the membership of the Council is appointed equally by both sides. And in Article 9(g) we will attempt to dilute the already weak functions of the Council. In any event, as we have explained to you on numerous occasions, it is obvious that the Council has no governmental authority.

-- With respect to North Vietnamese forces in South Vietnam, we will treat this problem in two ways. First, we will press for the de facto unilateral withdrawal of some North Vietnamese divisions in the northern part of your country. Secondly, we will introduce wording at the end of Article 9(h) which stipulates that troops should be demobilized on a one-to-one basis and that they should return to their homes.

-- With respect to the demilitarized zone, we will press in Chapter V for language that says it will be respected by the parties.

-- In Article 15(d) we will insist on deleting the inadvertent reference to "three Indochinese countries" and substituting "the Indochinese states."

-- In addition, we will do our best to obtain as many as possible of the changes in wording that your government suggests which are of a more technical nature.

We will use our maximum efforts to effect these changes in the agreement. I wish to leave you under no illusion, however, that we can or will go beyond these changes in seeking to improve an agreement that we already consider to be excellent.

It seems to me you have two essential choices. You could use the public support your recent actions have mobilized to claim the military victory the agreement reflects and to work in

---

Letter 12. Nixon to Thieu, November 8, 1972 (4 pages).
At the top Thieu wrote: "November 10, 1972. Read the letter to the National Security Council and the Task Force for them to work on these points." Question marks in the left margin were written by Thieu.

enemy is agreeing to conditions which any objective observer said were impossible four years ago. Our alliance and its achievements have been based on mutual trust. If you will give me continued trust, together we shall succeed.

Sincerely,

[signature]

His Excellency
Nguyen Van Thieu
President of the Republic of Vietnam
Saigon

3

unity with your strongest ally to bring about a political victory for which the conditions exist. You could take the political and psychological initiative by hailing the settlement and carrying out its provisions in a positive fashion. In this case I repeat my invitation to meet with you shortly after the signature of the agreement, in order to underline our continued close cooperation.

The other alternative would be for you to pursue what appears to be your present course. In my view this would play into the hands of the enemy and would have extremely grave consequences for both our peoples and it would be disaster for yours.

Mr. President, I would like you to tell General Haig if we can confidently proceed on this basis. We are at the point where I need to know unambiguously whether you will join us in the effort General Haig is going to outline or whether we must contemplate alternative courses of action which I believe would be detrimental to the interests of both of our countries.

I hope that you and your government are prepared to cooperate with us. There is a great deal of preparatory work that needs to be done, and we believe joint US-GVN task forces should begin working together so that we will be in the best possible position to implement the settlement.

It is my firm conviction that your people, your armed forces, and you have achieved a major victory which the draft agreement would ratify. It is my intention to build on these accomplishments. I would like to work with you and your government in my second term to defend freedom in South Vietnam in peacetime as we have worked during my first term to defend it in conflict.

In four years you and I have been close personal and military allies. Our alliance has brought us to a position where the

THE WHITE HOUSE
WASHINGTON

November 14, 1972

Dear Mr. President:

I was pleased to learn from General Haig that you held useful and constructive discussions with him in Saigon in preparation for Dr. Kissinger's forthcoming meeting with North Vietnam's negotiators in Paris.

After studying your letter of November 11 with great care I have concluded that we have made substantial progress towards reaching a common understanding on many of the important issues before us. You can be sure that we will pursue the proposed changes in the draft agreement that General Haig discussed with you with the utmost firmness and that, as these discussions proceed, we shall keep you fully informed through your Ambassador to the Paris Conference on Vietnam who will be briefed daily by Dr. Kissinger.

I understand from your letter and from General Haig's personal report that your principal remaining concern with respect to the draft agreement is the status of North Vietnamese forces now in South Vietnam. As General Haig explained to you, it is our intention to deal with this problem first by seeking to insert a reference to respect for the demilitarized zone in the proposed agreement and, second, by proposing a clause which provides for the reduction and demobilization of forces on both sides in South Vietnam on a one-to-one basis and to have demobilized personnel return to their homes.

Upon reviewing this proposed language, it is my conviction that such a provision can go a long way towards dealing with your concern with respect to North Vietnamese forces. General Haig tells me, however, that you are also

- 2 -

seriously concerned about the timing and verification of such reductions. In light of this, I have asked Dr. Kissinger to convey to you, through Ambassador Bunker, some additional clauses we would propose adding to the agreement dealing with each of these points. In addition, I have asked that Dr. Kissinger send you the other technical and less important substantive changes which General Haig did not have the opportunity to discuss with you because they had not yet been fully developed in Washington. With these proposed modifications, I think you will agree that we have done everything we can to improve the existing draft while remaining within its general framework.

You also raise in your letter the question of participation by other Asian countries in the International Conference. As you know, the presently contemplated composition are the permanent members of the United Nations Security Council, the members of the ICCS, the parties to the Paris Conference on Vietnam and the Secretary General of the United Nations. We seriously considered Cambodian and Laotian participation but decided that these would be unnecessary complications with respect to representation. We do not, however, exclude the possibility of delegations from these countries participating in an observer status at the invitation of the conference. As for Japan, this question was raised earlier in our negotiations with Hanoi and set aside because of their strenuous objections to any Japanese role in guaranteeing the settlement and also because it inevitably raises the possibility of Indian participation. I have, however, asked that Dr. Kissinger raise this matter again in Paris and he will inform your representative what progress we make on this. What we must recognize as a practical matter is that participation of Japan is very likely to lead to the participation of India. We would appreciate hearing your preference on whether it is better to include both countries or neither of them.

Finally, in respect to the composition of the ICCS, I must say in all candor that I do not share your view that its contemplated membership is unbalanced. I am hopeful that it

Letter 13. Nixon to Thieu, November 14, 1972 (4 pages).

- 3 -

will prove to be a useful mechanism in detecting and reporting violations of the agreement. In any event, what we both must recognize is that the supervisory mechanism in itself is in no measure as important as our own firm determination to see to it that the agreement works and our vigilance with respect to the prospect of its violation.

I will not repeat here all that I said to you in my letter of November 8, but I do wish to reaffirm its essential content and stress again my determination to work towards an early agreement along the lines of the schedule which General Haig explained to you. I must explain in all frankness that while we will do our very best to secure the changes in the agreement which General Haig discussed with you and those additional ones which Ambassador Bunker will bring you, we cannot expect to secure them all. For example, it is unrealistic to assume that we will be able to secure the absolute assurances which you would hope to have on the troop issue.

But far more important than what we say in the agreement on this issue is what we do in the event the enemy renews its aggression. You have my absolute assurance that if Hanoi fails to abide by the terms of this agreement it is my intention to take swift and severe retaliatory action.

I believe the existing agreement to be an essentially sound one which should become even more so if we succeed in obtaining some of the changes we have discussed. Our best assurance of success is to move into this new situation with confidence and cooperation.

With this attitude and the inherent strength of your government and army on the ground in South Vietnam, I am confident this agreement will be a successful one.

If, on the other hand, we are unable to agree on the course that I have outlined, it is difficult for me to see how we will be able to continue our common effort towards securing a just and honorable peace. As General Haig told you I would with

- 4 -

great reluctance be forced to consider other alternatives. For this reason, it is essential that we have your agreement as we proceed into our next meeting with Hanoi's negotiators. And I strongly urge you and your advisors to work promptly with Ambassador Bunker and our Mission in Saigon on the many practical problems which will face us in implementing the agreement. I cannot overemphasize the urgency of the task at hand nor my unalterable determination to proceed along the course which we have outlined.

Above all we must bear in mind what will really maintain the agreement. It is not any particular clause in the agreement but our joint willingness to maintain its clauses. I repeat my personal assurances to you that the United States will react very strongly and rapidly to any violation of the agreement. But in order to do this effectively it is essential that I have public support and that your Government does not emerge as the obstacle to a peace which American public opinion now universally desires. It is for this reason that I am pressing for the acceptance of an agreement which I am convinced is honorable and fair and which can be made essentially secure by our joint determination.

Mrs. Nixon joins me in extending our warmest personal regards to Madame Thieu and to you. We look forward to seeing you again at our home in California once the just peace we have both fought for so long is finally achieved.

Sincerely,

Richard Nixon

His Excellency
Nguyen Van Thieu
President of the Republic of Vietnam
Saigon

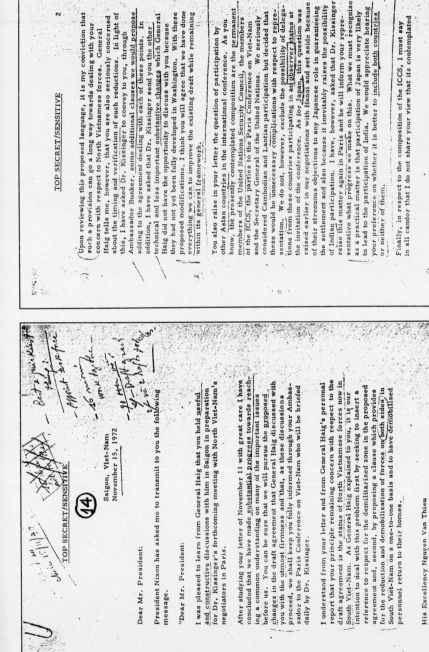

TOP SECRET/SENSITIVE

(14)

Saigon, Viet-Nam
November 15, 1972

Dear Mr. President:

President Nixon has asked me to transmit to you the following message.

"Dear Mr. President:

I was pleased to learn from General Haig that you held useful and constructive discussions with him in Saigon in preparation for Dr. Kissinger's forthcoming meeting with North Viet-Nam's negotiators in Paris.

After studying your letter of November 11 with great care I have concluded that we have made substantial progress towards reaching a common understanding on many of the important issues before us. You can be sure that we will pursue the proposed changes in the draft agreement that General Haig discussed with you with the utmost firmness and that, as these discussions proceed, we shall keep you fully informed through your Ambassador to the Paris Conference on Viet-Nam who will be briefed daily by Dr. Kissinger.

I understand from your letter and from General Haig's personal report that your principle remaining concern with respect to the draft agreement is the status of North Vietnamese forces now in South Viet-Nam. As General Haig explained to you, it is our intention to deal with this problem first by seeking to insert a reference to respect for the demilitarized zone in the proposed agreement and, second, by proposing a clause which provides for the reduction and demobilization of forces on both sides in South Viet-Nam on a one-to-one basis and to have demobilized personnel return to their homes.

His Excellency Nguyen Van Thieu
President of the Republic of Viet-Nam
Saigon, Viet-Nam

TOP SECRET/SENSITIVE

TOP SECRET/SENSITIVE

2

Upon reviewing this proposed language, it is my conviction that such a provision can go a long way towards dealing with your concern with respect to North Vietnamese forces. General Haig tells me, however, that you are also seriously concerned about the timing and verification of such reductions. In light of this, I have asked Dr. Kissinger to convey to you, through Ambassador Bunker, some additional clauses we would propose adding to the agreement dealing with each of these points. In addition, I have asked that Dr. Kissinger send you the other technical and less important substantive changes which General Haig did not have the opportunity to discuss with you because they had not yet been fully developed in Washington. With these proposed modifications, I think you will agree that we have done everything we can to improve the existing draft while remaining within its general framework.

You also raise in your letter the question of participation by other Asian countries in the international conference. As you know, the presently contemplated composition are the permanent members of the United Nations Security Council, the members of the ICCS, the parties to the Paris Conference on Viet-Nam and the Secretary General of the United Nations. We seriously considered Cambodian and Laotian participation but decided that these would be unnecessary complications with respect to representation. We do not, however, exclude the possibility of delegations from these countries participating in an observer status at the invitation of the conference. As for Japan, this question was raised earlier in our negotiations with Hanoi and set aside because of their strenuous objections to any Japanese role in guaranteeing the settlement and also because it inevitably raises the possibility of Indian participation. I have, however, asked that Dr. Kissinger raise this matter again in Paris and he will inform your representative what progress we make on this. What we must recognize as a practical matter is that participation of Japan is very likely to lead to the participation of India. We would appreciate hearing your preference on whether it is better to include both countries or neither of them.

Finally, in respect to the composition of the ICCS, I must say in all candor that I do not share your view that its contemplated

TOP SECRET/SENSITIVE

Letter 14.   Nixon to Thieu, November 15, 1972 (4 pages).
At the top Thieu wrote in English a note to convene a meeting: "Best and quickest thing: Appoint a task force, November 16 morning work together. Go over 1. Draft Agreement 2. And to draft protocol."

3

membership is unbalanced. I am hopeful that it will prove to be a useful mechanism in detecting and reporting violations of the agreement. In any event, what we both must recognize is that the supervisory mechanism in itself is in no measure as important as our own firm determination to see to it that the agreement works and our vigilance with respect to the prospect of its violation.

I will not repeat here all that I said to you in my letter of November 8, but I do wish to reaffirm its essential content and stress again my determination to work towards an early agreement along the lines of the schedule which General Haig explained to you. I must explain in all frankness that while we will do our very best to secure the changes in the agreement which General Haig discussed with you and those additional ones which Ambassador Bunker will bring you, we cannot expect to secure them all. For example, it is unrealistic to assume that we will be able to secure the absolute assurances which you would hope to have on the troop issue.

But far more important than what we say in the agreement on this issue is what we do in the event the enemy renews its aggression. You have my absolute assurance that if Hanoi fails to abide by the terms of this agreement it is my intention to take swift and severe retaliatory action.

I believe the existing agreement to be an essentially sound one which should become even more so if we succeed in obtaining some of the changes we have discussed. Our best assurance of success is to move into this new situation with confidence and cooperation.

With this attitude and the inherent strength of your Government and Army on the ground in South Viet-Nam, I am confident this agreement will be a successful one.

If, on the other hand, we are unable to agree on the course that I have outlined, it is difficult for me to see how we will be able to continue our common effort towards securing a just and honorable peace. As General Haig told you I would with great reluctance be forced to consider other alternatives. For this reason, it is

4

essential that we have your agreement as we proceed into our next meeting with Hanoi's negotiators. And I strongly urge you and your advisors to work promptly with Ambassador Bunker and our Mission in Saigon on the many practical problems which will face us in implementing the agreement. I cannot overemphasize the urgency of the task at hand nor my unalterable determination to proceed along the course which we have outlined.

Above all we must bear in mind what will really maintain the agreement. It is not any particular clause in the agreement but our joint willingness to maintain its clauses. I repeat my personal assurances to you that the United States will react very strongly and rapidly to any violation of the agreement. But in order to do this effectively it is essential that I have public support and that your Government does not emerge as the obstacle to a peace which American public opinion now universally desires. It is for this reason that I am pressing for the acceptance of an agreement which I am convinced is honorable and fair and which can be made essentially secure by our joint determination.

Mrs. Nixon joins me in extending our warmest personal regards to Madame Thieu and to you. We look forward to seeing you again at our home in California once the just peace we have both fought for so long is finally achieved.

Sincerely,

Richard Nixon"

With renewed assurances of my highest consideration,

Sincerely,

Ellsworth Bunker
Ellsworth Bunker
American Ambassador

(15)

THE WHITE HOUSE
WASHINGTON

November 18, 1972

Dear Mr. President:

I have read with great attention the November 18 memorandum from the Government of the Republic of Vietnam. I am sure you recognize the enormous difficulties posed to us by another set of extensive changes following the many proposed changes which we have already discussed. Nevertheless, I shall instruct Dr. Kissinger to seek to the maximum extent possible to incorporate your proposals. I must point out to you, however, first that the express references to North Vietnamese troops in the South that may remain and, secondly, as we have repeatedly pointed out are clearly unobtainable. Also, it is impossible at this point to change the composition of the International Control Group. As for the other changes, Dr. Kissinger will brief your Ambassador at the end of each day as to what progress is being made.

My instructions to Dr. Kissinger are to press to the maximum extent possible to incorporate your proposals. I must point out, however, that I am not prepared to scuttle the agreement or to go along with an accumulation of proposals which will have that practical consequence. It may therefore not be possible to get all the changes.

As for the proposal to send an emissary to Washington, I believe that after two visits by Dr. Kissinger and three by General Haig, three personal letters from me and numerous exchanges through Ambassador Bunker as well as my personal reading of all your communications, we have all of the suggestions that you have made fully in mind for this phase of the negotiations. I would therefore think that the best occasion for a meeting of your emissary with me would be immediately after the Paris phase when we have a new set of issues to consider jointly. I therefore suggest if you select Mr. Duc

- 2 -

as your emissary that he return to Washington on Dr. Kissinger's aircraft immediately upon the conclusion of the next Paris round. If, on the other hand, you prefer that Foreign Minister Lam serve as your emissary, I recommend that he proceed to Paris immediately and take part in the discussions which will follow each day's session and then return to Washington with Dr. Kissinger for a meeting with me.

I again urge you to join us in the course that I am determined to follow. I must once more impress upon you the enormous danger of losing public support in the United States with all the risks for continuing our joint effort. We will, of course, be in close touch after the completion of the negotiations in Paris.

Sincerely,

Richard Nixon

His Excellency
Nguyen Van Thieu
President of the Republic of Vietnam
Saigon

Letter 15.   Nixon to Thieu, November 18, 1972 (2 pages).

TOP SECRET/SENSITIVE

(16)

A.B. nao cayo
19/11/72
1200 G-

Saigon, Viet-Nam
November 19, 1972

Dear Mr. President:

President Nixon has asked me to transmit to you the following message.

"Dear Mr. President:

I have read with great attention the November 18 Memorandum from the Government of the Republic of Viet-Nam. I am sure you recognize the enormous difficulties posed to us by another set of extensive changes following the many proposed changes which we have already discussed. Nevertheless, I shall instruct Dr. Kissinger to seek to the maximum extent possible to incorporate your proposals, I must point out to you, however, first that the express references to North Vietnamese troops in the South have the disadvantage of legitimizing any forces that may remain and, secondly, as we have repeatedly pointed out are clearly unobtainable. Also, it is impossible at this point to change the composition of the international control group. As for the other changes, Dr. Kissinger will brief your Ambassador at the end of each day as to what progress is being made.

My instructions to Dr. Kissinger are to press to the maximum extent possible to incorporate your proposals. I must point out, however, that I am not prepared to scuttle the agreement or to go along with an accumulation of proposals which will have that practical consequence. It may therefore not be possible to get all the changes.

As for the proposal to send an emissary to Washington, I believe that after two visits by Dr. Kissinger and three by General Haig,

His Excellency Nguyen Van Thieu
President of the Republic of Viet-Nam
Saigon, Viet-Nam

TOP SECRET/SENSITIVE

TOP SECRET/SENSITIVE

2

three personal letters from me and numerous exchanges through Ambassador Bunker as well as my personal reading of all your communications, we have all of the suggestions that you have made fully in mind for this phase of the negotiations. Moreover, I'll be in Camp David all next week working on the reorganization of the Government. I would therefore think that the best occasion for a meeting of your emissary with me would be immediately after the Paris phase when we have a new set of issues to consider jointly. I therefore suggest if you select Mr. Duc as your emissary that he return to Washington on Dr. Kissinger's aircraft immediately upon the conclusion of the next Paris round. If, on the other hand, you prefer that Foreign Minister Lam serve as your emissary, I recommend that he proceed to Paris immediately and take part in the discussions which will follow each day's session and then return to Washington with Dr. Kissinger for a meeting with me. As you know, of course, I believe you and I should meet within a short time after the agreement is signed.

I again urge you to join us in the course that I am determined to follow. I must once more impress upon you the enormous danger of losing public support in the United States with all the risks for continuing our joint effort. We will, of course, be in close touch after the completion of the negotiations in Paris.

Sincerely,

Richard Nixon"

With renewed assurances of my highest consideration,

Sincerely,

Ellsworth Bunker
American Ambassador

TOP SECRET/SENSITIVE

In Vietnamese, Thieu wrote: "Nguyen Phu Duc (Foreign Affairs Advisor) to leave on time and to bring documents to follow up in Paris."

Letter 16. Nixon to Thieu, November 19, 1972 (2 pages).

TOP SECRET/SENSITIVE

Saigon, Viet-Nam
November 23, 1972

Dear Mr. President:

President Nixon has asked me to transmit to you the following message.

"Dear Mr. President:

I am increasingly dismayed and apprehensive over the press campaign emanating from Saigon. There are allegations that my associates are not informing me accurately of your views and that you have therefore dispatched a special emissary to Washington to accomplish this task. The unfounded attacks on the draft agreement have continued with increasing frequency.

In addition, I am struck by the dilatory tactics which we are experiencing from your side in Paris. It is evident that your representatives there have been unable to obtain with sufficient timeliness the answers to questions which we must have if we are adequately to represent your views during the negotiations, including the Protocols related to the draft agreement which were provided to your Government in Saigon some two weeks ago.

As I told you in my letters of November 8, 14, and 18, I will proceed promptly to a final solution if an acceptable final agreement is arrived at in Paris this week. Given my clear messages and those conveyed by my representatives these past several weeks, any further delay from your side can only be interpreted as an effort to scuttle the agreement. This would have a disastrous

His Excellency Nguyen Van Thieu
President of the Republic of Viet-Nam
Saigon, Viet-Nam

TOP SECRET/SENSITIVE

TOP SECRET/SENSITIVE　　2

effect on our ability to continue to support you and your Government.

I look forward to seeing your emissary in Washington as soon as the Paris sessions have been concluded, but in the interim I must urge you this one last time not to put ourselves irrevocably at odds. If the current course continues and you fail to join us in concluding a satisfactory agreement with Hanoi, you must understand that I will proceed at whatever the cost.

Sincerely,

Richard Nixon"

With renewed assurances of my highest consideration,

Sincerely,

Ellsworth Bunker
American Ambassador.

TOP SECRET/SENSITIVE

Letter 17.　Nixon to Thieu, November 23, 1972 (2 pages).

THE WHITE HOUSE
WASHINGTON

January 5, 1973

Dear Mr. President:

This will acknowledge your letter of December 20, 1972.

There is nothing substantial that I can add to my many previous messages, including my December 17 letter, which clearly stated my opinions and intentions. With respect to the question of North Vietnamese troops, we will again present your views to the Communists as we have done vigorously at every other opportunity in the negotiations. The result is certain to be once more the rejection of our position. We have explained to you repeatedly why we believe the problem of North Vietnamese troops is manageable under the agreement, and I see no reason to repeat all the arguments.

We will proceed next week in Paris along the lines that General Haig explained to you. Accordingly, if the North Vietnamese meet our concerns on the two outstanding substantive issues in the agreement, concerning the DMZ and the method of signing, and if we can arrange acceptable supervisory machinery, we will proceed to conclude the settlement. The gravest consequences would then ensue if your government chose to reject the agreement and split off from the United States. As I said in my December 17 letter, "I am convinced that your refusal to join us would be an invitation to disaster -- to the loss of all that we together have fought for over the past decade. It would be inexcusable above all because we will have lost a just and honorable alternative."

As we enter this new round of talks, I hope that our countries will now show a united front. It is imperative for our common objectives that your government take no further actions

- 2 -

that complicate our task and would make more difficult the acceptance of the settlement by all parties. We will keep you informed of the negotiations in Paris through daily briefings of Ambassador Lam.

I can only repeat what I have so often said: The best guarantee for the survival of South Vietnam is the unity of our two countries which would be gravely jeopardized if you persist in your present course. The actions of our Congress since its return have clearly borne out the many warnings we have made.

Should you decide, as I trust you will, to go with us, you have my assurance of continued assistance in the post-settlement period and that we will respond with full force should the settlement be violated by North Vietnam. So once more I conclude with an appeal to you to close ranks with us.

Sincerely,

Richard Nixon

His Excellency
Nguyen Van Thieu
President of the Republic of Vietnam
Saigon

Letter 18.   Nixon to Thieu, January 5, 1973 (2 pages).

19

THE WHITE HOUSE
WASHINGTON

January 17, 1973

Dear President Thieu:

I have received your letter of January 17, 1973, and I have studied it with the greatest care.

I must repeat what I have said to you in my previous communications: The freedom and independence of the Republic of Vietnam remains a paramount objective of American foreign policy. I have been dedicated to this goal all of my political life, and during the past four years I have risked many grave domestic and international consequences in its pursuit. It is precisely in order to safeguard our mutual objectives that I have decided irrevocably on my present course. I am firmly convinced that the alternative to signing the present Agreement is a total cutoff of funds to assist your country. We will therefore proceed to initial the Agreement General Haig has brought you on January 23, 1973 and sign it on January 27, 1973. Thus we have only one decision before us: whether or not to continue in peacetime the close partnership that has served us so well in war.

Let me comment on the specific concerns raised in your letter. With respect to the protocols, I am bound to point out that these criticisms come extremely late considering the fact that for two and a half months we have been asking for your Government's joint participation in the drafting of these documents and your comments upon them. As late as January 16 your representatives in Paris refused to give any comments to Ambassador Sullivan. In our negotiations on these documents we

have protected your interests and ensured that the protocols remain essentially technical instruments to help implement the Agreement. We believe the protocols are sound and serve further to strengthen the settlement.

With respect to the text of the Agreement, you list favorable provisions which you claim have been deleted from the Agreement. In reality, however, these provisions were never part of the Agreement; they were changes which we tried vigorously but without success to make in the text on your behalf. I might add that with respect to many of these issues, such as the political provisions, your January 5 letter had already accepted the outcome.

On the other hand, as you know, we have managed, through very strenuous negotiations, to incorporate many other of your Government's suggestions in the October draft. My January 14 letter, and General Haig's presentation highlighted these improvements. Significant changes we have achieved, in part due to your Government's policy, include the following:

-- In the document that your Government would sign, the PRG is not mentioned anywhere in the Preamble or text, while the Republic of Vietnam is mentioned.

-- Military assistance permitted under the replacement provision has been expanded to include material that has been "used up" and "destroyed" in addition to "damaged and worn out."

-- References to the U.S. being required to respect the political self-determination of South Vietnam have been expanded to include all countries.

-- The phrase "administrative structure" used to describe the National Council, whose Vietnamese translation suggested a somewhat "governmental structure," has been entirely deleted.

Letter 19.   Nixon to Thieu, January 17, 1973 (6 pages).

-- The role of the National Council has been further diluted by eliminating its role in the maintenance of a ceasefire and the preservation of peace.

-- The reduction of military effectives on both sides and their demobilization is now to be accomplished "as soon as possible."

-- South Vietnamese foreign policy is to be conducted on the basis of "mutual respect for independence and sovereignty," highlighting your country's sovereign status.

-- North Vietnam is now obligated to respect the demilitarized zone on either side of the provisional military demarcation line.

-- The ICCS "shall carry out its tasks in accordance with the principle of respect for the sovereignty of South Vietnam."

-- The four parties are obligated to strictly respect the 1954 and 1962 Geneva Agreements.

-- The reference to "three" Indochinese countries has been deleted.

-- The interval between the Vietnam ceasefire and the Laos ceasefire has been shortened from 30 to no more than 15 days.

-- The international control machinery has been fleshed out and will now be able to begin functioning immediately after the ceasefire.

All of these improvements in the October Agreement have been obtained without granting any changes favorable to the Communists.

In addition to strengthening the Agreement itself, as my January 14 letter pointed out, your overall political and security position has been bolstered in many ways in preparation for a ceasefire.

With respect to modifications you still seek in the Agreement, I must point out again that the text of the Agreement, the method for signing, and the protocols are the best obtainable. They can no longer be changed. On the signing procedure, General Haig has fully covered this issue with you. Your Government would sign a document which does not mention the PRG anywhere in the text. This Agreement would be signed first, with separate signature pages for the two sides, and it would make no reference to the two-party document. This is a major improvement over the previous procedure and one that fully protects your position.

In any event this discussion of specific provisions is to a large extent now irrelevant. As I have told you on many occasions, the key issue is no longer particular nuances in the Agreement but rather the postwar cooperation of our two countries and the need for continued U.S. support. It is precisely for this support that I have been fighting. Your rejection of the Agreement would now irretrievably destroy our ability to assist you. Congress and public opinion would force my hand. It is time, therefore, to join together at last and protect our mutual interests through close cooperation and unity.

As General Haig has told you, I am prepared to send Vice President Agnew to Saigon in order to plan with you our postwar relationship. He would leave Washington on January 28, the day after the Agreement is signed, and during his visit he would publicly reaffirm the guarantees I have expressed to you. Let me state these assurances once again in this letter:

-- First, we recognize your Government as the sole legitimate Government of South Vietnam.

It seems to me that you have two essential choices: to continue a course, which would be dramatic but short-sighted, of seeking to block the Agreement; or to use the Agreement constructively as a means of establishing a new basis for American-South Vietnamese relations. I need not tell you how strongly I hope that you will choose what I am firmly convinced to be the only possible path to secure our mutual objectives.

Sincerely,

Richard Nixon

His Excellency
Nguyen Van Thieu
President of the Republic of Vietnam
Saigon

-- Secondly, we do not recognize the right of foreign troops to remain on South Vietnamese soil.

-- Thirdly, the U.S. will react vigorously to violations to the Agreement.

In addition I remain prepared to meet with you personally three to four weeks later in San Clemente, California, at which time we could publicly reaffirm once again our joint cooperation and U.S. guarantees.

Against this background I hope that you will now join us in signing the Agreement. Because of the gravity of the situation and the consequences for the future, I have instructed General Haig to return to Saigon Saturday morning, January 20, 1973. This is the latest possible occasion for us to have your final position so that I will know whether we will be proceeding alone or together with you. The schedule is final and cannot be changed in any way. Dr. Kissinger will initial the Agreement in Paris on January 23; I will make a brief address to the American people that evening; and the formal signing will take place on January 27, 1973. If you refuse to join us, the responsibility for the consequences rests with the Government of Vietnam.

As I said in my previous letter, I would very much like to meet with Foreign Minister Lam on January 25 on his way to Paris for the signing ceremony, and I look forward to seeing you in the near future.

Let me close by saying that I respect the intensity with which you are defending the interests of your country. I recognize that the Agreement is not an ideal one, but it is the best possible one that can be obtained under present circumstances, and I have explained why these circumstances require a settlement now.

THE WHITE HOUSE
WASHINGTON

January 20, 1973

Dear President Thieu:

Thank you for your January 20 letter, which I have carefully read.

No point is served in reviewing the record of our exchanges, regarding the Agreement and the protocols. While it may be true that the latest texts of the protocols did not reach Saigon until January 11, it is also true that your representatives in Paris were continually without instructions during the various negotiating sessions in November and December. We were thus forced to proceed according to our own best judgment. During this process we kept your representatives fully informed, while continually asking in vain for your Government's suggestions.

In any event, all these considerations are now beside the point. The essential fact is that the situation in the United States makes it imperative to put our relationship on a new basis. It is obvious that we face a situation of most extreme gravity when long-time friends of South Vietnam such as Senators Goldwater and Stennis, on whom we have relied for four years to carry our programs of assistance through the Congress, make public declarations that a refusal by your Government of reasonable peace terms would make it impossible to continue aid. It is this situation which now threatens everything for which our two countries have suffered so much.

Let me now address the specific proposals you have made in your letter. We have made innumerable attempts to achieve the very provisions you have proposed with respect to North Vietnamese forces, both in the text of the Agreement and in

- 2 -

formal understandings. We have concluded that the course we have chosen is the best obtainable. While there is no specific provision in the text, there are so many collateral clauses with an impact on this question that the continued presence of North Vietnamese troops could only be based on illegal acts and the introduction of new forces could only be done in violation of the Agreement. It seems to me that the following clauses in the Agreement achieve this objective:

-- The affirmation of the independence and sovereignty of South Vietnam in Articles 14, 18(e), and 20.

-- The provision for reunification only by peaceful means, through agreement and without coercion or annexation, which establishes the illegitimacy of any use or threat of force in the name of reunification (Article 15).

-- The U.S. and DRV, on an equal basis, pledging themselves against any outside interference in the exercise of the South Vietnamese people's right to self-determination (Article 9).

-- The legal prohibition of the introduction of troops, advisers, and war material into South Vietnam from outside South Vietnam (Article 7).

-- The principle of respect for the demilitarized zone and the provisional military demarcation line (Article 15).

-- The prohibition of the use of Laotian and Cambodian territory to encroach upon the sovereignty and security of South Vietnam (Article 20).

-- The fact that all Communist forces in South Vietnam are subject to the obligation that their reduction and demobilization are to be negotiated as soon as possible (Article 13).

In addition, we are prepared to give you a unilateral U.S. note which sums up our understanding on this issue. Ambassador Bunker will show you a draft of a note which we will deliver in Saigon on the day of signature of January 27.

Letter 20.   Nixon to Thieu, January 20, 1973 (4 pages).

- 3 -

With respect to your concern about the protocols, it seems to us that Article 6 in the ceasefire/joint commission protocol would permit your police forces to continue carrying carbines and rifles since the continued presence of North Vietnamese forces obviously constitutes "unusual circumstances." Nevertheless, I shall instruct Dr. Kissinger to seek a change in this Article in an attempt to remove its ambiguity. I cannot, however, promise success.

The key issue is different, however. We have now reached a decisive point. I can no longer hold up my decision pending the outcome of further exchanges. When Dr. Kissinger leaves Washington Monday morning, our basic course must be set. As I have told you, we will initial the Agreement on January 23. I must know now whether you are prepared to join us on this course, and I must have your answer by 1200 Washington time, January 21, 1973.

I must meet with key Congressional leaders Sunday evening, January 21 to inform them in general terms of our course. If you cannot give me a positive answer by then, I shall inform them that I am authorizing Dr. Kissinger to initial the Agreement even without the concurrence of your Government. In that case, even if you should decide to join us later, the possibility of continued Congressional assistance will be severely reduced. In that case also I will not be able to put into my January 23 speech the assurances I have indicated to you, because they will not then seem to have been a voluntary act on my part. Needless to say, I would be most reluctant to take this fateful step.

Let me therefore sum up my position as follows: First, I welcome your decision to send Foreign Minister Lam to Paris, and I will instruct Dr. Kissinger to have the fullest and frankest discussion with him. Dr. Kissinger will see him both before and after his meeting with the North Vietnamese to make clear your Government's full participation in our actions. Secondly, I have instructed Dr. Kissinger to seek the change in the protocol regarding police forces. Thirdly, with respect to North Vietnamese forces, I can go no further than the draft note that I am asking Ambassador Bunker to transmit to you

- 4 -

and which we will hand over to you officially on January 27, the day of signing. Fourthly, if you join us we shall announce the Vice President's visit to Saigon before the date of signing though he could not leave Washington until January 28.

Finally, and most importantly, I must have your assurances now, on the most personal basis, that when we initial the Agreement on Tuesday we will be doing so in the knowledge that you will proceed to sign the Agreement jointly with us.

This Agreement. I assure you again, will represent the beginning of a new period of close collaboration and strong mutual support between the Republic of Vietnam and the United States. You and I will work together in peacetime to protect the independence and freedom of your country as we have done in war. If we close ranks now and proceed together, we will prevail.

Sincerely,

Richard Nixon

His Excellency
Nguyen Van Thieu
President of the Republic of Vietnam
Saigon

THE WHITE HOUSE
WASHINGTON

January 22, 1973

Dear President Thieu:

Thank you for your letter of January 21, 1973 and the promptness of your response. I want you to know that, despite all the difficulties and differences between our two governments in this recent phase, I have great respect for the tenacity and courage with which you are defending the interests of your people in our common objective to preserve their freedom and independence. I look forward to continuing our close association.

I shall now tell our Congressional leaders that we are proceeding on our course with your essential concurrence. With respect to the issue of North Vietnamese troops, we will send you a note in conformity with the language contained in your letter. Ambassador Bunker will give you a draft. In addition, we will find an occasion within a week of the initialing of the Agreement to state our views publicly along the same lines.

With respect to the issue of the police force, I have instructed that Ambassador Sullivan resume his meetings with the North Vietnamese immediately to seek some modification in the protocol. Dr. Kissinger will pursue this question further with your Foreign Minister and in his meetings with Special Adviser Le Duc Tho. In any event, however, we will have to proceed to initial the Agreement and the protocols on January 23 and sign them on January 27. If we fail to obtain the proposed modification, we will have to interpret the phrases in the protocol "unusual circumstances" in a way that gives us the latitude that we require.

2

On the general subject of the protocols, we do not agree that these documents are more legally binding in their obligations than the Agreement itself. Furthermore, you will note that we have purposely left many major issues in the protocol, such as points of entry and the status of Two-Party Commission, to be resolved between the two South Vietnamese parties, thus reflecting your basic approach of leaving questions to be negotiated among the South Vietnamese themselves.

Thus I am proceeding to prepare my January 23 speech along the outlines that General Haig gave you. It will include a strong reference to our essential unity and will also point out that your Foreign Minister personally participated in the final phase of the negotiations. As I mentioned in my previous letter, Dr. Kissinger will consult closely, and visibly associate himself with, your Foreign Minister while they are in Paris.

Our overwhelming mutual concern now must be to strengthen your government and people as we look toward implementation of the Agreement. From here on the emphasis must be on our close cooperation and a confident approach to implementing the settlement. With your strong leadership and with continuing strong bonds between our countries, we will succeed in securing our mutual objectives.

Sincerely,

Richard Nixon

His Excellency
Nguyen Van Thieu
President of the Republic of Vietnam
Saigon

Letter 21.   Nixon to Thieu, January 22, 1973 (2 pages).

THE WHITE HOUSE
WASHINGTON

May 21, 1973

Dear Mr. President:

In our correspondence before the Paris agreement, and when we met in San Clemente, I emphasized my determination to stand by your country and to see the agreement enforced. This is the effort in which we are now engaged.

I am writing to you with some concern because I am afraid that the reactions of some of your subordinates to the negotiations being conducted in Paris may produce a dangerous situation. As you know, I sent Dr. Kissinger to Paris in order to negotiate with the North Vietnamese an improved implementation of the ceasefire agreement. I need hardly emphasize the importance of this enterprise in the present climate of American opinion. As you know, I have publicly pressed for the strict implementation of the agreement and have both American prestige and American willingness to engage itself behind me. It would never be understood in America if the negotiation failed as a result of avoidable obstacles.

In this context, I am frank to say that your subordinates' procedural objections seem belated and obstructive. It has been known in Saigon since the middle of April that Dr. Kissinger would meet with Le Duc Tho. It is hard to understand why it was left for the last minute to raise procedural objections which make it impossible to sign a two-party document. It is absolutely impossible for us to bring about a four-party conference, as has been suggested. This has been repeatedly rejected by the other side. It would also have the practical consequence of forcing us to recognize the so-called PRG.

- 2 -

As for the substantive objections, it appears that some were sent to Paris by subordinates and not sufficiently considered by higher officials. For example, I do not see how the GVN can seriously object to an end of U. S. reconnaissance flights over North Vietnam when this was always part of the agreement and when these reconnaissance flights were reinstituted only after major DRV violations. This kind of objection simply cannot be seriously upheld.

Let me now turn to a more serious issue. I have asked Dr. Kissinger to send you immediately the latest document which is in the process of being discussed. As you will see, it has, these essential elements:

1. A new order for a ceasefire simultaneously but separately issued by the two South Vietnamese parties.

2. The effective coming into being of the two-party joint military commission at points which effectively remove them from the populated areas of South Vietnam.

3. The implementation of Article 7 of the agreement.

4. The reaffirmation of certain political provisions which leave the negotiations entirely to the South Vietnamese as provided for in Article 9 of the ceasefire agreement.

The document now being negotiated has the practical consequence of putting the establishment of the National Council of National Reconciliation and Concord into the indefinite future, of leaving the settlement of the internal questions entirely to the South Vietnamese, and of removing the NLF element of the two-party commission from your populated areas. In this context, the objection to placing the two-party commission teams along the demarcation lines existing in South Vietnam is difficult to comprehend. Is the GVN better off with NLF officials in provincial capitals? We will not insist on this provision, but we fail to understand your staff's objections.

Letter 22. Nixon to Thieu, May 21, 1973 (3 pages).

- 3 -

The most important concern we have now is that your side in fact carry out the agreed-to joint ceasefire announcement, which, if present plans materialize, should occur on Saturday, May 26, for implementation on Sunday, May 27. According to present plans, a joint communique may be issued on May 25 between our side and the DRV.

I want to reiterate that our only desire is to strengthen the agreement and to reaffirm our solidarity with you. I cannot believe you will put me into the position of having to explain to the American people a reason for the breakdown of negotiations, which would lead to an immediate cut-off of funds for Laos and Cambodia and ultimately for Vietnam.

When we talked together at San Clemente, I told you of the growing difficulties in obtaining adequate aid levels from the Congress. Nevertheless, I told you I would exert every effort to secure not only an aid level adequate for your immediate needs, but also enough additional aid to give an added momentum to the economic growth your just-announced program should put in motion. This effort to secure additional economic aid for Vietnam has been going well. It has clearly been given first priority. But I must frankly caution you that I can think of nothing that would so surely wreck this effort as to have even the appearance of disagreement between us just at this moment in time. I am certain you will keep this consideration very much in mind as you reflect on the contents of this message.

Sincerely,

Richard Nixon

His Excellency
Nguyen Van Thieu
President of the Republic of Vietnam

SECRET

Saigon, Vietnam
May 30, 1973

Dear Mr. President:

I have been asked to transmit the following message from President Nixon which has just been received.

"Dear Mr. President:

Once again I am writing you in connection with the draft communique which Dr. Kissinger and Le Duc Tho are negotiating in Paris. I wish to inform you of the action we have taken following the discussions which Ambassador Sullivan had with you and your representatives in Saigon last week.

We have examined with great care the various changes which your Government has proposed in the draft communique. On the basis of the negotiations which have brought the draft text to the form which was given to you on May 24, we know that some of your proposals would be completely rejected by the North Vietnamese, or would be accepted by them only at a price which would be higher than either you or we would be willing to pay. Others, which are of less intrinsic significance, might possibly be acceptable to them, but at the cost of long and tedious delays.

In the light of these considerations, I have directed

His Excellency
Nguyen Van Thieu
President of the Republic of Viet-Nam
Saigon, Viet-Nam

SECRET

SECRET

2

Dr. Kissinger to seek the agreement of Le Duc Tho to a number of the proposals you have made, either in the precise language you have suggested, or in modified versions which have been already discussed with you and Foreign Minister Lam. Ambassador Whitehouse can provide you the precise details of the proposals as we have put them forward.

I am not at all sanguine that we can obtain North Vietnamese concurrence in these changes. If we can obtain their concurrence even in part, the text would obviously be improved from your viewpoint. On the other hand, even if we obtain none of them, I feel very strongly that the text is, on balance, a document which is helpful to your Government and is useful to both of us. If it were a unilateral document, without North Vietnamese input, we would, of course, prefer to see it more positive and to have it contain more precise obligations for implementation of the Agreement.

However, given the circumstances of its negotiation, I believe it is the best we can obtain and that it contains nothing which could remotely occasion adverse effects for your Government. It will be enormously helpful to me to have the communique issued with the signature of your representative alongside that of Dr. Kissinger. We need an action of this kind if I am to be able to obtain from the Congress the sort of legislative cooperation which will be required to carry out the programs for peace and stability which you and I discussed in San Clemente.

Consequently, I seek your assurance that you will accept the text of the communique as it emerges from our negotiations with the North Vietnamese

SECRET

SECRET

Saigon, Viet-Nam
May 31, 1973

Dear Mr. President:

In his letter to you of May 30, 1973, President Nixon states that I can provide you the precise details of the proposals as we have put them forward.

The proposals, with our comments to the other side, are as follows:

3. In paragraph 3(a), it is proposed that the time for the issuance of the cease-fire orders be fixed at 0400 hours, GMT, which is 1200 noon Saigon time. A cease-fire taking effect at 1200 noon will discourage sneak attacks and other movements in the pre-dawn hours.

4. In the first sentence of paragraph 3(b), it is proposed to add the phrase "and the modalities of stationing". This is a direct quote from Article (B) of the Agreement and a useful clarification of the objectives which we both seek.

5. In paragraph 3(c), it is proposed to add the following phrase: "with a view to reaching an agreement on temporary measures to avert conflict and to ensure supply and medical care for these armed forces". Again, this text is taken directly from the protocol and provides a useful clarification of the purposes for the proposed meetings.

His Excellency
Nguyen Van Thieu
President of the Republic of Viet-Nam
Saigon, Viet-Nam

SECRET

SECRET

3

and that you will designate a representative to meet with the other three parties in Paris June 7 in order to sign the document on June 8.

Sincerely,

/s/ Richard M. Nixon"

With renewed assurances of my highest consideration.

Sincerely,

Charles S. Whitehouse

Charles S. Whitehouse
Chargé d'Affaires, a.i.

SECRET

6. It is proposed that the last sentence of paragraph 4(b) be broken into two sentences, to read as follows:

"In conformity with Article 15, the demilitarized zone shall be respected. Military equipment may transit the demilitarized zone only if introduced into South Vietnam as replacements pursuant to Article 7 of the Agreement and through a designated point of entry."

This is a more accurate statement of conformity with Article 15.

7. It is proposed that paragraph 7 be rewritten as follows:

"Consistent with the principles for the exercise of the Vietnamese people's right to self-determination stated in Chapter IV of the Agreement:

A. The National Council of National Reconciliation and Concord consisting of three equal segments shall be formed as soon as possible in conformity with Article 12 of the Agreement.

B. The two South Vietnamese parties shall sign an agreement on the internal matters of South Vietnam, including free and democratic general elections, as soon as possible, and shall do their utmost to accomplish this within 45 days from today.

C. The two South Vietnamese parties shall implement Article 13 of the Agreement, which reads as follows:

'The question of Vietnamese armed forces in South Vietnam shall be settled by the two South Vietnamese parties in a spirit of national reconciliation and concord, equality and mutual respect, without foreign interference, in accordance with the postwar situation. Among the questions to be discussed by the two South Vietnamese parties are steps to reduce their military effectives and to demobilize the troops being reduced. The South Vietnamese parties will accomplish this as soon as possible.'

This revised wording reintroduces a reference to elections which the GVN considers essential.

8. It is proposed that paragraph 8(b) be rewritten as follows:

"The headquarters of the central Two-Party Joint Military Commission shall be located in Saigon proper. Pending agreement on their permanent locations, the headquarters of the regional Two-Party Joint Military Commissions and the teams of the Joint Military Commissions, shall be provisionally located at places close to the headquarters and teams of the International Commission of Control and Supervision, as stipulated in article of the Protocol concerning the International Commission of Control and Supervision. Once the delimitation of the areas of control of the two South Vietnamese parties has been determined in conformity with Article 3(b) of the Agreement, the Two-Party Joint Military Commission shall agree upon permanent locations

SECRET

4

for its regional headquarters and teams, except
for teams at the points of entry, at places where
an area controlled by one of the two parties adjoins an area controlled by the other. The
accommodations of the military delegations of
each party shall be located in the area under
its control. The locations of these headquarters
and teams shall be determined by the Two-Party
Joint Military Commission within 15 days after
the delimitation of the areas of control has been
determined in conformity with Article 3(b) of
the Agreement."

This wording more accurately reflects the factual situation which will exist and the sequence of events which
will ensure after the issuance of the ceasefire orders.
It also conforms with the oral explanation of the anticipated sequence given by Mr. Le Duc Tho on May 22.

With renewed assurances of my highest consideration.

Sincerely,

Charles S. Whitehouse

Charles S. Whitehouse
Charge d'Affaires, a.i.

SECRET

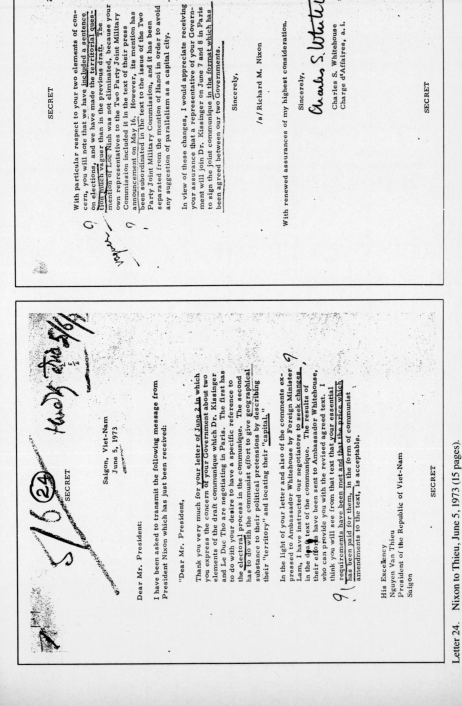

SECRET

Saigon, Viet-Nam
June 5, 1973

Dear Mr. President:

I have been asked to transmit the following message from President Nixon which has just been received:

"Dear Mr. President,

Thank you very much for your letter of June 2 in which you express the concern of your Government about two elements of the draft communique which Dr. Kissinger and Le Duc Tho are negotiating in Paris. The first has to do with your desire to have a specific reference to the electoral process in the communique. The second has to do with the communist effort to give geographical substance to their political pretensions by describing their "territory" and locating their "capital."

In the light of your letter and also of the comments expressed to Ambassador Whitehouse by Foreign Minister Lam, I have instructed our negotiators to seek changes in the draft text of the communique. The results of their efforts have been sent to Ambassador Whitehouse, who can provide you with the revised agreed text. I think you will see from that text that your essential requirements have been met and that the price which has been paid for them, in the form of communist amendments to the text, is acceptable.

His Excellency
Nguyen Van Thieu
President of the Republic of Viet-Nam
Saigon

SECRET

SECRET   2

With particular respect to your two elements of concern, you will note that we have included a sentence on elections, and we have made the territorial question much vaguer than in the previous draft. The mention of Loc Ninh was not eliminated, because your own representatives to the Two Party Joint Military Commission included it in the text of their press announcement on May 16. However, its mention has been subordinated in the text to the issue of the Two Party Joint Military Commission, and it has been separated from the mention of Hanoi in order to avoid any suggestion of parallelism as a capital city.

In view of these changes, I would appreciate receiving your assurance that a representative of your Government will join Dr. Kissinger on June 7 and 8 in Paris to sign the joint communique in the format which has been agreed between our two Governments.

Sincerely,

/s/ Richard M. Nixon

With renewed assurances of my highest consideration.

Sincerely,

Charles S. Whitehouse
Charge d'Affaires, a.i.

SECRET

Letter 24.   Nixon to Thieu, June 5, 1973 (15 pages).
Attached to the letter is the text of the draft Joint Communiqué (pp. 406 ff.). Thieu listed issues he did not want to renegotiate: the DMZ (demilitarized zone); North Vietnam infiltration; the issue of new infiltration after January 28 (after the Paris Agreement was signed, January 27, 1973); Cambodia and Laos ceasefire; Elections. Thieu listed what he felt the North Vietnamese had additionally gained from the June Joint Communiqué.—Cross the DMZ;—Article 11 separated;—Stationing of their troops at the delimitation

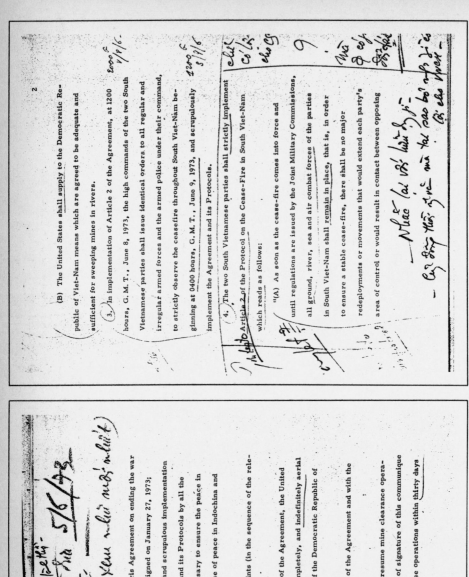

lines of the two territories;—Can go to Saigon and live there;—Elections become unclear. (Consider this text as the newest.)

At 4, Thieu commented: "Only beneficial to the Communists. Nothing in exchange for the GVN." At bottom he wrote: "What are the hidden motives of repeating this clause. Why leave out those clauses which are advantageous to the Republic of Vietnam?", referring to the Paris Agreement.

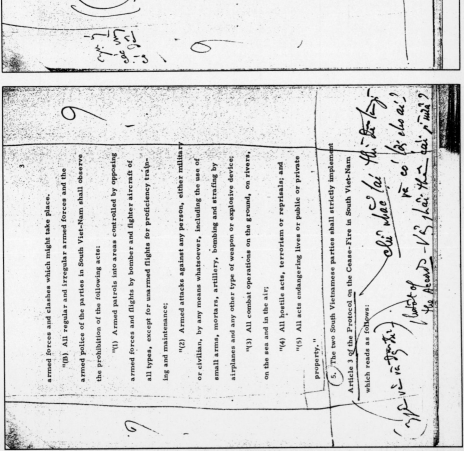

"(A) The above-mentioned prohibitions shall not hamper or restrict:

"(1) Civilian supply, freedom of movement, freedom to work, and freedom of the people to engage in trade, and civilian communication and transportation between and among all areas in South Viet-Nam;

"(2) The use by each party in areas under its control of military support elements, such as engineer and transportation units, in repair and construction of public facilities and the transportation and supplying of the population;

"(3) Normal military proficiency training conducted by the parties in the areas under their respective control with due regard for public safety.

"(B) The Joint Military Commissions shall immediately agree on corridors, routes, and other regulations governing the movement of military transport aircraft, military transport vehicles, and military transport vessels of all types of one party going through areas under the control of other parties."

armed forces and clashes which might take place.

"(B) All regular and irregular armed forces and the armed police of the parties in South Viet-Nam shall observe the prohibition of the following acts:

"(1) Armed patrols into areas controlled by opposing armed forces and flights by bomber and fighter aircraft of all types, except for unarmed flights for proficiency training and maintenance;

"(2) Armed attacks against any person, either military or civilian, by any means whatsoever, including the use of small arms, mortars, artillery, bombing and strafing by airplanes and any other type of weapon or explosive device;

"(3) All combat operations on the ground, on rivers, on the sea and in the air;

"(4) All hostile acts, terrorism or reprisals; and

"(5) All acts endangering lives or public or private property."

5. The two South Vietnamese parties shall strictly implement Article 3 of the Protocol on the Cease-Fire in South Viet-Nam which reads as follows:

Referring to 5, Thieu wrote: "Repeating this article for what purpose and beneficial to whom? This is *plutot* (more than) the Accords. If repeating must be textual and complete. What do we want to add to the text?"

Referring to A 1, Thieu wrote in the margin: "With the hidden implication of referring to the populated areas." On the bottom, he wrote: "Paragraph 4 and 5 of this communiqué must be accompanied by the issue of a political solution and the election."

6

(A) The two South Vietnamese parties shall not accept the introduction of troops, military advisers, and military personnel, including technical military personnel, into South Viet-Nam.

(B) The two South Vietnamese parties shall not accept the introduction of armaments, munitions, and war material into South Viet-Nam. However, the two South Vietnamese parties are permitted to make periodic replacements of armaments, munitions, and war material, as authorized by Article 7 of the Agreement, through designated points of entry and subject to supervision by the Two-Party Joint Military Commission and the International Commission of Control and Supervision.

In conformity with Article 15 (B) of the Agreement regarding the respect of the demilitarized zone, military equipment may transit the demilitarized zone only if introduced into South Viet-Nam as replacements pursuant to Article 7 of the Agreement and through a designated point of entry.

(C) Twenty-four hours after the entry into force of the cease-fire referred to in paragraph 3, the Two-Party Joint Military Commission shall discuss the modalities for the supervision of the replacements of armaments, munitions, and war

5

6. The Two Party Joint Military Commission shall immediately carry out its task pursuant to Article 3 (B) of the Agreement to determine the areas controlled by each of the two South Vietnamese parties and the modalities of stationing. This task shall be completed as soon as possible. The Commission shall also immediately carry out its task to agree on the corridors, routes, and other regulations on the movement of means of military transport of one party through areas of control of the other party. The Commission shall also immediately discuss the movements necessary to accomplish a return of the armed forces of the two South Vietnamese parties to the positions they occupied at the time the cease-fire entered into force on January 28, 1973.

7. Twenty-four hours after the cease-fire referred to in paragraph 3 enters into force, the commanders of the opposing armed forces at those places of direct contact shall meet to carry out the provisions of Article 4 of the Protocol on the Cease-Fire in South Viet-Nam with a view to reaching an agreement on temporary measures to avert conflict and to ensure supply and medical care for these armed forces.

8. In conformity with Article 7 of the Agreement:

In the left margin Thieu wrote: "The DMZ shall be respected." On the right he wrote: "No this is not balanced and just only advantages to the Communists. Why putting one thing in the text and not the other."

return of captured personnel, all captured and detained personnel covered by that Protocol shall be treated humanely at all times. The two South Vietnamese parties shall immediately implement Article 9 of that Protocol and, within fifteen days from the date of signature of this communique, allow National Red Cross societies they have agreed upon to visit all places where these personnel are held.

(D) The two South Vietnamese parties shall cooperate in obtaining information about missing persons and in determining the location of and in taking care of the graves of the dead.

(E) In conformity with Article 8 (B) of the Agreement, the parties shall help each other to get information about those military personnel and foreign civilians of the parties missing in action, to determine the location and take care of the graves of the dead so as to facilitate the exhumation and repatriation of the remains, and to take any such other measures as may be required to get information about those still considered missing in action. For this purpose, frequent and regular liaison flights shall be made between Saigon and Hanoi.

---

material permitted by Article 7 of the Agreement at the three points of entry already agreed upon for each party. Within fifteen days of the entry into force of the cease-fire referred to in paragraph 3, the two South Vietnamese parties shall also designate by agreement three additional points of entry for each party, in the territory controlled by that party.

9. In conformity with Article 8 of the Agreement:

(A) Any captured personnel covered by Article 8 (A) of the Agreement who have not yet been returned shall be returned without delay, and in any event within no more than thirty days from the date of signature of this communique.

(B) All the provisions of the Agreement and the Protocol on the return of captured personnel shall be scrupulously implemented. All Vietnamese civilian personnel covered by Article 8 (C) of the Agreement and Article 7 of the Protocol on the return of captured personnel shall be returned as soon as possible. The two South Vietnamese parties shall do their utmost to accomplish this within forty-five days from the date of signature of this communique.

(C) In conformity with Article 8 of the Protocol on the

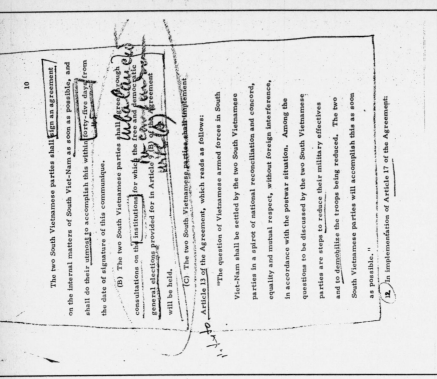

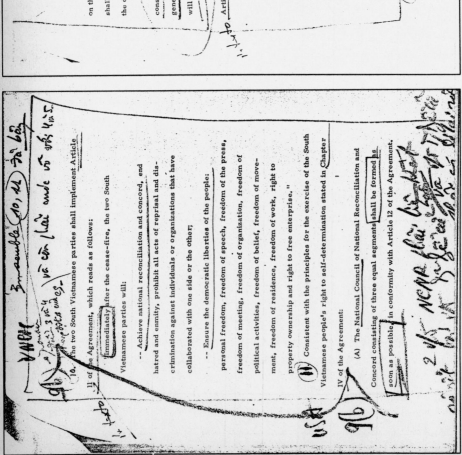

Thieu wrote in English: "Unbalanced in comparison with (A)."

At the top Thieu wrote: "Together items 10 and 11 were already bad for South Vietnam. It's even worse now that they are connected to 4 and 5." At the bottom he wrote: "The NCNR (National Council of National Reconciliation) must be linked with the issue of elections."

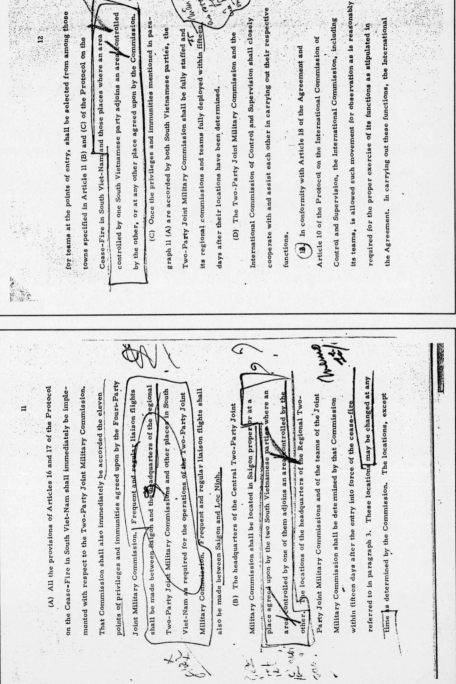

11

(A) All the provisions of Articles 16 and 17 of the Protocol on the Cease-Fire in South Viet-Nam shall immediately be implemented with respect to the Two-Party Joint Military Commission. That Commission shall also immediately be accorded the eleven points of privileges and immunities agreed upon by the Four-Party Joint Military Commission. Frequent and regular liaison flights shall be made between Saigon and the headquarters of the regional Two-Party Joint Military Commissions and other places in South Viet-Nam as required for the operations of the Two-Party Joint Military Commission. Frequent and regular liaison flights shall also be made between Saigon and Loc Ninh.

(B) The headquarters of the Central Two-Party Joint Military Commission shall be located in Saigon proper or at a place agreed upon by the two South Vietnamese parties where an area controlled by the other. The locations of the headquarters of the Regional Two-Party Joint Military Commission shall be determined by that Commission within fifteen days after the entry into force of the cease-fire referred to in paragraph 3. These locations may be changed at any time is determined by the Commission. The locations, except

12

for teams at the points of entry, shall be selected from among those towns specified in Article 11 (B) and (C) of the Protocol on the Cease-Fire in South Viet-Nam and those places where an area controlled by one South Vietnamese party adjoins an area controlled by the other, or at any other place agreed upon by the Commission.

(C) Once the privileges and immunities mentioned in paragraph 11 (A) are accorded by both South Vietnamese parties, the Two-Party Joint Military Commission shall be fully staffed and its regional commissions and teams fully deployed within fifteen days after their locations have been determined.

(D) The Two-Party Joint Military Commission and the International Commission of Control and Supervision shall closely cooperate with and assist each other in carrying out their respective functions.

13. In conformity with Article 18 of the Agreement and Article 10 of the Protocol on the International Commission of Control and Supervision, the International Commission, including its teams, is allowed such movement for observation as is reasonably required for the proper exercise of its functions as stipulated in the Agreement. In carrying out these functions, the International

In the left margin Thieu asks: "What does it say in the Vietnamese text?"

Referring to C, Thieu writes: "Contradictory to as soon as possible delimitation of the area under control by each party."

13

Commission, including its teams, shall enjoy all necessary assistance and cooperation from the parties concerned. The two South Vietnamese parties shall issue the necessary instructions to their personnel and take all other necessary measures to ensure the safety of such movement.

14. Article 20 of the Agreement, regarding Cambodia and Laos, shall be scrupulously implemented.

15. In conformity with Article 21 of the Agreement, the United States-Democratic Republic of Viet-Nam Joint Economic Commission shall resume its meetings four days from the date of signature of this communique and shall complete the first phase of its work within fifteen days thereafter.

Affirming that the parties concerned shall strictly respect and scrupulously implement all the provisions of the Paris Agreement, its protocols, and this communique, the undersigned representatives of the parties signatory to the Paris Agreement have decided to issue this communique to record and publish the points on which they have agreed.

Signed in Paris, June 8, 1973.

In the left margin referring to 14, Thieu wrote: "Unconditionally and immediately." In the right margin he wrote: "According to Ambassador Sullivan what have we gained from the Communist side on this issue?"

THE WHITE HOUSE
WASHINGTON

June 6, 1973

Dear Mr. President:

I was astounded to receive your letter of June 6 which seems to suggest that you will refuse to instruct your representative in Paris to sign the joint communique which Dr. Kissinger has negotiated with Le Duc Tho. As I made clear to you in my letter of June 5, the text of the Communique is final and is not subject to further detailed revision.

It is therefore absolutely unrealistic to suggest, as you do in your letter, that a great number of paragraphs in the text be reopened and that further efforts be made to change the language. I would like to remind you that every change you have previously requested has been included in one form or another. Moreover, the suggestions which you have made do not reflect certain fundamental facts which have been explained to members of your staff.

For example, you complain that the question of democratic liberties, which arises from Article 11 of the Agreement, appears in the Communique prior to the paragraph on the political process, which arises from Article 12 of the Agreement. It is impossible for me to comprehend the basis for this complaint, when it is clearly stipulated in the Preamble of the Communique that the subject matter it contains appears in the sequence of the relevant articles of the agreement. And in the agreement which you signed Article 11 precedes the discussions of the political process in Article 12.

Moreover, the language which the Communique employs is drawn from the language which your own representatives insisted should be inserted into the Agreement last winter. It is, therefore, doubly difficult for me to comprehend your current objections to it.

-2-

There are many other points of this nature. The last sentence of paragraph 8(c) to which you object is drawn from Article 7(b) of the ceasefire protocol which the GVN has signed.

Similarly, you expressed preference for Le Duc Tho's wording on the prohibition of introduction of military personnel and war material into South Vietnam ignores the fact that this wording makes no provision for the legitimate replacement of war material in accordance with Article 7 of the Agreement. Had we accepted it you would have been cut off from any U.S. military assistance.

I feel I must tell you, Mr. President, that we are now at a point where the text must be viewed as final. The decision you must make is to instruct your representatives in Paris to join with Dr. Kissinger in signing the Communique as it currently exists, despite the minor misgivings which you express, or else to refuse to sign, to scuttle the Agreement, and to face the inevitably disastrous consequences. In the latter case I will have no choice but to make a public explanation of the reason for the failure of the talks with obvious consequences for Congressional support. Phrased in these stark terms, which are my honest appraisal of the situation, the choice seems obvious to me. We have been through too much together to have our whole common enterprise collapse in this way on these points. I count on your broad understanding of your own interests and of ours to give me your urgent positive answer no later than noon Saigon time on June 7.

Sincerely,

Richard Nixon

His Excellency
Nguyen Van Thieu
President of the Republic of Vietnam
Saigon

THE WHITE HOUSE
WASHINGTON

June 7, 1973

Dear Mr. President:

Before I actually received your letter of June 7, before I could even consider a response to the points you raised in it, and while my negotiators in Paris were preparing for a session with the North Vietnamese, I was dismayed to learn that your Government had announced in Saigon that you would refuse to be a signatory to the document under discussion between Dr. Kissinger and Le Duc Tho.

On reading your letter, I was further troubled that you should accuse me of "undue haste" in these negotiations. The facts are that we consulted with you in April concerning our intentions, we briefed your representatives daily in Paris during our talks in May, we sent Ambassador Sullivan to Saigon to consult with you while the talks were in suspense, and we have been in almost daily correspondence with you since their resumption. All your views were taken into account and we have achieved the best consideration of them which was possible in a document which any objective observer will readily recognize as being favorable to your interests.

However, by your action, you have left me no choice as to the manner in which we must now proceed. I have instructed Dr. Kissinger to propose to Le Duc Tho that the two of them should sign the text of the communique as it now stands and that we and the North Vietnamese should issue a public appeal to the two South Vietnamese parties to carry out its terms. If Le Duc Tho refuses to do this, we will of course end our Paris talks in failure. If we fail, we will be forced to make a public explanation of our failure, which will involve the issuance of the aborted document, the record of our negotiations, and the record of our consultations with you.

-2-

If Le Duc Tho agrees to our proposal (and I assume he will) this will mean that the entire world will look immediately to you to issue the ceasefire order and to take the other measures stipulated in the communique. It will mean that all your actions will be scrutinized, not as voluntary steps being taken because you wish peace, but rather as concessions which you appear to be making with reluctance. It is a totally unfavorable posture you have chosen for yourself and your Government.

I regret also to inform you that your action has thwarted any realistic prospect we might have had for an agreement on Cambodia. The position you have chosen for yourself deprives the North Vietnamese of any possible motive to achieve an understanding with us on this key issue.

It is impossible for me to calculate the consequences which your action will have on public and Congressional opinion in the United States. These consequences will certainly be negative for you and it is quite likely that they will be disastrous. That fact is a cause of most serious regret to me and it saddens me to contemplate that the enterprise in which we have shared so much should seem doomed to collapse in this manner.

Because of these considerations, I have instructed Dr. Kissinger to delay the signing ceremony in Paris until Saturday in order that you may have time to re-examine your position. He will continue to hold open to Le Duc Tho the possibility of a four-party signature at that time. However, if your position remains unchanged at that time, he will proceed in accordance with the instructions I have described in the preceding paragraphs.

-3-

Please let me have your answer to this letter by 8:00 a.m. Paris time June 8, so that we can act in accordance with your decision.

Sincerely,

Richard Nixon

His Excellency
Nguyen Van Thieu
President of the Republic of Vietnam
Saigon

27

SECRET

Saigon, Viet-Nam
June 8, 1973

Dear Mr. Minister:

Since delivering President Nixon's letter to President Thieu to you in the middle of the night I have received further information from Dr. Kissinger in Paris.

In accordance with his instructions from President Nixon, Dr. Kissinger at yesterday's meeting made the proposal mentioned in President Nixon's letter to President Thieu for a two-party document accompanied by an appeal. No agreement could be reached on this formula. This leaves a four-party document as the only alternative to the collapse of the talks. Regardless of the restraint with which our government handles this matter, the public release by the DRV of the aborted communique will result in the Government of Viet-Nam being blamed for the failure to reach agreement. I need hardly repeat the dire consequences which will flow from this turn of events.

Once again I have been asked to urge you to reconsider your position and accept the present text.

Please accept, Mr. Minister, the renewed assurances of my highest consideration.

Sincerely,
Charles S. Whitehouse
Charge d'Affaires, a. i.

His Excellency Tran Van Lam
Foreign Minister of the Republic of Viet-Nam
Saigon, Viet-Nam

SECRET

TOP SECRET

Saigon, Viet-Nam
June 8, 1973

Dear Mr. Minister:

I have just received a letter from President Nixon for President Thieu with instructions to deliver it immediately. In my talk with President Thieu this afternoon he asked me to call you at any hour if a reply from President Nixon was received.

In the message which accompanied this letter, I was asked to bring to your attention that there is no longer a question of textual changes or other modifications in the Communique and the choices which confront us are those outlined in President Nixon's letter.

With renewed assurances of my highest consideration.

Sincerely,
Charles S. Whitehouse
Charge d'Affaires, a. i.

His Excellency Tran Van Lam
Foreign Minister of the Republic of Viet-Nam
Saigon, Viet-Nam

TOP SECRET

Letter 27. Nixon to Thieu, June 8, 1973 (9 pages).

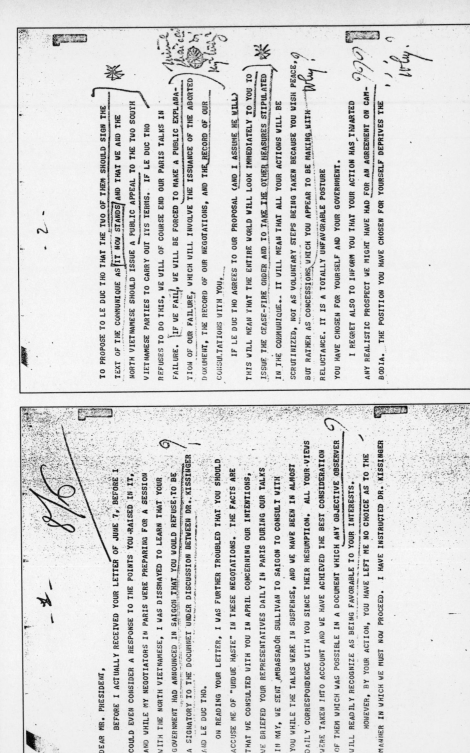

DEAR MR. PRESIDENT,

BEFORE I ACTUALLY RECEIVED YOUR LETTER OF JUNE 7, BEFORE I COULD EVEN CONSIDER A RESPONSE TO THE POINTS YOU RAISED IN IT, AND WHILE MY NEGOTIATORS IN PARIS WERE PREPARING FOR A SESSION WITH THE NORTH VIETNAMESE, I WAS DISMAYED TO LEARN THAT YOUR GOVERNMENT HAD ANNOUNCED IN SAIGON THAT YOU WOULD REFUSE TO BE A SIGNATORY TO THE DOCUMENT UNDER DISCUSSION BETWEEN DR. KISSINGER AND LE DUC THO.

ON READING YOUR LETTER, I WAS FURTHER TROUBLED THAT YOU SHOULD ACCUSE ME OF "UNDUE HASTE" IN THESE NEGOTIATIONS. THE FACTS ARE THAT WE CONSULTED WITH YOU IN APRIL CONCERNING OUR INTENTIONS, WE BRIEFED YOUR REPRESENTATIVES DAILY IN PARIS DURING OUR TALKS IN MAY, WE SENT AMBASSADOR SULLIVAN TO SAIGON TO CONSULT WITH YOU WHILE THE TALKS WERE IN SUSPENSE, AND WE HAVE BEEN IN ALMOST DAILY CORRESPONDENCE WITH YOU SINCE THEIR RESUMPTION. ALL YOUR VIEWS WERE TAKEN INTO ACCOUNT AND WE HAVE ACHIEVED THE BEST CONSIDERATION OF THEM WHICH WAS POSSIBLE IN A DOCUMENT WHICH ANY OBJECTIVE OBSERVER WILL READILY RECOGNIZE AS BEING FAVORABLE TO YOUR INTERESTS.

HOWEVER, BY YOUR ACTION, YOU HAVE LEFT ME NO CHOICE AS TO THE MANNER IN WHICH WE MUST NOW PROCEED. I HAVE INSTRUCTED DR. KISSINGER

- 2 -

TO PROPOSE TO LE DUC THO THAT THE TWO OF THEM SHOULD SIGN THE TEXT OF THE COMMUNIQUE AS [IT NOW STANDS] AND THAT WE AND THE NORTH VIETNAMESE SHOULD ISSUE A PUBLIC APPEAL TO THE TWO SOUTH VIETNAMESE PARTIES TO CARRY OUT ITS TERMS. IF LE DUC THO REFUSES TO DO THIS, WE WILL OF COURSE END OUR PARIS TALKS IN FAILURE. [IF WE FAIL,] WE WILL BE FORCED TO MAKE A PUBLIC EXPLANATION OF OUR FAILURE, WHICH WILL INVOLVE THE ISSUANCE OF THE ABORTED DOCUMENT, THE RECORD OF OUR NEGOTIATIONS, AND THE RECORD OF OUR CONSULTATIONS WITH YOU.

IF LE DUC THO AGREES TO OUR PROPOSAL (AND I ASSUME HE WILL) THIS WILL MEAN THAT THE ENTIRE WORLD WILL LOOK IMMEDIATELY TO YOU TO ISSUE THE CEASE-FIRE ORDER AND TO TAKE THE OTHER MEASURES STIPULATED IN THE COMMUNIQUE. IT WILL MEAN THAT ALL YOUR ACTIONS WILL BE SCRUTINIZED, NOT AS VOLUNTARY STEPS BEING TAKEN BECAUSE YOU WISH PEACE, BUT RATHER AS CONCESSIONS, WHICH YOU APPEAR TO BE MAKING WITH RELUCTANCE. IT IS A TOTALLY UNFAVORABLE POSTURE YOU HAVE CHOSEN FOR YOURSELF AND YOUR GOVERNMENT.

I REGRET ALSO TO INFORM YOU THAT YOUR ACTION HAS THWARTED ANY REALISTIC PROSPECT WE MIGHT HAVE HAD FOR AN AGREEMENT ON CAMBODIA. THE POSITION YOU HAVE CHOSEN FOR YOURSELF DEPRIVES THE

Thieu wrote in the right margin: "We must prepare very carefully for this eventuality."

Thieu wrote: "Who? If necessary must correct this and not let devious journalists damage our position."

-5-

NORTH VIETNAMESE OF ANY POSSIBLE MOTIVE TO ACHIEVE AN UNDERSTANDING WITH US ON THIS KEY ISSUE.

IT IS IMPOSSIBLE FOR ME TO CALCULATE THE CONSEQUENCES WHICH YOUR ACTION WILL HAVE ON PUBLIC AND CONGRESSIONAL OPINION IN THE UNITED STATES. THESE CONSEQUENCES WILL CERTAINLY BE NEGATIVE FOR YOU AND IT IS QUITE LIKELY THAT THEY WILL BE DISASTROUS.

THAT FACT IS A CAUSE OF MOST SERIOUS REGRET TO ME AND IT SADDENS ME TO CONTEMPLATE THAT THE ENTERPRISE IN WHICH WE HAVE SHARED SO MUCH SHOULD SEEM DOOMED TO COLLAPSE IN THIS MANNER

BECAUSE OF THESE CONSIDERATIONS, I HAVE INSTRUCTED DR. KISSINGER TO DELAY THE SIGNING CEREMONY IN PARIS UNTIL SATURDAY IN ORDER THAT YOU MAY HAVE TIME TO REEXAMINE YOUR POSITION. HE WILL CONTINUE TO HOLD OPEN TO LE DUC THO THE POSSIBILITY OF A FOUR-PARTY SIGNATURE AT THAT TIME. HOWEVER, IF YOUR POSITION REMAINS UNCHANGED AT THAT TIME, HE WILL PROCEED IN ACCORDANCE WITH THE INSTRUCTIONS I HAVE DESCRIBED IN THE PRECEDING PARAGRAPHS.

PLEASE LET ME HAVE YOUR ANSWER TO THIS LETTER BY 0800 PARIS TIME JUNE 8, SO THAT WE CAN ACT IN ACCORDANCE WITH YOUR DECISION.

SINCERELY, RICHARD NIXON.

TOP SECRET

Saigon, Viet-Nam
June 8, 1973

Dear Mr. Minister:

I have just received a letter from President Nixon for President Thieu with instructions to deliver it immediately. In my talk with President Thieu this afternoon he asked me to call you at any hour if a reply from President Nixon was received.

In the message which accompanied this letter, I was asked to bring to your attention that there is no longer a question of textual changes or other modifications in the Communiqué and the choices which confront us are those outlined in President Nixon's letter.

With renewed assurances of my highest consideration,

Sincerely,

Charles S. Whitehouse
Charles S. Whitehouse
Charge d'Affaires, a. i.

His Excellency Tran Van Lam
Foreign Minister of the Republic of Viet-Nam
Saigon, Viet-Nam

TOP SECRET

Thieu wrote: "You are sacrificing Vietnamese interests for Cambodian interests. Why?"

DEAR MR. PRESIDENT,

BEFORE I ACTUALLY RECEIVED YOUR LETTER OF JUNE 7, BEFORE I COULD EVEN CONSIDER A RESPONSE TO THE POINTS YOU RAISED IN IT, AND WHILE MY NEGOTIATORS IN PARIS WERE PREPARING FOR A SESSION WITH THE NORTH VIETNAMESE, I WAS DISMAYED TO LEARN THAT YOUR GOVERNMENT HAD ANNOUNCED IN SAIGON THAT YOU WOULD REFUSE TO BE A SIGNATORY TO THE DOCUMENT UNDER DISCUSSION BETWEEN DR. KISSINGER AND LE DUC THO.

ON READING YOUR LETTER, I WAS FURTHER TROUBLED THAT YOU SHOULD ACCUSE ME OF "UNDUE HASTE" IN THESE NEGOTIATIONS. THE FACTS ARE THAT WE CONSULTED WITH YOU IN APRIL CONCERNING OUR INTENTIONS, WE BRIEFED YOUR REPRESENTATIVES DAILY IN PARIS DURING OUR TALKS IN MAY, WE SENT AMBASSADOR SULLIVAN TO SAIGON TO CONSULT WITH YOU WHILE THE TALKS WERE IN SUSPENSE, AND WE HAVE BEEN IN ALMOST DAILY CORRESPONDENCE WITH YOU SINCE THEIR RESUMPTION. ALL YOUR VIEWS WERE TAKEN INTO ACCOUNT AND WE HAVE ACHIEVED THE BEST CONSIDERATION OF THEM WHICH WAS POSSIBLE IN A DOCUMENT WHICH ANY OBJECTIVE OBSERVER WILL READILY RECOGNIZE AS BEING FAVORABLE TO YOUR INTERESTS.

HOWEVER, BY YOUR ACTION, YOU HAVE LEFT ME NO CHOICE AS TO THE MANNER IN WHICH WE MUST NOW PROCEED. I HAVE INSTRUCTED DR. KISSINGER

TO PROPOSE TO LE DUC THO THAT THE TWO OF THEM SHOULD SIGN THE TEXT OF THE COMMUNIQUE AS IT NOW STANDS AND THAT WE AND THE NORTH VIETNAMESE SHOULD ISSUE A PUBLIC APPEAL TO THE TWO SOUTH VIETNAMESE PARTIES TO CARRY OUT ITS TERMS. IF LE DUC THO REFUSES TO DO THIS, WE WILL OF COURSE END OUR PARIS TALKS IN FAILURE. IF WE FAIL, WE WILL BE FORCED TO MAKE A PUBLIC EXPLANATION OF OUR FAILURE, WHICH WILL INVOLVE THE ISSUANCE OF THE ABORTED DOCUMENT, THE RECORD OF OUR NEGOTIATIONS, AND THE RECORD OF OUR CONSULTATIONS WITH YOU.

IF LE DUC THO AGREES TO OUR PROPOSAL (AND I ASSUME HE WILL) THIS WILL MEAN THAT THE ENTIRE WORLD WILL LOOK IMMEDIATELY TO YOU TO ISSUE THE CEASE-FIRE ORDER AND TO TAKE THE OTHER MEASURES STIPULATED IN THE COMMUNIQUE. IT WILL MEAN THAT ALL YOUR ACTIONS WILL BE SCRUTINIZED, NOT AS VOLUNTARY STEPS BEING TAKEN BECAUSE YOU WISH PEACE, BUT RATHER AS CONCESSIONS WHICH YOU APPEAR TO BE MAKING WITH RELUCTANCE. IT IS A TOTALLY UNFAVORABLE POSTURE YOU HAVE CHOSEN FOR YOURSELF AND YOUR GOVERNMENT.

I REGRET ALSO TO INFORM YOU THAT YOUR ACTION HAS IMPARTED ANY REALISTIC PROSPECT WE MIGHT HAVE HAD FOR AN AGREEMENT ON CAMBODIA. THE POSITION YOU HAVE CHOSEN FOR YOURSELF DEPRIVES THE

NORTH VIETNAMESE OF ANY POSSIBLE MOTIVE TO ACHIEVE AN UNDERSTANDING
WITH US ON THIS KEY ISSUE.

IT IS IMPOSSIBLE FOR ME TO CALCULATE THE CONSEQUENCES WHICH
YOUR ACTION WILL HAVE ON PUBLIC AND CONGRESSIONAL OPINION IN THE
UNITED STATES. THESE CONSEQUENCES WILL CERTAINLY BE NEGATIVE
FOR YOU AND IT IS QUITE LIKELY THAT THEY WILL BE DISASTROUS.
THAT FACT IS A CAUSE OF MOST SERIOUS REGRET TO ME AND IT SADDENS ME
TO CONTEMPLATE THAT THE ENTERPRISE IN WHICH WE HAVE SHARED
SO MUCH SHOULD SEEM DOOMED TO COLLAPSE IN THIS MANNER

BECAUSE OF THESE CONSIDERATIONS, I HAVE INSTRUCTED DR.
KISSINGER TO DELAY THE SIGNING CEREMONY IN PARIS UNTIL SATURDAY
IN ORDER THAT YOU MAY HAVE TIME TO REEXAMINE YOUR POSITION. HE
WILL CONTINUE TO HOLD OPEN TO LE DUC THO THE POSSIBILITY OF A
FOUR-PARTY SIGNATURE AT THAT TIME. HOWEVER, IF YOUR POSITION
REMAINS UNCHANGED AT THAT TIME, HE WILL PROCEED IN ACCORDANCE
WITH THE INSTRUCTIONS I HAVE DESCRIBED IN THE PRECEDING PARAGRAPHS.

PLEASE LET ME HAVE YOUR ANSWER TO THIS LETTER BY 0800 PARIS
TIME JUNE 8, SO THAT WE CAN ACT IN ACCORDANCE WITH YOUR DECISION.

SINCERELY, RICHARD NIXON.

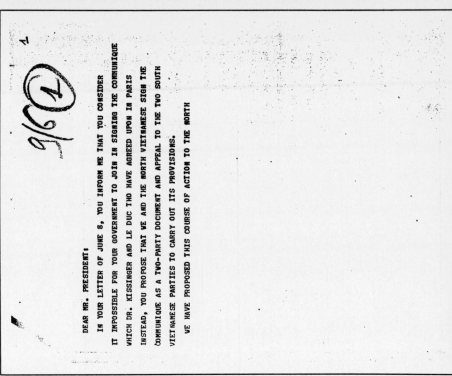

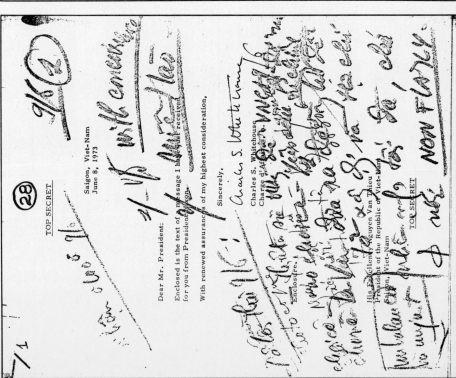

Letter 28.   Nixon to Thieu, June 8, 1973 (5 pages).
Thieu wrote over the cover letter: "Really the United States leaves the Republic of Vietnam with no choice. Propose amendments to show our cooperation and good will. Do not say no flatly." In the left hand corner Thieu wrote in English: "Unbalanced and unjust."

VIETNAMESE AND THEY HAVE REJECTED IT. THEY SAY THAT THERE MUST BE A FOUR-PARTY SIGNATURE OF THE COMMUNIQUE OR THE NEGOTIATIONS WILL COLLAPSE. IF THE NEGOTIATIONS COLLAPSE, THE NORTH VIETNAMESE WILL PUBLISH THE TEXT OF THE COMMUNIQUE AS IT HAD BEEN AGREED, BLAME ITS ABORTION ENTIRELY ON YOUR GOVERNMENT AND EXPLOIT THIS SITUATION TO YOUR CERTAIN DISASTER.

THEREFORE, AFTER SERIOUS REFLECTION, I FEEL THAT THERE IS NO ALTERNATIVE EXCEPT A FOUR-PARTY SIGNATURE OF THE COMMUNIQUE. I FIRMLY BELIEVE THAT IT WILL IMPROVE THE SITUATION, IN TERMS OF BOTH CONDITIONS WITHIN VIETNAM AND THE CONTINUATION OF THE PUBLIC SUPPORT NECESSARY TO MAINTAIN THE COURSE MY OWN GOVERNMENT HAS HERETOFORE PURSUED. EVEN IF YOU ARE CORRECT, HOWEVER, IN SOME OF YOUR CONCERNS, THEY CANNOT BE AS HARMFUL AS WOULD BE THE CONSEQUENCES OF NO AGREEMENT AT ALL BECAUSE OF THE GVN'S FAILURE TO ASSOCIATE ITSELF WITH OUR COURSE. THE WORST POSSIBLE CONSEQUENCES WHICH YOU CONJECTURE FOR YOUR GOVERNMENT RESULTING FROM THE SIGNATURE OF THIS DOCUMENT ARE PALE BY COMPARISON WITH THE CERTAINLY PREDICTABLE CONSEQUENCES WHICH WILL RESULT IF OUR NEGOTIATIONS FAIL AS A RESULT OF THE GVN'S FAILURE TO SIGN THE COMMUNIQUE.

IF THEY FAIL, THERE WILL BE AN INEVITABLE CONFRONTATION

BETWEEN YOU AND ME IN WHICH I SHALL HAVE TO DISAVOW YOUR REASONS FOR REFUSING TO SIGN AND IN WHICH I SHALL HAVE TO STATE PUBLICLY THAT YOU HAVE BLOCKED THE ACHIEVEMENT OF PROGRESS IN THE SEARCH FOR PEACE. IN YOUR LETTER YOU MENTION A PUBLIC EXPLANATION OF YOUR POSITION. YOU SHOULD KEEP IN MIND THAT IT WILL BE IN THE CONTEXT OF ATTACKING A DRAFT TO WHICH WE HAVE AGREED. UNLIKE OCTOBER, WE WILL OPPOSE AND NOT BACK YOUR POSITION.

YOU SHOULD ALSO KEEP IN MIND THAT THE SENATE AND HOUSE CONFEREES WILL BE VOTING ON MONDAY ON AN ABSOLUTE PROHIBITION OF FUNDS FOR MILITARY OPERATIONS IN OR OVER CAMBODIA AND LAOS. THE IMPACT ON YOUR COUNTRY OF AN IMMEDIATE CESSATION OF OUR AIR OPERATIONS IN CAMBODIA, AND THE INEVITABLE SUBSEQUENT EXTENSION SUCH A PROHIBITION TO ALL INDOCHINA SHOULD BE APPARENT TO YOU. FAILURE TO SIGN WILL THUS LEAD TO A SEQUENCE OF EVENTS WHICH CAN ONLY BECOME DISASTROUS FOR YOU AND YOUR GOVERNMENT. IN THE CONTEXT OF AMERICAN OPINION, EVERYTHING WHICH SUBSEQUENTLY GOES WRONG IN INDOCHINA WILL BE BLAMED ON THE GVN, NO MATTER WHAT ITS CAUSE. HANOI WILL DEMAND THAT WE FORCE YOU TO SIGN THE COMMUNIQUE. CONGRESS AND MUCH OF OUR PRESS WILL JOIN. THERE IS A HIGH PROB- ABILITY THAT THE CONGRESS WILL BLOCK ALL FUNDS FOR ECONOMIC OR

Thieu wrote: "Why? Between who and who? In October, the United States backed the Republic of Vietnam, when?"

MILITARY ASSISTANCE TO YOUR GOVERNMENT UNTIL YOU SIGN THE COMMUNIQUE.

THEREFORE, I MUST REITERATE, IN THE MOST INSISTENT WAY, THAT WE

NEED YOUR GOVERNMENT'S SIGNATURE ON THE COMMUNIQUE IF WE ARE TO

AVERT A DISASTER FOR YOU AND YOUR GOVERNMENT -- AND FOR EVERYTHING

WE HAVE SOUGHT TO ACHIEVE IN TEN YEARS OF COMMON EFFORT.

I WILL NEED YOU REPLY TO THIS MESSAGE, AGREEING TO THAT

SIGNATURE, IN TIME FOR ME TO INSTRUCT OUR NEGOTIATORS IN PARIS HOW

TO PROCEED BY 0700 PARIS TIME, JUNE 9.

THE FOUR-PARTY SIGNATURE OF THE COMMUNIQUE IS THE ONLY

ACCEPTABLE COURSE OPEN TO US. I ASK YOU TO CONSIDER, IN FORMULATING

YOUR ANSWER TO THIS LETTER, WHETHER YOU REALLY FEEL THAT A REJECTION

OF THAT COURSE FOR THE REASONS YOU HAVE ADVANCED IS WORTH GIVING

TOTAL SATISFACTION TO ALL THOSE WHO HAVE OPPOSED EVERYTHING WE

WORKED TOGETHER TO ACHIEVE IN OUR COMMON ENDEAVORS, AND FOR

WHICH SO MANY THOUSANDS OF OUR COUNTRYMEN HAVE ALREADY GIVEN THEIR

LIVES.

SINCERELY,

RICHARD NIXON

SECRET

(29)

Saigon, Viet-Nam
June 9, 1973

Dear Mr. President,

I enclose a message which I have just received for you from President Nixon.

Please accept the assurances of my highest consideration.

Very sincerely,

Charles S. Whitehouse

Charles S. Whitehouse
Charge d'Affaires, a.i.

Enclosure

His Excellency
Nguyen Van Thieu
President of the Republic of Viet-Nam
Saigon

SECRET

DEAR MR. PRESIDENT:

I WISH YOU TO KNOW THAT I APPRECIATE THE FACT THAT THE CHOICE WHICH HAS BEEN PLACED BEFORE YOU AS A RESULT OF DEVELOPMENTS IN OUR NEGOTIATIONS WITH THE NORTH VIETNAMESE ENTAILS A DIFFICULT DECISION FOR YOU. I UNDERSTAND YOU WILL BE MEETING WITH YOUR ADVISERS ON THE MORNING OF JUNE 9 TO FACE THIS DECISION. AS YOU ENTER THAT MEETING, THERE ARE SEVERAL CONSIDERATIONS I FEEL I SHOULD BRING TO YOUR ATTENTION.

THE FIRST CONSIDERATION CONCERNS ALL THOSE VARIOUS MATTERS WHICH I HAVE RAISED WITH YOU IN OUR EARLIER COMMUNICATIONS AS THEY AFFECT PUBLIC AND CONGRESSIONAL OPINION IN THE UNITED STATES. I REPEAT, ONCE AGAIN, THAT NO MATTER HOW STRONGLY YOU OR YOUR ADVISERS MAY FEEL ABOUT SOME OF THE MATTERS WHICH TROUBLE YOU, THEY CAN NOT COMPARE IN MAGNITUDE WITH THE PROBLEMS WHICH WILL BESET YOU BY YOUR REFUSAL TO SIGN THE COMMUNIQUE. THE MOOD IN OUR COUNTRY IS SUCH THAT I CAN PREDICT THAT THE CONSEQUENCES OF THAT REFUSAL WILL BE DISASTROUS.

THE SECOND CONSIDERATION, WHICH I WANT TO CONVEY TO YOU IN TOTAL CONFIDENCE, IS THAT WE HAVE AN ARRANGEMENT CONCERNING LAOS WHICH WILL INVOLVE THE WITHDRAWAL OF NORTH VIETNAMESE FORCES FROM THAT COUNTRY OVER A PERIOD OF SIXTY DAYS BEGINNING JULY 1.

Letter 29. Nixon to Thieu, June 9, 1973 (3 pages).

WE FEEL THIS IS OF PARAMOUNT IMPORTANCE TO YOU AND SHOULD NOT
BE LIGHTLY DISMISSED AS ONE OF THE ELEMENTS WHICH WILL BE LOST
IF THIS COMMUNIQUE IS NOT SIGNED.

FINALLY, I WANT TO INFORM YOU THAT WE ARE ENGAGED IN
A COMPLEX THREE CORNERED NEGOTIATION ON CAMBODIA. WE HAVE MADE
SOME PROGRESS IN THIS EFFORT AND WE HOPE TO BE ABLE TO EXPLOIT
IT FURTHER IN ORDER TO FORESTALL SOME OF THE SHORTSIGHTED STEPS
WHICH OUR CONGRESS IS PREPARED TO TAKE WITH RESPECT TO THAT
COUNTRY. WE WILL NEED SOME TIME FOR THAT PURPOSE AND THIS COMMUNIQUE
WILL BUY IT FOR US.

MR. PRESIDENT, THESE ARE THE THOUGHTS WHICH I WISH TO
IMPART TO YOU ON THIS FATEFUL MORNING IN OUR RELATIONS. I HOPE
THEY WILL PROVE OF VALUE TO YOU IN YOUR DELIBERATIONS.

SINCERELY,

RICHARD NIXON

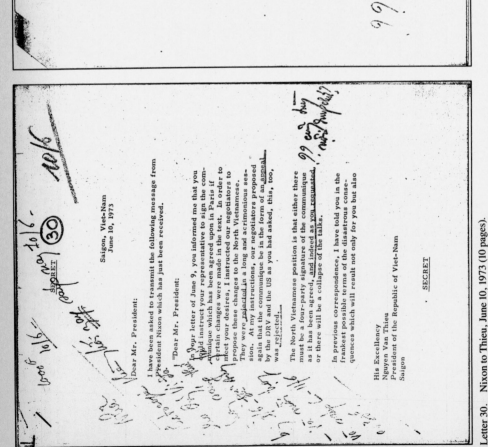

SECRET
2

for your Lao and Cambodian neighbors, if the talks collapse. In order to avoid those consequences, we have arranged a forty-eight hour delay during which Dr. Kissinger will be returning to Washington for consultations. At my instructions Dr. Kissinger agreed to return to Paris on Tuesday to sign the communique. We are now at the point where no further delay is possible.

During this same period, you will have an opportunity to reconsider your position. In this reconsideration, I trust you will reflect upon all those factors which I have previously cited, as well as a number of other factors which I wish to call to your attention in this letter.

There is, for example, the factor of the restraints which we hope to impose upon North Vietnam. These restraints can be effective only so long as you and we are clearly seen to be following a common policy and to share the same evaluation of events. If we are split by a public confrontation, the opportunity to insure the restraints vanish.

In a similar way, our ability to sustain international support for your position, even in such matters as obtaining satisfactory membership in the International Control Commission, will be weakened. The economic assistance group which we have been trying to mobilize among friendly nations to aid you in your economic program is also jeopardized.

All these results will flow from the fact that your Government refuses to accept language in a communique which neither adds to nor detracts from arrangements which you accepted in the January 27 Agreement, indeed which in its major provisions is drawn from that document.

SECRET

SECRET   30

Saigon, Viet-Nam
June 10, 1973

Dear Mr. President:

I have been asked to transmit the following message from President Nixon which has just been received.

"Dear Mr. President:

In your letter of June 9, you informed me that you would instruct your representative to sign the communique which has been agreed upon in Paris if certain changes were made in the text. In order to meet your desires, I instructed our negotiators to propose these changes to the North Vietnamese. They were rejected in a long and acrimonious session. At my instructions, our negotiators proposed again that the communique be in the form of an appeal by the DRV and the US as you had asked, this, too, was rejected.

The North Vietnamese position is that either there must be a four-party signature of the communique as it has been agreed, and indeed as you requested, or there will be a collapse of the talks.

In previous correspondence, I have told you in the frankest possible terms of the disastrous consequences which will result not only for you but also

His Excellency
Nguyen Van Thieu
President of the Republic of Viet-Nam
Saigon

SECRET

Letter 30.   Nixon to Thieu, June 10, 1973 (10 pages).
In the left margin Thieu wrote: "Make photocopies and distribute immediately this morning June 10 for those who have attended the meeting on June 8 so they can reflect on it and convene a meeting at 0830 on June 11." In the right margin: "Depending on the substance."

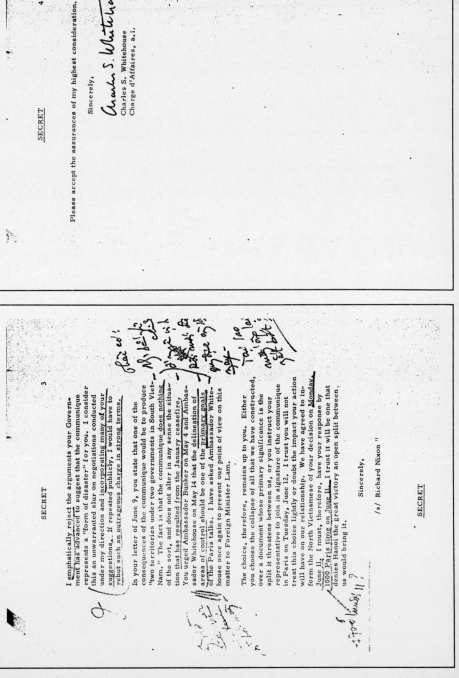

SECRET 4

Please accept the assurances of my highest consideration.

Sincerely,

Charles S. Whitehouse

Charles S. Whitehouse
Charge d'Affaires, a.i.

SECRET 3

I emphatically reject the arguments your Government has advanced to suggest that the communique represents a "form of disaster" for you. I consider this an unwarranted slur on negotiations conducted under my direction and incorporating many of your suggestions. If repeated publicly, I would have to rebut such an outrageous charge in strong terms.

In your letter of June 9, you state that one of the consequences of the communique would be to produce "two governments in South Viet-Nam." The fact is that the communique does nothing of the sort, and does not alter in any sense the situation that has resulted from the January ceasefire. You urged Ambassador Bunker on May 4 and Ambassador Whitehouse on May 14 that the delineation of areas of control should be one of the primary goals of the Paris talks. I have asked Ambassador Whitehouse once again to present our point of view on this matter to Foreign Minister Lam.

The choice, therefore, remains up to you. Either you choose the collapse of all that we have constructed, over a document whose primary significance is the split it threatens between us, or you instruct your representative to join in signature of the communique in Paris on Tuesday, June 12. I trust you will not treat this choice lightly or doubt the impact your action will have on our relationship. We have agreed to inform the North Vietnamese of your decision on Monday, June 11, 1000 Paris time on June 11. I trust it will be one that denies Hanoi the great victory an open split between us would bring it.

Sincerely,

/s/ Richard Nixon "

SECRET

In the left margin Thieu wrote: "Now we continue to maintain this demand." In the right margin: "There must be:—Serious ceasefire; —Remain in place; —Then immediate delimitation of the area under control by each side. Why do you skip some of these steps?"

SECRET   2

5) In short, a cease-fire in place automatically means that there are areas in South Vietnam which are not controlled by the GVN. These areas are ultimately to be delineated in accordance with the January 27 agreements. Nothing in the communique alters or modifies that concept. Paragraph 12 B concerning the location of TPJMC teams leaves the ultimate decision on their location up to the TPJMC as does the GVN draft of this paragraph.

6) The joint communique does not commit the GVN to stationing any teams of the TPJMC at a point located between an area controlled by one party and an area controlled by another or even to agreeing that there exists any area controlled by the communists. This is left strictly to the agreed decision of the two South Vietnamese parties.

7) There appears to us to be a good deal of merit in having TPJMC teams outside of population centers in which they wish to engage in subversive activities.

8) With respect to the paragraphs in the communique dealing with political matters, it is important to note that the agreement remains fixed and should not be superseded by the communique. There is no reason why the GVN cannot include setting a date for elections among those "internal matters" on which the parties are to reach agreement within 45 days. It should also be noted that the only reference to elections in the communique is taken directly from Article 12 B of the Agreement.

SECRET

SECRET

TALKING PAPER

Although the following points were not included in President Nixon's letter of June 10 to President Thieu, the President has asked me to go over in detail our answers to the concerns the Government of Vietnam has expressed with regard to portions of the draft communique.

1) It has been our understanding that the Government of Vietnam wished to achieve early agreement with the other, side on the delimitation of areas of control and hoped that the Paris negotiations would bring about subsequent detailed talks on this subject in the Joint Military Commission. This point has been stressed by President Thieu and by other senior officials.

2) The concept of stationing teams of the Two Party Joint Military Commission in certain places along boundaries of areas of control has been considered helpful by senior ARVN officers. As stated in the communique, this stationing would be only at places to which the GVN agreed and does not involve stationing teams along a theoretical frontier between two parts of South Vietnam.

3) The foregoing concept is consistent with concepts already spelled out in the Agreement and its Protocols. It is particularly noteworthy that there is no suggestion of a single "territory" controlled by the communists. Instead, reference is made to "areas" of control or in the case of paragraph 8 B to places "where an area controlled by one of them adjoins an area controlled by the other."

4) Similarly, the reference in paragraph 8 C to additional points of entry in "the territory controlled by that party" does not imply a territorial division of the country. This merely describes the location of the points in terms of military control,

June 10, 1973

SECRET

SECRET

for your Lao and Cambodian neighbors if the talks collapse. In order to avoid those consequences, we have arranged a forty-eight hour delay during which Dr. Kissinger will be returning to Washington for consultations. At my instructions Dr. Kissinger agreed to return to Paris on Tuesday to sign the communique. We are now at the point where no further delay is possible.

During this same period, you will have an opportunity to reconsider your position. In this reconsideration, I trust you will reflect upon all those factors which I have previously cited, as well as a number of other factors which I wish to call to your attention in this letter.

There is, for example, the factor of the restraints which we hope to impose upon Chinese and Soviet supplies of equipment to North Vietnam. These restraints can be effective only so long as you and we are clearly seen to be following a common policy and to share the same evaluation of events. If we are split by a public confrontation, the opportunity to insure the restraints will vanish.

In a similar way, our ability to sustain international support for your position, even in such matters as obtaining satisfactory membership in the International Control Commission, will be weakened. The economic assistance group which we have been trying to mobilize among friendly nations to aid you in your economic program is also jeopardized.

All these results will flow from the fact that your Government refuses to accept language in a communique which neither adds to nor detracts from arrangements which you accepted in the January 27 Agreement, indeed which in its major provisions is drawn from that document.

SECRET

SECRET

Saigon, Viet-Nam
June 10, 1973

Dear Mr. President:

I have been asked to transmit the following message from President Nixon which has just been received.

"Dear Mr. President:

In your letter of June 9, you informed me that you could instruct your representative to sign the communique which has been agreed upon in Paris if certain changes were made in the text. In order to meet your desires, I instructed our negotiators to propose these changes to the North Vietnamese. They were rejected in a long and acrimonious session. At my instructions, our negotiators proposed again that the communique be in the form of an appeal by the DRV and the US as you had asked, this, too, was rejected.

The North Vietnamese position is that either there must be a four-party signature of the communique, as it has been agreed, and indeed as you requested, or there will be a collapse of the talks.

In previous correspondence, I have told you in the frankest possible terms of the disastrous consequences which will result not only for you but also

His Excellency
Nguyen Van Thieu
President of the Republic of Viet-Nam
Saigon

SECRET

SECRET

I emphatically reject the arguments your Government has advanced to suggest that the communique represents a "form of disaster" for you. I consider this an unwarranted slur on negotiations conducted under my direction and incorporating many of your suggestions. If repeated publicly, I would have to rebut such an outrageous charge in strong terms.

In your letter of June 9, you state that one of the consequences of the communique would be to produce "two territories under two governments in South Viet-Nam." The fact is that the communique does nothing of the sort, and does not alter in any sense the situation that has resulted from the January ceasefire. You urged Ambassador Bunker on May 4 and Ambassador Whitehouse on May 14 that the delineation of areas of control should be one of the primary goals of the Paris talks. I have asked Ambassador Whitehouse once again to present our point of view on this matter to Foreign Minister Lam.

The choice, therefore, remains up to you. Either you choose the collapse of all that we have constructed, over a document whose primary significance is the split it threatens between us, or you instruct your representative to join in signature of the communique in Paris on Tuesday, June 12. I trust you will not treat this choice lightly or doubt the impact your action will have on our relationship. We have agreed to inform the North Vietnamese of your decision on Monday, June 11. I must, therefore, have your response by 1000 Paris time on June 11. I trust it will be one that denies Hanoi the great victory an open split between us would bring it.

Sincerely,

/s/ Richard Nixon "

SECRET

SECRET

Please accept the assurances of my highest consideration.

Sincerely,

Charles S. Whitehouse
Charge d'Affaires, a.i.

TOP SECRET

Saigon, Viet-Nam
June 13, 1973

Dear Mr. President:

I have received the enclosed letter from President Nixon with the request that it be delivered to you at once.

You will note that our negotiators have succeeded in obtaining the inclusion of paragraph 9 B of the Agreement in the Communique. The attachment to the President's letter gives the revised text of paragraph 11 of the English text of the draft communique.

The White House has asked me to inform you that if your Government agrees to sign the Communique today at 1600 Paris time, the cease-fire order will be issued at 1200 GMT June 14, 1973 and the cease-fire will become effective at 0400 GMT June 15, 1973.

The White House has confirmed that we would very much appreciate having your reply by 1300 Saigon time today.

Please accept renewed assurances of my highest consideration.

Sincerely,

Charles S. Whitehouse
Charge d'Affaires, a. i.

His Excellency Nguyen Van Thieu
President of the Republic of Viet-Nam
Saigon, Viet-Nam

TOP SECRET

TOP SECRET

Saigon, Viet-Nam
June 13, 1973

Dear Mr. President:

Your letter of June 12 came as a sharp and very painful blow to our friendship and mutual confidence, and to our common interests. In the light of the sacrifices we have made and the risks we have run in your behalf it seemed inconceivable that you would respond in such negative fashion. I cannot hide from you the strain on our relationship caused by the fact that you would totally ignore the offer of assurances I was prepared to make if you signed the Communique in its current form.

Nevertheless, because the consequences of failure of the negotiations risk making a mockery of so much heroism and suffering, I instructed Dr. Kissinger once again to delay his initialling of the text and to seek some satisfaction of your "minimum" conditions, even though I do not consider them of sufficient intrinsic merit to justify the risks you have pressed me to take or the attitude you have adopted toward my Government.

Dr. Kissinger spent a long and bitter session with Le Duc Tho in Paris today. In this session, he has been unable to achieve any change whatsoever in the paragraph concerning the location of the Two Party Joint Military Commission teams.

That paragraph, as it now stands, commits you to nothing concerning the team locations and preserves entirely your authority to control their location by stipulating that you

His Excellency Nguyen Van Thieu
President of the Republic of Viet-Nam
Saigon, Viet-Nam

TOP SECRET

Letter 31.   Nixon to Thieu, June 13, 1973 (5 pages).

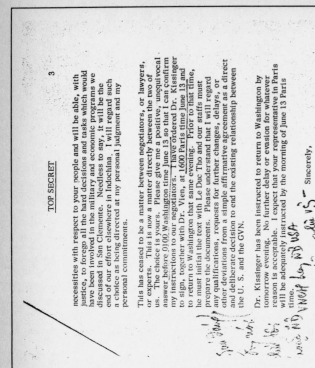

TOP SECRET

3

necessities with respect to your people and will be able, with justice, to forego all the hard decisions and tasks which would have been involved in the military and economic programs we discussed in San Clemente. Needless to say, it will be the end of our effort elsewhere in Indochina. I will regard such a choice as being directed at my personal judgment and my personal commitments.

This has ceased to be a matter between negotiators, or lawyers, or experts. This is now a matter directly between the two of us. The choice is yours. Please give me a positive, unequivocal answer before 0100 Washington time June 13 so that I can confirm my instructions to our negotiators. I have ordered Dr. Kissinger to sign, together with Dr. Vien, at 1600 Paris time June 13 and to return to Washington that same evening. Prior to that time, he must initial the text with Le Duc Tho and our staffs must prepare the documents. Please understand that I will regard any qualifications, requests for further changes, delays, or other deviations from a simple affirmative agreement as a direct and deliberate decision to end the existing relationship between the U. S. and the GVN.

Dr. Kissinger has been instructed to return to Washington by tomorrow evening. No further delay or evasion for whatever reason is acceptable. I expect that your representative in Paris will be adequately instructed by the morning of June 13 Paris time.

Sincerely,

Richard Nixon

TOP SECRET

TOP SECRET

2

must agree to the selection of their locations in the Commission itself. You do not have to agree either that any areas adjoin or that any teams should be stationed there. It is therefore inconceivable and unacceptable to my Government or U. S. public opinion that this paragraph should be made an issue of success or failure in these negotiations.

On the other hand, my negotiators have succeeded in obtaining a significant change in the paragraph concerning the South Vietnamese people's right to self-determination by obtaining a verbatim inclusion of Article 9 (b) of the Agreement in that paragraph. You suggested in your letter that this text precede the paragraph on democratic liberties, presumably because of the numerical sequence of articles in the Agreement. However, it is my sincere feeling that its location in the paragraph on self-determination is better. In that location, it is tied in directly with the functions of the National Council, and by having it precede the sub-paragraph on the Council, makes clear that functions of the Council are subordinate to the election process. Moreover, by disengaging it from the paragraph on democratic liberties, it deprives the communists of the tactic of using their own interpretation of democratic liberties as a block to the holding of elections. I am attaching the text of that paragraph.

Mr. President, this is frankly more than I thought we could achieve on your behalf. But, in order to accomplish this, I have had to give my personal word to the North Vietnamese, that this is the last change we will seek. If you refuse to accept these results and continue to decline to instruct your representative to sign the Communique, you will have repudiated my entire policy of constant support for you, your Government, and your country.

If you choose this course, Mr. President, you will have determined the future of my administration's policy with respect to Viet-Nam. I will be forced to follow American Congressional and public opinion by supporting only marginal humanitarian

TOP SECRET

Thieu wrote: "Excessive! This is what you say. Not what I say or the people of the Republic of Vietnam or the people of the United States of America."

No 1316

while 9 (b)
wa agud

TOP SECRET

ATTACHMENT

Consistent with the principles for the exercise of the South Vietnamese people's right to self-determination stated in Chapter IV of the Agreement:

(A) The South Vietnamese people shall decide themselves the political future of South Viet-Nam through genuinely free and democratic general elections under international supervision.

(B) The National Council of National Reconciliation and Concord consisting of three equal segments shall be formed as soon as possible, in conformity with Article 12 of the Agreement.

The two South Vietnamese parties shall sign an Agreement on the internal matters of South Viet-Nam as soon as possible, and shall do their utmost to accomplish this within forty-five days from the date of signature of this Joint Communique.

(C) The two South Vietnamese parties shall agree through consultations on the institutions for which the free and democratic general elections provided for in Article 9 (B) of the Agreement will be held.

(D) The two South Vietnamese parties shall implement Article 13 of the Agreement, which reads as follows:

-- The question of Vietnamese armed forces in South Viet-Nam shall be settled by the two South Vietnamese parties in a spirit of national reconciliation and concord, equality and mutual respect, without foreign interference, in accordance with the postwar situation. Among the questions to be discussed by the two South Vietnamese parties are steps to reduce their military effectives and to demobilize the troops being reduced. The two South Vietnamese parties will accomplish this as soon as possible.

TOP SECRET

Saigon, August 10, 1974

Dear Mr. President:

President Ford has asked me to transmit to you the following message:

"Dear Mr. President:

As I assume the office of President of the United States, one of my first thoughts concerns the savage attacks your armed forces are now successfully resisting with such courage and bravery. I do not think I really need to inform you that American foreign policy has always been marked by its essential continuity and its essential bipartisan nature. This is even more true today and the existing commitments this nation has made in the past are still valid and will be fully honored in my administration.

These reassurances are particularly relevant to the Republic of Vietnam. We have traveled a long and hard road together. I have listened to Ambassador Martin's report on the remarkable progress the Republic of Vietnam has made under your leadership. In the period since the signing of the Paris Agreements, I have been heartened by his report of your personal determination to continue the improvement of your governmental processes to insure that our aid, and the increasing aid we confidently expect from other donor countries, can be rapidly and effectively utilized to bring the South Vietnamese economy to a self-sustaining level in the next few years. As the professional efficiency, the high morale, and the combat effectiveness of the armed forces of the Republic of Vietnam

become increasingly evident to the leaders of the Democratic Republic of Vietnam in Hanoi, it is my earnest hope that they will agree to return to participation in the mechanisms set up by the Paris Agreements and begin to seriously work out with you modalities for the full and complete implementation of the Paris Agreements which I know is your desire.

I know you must be concerned by the initial steps taken by the Congress on the current fiscal year appropriations for both economic and military assistance to the Republic of Vietnam. Our legislative process is a complicated one and it is not yet completed. Although it may take a little time, I do want to reassure you of my confidence that in the end our support will be adequate on both counts.

In these important endeavors I shall look to Dr. Kissinger, whom I have asked to remain as Secretary of State, for guidance and support. He has my fullest confidence, as does Ambassador Martin.

Sincerely,

Gerald R. Ford"

With renewed assurances of my highest consideration,

Sincerely,

W. Y. Lehmann
Charge d'Affaires, a.i.

His Excellency
Nguyen Van Thieu
President of the Republic of Vietnam

Letter 32. Ford to Thieu, August 10, 1974 (2 pages).

THE WHITE HOUSE
WASHINGTON

October 24, 1974

Dear Mr. President:

I very much appreciated meeting with Foreign Minister Bac and receiving from him your letter of September 19.

American policy toward Vietnam remains unchanged under this Administration. We continue strongly to support your government's efforts to defend and to promote the independence and well-being of the South Vietnamese people. We also remain confident in the courage, determination and skill of the South Vietnamese people and armed forces.

I fully understand and share your concern about the current situation in the Republic of Vietnam, particularly the growing Communist military threat which you now face. I am also well aware of the critical necessity of American military and economic aid for your country. I give you my firm assurance that this Administration will continue to make every effort to provide the assistance you need.

Although I would welcome the opportunity to meet with you to discuss ways and means to achieve a genuine and lasting peace in South Vietnam, prior commitments preclude such a meeting at this time. But I hope that such a meeting can be arranged in the future.

I agree with you that it is essential that my government clearly indicate its support for your government

---

2

and for the full implementation of the Paris Agreements. I believe my public statement of October 9, my meeting with Foreign Minister Bac and Deputy Defense Secretary Clement's visit to Saigon all clearly demonstrate that we are standing firm in our commitments to you. We have also conveyed to other powers having an interest in Vietnam that we continue to support your government and that we favor a complete implementation of the Paris Agreements. I shall take advantage of other occasions to show my support for your government and for the peace that we achieved together.

Our countries have been through many difficult times together. It appears likely that we shall face other difficulties in the future. I am confident, however, that these problems can be overcome if we work together to meet them with strength and determination.

With best wishes for you and for the valiant people of the Republic of Vietnam.

Sincerely,

Gerald R. Ford

His Excellency
Nguyen Van Thieu
President of the Republic
of Vietnam
Saigon

Letter 33.   Ford to Thieu, October 24, 1974 (2 pages).

Saigon, Viet-Nam
February 26, 1975

Dear Mr. President:

President Ford has asked me to transmit to you the following message.

"Dear Mr. President:

Your thoughtful letters of January 24 and 25 come at a time when Viet-Nam is very much on my mind and on the minds of other people here and throughout the world, I share your concern about North Viet-Nam's failure to observe the most fundamental provisions of the Paris Agreement and about the heightened level of North Vietnamese military pressure, I wish to assure you that this Government will continue to press for the full implementation of this Agreement.

Once again the South Vietnamese people and Armed Forces are effectively demonstrating their determination to resist Hanoi's attacks. Despite your existing limitations on ammunition and other supplies, I was particularly impressed by the performance of your forces at the Phuoc Long province capital and at Ba Den Mountain, where they were overwhelmed only by greatly superior numbers after being cut off from resupply and reinforcement.

Even though your offers to reinstitute negotiations have been rejected thus far, they clearly demonstrate that it is the communist side -- not the Republic of Viet-Nam --

His Excellency
Nguyen Van Thieu
President of the Republic of Viet-Nam
Saigon

-2-

which is prolonging the war, We continue to believe that implementation of the Paris Agreement, with direct negotiations between the Vietnamese parties, is the quickest, most appropriate, and most effective way to end the bloodshed in Viet-Nam. We strongly support your efforts to resume negotiations and will make every effort to provide the assistance that is so necessary to your struggle until peace comes.

The path to peace is never easy. It has been extraordinarily long and difficult in Viet-Nam. But I remain hopeful that if we persevere we will yet reach our objective of a fair peace, a lasting peace and a peace which is consistent with the will of the South Vietnamese people -- justifying the sacrifices of the Vietnamese and American peoples,

Sincerely,

Gerald R. Ford"

With renewed assurances of my highest consideration,

Sincerely,

Graham Martin

Letter 34.   Ford to Thieu, February 26, 1975 (2 pages).

2

By the action, Hanoi is again seeking to undermine all that we have fought to achieve at enormous cost over the past ten years. Concurrently at stake is American resolve to support a friend who is being attacked by heavily armed forces in total violation of a solemn international agreement.

I, for my part, am determined that American shall stand firmly the RVN at this crucial hour. With a view to honoring the responsibilities of the US in this situation I am following developments with the closest attention and am consulting on an urgent basis with my advisors on actions which the situation may require and the law permit. With regard to the provision of adequate military assistance to your armed forces you can be sure that I shall send every effort to meet your material needs on the battlefields.

In closing I wish to repeat my continued high respect for your resolve and for the constancy and courage of your people.

Sincerely signed GR. R. FORD" The signed original letter will be sent to you by pouch next tuesday Stopend

Respects TRAN KIM PHUONG

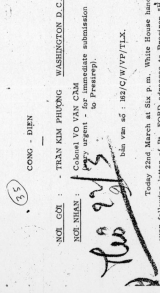

CONG - DIEN

NOI GOI : - TRAN KIM PHUONG   WASHINGTON D.C.
NOI NHAN : Colonel VO VAN CAM
           (very urgent - for immediate submission
            to Presirep)

bản văn số : 162/C/W/VP/TLX.

Today 22nd March at Six p.m. White House handed over following letter of Pt. FORD adresses to Presirep "H.E. NGUYEN-VAN-THIEU President of the RVN Saigon the White House Washington March 22nd 1975 :

Dear President THIEU,

The current North Vietnamese offensive against your country is profoundly disturbing and personally anguishing. It is my view that Hanoi's attack represents nothing less than an abrocation by force of the Paris Agreement.

This turn of events bears the most severe consequences for both our nations. For you and your countrymen it is a time of supreme sacrifice which will determine the very fate of your nation. I am confident that under your leadership the armed forces and people of the RVN will continue their tenacious defense against this new agression. I am equally confident that given additional external support you will prevail in your struggle for self determination.

As for the United States the issue is no less critical.

Letter 35.   Ford to Thieu, March 22, 1975 (2 pages).
The letter was encoded by the Vietnamese Embassy in Washington and decoded in Saigon in the Palace and contains several mistakes in English and spelling.

Appendix B

MEMORANDUM RE COMMUNIST PROPOSALS
AND US' MEMORANDUM OF SEPTEMBER 19, 72

As Dr. Kissinger is about to meet with Le Duc Tho we would like to stress the following points :

"1. The Communist September 15 proposals are even more arrogant than their August 1 proposals. The September 15 proposals show clearly the intention of the Communists who simply seek to force us to surrender unconditionally. Furthermore, they reveal the Communists' dark schemes which they have tried to conceal at the time of their August 1 proposals.

The Government of the Republic of Viet-Nam strongly rejects the Communist September 15 proposals, and considers that it does not serve any purpose to go over them.

2. We recognize that the US have all the right to conduct secret talks with the other side ; and we recognize also that any subject could be brought up in those exploratory talks. However, as far as the GVN is concerned, we wish to stress that our views with regard to the US counterproposals are contained in our September 13 Memorandum. These views are to be interpreted restrictively.

3. When the time is appropriate for the publication of the counter-proposals to the Communist IO points, we suggest that these counter-proposals would reflect the common stand of the USG and GVN on this subject to avoid the exploitation by the other side of possible variances between our two Government.

2

If the US counter-proposals, to be published, go beyond the GVN stand as embodied in the GVN Memo of September 13, we shall be obliged to clarify and defend publicly our views on this subject.

We feel that the suggestions we made in our Memo of Sept. 13 are sufficiently forthcoming, and contain important new elements in comparison with our proposals of January 27, and are convinced that they will earn the support of public opinion for the GVN and USG in the face of the stubbornness and arrogance of the Communist aggressors.

4. The GVN considers that the North Vietnamese proposals of September 15, 1972 are even harsher and even more absurd than their proposals of August 1. Their "proposals" amount to requiring from our side unconditional surrender while they are the aggressors and are unable to achieve their aims on the battlefields.

This attitude of Hanoi shows that they are not willing and ready to have a negotiated settlement of this conflict. The North Vietnamese Communists demonstrate again that they only try to obtain maximum concession from the USG in this electoral year in the US, on the basis of their experience in this matter in 1968.

On the fundamentals of a negotiated settlement of the Viet-Nam conflict, especially on the political aspects of it, it is the

Our position has also been backed up by the Geneva 1954 Agreements whose main features are the establishment of a demarcation line along the 17th parallel, and the strict obligation for the Administrations of each Zone in the North and in the South not to use force against each other, and not to interfere in the internal affairs of each other.

The participation of the US in this conflict and the presence of US troops in Viet-Nam are based on the request of the GVN which exercised its right of collective self-defense, recognized by the United Nations Charter.

In short, our position as a whole is very rational, reasonable, and quite defendable.

The "exploratory" Paris talks which began in March 1968, in which the GVN was excluded, has placed the USG, in our view, in an awkward position and allowed Hanoi to take continuously the offensive in portraying the US as the "aggressor".____

Instead of having to answer on its aggression of SVN, Hanoi has been able to revert the roles, and assumes for itself the role of an "heroic" victim of "US aggression". As a result of this, Hanoi has systematically refused the principle of reciprocity in the deescalation of the war, because to be consistent with itself Hanoi said that the US "aggressor" has no right to ask for reciprocity, a phraseology which corresponds to our statements that "aggression should not be rewarded". ...

considered view of the GVN that an honorable settlement could be achieved only if parallel to the Vietnamization of the war there is also the Vietnamization of peace. In other words, the other side should be brought to accept that the protagonist in the settlement is the GVN, and that it should negotiate directly with the GVN for a negotiated solution.

This is neither simply a matter of prestige or "face" for SVN, nor a "peripheral" question of forums. This is, in our view, the indispensable condition to break the deadlock generated by the circumstances under which the Paris talks began in their exploratory stage in early 1968. In our opinion, those "exploratory" talks should have been conducted by the GVN, or at least by the GVN concurrently with the USG, facing the Hanoi representatives.

We believe that by conducting the 1968 "exploratory" talks without the participation of the GVN, the USG lent itself to the description of the role which Communist propaganda has portrayed for many years, namely that the US is an aggressor in both South and North Viet-Nam, and that the GVN is only a "puppet" creature of the US, put up to materialize US "neo-colonialism".

Our common position, of course, is quite different. We consider that, pending reunification of the Viet-Nams by peaceful means, there are 2 international entities demarcated by the 17th parallel. In fact, the RVN has been recognized by a large number of countries, and is a member of numerous international organizations. Therefore the sending of troops and subversive cadres by NVN into SVN is an aggression, no less than the North Korean invasion across the 38th parallel in 1950.

These illogical foundations of the Paris talks led to the opening of the so-called "expanded" talks which materialized in January 1969. In these "expanded" talks the "inclusion" of the legal Government of the RVN was considered a "concession" by NVN, to be compensated by the participation of the NLF which, theretofore, was a very pale and shadowy façade organization, and whose nature as an instrument created by Hanoi had been clearly established.

Aside from the cessation of bombing of NVN which followed the "expanded" talks (the GVN preferred the term "new" talks to indicate a new phase), the net gain for the Communists was the officialized presence of the "NLF" at the talks. It is on that basis that a number of "non-aligned" governments have given recognition to the "NLF", and later to the so-called "PRG" after it has assumed that new name.

We understand the Anglo-Saxon pragmatism which seems to guide the US approach: This is a protracted conflict which should be terminated as soon as possible. As a beginning step, the opponents have to come to talk together, and we shall see what will develop. The modalities of the forum are considered of little importance.

In fact, as we have pointed out above, the circumstances leading to the official Paris talks, in which the GVN played no active part, have allowed Hanoi to take a "righteous" attitude of a victim of aggression and a most intransigeant stand which seriously hinders a negotiated settlement, as almost four years of completely fruitless exchanges in Paris have amply demonstrated.

On the other hand, the participation of the "NLF" in the official Paris talks helped the Communists to achieve on of its major political goals : the recognition of its political arm in SVN.

The Communist side does not even bother to be consistent with its own stand. It repeatedly proclaimed, as late as the NLF statement of Sept 11, 1972, that the Paris talks is a "four sides" talks. It dwelled on that description in order to emphasize the official presence of the NLF at the talks. However, in contradiction with that version of the talks, both Hanoi and the NLF pretend not to talk to the GVN, but only to the USG.

It is not difficult to understand this self-serving contradiction of the Communists : As long as Hanoi succeeds in placing the USG in the position of a protagonist in this war, it will be able to pursue its line in portraying the US as the "aggressor", and requiring the USG to make unilateral concessions.

Nothing illustrates better this approach of Hanoi to "negotiations" than its concept, in its lastest "Proposals", on the "conduct of negotiations" in which Hanoi and the USG will settle all the major questions, including the political problem of South Viet-Nam.

It is the view of the GVN that this formula is utterly unacceptable because it is severely detrimental to the common interests of the GVN and the USG, and will distort beyond recognition the role of the US in the Viet-Nam war.

As we pointed out in the beginning of this Memo, we are convinced that a chance for a negotiated settlement of the Viet Nam conflict, fair and honorable to both sides, lies in the Vietnamization of peace, in which the Communists must seek the talks with the legal Government of the RVN.

We shall not consider their acceptance to talk with us, when it materializes itself as a "concession" from them or an "honor" to us. But when they are brought to accept the realistic facts that there is a legal, elected Government of the RVN with which they must deal as the main protagonist, they will find us willing and ready to discuss the termination of this senseless war, and the ways to achieve national reconciliation.

The Communist "proposals" of September 15 are an insolent demand for surrender. It is our view that it does not serve any useful purpose by going over it point by point.

The GVN earnestly believes that a breakthrough in the negotiated settlement will be achieved when Hanoi finds that it has to discuss the major issues with the legal government of the RVN.

International public opinion will have an opportunity to judge when we publish our suggestions to the US counter-proposals in the various Memoranda we have given to the United States, the last of which is the September 13 Memorandum, and the Communist arrogant demands of August 1 and September 15, 72.

September 26, 72   TOP SECRET/SENSITIVE

TOP SECRET/SENSITIVE

MEMORANDUM

With regard to the NVN proposals of September 26, and the two US counter-proposals handed to the GVN on October 2, 1972, the GVN considers that it is important to lay down first the basic principles of a general settlement we hope to see accomplished.

The GVN feels that this is such a vital matter for the survival of the RVN and the future of Southeast Asia that it should be dealt with most carefully without any close deadline to meet. We feel that at least we should avoid giving to the other side the impression that we need to have a certain arrangement within a given frame of time.

More importantly, we need a clear concept of the kind of peace we consider to be a just and honorable peace, a peace which can endure and can safeguard the ideals and interests for which our two countries have been fighting for. The statements which the USG and the GVN have made on frequent occasions in recent years have established the fundamental positions of our two Governments on the issues involved in this war. We can always proudly defend them before public opinion.

TOP SECRET/SENSITIVE

2

The GVN therefore believes that we need not feel on the defensive if the other side makes proposals which go counter the basic principles we stand for.

In recent months, Hanoi made 3 proposals on August 1, September 15 and September 26. The characteristics of these proposals are that each of them is even more arrogant and more absurd than the previous ones. In this framework, the GVN is not convinced that we should match each of those proposals by a counter-proposal of our side which attempts to reflect as much as possible the new and increasing revendications of the Communist aggressors.

In case the USG has developed a new concept for a peace settlement, the GVN will greatly appreciate the necessary information from the USG, so that our two Governments can constructively exchange views on the fundamental questions, which would enable us to chart together a common course of action through various stages, in the same spirit of close cooperation we have had for many years.

In that spirit, the GVN takes this opportunity to convey to the USG our concept on the basic issues relating to a peace settlement :

1.- North Viet-Nam is the aggressor in this war. The Republic of Viet-Nam is the victim of aggression.   ...

TOP SECRET/SENSITIVE

President Thieu's memorandum to the U.S. Government on basic principles for a general peace settlement was given to General Alexander Haig at 1300 hours on October 4, 1972.

This is the more unacceptable that, in the case, the aggressor tries to impose unilateral obligations on the victim of aggression, under the guise of negotiations.

Therefore, the GVN would like to inquire whether the USG considers that NVN should assume any reciprocal actions toward a peace settlement, and what are the reciprocal actions and obligations by NVN which the USG contemplates.

We consider that these terms should be clearly spelled out in a general settlement.

6. - According to the areas of competence in the negotiations which the GVN defined in its Memo of August 17 to the USG, NVN is qualified to negotiate only on the military aspects of the war in a forum between all belligerents, and on the problems between NVN and SVN in a forum between the GVN and Hanoi.

The political problems in SVN are to be dealt with in a separate forum between the GVN and the NLF, in accordance with the GVN proposal of July 11, 1969. Any settlements in this area will be made in the spirit of national reconciliation in SVN, outside the sphere of competence of NVN.

Political settlements in SVN are to be made on the basis of the principle of self-determination of people.

October 4, 1972

3

North Viet-Nam must end its aggression.

2. - Pending the reunification of Viet-Nam, the reality is that there are two Viet-Nams, in the same way that there are two Koreas and two Germanys.

Differences between the two Viet-Nams should be solved by peaceful means, and through negotiations between the Governments effectively in control in North Viet-Nam and in South Viet-Nam.

3. - North Viet-Nam has no right to interfere in the internal affairs of South Viet-Nam, and vice versa.

The recent proposals made by Hanoi (Point 4) with regard to the modalities of Government in SVN go counter this important principle, and should be discarded.

4. - North Viet-Nam has invaded not only SVN but also Laos and Cambodia. It has made this war an Indochina war. Therefore, the Indochina aspects of this war are to be solved simultaneously, in a comprehensive settlement.

5. - The basic principle of negotiations is reciprocity. If one side seeks to impose obligations unilaterally on the other side without accepting any obligations in return, there can be no negotiations.

Appendix D

May 15, 1961

Dear Mr. President:

The gracious visit of Vice-President of the United States and Mrs. Johnson to Vietnam has brought to us an even warmer feeling of friendship for the American people and strengthened the bonds of friendship which had existed between our two countries since the birth of the Republic of Vietnam. The presence of your brother-in-law and your charming sister, Mr. and Mrs. Stephen Smith, brought to the Vietnamese people a warm feeling of your own personal interest in Vietnam, an interest which you may be sure will be long remembered.

Your thoughtful and understanding letter of May 8th, 1961, which was handed to me by Vice-President Johnson, contains wise and far-sighted proposals, many of which I myself have advocated for four years or more. I was accordingly glad to tell Vice-President Johnson without hesitation that the Government of Vietnam accepts the proposals in your letter to initiate, in collaboration with the Government of the United States, the series of joint, mutually supporting actions to win the struggle against communism in Vietnam and further the advancement of our country. Our agreement to these proposals was made public in the joint communique which was released to the press on Saturday morning 13th, just before Vice-President Johnson's departure from Saigon.

In the course of our frank and fruitful conversations, Vice-President Johnson graciously asked for my own suggestions as to the most urgent needs as we see them to save our country from the vicious communist aggression being waged against us, both within our borders and from every side today. I was most deeply gratified by this gracious gesture by your distinguished Vice-President, particularly as we have not become accustomed to being asked for our own views as to our needs. The recent developments in Laos have emphasized our grave concern for the security of our country with its long and vulnerable frontiers.

With the very real possibility that we may find ourselves faced with communist military forces pressing our borders not only from the north of the 17th parallel but from a possibly communist dominated Laos and a communist or neutral Cambodia on the west as well, we have undertaken urgent plans to determine the needs to save our country. These studies will be completed in preliminary form in about a week.

We now know that as a small nation we cannot hope to meet all of our defense needs alone and from our own resources. We are prepared to make the sacrifices in blood and manpower to save our country and I know that we can count on the material support from your great country which will be so essential to achieving final victory.

I was deeply gratified at Vice-President Johnson's assurances that our needs will be given careful consideration in Washington. An estimate of these needs as we see them will accordingly be furnished to you in a second letter which I shall write in about a week. The Government and people of Vietnam have been greatly heartened by the encouraging visit of your distinguished Vice-President and the members of his official party. I now feel confident that in the mutual interest of our two countries the sacrifices the Vietnamese people are prepared to make will find full support from the United States in our joint effort to save Vietnam and consequently Southeast Asia from being overwhelmed by communist aggression.

Please accept, Mr. President, this expression of my deep respect and friendship.

Sincerely,

[signature]

His Excellency
JOHN F. KENNEDY
President of the United States of America

President Ngo Dinh Diem to President John F. Kennedy, May 15, 1961.

Appendix E

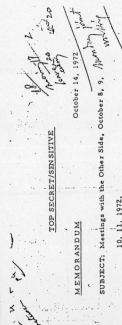

TOP SECRET/SENSITIVE

MEMORANDUM   October 14, 1972

SUBJECT: Meetings with the Other Side, October 8, 9, 10, 11, 1972.

1. I have had a further report from Dr. Kissinger on his four days of meetings with the other side.

2. The meetings were balanced between political and military discussions. While in the earlier meetings they put great emphasis on political issues, at the last meeting they displayed a far greater willingness to discuss military matters in some detail. Several of the meetings were lengthy and time consuming because of the other side's detailed presentations, especially in the political area. On the military side, they were insistent and unyielding in their demands that the United States end all supplies of military equipment to the South Vietnamese.

3. Dr. Kissinger reports that, from the first day through the fourth, there was decided movement in their position. In the earlier meetings they placed major emphasis on satisfying their political demands. In the later meetings they placed increasing emphasis on purely military conditions.

4. Dr. Kissinger's judgment is that the other side may be ready to accept a ceasefire in place in the not too distant future.

TOP SECRET/SENSITIVE   2

He emphasizes, therefore, the need for our side to regain as much territory as possible. He also emphasizes the fact that we need to have room for maneuver and for flexibility on the political side.

5. The other side tabled a political plan, a copy of which is attached.

6. Dr. Kissinger believes there is a possibility that the other side may come forward with more acceptable political proposals than those contained in the plan tabled at the recent meetings. He, therefore, thinks that we should be giving careful consideration to what political terms we are prepared to accept - we might examine again the proposals discussed when General Haig was here - with the understanding, of course, that we are not going to agree to anything which could result in your overthrow.

TOP SECRET/SENSITIVE

From South Vietnamese files, this is a copy of the memorandum from Ambassador Bunker to President Thieu describing in bare outline the meetings of Kissinger with the North Vietnamese in Paris on October 8–11, 1972.

Appendix F

COMMUNISTS' TEN-POINT PROGRAM **(MAY 9, 1969)**	**AGREEMENT ON ENDING THE WAR AND RESTORING PEACE IN** **VIETNAM** **(JANUARY 27, 1973)**
POINT 1 – To respect the Vietnamese people's fundamental national rights, i.e. independence, sovereignty, unity and terrirorial integrity as recognized by the 1954 Geneva Agreement on Viet Nam.	ARTICLE 1 – The United States and all other countries respect the independence, sovereignty, unity and terrirorial integrity of Vietnam as recognized by the 1954 Geneva Agreements on Viet Nam.
POINT 2 – The U.S. Government must withdraw fro- South Viet Nam all U.S. troops, military personnel, arms and war material, and all troops, military personnel, arms and war material of the other foriegn countries of the U.S. camp without posing any condition whatsoever;	ARTICLE 5 – Within sixty days of the signing of this Agreement, there will be a total withdrawal from South Vietnam of troops, military advisers, and military personnel, including technical military personnel associated with the pacification program, armaments, munitions, and war material of the United States and those of the other foreign countries mentioned in Article 3(a). Advisors from the above-mentioned countries to all paramilitary organizations and the police force will also be withdrawn within the same period of time.
(The United States must) liquidate all U.S. military bases in South Viet Nam; renounce all encroachments on the sovereignty, territory and security of South Viet Nam and the Democratic Republic of Viet Nam.	ARTICLE 6 – The dismantlement of all military bases in South Vietnam of the United States and of the other foriegn countries mentioned in Article 3(a) shall be completed within sixty days of the signing of this Agreement.
POINT 3 – The Vietnamese people's right to fight for the defense of their Fatherland is the sacred, inalienable right to self-defense of all peoples. The question of the Vietnamese armed forces in South Viet Nam shall be resolved by the Vietnamese parties among themselves.	ARTICLE 1 – (As above), and ARTICLE 13 – The question of Vietnamese armed forces in South Vietnamese parties in a spirit of national reconciliation and concord, equality and mutual respect, without foreign interference, in accordance with the postwar situation. Among the questions to be discussed by the two South Vietnamese parties are steps to reduce their military effectives and to demobilize the troops being reduced.

A comparison of the North Vietnamese Ten-Point Peace Plan offered to the Nixon administration on May 9, 1969, and the final Paris Agreement of January 27, 1973, which conformed to their demands. The comparison was prepared by Hung for President Thieu in 1973.

Communists' Ten-Point Program (May 9, 1969)	**Agreement on Ending the War and Restoring Peace in Vietnam** (January 27, 1973)
POINT 4 – The people of South Viet Nam settle themselves their own affairs without foreign interference. They decide themselves the political regime of South Viet Nam through free and democratic general elections, a Constituent Assembly will be set up, a Constitution worked out, and a coalition Government of South Viet Nam installed, reflecting national concord and the broad union of all social strata.	ARTICLE 9 (b) – The South Vietnamese people shall decide themselves the political future of South Vietnam through genuinely free and democratic general elections under international supervision. ARTICLE 12 (a) – Immediately after the cease fire, the two South Vietnamese shall hold consultation... to set up a National Council of National Reconciliation and concord of three equal segments. (See 12(a) below)
POINT 5 – During the period intervening between the restoration of peace and the holding of general elections, neither party shall impose its political regime on the people of South Viet Nam.	ARTICLE 9 (c) – Foreign countries shall not impose any political tendency or personality on the South Vietnamese people.
– The political forces representing the various social strata and political tendencies in South Viet Nam, that stand for peace, independence and neutrality, including those persons who, for political reasons, have to live abroad, will enter into talks to set up a provisional coalition government based on the principle of equality, democracy and mutual respect with a view to achieving a peaceful, independent, democratic and neutral South Viet Nam.	ARTICLE 12 (a) – Immediately after the cease-fire, the two South Vietnamese parties shall hold consultations in a spirit of national reconciliation and concord, mutual respect, and mutual non-elimination to set up a National Council of National Reconciliation and Concord of three segments. The Council shall operate on the principle of unanimity. After the National Council of National Reconciliation and Concord has assumed its functions, the two South Vietnamese parties will consult about the formation of councils at lower levels. The two South Vietnamese parties shall sign an agreement on the internal matters of South Vietnam as soon as possible and do their utmost to accomplish this within ninety days after the cease-fire comes into effect, in keeping with the South Vietnamese people's aspirations for peace, independence and democracy.
The provisional coalition government is to have the following tasks (NOTE: Change in order is made for the sake of comparison):	(b) – The National Council of National Reconciliation and Concord shall have the task of:

Communists' Ten-Point Program	Agreement on Ending The War and Restoring Peace in Vietnam
- To implement the agreements on the withdrawal of the troops of the United States and the other foreign countries.	- Promoting the two South Vietnamese parties' implementation of this Agreement.
- To achieve national concord, and a broad union of all social strata, political forces, nationalities	- Achievements of national reconciliation and concord and ensurance of democratic liberties.
- To hold free and democratic general elections in the whole of South Viet Nam with a view to achieving the South Viet Nam people's right to self-determination, in accordance with the content of Point 4 mentioned above.	- The National Council of National Reconciliation and Concord will organize the free and democratic general elections provided for in Article 9 (b) and decide the procedures and modalities of these general elections.
	ARTICLE 11 -Immediately after the cease-fire, the two South Vietnamese parties will (a change of order is made for the sake of comparison)
- To achieve broad democratic freedoms - freedom of speech, freedom of the press, freedom of gathering, freedom of belief, freedom to form political parties and organizations, freedom to demonstrate, etc.	(a) Ensure the democratic liberties of the people: personal freedom, freedom of speech, freedom of the press, freedom of meeting, freedom of organization, freedom of political activities, freedom of belief, freedom of movement, freedom of residence, freedom of work, right to property ownership, and right to free enterprise.
- To set free those persons jailed on political grounds; to prohibit all acts of terror, reprisal and discrimination against people having collaborated with either side, and who are now in the country or abroad, as provided for in the 1954 Geneva Agreements on Viet Nam.	(b) Achieve national reconciliation and concord, end hatred and enmity, prohibit all acts of reprisal and discrimination against individuals or organizations that have collaborated with one side or the other;
- To heal the war wounds, to restore and develop the economy, to restore the normal life of the people, and to improve the living conditions of the labouring people.	ARTICLE 8 - The question of the return of Vietnamese civilian personnel captured and detained in South Vietnam will be resolved by the two South Vietnamese parties on the basis of the principles of Article 2(b) of the Agreement on the Cessation of Hostilities in Vietnam of July 20, 1954.

POINT 6 - South Viet Nam will carry out a foreign policy of peace and neutrality:	ARTICLE 14 - South Vietnam will pursue a policy of peace and independence
To carry out a policy of good neighbourly relations with the Kingdom of Cambodia on the basis of respect for her independence, sovereignty, neutrality and territorial integrity within her present borders; to carry out a policy of good neighbourly relations with the Kingdom of Laos on the basis of respect for the 1962 Geneva Agreements on Laos.	ARTICLE 20(a) The parties participating in the Paris Conference on Vietnam shall strictly respect the 1954 Geneva Agreements on Cambodia and the 1962 Geneva Agreements on Laos, which recongized the Cambodian and the Laos peoples' fundamental national rights, i.e., the independence, sovereignty, unity, and territorial integrity of these countries. The parties shall respect the neutrality of Cambodia and Laos.
To establish diplomatic, economic and cultural relations with all countries, irrespective of political and social regime, including the United States, in accordance with the five principles of peaceful coexistence: mutual respect for the independence, sovereignty and territorial integrity, non-aggression, non-interference in the internal affairs, equality and mutual benefit, peaceful coexistence; to accept economic and technical aid with no political conditions attached from any country.	ARTICLE 14 - South Vietnam will pursue a policy of peace and independence. It will be prepared to establish relations with all countries irrespective of their political and social systems on the basis of mutual respect for independence and sovereignty and accept economic and technical aid from any country with no political conditions attached.
POINT 7 - "The reunification of Viet Nam will be achieved step by step, by peaceful means, through discussions and agreement between the two zones, without foreign interference."	ARTICLE 15 - The reunification of Vietnam shall be carried out step by step through peaceful means on the basis of discussions and agreements between North and South Vietnam, without coercion or annexation by either party, and without foreign interference. The time for reunification will be agreed upon by North and South Vietnam.
Pending the peaceful reunification of Viet Nam;	Pending reunification: (change of order)
the two zones reestablish normal relations in all fields on the basis of mutual respect.	(a) The military demarcation line between the two zones at the 17th parallel is only provisional and not a political or territorial boundary, as provided for in the Final Declaration of the 1954 Geneva Conference.
- The Military Demarcation line between the two zones at the 17th parallel, as provided for by the 1954 Geneva Agreements, is only of a provisional character and does not constitute in any way a political or territoral boundary.	(b) North and South Vietnam shall respect the Demilitarized Zone on either side of the Provisional Military Demarcation Line.

- (See "Pending the peaceful reunification"... above)

- The two zones reach agreement on the status of the Demilitarized Zone, and work out modalities for movement across the Provisional Military Demarcation line.

POINT 8 - As provided for in the 1954 Geneva Agreements on Viet Nam, pending the peaceful reunification of Viet Nam, the two zones North and South of Viet Nam undertake to refrain from joining any military alliance with foreign countries, not to allow any foreign country to maintain military bases, troops and military personnel on the respective soil.

POINT 9 - To resolve the aftermath of the war:

(a) The parties shall negotiate the release of the armymen captured in war.

(b) The U.S. Government must bear full responsibility for the losses and devastations it has caused to the Vietnamese people in both zones.

POINT 10 - The parties shall reach agreement on an international supervision about the withdrawal from South Viet Nam of the troops, military personnel, arms and war material of the United States and the other foriegn countries of the American camp.

(c) North and South Vietnam shall promplty start negotiations with a view to reestablishing normal relations in various fields. Among the questions to be negotiated are the modalities of civilian movement across the Provisional Military Demarcation Line.

(d) North and South Vietnam shall not join any military alliance or military bloc and shall not allow foreign powers to maintain military bases, troops, military advisers, and military personnel on their respective territories, as stipulated in the 1953 Geneva Agreements on Vietnam.

ARTICLE 8(a) The return of captured military personnel and foreign civilians of the parties shall be carried out simultaneously with and completed not later than the same day as the troops withdrawal mentioned in Article 5.

ARTICLE 21 - The U.S. will contribute to the healing of war and postwar reconstruction of the Democratic Republic of Vietnam and throughout Indochina.

[AUTHOR'S NOTE: There is no need for international supervision of U.S. troops withdrawal because Article of 8(a) above, which, in effect, programs Hanoi's release of P.O.W.'s to coincide with U.S. withdrawal; the two actions were to reach the same terminal date.]

Appendix G

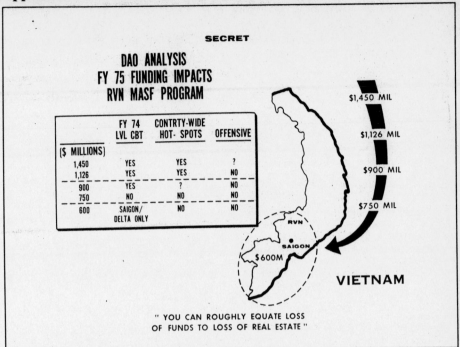

This analysis, from South Vietnamese files, was presented to President Thieu by the U.S. Defense Attache's Office in Saigon of the fiscal year 1975 funding impacts on the Republic of Vietnam Military Assistance Fund Program.

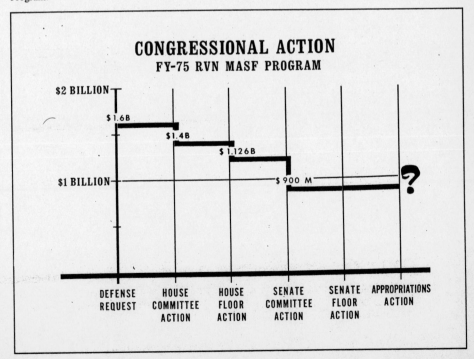

SECRET

RVNAF EQUIPMENT REPLACEMENT
—FY-75 MASF PROGRAM—

FY-75 FUND LEVELS
($ MILLION)

	ARVN	VNN	VNAF
1,450	1 FOR 1	<1 FOR 1	<1 FOR 1
1,126	<1 FOR 1	NONE	ESSENTIAL AIRCRAFT
900	ESSENTIAL WEAPONS	NONE	NONE
750	NONE	NONE	NONE
600	NONE	NONE	NONE

UNREPLACED RVNAF LOSSES - FY 74

1,132 1/4 TON TRKS	58 SHIPS/	281 A/C
904 3/4 TON TRKS	BOATS/CRAFT	
1,374 2 1/2 TON TRKS		

SECRET

SECRET

OPERATIONS & MAINTENANCE I

EST LEVEL OF SUPPORT

FY 75 FUND LVLS ($ MIL)	O&M FUNDS ($ MIL)	POL	AMMO	COM-EL	QM
1,450	1,130	< FULL*	< FULL*	FULL	< FULL*
1,126	983	49%	60% REDUCTION IN TNG	INTER-REGIONAL COMMO IMPACT	IMPAIR MAINTENANCE
900	870	45%	75%	TACTICAL COMMO IMPACT	ONLY CRITICAL SUPPLIES
750	750	38%	62%	INEFFECTIVE	NON-SUPPORTIVE
600	600	33%	50%	INEFFECTIVE	EMERGENCY ITEMS ONLY

* REDUCED PROCUREMENT DUE TO INFLATION

SECRET

OPERATIONS & MAINTENANCE II

EST LEVEL OF SUPPORT

FY 75 FUND LVLS ($ MIL)	O&M FUNDS ($ MIL)	MEDICAL	AC ENGINES	CONTRACTS	OFF SHORE TRAINING
1, 450	1, 130	FULL	FULL	FULL	FULL
1, 126	983	FULL	FULL	FULL	FULL
900	870	CURTAIL PREV MED BLOOD BK PLAGUE MALARIA	FULL	FULL	FULL
750	750	REDUCE CBT MED SPT	GROUND SOME A/C	REDUCE FLYING HRS BY 30%	CURTAIL
600	600	NON SUPPORTING	ELIMINATE CONUS OVERHAUL	REDUCE FLYING HRS BY 55%	FURTHER CURTAIL

OPERATIONS & MAINTENANCE III

EST LEVEL OF SUPPORT

FY 75 FUND LVLS ($ MIL)	O&M FUNDS ($ MIL)	IN-COUNTRY REBUILD	OFFSHORE REBUILD	CONST	AIR FAC
1,450	1,130	< FULL *	FULL	< FULL *	FULL
1, 126	983	LOSE 34% OF FY 76 REBUILD	LOSE HVY ENGINE REBUILD	ELIMINATE MINOR CONST MAT'L	FULL
900	870	LOSE 55% OF FY 76 REBUILD	ELIMINATE APC REDUCE TK	REDUCE ALL CONST MAT'L 50%	DEGRADE AIR CONTROL & A/C SORTIES
750	750	LOSE 75% OF FY 76 REBUILD	NONEXISTENT	ELIMINATE US SPT OF RVN LOC	REDUCE AIR FAC SPT BY 46%
600	600	NONEXISTENT	NONEXISTENT	ROADS & FAC DETERIORATE	SELECTED BASES INEFFECTIVE

* REDUCED PROCUREMENT DUE TO INFLATION

Appendix H

Kính Gửi Tổng Thống Hoa Kỳ

Phủ Tổng Thống   Saigon, the 9th of June, 1961

Dear Mr. President:

In reference to my letter dated 15 May 1961 and in reply to the invitation that was made to me in your name by Vice President Johnson, I have the honor to send you a study on our needs to meet the new situation.

As I expressed verbally to your eminent representative, it pertains to a situation which has become very much more perilous following the events in Laos, the more and more equivocal attitude of Cambodia and the intensification of the activities of aggression of international communism which wants to take the maximum advantage to accelerate the conquest of Southeast Asia. It is apparent that one of the major obstacles to the communist expansion on this area of the globe is Free Vietnam because with your firm support, we are resolved to oppose it with all our energies. Consequently, now and henceforth, we constitute the first target for the communists who overthrow at any cost. The enormous accumulation of Russian war material in North Vietnam is aimed, in the judgement of foreign observers, more at South Vietnam than at Laos. We clearly realize this dangerous situation but I want to reiterate to you here, in my personal name and in the name of the entire Vietnamese people, our indomitable will to win.

On the second of May, my council of generals met to evaluate the current situation and to determine the needs of the Republic of Vietnam to meet this situation. Their objective evaluation shows that the military situation at present is to the advantage of the communists and that most of the Vietnamese Armed Forces are already committed to internal security and the protection of our 12 million inhabitants. For many months the communist-inspired, fratricidal war has taken nearly one thousand casualties a month on both sides. Documents obtained in a recent operation along route No. 9 which runs from Laos to Vietnam, contain definite proof that 2,360 armed agents have infiltrated among us in the course of the last four months. It is certain that this number rises each day. Moreover, the Vietnamese people are showing the world that they

- 2 -

are willing to fight and die for their freedom, not withstanding the temptations to neutralism and its false promises of peace being drummed into their ears daily by the communists.

In the light of this situation, the council of generals concluded that additional forces numbering slightly over 100,000 more than our new force level of 170,000 will be required to counter the ominous threat of communist domination. The 100,000 reservists to be called up according to the plan of my council of generals were to meet the requirement for an augmentation of the Vietnamese Army by nine infantry divisions plus modest naval and air force increases. First priority called for one division to reinforce each of the three Army Corps in Vietnam plus a two divisional general reserve for a total of five divisions. In second priority, an additional division for each of the three Army Corps plus one in general reserve brought the total to nine new divisions. With the seven existing divisions, fragmented in anti-guerilla operations, the Army of Vietnam would thus have a strength of 16 divisions of slightly less than 10,000 men each plus appropriate combat and logistic support units.

We have now had an opportunity to review this initial force requirement with General McGarr and the MAAG staff who have recommended certain modifications which are basically in consonance with our plan and with which we agree.

After considering the recommendations of our generals and consulting with our American military advisors, we now conclude that to provide even minimum initial resistance to the threat, two new divisions of approximately 10,000 strength each are required to be activated at the earliest possible date. Our lightly held defensive positions along the demilitarized zone at our Northern border is even today being outflanked by communist forces which have defeated the Royal Laotian Army garrisons in Tchepone and other cities in Southern Laos. Our ARVN forces are so throughly committed to internal anti-guerilla operations that we have no effective forces with which to counter this threat from Southern Laos. Thus, we need immediately one division for the First Army Corps and one for the Second Army Corps to provide at least some token resistance to the sizeable forces the communists are capable of bringing to bear against our Laotian frontier. Failing this, we would have no recourse but to withdraw our forces southward from the demilitarized zone and sacrifice progressively greater areas of our country to the communists. These divisions should be mobilized and equipped, together with initial logistic support units immediately after

168

President Ngo Dinh Diem to President John F. Kennedy, June 9, 1961.

– 3 –

completion of activation of the presently contemplated increase of 20,000 which you have offered to support.

Following the activation of these units, which should begin in about five months, we must carry on the program of activation of additional units until over a period of two years we will have achieved a force of 14 infantry divisions, an expanded airborne brigade of approximately division strength and accompanying supporting elements of logistical, naval and air units. In other words, our present needs as worked out with General McGarr's advice and assistance call for a total force of 15 divisional equivalents plus combat and logistic support units instead of our original plan for a 16 division force. The strategic concept and mission of this total 270,000 man force remains the same, namely, to overcome the insurgency which has risen to the scale of a bloody, communist-inspired civil war within our borders and to provide initial resistance to overt, external aggression until free world forces under the SEATO agreement can come to our aid. The question naturally arises as to how long we shall have to carry the burden of so sizeable a military force. Unfortunately, I can see no early prospects for the reduction of such a force once it has been established, for even though we may be successful in liquidating the insurgency within our borders, communist pressure in Southeast Asia and the external military threat to our country must be expected to increase, I fear, before it diminishes. This means that we must be prepared to maintain a strong defensive military posture for at least the foreseeable future in order that we may not become one of the so-called "soft spots" which traditionally have attracted communist aggression. We shall therefore continue to need material support to maintain this force whose requirements far exceed the capacity of our economy to support.

To accomplish this 100,000 man expansion of our military forces which is perfectly feasible from a manpower viewpoint will require a great intensification of our training programs in order to produce, in the minimum of time, those qualified combat leaders and technical specialists needed to fill the new units and to provide to them the technical and logistic support required to insure their complete effectiveness. For this purpose a considerable expansion of the United States Military Advisory Group is an essential requirement. Such an expansion, in the form of selected elements of the American Armed Forces to establish training centers for the Vietnamese Armed Forces, would serve the dual purpose of providing an expression of the United States' determination to halt the tide of communist aggression and of preparing our forces in the

– 4 –

minimum of time.

While the Government and people of Vietnam are prepared to carry the heavy manpower burden required to save our country, we must know that we cannot afford to pay, equip, train and maintain such forces as I have described. To make this effort possible, we would need to have assurances that this needed material support would be provided. I have drawn on our past experience of United States support we have received to make some extremely rough estimates of the costs of these proposals.

The costs of providing essential initial equipment to the added forces under the Military Assistance Program would probably be in the neighborhood of $175,000,000 with deliveries to be distributed over the next two and one-half years as units can be activated. If the United States assumes the task of providing this initial equipment for the additional forces, I understand that the annual Military Assistance Program for force maintenance will increase by about $20 million above the level of MAP support for the presently authorized 170,000 force.

The Vietnamese Military Budget, which includes piaster requirements, must also be supplemented. As you know, Vietnam contributes to this budget to its fullest capability now with respect to existing forces. Despite our best efforts, your Government has largely supported this budget through Defense Support Assistance. Although we have made significant progress in developing our economy in the last four years, the support of even the inadequate armed forces we have has far exceeded the modest capabilities of the economy of our small country. In order to carry out the expansion of forces, the piaster military budget now averaging nearly 7.0 billion piasters a year will have to be supplemented. As I see it, the annual maintenance cost will increase gradually during the force implementation and will ultimately level off at approximately 10.60 billion piasters.

This program, I realize, will be expensive in money, equipment and personnel. The benefits to be gained, however, in preventing the subjugation of our free people and in establishing a solid obstacle to the advance of communism, I know you will agree, far outweigh the cost. With your support, we stand determined to survive in independence and freedom.

It goes without saying that in the face of the extremely serious situation created by the communist aggressor, we must temporarily

- 5 -

accord priority to the military problems. However, my Government does not attach less importance to economic, political and social problems. At this point the doctrinal position which pertains to South Vietnam is clear and clean. It was expressed in a free and sincere manner in my message to the American Congress in April 1957. It has not varied since. Neither did it vary during the recent presidential campaign when I was elected by a very large majority.

Presently, it is necessary not to be maneuvered by the communists, who exploit our tendency to consider military efforts as reactionary and fruitless, to divert our effective action, which is necessitated by the mortal communist attacks, toward a long range project of economic and social improvement, and which, of course, supposes that we are still alive. We see for the army an economic and social mission along with military role, a conception which rationally responds to the double challenge which the newly independent countries of Africa and Asia have had to face : underdevelopment and communist subversive war. It is along this line that, since my taking office in July 1954, I have undertaken to create an economic infrastructure throughout the country, including the least inhabited regions : to develop the lines of communication with the double purpose of facilitating intercourse and facilitating the mobility of our troops ; to increase and diversify the agricultural production ; to give each family a tract of land which will belong to them ; to create each day more employment by industrializing the country ; in brief to open new horizons to the rural masses, the determining factor in the struggle against communism. It is sufficient to consider the product of our exportation these last two years, the reduction of our importation program, to count the factory chimneys which make their appearance to realize the progress already made . On the other hand, in spite of its lack of resources, the Government increases the social investments to respond to the diversified needs of a population which increases at the rate of 3% per year : hospitals in the towns, dispensaries in the villages, primary schools in each commune, secondary schools in each city of whatever importance. Education is developing at the annual rate of 20% while in the domain of public health, we have a hospital bed available for each thousand inhabitants. We want to progress more rapidly but, in addition to the budgetary limitations which constitute a primary obstacle, the lack of trained personnel has made itself felt despite our accelerated training programs . The agrovilles, which I have built in the last year, are another proof of the Government's efforts : These are agricultural communities located between two urban centers to give the rural population the benefits of the commodities of modern life and to correct the extreme dispersion of the

- 6 -

population. All foreign observers who travel in the country are struck by the standard of living enjoyed by the mass of peasants: sewing machine, bicycle, transistor radio for each family in more or less comfortable circumstances, theater, movies in the most backward areas, motor boats on the innumerable canals, tricycle busses on all passable roads. And it is precisely in order not to interrupt this development program that we ask for supplementary aid to finance our war effort; otherwise we will be forced to make the tragic decision to abruptly cease all out social and economic programs.

Concerning Cambodia, our diplomatic efforts would have results only if we recognize our adversary.

The idea of Cambodia being afraid of Vietnam is a myth. For 7 years, Sihanouk has not missed one chance to provoke South Vietnam, of which he has militarily occupied six islands. Having no reason to fear a Vietnam, divided and weakened by the subversive communist war, Sihanouk has nothing to fear at all. However, this idea would be pleasing to those who would seek to arbitrate between Cambodia and South Vietnam. It would also be pleasing to certain Vietnamese because this idea is flattering to their vanity and to their infantilism which consists of minimizing the difficulties and proposing any solutions. It would also be pleasing to Sihanouk who has a need to give substance to another myth that of encirclement which he needs to excuse his internal failures in order to justify his presence in power, to accuse the Americans and to court the communists. In reality, Sihanouk is committed intellectually and morally to communism, which he considers the stronger party and the inevitable victor in the future. In spite of the aid which he receives from America, has Sihanouk ever aided the US in the battle with the communists? He always takes positions favorable to the communists against the USA. His conduct in the Laotian affair is clear. Not only does he serve the communists, but he is proud to serve a stronger master. On the other hand, Cambodia, like Laos, is unable to ensure the security of her territory from the communist guerillas because he will not or does not wish to make the appropriate efforts. It is for this reason that he takes refuge in communist servitude under the guise of a neutralist. It is also for that reason that he has always refused to accept any arrangement for the effective control of the Cambodian-Vietnamese border under the fallacious pretext of neutrality.

From the political point of view, the reforms that I have anticipated,

-7-

that is to say the elective system established at the village level, the creation of the provincial councils, the institution of a High Economic Council, of a National and Social Council - all these measures are tending to insure more and more active participation by the population in public affairs, in the dramatic situation of an underdeveloped country, divided and mortally menaced by communism.

Such is the direction of my efforts and such is our regime - a regime open to progress and not a closed system. I am convinced that with your support and so generously aided by your great, friendly nation, I will manage to reestablish law and order in our provinces, in our villages, to accelerate progress in all other areas for the edification of a society of free men, happy and prosperous. Vietnam thus constitutes a pole of attraction for the countries of Southeast Asia, for those who fight communism as well as for those who still doubt the future of the free world.

I wish to assure you, Mr. President, of the sincerity of my sentiments and most cordial wishes.

His Excellency JOHN F. KENNEDY
United States of America
Washington, D.C.

Appendix I

Excellencies
Gentlemen:

Two years have elapsed since the Agreement on Ending the War and Restoring Peace in Vietnam came into being, but peace has yet to be seen in this land of constant suffering. The Communists have continued their attacks throughout the Republic of Vietnam and their belligerency has increased with each passing day.

Indeed, the record shows that in 1973, the first year of "peace" enemy forces perpetrated an average of 2,900 military offensive violations a month. In 1974, the monthly average increased to 3,300.

Another indication of growing enemy belligerency is the size of Communist attacks over the past two years. Immediately after the conclusion of the Paris agreement, we were subjected to small-unit and occasionally battalion-size attacks. Now, entire divisions of the North Vietnamese Army (NVA) are committed to campaigns involving infantry, artillery, and armored units.

This is all the more visible in the type of targets the enemy has been coveting, too. From such small targets as outposts, hamlets, and villages, NVA forces are now trying to capture bigger installations and population centers. They have recently assaulted a number of depots and airfields. More recently, they have seized six district towns and the province of Phuoc Long and are presently concentrating to attack other provincial capitals and a number of big cities, including Saigon itself.

From captured documents, we also know the enemy has never had any intention of complying with the provisions of the Paris agreement. In the immediate aftermath of the ceasefire agreement, his forces were instructed to maintain a state said of "derniere var, comme peace." Beginning in April 1973, this became "peace in war." By October 1973, the Communist guideline for NVA forces was "attack in peace." And in the future, it is said to be "war to maintain peace."

- 2 -

Although Communist, especially Vietnamese Communist, terminology is rather difficult to comprehend, all of these mottos simply mean that it has never been the intention of the Hanoi leadership to fully implement the Paris agreement, which, in their eyes, only represents an instrument with which they can fulfill their dream of hegemony over the entire Indochinese peninsula.

Enemy Activity

For an understanding of what the enemy has been trying to do over the past two years, let it be reported that while mounting innumerable land and people-grabbing campaigns, NVA units have endeavored to build and develop their strength in preparation for subsequent campaigns of aggression.

This is rather obvious in the number of units and men the NVA command now has in South Vietnam, which by far surpass what it had before the ceasefire agreement. Significantly, it has formed three Army Corps commands—Corps 2 and 3 in the First Military Region and Corps 301 in the Third Military Region—and four new infantry divisions, two in the Third Military Region and two in the Mekong delta.

In order to do this, Hanoi has had to increase its infiltration of men to an unprecedented level. An estimated 240,000 North Vietnamese recruits have reached South Vietnam on battlefields during the past 25 months. By ceasefire day, the enemy had an estimated 90 to 115 tracked vehicles left in South Vietnam. With the infiltration of an additional 660 to 885, enemy tracked vehicles now number 750 to 1,000.

At the time of the ceasefire enemy 122mm and 130mm field guns numbered 100 to 120. An additional 350 to 490 have been infiltrated since then, bringing the total of these field guns to 450-610. All the artillery pieces put together would give the enemy a force of an estimated 1,000 heavy guns.

In air-defense, 20 additional regiments have infiltrated with an estimated 1,000 guns ranging in caliber from 37 to 100 millimeters, including the modified SA-7. Moreover to reads that the enemy had only 720 anti-aircraft guns at the time of the ceasefire.

A network of assorted radars gives the NVA a degree of control over the entire airspace of the First and Third Military Regions and most of the Second and Fourth Military Regions.

Of course, much of this equipment has been brought into our country after the conclusion of the Paris agreement, which forbids

The text of a secret briefing prepared by General Cao Van Vien, Chairman of the Joint General Staff, for the United States, warning of Communist preparations for a large-scale offensive in 1975. The briefing was prepared on January 9, 1975.

- 3 -

the introduction of new weapons into South Vietnam. The following chart will give you an idea of this serious violation of the Paris agreement.

To maintain such a big expeditionary force, the Hanoi command has had to make a big logistics effort, which is particularly conspicuous in its road construction endeavor. Its engineers have completed, among other things, the construction of the so-called Truong Son corridor, which extends over nearly 1,600 kilometers. NVA vehicles can now be driven all the way from the 17th Parallel to the Northern edge of Tay Ninh province. This corridor has innumerable tentacles, which link it to the network. In all, the NVA can be said to control over 5,500 kilometers of road.

The enemy has rehabilitated 17 airfields in overrun areas. Among these, the ones at Kho Sanh and Loc Ninh may be modified to accommodate jet fighter aircraft.

The NVA modernization effort is also rather visible in an enormous, costly network of fuel storage and pipeline and pumping facilities, which now contains over 13.6 million liters or 3.5 million gallons of fuel. Prior to the Paris agreement, it had only just over one million liters or 264,000 gallons. The NVA pipeline network, some 560 kilometers long, runs from the demilitarized zone to the Western portion of Quang Nam province and to the Western edge of Quang Duc province (Dakdam).

Mention finally must be made of the 45,000 structures which the enemy presently has in South Vietnam, which represents a fourfold increase over what it had before the ceasefire agreement.

In brief, enemy capabilities increased considerably compared to the level of the pre-ceasefire days. Especially, artillery increased from 350 to 400%; armor increased from 730 to 760%; A.A. Artillery increased about 150%; POL increase about 1,150%.

The Communists are able to increase their potential in the North and infiltrate large quantities of supplies and war materiel into South Vietnam, because they continue to receive economic aid and support from the Communist Bloc. Hanoi received 1.2 to 1.3 billion U.S. dollars of aid in 1974. This aid is larger than what it received in 1967, i.e. prior to the 1968 Offensive.

All of this build-up apparently must serve some purpose. According to Resolution 21 of the Lao Dong Party Central Committee and Resolution 12 of the Central Office for South Vietnam, the Communist leadership seek to disrupt the current pacification and develop-

- 4 -

ment plans of the Republic of Vietnam (1), consolidate and expand Communist-controlled areas (2), build up their military forces in every respect (3), promote an anti-Government movement in the urban areas (4), and step up their attacks on the military and political fronts (5).

To achieve whatever they might have in mind, they reckon they have to extend their control over an additional 2,000,000 people, especially through destroying a significant portion of the Republic of Vietnam armed forces and destroying some 4,000 outposts scattered all over the country. The aforementioned enemy strategem is primarily aimed at deviating the balance of force in favor of the Communists.

There are presently numerous indicators of enemy preparations for large-scale attacks in 1975 :

(a) The enemy has renamed the territorial command structure for his Military Regions from NVN through SVN.

(b) He has organized Army Corps to meet the needs of a large theater.

(c) He has activated new divisions such as the 3rd and 6th in MR 3 and the 4th and 6th in the delta.

(d) The 968th Division has redeployed from Lower Laos to Pleiku in the Highlands.

(e) The 320th Division has redeployed from Pleiku to Northern Darlac to assume responsibility for operations in the Southern Highlands.

(f) Three of the seven divisions of Hanoi's strategic reserves are prepared to move South.

(g) In the North, an entire Air Regiment has left the Ta Ngan (Western Bank) Military Region to redeploy further South.

(h) Massive flows of supplies are leaving North Vietnam for the South in a high point of logistical operation of the 559th Transportation Corps.

Overall, Communist efforts for an intensified war will give them an option from two capabilities :

. The first capability presumes a deterioration of the situation in South Vietnam, which NVA forces would try to speed up by a general attack.

. The second capability presumes a vigorous reaction of the Republic of Vietnam armed forces to the current high level of Communist

- 6 -

We believe we are, in fact, getting more combat power today for every dollar spent than we got two years ago. However, in spite of improved efficiency and stringent conservation measures we simply do not have the material resources to stop the North Vietnamese from continuing their seizure of our land and population, much less sufficient resources to eject the invaders from our country.

- 5 -

munist truce violations, which would then be presented by the Communist as a South Vietnamese effort at resuming the war and violating the Paris agreement. In this case, they will counter-attack with great vigor while recint themselves for seizing what they call a "strategic opportunity" to launch a big offensive of the type seen in 1972.

In Capability One, they also reckon, the United States will be denied any good reason to provide additional aid as the Hanoi command will only commit these augmented units already in the South and in so doing present the new conflict as a civil war that comes about as a result of more serious truce violations. In Capability Two, in order to deny the United States the opportunity for timely assistance, they will launch a Blitzkrieg-like attack with every means at their disposal, including their general reserve presently in North Vietnam, in order to gain control over large portions of the territory of South Vietnam.

In sum, one can say that both capabilities involve a military offensive of major proportions.

Friendly Activity

While the North Vietnamese invaders have been increasing their war-making capability both within and outside of South Vietnam, our own capabilities for self-defense have been seriously limited by three factors: our respect for the various provisions of the Paris Agreement; reduced U.S. military assistance; and, a galloping inflation.

Indeed, the North Vietnamese have, in the past two years, increased their combat strength in South Vietnam by about a third; that is, the combined strength of their combat units has increased by some 120,000 over the 240,000 mark recorded two years ago. We, on the other hand, have been barely able to hold our own in terms of combat strength. They have over eight times as many tracked vehicles in South Vietnam today as two years ago; we, on the other hand, have a slightly decreased inventory. Their heavy artillery increased by a factor of 4,000; we, again, have been unable even to replace our losses.

However, we have made steps to increase the effectiveness of our forces.

We have made a concerted effort to upgrade the training, organization and equipment of our territorial forces.

We have deactivated units no longer required, such as railway security forces and POW-camp guard units, while converting the spaces from those units into combat units, specifically Marine, Airborne and Ranger battalions,.. a total of nine newly formed light infantry battalions.

- 7 -

Logistics

In the new context of the continuing military struggle, the South Vietnamese high command has had to take quite a few measures to improve its logistics organization and reduce expenditure.

Without going into the details, let me simply say that a major effort has been made to reorganize all logistics support units with the purpose of reducing overhead costs. This endeavor, which mainly involves a shift from the technical organization concept to the functional organization concept, has resulted in simplifying to a great extent the procedure for requesting supplies and maintenance. As a matter of fact, while a combat unit used to have to contact six separate agencies for one case of supply and maintenance, it now has to contact only one.

This and other measures have resulted in saving a lot of time and energy--and what is possibly more important a lot of money. For example, if you should compare the trend of enemy activities (red line) and that of ammunition consumption (blue line) and on the basis of what was recorded in 1972, it can be said the Republic of Vietnam armed forces has been able to conserve up to 75 per cent of what it used to expend.

The same thing can be said of fuel. Indeed, on this chart, which shows the gradual reduction of the POL consumption rate (blue line) and the gradual increase of enemy activities (red line), note can be made of a considerable fuel consumption reduction--by some 45 per cent. This POL reduction, however, has had a nefarious impact on the mobility of the South Vietnamese Army.

Of much more importance to the course of events in South Vietnam is the matter of ammunition supply. As presented on this chart, you have here an analysis of the ammunition status in different rates: the available supply rate (ASR) dictated by the military assistance fund, the theater sustaining rate (TSR), and the Vietnam supply rate (VSR), which is the intensive combat rate based on the pre-ceasefire day level of fighting and ammunition consumption.

For a better view of this most important aspect of the continuing crisis, we should like to invite you have a look at this chart, which compares the available supply rates for U.S. and South Vietnamese troops on the Vietnam theater of operation.

And this chart, which shows the firepower of combined allied forces in 1969, which was 6,439 short tons, and that of the Vietnamese armed forces at present: 767 short tons. Note possibly should be made that in 1972, the firepower capabilities of the South Vietnamese armed forces was 2,200 short tons.

- 8 -

Now, a few remarks on the on-hand ground ammunition stock, which, at the beginning of the fiscal year, were 129,000 tons. This balance was drawn down to 104,000 tons at the end of September because of the high consumption rate of 20,797 tons per month experienced during the first quarter.

The balance on hand 31 December has increased to a level just below the beginning FY.75 position. During the past three months our goal has been to have on hand at least 60 days of supply at the intensive combat rate (ICR) for all key items. This increase results from a combination or reduced consumption during the second quarter and receipt of requisitions placed earlier for delivery during this period.

Issues for the remaining two quarters have been projected at 19,481 tons per month, which is the average consumption rate for the past seven months.

As can be seen, the funding level will not support consumption requirements for the remaining two quarters. Accordingly, we will have an end-year balance of 79,000 tons which is 2%,000 tons or 27% below the 60-day intensive combat rate and 50,000 tons below the beginning FY.75 level (39%).

To give you an example how serious this is, let me simply say that the artillery ammunition stock has greatly decreased with the result that the daily allocation for each 105mm howizer has dropped from 30 rounds in 1972 to 11 rounds in 1973 and only eight rounds last year. The daily allocation for each 155mm gun has dropped from an initial 18 rounds to eight and more recently to seven rounds.

It can be said that this drastic reduction of firepower has had a serious impact on the casualty rates, including the killed and wounded categories. On this chart, the blue line represents the ammunition consumed and the red line the casualties suffered by the Republic of Vietnam Armed Forces. In 1972 and until the Paris agreement was signed, the level of ammunition consumption appears to follow more or less the trend of casualties. After the conclusion of the Paris treaty, at which point the ammunition consumption rate started being reduced, the casualty trend shot up dramatically far above the ammunition consumption rate.

Let us now go back a few years' time and have a look at South Vietnamese fatality rates from 1966 to date. On the basis of these figures, it can be said the Paris agreement has failed to bring the bloodshed to an end. Indeed, there were in 27,901 KHA in 1973 31,219 KHA in 1974. At present, this stands at about 3,000 per month.

- 9 -

The problems you have just heard about are only parts of the impacts of the 700 million security assistance appropriation. This level of appropriation supports only 53% of our operating cost requirements.

Of this 460 million or 66% is slated for the Army, 185 million or 27% for the Air Force and 15 million or 2% for the Navy.

With the present program level, there will necessarily be serious impacts on the Army. We foresee critical shortages of ammunition, POL, medical supplies and repair parts. Communication capabilities may also be seriously affected and drastic reductions in support levels are being made across the board.

The impacts on the Air Force are no less serious. The total Air Force operating requirements are supported at only 47%.

Navy operating requirements can be financed at only 52% of the total need.

Finally, this chart will show you the one-for-one status of essential major items. The funds for tactical vehicles, combat vehicles, artillery, signal equipment, and small arms are only approximately 50 per cent of the requirement. There are no funds for aircraft and ships. The funds for ammunition is 85 per cent of the requirements. In short, with the cost of these for the period from Jan. 28, 1973 to Jan. 31, 1975 estimated at 1,141.4 million and with the authorized cost for replacement at 765.4 million only, the remaining cost not funded is 376 million.

Conclusion

In summary, it can be said the North Vietnamese leadership have yet to give up their attempt at conquering South Vietnam by force of arms. As a matter of fact, immediately following the conclusion of the Agreement on Ending the War and Restoring Peace in Vietnam, they issued a number of policy documents, including the Twelfth COSVN Resolution, which seeks above all to tip the balance of military force in their favor.

- 10 -

Since then, all that the Communists have done appears to be aimed at strengthening their hands and weakening the self-defense capabilities of South Vietnam, in so doing, they also appear to be preparing for what Communist documents have been referring to as "a new opportunity" with which they think they can secure important concessions from South Vietnam. Indeed, speaking last September 2 in Hanoi, North Vietnamese Premier Pham Van Dong himself predicted that "the people of South Vietnam will witness major developments in 1975," probably meaning that the Communists will do their best this year to conquer South Vietnam by force of arms.

According to a couple of documents captured very recently, it also appears that the Communists, while still seeking to expand and modernize their armed forces to ensure a degree of success in limited military campaigns, are also preparing for a general offensive if and when they feel ready for it.

To cope with this threat, the Republic of Vietnam Armed Forces has done its best. It will continue to do its best. We in the South Vietnamese military very deeply appreciate the help the American nation has given us. But a steady flow of U.S. military assistance is a prerequisite for success until the North Vietnamese return to their own country and cease their military activities in South Vietnam.

With that basic verity of the Vietnam situation in mind, this headquarters has a few suggestions for your consideration. In the first place, we should like to request the United States Congress for a supplemental military assistance program of 300 million dollars, which constitutes we think the minimum requirement in the present situation of the land and without which difficulties of the gravest nature cannot be avoided. In the second place, we should like to request a 400 million fund for the replacement of materiel, lost or worn out, as provided for by the one-for-one provision of the Paris agreement. In the third place, we should like to suggest that the United States develop a contingency plan for use in the event of an enemy general offensive.

Excellencies
Gentlemen

What we have presented to you in the first part of this briefing clearly demonstrates that the Paris agreement has not only failed to deter but has, in fact, facilitated Communist efforts to gain control over South Vietnam. The continuous build-up of Communist manpower, materiel, and logistics assets since that time

- 11 -

has progressed unhindered to any significant degree.

Moreover, a renewed emphasis on major military attacks since the middle of last year signals a positive enemy commitment to a primarily military course of action, whether Hanoi chooses to continue the current level of military activity or escalate that activity to a general offensive, the primary emphasis on military means to defeat the Government of the Republic of Vietnam is readily apparent.

Thank you for your attention.

Appendix J

The March 24, 1975 letter from the Speaker of the House of Representatives of the Republic of Vietnam and the President of the Senate of the Republic of Vietnam to President Ford, and the March 25, 1975 letter which was sent to Nelson Rockefeller, President of the U.S. Senate. A letter similar to the one to Rockefeller was also sent to Carl Albert, Speaker of the House of Representatives. There is no trace that members of both houses actually saw the two letters.

- 3 -

people in order to fight the Communist aggression; from now on, all able-bodied South Vietnamese men from 17 up to 43 will be drafted to serve in the Armed Forces. At the same time, we have put a ban on all non essential foreign imports to devote most of our resources to our struggle to preserve our liberty.

Over the past two decades, the United States, by actions and words, have persuaded the South Vietnamese people to take a stand against the Communist. Because of their faith in America, they have staked their lives and the lives of their families on the sincerity of American promises. It is beyond the state of a doubt that the Communist will never forgive our population for their choice of taking side with the Free World, with America.

Indeed, the prospect of a bloodbath is real if and when the Communist take over South Vietnam. Evidences of this assertion are ample; the 1968 Tet offensive and the massacres in Hue, the 1972 Easter offensive, and most recently, the battles of Phuoc Long and Ban Me Thuot. Whenever the Communist came, they systematically executed all government officials, soldiers, police, churchmen, and those who have been directly or indirectly involved with the U.S. Moreover, the manner in which they have carried out the execution is beyond human imagination and is unworthy of even mentioning it here.

As results of the enemy's recent attacks, thousands of innocent civilians have lost their lives amidst

- 4 -

war flames and around a million have fled their hometowns, leaving behind all their properties to seek refuge in government controlled areas; they are, by action, participating in a very active election; they are voting by their feet, and voting for freedom.

The huge column of refugees who make up the largest exodus ever known in the Vietnam history has clearly manifested the most dramatic rejection of North Vietnam's Communism.

Mr. President,

At this time, the only question that arises in everyone's mind - and not only in South Vietnam - is what the United States is going to do about all this. The United States is a signatory to the Paris Agreement of January 27, 1973. It has formally endeavored to guarantee the implementation of that Agreement. Will it then stand meekly aside while the Agreement is torn to pieces by Hanoi? Will it renege from its responsibilities to the people of South Vietnam?

Therefore, in the face of the current perilous situation, we believe it necessary to raise our voice again and appeal to the U.S. Congress and Government to honor the commitments to its ally.

We solemnly reiterate here that the U.S. had promised to our country at the signing of the Paris Accord on January 27, 1973 in order to get over five hundred thousand American troops out of Vietnam; that the U.S. will provide adequate military aid to the Republic of Vietnam

- 5 -

for her self-defense and exercise of the right of self-determination. The U.S. will also provide the Republic of Vietnam with replacement of destroyed or worn-out weapons and ammunitions on a one-for-one basis.

In order to prevent the Communist from halting their strength, the U.S. also gave us assurances that 15 days after the signing of the Paris Accord Communist North Vietnam will stop her encroachments of the territories of Laos and Cambodia which she had been using as a springboard to attack the Republic of Vietnam.

In face of the enemy's direct attack on the foundation of the Paris Agreement, and on the basis of these pledges as well as on the previous commitments which were made by four Presidents of the United States to Vietnam, we solemnly appeal to the U.S. Congress and Government to take immediate and drastic measures to restore the Paris Agreement as it was in January 27, 1973, that is:

(1) to force the North Vietnamese back to their initial positions at the time of signing of the Paris Agreement, and

(2) to deliver to us on time all the necessary means to redress the balance of forces and for us to defend ourselves.

We know that only your prompt actions can save the Paris Agreement, only your drastic measures can save the people of South Vietnam.

- 6 -

We would very much appreciate, Mr. President if you could communicate the contents of this letter to your colleagues in the Senate.

Sincerely yours,

TRAN-VAN-LAM
President of the
Senate of the
Republic of VN

NGUYEN-BA-CAN
Speaker of the House
of Representative of the
Republic of Vietnam.

The Honorable NELSON ROCKEFELLER
President of the Senate
Of the United States of America
Washington D.C.

REPUBLIC OF VIET-NAM

SENATE
☆

SAIGON, March 24, 1975

Dear Mr. President:

Representing the two chambers of the Vietnamese National Assembly, we make bold in writing to you on behalf of twenty million South Vietnamese, including more than half a million new refugees caused by the recent Communist attacks in our country.

We are writing to you also as allies since this war which was started, perpetuated and nurtured neither by the United States nor by South Vietnam has bound the destinies of our two nations together in the last two decades. We accepted the challenge together and it is only fitting that we tried to solve the problem together. Together the U.S. and South Vietnam went to Paris, together we signed the Agreement on Ending the War and Restoring Peace in Vietnam, together we gave our word and guarantee that we would respect it and fulfill our commitments as they are defined by the Paris Agreement. The Agreement was followed by a International Conference with an International Act which made explicit all the great powers' guarantees of its validity.

President GERALD FORD
The White House
WASHINGTON D.C.

- 2 -

It was in this belief that we in the Vietnamese legislative branch strongly urged our President to sign the Paris Agreement, thus bringing an honorable end to the direct commitment of American troops in Vietnam. Thus, no one can blame us for wanting to prolong the war or not keeping our end of the bargain.

At that time, we were given assurances by the United States that the Soviet Union and Red China will gradually reduce their military aid to North Vietnam. But the experience of the last two years since the ceasefire showed instead an unprecedented building up Hanoi's military arsenal.

We were also given assurances that the United States would continue using its power, in combination with the persuasive power of Peking and Moscow, to restrain North Vietnam and enforce the respect of the ceasefire agreement. Hanoi, of course, went on flaunting every provision of the ceasefire agreement ever since.

Another commitment was even incorporated into the text of the Agreement: Fifteen days after the ceasefire went into effect, all North Vietnamese troops were to be removed from Laos and Cambodia. How more than two years have elapsed and tens of thousands of them are still in these neighboring countries.

Knowing full well what the Communist

- 3 -

leaders in Hanoi were up to, the United States has, on several occasions, promised vigorous and immediate reaction in case North Vietnam launched an offensive. Now they have accumulated more than eighty thousand violations of the ceasefire and are launching what is being the largest and most powerful offensive of the entire war.

The United States also promised us to continue to provide substantial military and economic aid, not for the purpose of lengthening the war but simply because the defense of peace must rest on armed and economic strength. The right of self-determination of the South Vietnamese people that was solemnly upheld and guaranteed by the Paris Agreement would turn out to be empty words if it cannot be assured the conditions in which it can be expressed fully and freely, not under the threat of naked force. Thus American continued aid to maintain a certain degree of balance of forces is a sine qua non condition of peace in our tortured land.

This in fact was even written into the Agreement under the clause of one-to-one replacement of ARVN equipment. The very provision of one-to-one replacement reflected our goodwill for peace since it precluded any escalation in the aid. Instead of tying the question of military aid that comes to Saigon to the level of aid received by Hanoi, the one-to-one replacement provision in itself represented a ceiling of aid to South Vietnam. Yet we have

- 4 -

not received anything approaching one-to-one replacement, thus resulting drastic reduction of our capabilities. Now, six out of seven airplanes in our armed forces are grounded for lack of fuel or spare parts. Others were destroyed by enemy anti-aircraft without getting replaced. Our firepower and mobility have all been severely limited resulting in an unprecedented low-level capacity. And all of this happened not because we do not have the manpower (all our pilots are still there) or because we are unwilling to fight for our survival.

As a result of the above-said defection, what can now be seen clearly in South Vietnam is the increasing deterioration of the situation. Thousands of persons have been killed and hundreds of thousands of others have fled to the government controlled areas, leaving behind all their properties.

Given the Communist superiority in firepower and manpower as a result of their violations of the Peace Agreement with impunity, the greatest concern now prevailing in South Vietnam is the direct threat of a quick over-running of many areas in the country by Communist forces.

When the Paris Agreement was signed, it was hailed as a foundation of a peace with honour, since it was entirely built on the principle of self-determination of the South Vietnamese people. We ourselves would continue to believe so, had it been scrupulously respected by North Vietnam, just as the United States and the Republic of Vietnam have done.

- 5 -

But contrary to our hope the foundation of peace is severely threatened because the North Vietnamese have once again decided to seek a military conquest of South Vietnam.

As a matter of emergency, therefore, we respectfully urge you to take all the necessary actions to preserve the peace and to deter North Vietnam once and for all from carrying out its ambition. We respectfully request that you do whatever is required to:

1. Restore the Paris Agreement to the initial condition, that is to force the Communist back to their positions which existed on January 27, 1973 and

2. Promptly supply us with urgent means to counter attack the offensive.

In this, you can only be right, for in doing so you will be upholding the two most sacred rights of all nations: the right to self-defense consecrated in the United Nations Charter and the right to self-determination of a people - the very root of American democracy.

In closing, we would like to thank you for your generous and kind support to our common struggle and we wish you every success in the heavy responsibilities that your high office, Mr. President, devolves upon your person.

Sincerely yours,

President GERALD FORD
The White House
WASHINGTON D.C.

NGUYEN BA CAN
Speaker of the House
of Representatives of
the Republic of Vietnam.

TRAN VAN IAM
President of the Senate
of the Republic of VN

Appendix K

UNITED STATES ARMY
THE CHIEF OF STAFF

4 April 1975

MEMORANDUM FOR THE PRESIDENT
SUBJECT: Vietnam Assessment

In accordance with your instructions, I visited South Vietnam during the period 28 March-4 April. I have completed my assessment of the current situation there, analyzed what the Government of the Republic of Vietnam intends to do to counter the aggression from the North, assured President Thieu of your steadfast support in this time of crisis, and examined the options and actions open to the United States to assist the South Vietnamese.

The current military situation is critical, and the probability of the survival of South Vietnam as a truncated nation in the southern provinces is marginal at best. The GVN is on the brink of a total military defeat. However, the South is planning to continue to defend with their available resources, and, if allowed respite, will rebuild their capabilities to the extent that United States support in materiel will permit. I believe that we owe them that support.

We went to Vietnam in the first place to assist the South Vietnamese people--not to defeat the North Vietnamese. We reached out our hand to the South Vietnamese people, and they took it. Now they need that helping hand more than ever. By every measure we have been able to apply 20,000,000 people have told the world they fear for their lives, they cherish values that are closely allied with those of non-communist systems, they desperately seek the opportunity to continue their development of a way of life different from those who now live under North Vietnamese rule.

The present level of U.S. support guarantees GVN defeat. Of the $700 million provided for FY 1975, the remaining $150 million can be used for a short time for a major supply operation; however, if there is to be any real chance of

SECRET

DECLASSIFIED
Authority NLF MR 90-16 Doc.#1
By _____ NLF Date 04/7/95
Copy from
Gerald R. Ford Library

success, an additional $722 million is urgently needed to bring the South Vietnamese to a minimal defense posture to meet the Soviet and PRC supported invasion. Additional U.S. aid is within both the spirit and intent of the Paris Agreement, which remains the practical framework for a peaceful settlement in Vietnam.

The use of U.S. military airpower to reinforce Vietnamese capabilities to blunt the North Vietnamese invasion would offer both a material and psychological assist to GVN and provide a much needed battlefield pause. I recognize, however, the significant legal and political implications which would attend the exercise of this option.

Given the speed at which events are moving, there is one other matter you should consider. For reasons of prudence, the United States should plan now for a mass evacuation of some 6,000 U.S. citizens and tens of thousands of South Vietnamese and Third Country Nationals to whom we have incurred an obligation and owe protection. The lessons of Danang indicate that this evacuation would require as a minimum a U.S. task force of a reinforced division supported by tactical air to suppress North Vietnamese artillery and anti-aircraft, as required. At the appropriate time, a public statement of this policy should be made and the North Vietnamese clearly warned of U.S. intention to use force to safely evacuate personnel. Authority should be obtained to authorize appropriate use of military sanctions against North Vietnam if there is interference with the evacuation.

United States credibility as an ally is at stake in Vietnam. To sustain that credibility we must make a maximum effort to support the South Vietnamese now.

A more detailed analysis is contained in the attached report.

Respectfully,

[signature]

FRED C. WEYAND
General, United States Army
Chief of Staff

1 Incl
As stated

SECRET

2

Copy from
Gerald R. Ford Library

The *Report to the President of the United States on the Situation in South Vietnam* was prepared for President Ford by General Fred C. Weyand, Chief of Staff of the U.S. Army. Weyand visited the Republic of Vietnam from March 28 to April 4, 1975 with Eric Von Marbod, Principal Deputy Assistant Secretary of Defense/Comptroller, Theodore Shackley and George Carver, Vietnam specialists in the CIA, who contributed to the report. The report is declassified and is on file in the Gerald R. Ford Library.

REPORT TO THE PRESIDENT OF THE UNITED STATES

ON THE SITUATION IN SOUTH VIETNAM

CONTENTS

INTRODUCTION

On 24 March 1975 you directed me to conduct a fact finding mission to the Republic of Vietnam. My task was to:

Assess the current military situation and probable North Vietnamese intentions during the current offensive.

Determine and assess what the Government of the Republic of Vietnam is now doing and intends to do in coping with this offensive and with its impact on both the military and civilian sectors.

Determine what the United States Government can do to to bolster South Vietnamese military capabilities and to alleviate suffering among the civilian population.

Assure President Thieu that this Administration remains steadfast in its support of the efforts by the Republic of Vietnam to resist North Vietnamese aggression and that it will do what it can to provide the materiel assistance necessary for the defense of the republic.

S.E.C.R.E.T

I. THE CURRENT SITUATION

   A. The Background

The Paris Agreement of 27 January 1973 marked not the beginning of peace in Vietnam, but instead the beginning of a Communist build-up of supplies and equipment for continued North Vietnamese military aggression in Vietnam. In the ensuing 26 months since the Agreement was signed, North Vietnam rebuilt the Ho Chi Minh Trail into a major all-weather supply artery. They built pipelines extending 330 miles into South Vietnam for movement of their POL. With this major supply system in full operation, they quadrupled their field artillery, greatly increased their anti-aircraft and sent six times as much armor into South Vietnam as they had in January 1973 (See Table A). At the same time, they increased their troop strength by almost 200,000 men. All of these actions were in direct violation of the Paris Agreement. The US, by contrast, did not fulfill its obligations to maintain South Vietnamese equipment and materiel levels as they were authorized to do under the Agreement. Ground ammunition declined by 30% from 179 thousand short tons at the cease fire to 126 thousand short tons when the current NVA offensive began. Shortages of POL and spare parts curtailed operations of the South Vietnamese Air Force by 50%.

The historical record outlined above set the stage for the current situation in South Vietnam. This situation is both fluid and fragile. It changed markedly during the month of March and has the potential for further rapid change in the weeks, or even days, immediately ahead.

On 10 March, the Communists launched "Phase II" of their 1975 campaign. Two North Vietnamese Army Divisions assaulted Ban Me Thuot, a strategic cross-roads in the western highlands, which was lightly defended by ARVN. At about the same time, North Vietnamese Army units west of Saigon initiated a systematic effort to eliminate the GVN presence, give the Communists a shortened, more secure infiltration corridor south into the Mekong Delta and, simultaneously, to interdict the only two roads between Saigon and Tay Ninh.

In mid-February, President Thieu sent Senator Tran Van Lam to the US as a private emissary to assess the mood of Congress with respect to Vietnam and the prospects for favorable Congressional action on aid legislation. Lam submitted a very pessimistic appraisal, which Thieu felt was confirmed by the early March votes of the House Democratic caucus. Thieu was digesting Lam's bleak estimate when the Communists launched the afore-mentioned "phase II" attacks. Thieu saw his country faced with a major Communist offensive coinciding with a curtailment, and possible cessation, of US aid. He and his military advisors therefore decided that a drastic strategic retrenchment was essential to the GVN's survival.

2

SECRET

This new strategic concept entailed writing off most of the mountainous, sparsely populated portions of MR's 1 and 2 to concentrate the GVN's assets and resources on defending MR's 3 and 4 plus the coastal lowlands of MR's 1 and 2, the agriculturally productive areas of South Vietnam in which the bulk of the population resided. This strategy was sound in concept and Thieu's estimate of its necessity was correct. Its execution, however, was disastrous.

In a 13 March meeting with his MR 1 Commander, General Truong, President Thieu outlined his new strategic concept and his resultant decision to withdraw the Airborne Division from MR 1 to MR 3, despite General Truong's strong objection that the withdrawal of the airborne division would make the GVN's position in MR 1 untenable. During the next twelve days (13-25 March) there was vacillation, both in MR 1 and in Saigon, over what portions of MR 1 were to be held--and particularly, whether any attempt should be made to defend Hue. As a result of the changing orders he was receiving from Saigon, General Truong had to revise his troop deployment plans at least three times, even as the North Vietnamese Army attack was steadily increasing in intensity. Quang Tri City was evacuated in orderly fashion on 19 March, but before a new GVN defense line could be stabilized along the My Chanh River, territorial forces in the area began evaporating in the face of North Vietnamese pressure; Saigon recalled the last airborne brigade in MR 1, and an unravelling process began. North Vietnamese pressure mounted daily at a sharply increasing rate. Hue was evacuated on 25 March, but by then NVA units had cut Route 1 south of the city and the removal of Hue's 20,000 defenders, including most of ARVN's 1st Division, became largely dependent on haphazard, improvised sealift operations. During this same period, over-extended GVN units in Quang Nam, Quang Tin, and Quang Ngai Provinces, were being dispersed or defeated piecemeal by advancing NVA forces.

The GVN's presence in MR 1 collapsed into an enclave at Da Nang. What was left of the GVN's effective strength in that region--basically the Marine Division and a part of the 3rd ARVN Division--tried to set up a defense of Da Nang, but the effort was not successful. Arrayed against the GVN's 10,000 odd organized defenders were over 30,000 NVA troops advancing with the momentum of success. Further compounding the situation's problems was the influx of more than a million refugees. With a total of close to 2 million people increasingly desperate to get out, panic spread and on 28 March order collapsed. NVA tanks began moving into the town soon thereafter. No more than 50,000 refugees were brought out by air or by sea, and the GVN succeeded in extracting approximately 22,000 troops, including about 9,000 marines and 4,000 -5,000 troops from the 2nd and 3rd ARVN divisions, but the fate of the remainder of Da Nang's civil and military population is unknown.

In MR 2, President Thieu and his regional commander, General Phu, met at Cam Ranh Bay on 14 March to discuss the situation in light of the loss of

Ban Me Thuot. At that meeting, President Thieu outlined his new strategic concept to withdraw from the highlands and consolidate GVN forces for defense of vital coastal areas. The exact wording of the President's orders are not known, but General Phu interpreted them as authorizing at his discretion the immediate, total evacuation of Pleiku and Kontum Provinces, for which no plans or preparations had been made. The exodus began in the next two days, with the evacuating ARVN forces following Highway 14 and Route 7B across Phu Bon and Phu Yen Provinces to the coast at Tuy Hoa. Compounding the already severe difficulties inherent in this unplanned exodus, 7B was a secondary road, virtually unused for years, with many bridges out and no fords prepared. Command and control broke down. The six ranger groups and one infantry regiment from Kontum and Pleiku became interspersed among the increasingly desperate 200,000 odd civilians fleeing with the exfiltrating column. At least two and possibly three NVA regiments wheeled northward from Darlac to Phu Bon and Phu Yen Provinces to harass the column, systematically and methodically engaging the dispersed ARVN military units, none of which were combat effective when the column's lead elements entered Tuy Hoa City on 26 March. The carnage inflicted en route on the hapless civilian refugees was horrendous.

While the above events were in train, the GVN diverted one airborne brigade from the Hue area to Khanh Hoa Province to block the two to four NVA regiments pursuing the remnants of the 23rd ARVN eastward from Ban Me Thuot across Darlac Province. The 23rd Division already battered by its stand at Ban Me Thuot, had virtually ceased to exist as an organized unit by the time its survivors began trickling into Nha Trang.

B.   The Present Situation

The military situation existing in the first week in April has to be assessed in light of what happened in March. Amid the general chaos in MR's 1 and 2, a number of ARVN units performed well. Without the effectiveness of the Marines and some elements of the 3rd ARVN, no one would have gotten out of Da Nang. In Ban Me Thuot, elements of the 23rd ARVN held out for more than a week against two NVA divisions. The 40th and 41st regiments of ARVN's 22nd division fought savagely to delay superior NVA forces from breaking through to the coast at Qui Nhon in Binh Dinh Province. The net effect of March's events, however, has been severely adverse both in concrete terms and, even more, in psychological terms.

Communist forces have the momentum of success and though they have suffered casualties which may have been heavy, they are being augmented daily by fresh replacements and supplies from North Vietnam (Table, TAB A). During the last three weeks in March, five ARVN divisions, twelve Ranger Groups and two brigade equivalents of armor have been rendered combat ineffective. Officers and men from these units can be regrouped into new formations, but virtually all of their equipment has been lost. Many other GVN units have suffered heavy losses in personnel and equipment.

As of 1 April, Communist combat forces in South Vietnam, predominately North Vietnamese Army units and personnel, totalled over 200,000 organized

ARVN forces or a significant further increase in Communist strength beyond that of the past week, the GVN should be able to hold the situation in MR 3 about as it stood on 3 April, at least for the immediate future.

In the Mekong Delta (MR 4), the past several weeks have not seen any appreciable change. Opposing regular combat forces are about evenly matched (See Tables, Tabs B & C). The tactical situation could deteriorate rapidly if additional Communist units come into the area or if the GVN should redeploy to MR 3 any one of the three ARVN divisions now assigned to MR 4.

Militarily, the GVN is on the defensive and beleaguered. March's military reverses and their attendant consequences--the loss of territory, military and civilian casualties, and the enormous population dislocation of the more than two million civilian refugees--have had a heavy, adverse impact on the whole political and social structure of South Vietnam. Just how heavy, extensive or lasting is hard to tell, partly because the South Vietnamese people are in a state of shock and because a full knowledge of what actually has happened in MR's 1 and 2 is not yet widespread, even in Saigon, let alone the populated rural areas in MR 3 or the still prosperous and agriculturally busy Mekong Delta.

C. North Vietnamese Plans and Intentions

North Vietnam's intentions are hard to discern and its next moves are probably the subject of active discussion now being conducted by the Lao Dong Politburo in Hanoi. Such evidence as is available suggests that Hanoi is weighing two broad options:

a. Exert a maximum effort to exploit the recent tactical successes and present battlefield advantage of the North Vietnamese Army in an all out effort to collapse the GVN and eliminate it as a functioning political entity.

b. Consolidate recent gains and try for one or two more major victories (e.g., disperse the 25th ARVN Division and/or capture Tay Ninh), then call for negotiations on terms tantamount to a GVN surrender, planning to try again for military victory later in 1975 or 1976 if the GVN can not be pressured politically into accepting some form of "coalition government" that would give the Communists de facto political control over South Vietnam.

From the time the Paris Agreement was signed in 1973, Hanoi has been steadily improving its military capabilities in South Vietnam through a continuous improvement of its logistic infrastructure (roads, trails, depots, etc., in both Laos and South Vietnam) and a continuous infusion of supplies, equipment and troops--all in direct violation of Article 7 of the 1973 Agreement. This flow has peaked and valleyed over the past 26 months, but it has never stopped.

SECRET

6

---

into 123 regiments--71 infantry, 7 sapper, 4 armor, 16 artillery and 25 AAA*.

Comparable, currently effective ARVN ground combat forces total just over 54,000 troops, organized in 39 regiments/brigades or equivalents--18 infantry regiments, 2 armored brigades, 5 ranger groups, 3 airborne and 2 marine brigades**. Given replacement equipment, effective ARVN combat manpower and unit strengths can be augmented by new units formed out of the personnel remnants of the units dispersed during the March battles in MR's 1 and 2, but this will take time. As of 1 April, the predominantly North Vietnamese Communist combat force in South Vietnam outnumbers equivalent GVN forces just under 3 to 1 in size.

Territorially, all of MR 1 has been lost by the GVN, along with most of MR 2***. The GVN currently holds a coastal lowland strip running southward from about Cam Ranh to the MR 3 border, plus the southern portion of Tuyen Duc Province. Lam Dong Province fell on 1 April, Dalat City was evacuated on 2 April and what is left of Tuyen Duc Province is disintegrating.

In MR 3, Phuoc Long Province was lost in January. In March there was further territorial erosion in a broad arc about 50 miles west, north and east of Saigon. The fighting in MR 3 has been sporadic and, on occasion, heavy but there, the ARVN has basically held its own during the past three weeks. In MR 3, ARVN forces do not yet face the problem of being significantly outnumbered. Though the Communists are already applying severe pressure in several areas (e.g., Tay Ninh and around Xuan Loc) and are clearly planning a round of new attacks, GVN forces by and large are holding their own and fighting well, and in the process have badly mauled a few Communist units. Barring a wholesale morale erosion on the part of

*See Table, Tab B, for details. This does not include administrative service and combat support personnel, nor does it include Viet Cong provincial and district territorial units.

**See Table, Tab C, for details. These figures do not include the South Vietnamese Air Force or Navy, nor do they include the Regional and Popular Forces, Police Field Forces or other miscellaneous non-ARVN units. Strength estimates for the GVN Regional Forces are included in the table as part of the GVN's overall armed strength. With some specific exceptions, these territorial units, however, were ineffective during the March campaigns in MR's 1 and 2, often dispersing and dissolving at the first serious probes (or even appearance) of North Vietnamese Army line units. ARVN commanders in MR's 3 and 4 generally doubt the territorials would be more effective in the face of heavy North Vietnamese attacks in the lower half of the country. As a consequence, territorial forces are being upgraded into the regular ARVN structure.

***See Maps (Tab D).

S E C R E T

5

In the summer of 1974, when the GVN's overall position looked promising, this manpower and supply flow augmenting North Vietnam's invading expeditionary force in the South was down. It began to pick up soon after last summer's political developments within the United States and diminishing Congressional support for continued assistance to South Vietnam. The logistic flow of men and materiel out of North Vietnam--and, hence, the North Vietnamese Army's capabilities in the south--began to pick up in the latter part of 1974. The pace has been intense since the beginning of 1975, was increased in February and March, and is now going at full throttle.

Hanoi certainly had planned a significant level of offensive action this spring. In retrospect, the "Phase I" January campaign (which overran Phuoc Long Province), among other things, seems to have been a test of whether the US would react to what even Hanoi must have considered a blatant violation of the 1973 Paris Agreement. Judging from the Communists subsequent behavior--e.g., the sharply rising build-up, introduction of North Vietnamese strategic reserve units, the assault on Ban Me Thuot with two NVA divisions (one recently brought south from Hanoi's strategic reserve) and the increasing stridency with which the Communists have played the propaganda theme of US "impotence"--Hanoi seems to have decided that the US was too preoccupied with other problems to react significantly to anything North Vietnam did in Indochina.

Official party directives and high level instructions issued in January and February and even through the third week in March suggest that at least the initial objectives of the 1975 campaign were something less than near term total victory--i.e., an improved territorial position (probably including capture of Tay Ninh City), harassment and attrition of ARVN, and heavy overall pressure on the GVN. The main goal of this campaign appeared to be that of putting the Communists in a commanding position from which they could demand negotiations leading to a coalition government, and, if such were not forthcoming, from which they could launch a "final" assault in 1976.

How much Hanoi's goals may have escalated or its appetite been whetted by the past month's events in South Vietnam--and in the United States--is impossible to tell, particularly since even Hanoi has not had time to digest the most recent developments. The rate at which men and supplies are coming down from North Vietnam into South Vietnam, however, certainly suggests that Hanoi intends to keep pressing its invading expeditionary force's attacks.

II. MAJOR PROBLEM AREAS

The GVN is faced with an interlocking web of rapidly mounting problems which fall into three broad areas.

First, there are physical or concrete problems. The most important of these is the North Vietnamese Army--including its present size, increasing

7

strength and aggressive activity. Then, there is the sheer magnitude of the past three weeks' losses in personnel and equipment which--unless or until replaced--puts an increasingly debilitated ARVN in a worsening position against a growing North Vietnamese threat. In the civil sphere, there is the concomitant magnitude of the refugee flow, uprooting close to ten per cent of the entire population, whose urgent needs for food, clothing, shelter, and medical care place enormous strains on the machinery of government. Meeting these refugees' immediate needs is in itself a massive problem but resettling them and absorbing them in the areas still under GVN control is an even more formidable task.

There are many other concrete problems that are intrinsically important (e.g., keeping the roads and lines of communication open, food supplies moving, maintaining basic law and order in areas inundated with refugees, controlling or checking Viet Cong subversion and terrorism in areas not under immediate conventional attack), but these are overshadowed by the three "physical" problems mentioned above.

In addition, there are a host of burgeoning, related problems which might be termed "administrative". These involve providing the leadership, guidance and direction necessary to cope with the physical problems noted above. They also involve the leadership and administration, military and civil, necessary to rally a nation after a series of defeats, check the spread of despondency and hopelessness, develop a sense of national unity and common purpose, and wage a war for survival. In a Vietnamese context, the situation requires the kind of leadership and effective administration Churchill and his War Cabinet gave Great Britain after Dunkirk and the fall of France. To date (as outlined in Section III below) this kind of leadership and administration is not evident--and in Vietnam, there is no English Channel to check the onrushing tide of invasion or provide a respite for regroupment.

Then there is a complex of psychological and attitudinal problems which, in the end, may prove the most important of all. In refugee-clogged coastal MR 2, the kind of fear and panic which erupted in Da Nang also rose to the surface before the GVN's position north of Cam Ranh collapsed. In MR 3 and Saigon, the people are shocked and bewildered. They may not yet have a sense of immediate personal danger and crisis, but that emotion is beginning to spread with increasing rapidity. In the Delta, where news of northern developments takes time to circulate, life is prosperous and there is no change in the pattern of the past two years' events yet perceptible to the ordinary citizen, people are perplexed and troubled but do not yet feel immediately threatened. The GVN has a little time in which to act before the full story of what has happened in MR 1 and MR 2 becomes widely known throughout the rest of the country; but the time is very short.

In the Army, the psychological problems are more focused and more intense. Army units in coastal MR 2 know they may soon be overwhelmed. Despite certain local tactical successes, the units in MR 3 could fall prey to a

8

sense of defeatism and hopelessness. In the Delta, senior ARVN commanders assert that the morale of their troops is still good and that when attacked they will fight, but when talked to privately by Americans they know, and whose discretion they trust, these same commanders caution that their troops' morale could not stand the news of major defeats in MR 3.

One of the most serious psychological and attitudinal problems at all levels, military and civilian, is the belief that the South Vietnamese have been abandoned, and even betrayed, by the United States. The Communists are using every possible device of propaganda and psychological warfare to foster this view. The higher one goes in the social or hierarchical scale the greater the degree of sharpness and focus to such sentiments. Much of this emotion is keyed on the 1973 Paris Agreement and subsequent US withdrawal. It is widely believed that the GVN was forced to sign this agreement as a result of a private US-North Vietnamese deal under which the US was allowed to withdraw its forces and get its prisoners back in return for abandoning South Vietnam. This sense of abandonment has been intensified by what is widely perceived as a lack of public US acknowledgement of South Vietnam's current plight or willingness to provide needed support.

All of the above problems are interacting. One result of this interaction is a spreading loss of confidence in the GVN's top leadership, a sentiment felt throughout the politically aware population and mounting rapidly in the Army. President Thieu's inner core of senior advisors is felt to be disgraced. With every passing day, more of this bitterness and resentment is being focused on President Thieu himself. There is a general awareness that any coup attempt, even if successful, would probably be the ultimate disaster; but the odds are mounting that unless this crisis of confidence is dispelled, President Thieu will have to step down.

III. CURRENT GVN PLANS AND INTENTIONS

The GVN has what it calls a "strategic plan" but it is being revised almost daily in the light of events. A week ago (25 March) it envisioned an enclave at Da Nang and a southern defense line anchored on the coast at Binh Dinh or, failing that, just below Tuy Hoa in Phu Yen Province. The contemplated line was to swing through Tuyen Duc and over to Tay Ninh. Since the plan was developed, Da Nang has fallen, the GVN's position in coastal MR 2 has collapsed north of Cam Ranh.

The GVN intends to reorganize and refit the ARVN and Marine units decimated in last month's battles with all possible speed. It also intends to take other steps to augment ARVN's strength by upgrading significant numbers of territorial forces and Ranger groups. The success of all of this will depend on the degree to which RVNAF is able to correct serious deficiencies in command and control and its capacity to translate plans into coordinated action. President Thieu and General Vien are aware of the need and have promised corrective action.

The refugee problem reflects similar deficiencies in planning and administration. There is a concern and desire to be helpful and sources of international sympathy and support which could be tapped, including funds, medical personnel, supplies, etc. Dr. Dan—the Deputy Prime Minister responsible for refugees—is doing what he can, but there is, as yet, no internal GVN mechanism capable of addressing the intricate details and systematic follow through this enormous and complex problem requires. As a result, the burden tends to fall on a few officials, including local provincial ones, some of whom have been imaginative in coping with immediate crises but whose efforts are individual, fragmented and not part of an integrated whole.

Propaganda and psychological warfare and even essential governmental communication with the GVN's own people show similar deficiencies in overall concept and systematic follow through.

The GVN, in short, has hopes and aspirations, and a desire to cope, but few of these are focused, channeled or truly organized. The government, especially the bureaucracy, is in a state of shock and bewilderment and the top echelons do not seem to have a full realization or comprehension of the magnitude of the GVN's many problems.

IV. CURRENT PROSPECTS

What happens in South Vietnam over the next month or so, let alone a longer time frame, depends very much on what is done—or not done—by North Vietnam, the GVN, and the United States during the next two to three weeks and even the next few days.

Unless North Vietnamese Forces are somehow checked in battle or Hanoi induced to pause by some form of diplomatic or other suasion, the North Vietnamese will defeat the GVN militarily. There is no evidence that the North Vietnamese are developing logistic problems or beginning to outrun their supplies. The southward march of one, let alone two, of Hanoi's five divisions now in MR 1 would be enough to seal the fate of the GVN's hold on coastal MR 2. If one of Hanoi's five divisions already in MR 2 were brought down into MR 3, particularly if augmented with more armor and artillery, that would tilt the present balance of forces in MR 3. The GVN's forces in the Delta have all they can handle with the North Vietnamese troops already in that region, and MR 4 could not hold if MR 3 collapsed in the wake of defeats in MR's 1 and 2.

The above picture may be altered as the GVN deploys into MR 3 units reconstituted from the remnants of the ones recovered from MR 1 and MR 2. This, however, requires time to reorganize and equip. The odds are that in pure capability terms, the North Vietnamese can move and commit existing divisions within SVN faster than the GVN can form new ones.

As for the GVN, some steps—dramatic and demonstrably effective—have to be taken not just to prevent any near term deterioration in the GVN's military position in MR 3, but also--and perhaps more important--to give the population, and the RVNAF, a psychological lift and confidence in the GVN's top leadership. In the morale sphere, South Vietnam--at least in MR 3, including Saigon--is very near the brink of a slide into the kind of hopelessness and defeatism that could rapidly unravel the whole structure.

V. THE US ROLE AND POSSIBLE COURSES OF ACTION

What the US does, or does not do, in the days immediately ahead will probably be as critical a determinant of the next few weeks' events as the actions or non-actions of Saigon or Hanoi. The US, alone, can not save South Vietnam but it can, however inadvertently, seal its doom.

My specific recommendations fall into two different categories. There are short term actions--partly physical but primarily psychological-- needed to give South Vietnam a morale lift and, if possible, to induce Hanoi to pause. This buys nothing but time, but at the moment that time is urgently needed. Secondly, there are longer term actions, mainly material though still with a strong psychological dimension, which are necessary if South Vietnam is to have any hope of physically surviving the North Vietnamese onslaught or negotiating any settlement short of unconditional surrender.

The essential and immediate requirement is Vietnamese perception of US support. Perceptions are important in every respect. A perception of diminishing US support for South Vietnam encouraged the North Vietnamese to launch their current offensive. It was this same perception that caused the Republic of Vietnam to begin withdrawal from the dispersed and exposed positions in the northern provinces. These perceptions were shaped by the following actions: Immediately following the signing of the Paris Agreement, $1.6 billion was requested to meet the requirements of the South Vietnamese in FY 1974; $1.126 billion was provided--70% of the needs. A subsequent request for a $500 million supplemental was ultimately turned down. For the current fiscal year, $1.6 billion was requested to maintain a viable Vietnamese military capability for defense; $700 million was provided--44% of the stated requirement. These and related actions helped generate the crisis of confidence that precipitated the GVN strategy of retrenchment.

Now, the key to Vietnamese national survival is the GVN's ability to stabilize the situation, and to bring their military resources to bear in blunting the North Vietnamese offensive. Their ability to stabilize the situation hinges, to a very large extent, on the ability to convince the average soldier and citizen that all is not lost, and that the North Vietnamese can be stopped. Though this is largely a task for the Government of Vietnam, the actions of the US are vital in restoring confidence.

SECRET

11

The action which the US could take which would have the greatest immediate effect on Vietnamese perceptions--North and South--would be the use of US air power to blunt the current NVA offensive. Even if confined to South Vietnam and carried out for only a limited time, such attacks would take a severe toll on the North Vietnamese expeditionary force's manpower and supplies, and have a dramatic morale impact on North Vietnam's invading troops. These attacks would also give Hanoi's leaders' pause and raise concerns, which do not now exist, about the risks involved in ignoring a formal agreement made with the United States.

South Vietnamese military leaders at all levels have repeatedly cited the importance of B-52 attacks to the conduct of a successful defense against superior enemy forces and there is sound military justification for such a point of view.

The above comments convey only a military assessment. I recognize, however, the significant legal and political implications which would attend the exercise of such an action.

One important step that the US should take is to make it clear that the US supports South Vietnam. This should include positive statements by the President and other senior US officials. Sagging Vietnamese morale was clearly bolstered by the arrival of the United States team sent by the President to investigate the situation. Additional US actions of this nature would highlight US concern. In addition to statements from the Executive Branch, there should be an effort to insure that a broad spectrum of concern is evident in the United States. Support from Members of Congress; public statements from responsible individuals both in and outside of the Government; and understanding in the US press will foster changing US perceptions of the situation in Vietnam.

This effort could stress three principal themes:

--The Vietnamese people, with first-hand knowledge of life under both the Thieu Government and Communism, have clearly indicated their choice by "voting with their feet," as the East Germans did before the intro- duction of the Berlin Wall. The mass exodus from the northern provinces, in the face of hardships, danger and intense human suffering, is a true sign of their feelings. In their choice, none have fled north to Hanoi and North Vietnam--where there is no fighting, where there are no 'refugee columns, and where war has not touched since the Paris Agreement. The question is not an academic one to the individual Vietnamese; it is one of life and death. By their actions they have chosen liberty and possible death.

--South Vietnam is fighting a defensive war. US materiel is used to defend South Vietnam, while Soviet and Chinese tanks and war materiel are being used by the North Vietnamese for open, naked, defiant aggression. It is this North Vietnamese invasion, not the actions of the South Vietnamese, that has already required the Administration to seek additional support from the Congress.

SECRET

12

--We should continue to emphasize the effect of Vietnam on the credibility of any US commitment. The world clearly understands past US commitments to Vietnam. Our expenditure of lives and resources in pursuit of this commitment is well known to all. The governments of the world know the past, but will see any present inability to support the Vietnamese in their crisis of survival as a failure of US will and resolve. If we make no effort, our future credibility as perceived by ally and potential adversary alike will be lost for years to come.

Statements of US support are important, but it is also essential that the message be validated with concrete actions to demonstrate that the United States stands behind her ally. While the ultimate availability of military resources will rest with supplemental appropriations in the Congress for the current fiscal year, there is more than $150 million available from the $700 million voted in the Defense Appropriations Act. This money can be used to meet the most immediate needs now and in the next few weeks. However, the rapid expenditure of the remaining funds will soon exhaust US capabilities to provide support. A supplemental appropriations bill, probably for about $722 million, is urgently needed for basic military necessities to provide a chance for the survival of the Republic of Vietnam. Details of the requirement follow:

The present offensive campaign by the NVA has caused serious materiel losses which must be replaced now:

--Five ARVN Divisions have been destroyed or rendered combat ineffective and another division has been only partially salvaged. While at this writing an exact numerical count of personnel and equipment losses is impossible to obtain, the following are the presently known materiel losses:

GROUND MUNITIONS (DEPOT STOCKS ONLY)	$ 129.0 M
INDIVIDUAL & CREW SERVED WEAPONS	24.6 M
ARTILLERY	16.0 M
TRACK VEHICLES	85.0 M
WHEEL VEHICLES	77.0 M
COMMUNICATIONS EQUIPMENT	15.6 M
POL	6.3 M
MEDICAL	7.9 M
ENGINEER	1.8 M
GENERAL SUPPLY STOCKS	110.5 M
TOTAL	$ 473.7 M

--In addition the VNAF has lost 393 aircraft valued at $176.3 million, $52.8 million of air munitions, and $68.6 million of spare parts and support equipment.

--During the current offensive the Vietnamese Navy lost three craft valued at $2.4 million and $5.4 million in supplies and support equipment.

The total estimated cost for RVNAF military supplies and equipment lost in the current offensive is $779.2 million. These losses do not include basic load munitions, non-divisional support units or fixed facilities such as airfields, ports and military installations.

The GVN believes the current offensive can be blunted with military forces currently available and to be reconstituted. They contemplate retaining a reduced RVN consisting of the southeastern portion of the MR 2 lowlands, the southern two-thirds of MR 3 and all of MR 4. The territory to be held contains the bulk of the population and has the requisites for a viable political and economic entity. They are working on a reorganization plan which, if successfully implemented, could provide military protection for this truncated RVN.

At this writing, the GVN reorganization plan envisages reconstitution of four infantry divisions, conversion of 12 ranger groups into four ranger divisions and the upgrading of 27 mobile Regional Force Groups into 27 infantry regiments. To be effective, implementation must begin immediately. Under the critical assumption that the GVN can stabilize the present military situation, with the material and manpower resources presently at their disposal and within the limited remaining FY75 appropriation, they need immediate additional materiel replenishments which will require new authorizations and appropriations. Our estimate of these immediate requirements is:

--Equipment for four infantry divisions:	$ 138.6 M
--Conversion of 12 ranger groups to four divisions:	118.0 M
--Conversion of 27 RF groups to 27 ARVN Regiments:	69.6 M
--Ground munitions to sustain combat operations and reconstitute stockage levels:	198.0 M
--Air munitions to sustain combat operations and reconstitute stockage levels:	21.0 M
--POL products to sustain combat operations and insure adequate stockage levels:	10.4 M
--General supplies and repair parts:	21.0 M

--Medical Support (Hospitals & Supplies): $ 7.0 M

--Aircraft (two C-130's), spares, ground
support equipment, and airfield repairs: 44.9 M

--Cost of transportation of supplies and
equipment: 93.7 M

TOTAL $ 722.2 M

We estimate that the bulk of the above materials can be delivered to RVN within 45 days of availability of funds. It must be understood that without this supplemental funding, RVNAF's ammunition supply will be exhausted before the end of this fiscal year at the present level of combat. Reconstitution of combat ineffective units will not be possible without supplemental funding.

Beyond satisfying these immediate military requirements we should seek separate appropriations for refugee relief. The GVN should not be burdened with the expense of resettling over one million refugees when its resources are already needed for its fight for survival.

There is not and can not be any guarantee that the actions I propose will be sufficient to prevent total North Vietnamese conquest. The effort, however, should be made. What is at stake in Vietnam now is America's credibility as an ally. We must not abandon our goal of a free and independent South Vietnam.

15

SECRET

NVA/INCREASED NVA WEAPONS
IN RVN SINCE CEASEFIRE
(All Numbers Rough Estimates)

WEAPONS	ON HAND 23 JAN 73	MOVED IN THRU 1 MAR 75	TOTAL 1 MAR 75	MOVED IN 1 MAR-1 APR 75	TOTAL INCREASE 23 JAN 73-1 APR 75	MOVING SOUTH 1 APR 75
Field Arty Pieces (85, 122, 130MM)	85-105	270-380	355-485	15	285-395	30-40
Anti-Aircraft 12.8, 14.5, 23, 37, 57, 100MM	700	800	1500	250	1050	250
SA-2	----	15-25 LCHRS	15-25 LCHRS	16-25 LCHRS	31-50 LCHRS	Poss 50-75 LCHRS
SA-3	----	-----------	-----------	-----------	-----------	
ARMOR PT76, T54, T63, etc.	90-115	575-635	665-750	20-30	595-665	Unk

	APRIVED BETWEEN 28 JAN 73 AND 1 MAR 75	ARRIVED DURING MARCH 1975	DETECTED APRIL ARRIVALS	ESTIMATED ADDITIONAL APRIL ARRIVALS	TOTAL
PERSONNEL INFILTRATION ARRIVALS IN RVN	195,400	19,400	23,400	10,000	248,300

SECRET

'GD

SECRET-SENSITIVE

DAO VC/NVA OB
MAJOR COMBAT UNITS IN RVN

	JAN 73 DIVS	REGTS	MAR 75 DIVS	BDES	Regts	APR 75 (Change over Mar 75) DIVS	Bdes	REGTS	Moving t DIVS
COUNTRY-WIDE	17 (16 Inf, 1 AA)	97 (85 Inf, 12 AA)	20 (+3) (15 Inf, 1 Arty 3 AA, 1 Sap)	4 (+4) (1 Inf, 2 Arty, 1 Armor)	117 (+20) (65 Inf, 16 Arty, 4 Armor, 24 AA, 1 SAM, 7 Sap)	22 (+2 Inf)	4 (No Change)	123 (+6 Inf)	4 (3 Inf, 1 AA)
MR-1	9 (8 Inf, 1 AA)	50 (39 Inf/ Arty, 11 AA)	6 (-3) (4 Inf, 2 AD)	4 (+4) (1 Inf, 2 Arty, 1 Armor)	46 (-4) (20 Inf, 6 Arty, 2 Armor, 17 AA, 1 SAM)	6 (No Change)	4 (No Change)	50 (+1 Inf)	
MR-2	3 Inf	10 Inf/ Arty	4 Inf (+1)	-	23 (+15) (15 Inf, 3 Arty, 1 Armor, 4 AA)	6 (+2) (1 Inf, 1 AA)	-	27 (+4) (3 Inf, 1 AA)	
MR-3	2 Inf	17 (16 Inf/ Arty, 1 AA)	7 (+5) (4 Inf, 1 Arty, 1 Sap, 1 AA)	-	31 (+14) (15 Inf, 5 Arty, 1 Armor, 1 Sap, 3 AA)	8 (+1 Inf)	-	34 (+3 Inf)	
MR-4	3 Inf	20 Inf	3 Inf (No Change)	-	18 (-2) (15 Inf, 1 Sap, 2 Arty)	3 Inf (no Change)	-	18 (No Change)	

SECRET-SENSITIVE

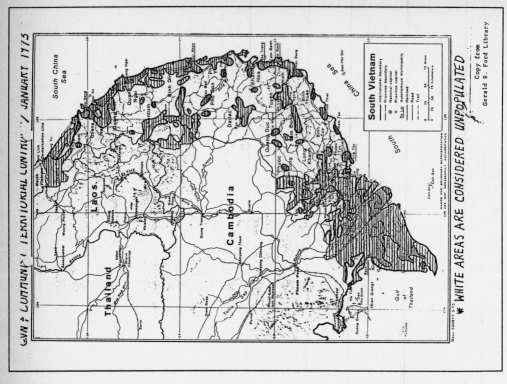

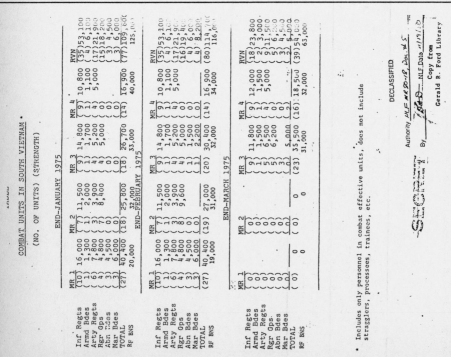

Appendix L

President Duong Van Minh's letter to Ambassador Graham Martin was the last communication from the government of the Republic of Vietnam.

The letter reads:

Dear Mr. Ambassador:

I respectfully request His Excellency to please issue an order for the personnel of the Defense Attache's Office to depart from Viet Nam within 24 hours beginning April 29, 1975 so that the question of peace in Viet Nam can be settled early.
With my Highest Regards,

Saigon, 28 April 1975

/s/ General Duong Van Minh

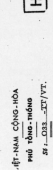

VIỆT-NAM CỘNG-HÒA
PHỦ TỔNG-THỐNG
Số : 033...TT/VT.

MẬT
HỎA-TỐC

TỔNG - THỐNG VIỆT - NAM CỘNG - HÒA

Kính gởi

Ong Đại-Sứ Hoa-Kỳ

tại Việt-Nam

Thưa Ong Đại-Sứ,

Tôi trân trọng yêu cầu Ong Đại-Sứ vui lòng ra chỉ thị cho các nhân-viên của Cơ-Quan Tùy-Viên Quân-Sự DAO rời khỏi Việt-Nam trong 24 giờ đồng hồ kể từ ngày 29-4-1975 về vấn đề Hòa-Bình Việt-Nam sớm được giải-quyết.

Trân trọng kính chào Ong Đại-Sứ.

SAIGON, ngày 28 tháng 4 năm 1975

Đại-tướng DƯƠNG VĂN MINH

MẬT

Notes

Chapter 1
The Turning Point

1. In 1954 General Paul Ely, High Commissioner for Indochina, transferred the Norodom Palace, named for the ancient King of Cambodia, to Ngo Dinh Diem and his government. Diem renamed it the Independence Palace and took up residence there. When the Palace was bombed by two dissident pilots in 1962, Diem moved into the Gia Long Palace, three hundred yards away, which had been the residence of the French Governor General of Cochin China. It was then the home of Diem's brother, Ngo Dinh Nhu.

   After the Independence Palace was rebuilt, Thieu took a small apartment on the second floor.

2. Diem's monologues were a trademark of his Mandarin style and there was never any give and take with the pudgy leader; Hung's elder brother, who had served in the Diem government, told him about them. Hung recalled the story of his law professor, who was considered a stern and formidable man. He had an audience with Diem and was so intimidated by Diem's aloof manner that he did not turn his back to him as he left the room. He backed out bowing, and crashed into an antique vase. Stanley Karnow, *Vietnam: A History,* p. 214, also describes his experience with a Diem monologue.

3. Henry Kissinger, *The White House Years,* argues: "Whatever the conclusions of systems analysts, there was no significant combat for nearly two years thereafter in the areas of South Vietnam that had been most exposed to attacks from the sanctuaries. The Mekong Delta and the heavily populated areas were effectively secured. And when Hanoi launched a nationwide offensive in the spring of 1972, its major thrust came across the DMZ, where its supply lines were shortest; its attacks from Cambodia were the weakest and most easily contained" (p. 508).

4. The Soviet Union and China were in open conflict on the Ussuri River border between their two countries in the winter of 1969–70. The Russians had even made informal attempts to see how the United States would respond to a Soviet attack on Chinese nuclear installations.

   During the 1960s Sino-Soviet relations openly and steadily worsened. In 1961, the Soviet Union withdrew its economic aid advisers from China; in September 1964, the Chinese exploded their first nuclear bomb and Soviet concerns deepened. During the Cultural Revolution in 1965 and 1966 the Soviet Embassy was a frequent target of Chinese demonstrators. Beginning in 1967, the Soviet Union reinforced its forces in the Far East. On March 2, 1969, some three hundred Chinese troops ambushed and killed an estimated thirty Soviet border guards on disputed Damansky Island in the Usurri River. On March 15, a Soviet battalion, equipped with mortars, artillery, and supported by helicopters and jet fighters, attacked the Chinese and inflicted heavy losses estimated in the hundreds. The same day a Radio Moscow commentary entitled "Is the Soviet Union Afraid of China?" stressed the overwhelming nuclear superiority of the Soviet Union over China. The Soviet Union called for negotiations over the disputed island in April and again in June. In September 1969, Premier Alexsei Kosygin met Zhou Enlai after attending Ho Chi Minh's funeral in Hanoi. On September 16 the London *Evening News* carried an article by Victor Louis headlined "Will Russian Rockets Czech-Mate China?" The article noted that the Brezhnev doctrine could be applied to China, especially since a unified anti-Mao group was eagerly awaiting Soviet help—"Nobody here has a shadow of a doubt that Russian nuclear installations stand aimed at Chinese nuclear facilities." See Morris Rothenberg, *Whither China: The View from the Kremlin,* p. 93, and Jonathan R. Adelman, *Crossroads,* "The Soviet Use of Force: Four Cases of Soviet Crisis Decision Making," pp. 545–556.

5. Thieu was compiling a library in the Independence Palace in the summer of 1973 and he asked Hung to suggest books. During the discussion, Thieu showed Hung his file of clippings on Nixon's comments on China and recalled reading and studying the file after Nixon announced Kissinger's trip to China.

6. Lloyd C. Gardner, *The Great Nixon Turnaround.* The speech was given to the Commonwealth Club of California, April 2, 1965. Nixon said: "If the United States gives up on Vietnam, Asia will give up on the United States and the Pacific will become a Red Sea. These are the stakes. And this is the reason the Johnson administration has decided to win in Vietnam—no more, no less." (pp. 50–51).

7. Hung conversation with Col. Vo Van Cam, Thieu's cabinet director, July 19, 1974.

8. Interview with Nguyen Van Thieu, May 3, 1985.

9. Hung conversation with Nguyen Van Thieu, in early September 1973.

10. When he left the Palace, Hung recalled the story in his North Vietnamese grade-school textbook. The famous French general, Lazare Nicholas Marguerite Carnot, returned to Nolay, his native village in Burgundy, after organizing the victory for the revolutionary armies during the French Revolution. At his old school his teacher lined up the pupils to salute him. Instead, Carnot took off his cap and bowed to his teacher. "This is my master, you should salute him," said General Carnot. Upon leaving the Palace in his own small triumph, Hung returned to his high school in Saigon and greeted his former teachers.

11. Interview with Nguyen Van Thieu, June 13, 1985. Hoang Duc Nha said it was suspected in Saigon that Big Minh had kept $2 million and sent $3 million via the Bank of Tokyo to his son who was a medical student in Paris. Frank Snepp, in *Decent Interval,* says plainly that Ambassador Bunker "decided to bribe the moderate opposition figure, General Duong Van 'Big' Minh, to stay on the slate for the sake of appearances. The caper would have worked—Bunker made his overture with typical diplomacy—had not Minh ultimately concluded that the three million dollars offered him for his campaign were less compelling than the

prospect of assured defeat" (p. 11). Seymour Hersh, *The Price of Power,* notes that despite heated denials by Bunker and others, the deposition of a CIA official taken in 1978 in a Freedom of Information lawsuit by Frank Snepp disclosed that "the basic report by Snepp is true." The deposition also confirmed reports that Thieu's private quarters, his office, and Minh's residence were wiretapped by the CIA (pp. 437–438).

12. Interview with Nguyen Van Thieu, June 13, 1985.

13. Interview with Vuong Van Bac in Paris, August 23, 1985.

14. Interview with Nguyen Van Thieu, June 13, 1985. Thieu also mentioned these thoughts to Hung on several occasions in Saigon in 1974 and 1975. "I was ready to step down provided the peace agreement was a good one, a durable one, that the Viet Cong would respect. It would be over for me and I would withdraw to the country. It is better to live as a peacemaker and a national hero. There are more problems in peacetime."

16. Hersh, *The Price of Power,* p. 440, quotes Robert Shaplen, the *New Yorker* magazine's respected Southeast Asian correspondent, as noting that "Very few observers here, Vietnamese or foreign, believe . . . the official figures. The best estimates are that in the countryside fifty or sixty percent of those eligible voted and in Saigon and other major cities something like thirty or forty percent."

17. Hung, *Economic Development of Socialist Vietnam, 1955–80,* p. 14.

18. The Chinese Nationalist general Lu Han, commander of the Chinese forces, was persuaded to withdraw his support from Vietnamese nationalist factions that opposed Ho Chi Minh by a present of a solid gold opium smoker's set from Ho. The Gold Week funds were used to buy Chinese connivance in Ho's seizure of power. See Donald Lancaster, *The Emancipation of French Indo-China,* p. 126, and Philippe Devillers, *Histoire du Viet-Nam de 1940 à 1952,* p. 193.

19. Kissinger, *White House Years,* p. 1043.

20. *U.S. Foreign Policy for the 1970's, The Emerging Structure of Peace, A Report to the Congress by Richard Nixon, President of the United States, February 9, 1972,* p. 115. "In order to speed negotiations, we agreed to depart from the approach of our May 31 proposal [offering a total U.S. withdrawal in return for a prisoner exchange and an Indochina cease-fire] and to deal with the political as well as the military issues."

21. Hung interview with Nguyen Van Thieu, London, November 26, 1976, and interview with the authors, May 3 and June 13, 1985.

22. Oriana Fallaci, *Interview with History.* See Thieu's interview with Fallaci in Saigon, January 23, 1973. When asked if he had counted too much on the Americans, Thieu replied: "I still can't make such a judgment, Mademoiselle! The moment still hasn't come for me to say, 'I've been abandoned.' I have to go on explaining myself to the Americans who look too far ahead, if you see what I mean. Maybe I've counted on them for too much, it's true. But in my place you would have done the same. A small country like mine, to keep its independence needs everything—from military aid to economic. Oh, sure I counted a lot on the Americans, sure! I still count on them despite everything! If you don't trust your friends then who should you trust? A friend is like a wife. Until the day she abandons you or you abandon her, until the day you get a divorce there has to be trust, doesn't there?" (p. 57).

Thieu often used the analogy of the United States and South Vietnam being married. To argue in public with President Nixon, he told his close aides, was like having a fight with one's wife in front of the children. "If you want to argue with your wife, you shut the door so the children cannot hear you," Thieu said.

23. Fallaci, *Interview with History*, p. 49.
24. John Prados, *The Sky Would Fall*, p. 170, discusses Nixon's arguments in support of the Dien Bien Phu bombing in detail.
25. Interview with Hoang Duc Nha, July 23, 1985.
26. H. G. Creel, *Chinese Thought from Confucius to Mao Tse-tung*, discusses the origins of the Mandate of Heaven or the Decree of Heaven as the justification for rule in Chinese history dating back to the Shang kings in 1400 B.C. Heaven was seen by Confucius as "a vaguely conceived moral force in the universe." The king possessed this force on earth. Heaven rejected rulers who did not treat the people well (pp. 30–31 and 50).

The Vietnamese adopted the concept from the Chinese and it remained a part of their political style. Thus, for example, Diem and Thieu had no sense of a permanent political opposition as part of a democratic process. They saw their power as absolute in the sense of being granted the right to rule from Heaven. Diem said that "the Confucian mandate of heaven held by the sovereign was revocable only if he proved himself unworthy thereof; the voice of the people was the voice of heaven." See Schecter, *The New Face of Buddha*, p. 187.

27. Interview with Nguyen Van Thieu, June 13, 1985, and Hung conversations with Thieu, Saigon, 1974.

Chapter 2
Nixon and Thieu: A Political Debt

1. During our interviews we asked Thieu if he felt Nixon owed a debt to him because of his support for Nixon during the 1968 campaign. "Naturally, naturally," replied Thieu. Given his pride and restrained nature, Thieu never discussed the 1968 campaign with Nixon, nor did Nixon raise it with him.
2. Interview with Nguyen Van Thieu, May 3, 1985.
3. Interview with Ted Van Dyk, December 17, 1985.
4. Interview with Nguyen Van Thieu, May 3, 1985.
5. Johnson, *The Vantage Point*, p. 524.
6. Interview with Anna Chennault, February 23, 1986.
7. Interviews with Mrs. Chennault, May 3 and 5, 1985.
8. Chennault, *The Education of Anna*, quoted by Seymour M. Hersh in *The Price of Power*, p. 21. See also Karnow, *Vietnam: A History*, pp. 585–586.
9. Nixon, *Memoirs*, p. 324.
10. Hersh, *The Price of Power*, documents how Kissinger had a foot in both the Humphrey and Nixon campaigns while working for Nelson Rockefeller as a foreign policy adviser. Early in the campaign Kissinger offered to provide his files on Nixon to the Humphrey campaign, but then withdrew the offer. However, as the race drew closer, Kissinger wrote the Humphrey camp and offered his services in a Humphrey administration. When the Hersh book was published, Kissinger called him a "slimy liar." He tried to get Zbigniew Brzezinski, who was a key foreign policy adviser to Humphrey in 1968, to refute the Hersh charges. Brzezinski, along with Samuel P. Huntington, a Harvard professor of government, and Robert Hunter, a former staff aid to Senator Edward Kennedy,

all worked on the Humphrey campaign and recalled Kissinger's offer of help to Humphrey. So does Ted Van Dyk, who received the letter from Kissinger offering to work in a Humphrey administration. "I would not lie for Henry," Brzezinski said. The incident left a permanent strain between the two men (pp. 14, 20–24).

11. See Karnow, *Vietnam*, p. 586.

12. While seeking to limit the role of the Provisional Revolutionary Government, Thieu projected his own flexibility by recalling General Big Minh from exile in Thailand to be an adviser. Minh was favored by the Communists to head a South Vietnamese delegation to the peace talks. As a native southerner, Minh had links to the PRG and was believed to favor a neutralist solution in the South. All of these diversionary tactics were aimed at slowing Johnson's momentum toward declaring a bombing halt.

13. Nixon, *Memoirs*, p. 326. Nixon quotes a memorandum on October 22, 1968, from his political aide Bryce Harlow on Johnson's plans. Nixon read the memo several times and with each reading became "angrier and more frustrated." Harlow wrote:

"The President is driving exceedingly hard for a deal with North Vietnam. Expectation is that he is becoming almost pathologically eager for an excuse to order a bombing halt and will accept almost any arrangement . . . Careful plans are being made to help HHH exploit whatever happens. White House Staff liaison with HHH is close. Plan is for LBJ to make a nationwide TV announcement as quickly as possible after agreement; the object is to get this done as long before November 5 as they can. . . . White Housers still think they can pull the election out for HHH with this ploy; that's what is being attempted."

After reading the memo, Nixon moved to confront Johnson. He ordered John Mitchell to check with Kissinger, have Senators Everett Dirksen and John Tower "blast the moves by the White House," and have Dirksen, the Senate Minority Leader, call Johnson and "let him know we are onto his plans." Anna Chennault immediately sent an emotional appeal to Thieu urging him "to hold firm."

14. Nixon, *Memoirs*, p. 327.

15. Johnson, *The Vantage Point*, pp. 520–521.

16. *Ibid.*

17. *Ibid.*, p. 524.

18. White, *The Making of the President 1968*, p. 446.

19. Hung conversation with Nguyen Van Thieu, Nov. 25, 1976. Thieu ordered that the secretaries be kept in a small room on the second floor of the Independence Palace where they typed the speech until after his delivery. They were not permitted to leave the room even to use the toilet. Thieu wanted to take no chances that they might try to communicate with a CIA control officer through a concealed transmitter. Thieu did not know if any of his employees were working for the CIA, but he assumed the worst with his suspicious nature. Food and plastic utility bags were provided and an officer remained in the room with the secretaries until Thieu finished his speech and they could leave.

20. Hung conversation with Thieu, November 25, 1976.

21. President Johnson was furious with Ambassador Bunker, who had assured Washington, on Thieu's word, that South Vietnam would take part in the Paris Talks. Some embassy staffer like Vietnamese-speaking political officer John Negroponte had predicted Thieu would not go along, but he was overruled when

Bunker spoke with Thieu. Interview with Richard Holbrooke, April 26, 1985. Holbrooke was then a junior staffer working for Averell Harriman at the Paris Peace Talks.

22. White, p. 447.
23. Nixon, *Memoirs,* p. 328.
24. *Ibid.*
25. Hung conversation with Thieu, London, November 26, 1976.
26. Interview with Nguyen Van Thieu, June 13, 1985.
27. Hoang Duc Nha interview with the authors, July 23, 1985.
28. White, p. 447.
29. Humphrey, although advised by Johnson of the role of Mrs. Chennault in trying to influence Thieu, never went public with the information. The Nixon-Mitchell connection to Mrs. Chennault was so carefully guarded that Nixon's campaign headquarters could tell author Theodore White that they were appalled to learn of her intervention. White explains: "for the sake of the record, I must add that in probing this episode during the weekend of its happening, this reporter's judgment was that Humphrey's decision was morally, if not tactically correct. At the first report of Republican sabotage in Saigon, Nixon's headquarters had begun to investigate the story; had discovered Mrs. Chennault's activities; and was appalled. The fury and dismay at Nixon's headquarters when his aides discovered the report were so intense that they could not have been feigned simply for the benefit of this reporter. Their feeling on Monday morning before the election was, simply, that if they lost the election, Mrs. Chennault might have lost it for them. She had taken their name and authority in vain; if the Democrats now chose to air the story, no rebuttal of the Nixon camp would be convincing; and they were at the mercy of Humphrey's good-will" (p. 445). Nixon's *Memoirs,* published in 1979, ten years later, make it clear that the President and his top aides, Haldeman and Mitchell, worked directly on the problem and knew of Johnson's plan through Henry Kissinger and an unnamed source close to Johnson. Nixon never mentions Mrs. Chennault by name in his memoirs, but she names Mitchell in hers—*The Education of Anna,* p. 190.
30. *The Washington Post,* November 12, 1966.
31. Mrs. Chennault was offered an ambassadorial post by Nixon but declined. Johnson never publicly acknowledged Mrs. Chennault's role. In his memoirs, Johnson says only that "we had received information that people who claimed to speak for the Republican candidate were still trying to influence the South Vietnamese to drag their feet on the peace talks" (p. 521).

     Humphrey and Johnson both considered breaking the story of Mrs. Chennault's efforts to influence Thieu but decided against making any public charges against her. According to Ted Van Dyk, Humphrey's chief speechwriter, President Johnson decided not to go public because he would have had to explain that the information on Mrs. Chennault's actions had been obtained from an illegal intercept of her phone calls. In addition, President Johnson did not want to hurt Thomas Corcoran (Tommy the Cork), a long-time friend and associate of LBJ who was a very close personal friend of Mrs. Chennault. Johnson also remained ambivalent over Humphrey and his desire to end the Vietnam War.

     Humphrey had urged James Rowe, Corcoran's law partner and a major Humphrey supporter, to get to Mrs. Chennault and call her off. Word came back to Humphrey from Rowe that "it is no go; Thieu will hold on." Humphrey was aboard his campaign plane when Van Dyk gave him the news and told him: "In 1968 the old China Lobby is still alive." Humphrey stormed up and down the aisle and shouted, "I'll be God-damned if the China Lobby can decide this government." He ordered Van Dyk to issue a statement withholding his support from the Thieu regime. Instead, Van Dyk released a statement saying that if the South Vietnamese did not go to the conference table in Paris, the United States would go without them. After the election Humphrey was praised for not bringing the efforts of Mrs. Chennault into the campaign. Van Dyk believes that "if Mrs. Chennault and Nixon had not intervened with Thieu, we might have won the election because the momentum was in Humphrey's favor." Interview with Ted Van Dyk, December 17, 1985.

32. Interview with Anna Chennault, March 2, 1986. Mrs. Chennault recalls that Lyndon Johnson told Tom Corcoran that he was concerned that his efforts to bring peace in Vietnam not be thwarted. LBJ told this to Nixon during their meeting in the White House and Nixon, apprehensive that LBJ not make a public issue of Mrs. Chennault's liaison with Thieu, agreed to urge Thieu to go to Paris. Having accomplished his goal of winning the Presidency Nixon was less worried about Thieu going to Paris than he was of having LBJ upset his victory.

33. Interview with Hoang Duc Nha, May 23, 1985.

34. Thieu's Resignation Address, April 21, 1975, in Saigon. Federal Broadcast Information Services (FBIS) copy.

35. Both Nixon and Kissinger discuss the EC-121 incident in detail. See Nixon, *Memoirs,* pp. 382–385; Kissinger, *White House Years,* pp. 313–321.

36. Stephen E. Ambrose, *Eisenhower,* vol. 2, pp. 97–99; U. Alexis Johnson, *The Right Hand of Power,* p. 160—"Eisenhower thought we should even consider using tactical nuclear weapons there if the armistice talks continued to languish."

37. The secret bombing of Cambodia was revealed in *The New York Times* by William Beecher in a detailed story on May 9.

38. Nixon, *Memoirs,* p. 385.

39. Interview with Alexander Haig, January 14, 1986. Haig said that as Secretary of State he advised President Reagan to act firmly against Cuba shortly after he took office in January 1981 to stop Cuban support for the Sandinistas in Nicaragua. Haig said he was "thinking back to taking a page from Eisenhower."

40. Kissinger, *White House Years,* p. 272, notes that "it was a symptom of the morass into which the Vietnam war had plunged our society that a meeting between the President and the leader for whose country over thirty thousand Americans had died had to take place on an uninhabited island in the middle of the Pacific."

41. Hung conversation with Thieu, London, November 24, 1976.

42. Interview with Nguyen Van Thieu, May 3, 1985.

43. Interview with Nguyen Van Thieu, May 3, 1985.

44. Kissinger, *White House Years,* p. 274.

45. Conversation between Thieu and Hung in London, November 26, 1976. Thieu was referring to Ngo Dinh Diem, who led the Republic of Vietnam from 1954 until he was murdered in a coup in November 1963.

46. Unification of North and South was decided on in June 1975 and put into effect in November 1975. In February 1977 the National Liberation Front was merged

out of existence into the Vietnam Fatherland Front run from Hanoi. See Truong Nhu Tang, *A Vietcong Memoir*, pp. 259–266 and Hung, *Economic Development of Socialist Vietnam, 1955–1980*, pp. 155, 170–171.

47. P. J. Honey study on the development of the North Vietnamese Communist Party, printed in Saigon in 1967. Honey is a British expert on North Vietnam.

48. Philippe Devillers, *Histoire du Viet-Nam de 1940 à 1952*. According to Ngo Ton Dat, the son of a prominent Vietnamese Nationalist leader, during the two-month period in the fall of 1945, "some 10,000 people were killed in Hanoi and its immediate environs." Cited in U.S. Senate, Committee on the Judiciary, *The Human Cost of Communism in Vietnam* (Washington, D.C.: Government Printing Office, 1972), p. 5.

49. Robert F. Turner, *Vietnamese Communism: Its Origins and Development*, pp. 58–59.

50. For more details, see Turner, *ibid.,* and Hoang Van Chi, *From Colonialism to Communism*. North Vietnamese atrocities against landlords became part of the emotional fear of the Communists. In the Khu Tu (Zone Four), including Hung's own village, the Viet Minh cadres buried landowners alive with only their heads uncovered. After the People's Court verdict was handed down, they would run a plow through the heads of the condemned victims to execute them.

51. Interview with Nguyen Van Thieu, May 3, 1985.

52. Thieu and Hung discussed the Midway meeting, Thieu's visit to Taiwan, and his return to Saigon for the first time in the fall of 1971, when Hung visited Thieu as a private consultant. They discussed Midway again in London in 1976.

53. Thieu gave April 5, 1923, as his birth date when he registered for school. He said he picked the date when his parents were not available to give the correct one. Thus his date of birth is sometimes listed as April 5, 1923, but he was actually born on December 24, 1924.

54. Confucius stressed the importance of *jen,* or virtue, which included filial piety, courage. When asked to define *jen,* Confucius listed five characteristics. He said: "With respect you will avoid insult; with magnanimity you will win over everyone; with sincerity men will trust you; with earnestness you will have achievement; and with kindness you will be fitted well to command others." See Fung Yu-Lan, *A History of Chinese Philosophy,* vol. I, pp. 72–73.

55. Tran Van Don, *Our Endless War Inside Vietnam*, p. 168, and Karnow, *Vietnam,* pp. 384–386.

56. Former Foreign Minister Vuong Van Bac recalled that LBJ "treated Marcos, Chung Hee Park, and Thieu as leaders of conquered territories." Interview with Bac in Paris, August 23, 1985.

57. Interview with General Lu Lan, December 20, 1984.

58. Thieu conversation with Hung, London, April 30, 1978, and later repeated in *Der Spiegel* interview, December 1, 1979.

59. Nixon speech on May 14, 1969.

60. Kissinger, p. 277. Kissinger's version sharply contrasts with Thieu's, who insisted there was no discussion of any systematic timetable for withdrawals at the American initiative. Thieu said he saw Nixon as moving slowly to develop a strategy that would gather public support at home while moving toward negotiations with Hanoi on favorable terms to Saigon.

Chapter 3
No Secret Deals

1. Nixon, *Memoirs,* pp. 394–395. Nixon flew to Guam on July 23, 1969, and announced his doctrine in a speech there. He had flown to the Pacific to greet the Apollo XI astronauts on their return from the moon, the first time man had landed on the moon, a round trip of nearly half a million miles. They landed less than two miles from the prearranged target in the Pacific Ocean a thousand miles southwest of Hawaii.

    In Saigon the Vietnamese, who observe the cycles of the lunar calendar and believe strongly in the power of the moon, were deeply impressed. There were rumors of how strong the Americans were and how they had broken the sacred powers of the moon. The Chinese too, who originated the lunar calendar and stress the importance of the moon on the cycle of life, were impressed by the American feat. This technological marvel had deep overtones in Asia where social, cultural, and economic cycles are related to the phases of the moon. For the Americans to demystify the moon commanded great respect.

2. Alan Goodman, *The Lost Peace,* p. 59. Goodman also notes that "By the end of 1971 there were many in Washington and Saigon who thought that the war would be ended without a negotiated settlement or with, at most, a secret agreement between Hanoi and Washington for the return of American prisoners of war."

3. Kissinger, *Memoirs, p. 1002.* Kissinger says the operation, "conceived in doubt and assailed by skepticism, proceeded in confusion." He provides an extensive analysis critical of all those involved except himself.

4. Interview with Lieutenant Colonel Lam Duy Tien, December 5, 1984.

5. Interview with Nguyen Van Thieu, May 3, 1985.

6. Hung conversation with Nguyen Van Thieu, London, November 26, 1976.

7. Kissinger, *Memoirs,* p. 1005. Kissinger describes the American side of the Lam Son operation in excruciating detail, emphasizing how bureaucratic infighting and indecision hampered the effectiveness of American planning and assistance to the South Vietnamese.

8. *Ibid.,* p. 1004. "Given Hanoi's probable penetration of the South Vietnamese high command (far better placed than we were to understand its workings), this had to be known to the enemy, who therefore could organize a response designed to maximize the casualties rather than contest territory. We would never have approved the Tchepone plan in the White House had such a restriction been communicated to us."

9. Interview with Nguyen Van Thieu, May 3, 1985.

10. Interview with Alexander Haig, November 13, 1985.

11. Thieu interview with *Der Spiegel,* December 1, 1979; also conversation with Hung in London, November 26, 1976.

12. It was the first time the South Vietnamese knew exactly how many secret meetings Kissinger had held with the North Vietnamese. Most of the secret talks took place during weekends; Kissinger flew to Europe, had four or five hours of discussions with Special Adviser Le Duc Tho, the North Vietnamese Politburo member in charge of the war in the South, and returned to Washington in time to be at his desk in the West Wing of the White House on Monday morning. On other occasions Kissinger would slip away from formal diplomatic

meetings or pretend to be dining with attractive female friends. See "Nixon's Secret Agent," *Time,* February 7, 1972.

13. The first time the United States offered a cease-fire in place was in the fall of 1970. At the same time as he was maneuvering to open relations with China, Kissinger had come to the conclusion that short of eliminating Thieu, a cease-fire in place was the only concession the United States could reasonably offer to get Hanoi to sign an agreement. In September 1970 Kissinger proposed a cease-fire in place in a secret meeting with Xuan Thuy, head of the North Vietnamese delegation in Paris. Hanoi did not respond to the offer. See Allan Goodman, *The Lost Peace,* p. 109. Goodman quotes a member of the U.S. delegation: "We wanted to convey the impression that what we were offering to give Hanoi a fair crack at the South but that they could not expect us to abandon an ally of some twenty years and install a replacement government before our offer would be acceptable."

In October 1970 Ambassador David Bruce, the newly appointed head of the U.S. delegation to the public Paris Talks, announced the cease-fire in place proposal and called for an immediate and unconditional prisoner release, to be followed by a total withdrawal of U.S. forces and an international conference to guarantee the settlement. The North Vietnamese again refused to consider the offer, insisting on the resignation of Thieu and the creation of a coalition government before a cease-fire. Goodman, p. 110, notes that "Hanoi's refusal to consider the American offer in private or public was consistent with its own sense of timing and strategy. Internal communist documents from this period suggest that from the leadership in Hanoi down to the local cadres the growing strength of the GVN and its increasing administrative presence throughout the countryside alarmed the PRG. Saigon's counterintelligence program was beginning to take its toll of the indigenous PRG left after the Tet offensive, and in general the Politburo was dissatisfied with the weaknesses in its own movement. The significance of this is that, however much an agreement specified that there would be peaceful political evolution after the U.S. withdrawal, Hanoi knew that Saigon would never implement it. 'It would also be,' one Communist diplomat told me, 'absurd to expect that in life-and-death struggle both sides would renounce the use of force if they appeared to be losing. Then what guarantee have we that the Americans will not reintervene?' Only through expansion and consolidation of control in the countryside would the PRG be assured of a secure base of operations; this would take time."

14. By playing on Leonid Brezhnev's desire for an agreement to limit strategic nuclear weapons, and his lust for increased trade and credits with the United States, Nixon hoped to induce him to serve his own national interests before those of North Vietnam. The contrasting negotiating styles of the Chinese and Russians afforded Kissinger the opportunity to win support for Nixon's China initiative and to exploit Sino-Soviet tensions while skillfully denying that he was playing "the China Card." In press interviews after his trips to Beijing, Kissinger gushed over how impressed he had been with Prime Minister Zhou Enlai during their seventeen hours of talks. In private, Kissinger would confide how much he preferred to negotiate with the Chinese compared to the Russians. The Chinese, personified by Zhou, had a world view. They knew where they wanted the negotiations to proceed and, unlike the Russians, they would indicate where the areas were for compromise. With the Russians any early sign of compromise was taken as weakness and the negotiations had to proceed through what Kis-

singer called "a rigid and disagreeable set of stages before the actual give and take could commence." The Chinese never bargained to score petty points. They perceived the Soviet Union, with one million troops along the Sino-Soviet border, as a threat to their security and at the same time feared a dominant Soviet influence in Vietnam. The Chinese were not in a position to exert pressure on the Vietnamese and were careful not to publicly undermine the North Vietnamese. To the North Vietnamese, the act of meeting with the Americans was taken as a sign of betrayal of socialist solidarity. Still, Zhou left the impression that the Chinese did not want to see the United States defeated in Vietnam or to withdraw from Southeast Asia. See Kissinger, *White House Years,* pp. 792–393 and p. 1056, and Haig, *Caveat,* pp. 201–202; Schecter's notes on interview with Kissinger, August 1971, and interview with Alexander Haig, November 13, 1985.

15. Other main points of the proposal called for: a cease-fire throughout Indochina; exchange of all prisoners; respect for the Geneva Accords of 1954 and the Laos Agreement of 1962; settlement by the Indochinese parties themselves of problems existing between them, including the role of North Vietnamese forces; international supervision of the agreement; and U.S. willingness to undertake a reconstruction program over five years for $7.5 billion of which North Vietnam would share up to $2.5 billion. See *U.S. Foreign Policy for the 1970's, The Emerging Structure of Peace, A Report to the Congress by Richard Nixon, President of the United States, February 9, 1972,* pp. 117–119.

16. Interview with Hoang Duc Nha, May 24, 1985.

17. Interview with Nguyen Van Thieu, May 3, 1985. Thieu used the analogy of a man fighting an opponent with a pistol. When he found a machine gun, he threw away the pistol. "This is unwise because the pistol can be used against you by your enemy," Thieu said. "Even with a pistol you can be killed. A wise man keeps all his weapons." Cam Ranh Bay is now being used as a major Soviet naval base in Southeast Asia and provides an important strategic reach for the Soviet fleet into Asian waters.

18. A White House press release dated January 25, 1972, explained: "There will be international supervision of the military aspects of this agreement, including the ceasefire and its provisions, the release of prisoners of war and innocent civilians, the withdrawal of outside forces from Indochina and the implementation of the principle that all armed forces of the countries of Indochina must remain within their frontiers." In interpreting the speech, *Time* magazine said, "Nixon did not mention it in his address, but the formal eight-point U.S. plan would require the later withdrawal of all North Vietnamese troops from Laos, Cambodia and South Viet Nam, although the U.S. withdrawal would proceed first."

19. Kissinger offers the text of his May 31 proposal in a footnote on pp. 1488 and 1499 of *White House Years.* While agreeing to set a terminal date for withdrawal of all American and Allied forces from South Vietnam, it avoids the issue of North Vietnamese troop withdrawals by providing that "the Vietnamese and the other peoples of Indochina should discuss among themselves the manner in which all other outside forces would withdraw from the countries of Indochina." Nixon's eight points do not directly address the question of the withdrawal of North Vietnamese troops. See Kissinger, pp. 1489 and 1490.

20. Kissinger, p. 1043.

21. Oriana Fallaci, *Interview with History,* p. 57.

22. Kissinger, *White House Years,* p. 282, says he kept Thieu "thoroughly briefed

on my secret negotiations from the beginning." Thieu, in an interview with the authors on June 13, 1985, said, "The Americans did brief me on several occasions, but they only informed me of what they saw fit."

23. Kissinger, p. 1045.

24. Nixon, *Memoirs*, pp. 568–569.

25. In the joint communiqué, each side stated its own views on Vietnam. "The U.S. side stated: Peace in Asia and peace in the world requires efforts both to reduce immediate tensions and to eliminate the basic causes of conflict. . . . The United States stressed that the peoples of Indochina should be allowed to determine their destiny without outside intervention; its constant primary objective has been a negotiated solution; the eight-point proposal put forward by the Republic of Vietnam and the United States on January 27, 1972 represents a basis for the attainment of that objective; in the absence of a negotiated settlement the United States envisages the ultimate withdrawal of all U.S. forces from the region consistent with the aim of self-determination for each country of Indochina.

"The Chinese side stated: Wherever there is oppression, there is resistance. Countries want independence, nations want liberation and the people want revolution—this has become the irresistible trend of history. . . . The Chinese side expressed its firm support to the people of Vietnam, Laos and Cambodia in their efforts for the attainment of their goal and its firm support to the seven-point proposal of the Provisional Revolutionary Government of the Republic of South Vietnam and the elaboration in February this year of the two key problems in the proposal and to the Joint Declaration of the Summit Conference of the Indochinese Peoples."

26. Authors' interviews; see also Tad Szulc, *Foreign Policy* (Spring 1974), pp. 44–45.

27. Nixon, *Memoirs*, pp. 562–563, 567–569.

28. Hersh, *The Price of Power*, pp. 496–499, discusses Green's critique of the Shanghai Communiqué. Schecter covered the Nixon trip for *Time* magazine. At the press conference releasing the Shanghai Communiqué, the question of the U.S. commitment to Taiwan was raised by correspondents, but there was no questioning of the American commitment to the Republic of Vietnam.

29. *New York Times*, May 2, 1975, "Saigon Endorses Nixon China Trip, In Official Comment It Says Visit Eased Tensions."

30. Interview with Marshall Green, Washington, D.C., May 16, 1985.

31. *Washington Post Magazine*, April 21, 1985, p. 30.

32. Tad Szulc, *The Illusion of Peace*, p. 523.

33. Hersh, p. 442.

34. Quoted in Hersh, p. 506, from a tape recording made public during the impeachment proceedings.

35. Nearly 350 Soviet ships brought one million tons of cargo to North Vietnamese ports in 1971. The 130mm long-range cannon provided the North Vietnamese a capability surpassing the South's and the Russian T-54 tanks were a match for the U.S. M-48 tanks used by the South Vietnamese. See Dave Richard Palmer, *Summons of the Trumpet*, p. 248.

36. Nixon, *Memoirs*, p. 594.

37. *Ibid.*, p. 600.

38. See Palmer, *Summons of the Trumpet*, pp. 253–254, for details.

39. Nixon, *Memoirs*, p. 592.

40. *Ibid.* Nixon on balance was pleased with the results of Kissinger's meeting with

Brezhnev and says, "Given Kissinger's achievements on the summit issues, I felt that there was no point in gainsaying his performance after the fact."

41. Interview with Alexander Haig, November 13, 1985. Interview with Peter Rodman, January 7, 1986. Kissinger told the Russians that the U.S. would not tolerate the North Vietnamese invasion and warned of American retaliatory action. At the same time he indicated that if the North Vietnamese removed the invading troops, they could retain in the South their troops that had been infiltrated earlier, prior to the invasion. This set the stage for a cease-fire in place and was a clearer definition of what the U.S. would accept than earlier, more general formulations. Although the U.S. was negotiating directly with Hanoi, Kissinger hoped to use the Soviet Union to exert influence on Hanoi to move the negotiations forward and accept a cease-fire in place.

See also Szulc, *The Illusion of Peace,* pp. 544–573, and Hersh, *The Price of Power,* pp. 517–518. In addition to the January 25, 1972, public eight-point peace plan, there were earlier secret proposals on May 31, 1971, June 26, 1971, July 12, 1971, and August 16, 1971, which moved away from mutual withdrawal. They were not accepted by the North Vietnamese because they remained unclear on defining total withdrawal. The January 25 proposal was still ambiguous on the issue of removing "other outside forces"—the code name for North Vietnamese troops. In his talks with Brezhnev, Kissinger removed the ambiguity.

Richard Nixon, *No More Vietnams,* pp. 152–153, defends his decision to allow the North Vietnamese to maintain their troops in South Vietnam. "We knew there was no way to force them to concede this point. It is an axiom of diplomacy that one cannot win at the conference table what one could not win on the battlefield. Although South Vietnam had reversed the tide of battle before the monsoons set in, the North Vietnamese continued to occupy large areas of South Vietnam along the demilitarized zone and in the central highlands. We had to consider how Hanoi viewed its options. We knew that if reaching a settlement required the North Vietnamese to give away territory that South Vietnam had been unable to take away, they would calculate that they were better off *not* concluding an agreement. If we had stood firm in demanding North Vietnam's withdrawal, there would have been no peace agreement.

"In resolving the issue, we never conceded the legitimacy of North Vietnam's military presence in South Vietnam. Our tactic was to write a formulation that tacitly required the enemy to withdraw. We demanded that Hanoi pledge to stop the infiltration of men into South Vietnam. If the promise was kept, enemy forces in the South would have to withdraw or else wither away. When the North Vietnamese agreed to this, we set a timetable for signing a completed agreement by October 31."

Given President Nixon's sophisticated views on the use of power and military force, this explanation begs the question of enforcement and neglects to say that the decision was made without consultations with President Thieu, which Nixon had repeatedly promised in his letters to Thieu.

42. Interview with Nguyen Van Thieu, June 13, 1985.
43. Schecter interview with Kissinger, April 28, 1972.
44. Nixon, *Memoirs,* p. 594.
45. *Ibid.,* p. 601.
46. Nixon, *No More Vietnams,* p. 145.
47. Nixon, *Memoirs,* p. 602.

48. *Ibid.*, p. 603.
49. *Ibid.*, p. 605. The terms were:
    "First, all American prisoners of war must be returned.

    "Second, there must be an internationally supervised cease-fire throughout Indochina.

    "Once prisoners of war are released, once the internationally supervised cease-fire has begun, we will stop all acts of force throughout Indochina, and at that time we will proceed with a complete withdrawal of all American forces from Vietnam within four months.

    "Now these terms are generous terms, They are terms which would not require surrender and humiliation on the part of anybody. . . . They deserve immediate acceptance by North Vietnam."
50. In a fifty-five-minute press conference in the East Room of the White House on May 9, 1972, following President Nixon's speech, Kissinger was not asked a single question about mutual withdrawal, nor did he elaborate on the shift from the earlier American insistence on mutual withdrawal.

Chapter 4
Threats of Assassination

1. Richard Nixon, *No More Vietnams,* p. 147, says Brezhnev decided to go ahead with the summit for two reasons. "First, he wanted and needed better relations with the United States, particularly in view of our China initiative. Second, he knew we were worth talking to, because our actions in Vietnam had demonstrated that we had not only the power to defend our interests but also the will to use it."
2. Nixon, *Memoirs,* p. 613.
3. *Ibid.*
4. Szulc, *Foreign Policy* (Spring 1974), *"Behind the Vietnam Ceasefire Agreement,"* pp. 44–45. Zhou told Kissinger that China would not press Hanoi one way or another, even though it did not necessarily approve of the North Vietnamese strategy of invading the South with conventional forces. He offered the opinion that history was against the United States and that communism would prevail in Vietnam and Cambodia, but that Laos would continue to be ruled by its king. Zhou was very cautious and restrained in his remarks about Vietnam. He never said anything that would appear to be disloyal to Hanoi. Zhou was concerned that the record of his talks would be leaked, as in the case of the Pentagon Papers, and that his internal enemies in China would use his statements against him. Zhou was careful not to further strain China's relations with Hanoi in his remarks.
5. Kissinger, *White House Years,* p. 1310.
6. *Ibid.*, p. 1211.
7. Congressional Record, January 15, 1973, pp. E191–E192. Hung's analysis and research were also sent to President Thieu.
8. Kissinger, p. 1315.
9. *Ibid.*, pp. 1316–1317.
10. Bunker letter to Thieu, August 15, 1972, in authors' possession.
11. Kissinger, p. 1319.
12. *Ibid.*, p. 1320.

13. *Ibid.*, p. 1324.

14. *Ibid.*, p. 1325.

15. Interview with Hoang Duc Nha, May 24, 1985. Such answers from Kissinger "were standard," said Nha. "The Americans always said: 'We'll try, but we don't know how far we can get.' That's when we discovered formally that they didn't honor our request in April." Whether or not Nixon approved of this position on bypassing mutual withdrawal was unclear to the Vietnamese. "We suspected all along that Kissinger played his cards close to his chest and was not apprising Nixon of all the facts. It was a suspicion on our part. We couldn't prove anything."

16. Interview with Nguyen Van Thieu, June 13, 1985.

17. Interview with Hoang Duc Nha, July 23, 1985.

18. Kissinger, p. 1327.

19. Truong Nhu Tang, *A Vietcong Memoir,* p. 240, Thieu told the daughter Loan that although he and her father were enemies, "that makes absolutely no difference as far as your welcome in my home is concerned."

20. Interview with Nguyen Van Thieu, June 13, 1985.

21. Kissinger, p. 1327.

22. *Ibid.*, pp. 1327–1328.

23. *Ibid.*, p. 1330.

24. *Ibid.*, p. 1334.

25. *Ibid.*, p. 1331; see chapter XXXI, p. 1494, note 1, for the differences between the American and South Vietnamese drafts.

26. *Ibid.*, p. 1329.

27. Quoted in *ibid.*, p. 1334.

28. *Ibid.*, p. 1335.

29. *Ibid.*, p. 1338.

30. Republic of Vietnam, September 13, 1972, Memorandum to the U.S. Government. See Appendix B.

31. Nixon, *Memoirs,* p. 690.

32. It was American policy to conduct all negotiations involving South Vietnam directly between Washington and Hanoi. A draft position paper of November 29, 1964, produced by a working group under the direction of Assistant Secretary of State for East Asia and Pacific Affairs William Bundy, included the statement: "The U.S. would seek to control any negotiations and would oppose any independent South Vietnamese efforts to negotiate." The United States was prepared to explore negotiated solutions that would "attain U.S. objectives in an acceptable manner." This was to remain American policy until the fall of South Vietnam. See *Pentagon Papers, New York Times* edition, document 88, p. 375.

33. Interview with Nguyen Van Thieu, May 3, 1985.

34. Interview with General Tran Van Don, February 14, 1985.

35. Interview with Lieutenant Colonel Lucien Conein, October 30, 1985.

36. Nhu had also ordered an attack on the Buddhist pagodas with U.S. trained special forces under his control.

37. *The Pentagon Papers,* Gravel Edition, vol. II, pp. 234–235.

38. Interview with Tran Van Dinh, November 24, 1985, and Gareth Porter, *A Peace Denied,* p. 19.

39. Interview with Nguyen Van Thieu, May 3, 1985.

40. Suspicion among the officers was rife even before the coup. In his account,

General Tran Van Don describes a call from General Dinh after his meeting with Khiem, "who seemed discouraged." Dinh urged Don to be cautious but to receive General Khiem, who was on his way to Don's office. Khiem reported on his meeting with Dinh. "He [Khiem] told me [Don] he had put some irritating ointment in his eyes to make Dinh believe he had been crying. Khiem had suggested to Dinh that we give up the plan because he felt sorry for the President and did not want harm to come to him. He was pleased that Dinh did not agree. Apparently Dinh and Khiem were afraid of each other's loyalties and wanted to have some definite checks made on each other" (p. 103).

41. Interviews with General Ton That Dinh, October 18, 1985, and November 20, 1985.

42. Hung conversation with Thieu, London, November 26, 1976.

43. Cao The Dung and Luong Khai Minh (pen name for Dr. Tran Kim Tuyen), *How to Kill a President (Lam The Nao De Giet Mot Tong Thong)* (Saigon, 1970), pp. 640–641.

44. Article in *Dong Nai,* Vietnamese magazine printed in California, taken from *Viet Hoa* Chinese community magazine in Los Angeles, in author's possession. See account by General Tran Van Don, *Our Endless War,* pp. 101–118, and Karnow, *Vietnam,* pp. 308–309.

45. The order to kill Diem was given by General Minh before the group left the JGS headquarters. Captain Nhung was the man who killed Diem and Nhu. He was shot to death in his home by an unknown assassin in 1964. Interview with Tran Van Don, January 23, 1985.

46. Karnow, pp. 277–311, has a detailed account of the coup. Thieu's account comes from him in interviews with Hung and Schecter. Karnow explains in detail how Diem and Nhu were murdered by order of General Minh. The three officers who brought Diem and Nhu back executed them in the back of the armored personnel carrier.

47. Interview with Lieutenant Colonel Lucien Conein, October 30, 1985.

48. Quoted in Karnow, *Vietnam,* p. 307.

49. See Footnote 44.

50. Tran Van Don, *Our Endless War,* pp. 111–112. Don says, "I can state without equivocation that this was done by General Big Minh and by him alone. I base this in part on my conversations with Minh, and on hearing General Xuan's report to Minh that his mission had been accomplished. . . . In addition I received two reports from eyewitnesses."

51. Nixon first met Kissinger at a party in the New York apartment of Clare Booth Luce. Nixon was familiar with Kissinger's writings. The late Henry Cabot Lodge, who served two terms as Ambassador to Vietnam (1963–64 and 1965–67) met with President-elect Nixon at his home in Key Biscayne, Florida, after the election and suggested that Nixon establish a cabinet-level Vietnam coordinator in the White House. He proposed Henry Kissinger for the job. Nixon asked Lodge about Kissinger and said, "Wasn't he a Rockefeller person?" When Kissinger was named to the National Security job, Lodge took credit for getting him together with Nixon, according to Peter Tarnoff, a long-time aide of Lodge, now president of the Council on Foreign Relations. Interview with Tarnoff, January 21, 1986.

52. Hersh, *The Price of Power,* pp. 22–23. Interview with William Buckley, January 8, 1986. Buckley said he recalled his conversation with Kissinger well. "There was no talk of assassination. Kissinger told me he had heard that President

Johnson was planning to dump Thieu before the inauguration. The inference was that the U.S. would cooperate with and back a coup against Thieu by his own military,'' said Buckley.

53. Interview with Robert Komer, April 15, 1985.
54. Interview with Clark Clifford, December 10, 1985.
55. Quoted in Hersh, *The Price of Power,* p. 128.
56. Tran Van Don, *Our Endless War,* p. 53.
57. Interview with Nguyen Van Thieu, June 13, 1985.

Chapter 5
Kissinger's Design

1. Kissinger, p. 1363. Kissinger quotes his instructions to Bunker "to give Thieu a summary of where we are heading." His message reads: "Prior to my arrival in Saigon, now tentatively scheduled for Wednesday night, I will be seeing Minister Xuan Thuy and anticipate that the other side will propose a political formula which will require far less of Thieu than the alternate arrangements outlined to him by Haig during his recent visit. This would be combined with a cease-fire in place to go into effect as early as two weeks from the time that an overall agreement in principle is arrived at. In view of this likelihood, it is essential that Thieu understand now that we could have settled the conflict a long time ago under terms which would have removed him from power. Therefore, he cannot approach his upcoming meeting with me in the context of confrontation but rather with a positive attitude in which we can confirm arrangements which will consolidate and solidify his future control. I am confident that such political arrangements are in the offing from Hanoi and Thieu must be put off his current confrontation course with us and at the same time be prepared, in return for Hanoi's political concessions, to show a reasonable flexibility on the modalities of a cease-fire in place."
2. Interview with Nguyen Van Thieu, May 3, 1985.
3. Thieu's October 4, 1972, memorandum, in authors' possession.
4. Bunker's October 14, 1972, letter to Thieu, in authors' possession. Bunker's letter does not mention the specifics of a cease-fire in place as Kissinger had advised him in his instructions. See note 1.
5. Kissinger, p. 1365.
6. The U.S. delegation included Ambassador Ellsworth Bunker, Deputy Ambassador Charles Whitehouse, General Creighton Abrams, Deputy Assistant Secretary of State William Sullivan, Winston Lord, and David Engel, the interpreter.
    The Vietnamese at the meeting were Thieu, Vice President Tran Van Huong, Prime Minister Tran Thien Khiem, Foreign Minister Tran Van Lam, Chairman of the Joint General Staff Cao Van Vien, Nguyen Phu Duc, and Hoang Duc Nha.
7. General Cao Van Vien, *The Final Collapse,* p. 19.
8. Interview with Hoang Duc Nha, July 23, 1985.
9. *Ibid.*
10. Henry Kissinger, *A World Restored,* p. 329.
11. Oriana Fallaci, *Interview with History,* pp. 40–41.
12. Schecter notes, October 4, 1972. Those attending the lunch were Hedley Dono-

van, Henry Grunwald, Hugh Sidey, Louis Banks, and Richard Campbell of *Fortune*.

13. H. R. Haldeman, *The Ends of Power*, p. 177.
14. See Arthur Woodstone, *Nixon's Head*, p. 122.
15. U. Alexis Johnson, *The Right Hand of Power*, pp. 534–535.
16. *Ibid.*, p. 535.
17. Kissinger, *White House Years*, pp. 1184–1185.
18. Alan E. Goodman, *The Lost Peace*, p. 81.
19. *Foreign Policy Report*, February 18, 1970, p. 68.
20. Landau, *Uncertain Greatness*, p. 156, quotes Nixon telling Kissinger at the end of the first meeting of the National Security Council staff: "And you and I will end the war."
21. Kissinger, *White House Years*, p. 1025.
22. *U.S. Foreign Policy for the 1970s: A Report to the Congress by Richard Nixon, President of the United States, February 9, 1972*, p. 113.
23. Nixon, *Memoirs*, p. 409–410. This was Nixon's famous November 3, 1969, Silent Majority speech. "Very few speeches actually influence the course of history," writes Nixon. "The November 3 speech was one of them. Its impact came as a surprise to me; it was one thing to make a rhetorical appeal to the Silent Majority—it was another actually to hear from them."
24. Goodman, *The Lost Peace*, p. 57.
25. *Ibid.*, p. 87.
26. *Foreign Policy* (January 1969), "The Vietnam Negotiations," p. 214.
27. Kissinger, p. 262.
28. Ho Chi Minh, *Selected Writings*, p. 356.
29. *Ibid.*, p. 361.
30. *Foreign Policy* (January 1969), "The Vietnam Negotiations," p. 230.
31. Kissinger, *White House Years*, p. 280.
32. Goodman, *The Lost Peace*, p. 89.
33. Guenther Lewy, *America in Vietnam*, pp. 279–285. Lewy offers a critical assessment of the Phoenix Program, noting that in a 1970 study for the Rand Corporation, Robert Komer called Phoenix a "poorly managed and largely ineffective effort, and this can probably serve as an accurate overall appraisal."
34. *U.S. Foreign Policy for the 1970s: The Emerging Structure of Peace—A Report to the Congress by Richard Nixon, President of the United States, February 25, 1971*, p. 72.
35. Cao Van Vien, *The Final Collapse*, p. 21.
36. Interview with Nguyen Van Thieu, June 13, 1985.
37. Interview with Hoang Duc Nha, July 23, 1985.
38. *Ibid.*
39. Marvin Kalb and Bernard Kalb, *Kissinger*, p. 371.
40. Don, *Our Endless War*, p. 206.
41. Nixon, *Memoirs*, p. 699.
42. *Ibid.*, p. 700.
43. Seymour Hersh, in *The Price of Power*, p. 564, discusses the North Vietnamese strategy for a coalition in detail. When the North Vietnamese failed in their efforts to remove Thieu and impose a coalition government during the August and September negotiations with Kissinger in Paris, their alternative position was to negotiate for a coalition government with two regional governments in the South, the Provisional Revolutionary Government (PRG) and Saigon oper-

ating at a lower level. That was also rejected by Kissinger. Hanoi's fall-back position was presented in its draft of the peace agreement handed to Kissinger in Paris on October 8, 1974. It called for "two governments with a loose form of government on top—the Council for Concord and Reconciliation." After Thieu's objections, Kissinger then worked to dilute the functions of the Council and make it merely an advisory body with no legal governmental status. In an interview with Hersh in Hanoi, Nguyen Co Thach, a key aide to Le Duc Tho during the negotiations and now foreign minister, said all three variations proposed had a single goal: "It is to not have the Saigon government *uniquely* lawful. That is the one important thing for all the options—there is to be no lawful Saigon government. There are to be two lawful governments and not only one."

"This was the minimum," Thach said of the third option. "This reflected the reality of the time."

44. Interview with Hoang Duc Nha, December 19, 1985.
45. Kissinger, p. 1382.
46. Tran Van Don, *Our Endless War,* p. 209, and Hersh, *The Price of Power,* pp. 398–399. In *White House Years,* Kissinger describes the meeting with Lon Nol as "a shaming encounter." Kissinger writes: "Though Lon Nol had genuine cause for uneasiness, there was none of the nitpicking of Saigon, or the insolence." Insolence is a favorite Kissinger expression used to describe those who do not accept his authority. Kissinger said Lon Nol continued to place his trust in the United States "even though he understood that his was the one country in Indochina not given a specific date for a ceasefire—though the North Vietnamese were obligated to withdraw. Lon Nol even promised to put out a statement of strong support for the agreement when it was announced." Kissinger admits that Lon Nol was "shortchanged," but blames it on the North Vietnamese, not himself (p. 1384).
47. Interview with Hoang Duc Nha, January 19, 1986.
48. Interview with Nguyen Van Thieu, June 13, 1985.
49. Kissinger, p. 1385.
50. *Ibid.,* pp. 1385–1386.
51. Kissinger called Nha a "master of contraction." Nha insists he was following the spirit and intent of Thieu's remarks but was seeking a greater impact on Kissinger by using strong language and greater emphasis than Thieu's more circumspect usage in Vietnamese. Interview with Hoang Duc Nha, July 23, 1985.
52. Interview with Nguyen Van Thieu, May 3, 1985.
53. Kalb and Kalb, in *Kissinger,* p. 375.
54. Thieu conversation with Hung, Summer 1973. Thieu said: "I could have built a big statue of Kissinger along the Saigon river front." Thieu told Hung he was thinking of General Douglas MacArthur's statue in Manila.
55. Quoted by the Kalbs, p. 376.
56. Interview with Hoang Duc Nha, July 23, 1985.

Chapter 6
Peace Out of Hand

1. Kissinger, *White House Years,* p. 1390.
2. Interview with Hoang Duc Nha, December 19, 1985. Nha recalled that "we

debated the issue and Thieu decided not to tell Kissinger. He did not want to embarrass him any further in our meetings and we did not want to argue with Kissinger over the captured documents which he might say were a fabrication. We decided to save the documents as evidence for our case. To have told him about the documents would only have produced another confrontation at a very difficult time and detracted from our basic arguments against the draft treaty he presented us.''

3. Hung's conversations with Nguyen Van Thieu, London, November 25–27, 1976, March 4, 1978, and August 8, 1978. Also interview with Hoang Duc Nha, July 23, 1985.

4. Kissinger, *Foreign Affairs* (January 1969), "The Vietnam Negotiations," pp. 217–218.

5. See Appendix B for full text.

6. Major General Nguyen Duy Hinh, *Vietnamization and the Cease-Fire,* Indochina Monographs, U.S. Army Center of Military History, Washington, D.C., p. 186.

7. Schecter interview with Kissinger in Paris, December 7, 1972.

8. Kissinger, *White House Years,* p. 1393.

9. Interview with Nguyen Van Thieu, May 3, 1985.

10. *Ibid.*

11. Allan Goodman, *The Lost Peace,* p. 137, quotes from Chinh Luan, October 20, 1972, p. 1.

12. After the Tet Offensive in 1968 the Viet Cong forces in the South were seriously decimated. During the offensive North Vietnamese regular troops took part and remained in the South to fight with Viet Cong units and reorganize them. The North Vietnamese build-up continued. It was estimated at 200,000 at the time of the Easter offensive in 1972 when more than 150,000 North Vietnamese troops invaded the South across the demilitarized zone and the Cambodian and Laotian borders.

13. Goodman, pp. 137–138.

14. Tran Van Don, *Our Endless War Inside Vietnam,* p. 207.

15. One American Embassy Political Officer said that he was instructed to tell the South Vietnamese that the North Vietnamese soldiers would wither away and return to North Vietnam. He spoke good Vietnamese and was embarrassed because he knew the South Vietnamese were not so naive. The Vietnamese compared the story to the traditional Vietnamese saying that children are fooled by saying chicken dung is candy. Literally, *xui tre con an cut ga,* or to tempt little children with chicken dung by saying it is candy.

16. Interview with Vuong Van Bac, August 22, 1985.

17. Kissinger at lunch with *Time* magazine editors, September 29, 1972.

18. White House Press Office, Kissinger press conference, October 26, 1972, p. 8.

19. Thieu's memorandum to Nixon dated October 4, 1972.

20. Thieu interview with *Der Spiegel,* December 1, 1979.

21. Szulc, *The Illusion of Peace,* p. 633.

22. Nixon, *Memoirs,* p. 697.

23. Hersh, *The Price of Power,* pp. 563–564.

24. Kissinger, *White House Years,* p. 973, says that in May 1970 he ordered a special study on the consequences of North Vietnamese troops remaining in the South after a cease-fire. "Everyone agreed that Hanoi would reject a ceasefire including regroupment or withdrawal; the only kind with any chance of being accepted

by the other side was a ceasefire in place." Kissinger added that the success of the Cambodian invasion "made the risks tolerable." He also notes that with a cease-fire in place, "Saigon's control over the population would erode by at least six percent."

Chapter 7
Nixon's Second Term

1. Schecter interview with Haig for *Time,* October 20, 1972.
2. Nixon, *Memoirs,* p. 718.
3. Interview with Hoang Duc Nha, May 23, 1985. Nha explained that the reason he and President Thieu laughed was that they had anticipated that Haig might make a threat of a coup or worse during the meeting, and they had decided the only way to deal with such a threat was to laugh it off and ignore it.

     During President Thieu's visit to Washington in April 1973, Nha sat next to Deputy Assistant Secretary of State for Far Eastern Affairs William Sullivan at a lunch given for Thieu at the State Department. In a conversation between the two men, Nha says he told Sullivan: "Remembering the past year, you were not very clever. What is this bullshit about brutal action?"

     "Well, we didn't mean that," replied Sullivan. "What do you think we meant?"

     "We thought you were either going to throw us out or assassinate us," replied Nha.

     "What?" answered a surprised Sullivan. "Oh, we'd never do things like that."

     "Bill, I'm not a choirboy," snapped Nha. Interview with Hoang Duc Nha, July 23, 1985.
4. See Thieu's handwritten notes on letter in Appendix A.
5. Schecter, then *Time* White House correspondent, was backgrounded on Kissinger's overstepping his role and not giving proper credit to President Nixon by John Scali, then a counsellor to the President. Scali took his lead from Haldeman.
6. Interview in *Der Spiegel,* December 1, 1979, and recalled by Thieu during his interview with the authors on May 3, 1985.
7. Nixon, *Memoirs,* p. 718.
8. *Ibid.*
9. Kissinger, *White House Years,* p. 1413.
10. Nixon, *Memoirs,* p. 719.
11. Interview with Hoang Duc Nha, May 23, 1985.
12. Hung's conversation with Nutter on November 18, 1972.

Chapter 8
The Christmas Bombing

1. Interview with Nguyen Van Thieu, June 13, 1985.
2. Kissinger, *White House Years,* p. 1398; Hersh, *The Price of Power,* pp. 606–607.
3. Kalbs, quoted in *Kissinger,* p. 395.

4. *Ibid.,* p. 396.
5. It also appeared in *The Washington Post,* Outlook Section, pp. B-1 and B-4, 1973.
6. Interviews with Vuong Van Bac in Paris, August 23, 1985, and Tran Kim Phuong, July 10, 1985.
7. Interview with Vuong Van Bac, Paris, August 23, 1985.
8. Kissinger, *White House Years,* p. 1420. Nixon, *Memoirs,* p. 723. Nixon says Kissinger favored breaking off the talks and resuming the bombing. Nixon takes credit for continuing the talks for another round while Kissinger says that evidence does not sustain Nixon but he gives no evidence to support his claim. General John W. Vogt, Jr., the U.S. Seventh Air Force commander and deputy commander of the U.S. Military Advisory Group, recalled that he opposed the bombing halt in October. "I protested and said, 'You know our history with Communists is one of having to keep the heat on them in order to get them to do anything. If you take the heat off them, they may never sign.' " Vogt said: "I sent reconnaissance planes up there and I could see them rebuilding the power plants; Soviet airplanes were landing and unloading equipment. The railroads were being rebuilt with China and trains were coming back down. They didn't want an agreement at this point. They thought that, politically, it would be impossible, having stopped the bombing, for the President to do it again, and they were sitting there thinking they had it made. Then the President had to make the very, very tough decision to go to the use of B-52s, which incurred some risks and which, of course, aroused public opinion against him all over the world, and especially in this country." See Vogt, *Oral History,* pp. 88–89.
9. In the Palace, Thieu and his aids would joke about Kissinger's fancy phrases and his overuse of the terms "conceptual overview," "structure of peace," and "framework for negotiations." They were impressed, recalls Hung, by how this placed Kissinger in a superior position with a lofty, theoretical plan that ignored the practical realities to be faced in the countryside.
10. Nixon, *Memoirs,* p. 723.
11. Kalbs, *Kissinger,* p. 402.
12. Kissinger, p. 1425.
13. *Ibid.*
14. Nixon, p. 724.
15. Kissinger, p. 1426.
16. The U.S. commander at Nakorn Phanom, General John Vogt, flew South Vietnamese Corps commanders to Thailand to see the base command facilities and coordinate targeting information after the agreement was signed. Vogt's mission was to keep the Joint Chiefs of Staff informed of developments in the area after the cease-fire. In his *Oral History,* Vogt notes: "I still had responsibility for the entire area, including responsibility for the possible resumption of bombing in Vietnam if and when the situation arose which required it" (p. 263).
17. Kissinger, p. 1426.
18. *Ibid.,* p. 1435.
19. *Ibid.*
20. Interview with John Negroponte March 20, 1985, quoting Kissinger in Paris.
21. Nixon, pp. 722–723; Kissinger, p. 1421.
22. Kissinger, p. 1437.
23. *Ibid.,* p. 1441.
24. Interview with Nguyen Van Thieu, June 13, 1985.
25. Kissinger, p. 1448.

26. *United States Foreign Policy, 1972, A Report of the Secretary of State*, pp. 661–665.

27. Nixon, p. 737. Nixon was referring to a message delivered to Cuban General Calixto Garcia from President McKinley in 1898. McKinley sent Lieutenant Andrew Summers Rowan to advise Garcia of the imminent landing of U.S. troops in Cuba after the sinking of the American battleship *Maine* in Havana Harbor on February 15, 1898. Lieutenant Rowan took the President's letter, sealed in an oilskin pouch, and strapped it over his heart when he landed on the west coast of Cuba. He was met by Cuban guerrillas opposed to the Spanish. They disappeared into the jungle and crossed the country. Three weeks later Rowan delivered the "message to Garcia," the commander of the Cuban forces in Oriente Province.

28. Kissinger, p. 1460.

29. Nixon, p. 737.

30. Kissinger, p. 1460.

31. Vogt, *Oral History*, pp. 89–90, and interview, December 20, 1985.

32. *Ibid*. Of an estimated 884 SAM missiles fired, only 24 hits were scored, of which 15 resulted in downed aircraft. This is a 1.7 percent kill rate for the number of SAMs launched. There are other estimates that between 914 and 1,042 SAMs were fired. Of the total sortie count of 729 B-52s, 498 penetrated the especially high threat zones immediately surrounding Hanoi and Haiphong. These aircraft had a 4 percent loss rate. See *Linebacker II: A View from the Rock*, USAF Southeast Asia Monograph Series, vol. VI, Monograph 8, pp. 171–175. Also see Major Karl J. Eschmann, Report Number 85-0765, *The Role of Tactical Air Support: Linebacker II*, Air Command and Staff College Air University, Maxwell AFB, Alabama, pp. 97–109.

33. Interview with Finance Minister Chau Kim Nhau, October 23, 1985.

34. Vogt, *Oral History*, p. 257.

35. Interview with Alexander Haig, November 13, 1985.

36. Nixon, p. 744.

37. Interview with Vuong Van Bac in Paris, August 23, 1985.

38. Interview with Nguyen Van Thieu, May 3, 1985.

Chapter 9
The Real Agreement

1. Interview with John Negroponte, March 20, 1985.

2. Congressional Record, Extension of Remarks, January 15, 1973, pp. E191–192. Hung analyzed all the public peace proposals and concluded that the United States had opposed the continued presence of North Vietnamese troops in the South. Hung wrote: "More than anyone else, President Nixon foresaw the impossibility of South Vietnam's exercising its own free will in the presence of non-South Vietnamese forces. Thus in his first proposal on May 14, 1969, he was most specific about this question: 'What kind of a settlement will permit the South Vietnamese people to determine freely their political future? Such a settlement will require the withdrawal of all non-South Vietnamese forces from South Vietnam and procedures for political choice that give each significant group in South Vietnam a real opportunity to participate in the political life of the nation.'

"One of the most difficult problems in the recent peace negotiations has been the fact that, in spite of the invasion, Hanoi has not publicly admitted the presence of its troops in the South. Nevertheless, the answer to this question has already been provided by President Nixon four years ago, also in his first peace plan cited at the beginning of this article. He said, 'If North Vietnam wants to insist that it has no forces in South Vietnam, we will no longer debate the point provided that its forces cease to be there and that we have reliable assurances that they will not return.'

"Indeed, it may be in the context of this very statement that an answer may be found for the Paris deadlock, since obviously one of the assurances would be Hanoi's intention to respect the DMZ."

3. In his December 16, 1972, press conference, Kissinger said that the U.S. position with respect to a cease-fire in place "had been made clear in October 1970. It had been reiterated in the President's proposal of January 25, 1972. It was repeated again in the President's proposal of May 8, 1972. None of these proposals had asked for a withdrawal of North Vietnamese forces. Therefore, we could not agree with our allies in South Vietnam when they added conditions to the established positions after an agreement had been reached that reflected these established positions." In an analysis published in the Congressional Record on January 15, 1973, p. E-191, Hung argued that "a thorough analysis of peace proposals over the past four years suggests that contrary to Dr. Kissinger's statement, the United States' established position has consistently been that all outside forces, including the North Vietnamese, must depart from South Vietnam as part of a final solution."

4. Kissinger, *The White House Years,* p. 1469.

5. Nixon, *Memoirs,* pp. 749–750.

6. Article One stipulates: "The United States and all other countries respect the independence, sovereignty, unity, and territorial integrity of Vietnam as recognized by the 1954 Geneva Agreements on Vietnam." To the North Vietnamese this meant South Vietnam was a part of Vietnam, not the independent Republic of Vietnam with its capital in Saigon.

7. United States–Vietnam Relations, 1945–1967, Study prepared by the Department of Defense, Book 3 of 12, p. 23.

8. Interview with Hoang Duc Nha, July 23, 1985.

9. Interview with Nguyen Van Thieu, June 13, 1985.

10. General John Vogt recalls that during the time General Haig was in Saigon to "reassure and threaten Thieu into signing the agreement," Haig and others came to him and said, " 'We would like you to go to your military counterparts, the people that you have been fighting with and supporting here for the last year, and convince them that we will in fact remain steadfast. You know, if you tell them now that the United States is serious in its determination to back up our guarantees, they will probably listen to you.' I refused to do this. I am sure it didn't make Washington happy to find out that General Vogt was not going to go around to Vietnamese generals who had confidence in him and assure them that we would take the political action necessary to turn on the bombing again when the time came. I refused to do it." Vogt added that Thieu "finally did agree to the signing after he received iron-clad guarantees that we would, in fact, be there in the event of a major attack." See Vogt, *Oral History,* p. 276.

11. Interviews with Hoang Duc Nha, July 23, 1985, and January 19, 1986.

12. Thieu made this point in meetings with Hung in Saigon in 1975 and again in conversations with Hung in London in 1976.
13. Interview with Nguyen Van Thieu, May 3, 1985.
14. Another version is "once a word flies from your mouth even the horses from Sichuan province (Tu Xuyen) cannot catch it."
15. Nixon, *Memoirs,* p. 751.
16. Quoted in an article by Hong Ha on Hanoi Radio January 27, 1974. JPRS 61277, February 20, 1974.
17. Schecter file to *Time* magazine based on interview with CIA and State Department sources, January 25, 1972.
18. Interview with Vuong Van Bac, November 27, 1985.
19. Thieu in retrospect called Enhance Plus "a joke." Interview with Thieu, May 3, 1985.
20. General John E. Murray, Vietnam Report, December 12, 1972, to August 21, 1974, pp. 61–62.
21. The other countries that signed the International Act on Vietnam were Hungary, Indonesia, Poland, Canada, People's Republic of China, Republic of Vietnam, Democratic Republic of Vietnam, and the Provisional Revolutionary Government of the Republic of South Vietnam.

Chapter 10
San Clemente and Watergate

1. Vogt, *Oral History,* pp. 239–240.
2. Thieu's Farewell Address, FBIS text.
3. Interview with Hoang Duc Nha, May 13, 1985.
4. Kissinger, *Years of Upheaval,* p. 310.
5. In April 1986 there were still 2,436 American servicemen listed as missing in action or unaccounted for in Indochina. There were 695 missing in North Vietnam, 1,097 in South Vietnam, 82 in Cambodia, 556 in Laos and 6 off the coast of the People's Republic of China. There are also 42 American civilians listed as missing or unaccounted for in Indochina, according to the Defense Department.
6. Nixon, *Memoirs,* pp. 842–843.
7. Interview with Hoang Duc Nha, July 23, 1985.
8. Interview with Hoang Duc Nha, July 23, 1985.
9. Interview with Nguyen Van Thieu, June 13, 1985.
10. Interview with Hoang Duc Nha, July 23, 1985.
11. Interview with Hoang Duc Nha, July 23, 1985.
12. Interview with Nguyen Van Thieu, March 4, 1978.
13. *The Fall of South Vietnam,* p. 38.
14. Kissinger, *Years of Upheaval,* p. 310. Totally ignoring his own previous actions against Thieu, Kissinger says, "In my days in Washington, several Communist leaders had been received with honor. Senior officials had vied to attend State dinners in honor of neutralist leaders who specialized in castigating the United States. But the staunch President of a friendly country was a pariah. His alleged failings as a democrat were, for a decade, used as an excuse—by those who wished us to abandon his people to the enemies of democracy. There were no boat people fleeing from Vietnam while Thieu was there. Vietnamese by the

million voted with their feet during his rule, pouring into areas under his control and away from Communist-held territory. Conventional wisdom blamed this on our bombing; since it continued after our bombing ended, it was almost certainly a reaction to the brutality of Communist rule. Thieu took steps to liberalize his government—however inadequately—even in the midst of Communist terrorism of which his best officials were the primary targets. None of this profited him with his critics.

"To be sure, South Vietnam was hardly a democracy in our sense. There were justified criticisms of harshness and corruption. But when Thieu's opponents in Saigon's turbulent pluralistic politics expressed these to our press, no contrast was drawn with Hanoi, where no opposition was tolerated, the press was controlled, and access to foreign media was prohibited. It was not, in short, a fastidious assessment of degrees of democracy that was at work on American emotions about Thieu. He was the victim of a deeper, more pervasive confusion that manifested itself in double standards in all the democracies."

15. Hung visited Con Son Island in 1974. The Tiger Cages had been cleaned up and prisoners were no longer shackled to bars in their cells.

16. Arnold Isaacs, *Without Honor*, pp. 108–109, discusses the Phoenix Program in detail and notes that more than 20,000 "eliminations" "were achieved by Phoenix—Phung Hoang, in Vietnamese—raised the image of an indiscriminate CIA controlled Murder, Inc. in Vietnam. . . . The claimed 20,000 eliminations made Phoenix sound very efficient or very sinister, depending on your viewpoint, but in fact about 90 percent of them were actually casualties in normal battlefield combat. After the fact, and on the flimsiest evidence or sometimes on none at all, bodies were declared to be Viet Cong agents and labeled as a Phoenix 'kill' in order to meet the quotas assigned to province and district officials." He adds that "Phoenix . . . must have made enemies of many who passed through its jails and interrogation cells."

17. Guenter Lewy, *America in Vietnam*, p. 294.

18. Isaacs, *Without Honor*, pp. 106–107. He also critically analyzes the *an tri,* or security placement system, a preventive detention program to hold suspected Communists or anyone else considered "dangerous to the national defense, national security and public order." Detainees could be held for two years without a trial. The official American position on this procedure was contained in a U.S. Embassy "Analysis of Province Security Committees." The committees, which placed people in preventive detention, said the analysis, were "extra-constitutional and non-judicial, based on the right of the state to survive." The detention process reflected "the political 'facts of life' in a country at war . . . the nature of these committees and their strictly political function dictate a 'hands-off' policy by all U.S. personnel and agencies." The U.S. Embassy in the summer of 1973 estimated that there were 500 to 1,000 political detainees. Lewy, *America in Vietnam*, p. 294, notes that "By 1972–73 the *an tri* procedure had become a favorite target of attack of Hanoi's sympathizers in the U.S., and the existence of such a system of detention was cited as proof of the repressive character of the Thieu regime. The logic of this argument was surely fallacious . . . emergency detention has been used by democratic nations and the practice in and of itself is not necessarily to be regarded as an unacceptable violation of individual liberty. It is also necessary to reject as a fabrication the allegation that the GVN imprisoned hundreds of thousands of political prisoners."

19. Schecter's notes from breakfast with Thieu, April 5, 1973.
20. Vogt, *Oral History,* pp. 254–256. Vogt argues that "this was no substitute for the former close relationships I had had where I could actually go into the country and talk to these people and find out what was happening.

    "So, we willfully cut off the flow of information that would have helped us in our efforts to see what was happening and which may have led us to understand what the enemy was up to. And, once again, the reason for it, apparently, was it was the kind of thing they didn't want to hear in Washington which was now beset with the problems of Watergate, growing unhappiness in Congress of our handling of the situation down there. It was just ironic that after having forced the enemy into a hard agreement, which if it had been adhered to would have preserved all our holdings in the South, we were now giving it all away. Having won the military victory, we were now giving it all away by our unwillingness to enforce the very agreement we had insisted upon. I think the American public ought to hear this story" (p. 256).
21. Goodman, *The Lost Peace,* p. 84.
22. *Ibid.,* p. 85.
23. Nixon, pp. 374–375.
24. In the summer of 1974 Thieu confided to Hung on several occasions that he was deeply concerned by the Pope's lack of understanding for the danger of communism in South Vietnam. Thieu told Hung that the Vatican's representative in Saigon had indicated that Thieu should find a way to reach an accommodation with the Provisional Revolutionary Government.

Chapter 11
Coming Home

1. In the Vietnamese tradition the rule of *tam tong,* the three obediences, required that a woman when at home had to obey her father, when leaving home for marriage to obey her husband, and when her husband died to obey the eldest son. Hung's mother was not the head of the family, but had to defer to her eldest son.
2. Dr. Tuyen, a medical doctor, also had a law degree. In the period after the Viet Minh took power, he tried to coordinate and build an anti-Communist nationalist opposition among the Catholics in the North. With his younger brother he was carrying messages by bicycle on a back road he thought was deserted when he saw a Viet Minh checkpoint in the distance. Tuyen sent his younger brother running ahead to the checkpoint with a bicycle pump in his hands. Then he deflated the air in his back tire and limped up to the checkpoint, where he asked the guards to help him. "My wife is about to give birth—I need to find help," he pleaded. The guards passed him through and told him to try to catch up with a small boy who had just gone through with a bicycle pump. Tuyen barely escaped from Saigon in 1975. Today, he lives in London with his family.
3. Interview with Hoang Duc Nha, July 23, 1985.
4. Karnow, *Vietnam: A History,* notes that in several places, including Saigon, the number of votes for Diem exceeded the number of registered voters. Diem claimed to have won 98.2 percent of the vote—having spurned American advice to aim for a more plausible 60 or 70 percent. What Americans failed to under-

stand was that his mandarin mentality could not accept the idea of even minority resistance to his rule. "Diem renounced the elections prescribed by the Geneva agreement because, he said, they could not be 'absolutely free' " (pp. 223–224).

5. Snepp, *Decent Interval,* p. 14, and interview with Hoang Duc Nha, July 23, 1985.
6. Interview with General Tran Van Don, December 15, 1985.

Chapter 12
Fatal Concession

1. Kissinger, *Years of Upheaval,* p. 319.
2. Nixon, *Memoirs,* p. 786.
3. Interview with Alexander Haig, January 14, 1986.
4. Kissinger, p. 318.
5. Interview with Hoang Duc Nha, July 24, 1985.
6. Kissinger, p. 326.
7. Interview with Henry Kissinger, March 3, 1986.
8. Interview with General Ngo Quang Truong, March 10, 1985.
9. The aid figures for North Vietnam were never officially released. In *U.S. Foreign Policy for the 1970's, The Emerging Structure of Peace, A Report to the Congress by Richard Nixon, President of the United States, February 9, 1972,* Nixon says, "We are prepared to undertake a massive 7½ billion five-year reconstruction program in conjunction with an overall agreement in which North Vietnam could share up to two and a half billion dollars."

In a secret letter to Pham Van Dong, drafted by Kissinger and his staff and delivered on January 30, 1973, Nixon suggested the procedures for setting up a Joint Economic Commission and said, "Preliminary United States studies indicate that the appropriate programs for the United States contributions to postwar reconstruction will fall in the range of $3.25 billion of grant aid over five years. Other forms of aid will be agreed upon between the two parties.

"The estimate is subject to revision and to detailed discussion between the government of the United States and the government of the Democratic Republic of Vietnam."

A second separate page at the end of the agreement spells out the $1 billion to $1.5 billion, "depending on food and other commodity needs of the Democratic Republic of Vietnam." In his memoirs Kissinger says the food aid was to be included in the $3.5 billion total. The Commission was set up during Kissinger's trip to Hanoi, but Kissinger returned with a sober estimate that the North Vietnamese would violate the agreement and seek to get U.S. economic aid." Our essential task is to convince them they must make a choice between, the two. That was the essential objective of my trip." *Years of Upheaval,* pp. 23–43.

The actual dollar amounts discussed with Hanoi were not revealed until 1977, when Congressman Lester Wolff released the Nixon message with the intent of laying to rest any U.S. commitment to North Vietnam because of gross violations of the Paris Accords and the invasion of the South in 1975. See *The Washington Post,* May 20, 1977, p. 1.

10. *New York Times,* June 12, 1973, p. 2.
11. Snepp, *Decent Interval,* p. 52.
12. CBS News Special Report, "A Conversation with Henry Kissinger," February 1, 1973.
13. Interview with Henry Kissinger March 3, 1986.
14. Goodman, *The Lost Peace,* pp. 100–101.
15. *Idem.*
16. Kissinger, p. 302.
17. Snepp, p. 50.
18. This view was known to the American Embassy. See Colonel William E. Le Gro, *Vietnam from Cease-Fire to Capitulation,* pp. 50–51.
19. Daniel Rapoport, *Inside the House,* p. 238.
20. The scrapbook with the notes is in the Gerald R. Ford Library and is available.
21. Rapoport, *Inside the House,* pp. 240–243, discusses the episode in detail and interviewed Ford a week after the vote.
22. Interview with Alexander Haig, November 13, 1985. Laird insists that "I didn't get Ford to say that. Ford went a little further when he included all of Southeast Asia. He asked me what to do and I told him, 'You can't back up from it.' The President was madder than hell, but Congress felt misled by promises that had been made to Thieu which they had not been informed about. When I was Secretary of Defense I kept my committees advised. They broke that rule and did not tell the committee. Haig's promises to Thieu sent them up the wall. They did not know the specific content of the promises but they believed promises had been made to bomb without consulting them. Senator Stennis got angry and we lost Mike Mansfield and Carl Albert." Interview with Melvin Laird, December 4, 1985.

Chapter 13
Standing Alone

1. Interview with Vuong Van Bac, August 24, 1985. Bac was then foreign minister and was infuriated by Khiem's refusal to take responsibility on simple matters that he should have dealt with instead of burdening Thieu.
2. The French ambassador complained to Thieu that it was difficult for the French to provide aid for Saigon in 1974 because the 1973 aid package could not be agreed upon. Thieu urged Hung to compromise with the French, but they never could agree on the contents of the package. The French would provide only what they wanted to send, not what Hung requested.
3. Charles J. Timmes, *Military Review* (August 1976), "Vietnam Summary: Military Operations After the Ceasefire Agreement," p. 66.
4. Ehrlichman, *Witness to Power,* p. 288.
5. *Vietnam Bulletin,* April 15 and May 1, 1974.
6. Fung Yu-Lan, *A History of Chinese Philosophy,* pp. 74–75, discusses Confucius' view of profit and quotes him as saying: "The Superior Man is informed in what is right. The Inferior Man is informed in what is profitable."
7. Interview with Vuong Van Bac, November 27, 1985. Bac was referring to his notes from a meeting with Kissinger in Paris on January 12, 1973.
8. Cao Van Vien, *The Fall of South Vietnam,* pp. 42–43, describes the South Vietnamese belief in the investment theory.

9. Interview with Graham Martin, March 27, 1985.
10. James Gavin, "A Communication on Vietnam," *Harper's* (February 1966), pp. 16–21.
11. Westmoreland, *A Soldier Reports,* pp. 128–129.
12. See William Safire, *Safire's Political Dictionary,* p. 763.
13. *Ibid.*
14. Hinh, *Vietnamization and the Cease-Fire,* chapter VII, especially p. 183.
15. Vien, *The Fall of South Vietnam,* p. 133.
16. *Ibid.,* p. 169.
17. Interview with General Ngo Quang Truong, February 21, 1985.
18. In February 1973 Hanoi's 2nd Division attacked Sa Huynh in Quang Ngai Province and was repulsed by Saigon's 2nd Division. In April 1973 the North Vietnamese 9B Division attacked Kien Phong Province to gain control of a part of the Mekong River but was pushed back to Cambodia by the ARVN 9th Division. The third attack by the NVA F10 Division struck near Kontum and was held to a standstill and forced to withdraw by the 23rd Division.

Chapter 14
Promises to Keep

1. Interviews with General John Murray, May 10, 1985, and February 12, 1986. "It was an arbitrary move, a lousy bookkeeping system in the army and their concern for running out of funds," explained Murray.
2. Interview with General John Murray, May 10, 1985.
3. See Le Gro, *Vietnam from Cease-Fire to Capitulation,* pp. 81–82.
4. *Ibid.,* p. 80.
5. Statement by General John Murray in Congressional Record, March 6, 1975, pp. H1454–H1455.
6. Cao Van Vien, *The Final Collapse,* pp. 53–54.
7. *Ibid.,* pp. 54–55.
8. Interview with General John Murray, May 10, 1985.
9. Quoted in *Vietnam at the Balance,* Special Report for the Republican Steering Committee, U.S. House of Representatives, by James Cowin, pp. 1–2, in author's possession.
10. The Indochina Resources Center was a center for anti-war activities in Washington. Its main goal was to lobby in Congress to cut economic and military aid to South Vietnam. The group prepared position papers against the war and lobbied individual staff members and congressmen to turn against South Vietnam.
11. Hung's notes from Saigon. Thieu repeated these remarks to others in his cabinet.
12. When he visited Vietnam in 1964, McNamara tried to boost the fortunes of Prime Minister and head of the junta General Nguyen Khanh. He would hold Khanh's hands high and shout, "Long Live Vietnam!" in Vietnamese. *Muon Nam,* which literally means one thousand years, would come out of McNamara's mouth with the wrong inflection so that it sounded like "The lying duck wants to go to sleep."
13. Thieu used the French, *clair précis et concis.*
14. See Appendix G. Ngo Dinh Diem, letter to John F. Kennedy dated June 9, 1961.
15. *Vietnam Bulletin,* IX, no. 12 (Aug. 31, 1974), p. 8.

16. Nutter memo to Marsh, October 1, 1974, in Hung's possession.
17. Hung was note taker at the meeting.
18. Interview with Morton Abramowitz, March 11, 1986.
19. Major General Charles J. Timmes, *Military Review* (September 1976), pp. 71–75.
20. Bac recalls his days in Washington as being lonely. Most Americans he met in 1956 had no idea where Vietnam was. "I would say I was from China. It was easier than explaining about Vietnam whenever I met somebody." Interview with Vuong Van Bac, August 22, 1985.
21. Interviews with Vuong Van Bac, August 22 and 23, 1985.
22. Interview with Vuong Van Bac, August 23, 1985.
23. Interview with Vuong Van Bac, November 27, 1985.

Chapter 15
Twilight of the Republic

1. Van Tien Dung, *Our Great Spring Victory*, pp. 17–18.
2. Major General John E. Murray, Defense Attaché, Saigon, *Vietnam Report, 21 August 1974*, pp. 62–63. Murray was particularly concerned with the growing shortage of ammunition in his final report. He noted that "the ARVN was shorted on ammunition by the Cease-Fire edict. There were six fully-loaded ammunition ships steaming toward Vietnam ports that had to be turned around. Their wealth of indispensable ammunition was not counted against the ordnance ceiling due to the Peace Agreement."
3. An unedited copy of "Briefing on the Military Situation in South Vietnam by the Joint General Staff, Republic of Vietnam Armed Forces," dated January 9, 1975, is in Hung's possession. An edited version, which eliminates the detailed intelligence data on North Vietnamese troop and supply movements, is in Appendix I. The JGS Briefing discussed the North Vietnamese options or Capabilities, and said:
    "In Capability One, they also reckon the United States will be denied any good reason to provide additional aid as the Hanoi command will only commit those augmented units already in the South and in so doing present the new conflict as a civil war that comes about as a result of more serious truce violations. In Capability Two, in order to deny the United States the opportunity for timely assistance, they will launch a Blitzkrieg like attack with every means at their disposal, including their general reserves presently in North Vietnam in order to gain control over large portions of the territory in South Vietnam. In sum, one can say that both capabilities involve a military offensive of major proportions."
4. See Briefing document cited above, and General Cao Van Vien, *The Final Collapse*, pp. 33–36.
5. Interview with General Tran Van Don, April 10, 1985.
6. Interview with General Brent Scowcroft, November 25, 1985.
7. Hung's personal notes after talking to friends and politicians, including Vice President Huong, in Saigon during the Tet holidays in February 1975.
8. Vien, *The Final Collapse*, pp. 62–68.
9. Extract from News Conference with Secretary of Defense James R. Schlesinger, January 14, 1975, Department of Defense.

10. *Ibid.*

11. *Ibid.* In an interview on November 27, 1985, Schlesinger said: "The Secretary of Defense had been bluffing. He had been bluffing in what I regarded as a good cause, which was to try and hold Hanoi back, but they saw that we were not responding to the tests."

   By warning the North Vietnamese of a possible resumption of bombing, Schlesinger hoped to restrain them. But when the United States failed to come to the aid of South Vietnam after the loss of Phuoc Long in January 1975, it became clear to the North Vietnamese that the United States would not resume bombing, despite Schlesinger's threats.

12. Dung, *Our Great Spring Victory,* pp. 22–23.

13. Interview with Alexander Haig, January 13, 1986. Haig said that he asked Kissinger to join him in making the appeal to Ford, but that Kissinger said he could not join him. Kissinger said he had no recollection or record of Haig's request.

14. Interview with Vuong Van Bac, Paris, August 23, 1985.

15. General John W. Vogt, Jr., *Oral History,* pp. 145–146. On an earlier trip Mrs. Abzug sent word to General Vogt, commander of the U.S. Seventh Air Force based at Nakorn Phanom, Thailand, that she wanted to meet him for a briefing. He provided a plane, but when it arrived in Saigon Mrs. Abzug insisted on being taken to Vientiane, Laos, to meet with American Ambasssador Godley. The next morning the pilot of her plane called General Vogt and said, "She wants me to fly her and her husband and secretary directly to Hong Kong." Vogt refused to fly Mrs. Abzug to Hong Kong and she never received the briefing she requested from him. General Vogt was angry with Mrs. Abzug for not accepting his briefing. "I don't know why or what she had in mind, whether it was urgent business or a shopping tour or what, but she couldn't find time now to come down to talk to me to find out what we were doing and why we were doing it. And as I say, I left her there. Godley had to make arrangements to get her on commercial air up to Hong Kong. That's the sort of thing you run into with people with their minds made up who don't want to really see the facts and who won't listen or go through the motions of just sleeping through it. It was disconcerting because we had a real story to tell" (p. 146).

16. Guenter Lewy, *America in Vietnam,* p. 296.

17. Tiziano Terzani, *Giai Phong! The Fall and Liberation of Saigon,* pp. 257–259.

18. From 1970 to 1973 Saigon redistributed 2,500,000 acres of land to over 800,000 tenant farmers so that 90 percent of the arable land was now worked by individual farmers who owned their land. See Nixon, *No More Vietnams,* p. 133.

19. Lewy, p. 90.

20. Interview with Vuong Van Bac, Paris, August 23, 1985.

21. Le Loi proclaimed himself king in 1428. He is considered to be an architect of national unity and a pioneer in the art of guerrilla warfare. See Joseph Buttinger, *The Smaller Dragon,* pp. 157–159 and 190.

Chapter 16
The Last Enclave

1. Animosity between the Vietnamese and the *montagnards* occasionally broke into open warfare. In September 1964, 3,000 heavily armed *montagnards* rebelled against the Vietnamese, killing 29 and capturing hundreds of Vietnamese. Only the intervention of American Special Forces officers prevented a major bloodbath. See Howard Sochurek, "American Special Forces in Action in Viet Nam," *National Geographic* (January 1965), pp. 38–64.
2. Major General Charles J. Timmes, *Military Review* (September 1976), Military Operations After the Cease-Fire Agreement, Part II, p. 22. Timmes notes that the JGS suggested General Phu move his troops to reinforce Ban Me Thuot but had no authority to order him to do so.
3. General Cao Van Vien, *The Final Collapse,* pp. 68–69.
4. *Ibid.,* p. 102.
5. Vien, *The Final Collapse,* provides details of improved Soviet equipment supplied to the North Vietnamese, including SAM-2 and SAM-3 missiles, a new heat-seeking SA-7 missile, and a new artillery capability of 430 122mm and 130mm guns. The Soviet Union also supplied the North Vietnamese with an estimated 655 armored vehicles, including portable bridge carriers and armored personnel carriers for the first time. For full details, see pp. 33–36.
6. *Ibid.,* p. 78.
7. General Tran Van Don was asked in 1971 by President Thieu to approach General Vien and "ask him to work a little harder and spend more time in the field with his officers." Interview with Tran Van Don, January 23, 1986.
8. See Vien, pp. 112–113, for details on what happened to the reserve units and how they were deployed. As the North Vietnamese troop build-up grew, Thieu's reserves were quickly exhausted. In his largely self-serving account, Vien insists that Thieu was in control and made the decisions and that the JGS was only serving him in an advisory capacity. When Thieu asked Vien if there were any reserves available, Vien says, "It was as if President Thieu, by asking something he had known all along, just wanted to call everyone present to witness the impasse in which we had found ourselves and what was going to dictate the next move."
9. Hung conversation with Nguyen Van Thieu, London, March 4, 1978.
10. Bernard B. Fall, *Street Without Joy,* pp. 27–35. The French used napalm against the Viet Minh and the Communists lost 6,000 dead and 500 prisoners.
11. Interview with Nguyen Van Thieu, June 13, 1985. See B. H. Liddell Hart, *History of the Second World War,* chapter 31, pp. 543–567, for a discussion of Allied strategy.
12. Hung conversation with Nguyen Van Thieu, London, March 4, 1978.
13. See Fall, *Street Without Joy,* chapter 9, pp. 185–250.
14. For a detailed account, see Vien, report pp. 110–132, and Snepp, *Decent Interval,* pp. 192–216; also Timmes, *Military Review* (September 1976), "Military Operations After the Cease-Fire Agreement, Part II," pp. 21–29.
15. Snepp, p. 208.
16. Lieutenant General Ngo Quang Truong, *RVNAF and U.S. Operational Cooperation and Coordination,* U.S. Army Center of Military History, Washington, D.C., notes that "The division of tasks between US and ARVN forces no doubt

spared the ARVN Corps commanders the major war burden. It was also a reflection of the prevalent political situation in which Corps commanders played a preeminent role. . . . As a result ARVN field commanders were sometimes more preoccupied with politics than combat operations" (p. 59).

17. General William C. Westmoreland, *A Soldier's Report,* discusses the importance of obtaining "the unity of command that military history through the years has shown to be essential." Both the United States and South Vietnam were sensitive to placing their troops under another nation's command. No parallel with the Korean War existed, "for even though the overall command in Korea was essentially American, it was under the aegis of the United Nations, which had no role in Vietnam." Westmoreland notes that the South Vietnamese were "jealous of their sovereignty while at the same time wary of providing verisimilitude to Communist charges that they were puppets of the United States." Westmoreland dropped the idea of a formal unified command, adding that "I never encountered serious disagreement with senior South Vietnamese officers. . . . In the final analysis I had the leverage to influence the South Vietnamese and they knew it, and both sides exercised a rare degree of tact" (pp. 133–134).

18. Lieutenant General Ngo Quang Truong, *RVNAF and U.S. Operational Cooperation and Coordination,* notes: "When US combat units were introduced into South Vietnam to fight the war, their role overshadowed the advisory effort because they held the initiative on the battlefield and coordinated all military efforts. . . . Because of the plentiful and sometimes lavish support provided by US units, the morale and combat effectiveness of ARVN units was very high. . . . In time, they came to regard Americans as protectors and providers instead of advisers and comrades-in-arms" (pp. 163–164; see also pp. 165–171).

19. Vien, *The Final Collapse,* Appendix A, pp. 169–171. Vien argues that President Thieu for all practical purposes was the supreme commander of the armed forces and "the JGS did not make any decisions on the war it had been created to fight." Among his Vietnamese colleagues and American counterparts, Vien emerged as a general who never took the initiative and failed to fulfill his acknowledged mission of "employment of the armed forces for national defense and territorial pacification."

20. Interview with General Ngo Quang Truong, May 21, 1985. Truong recalled that President Thieu always respected and followed the recommendations of the JGS, when he could get them to make recommendations.

21. Interview with Eric Von Marbod, May 10, 1985.

22. Hung conversation with Nguyen Van Thieu, London, April 3, 1978.

23. Interview with General Ngo Quang Truong, May 21, 1985.

24. Snepp, *Decent Interval,* pp. 210–211.

25. Interview with General Ngo Quang Truong, May 31, 1985.

26. Hung conversation with Nguyen Van Thieu, London, March 4, 1978.

27. Hung interview with General Ngo Quang Truong, February 21, 1985.

28. According to Thieu, on the evening of March 19, when Truong had returned from Saigon, he called Thieu and asked him to hold back on the radio speech until the situation was clarified. At that point Thieu detected hesitation on the part of Truong in his ability to hold Hue. This was a factor which Thieu said influenced his decision "to give Truong flexibility" to hold Danang alone. Hung conversation with Thieu, August 4, 1978.

29. Interview with General Ngo Quang Truong, May 21, 1985.
30. Interview with Thomas Polgar, former Saigon station chief, Central Intelligence Agency, November 5, 1975.
31. Hung conversation with Nguyen Van Thieu, London, November 25, 1976.
32. Hung conversation with Nguyen Van Thieu, London, November 25, 1976.
33. Interview with James Schlesinger, November 27, 1985. Schlesinger was referring to Winston Churchill's *Their Finest Hour* (Boston: Houghton Mifflin), pp. 3–301. Churchill describes the French efforts to evacuate their troops: "At Brest and the Western ports the evacuations were numerous. The German air attack on the transports was heavy. One frightful incident occurred on the 17th at St. Nazaire. The 20,000 ton liner *Lancastria* with five thousand men on board was bombed and set on fire just as she was about to leave. A mass of flaming oil spread over the water round the ship, and upwards of three thousand men perished. The rest were rescued under continued air attack by the devotion of the small craft. When this news came to me in the quiet of the Cabinet Room during the afternoon, I forbade its publication, saying, 'The newspapers had got quite enough disaster for today at least.' I had intended to release the news a few days later, but events crowded upon us so black and so quickly that I forgot to lift the ban, and it was some years before the knowledge of this horror became public" (p. 194).

    The fall of Danang and the horror of Vietnamese clawing their way aboard aircraft and ships only to be shot or pushed off by soldiers seeking escape could not be kept secret and it played on the evening television news every day, as had most of the war. There was no forbidding publication. The public perception of the war for the first time was based on real events and reactions. In a political sense a war, for the first time, was fought on television.
34. Interview with James Schlesinger, November 27, 1985, and interview with Gerald R. Ford, February 10, 1986. Ford said that Schlesinger never made a written recommendation on his own or with the Joint Chiefs of Staff to him to use tactical nuclear weapons. Ford indicated that Schlesinger had raised the possibility in conversation.

Chapter 17
The Final Appeal

1. During the 1968 Tet Offensive against Hue, 5,800 civilians were killed or abducted; most of the missing are considered dead. Mass graves containing some 2,800 bodies were uncovered over a period of eighteen months after Hue was retaken. See Guenter Lewy, *America in Vietnam,* p. 274, and Don Oberdorfer, *Tet,* pp. 198–235.
2. Interview with Vuong Van Bac in Paris, August 23, 1985.
3. John H. Sullivan, *The War Powers Resolution, A Special Study of the Committee on Foreign Affairs,* p. 148.
4. *Ibid.,* p. 170.
5. *Ibid.,* p. 179.
6. *Ibid.*
7. *Ibid.,* p. 284.
8. All of the other letters were sent directly from the White House to the American ambassador in Saigon for delivery to President Thieu.

Chapter 18
The Weyand Mission

1. Interview with Gerald R. Ford, February 10, 1986. When asked why he did not reply to Thieu's letter of March 25, 1975, Ford replied: "I sent General Weyand to Saigon." At a White House meeting to discuss the mission, attended by Eric Von Marbod with the President, Thieu's letter of appeal was not mentioned, according to Von Marbod. Interview with Eric Von Marbod, January 2, 1986.
2. Ford, *A Time to Heal,* pp. 250–251.
3. Interview with Gerald R. Ford, February 10, 1986.
4. Memorandum for the President from General Fred C. Weyand, 4 April 1975.
5. Weyand had been called to the White House on Tuesday, March 25, to meet with President Ford, Secretary of State Kissinger, National Security Advisor Brent Scowcroft, and Ambassador Martin before departing for Saigon. There had been no discussion of the presidential letters and their promises.
6. Tran Van Don, *Our Endless War Inside Vietnam,* p. 242, describes Khiem's efforts to send nine tons of his possessions to the Vietnamese ambassador in Paris, who was a relative by marriage.
7. On the American side the team was led by Ambassador Martin who made sure to assert his top protocol position. Next to him came Weyand and Von Marbod, then General Homer Smith, head of the DAO, and George Carver and Ted Shackley of the CIA. On the Vietnamese side along with Thieu there was Vice President Huong; Prime Minister Khiem, who attended despite his resignation earlier in the day; General Vien, chairman of the JGS; Hung and General Quang.
8. Interview with Graham Martin, March 27, 1985.
9. The Daisy Cutter is the nickname for the BLU-82, designed to clear helicopter landing pads in the jungle. It explodes a cloud of fuel fifty feet in diameter and eight feet thick that scorches the ground for one hundred yards. The cloud generates a down pressure of some 300 pounds per square inch, sufficient to crush anything in its field. Survivors of the initial blast suffocate in the post-explosion vacuum. Six Daisy Cutters were shipped to Saigon and three were dropped in a makeshift arrangement from C-130 aircraft. The North and South Vietnamese thought that B-52 raids had been resumed when the first bombs were dropped. The three unused bombs were captured by the North Vietnamese and were put on display in Ho Chi Minh City.

Chapter 19
Playing to the Congress

1. Interview with Morton Abramowitz, January 26, 1986.
2. Interview with Eric Von Marbod, October 2, 1985.
3. Nessen, *It Sure Looks Different from the Inside,* p. 98.
4. *Idem.*
5. Butler, *The Fall of Saigon,* p. 129.
6. Interview with Eric Von Marbod, October 25, 1985. Schlesinger said, "When somebody asks me about the strategic importance of Vietnam, I say that inherently it is not strategically important, but that the U.S. investment, over time, of prestige had created a strategic importance that was not there inherently.

That was my usual response." Interview with James Schlesinger, November 27, 1985.

7. Le Gro, *Vietnam from Cease-Fire to Capitulation*, quotes the cable in full, pp. 171–172.

8. General Van Tien Dung, *Our Great Spring Victory*, pp. 151–153.

9. Carver recalls that "the Vietnamese asked for the B-52s as a big panacea. We felt that at best the renewal of bombing could create a pause, but it would not solve the problems by itself. Our best hope was for truncation, saving Military Regions III and IV and the delta." Interview with George Carver, January 7, 1986.

10. Nessen, *It Sure Looks Different from the Inside* p. 106.

11. Interview with James Schlesinger, November 27, 1985. Schlesinger made a public effort to prevent recriminations between the White House and Congress and to prevent Ford and Kissinger from blaming the defeat of South Vietnam on the Congress. On *Face the Nation*, April 6, 1975, Schlesinger was asked why the administration seemed not to let an opportunity go by without blaming Congress. Schlesinger replied: "Let me state categorically the question of who is to blame is a simplistic question in a very complex set of events. . . . I would hope that we can get these issues behind us. There is nothing that this country needs less at this time than an extended post-mortem on Vietnam that is as divisive as the Vietnam episode itself; and the only thing that we need less than that is a major confrontation between the Executive and the Legislature."

12. Nessen, *It Sure Looks Different from the Inside* p. 106.

13. *Idem.*, p. 106.

14. *Ibid.*

15. *Ibid.*, p. 107.

16. Interview with Gerald R. Ford, February 10, 1986.

17. Interview with Dorothy Fosdick, May 22, 1985. Fosdick was a key aide to Senator Jackson.

18. Nessen, pp. 99–100. Nessen writes at length about a dinner Ford was supposed to attend at Kissinger's house in Palm Springs with Frank Sinatra. Bob Hartmann, Ford's chief speechwriter and long-time adviser, urged Nessen to tell Kissinger to turn down Sinatra because it would damage Ford's image "at the end of a week in which the president had been criticized daily for lazing in the millionaires' playground while Vietnam burned." Sinatra was a friend of Agnew and, said Nessen, "had a questionable reputation." Nessen phoned Kissinger and asked him to turn Sinatra down. Kissinger agreed. Then ten minutes later Kissinger called Ford and got him to agree to go to dinner with Sinatra. Nessen thought he had lost, but "at that point Kissinger gave an illuminating insight into his character and methods. Having demonstrated his power by winning Ford over to his view in a clash with rivals on the staff, with his clout reaffirmed and his ego boosted, Kissinger then did what was best for the president and told Sinatra not to come to dinner."

19. Ford, *A Time to Heal*, pp. 253–254.

20. *New York Times*, April 11, 1973, p. 10, from transcript of the President's speech.

21. *Ibid.*

22. Interview with Brent Scowcroft, March 5, 1986. Scowcroft was Deputy Assistant to the President for National Security Affairs at the time. After he became Secretary of State in November 1973, Kissinger retained his title as Assistant to the President for National Security Affairs and divided his time between his

office in the White House and the State Department. In November 1975 Kissinger relinquished his White House office to Scowcroft, who took over as Ford's Assistant for National Security Affairs.

23. *New York Times,* April 11, 1975, p. 1.
24. Martin's memo to Thieu, in author's possession.
25. Hung conversation with Nguyen Van Thieu, London, August 8, 1978.
26. Interview with Vuong Van Bac, Paris, August 22, 1985.
27. The Chinese supported Prince Norodom Sihanouk in Cambodia and the Khmer Rouge in an effort to gain influence against the North Vietnamese. The Chinese had continued this support despite the Khmer Rouge's massacre of more than one million Cambodian citizens when they took power in 1975. The Chinese still support Sihanouk and the Khmer Rouge as they continue to oppose Hanoi's control of Cambodia with American aid.
28. Interviews with Vuong Van Bac, Paris, August 22 and 23, 1985.
29. Interview with Tran Van Don, February 14, 1985.
30. *Ibid.*
31. *Washington Post,* March 9, 1975.
32. Bernard Fall, *The Two Vietnams,* p. 117. Hung was told of Bernard de Lattre's mutilation by a friend who was stationed in the area at the time.
33. Joseph Buttinger, *The Smaller Dragon,* pp. 30–35. Buttinger estimates the size of the remaining Cham community in South Vietnam as about 20,000 in 1958. The Chams, who derived their cultural and commercial values from India, left a legacy of sculpture that was preserved by the French at the Museum of Tourane, the French name for Danang. There are also the ruins of a Cham city in Quang Nam Province.

Chapter 20
The Last Mission

1. Arnold R. Isaacs, *Without Honor,* says: "Little known and little regarded, Can was chiefly reputed as a dutiful follower of Thieu in the past; clearly, he was neither a potential negotiator for peace nor the leader who could reawaken his country's devastated spirit" (p. 414).
2. Ford, *A Time to Heal,* p. 255.
3. Thieu told Hung about his plan for a defense line at Ben Luc in a conversation in London in April 1976. At the time he went to Washington, Hung was only told by Thieu that if American aid was continued, "we still have some chance." Hung believed that it might be possible to divide the country again or form a coalition government.
4. The choir learned to sing "Hail Mary, Full of Grace" in English. It was the first time that English was sung in the cathedral and Cardinal Spellman was pleased.
5. Ron Nessen, *It Sure Looks Different from the Inside,* describes his own opposition to the war and how he tried to convince Ford against further aid to Saigon. Those strongly urging Ford to disassociate himself from Vietnam included Counsellor to the President Robert Hartmann, speechwriter Milton Friedman, and Donald Rumsfeld who was named to replace Al Haig as White House coordinator. Rumsfeld hoped to be named Ford's vice-presidential running mate in 1976.
6. Interview with Graham Martin, March 26, 1985.

7. Ambassador Martin brought with him impressive evidence of the deteriorating military situation and the bleak outlook for a defense of Saigon. Colonel Vo Van Cam, Thieu's director of cabinet, said that when he came to clear Thieu's desk after Martin left, he saw the maps and briefing materials the ambassador had brought with him. Cam thought "the briefing materials portrayed the situation as more serious than it actually was at the time." The briefing was prepared by Frank Snepp, who describes Thomas Polgar, the CIA station chief, ordering him to make a field appraisal of the military situation. "Make it as bleak as you can," Polgar said. "The Ambassador is going to use it to convince Thieu it's time for him to go." Snepp added that he needed no prompting to write the appraisal as Polgar wanted. "Its bleakness was a simple reflection of the facts." Snepp, p. 382.

8. Interview with Graham Martin, March 26, 1985. President Thieu told the authors that Ambassador Martin told him "there might be some chance" for aid if he stepped down. In his testimony before the Special Committee of Investigations of the Committee on International Relations, House of Representatives, on January 27, 1976, Ambassador Martin said: "President Thieu asked whether his leaving would affect the vote in Congress. I said it might have changed some votes some months ago, it could not now change enough to affect the outcome.

"In other words, if his thought was to offer to resign if Congress assured a level sufficient for South Vietnamese survival, that was a bargain whose day had passed, if indeed it had ever existed.

"After all, his opponents would accept just as easily the distortions that would be fed to them about his successor as they had about him. The important thing was perhaps the effect his leaving would have on the other side.

"I said I did not know the answer, but it seemed that most South Vietnamese now seemed to think it would facilitate negotiations.

"I personally thought it would make little difference. Hanoi would be opposed to any strong leader. They would insist on a much weaker man, if indeed they were really interested in negotiating. But his colleagues felt it might buy time which was now the essential commodity for Vietnam.

"Some felt if the destruction of Saigon could be avoided, if an independent Vietnam could continue to exist, one might hope, even if reason recognizes the dimness of the hope, that things might improve." The conversation went on for about an hour and a half (p. 547).

In Thieu's mind it was the Americans who were pressing for the negotiations and his removal. Thieu told Hung in November 1976 that he decided to step down "because everybody, the French, the Americans, and the people, accused him of being an obstacle to renewed American aid and a political solution with the Communists."

9. Interview with Graham Martin, March 27, 1985.

10. Chiang was a favorite of Thieu's. Only Chiang's photograph and a portrait of South Korean President Park Chung Hee hung in his office. When the news of Chiang's death was received in the Palace, it seemed yet another omen of disaster for the Republic of Vietnam. Coming on the heels of King Faisal's assassination and the crumbling military situation, the Vietnamese felt they were doomed, out of favor and balance with the heavens. "We were reminded of the saying, 'troi sa dat lo' ('The sky falls and the earth splits open')" recalled Hung.

11. Frank Snepp, Decent Interval, pp. 433–437, describes Thieu's departure. He was one of the drivers.

12. Interview with Thomas Polgar, March 6, 1986. Polgar's account differs from

Snepp, who said that heavy suitcases were loaded into the car. Polgar insists that there was no additional luggage because he wanted "to make the move as swift and as smooth as possible."

13. Interview with Thomas Polgar, March 6, 1986, and David Butler, *The Fall of Saigon,* p. 347.

14. Interview with Anna Chennault, March 2, 1986. Thieu and his family settled in London. His children attended school in the United States and his daughter settled there. He visits them occasionally. Mrs. Chennault also met separately with former Prime Minister Khiem, who asked to come to the United States. Khiem now lives in Arlington, Va.

Chapter 21
The Exodus

1. Interview with Graham Martin, March 27, 1985. Martin mused about the gold and said: "At the very end I thought about calling up my old friend in Thailand Air Marshall Dhawee Chulasapaya and having some Thai marines come in and sort of liberate the gold and take it out; but not seriously. You see it stayed there. Had the gold been stored in the account of the Republic of Vietnam at the Federal Reserve Bank in New York, as was intended, the United States would have been in a strong position to negotiate for information and the return of the remains of Americans missing in action in Vietnam.

2. Interview with Chau Kim Nhan, December 9, 1985. David Butler, *The Fall of Saigon,* pp. 350–352. Hao had publicly broadcast that he would not leave the country. After the fall of Saigon Hao was well treated by the Communists who used him as an adviser until they permitted him to depart. Hao left Saigon in 1982 and now lives in Houston, Texas, with his wife and children. He has an unlisted telephone number.

3. Butler, pp. 244–250, describes being flown into Xuan Loc for a briefing and then leaving by helicopter in a mad scramble when he "finally realized that the helicopters were the only way out."

4. Le Gro, *Vietnam from Cease-Fire to Capitulation,* p. 174.

5. *Ibid.,* pp. 173–177.

6. See Emergency Supplemental Appropriations for Assistance to the Republic of Vietnam for Fiscal Year 1975, Hearings Before Subcommittees of the Committee on Appropriations, House of Representatives, Ninety-Fourth Congress, First Session, Monday April 21, 1975, p. 20.

7. Interview with Philip C. Habib, December 30, 1985. Habib recalls being constantly refused when requesting aid funds on the Hill in the final days of the war. "The American people had gotten out of the war and didn't want to get back in. Nobody wanted to get reinvolved. We forgot our obligations," said Habib.

8. See Note 6, p. 25.

9. *Ibid.,* p. 26.

10. Interview with Eric Von Marbod, May 10, 1985.

11. Hung's brother-in-law was able to save some of his notebooks with the minutes of meetings with Thieu and the cabinet in the Independence Palace.

12. Interview with Brent Scowcroft, November 25, 1985.

13. Interview with Graham Martin, March 26, 1985.

14. Interview with Eric Von Marbod, October 2, 1985 and January 2, 1986.

15. *Ibid.*
16. Historical Monograph: *The Fall and Evacuation of South Vietnam,* Department of the Air Force, pp. 114–117, and Snepp, *Decent Interval,* pp. 318–328 and 366–368.
17. Interview with Eric Von Marbod, January 2, 1986.
18. General Van Tien Dung, *Our Great Spring Victory,* p. 209.
19. *Ibid.,* p. 215. There was no suggestion in the plan for a coalition government or possible last minute negotiations. The plan called for "total victory."
20. Butler, *The Fall of Saigon,* p. 386.
21. The two marines were Lance Corporal Darwin Judge of Marshaltown, Iowa, and Corporal Charles McMahon, Jr., of Woburn, Massachusetts. Both were part of a U.S. Embassy security force brought in to protect the evacuation airlift from Tan Son Nhut. They were the last U.S. casualties of the war.
22. In his testimony before the House International Relations Committee in January 1976, Ambassador Graham Martin charged that Von Marbod's decision to take out the planes on April 28, 1975, led to the North Vietnamese decision to shell the runways. "My own perception of the reasons for the rocketing on the morning of the 29th was because the day before we had begun to move out the elements of the Vietnamese Air Force, and I think it was designed to impede that option that the shelling took place. I do not think it was specifically designed to interfere with our evacuation," Martin said.

    In a note to Martin after his testimony, Von Marbod told him that he was pleased his testimony had gone well and said: "I don't believe that our conversation that hectic morning is important because the situation changed so drastically after I departed your office. I certainly did not hold to your early morning guidance for long, because the enemy situation forced me to take new initiatives to remove operationally ready equipment."

    Martin refused to believe that he was no longer in control of the situation. During our interviews with him in March 1985 Martin maintained that the North Vietnamese were "mad" because the planes were flown out "so they shelled the airport." Dung's memoirs make no mention of the planes being flown out, but indicates that the air attack on April 28 and the shelling on April 29 were pre-planned as part of the Ho Chi Minh campaign.
23. Butler, *The Fall of Saigon,* p. 390. See Le Gro, *Vietnam from Cease-Fire to Capitulation,* p. 172, for an evaluation of the JGS failure to provide the planning necessary for reorganization and regrouping the ARVN in the final days.
24. For detailed accounts of the final evacuation see Snepp, *Decent Interval* and Butler, *The Fall of Saigon.*
25. Interview with General John E. Murray, April 20, 1985.
26. Von Marbod personally sponsored a group of pilots in the United States and paid their initial resettlement expenses.
27. *TIME,* May 12, 1975, p. 26.
28. *Ibid.*

Chapter 22
Reflections

1. Truong Nhu Tang, *A Vietcong Memoir,* describes with bitterness the Political Conference for the Reunification of the Country held in Ho Chi Minh City (Saigon) on November 17, 1975. It was the end of the PRG and the NLF roles

in governing the South. Truong Nhu Tang, the Minister of Justice in the PRG, recalls how North Vietnamese Politburo Member Truong Chinh had hugged him and wished him success before he returned to Saigon in 1975. When he met Truong Chinh 15 months later Chinh greeted him: " 'Excuse me, comrade, you look familiar to me. Who are you again?' For a moment I was nonplussed—to say the least," wrote Tang. "When I answered that I was the minister of justice for the South, Chinh's eyes lit up. 'Oh, really?' he said. 'What's your name, and what are you doing now?' I don't think there was anything intentionally malicious in this, only an old man's forgetfulness. But as a final comment on the South's revolution, the remark spoke volumes" (pp. 259–262).

2. Dayan said this to his Vietnamese hosts when he visited Saigon in the late 1960s and it was widely quoted among the Vietnamese. Hung heard it repeated in a conversation with military officers. The implication was that the North Vietnamese might win in war but they would be defeated in peace because the Communists would never be able to successfully impose their system on the South.

3. Federal Broadcast Information Service Daily Report on Asia, October 3, 1985.

4. Interview with James Schlesinger, November 27, 1985. See Omar N. Bradley and Clay Blair, *A General's Life,* pp. 558–559, for a discussion of Rusk's views that the 38th parallel could be crossed without the Chinese intervening. George Kennan and Charles Bohlen were opposed to crossing the 38th parallel. Paul Nitze, then head of the State Department's Policy Planning Staff, produced a paper recommending that the United States should "should make every effort to restrict military ground action to the area south of the 38th parallel." They were outweighed by Secretary of State Dean Acheson, Rusk and John Allison.

5. United States–Vietnam Relations 1945–1967. Book 3 of 12, Military Pressure Against North Vietnam Actions and Debate, Feb.–June 1964, pp. 31–32. At the Honolulu Conference, June 1–2, 1964, General Maxwell Taylor said seven American divisions would be needed if the Chinese Communists employed their full capabilities in the dry season, and five divisions even in the wet season.

6. Gravel Edition *The Pentagon Papers,* Vol. III, p. 354.

7. Interview with Nguyen Van Thieu, June 13, 1985.

8. The North Vietnamese policy of trading the remains of Americans for diplomatic recognition has won little sympathy or respect. Henry Kissinger believes that, "They (the North Vietnamese) have learned that the Russians are no help in developing an economy. I think there is something indecent to let them sell us a few bones. They must have a warehouse of bones out of which they produce a few examples every few months. What we have to keep in mind is the impact of this on the Chinese. Whether we normalize or don't normalize I would judge this from its impact on the Chinese. What do we get out of it? What can the North Vietnamese do for us?" Interview with Henry Kissinger, March 3, 1986.

9. Kissinger, *White House Years,* p. 1373.

10. McGeorge Bundy, *Foreign Affairs,* "Vietnam and Presidential Power," pp. 397–407. Based on the two letters that Hung released in 1975, Bundy says, "So it is clear that the public record and the private assurances are poles apart." Bundy looks at the eight public statements Kissinger refers to in his memoirs (*White House Years,* p. 1495, footnote 2, Ch. XXXII) as assuring Thieu publicly of the American commitment. He concludes that Nixon's language is "Delphic, not categorical" and "None of these statements suggests a definite U.S. commitment to use force in reply to violations." Kissinger's own language in public is vague and shies away from the return of U.S. troops or a resumption of bombing.

For example, in an interview with Marvin Kalb, Kissinger is asked: "So that for the next year or two, if I understand you right, there would be no need for a reinvolvement of American military power?"

Kissinger: "Marvin, we did not end this war in order to look for an excuse to reenter it. But it would be irresponsible for us, at this moment, to give a precise checklist to potential aggressors as to what they can or cannot safely do."

In his press conference explaining the Paris Accords Kissinger made no mention of any U.S. commitment to go back to war, or to attack North Vietnam if the ceasefire was violated. As Bundy notes, "Indeed, Dr. Kissinger, at this most public and dramatic moment of all, took great pains to draw attention away from any such prospect. Here are two questions and his answers:

Q. If the peace treaty is violated and if the ICC proves ineffective, will the United States ever again send troops to Vietnam?

A. I don't want to speculate on hypothetical situations that we don't expect to arise.

Q. What is now the extent and the nature of the American commitment to South Vietnam?

A. The United States, as the President said, will continue economic aid to South Vietnam. It will continue that military aid which is permitted in the agreement. The United States is prepared to gear that military aid to the actions of other countries and not to treat it as an end in itself and the United States expects all countries to live up to the provisions of the agreement." (*New York Times*, January 25, 1973, p. 21.)

As Bundy concluded, "It would take a most remarkable interpreter to reconcile these comforting words with the plain language of the assurances of Thieu."

11. Interview with Elliot Richardson, December 16, 1985, and Bundy, *Foreign Affairs*, "Vietnam and Presidential Power," p. 401.

12. Interview with James Schlesinger, November 27, 1985.

13. Interview with Melvin Laird, December 4, 1985.

14. Bundy, *Foreign Affairs*, p. 404.

15. *New York Times*, April 11, 1975, p. 1.

16. Interview with John Negroponte, March 20, 1985.

17. Interview with Henry Kissinger, March 3, 1986.

18. *Ibid*.

19. General John E. Murray in Braestrup, *Vietnam As History*, p. 143.

20. Nixon, *No More Vietnams*, pp. 12–13.

21. The debate on how much to escalate the war against North Vietnam was always present. When the decision was made to change the role of U.S. ground forces from static defense to active combat operations against the Viet Cong in April 1965, then CIA director John McCone insisted the bombing tactics also be changed. McCone argued that the "slowly ascending tempo" of the Rolling Thunder (bombing) operations were modest in scale and would not impose "unacceptable damage" on North Vietnam, "nor will they threaten the DRV's vital interests." McCone insisted that a change in ground force mission "is correct only if our air strikes against the North are sufficiently heavy and damaging really to hurt the North Vietnamese." He also warned that pressure would increase to stop the bombing. "Therefore time will run against us in this operation and I think the North Vietnamese are counting on this."

Gravel Edition, *The Pentagon Papers,* Vol. III, pp. 352–353. Also see Vol. IV, pp. 183–198, for a breakdown on the same debate in 1968, especially p. 188 where complete disarray is indicated over whether the Chinese will intervene and whether all worthwhile targets had been struck. Under LBJ the bombing was used to bring North Vietnam to the conference table. Under Nixon it was used finally to change the order of battle and count in the military equation to the point that the damage was "unacceptable" to Hanoi. At that point, despite the military success recognized by Hanoi, the political costs of the war were too high to continue the bombing. Time had run out on Nixon.

Interviews

Morton Abramowitz, January 26, March 11, 1986.
Richard Allen, February 20, 1986.
Vuong Van Bac, August 22 and 23, 1985, and November 27, 1985.
William Buckley, January 8, 1986.
George Carver, January 7, 1986.
Anna Chennault, May 2, 1985, January 17, 1986, February 23, 1986, March 2, 1986.
Clark Clifford, December 10, 1985.
Lucien Conien, October 30, 1985.
Arnaud de Borchgrave, January 23, 1986.
Bui Diem, March 18, 1986.
Tran Van Dinh, July 31 and November 24, 1985.
Ton That Dinh, October 18, 1985, November 20, 1985.
Tran Van Don, February 14, April 10, December 15, 1985 and January 23, 1986.
Gerald R. Ford, February 10, 1986.
Dorothy Fosdick, May 22, 1985.
Marshall Green, May 16, 1985.
Philip C. Habib, December 30, 1985.
Alexander Haig, November 13, 1985, January 14, 1986.
Morton Halperin, January 15, 1986.
Tom Harkin, December 19, 1985.
Bryce Harlow, February 21, 1986.
Richard Holbrooke, April 26, 1985.
George Jacobsen, March 13, 1986.
U. Alexis Johnson, May 15, 1985.
Henry A. Kissinger, March 3, 1986.
Robert Komer, April 15, 1985.
Melvin Laird, December 4, 1985.
Lu Lan, December 20, 1984.
Wolf Lehmann, December 12, 1985.
Graham Martin, March 26 and 27, 1985.
Stuart E. Methven, October 15, 1985.
Robert M. Montague, April 15, 1985.
John E. Murray, April 20 and May 10, 1985.
John Negroponte, March 20, 1985 and April 16, 1986.
Hoang Duc Nha, July 23 and 24, December 19, 1985, January 19, 1986.
Chau Kim Nhan, October 23 and December 9, 1985.
Tran Kim Phuong, July 10, 1985, July 22, 1985.

Thomas Polgar, November 5 and December 9, 1985, March 6 and 19, 1986.
Elliot Richardson, December 16, 1985.
Peter Rodman, January 7, 1986.
Jean A. Sauvageot, July 9, 1985.
James Schlesinger, November 27, 1985.
Brent Scowcroft, November 25, 1985, March 5, 1986.
Theodore Shackley, January 9, 1986.
Peter Tarnoff, January 21, 1986.
Nguyen Van Thieu, May 3, 1985, June 13, 1985.
Lam Duy Tien, December 5, 1984.
Charles J. Timmes, March 10, 1986.
Ngo Quang Truong, February 21, March 10, and May 21, 1985.
Ted Van Dyk, December 17, 1985.
John W. Vogt, October 10, 1985.
Eric Von Marbod, May 10, October 2 and 25, 1985, January 2, 1986.
Fred Weyand, February 19, 1986.
Charles Whitehouse, March 5, 1985.

Selected Readings

Bao Dai, S. M. *Le Dragon d'Annam*. Plon, 1980.

Berman, Larry. *Planning a Tragedy: The Americanization of the War in Vietnam*. New York: W. W. Norton & Company, 1982.

Blumenthal, Ralph. The Staff and Editors of *The New York Post*. *Henry Kissinger: The Private and Public Story*. New York: New American Library, 1974.

Bowman, John S., ed. *The Vietnam War: An Almanac*. New York: World Almanac Publications, 1985.

Braestrup, Peter, ed. *Vietnam As History: Ten Years After the Paris Peace Accords*. Washington, D.C.: The Wilson Center/University Press of America, 1984.

Bundy, McGeorge. "Vietnam, Watergate and Presidential Powers," *Foreign Affairs*, Vol. 58, No. 2 (Winter 1979–1980), pp. 397–407.

Butler, David. *The Fall of Saigon: Scenes from the Sudden End of a Long War*. New York: Simon and Schuster, 1985.

Buttinger, Joseph. *Vietnam: A Dragon Embattled*, Vols. I and II. New York: Praeger, 1967.

Cao The Dung and Luong Khai Minh (pen name for Dr. Tran Kim Tuyen). *Lam The Nao De Giet Mot Tong Thong, (How to Kill a President)*. Saigon, 1970.

Chennault, Anna. *The Education of Anna*. New York: Times Books, 1980.

Colby, William. *Honorable Men*. New York: Simon and Schuster, 1978.

Committee on Foreign Affairs. *The War Powers Resolution: A Special Study of the Committee on Foreign Affairs*. Washington, D.C.: U.S. Government Printing Office, 1982.

Cooper, Chester L. *America in Vietnam*. New York: Fawcett, 1972.

Crawford, Ann Caddell. *Customs and Culture of Vietnam*. Rutland, VT & Tokyo, Japan: Charles E. Tuttle Co., 1966.

Creel, H. G. *Chinese Thought: From Confucius to Mao Tse-tung*. London: Eyre & Spottiswoode, 1954.

Department of Defense, The. *United States–Vietnam Relations: 1945–1967*, Books 3, 11 and 12. Washington, D.C.: U.S. Government Printing Office, 1971.

Don, Tran Van. *Our Endless War: Inside Vietnam*. Novato, CA: Presidio Press, 1978.

Duiker, William J. *The Communist Road to Power in Vietnam*. Boulder, CO: Westview Press, 1981.

Dung, Van Tien. *Our Great Spring Victory*. London: Monthly Review Press, 1977.

Eagleton, Thomas F. *War and Presidential Power*. New York: Liveright, 1974.

Ehrlichman, John. *Witness to Power: The Nixon Years*. New York: Pocket Books, 1982.

Fall, Bernard B. *Street Without Joy: Indochina at War, 1946–1954*. Harrisburg, PA.: Stackpole Company, 1961.

——. *The Two Vietnams*. New York: Praeger, 1963.

——. *Vietnam Witness: 1953–66*. New York: Praeger, 1966.

Fallaci, Oriana. Trans. by John Shepley. *Interview with History*. Boston: Houghton Mifflin Company, 1976.

Ford, Gerald R. *A Time to Heal*. New York: Harper & Row, 1979.

Franck, Thomas M., and Weisband, Edward. *Foreign Policy by Congress*. New York: Oxford University Press, 1979.

Fung Yu-Lan. Trans. by Derk Bodde. *A History of Chinese Philosophy, Vol. I: The Period of the Philosophers (from the Beginnings to Circa 100 B.C.)*. Princeton, NJ: Princeton, University Press, 1952.

Gallucci, Robert L. *Neither Peace Nor Honor*. Baltimore and London: Johns Hopkins University Press, 1975.

Gardner, Lloyd C. *The Great Nixon Turnaround*. New York: New Viewpoints, 1973.

Gelb, H. Leslie, with Betts, Richard K. *The Irony of Vietnam*. Washington, D.C.: Brookings Institute, 1978.

Goodman, Allan E. *The Lost Peace: America's Search for a Negotiated Settlement of the Vietnam War*. Stanford, CA: Hoover Institution Press, 1978.

Gras, Yves. *Histoire de la Guerre D'Indochine*, 1979.

Gravel Edition, The Senator. *The Pentagon Papers: The Defense Department History of United States Decisionmaking on Vietnam*. Vol. III. Boston: Beacon Press, 1971.

Grey, Anthony. *Saigon*. New York: Dell, 1982.

Haig, Alexander M., Jr., *Caveat: Realism, Reagan, and Foreign Policy*, New York: Macmillan, 1984.

Halberstam, David. *The Best and the Brightest*. New York: Fawcett Crest, 1969.

Haldeman, H. R., with Joseph DiMona. *The Ends of Power*. New York: Times Books, 1978.

Hammer, Ellen. *The Struggle for Indochina*. Stanford, CA: Stanford University Press, 1967.

Hersh, Seymour M. *The Price of Power*. New York: Summit Books, 1983.

Herz, Martin F., assisted by Leslie Rider. *The Prestige Press and the Christmas Bombing, 1972: Images and Reality in Vietnam*. Washington, D.C.: Ethics and Public Policy Center, 1980.

Hinh, Major General Nguyen Duy. *Lam Son 719*. Indochina Monographs, U.S. Army Center of Military History, 1979.

Honey, P. J. *Vietnamese Communism—The Formative Years*. Saigon: Council on Foreign Relations, 1972.

Hosmer, Stephen; Kellen, Konrad; Jenkins, Brian M. *The Fall of South Vietnam: Statements by Vietnamese Military and Civilian Leaders*. New York: Crane Russak, 1980.

Hung, G. Nguyen Tien. *Economic Development of Socialist Vietnam. 1955–1980*. New York: Praeger, 1977.

Isaacs, Arnold. *Without Honor: Defeat in Vietnam and Cambodia*. New York: Vintage Books, 1983.

Johnson, Lyndon Baines. *The Vantage Point: Perspectives of the Presidency, 1963–1969*. New York: Holt, Rinehart and Winston, 1971.

Johnson, U. Alexis, with Jeff Olivarius McAllister. *The Right Hand of Power: The Memoirs of an American Diplomat*. Englewood Cliffs, NJ: Prentice-Hall, 1984.

Kahin, George M., et al. *The United States in Vietnam*. New York: Dell, 1969.

Kalb, Marvin, and Kalb, Bernard. *Kissinger*. Boston: Little, Brown, 1974.

Kaplan, Morton; Chayes, Abram; Nutter, G. Warren; Warnke, Paul C.; Roche, John P.; Fritchey, Clayton. *Vietnam Settlement: Why 1973, Not 1969?* Washington, D.C.: American Enterprise Institute for Public Policy Research, 1973.

Karnow, Stanley: *Vietnam: A History.* New York: Viking, 1983.

Kissinger, Henry A. *The Necessity for Choice.* London: Chatto and Windus, 1960.

———. *A World Restored: The Politics of Conservatism in a Revolutionary Age.* New York: Grosset & Dunlap, 1964.

———. *American Foreign Policy.* New York: Norton, 1974.

———. *The White House Years.* Boston: Little, Brown, 1979.

———. *Years of Upheaval.* Boston: Little, Brown, 1982.

Landau, David. *Kissinger: The Uses of Power.* Boston: Houghton Mifflin, 1982.

Laqueur, Walter. *A World of Secrets: The Uses and Limits of Intelligence.* New York, Basic Books, 1985.

Lau, Theodora. *The Handbook of Chinese Horoscopes.* New York: Harper & Row, 1979.

LeGro, Col. William E. *Vietnam from Cease-Fire to Capitulation.* Washington, D.C.: U.S. Army Center of Military History, 1981.

Lewy, Guenter. *America in Vietnam.* New York: Oxford University Press, 1978.

McCarthy, Brigadier General James R. *Linebacker II: A View from the Rock.* U.S.A.F. Southeast Asia Monograph Series, Vol. VL, Monograph 8, 1979.

Maclear, Michael. *The Ten Thousand Day War: Vietnam, 1945–1975.* New York: St. Martin's Press, 1981.

Marr, David G. *Vietnamese Anticolonialism: 1885–1925.* Berkeley: University of California Press, 1971.

Minh, Ho Chi. *Selected Writings: 1920–1969.* Hanoi: Foreign Languages Publishing House, 1973.

Momyers, General William W. *The Vietnamese Air Force, 1951–1975.* Vol. 3, Monograph 4, U.S.A.F. Southeast Asia Monograph Series. Office of Air Force History, 1975.

Morris, Roger. *Uncertain Greatness.* New York: Harper & Row, 1977.

———. *Haig: The General's Progress.* Playboy Press, 1982.

Nalty, Bernard C. *Airpower and the Fight for Khe Sanh.* Washington, D.C.: USAF, History Branch, 1973.

Nixon, President Richard. *U.S. Foreign Policy for the 1970s: The Emerging Structure of Peace. A Report to the Congress.* Washington, D.C.: U.S. Government Printing Office, February 9, 1972.

Nixon, Richard. *The Memoirs of Richard Nixon.* New York: Grosset and Dunlap, 1978.

———. *The Real War.* New York: Warner Books, 1980.

———. *No More Vietnams.* New York: Arbor House, 1985.

Nessen, Ron. *It Sure Looks Different from the Inside.* Chicago: Playboy Press, 1978.

Nutter, G. Warren. *Kissinger's Grand Design.* Washington, D.C.: American Enterprise Institute for Public Policy Research, 1975.

Oberdorfer, Don. *TET!* Garden City, NY: Doubleday, 1971.

Palmer, Dave Richard. *Summons of the Trumpet: U.S.–Vietnam in Perspective.* San Rafael, CA: Presidio Press, 1978.

Palmer, General Bruce, Jr. *The 25-Year War: America's Military Role in Vietnam.* New York: Simon & Schuster, 1984.

Porter, Gareth. *A Peace Denied: The United States, Vietnam, and the Paris Agreement.* Bloomington: Indiana University Press, 1975.

——, ed. *Vietnam: A History in Documents*. New York: New American Library, 1981.

Prados, John. *The Sky Would Fall—Operation Vulture: The U.S. Bombing Mission in Indochina, 1954*. New York: Dial Press, 1983.

Pratt, John Clark, ed. *Vietnam Voices: Perspectives on the War Years, 1941–1982*. New York: Penguin Books, 1984.

Rapoport, Daniel. *Inside the House*. Chicago: Follett Publishing Company, 1975.

Robequain, Charles. *The Economic Development of French Indo-China*. London: Oxford University Press, 1944.

Rothenberg, Morris. *Whither China: The View from the Kremlin*. Miami: Center for Advanced International Studies, 1974.

Rust, William J., and the Editors of U.S. News Books. *Kennedy in Vietnam*. New York: Charles Scribner's Sons, 1985.

Safire, William. *Safire's Political Dictionary: An Enlarged, Up-to-Date Edition of the New Language of Politics*. New York: Random House, 1960.

——. *Before the Fall*. New York: Tower Publications, 1975.

Santoli, Al. *To Bear Any Burden: The Vietnam War and Its Aftermath in the Words of Americans and Southeast Asians*. New York: E. P. Dutton, 1985.

Shawcross, William. *Sideshow: Kissinger, Nixon and the Destruction of Cambodia*. New York: Simon and Schuster, 1979.

——. *The Quality of Mercy: Cambodia, Holocaust and Modern Conscience*. New York: Simon & Schuster, 1984.

Schecter, Jerrold. *The New Face of Buddha: Buddhism and Political Power in Southeast Asia*. New York: Coward-McCann, 1967.

Snepp, Frank. *Decent Interval: An Insider's Account of Saigon's Indecent End, Told by the CIA's Chief Strategy Analyst in Vietnam*. New York: Random House, 1977.

Summers, Harry G., Jr. *On Strategy: A Critical Analysis of the Vietnam War*. Novato, CA: Presidio Press, 1982.

Szulc, Tad. *The Illusion of Peace*. New York: Viking, 1977.

Terzani, Tiziano. Trans. by John Shepley. *Giai Phong!: The Fall and Liberation of Saigon*. New York: St. Martin's Press, 1976.

Thai, Nguyen. *Is South Vietnam Viable?*, Manila, Philippines, Makati, Rizal: Carmelo & Bauermann, Inc., 1962.

Thompson, Sir Robert. *Peace Is Not at Hand*. London: David McKay Co., 1974.

Timmes, Major General Charles J. "Vietnam Summary: Military Operations After the Cease-Fire Agreement." *Military Review*. Leavenworth, KS (August, September 1976).

Tobin, Lt. Col. Thomas G., et al. *Last Flight from Saigon*. Vol. 4, Monograph 6, U.S.A.F. Southeast Asia Monograph Series. Office of Air Force History, 1975.

Truong, Lt. General Ngo Quang. *The Easter Offensive of 1972*. Indochina Monographs, U.S. Army Center of Military History, 1980.

Turner, Robert F. *Vietnamese Communism: Its Origins and Development*. Stanford, CA: Hoover Institution Press, 1975.

U.S. Congress. House Committee on International Relations. *The Vietnam–Cambodia Emergency, 1975*. Parts 1, 2, 3, and 4. 94th Congress, 2nd session, April 1975–May 1976.

Vanuxem, François. *La Mort du Vietnam: les faits, les causes externes et internes, les consequences sur le Vietnam, la France, et le Monde*. Editions de la Nouvelle Aurore.

Vien, General Cao Van. *The Final Collapse*. Indochina Monographs. Washington, D.C.: U.S. Army Center of Military History, 1983.

——. *Leadership*. Indochina Monographs, Washington, D.C.: U.S. Army Center of Military History, 1983.

Vogt, John W. Oral History, U.S. Air Force Historical Research Center Collection, Maxwell Air Force Base, AL, 1973–1978.

Walters, Major General Vernon. *A Silent Mission*. Garden City, NY: Doubleday, 1978.

Westmoreland, General William C. *A Soldier Reports*. Garden City, NY: Doubleday, 1976.

White, Theodore H. *The Making of the President 1968*. New York: Atheneum Publishers, 1969.

Williams, William Appleman; McCormick, Thomas; Gardner, Lloyd; LaFeber, Walter, eds. *America in Vietnam: A Documentary History*. Garden City, NY: Anchor Press/Doubleday, 1985.

Woodstone, Arthur. *Nixon's Head*. London: Olympia Press, 1972.

Index